The Problem of Evil

THE PROBLEM OF Evil

Slavery, Freedom, and the Ambiguities of American Reform

Edited by Steven Mintz and John Stauffer

UNIVERSITY OF MASSACHUSETTS PRESS

Amherst and Boston

Copyright © 2007
by University of Massachusetts Press
All rights reserved
Printed in the United States of America
LC 2006037069
ISBN 10: 1-55849-570-3 (paper); 569-X (library cloth ed.)
ISBN 13: 978-1-55849-570-8 (paper); 569-2 (library
cloth ed.)
Designed by Rich Hendel
Set in Quadraat and Eqiziano types
Printed and bound by The Maple Vail Book
Manufacturing Group

Library of Congress Cataloging-in-Publication Data

The problem of evil : slavery, freedom, and the
ambiguities of American reform / edited by Steven
Mintz and John Stauffer.
    p. cm.
  Includes bibliographical references and index.
  ISBN-13: 978-1-55849-569-2 (library cloth : alk. paper)
  ISBN-10: 1-55849-569-X (library cloth : alk. paper)
  ISBN-13: 978-1-55849-570-8 (pbk. : alk. paper)
  ISBN-10: 1-55849-570-3 (pbk. : alk. paper)
  1. Slavery—United States—History. 2. Slavery—Moral
and ethical aspects—United States—History.
  3. Antislavery movements—United States—History.
  4. Slavery—United States—Psychological aspects.
  I. Mintz, Steven, 1953– II. Stauffer, John.
  E441.P957 2007
  306.3'620973—dc22
                        2006037069

British Library Cataloguing in Publication data are
available.

For David Brion Davis,
who through his scholarship and teaching,
generosity and curiosity, has been a brilliant
guide and beacon for exploring the ironies and
moral ambiguities of the past.
You are the mentor of us all.

The Editors and Contributors

The children of darkness are evil because they know no law beyond the self. They are wise, though evil, because they understand the power of self-interest. The children of light are virtuous because they have some conception of a higher law than their own will. They are usually foolish because they do not know the power of self-will.... The preservation of a democratic civilization requires the wisdom of the serpent and the harmlessness of the dove. The children of light must be armed with the wisdom of the children of darkness but remain free from their malice. They must know the power of self-interest in human society without giving it moral justification.

—REINHOLD NIEBUHR, *The Children of Light and the Children of Darkness* (1944)

Contents

Introduction, Steven Mintz 1

Part I. Slavery and Freedom as Moral Problems

Introduction to Part I 23
  Steven Mintz

The Ancient and Medieval Origins of Modern Freedom 31
  Orlando Patterson

Slavery and Evil 67
  Stanley L. Engerman and David Eltis

Twin Evils? Slavery and Homicide in Early America 74
  Randolph Roth

The Transformation of Slavery in the United States, 1800–1863 89
  Ira Berlin

The Significance and Persistence of Proslavery Thought 95
  Paul Finkelman

Confederate Racialism and the Anticipation of Nazi Evil 115
  Robert E. Bonner

Part II. The Antislavery Impulse

Introduction to Part II 127
  Steven Mintz

Icarus Unbound:
  Ambition and Sin in Anglo-American Culture, 1560–1776 138
  William Casey King

Timothy Dwight, Congregationalism, and Early Antislavery 148
  Peter Hinks

Benjamin Franklin, Religion, and Early Antislavery 162
  David Waldstreicher

The Specter of White Chatellization:
  William Goodell's Abolitionist Thought 174
  Jonathan A. Glickstein

The Oriental Imaginary:
   Constructions of Female Bondage in Women's Antislavery Discourse 183
   Margaret M. R. Kellow

The Supernatural and Slavery:
   Catholics, Power, and Oppression 199
   Paula Kane

Souls of Darkness:
   Dominance and Submission in the Narratives of Frederick Douglass
   and Harriet Jacobs 210
   Catherine Clinton

Part III. Imagining Emancipation

Introduction to Part III 221
   John Stauffer

Political Evil and the Body Politic in Mid-Nineteenth-Century America 231
   Iver Bernstein

Labor, Race, and Colonization:
   Imagining a Post-Slavery World in the Americas 260
   Sharon Hartman Strom

Bankruptcy and Bondage:
   The Ambiguities of Economic Freedom in the Civil War Era 276
   Edward Balleisen

More Meteor than Martyr:
   The Legacy of John Brown 287
   Laura L. Mitchell

Performing Emancipation 298
   Richard Wightman Fox

Part IV. Post-Emancipation America

Introduction to Part IV 315
   John Stauffer

The Transferability of Otherness:
   American Expansionists Greet the Filipinos, 1898–1902 337
   Michael Fellman

Liberal Victorians and War in the Age of Empire 353
   Leslie Butler

Psychiatry and the Black Soldier during World War II 366
   Ellen Dwyer

Dwight D. Eisenhower:
   Religion, Politics, and the Evils of Communism 382
   Jack M. Holl

Contributors 397

Acknowledgments 401

Index 403

The Problem of Evil

STEVEN MINTZ

Introduction

Following World War II, West Germans coined the tongue-twisting term *Vergangenheitsbewaltigung* to describe the wrenching process of coming to terms with the Nazi past. Confronted with the horrors of the holocaust, *Vergangenheitsbewaltigung* entailed a lengthy and painful process of wrestling with the demons of German history through reflection, remembering, and moral reckoning. Only then would a new generation of Germans truly be free from the burden of historical guilt.[1]

There is no precise English equivalent to the word *Vergangenheitsbewaltigung* and its insistence that past evils must be faced and overcome before one can move forward. Certainly, Americans would benefit from such a process of self-analysis. This volume represents an effort to confront certain fundamental moral issues raised by American history, above all, the problem of slavery and its legacies of racism, racial exclusion, and racial inequality.

This volume reflects five basic commitments. The first is to a history that wrestles with fundamental moral problems. All of the contributors believe that history without a moral dimension is antiquarianism. They consider history a moral enterprise, an undertaking that seeks to understand the circumstances that allow evil to happen; asks how people, as intelligent and moral beings, could participate in the most horrendous evils; and how, at certain historical moments, some individuals have been able to rise above their circumstances, address evil in fundamental ways, and expand our moral consciousness. Many of the essays focus on the problems of slavery and racial prejudice, and on the ways that these evils have been rationalized and masked or confronted and challenged.

A second commitment is to the centrality of ideas. The forms and varieties of history represented in this volume have in common that they emphasize perception and meaning, both the meanings that people assigned at the time and the meanings that can be ascribed in retrospect. Religious ideas occupy a particularly important place in this moral history, since religion has been the vehicle through which most people in the past made sense of the world and their place in it. Ideas are indispensable in studying the past because human beings have minds, and their perceptions and value commitments guide their behavior. All of the contributors, however, reject the notion that ideas can be treated as free-floating entities that can be studied apart from their social, economic, and political settings. To connect economic and political interests and the realm of ideas, many contributors invoke the concept of ideology. Ideology, in their view, is not a deliberate distortion of reality or a façade for material interests. Rather, it provides the conceptual lens through which historical actors perceive the world around them.

A third commitment is to a conception of culture as a process involving conflict, resistance, accommodation, and, above all, power, including the power of moral ideals. American culture has always involved a cacophony of contending voices, social groups, and points of view. The essays focus not only on elites and intellectuals but on enslaved African Americans, artisans, serfs, women, and many other groups. The ways that each resisted various forms of economic and cultural oppression are closely examined.

A fourth commitment is toward overcoming the parochialism of narrow national histories. Only by bridging the boundaries of nations and time can we understand how the history of the United States fits into the larger process of modernization. Only by re-situating American history in a broader multinational frame can we understand what is distinctive about the construction of race in the United States, the nature of American slavery, and the limits of American social reform.

Finally, the contributors regard the problem of slavery as lying at the core of any thorough understanding of modernity. Not only was the institution of slavery indispensable to the emergence of modern consumer societies and the settlement and development of the New World, it was also connected to the emergence of new conceptions of racial identity and to the rise of new notions of liberty and equality. Equally important, the struggle against slavery was part of a much broader revolution in intellectual and moral life. In condemning slavery, abolitionists and their allies developed new notions of contract and consent that radically reshaped attitudes toward poverty, cruelty, labor, the Bible, and marriage.

THE PROBLEM OF EVIL

Evil pervades American popular culture. Popular films and television programs present an endless parade of serial killers, vampires, maniacs, psychopaths, and sociopaths. Much popular music, from gangsta rap to heavy metal, self-consciously appeals to the allure of evil. A surprising number of young people have embraced the trappings of evil, by wearing Goth fashions or taking up witchcraft or satanism. Meanwhile, our political culture is also obsessed with evil. For more than two centuries, Americans have frequently viewed politics as a contest between a virtuous us and an immoral other, and reform efforts have tended to take on the aura of moral crusades, whether this involved defeating the so-called slave power, banning the manufacture and sale of liquor, or locating and prosecuting Communists in our midst. Today, our political leaders describe the war against terrorism as a struggle against evildoers. It is an unfortunate fact that Americans' intense moralism has been as likely to lead to censoriousness and discrimination as to visionary hopes for social improvement or strivings for reform.[2]

No doubt the popular fascination with evil reflects the fact that the last century, like no other in human history, dramatized the human capacity for radical evil. Genocide, ethnic cleansing, lynching, concentration camps, and involuntary sterilization scarred the twentieth century. To magnify the horror, such evils often were perpetrated in the name of some higher good. It makes one wonder whether Carl Jung was correct when he described the Shadow, the portion of the self that people considered shameful and projected onto others; and whether Sigmund Freud was right when he posited that human beings possessed a "death instinct" that could be as readily directed outward as inward.[3]

The pervasiveness of the language and imagery of evil in contemporary culture makes it hard to remember that, as recently as the mid-1990s, popular writers and scholars decried the absence of a language to address evil. In not atypical terms, Andrew Delbanco, in 1995, lamented that Americans had "lost their sense of evil" under the pressures of modernity. Secular rationality, liberal relativism, modern cynicism, a sensibility emphasizing irony, and a loss of fear of perpetual damnation, he argued, had eroded the vocabulary for discussing evil. After September 11, 2001, however, the discourse of evil reasserted itself with a vengeance. The indiscriminate killing on airliners and at the World Trade Center and the Pentagon reinvigorated an older language of evil that pitted the children of light against the children of darkness.[4]

For more than two millennia, dramatists, theologians, philosophers, and their modern counterparts have pondered the problem of evil. Many of Western culture's foundational myths and greatest works of literature are accounts of the sources and nature of evil, from the biblical book of Genesis to the story of Job, from Dante's *Inferno* and Goethe's *Faust* to Dostoevsky's *Crime and Punishment*. The Old Testament begins with stories of evil, sin, and disobedience: the Temptation and the Fall in Eden, conflict among brothers leading to murder, and sexual sin, apostasy, and heresy; all result in divine punishment extending across generations. Classical drama, too, was preoccupied with the themes of corruption, dishonor, pollution (*agos* and *miasma*), hubris, rashness (até), jealousy (phthonos), suffering (pathos), revenge, and injustice. From *Beowulf*, with its vivid depiction of Grendel's lust for power, and Chaucer's "Pardoner's Tale," with its theme of "*Radix malorum est cupiditas,*" or "Greed is the root of all evil," English literature, then as in more recent times, has been engrossed with issues of corruption, vengeance, vice, villainy, violence, and human frailty. Outcasts, monomaniacs, and murderers stand at the heart of canonical literature, and evil is frequently represented as cunning, imaginative, and adaptive.[5]

Philosophy, like literature, has been preoccupied with the problem of evil: its origins, nature, and effects. Philosophers have tried to define evil, to assess the utility of the moralistic language of evil, and to ask what the existence of evil says about human nature. Philosophic works have also pondered whether malevolence is an essential ingredient in evil acts; whether rational explanations of evil diminish personal responsibility; and whether people can be held accountable for acts committed as a result of unconscious drives.[6]

Religious thinkers have asked how an all-powerful and benevolent God can tolerate evil and undeserved suffering; whether evil is intelligible and serves some rational purpose or is utterly inexplicable; and whether evil is intractable or can be eradicated or overcome. Theologians like St. Augustine and Reinhold Niebuhr stressed evil's inward character, its roots in human pride, arrogance, sensuality, selfishness, and alienation from the divine. Drawing upon the notion of original sin, this perspective sees the capacity for sinfulness as omnipresent, lying ultimately in the human capacity for self-deception and the tendency to confuse self-interest with righteousness. Other theologians have adopted a Manichean perspective, regarding evil as an entity outside the self. Ironically, the waning of belief in original sin and liberal theology's emphasis on the essential goodness of human nature made it easier to regard evildoers as moral monsters or as licentious inferiors who were not wholly human. If liberal theology could inspire dreams of individual and collective perfection, it could also inspire crusades to purify society of evil by patrolling the boundaries of personal conduct, driving feverish crusades against prostitution, gambling, drug use, smoking, and drinking. Yet a religious consciousness also inspired recurrent efforts at "disinterested benevolence." The antinomian impulse—the intense identification with God's will and the quest to become one with the divine—has lain behind many reform movements. Throughout American history, antinomian perfectionism has repeatedly ignited powerful challenges to entrenched injustice, from abolitionism in the early nineteenth century to the Civil Rights and environmentalist movements more recently.[7]

In the twentieth century, secular explanations of evil, attributing evil to environmental or psychological defects, tended to replace religious and philosophic ones, at least among intellectuals. Psychologists and sociologists blamed evil on such factors as mental disease, past abuse, psychological desensitization, and dysfunctional patterns of development; social, demographic, economic, and political stresses, frustrations, inequalities, and dislocations; flawed ideologies and misplaced idealism; and such social-psychological factors as xenophobia, peer pressure, obedience to authority, scapegoating, and threats to an individual or group's self-image. Unfortunately, many of the most profound psychological and sociological studies of evil have fixated on individual acts of human violence and cruelty, much as theological accounts have tended to focus on explaining undeserved evil.[8]

Historical studies are distinctive in their emphasis on specific and unique examples of evil and on the diversity of the motives, aims, dynamics, and consequences of various collective evils. Contingency is a hallmark of many historical accounts of evil. A key goal of a moral history of evil must be to understand the social, economic, cultural, and political conditions and ideologies that misshape societies and allow collective evil to develop, take root, and flourish. Any reasonable account must recognize that most acts of collective evil are perpetrated not by moral monsters but by ordinary people going about their ordinary lives. Historical evils have resulted from forces as diverse as racial and religious intolerance, difficult economic circumstances, the untrammeled workings of the free market, and utopian and messianic ideas.[9]

THE PROBLEM OF SLAVERY

Slavery is a historical evil that the United States has never properly acknowledged or atoned for. Even those who think that they know something about this nation's past tend to misunderstand slavery's cruelties and its central role in the nation's politics and economic development. Even though enslaved African Americans were physically larger than their counterparts in West and West Central Africa and the Caribbean, they suffered grievously under slavery. Infant and child death rates were twice that of white southerners. Fully half of all slave children grew up apart from their father, either because he resided on another farm or plantation or because he was white and refused to acknowledge his fatherhood. By the age of sixteen, half of all slave children were forcibly separated from their mother and siblings. Probably a third of all slave marriages were broken by sale. Meanwhile, fewer than 10 percent of slaves learned to read and substantially fewer to write.[10]

Yet many of slavery's worst horrors were psychological. At least some slaveholders sought self-consciously to strip enslaved African Americans of a distinctive culture and identity and instill a sense of dependency. Many slaveowners sought to weaken the role of parents, striving to make slave children feel that their primary loyalty was to their master and mistress. Above all, American slavery was buttressed by a system of racism that has persisted long after the institution of slavery collapsed and that continues to shape public perceptions. Even after its abolition, slavery has left a legacy of racial prejudice, economic inequality, and underdevelopment. Vestiges of slavery—substandard education, employment discrimination, housing discrimination, racial profiling—persist.

Although this fact is often denied or evaded, slavery occupied a central place in America's past. A majority of the 650 workers who built the White House and the U.S. Capitol were enslaved African Americans. Yet no marker acknowledges their contribution to the construction of the two key symbols of American nationhood. Slave-grown cotton constituted 75 percent of the value of the nation's exports in the decades before the Civil War, and it paid for the capital that financed canals, railroads, and textile factories. Slaveowners (who made up nine of the first fifteen presidents) occupied the presidency for approximately fifty of the nation's first seventy-two years. Two slaveholders served as Chief Justice of the United States from 1801 to the Civil War and presided over a court made up of a majority of slaveowners. Yet, despite a steady outpouring of scholarship on slavery, our society has not faced up to slavery at our most important public sites. Not until 2011—150 years after the beginning of the Civil War—will a Congressional mandate require the National Park Service to discuss the role of slavery at Civil War battlefields. Americans need to overcome the moral immaturity that denies responsibility for past injustice.[11]

Since the late 1970s, slavery studies have undergone four sweeping upheavals that have fundamentally altered our understandings. First, American slavery has been located in global and comparative perspectives. Scholars have recognized that southern slavery was one manifestation of an institution and a system of exploitation that could be found in diverse societies and cultures at very different time periods. Of course, there were earlier attempts at comparison, notably the works of Frank Tannenbaum and Stanley Elkins, and the criticism that their works inspired. But what is especially exciting about more recent scholarship is the way that the global development of slavery is now tied to larger themes in world history, including the construction of racial identities, the emergence of multinational industries serving a consumer market, and European expansion and colonialism.[12]

Equally significant is the discovery that American slavery was a dynamic and a national institution. Instead of focusing simply on the antebellum period, scholarship has shown how the institution of slavery evolved over a period of more than two centuries. Rather than focusing exclusively on the South, scholarship has also examined slavery in the North, the linkages between northern economic development and slavery, and the centrality of slavery in American politics.[13]

Meanwhile, our understanding of slave culture and resistance has been radically reshaped. Historians of slavery in conjunction with archaeologists, historical sociologists, and folklorists, have rethought older ideas about cultural persistence and retention. Especially impressive are works that have revealed the ongoing significance of Africans' ethnic and national identities in colonial America as well as studies that have traced the emergence of distinctive African American styles of dress, expression, and presentation of self. On resistance, recent scholarship has built on older notions of cultural resistance and day-to-day resistance to show that slavery involved a constant process of negotiation in which all power did not reside with the masters.[14]

Perhaps the most important development, however, is the emergence of a moral history of slavery. After decades of reconstructing the contours of slavery—in terms of demography, economics, gender, family, health, labor, and other aspects—historians have increasingly dwelt on the moral and philosophical issues raised by slavery. They have explored the evolution of moral sensibilities and the development of ideals of freedom and equality; questions of complicity and moral responsibility; slavery's legacies and modern societies' historical debts; and issues of meaning, including African Americans' shifting and contested memory of enslavement.[15]

The moral history of slavery is quite different from the superficial forms of moralizing that slavery prompted in the past. It asks why, if slavery's evil is self-evident to us, this wasn't apparent to our forebears? It prompts us to ask why slavery's abolition was followed by a century-long backlash. By problematizing moral issues, by connecting philosophic and historical issues—by asking, what are the circumstances and ideologies that make horrendous collective forms of evil possible?—history acquires a much more profound meaning.

THE PROBLEM OF RACE

The problem of slavery is inseparable from the problem of race, which it helped create. Race represents one of the most important, pervasive, misused, and pernicious modern ideas. On one level, race is a fiction. Human beings are a single species. There is scant genetic difference among people, and all human population groups are historical mixtures of different ethnicities. As Samuel Stanhope Smith wrote in 1787: ". . . it is impossible to draw the line precisely between the various races of man, or even to enumerate them with certainty . . ."[16] Yet this does not mean that race is entirely fictitious. Racial categories profoundly affect individual lives. Racial identities shape peoples' lived experience and cultural perceptions; race also maintains social barriers and reinforces economic inequality. Above all, racial ideas have driven public behavior. The idea of race played a crucial role in justifying slavery, the dispossession of Native Americans, and the deprivation of citizenship rights among Americans of color.[17]

Recent scholarship regards race not as a biological category grounded in genetics but as a historically shaped and highly contested cultural construct. It is commonplace to think of modern science as a force eroding superstition and outmoded ideas, but, in fact, the early scientific notion that differences in physiognomy, skin color, hair texture and color, and facial characteristics (such as the shape of the jaw, chin, lips, nose, or eyes) were linked to intelligence, temperament, and aptitude gave rise to modern racial categories.[18]

Beginning in the late eighteenth century, a group of highly influential natural scientists and ethnologists challenged the biblical notion that all humans were made in the image of God. In doing so they drew on derogatory classical and early Arabic stereotypes about black slaves, elitist European notions about the lower classes (as animalistic and incapable of higher thought or fully human emotions), sixteenth-century Spanish conceptions regarding purity of blood, and new ideas about animal breeding. "Modern" science thus embraced several ideas that carried profoundly negative consequences for the future. Chief among these consequences was the growing assumption that human beings could be classified into distinct racial groups based on physiognomy; that those races could be ranked hierarchically from superior to inferior; and that intellectual, moral, and physiological characteristics were passed down through the blood. Such ideas contributed to the rise of modern racism and paved the way for the horrors conducted in the name of eugenics, such as the involuntary sterilization of some sixty thousand Americans as "defectives."[19]

Anything but a static category, race has shifted dramatically in meaning over time, a fact that is evidence in changes in English usage. During the colonial and antebellum eras, there was a tendency to conflate many nonwhite groups; as a result, African Americans were generally referred to as "colored" or as "people of color." In the late eighteenth and early nineteenth centuries, as ethnological categories hardened, there was an increasing tendency to use the racial label of "Negro." Adoption of the term "African American" in the late twentieth century, in turn, reflected a shift away from racial categorization toward an emphasis on ethnicity. Unlike race, which carries connotations of innate physical, cultural, and intellectual characteristics, ethnicity refers to cultural differences in national origin, religion, and traditions. It is regarded as more changeable and less ineradicable than is race.[20]

Though the initial drift was toward fixed racial distinctions that can be ranked in order of intellectual, moral, and cultural achievement, in fact race had a bitterly contested history. Following the Revolution, racial theories evolved out of a debate over the status of African Americans in the new republic. Elaborate theories arose about racial degeneration and adaptation. Disputes arose about whether external physical differences gave rise to differences in mental and emotional traits or in social rights; whether race was a product of environment or of what would later be called heredity; and whether humanity shared a common ancestry or had resulted (according to elaborate theories of polygenesis) from separate creations.[21]

Controversies over race were not confined to the realm of theology, ethnology, or natural science, either. In the American colonies, the need for labor fostered an ideology that inborn characteristics made some peoples more exploitable than others. The Haitian Revolution encouraged apologists for slavery to link African ancestry with savagery and animality. During the antebellum era, some southern apologists for slavery eagerly embraced theories of racial difference propounded by northern and European scientists, who provided pseudoscientific legitimation for imperialism.[22]

Yet it is essential not to assume that social thought was moving monolithically toward rigid racial categorization. The theories that emphasized fixed racial categories and an inflexible racial hierarchy underwent heated challenge, especially from those who continued to embrace the biblical view of a common human ancestry. It is notable that it was among colonizationists, who believed that entrenched racial prejudice would not allow blacks and whites to coexist on a level of social and political equality, that one sees the earliest unambiguous ideas about the glories of early African civilizations, including positive portrayals of Ethiopian achievement.[23] Meanwhile, African Americans responded to the sciences of race advanced by white scientists, politicians, and proslavery polemicists by creating alternate ethnological discourses that sought to explain why white Americans were so eager to embrace ideas about racial difference and to discriminate on the basis of race.[24] But even critics of racist assumptions advanced by the American school of ethnology proved to be susceptible to notions of racial difference. Harriet Beecher Stowe, for example, embraced a romantic racial paternalism that regarded suffering under slavery as redemptive and portrayed enslaved African Americans as more pious than whites.[25]

THE AMBIGUITIES OF REFORM

Americans often conceive of their country's history as a history of reform, as an ongoing struggle to realize the ideals of the Declaration of Independence by extending the boundaries of those who are "created equal and endowed with certain inalienable rights." In fact, the birth of the American reform tradition coincided with the birth of the republic. In the late eighteenth and early nineteenth centuries, the first secular movements in history arose to improve society through reform. Unprecedented campaigns sought to ensure universal literacy, educate the deaf and blind, cure mental illness, rehabilitate criminals, extend equal rights to women, achieve world peace, and abolish slavery.[26]

The roots of the reform impulse lay in a mixture of anxiety and hope. In part, modern humanitarianism was a self-conscious alternative to revolutionary upheaval and a response to deep-seated fears of social disorder, family fragmentation, and widening class divisions. The period of the late eighteenth and early nineteenth centuries was one of rapid and unsettling social changes: the expansion of a market economy, the beginnings of rapid urban and industrial growth, the breakdown of household industries, the decline of social deference, the spread of democratic politics, an increasingly unequal distribution of wealth and income, and radical shifts in women's roles. The disintegration of an older patriarchal, hierarchical social order contributed to a profound sense of anxiety—that democracy would degenerate into anarchy, that self-seeking individualism would erode traditional morality, that commercialism would undermine national ideals. Earlier mechanisms for dealing with dependence and deviance, such as indentured servitude and the apprenticeship system, were breaking down. Many reformers were convinced that the only way to stabilize the social order was to internalize self-restraints within the depths of individual character through religion, more intensive forms for childrearing and education, and moral reform.

But the roots of reform did not lie exclusively in fear and anxiety. Reform also arose out of a millennialist sense of possibilities that was both secular and religious in origins. America's revolutionary heritage, the philosophy of the Enlightenment, and religious zeal all contributed to a heightened sensitivity to human suffering and a boundless faith in humankind's capacity to improve social institutions. Especially important contributions to the reform impulse came from two religious currents: a liberal religion that stressed the power of reason, the malleability of human nature, and humanity's capacity to imitate Christ's example; and an evangelical Protestantism that defined sin not as a metaphysical abstraction but as concrete social evils that needed to be suppressed and that warned of collective punishment if the nation failed to eradicate sinful behaviors.

Since the early nineteenth century, the American reform impulse has taken expanding forms, even as it has grown more professionalized and institutionalized. While the issues that antebellum reformers addressed, such as moral reform, education, poverty, disability, and crime, persisted, subsequent generations of reformers also confronted the distinctive problems created by urbanization and industrialization: corrupt business practices, health hazards, inadequate housing, and unsafe working conditions. Along with earlier traditions of moral and cultural reform, which sought to reshape behavior and uplift moral character, came an increasing willingness to use government as an instrument of reform and as a means of addressing the structural flaws and inequalities in American society.[27]

How historians have explained and interpreted reform has evolved through a series of interpretive cycles. For many years, the history of reform was treated from a liberal, progressive, Whiggish perspective. According to this view, the history of reform was essentially a story of progress: an advance from barbarism, cruelty, ignorance, and brutality to humanitarianism. After World War II, however, a new generation of historians looked at reform more skeptically. Shaken by the horrors of fascism, the Holocaust, and the gulag, revisionists adopted a more critical perspective on perfectionism, utopianism, and social engineering. The reformers' optimistic convictions about human innocence and perfectibility seemed sadly out of date. The revisionists were particularly likely to depict reformers as psychological deviants and fanatics and to seek the origins of the reform impulse in the reformers' declining class status.[28]

Beginning in the mid-1960s, historical approaches shifted in two very different directions. Many New Left historians celebrated the nation's pioneering reformers as the forerunners of later struggles for social change in American. Unlike the revisionists, who criticized the reformers' moralism and fanaticism, New Left historians viewed the abolitionists and women's rights advocates as models of uncompromising integrity, high moral idealism, and passionate commitment. According to the New Left argument, reformers' extremism and tactics of confrontation, far from being symptoms of a deep-seated irresponsibility, were in fact pitched to the level of evil in their society.[29]

At the same time, another group of historians began to criticize reform as an instrument of social control and class domination. Far from being idealistic altruists, reformers were motivated by class and professional self-interest. Rather than concerted efforts to uplift and rehabilitate, reform instead sought to suppress an autonomous working-class culture, impose bourgeois values, and repress and isolate deviants. All efforts at reform, from this perspective, were parts of a vast campaign to impose order on society by increasing the power of the state.[30]

In recent years, there has been a growing tendency to explore the ambiguities of reform, to show that, even as reform expanded public responsibility for the vulnerable, it served ulterior functions and helped legitimate new forms of exploitation and social control. Recent scholarship has cut across the boundaries dividing the antebellum and postbellum eras, and between the nineteenth and twentieth centuries; questioned and modified the social control thesis; scrutinized the role of reform in the creation of the distinctive American welfare state; and analyzed the role of race and gender in shaping reform. Five key themes stand out in the new scholarship of reform. The first involves the discursive definition and redefinition of social problems. Discursive analysis addresses two fundamental problems. One is a problem of perception—why longstanding social realities (such as poverty, delinquency, or domestic violence) become defined as social problems only at particular historical moments. The second is a problem of social praxis—how shifting perceptions lead to collective action. Discursive analysis suggests that how social problems are framed and understood has varied radically over time, according to public sensibilities and the political and social climate; that new ways of perceiving social conditions give rise to new forms of knowledge; and that this knowledge, in turn, compels attempts to apply it and shapes proposed solutions.[31]

A second development involves the gender dimensions of reform. Although women lacked the vote and formal political influence, they were crucial actors in promoting reform. During the antebellum era, women made up the grassroots support for many reforms, including abolition. A belief in women's moral superiority and natural benevolence encouraged many to take an active role in movements to establish orphan asylums, houses of refuge, and asylums for the mentally ill; suppress the drinking of hard liquor; and abolish slavery. Even though most antebellum women reformers disavowed any interest in involvement in partisan politics, they nevertheless engaged in petition campaigns and lobbied legislators. Yet, even as gender identification encouraged middle-class female reformers to reach out to poor women and women of color, the ideology of sisterhood sometimes blinded them to the realities of social class and led many to assume that all women should meet the standards of middle-class respectability.[32]

Women's activism was also responsible for many social reforms of the

Gilded Age and Progressive era, including expanded public efforts to address problems of infant and child mortality, child labor, juvenile crime, domestic violence, and poverty. Female reformers were at the forefront of efforts to establish kindergartens, playgrounds, expand high schools, establish juvenile courts, abolish child labor, and provide aid to single mother's with dependent children. But by basing their claims to influence on women's special characteristics as nurturers, female reformers inadvertently reinforced gender assumptions, encouraging protective legislation, mothers' pensions, and other legislations that assumed that most women would be family caretakers and should depend on male breadwinners for their support. Later, when the New Deal greatly expanded the federal role in welfare provision, the result was a two-tiered system, with Old Age Pensions and Unemployment Compensation based on labor-force participation (not economic means) and carrying relatively high benefits, while Aid to Dependent Children (or what would later be referred to as "welfare") was means- and morals-tested and offered lower benefits.[33]

A third key theme in the history of reform involves the importance of politics: how particular issues reach the public agenda and how reform measures are formulated, enacted, implemented, and administered.[34] Although reform agitation repeatedly brought social issues to public attention, reformers lacked the power to shape the political outcome on their own. Another key development in our understanding of reform involves increasing interest in the interactions and tensions between reformers and those they intended to help.[35] Reform invariably involves two-way, dialectical relationships, involving intricate processes of cooptation, resistance, negotiation, and subversion. Far from being the passive recipients of benevolence, the objects of reform have proven to be active agents who are far more resourceful than previously assumed. Finally, scholars have examined the extent to which reforms actually met the needs of those whom they sought to help and whether specific reform challenged or reinforced existing inequalities and power relationships. A major challenge has been to explain the gulf between the reformers' high aims and the failure of many of the reforms that have been instituted. Why, we must ask, have reforms often resulted in unforeseen and unintended consequences? Does this reflect the opposition of entrenched interests, the limitations of the reformers' vision, or some other factors?

Many of the essays in this volume examine reformers' diverse backgrounds, motives and objectives, and the ambiguous consequences of their reform efforts. The authors explore the paradoxes and ironies of reform, such as the tension between reform's religious roots and the secular form it generally took. They also explore the ways in which women and racial and cultural minorities deployed reform to challenge traditionally defined roles and constraints, and reformers' roles in modernizing and rationalizing society by creating enduring social institutions and bureaucracies and strengthening the role of the state. Above all, these essays explore the tension between humanitarianism and social control, suggesting new ways to conceptualize the ideological, cultural, and social significance of reform.

It is certainly true that American reformers have, at times, been morally self-righteous and paternalistic; that they have often acquiesced in the inequities of the wage system; and that their reforms have increased the state's power to discipline and control the poor and deviant. Nevertheless, it would be a mistake of the highest magnitude to cynically conclude that reform has, in its essence, been an instrument of class hegemony and control. Reformers were those Americans who refused to accept the idea that the existing social order was the best possible one and that society must acquiesce in its greatest evils. They viewed reform as society's highest endeavor, a means to bring social realities in line with our country's highest aspirations. They created notions of civic and communal responsibility that remain deeply meaningful as Americans embark upon a new century.

NOTES

1 Ingrid Strobl, *Das Feld des Vergessens: Jüdischer Widerstand und deutsche "Vergangenheitsbewaltigung"* (Berlin: ID-Archiv, 1994); Thomas McCarthy, "Vergangenheitsbewaltigung in the USA: On the Politics of the Memory of Slavery," *Political Theory* 30 (2002): 623–48.
2 James A. Morone, *Hellfire Nation: The Politics of Sin in American History* (New Haven: Yale University Press, 2003).
3 Carl G. Jung, *Jung on Evil*, ed. Murray Stein (Princeton: Princeton University Press, 1995); Eli Sagan, *Freud, Women, and Morality: The Psychology of Good and Evil* (New York: Basic Books, 1988).
4 Andrew Delbanco, *The Death of Satan: How Americans Have Lost the Sense of Evil* (New York: Farrar, Straus and Giroux, 1995); Ron Rosenbaum, "Staring into the Heart of the Heart of Darkness," *New York Times*, June 4, 1995, sec. 6, 36. On the recent outpouring of works on evil, see Lance Morrow, *Evil: An Investigation* (New York: Basic Books, 2003); Judith Shulevitz, "There's Something Wrong with Evil," *New York Times*, October 6, 2002, sec. 7, 39; "Research on Evil: An Annotated Bibliography," *Hedgehog Review* (Summer 2000), http://religionanddemocracy.lib.virginia.edu/hh/summeroo/ThrBiblVol2–2.html.
5 On evil in literature, see George Bataille, *Literature and Evil*, trans. Alastair Hamilton (New York: Marion Boyars, 1985); Mark Edmundson, *Nightmare on Main Street: Angels,*

Sadomasochism, and the Culture of Gothic (Cambridge: Harvard University Press, 1997); Neil Forsyth, *The Satanic Epic* (Princeton: Princeton University Press, 2003); Karen Halttunen, *Murder Most Foul: The Killer and the American Gothic Imagination* (Cambridge: Harvard University Press, 1998); Colin McGinn, *Ethics, Evil, and Fiction* (Oxford: Clarendon, 1997); Peter A. Schock, *Romantic Satanism: Myth and the Historical Moment in Blake, Shelley, and Byron* (New York: Palgrave Macmillan, 2003); Paul Ricoeur, *The Symbolism of Evil*, trans. Emerson Buchanan (Boston: Beacon, 1967); Roger Shattuck, *Forbidden Knowledge: From Prometheus to Pornography* (New York: St. Martin's Press, 1996).

6 On the philosophy of evil, see C. Fred Alford, *What Evil Means to Us* (Ithaca: Cornell University Press, 1997); Hannah Arendt, *Eichmann in Jerusalem: A Report on the Banality of Evil*, rev. ed. (New York: Viking, 1965); Joan Copjec, ed., *Radical Evil* (London: Verso, 1996); John Kekes, *Facing Evil* (Princeton: Princeton University Press, 1990); Mary Midgley, *Wickedness: A Philosophical Essay* (London: Routledge, 1984); Susan Neiman, *Evil in Modern Thought: An Alternative History of Philosophy* (Princeton: Princeton University Press, 2002); Amélie Oksenberg Rorty, *The Many Faces of Evil: Historical Perspectives* (New York: Routledge, 2001); Richard Taylor, *Good and Evil*, rev. ed. (Amherst, N.Y.: Prometheus Books, 2000). Laurence Mordekhai Thomas, *Vessels of Evil: American Slavery and the Holocaust* (Philadelphia: Temple University Press, 1993), analyzes institutionalized evil and the problem of comparing moral evils and suffering by examining differences in motives, magnitude, dynamics, intent, and consequences.

7 On evil in religious thought, see Marilyn McCord Adams, *Horrendous Evils and the Goodness of God* (Ithaca: Cornell University Press, 1999); Marilyn McCord Adams and Robert Merihew Adams, eds., *Problem of Evil* (Oxford: Oxford University Press, 1990); Edward Farley, *Good and Evil: Interpreting a Human Condition* (Minneapolis: Fortress, 1990); Wendy Farley, *Tragic Vision and Divine Compassion: A Contemporary Theodicy* (Louisville: Westminster/John Knox, 1990); David Rey Griffin, *Evil Revisited: Responses and Reconsiderations* (Albany: State University of New York Press, 1991); John Hick, *Evil and the God of Love*, rev. ed. (San Francisco: Harper & Row, 1978); Oliver Leaman, *Evil and Suffering in Jewish Philosophy* (Cambridge: Cambridge University Press, 1995); Jon D. Levenson, *Creation and the Persistence of Evil: The Jewish Drama of Divine Omnipotence* (Princeton: Princeton University Press, 1988); Michael L. Peterson, ed., *Problem of Evil: Selected Readings* (Notre Dame: University of Notre Dame Press, 1992); Anthony B. Pinn, *Why, Lord?: Suffering and Evil in Black Theology* (New York: Continuum, 1995); Alvin Plantinga, *God, Freedom, and Evil* (New York: Harper & Row, 1974); Kenneth Surin, *Theology and the Problem of Evil* (Oxford: Basil Blackwell, 1986); Richard Swinburne, *Providence and the Problem of Evil* (Oxford: Clarendon, 1998); Terence Tilley, *Evils of Theodicy* (Washington, D.C.: Georgetown University Press, 1991). On antinomian perfection and evil, see Jackson Lears, "Sanctimonies," *New Republic* (June 19, 2003), http://www.tnr.com/doc.mhtml?i=20030630&s=lears063003.

8 Among the works that examine the psychological states and social and economic

circumstances that contributed to mass violence during the twentieth century are Roy F. Baumeister, *Evil: Inside Human Violence and Cruelty* (New York: W. H. Freeman, 1996); Stephen A. Diamond, *Anger, Madness, and the Daimonic: The Psychological Genesis of Violence, Evil, and Creativity* (Albany: State University of New York Press, 1996); Jonathan Glover, *Humanity: A Moral History of the Twentieth Century* (New Haven: Yale University Press, 1999) Barrington Moore Jr., *Moral Purity and Persecution in History* (Princeton: Princeton University Press, 2000); Ervin Staub, *The Roots of Evil: The Psychological and Cultural Origins of Genocide* (Cambridge: Cambridge University Press, 1989). For the perspectives of sociobiology and evolutionary psychology, see Lyall Watson, *Dark Nature: A Natural History of Evil* (New York: HarperCollins, 1995).

9 A sophisticated historical study that critically evaluates psychological and sociological theories of evil is Christopher R. Browning, *Ordinary Men: Reserve Police Battalion 101 and the Final Solution in Poland* (New York: HarperCollins, 1992), which asks how a group of middle-aged men from Hamburg with no previous experience with violence could participate in the massacre of Polish Jews during World War II. Browning attributes this to Nazi indoctrination; peer group pressure and male bonding; careerism; obedience to authority; moral cowardice; fear of appearing weak; uprooting from a familiar environment; and the wartime suspension of conventional morality. Essays that identify similarities and differences between the Holocaust and other historical examples of institutionalized evil can be found in Alan S. Rosenbaum, ed., *Is the Holocaust Unique?: Perspectives on Comparative Genocide*, 2nd ed. (Boulder: Westview Press, 2001).

10 Robert William Fogel, *The Slavery Debates, 1952–1990* (Baton Rouge: Louisiana State University Press, 2003); Fogel, *Without Consent or Contract: The Rise and Fall of American Slavery* (New York: Norton, 1989); Peter Parish, *Slavery: History and Historians* (New York: Harper & Row, 1989).

11 Ira Berlin, *American Slavery in History and Memory* ([Gettysburg, Pa.]: Gettysburg College, 2001); Don Edward Fehrenbacher, *The Slaveholding Republic: An Account of the United States Government's Relations to Slavery*, completed and edited by Ward M. McAfee (New York: Oxford University Press, 2001); Garry Wills, *"Negro President": Jefferson and the Slave Power* (Boston: Houghton Mifflin, 2003).

12 Robin Blackburn, *The Making of New World Slavery: From the Baroque to the Modern, 1492–1800* (New York: Verso, 1997); Philip D. Curtin, *The Rise and Fall of the Plantation Complex: Essays in Atlantic History*, 2nd ed. (Cambridge: Cambridge University Press, 1998); David Eltis, *The Rise of African Slavery in the Americas* (Cambridge: Cambridge University Press, 2000).

13 Ira Berlin, *Generations of Captivity: A History of African-American Slaves* (Cambridge: Harvard University Press, 2003) and *Many Thousands Gone: The First Two Centuries of Slavery in North America* (Cambridge: Harvard University Press, 1998); Sylvia R. Frey, *Water from the Rock: Black Resistance in a Revolutionary Age* (Princeton: Princeton University Press, 1991); Kenneth Morgan, *Slavery and Servitude in Colonial North America:*

A Short History (New York: New York University Press, 2001); Phillip D. Morgan, *Slave Counterpoint: Black Culture in the Eighteenth-Century Chesapeake and Lowcountry* (Chapel Hill: University of North Carolina Press, 1998); Betty Wood, *The Origins of American Slavery: Freedom and Bondage in the English Colonies* (New York: Hill and Wang, 1997).

14. John Thornton, *Africa and Africans in the Making of the Atlantic World, 1400–1800*, 2nd ed. (New York: Cambridge University Press, 1998); Shane White, *Somewhat More Independent: The End of Slavery in New York City, 1770–1810* (Athens: University of Georgia Press, 1991); Shane White and Graham White, *Stylin': African American Expressive Culture from its Beginnings to the Zoot Suit* (Ithaca: Cornell University Press, 1998).

15. David Brion Davis, *Challenging the Boundaries of Slavery* (Cambridge: Harvard University Press, 2003) and *In the Image of God: Religion, Moral Values, and Our Heritage of Slavery* (Cambridge: Harvard University Press, 2001); Orlando Patterson, *Freedom in the Making of Western Culture* (New York: Basic Books, 1991).

16. Smith, *An Essay on the Causes of the Variety of Complexion and Figure in Human Species*, quoted in Alain F. Corcos, *The Myth of Human Races* (East Lansing: Michigan State University Press, 1997), 18.

17. Corcos, *The Myth of Human Races*, 3.

18. "Constructing Race," a special issue of the *William and Mary Quarterly* 54 (January 1997); Michael A. Morrison and James Brewer Stewart, *Race and the Early Republic: Racial Consciousness and Nation-Building in the Early Republic* (Lanham, Md.: Rowman & Littlefield, 2002).

19. Corcos, *The Myth of Human Races*, 1; Bruce R. Dain, *A Hideous Monster of the Mind: American Race Theory in the Early Republic* (Cambridge: Harvard University Press, 2002), 7.

20. A valuable guide to the contrasts between Anglo-American and Latin American conceptions of race is Thomas M. Stephens, *Dictionary of Latin American Racial and Ethnic Terminology*, 2nd ed. (Gainesville: University Press of Florida, 1999).

21. Bruce R. Dain, *A Hideous Monster of the Mind: American Race Theory in the Early Republic* (Cambridge: Harvard University Press, 2002); George M. Fredrickson, *Racism: A Short History* (Princeton: Princeton University Press, 2002) and *The Black Image in the White Mind: The Debate on Afro-American Character and Destiny, 1817–1914* (Middletown, Conn.: Wesleyan University Press, 1987); Ivan Hannaford, *Race: The History of an Idea in the West* (Washington, D.C.: Woodrow Wilson Center Press; Baltimore: The Johns Hopkins University Press, 1996); Pat Shipman, *The Evolution of Racism: Human Differences and the Use and Abuse of Science* (Cambridge: Harvard University Press, 2002).

22. Joyce Chapin in David Armitage and Michael J. Braddick, eds., *The British Atlantic World, 1500–1800* (New York: Palgrave Macmillan, 2002); Dain, *A Hideous Monster of the Mind*, 81–111; Fredrickson, *Black Image in the White Mind*.

23. Dain, *A Hideous Monster of the Mind*, 105.

24 Mia Bay, *The White Image in the Black Mind: African-American Ideas about White People, 1830–1925* (New York: Oxford University Press, 2000).

25 Fredrickson, *Black Image in the White Mind*, 102, 124.

26 On the origins of the American reform tradition, see Robert H. Abzug, *Cosmos Crumbling: American Reform and the Religious Imagination* (New York: Oxford University Press, 1994); Steven Mintz, *Moralists & Modernizers: America's Pre–Civil War Reformers* (Baltimore: Johns Hopkins University Press, 1995); Ronald G. Waters, *American Reformers, 1815–1860*, rev. ed. (New York: Hill and Wang, 1997).

27 LeRoy Ashby, *Endangered Children: Dependency, Neglect, and Abuse in American History* (New York: Twayne, 1997); Judith Sealander, *The Failed Century of the Child: Governing America's Young in the Twentieth Century* (Cambridge: Cambridge University Press, 2003).

28 David Brion Davis, *Ante-Bellum Reform* (New York: Harper & Row, 1967).

29 Martin B. Duberman, ed., *The Antislavery Vanguard: New Essays on the Abolitionists* (Princeton: Princeton University Press, 1965).

30 David J. Rothman, *The Discovery of the Asylum: Social Order and Disorder in the New Republic*, rev. ed. (New York: Aldine de Gruyter, 2002) and *Conscience and Convenience: The Asylum and its Alternatives in Progressive America*, rev. ed. (New York: Aldine de Gruyter, 2002).

31 Martin J. Wiener, *Humanitarianism or Control?: A Symposium on Aspects of Nineteenth-Century Social Reform in Britain and America* (Houston: William Marsh Rice University, 1981).

32 Anne M. Boylan, *The Origins of Women's Activism: New York and Boston, 1797–1840* (Chapel Hill: University of North Carolina Press, 2002); Lori D. Ginzberg, *Women in Antebellum Reform* (Wheeling, Ill.: Harlan Davidson, 2000) and *Women and the Work of Benevolence: Morality, Politics, and Class in the Nineteenth-Century United States* (New Haven: Yale University Press, 1990); Nancy A. Hewitt, *Women's Activism and Social Change: Rochester, New York, 1822–1872* (Lanham, Md.: Lexington Books, 2001); Susan Zaeske, *Signatures of Citizenship: Petitioning, Antislavery, & Women's Political Identity* (Chapel Hill: University of North Carolina Press, 2003).

33 Elizabeth J. Clapp, *Mothers of All Children: Women Reformers and the Rise of Juvenile Courts in Progressive Era America* (University Park: Pennsylvania State University Press, 1998); Judith Ann Giesberg, *Civil War Sisterhood: The U.S. Sanitary Commission and Women's Politics in Transition* (Boston: Northeastern University Press, 2000); Robyn Muncy, *Creating a Female Dominion in American Reform, 1890–1935* (New York: Oxford University Press, 1991); Alison M. Parker, *Purifying America: Women, Cultural Reform, and Pro-Censorship Activism, 1873–1933* (Urbana: University of Illinois Press, 1997); Daphne Spain, *How Women Saved the City* (Minneapolis: University of Minnesota Press, 2001).

34 Colin Gordon, *Dead on Arrival: The Politics of Health Care in Twentieth-Century America* (Princeton: Princeton University Press, 2003); James T. Patterson, *America's Struggle Against Poverty in the Twentieth Century* (Cambridge: Harvard University Press, 2000);

Theda Skocpol, *Protecting Soldiers and Mothers: The Political Origins of Social Policy in the United States* (Cambridge: Belknap Press, 1992).

35 Linda Gordon, *Heroes of Their Own Lives: The Politics and History of Family Violence: Boston, 1880–1960* (Urbana: University of Illinois Press, 2002); Eric C. Schneider, *In the Web of Class: Delinquents and Reformers in Boston, 1810s–1930s* (New York: New York University Press, 1992).

Slavery and Freedom as Moral Problems

STEVEN MINTZ

Introduction

Nearly a century and a half after the Emancipation Proclamation, slavery continues to haunt American society. Controversy rages over whether the federal government should issue an official apology for slavery, construct a national museum to memorialize the history of slavery, or pay reparations to the descendants of slaves. The shadow of slavery still lingers in the persistence of racial stereotypes and the gulf between blacks and whites in income, wealth, education, and healthcare.

The significance attached to slavery today makes it all the more surprising to discover that, for many years, slavery was treated as a marginal aspect of American history. Slavery was regarded as a subset of southern or African American history rather than as central to the nation's history and its economic and political development. Selective amnesia allowed Americans to downplay slavery's significance. Sectional reconciliation in the wake of the Civil War and Reconstruction was achieved in part by minimizing slavery's role in the coming of the Civil War, which was treated as a dispute over states' rights or as a conflict between an industrial and an agrarian civilization. Meanwhile, Reconstruction, rather than being treated as a momentous struggle to define the legal, social, and economic position of former slaves, was instead regarded as a mistake, a flawed attempt to revolutionize the South by overturning the power of the region's natural leaders.

In the course of a generation, a revolution has taken place in our understanding of slavery's history and its centrality in American society. We now recognized that slavery was anything but a static institution and that it underwent a series of disjunctive transformations during the seventeenth, eighteenth, and early nineteenth centuries. The first was a demographic revolution. As early as the 1720s in the Chesapeake colonies of Virginia and Maryland, and by the 1750s in the Carolinas and Georgia, a majority of slaves had been born in the New World and were capable of increasing their numbers by natural reproduction. The second was the plantation revolution. Instead of working on small farms, the enslaved toiled in growing numbers on much larger units, within which they were subject to increasingly strict discipline and regimentation. A third revolution was religious. During the colonial period, many planters resisted the idea of converting slaves to Christianity out of a fear that baptism would change a slave's legal status. By the early nineteenth century, slaveholders increasingly adopted the view that Christianity would make slaves more submissive, orderly, and conscientious and encouraged missionary activities among slaves. Slaves themselves found in Christianity a faith that could give them hope in an oppressive world.

Not only was slavery a dynamic, evolving institution, it was a national, not simply a regional, institution. Prior to the Revolution, slavery could be found in each of the thirteen colonies. Even after the northern states abolished slavery or adopted gradual emancipation plans, slavery remained the cornerstone of the new nation's economy. Not only was the fortune of almost all influential southern families tied up in slavery, but slave-grown cotton was also the nation's chief export, and the manufacture of cotton was a principal foundation of northern economic prosperity. Precisely because the South specialized in the production of cash crops, the North was able to develop lucrative industries that provided services that the slave South needed, including banking, insurance, meat-packing, railroads, shipping and ship-building, and textiles.

Slavery was firmly implanted not only in the nation's economy but also in its religious denominations. Abolitionists quickly discovered that they faced strong theological and institutional barriers in spreading their message through the churches. Most denominations strongly resisted abolitionist efforts to embrace the antislavery cause or declare slaveholders sinners who should be excommunicated. Only a small number of sects, notably the Quakers and the Freewill Baptists, openly condemned slaveholding as a sin. Episcopalian and Roman Catholic bishops barred clergy from participating in antislavery activities, and Methodists bishops convinced local conferences to discipline or expel antislavery preachers and prevented antislavery articles from appearing in Methodist periodicals. Fearful of losing southern financial support, most Bible and missionary societies eschewed antislavery.[1]

It proved impossible to insulate the churches from the escalating controversies over slavery. In 1837, the Presbyterian church divided partly over the issue of slavery. The Methodist and Baptist churches split partly over the slavery issue in 1844 and 1845, and the New School Presbyterians in 1857.[2] The struggle over slavery within the churches carried profound consequences for the future of American religion. It contributed to a deepening gulf between evangelical Protestantism and liberalism that had temporarily been bridged during the antebellum era.[3]

As in the economy and the churches, slavery was securely entrenched in politics. Southern slaveholders exerted a disproportionate influence over national politics from the drafting of the Constitution until the election of Abraham Lincoln. The slave South's political influence rested on several elements, including the Constitution's Three-Fifths clause, which increased the South's representation in the House of Representatives and the Electoral College; the sectional balance of power in the U.S. Senate (despite a free population that was just half that of the North as early as 1812); and the South's overrepresentation on the Supreme Court, where slaveholders comprised eighteen of the first thirty-one justices. Southern slaveholders held such key congressional positions of power as speakers of the House, chairmen of the House Ways and Means Committee, and presidents pro tem of the Senate two-thirds of the time; they accounted for just under 60 percent of all Supreme Court justices; dominated the Democratic Party caucus; and received (relative to the South's free population) twice as many major cabinet and diplomatic appointments as northerners. Especially important was the South's ability to mobilize the support of northern "doughfaces," who sided with the South on divisive sectional issues. Their support was instrumental in the adoption of Indian Removal Act of 1830, the annexation of Texas, enactment of the gag rule, tabling antislavery petitions to Congress, the defeat of the Wilmot Proviso in the U.S. Senate, and passage of the Kansas-Nebraska Act.[4]

Southern dominance of American politics gave rise to the myth of a slave power conspiracy, the notion that a small group of large slaveowners had fomented revolution in Texas and war with Mexico and manipulated American politics to expand the South's slave empire. In his "House Divided" speech in 1858, Abraham Lincoln advanced a particularly influential version of this myth when he asserted that the Compromise of 1850, the Kansas-Nebraska Act, and the Dred Scott decision were part of a concerted plan to make slavery legal in all the states. In its most extreme form, proponents of the slave power conspiracy argued that slaveholders had conspired in the murder of two presidents (William Henry Harrison and Zachary Taylor) and the attempted assassination of three others (Jackson, Pierce, and Buchanan). It seems plausible that fears of the slave power conspiracy and its threat to republican government, rather than concern over the morality of slavery, convinced hundreds of thousands of northerners to turn against slavery.[5]

Even as scholars have underscored slavery's evolution as an institution and its significance in the nation's economy, religion, and politics, attention has also turned ever more intensively to the world of the enslaved. Special emphasis has been placed on African cultural survivals and on acculturation and cultural adaptation; family life under bondage; women's lives within slavery; and modes of accommodation and resistance. A key question is how the slave system was able to function productively when there was an average of just two adult white males on plantations with more than twenty slaves.

During the colonial period, enslaved Africans and African Americans regarded themselves as members of two distinct communities: the plantation unit and the national or ethnic group. National identity was particularly important in funerals, religious rituals, and in rebellions against slavery. During the mid-eighteenth century, as a result of the massive importation of slaves into the American colonies, a more inclusive sense of pan-African identity emerged, evident in the founding of churches and other communal institutions with the word *African* in their name. Certain elements of African cultures were more likely to survive the transit to the colonies than were others. Aesthetic ideals and cosmological assumptions proved to be more persistent than did language or specific religious practices. Cultural blendings and syncretisms were especially evident in naming patterns, music, and cuisine. Nevertheless, distinctive Africanisms were evident in forms of dance, diction, dress, hairstyling, vocabulary, and other elements of expressive culture.[6]

Out of fear that baptism might affect slaves' legal status, efforts to Christianize the slave population were limited before the Great Awakening of the 1730s and 1740s. When growing numbers of enslaved African Americans did begin to embrace Protestantism during the eighteenth century, most adopted forms of revivalistic religion with affinities to religious notions (such as spirit possession) found in West and West Central Africa. Indeed, it seems clear that the lines of influence were not simply one-way. African American preachers, such as Harry Hoosier, were active participants in the spread of evangelical religion. Meanwhile, a significant number of enslaved African Americans did not embrace Protestant Christianity, even during the antebellum period. In short, acculturation was selective and its extent was defined by the enslaved themselves.

Despite a lack of legal sanction for marriage, enslaved African Americans did marry, and most slave marriages lasted, unless broken by sale, until a partner's death. Slave families, however, were much more than havens in a heartless world. Parents transmitted craft skills and even property to their offspring. Children, in turn, contributed to their family's well-being through fishing and hunting and by assisting their parents in work routines. Nevertheless, slave families were highly vulnerable to disruption. About a third of all marriages were broken by sale or transfer of ownership, and over half of all slave children were sold away from their parents during their teen years. On larger plantations, about a third of husbands lived apart from their families on a neighboring unit; on smaller farms, the figure was about two-thirds.[7]

Property ownership was widespread among slaves across the antebellum South, as slaves seized the small opportunities for ownership permitted by their masters. While there was no legal framework to protect or even recognize slaves' property rights, an informal system of acknowledgment recognized by both blacks and whites enabled slaves to mark the boundaries of possession.

Family units within slavery did not fit the nuclear pattern common among whites. Families tended to be more inclusive, diverse, and flexible or permeable in structure. Single-parent families, multiple-generation families, and stepparenting relations were much more common among the enslaved than among whites. Nevertheless, this does not mean that slave families were weak, dysfunctional, or pathologically disorganized. Rather, slave families were highly supportive for their members. Slave families were less isolated from the broader kin group or the community, which was expected to help out whenever a child was separated from a parent. Precisely because enslaved families did not conform to a nuclear definition, many white observers questioned whether slaves had families at all. After the Civil War, there were repeated legal efforts to force former slaves to adopt the father-centered, nuclear patterns found among whites.

In reconstructing slave women's lives, much attention has focused on whether gender differences blurred under slavery, whether matricentric family relations prevailed, and whether there was greater gender equality in slave than in free families. Enveloped in stereotypes—such as the sexless, loyal Mammie or the sexually impure, lusty Jezebel—slave women's lives differed sharply from those of white women. They gave birth earlier (at an average age of nineteen, two years earlier than southern white women) and were much more likely to live in a female-headed family. On two-thirds of small farms and one-third of larger plantations, there was no adult male in a slave family, either because he resided on neighboring plantation or because he was dead, absent, or white. Within individual families, gender roles were defined differently than among whites. Under slavery, women were much more likely to earn an independent income or to independently own property than white women.[8]

Nevertheless, slave women led far more circumscribed lives than did enslaved males, since they had less access to skilled or supervisory jobs, fewer chances to travel outside of individual plantations, and less opportunity to sell their time or to engage in urban occupations, though in many locales, slave women dominated local markets. Enslaved women lived under a dual burden, as both their labor and their sexuality and childbearing capacity were exploited. Girls frequently entered into productive labor even earlier than boys, and, as they grew older, they were expected to sew, weave, cook, clean, and care for children in addition to performing fieldwork.

Motherhood was an especially important aspect of a slave women's identity. Their birth rate was significantly higher than southern white women's; but enslaved mothers suffered an appalling infant and child death rate that was twice that of their southern white counterparts. Sexual abuse was a haunting reality, and it appears in almost every published slave narrative. The WPA oral histories collected in the 1930s indicate that five percent of those interviewed said that they had a white father. Yet within the slave community, the most stable relationships tended to revolve around women. Enslaved women worked in sex-segregated gangs, participated in group activities such as quilting or clothes washing, and, in a hostile environment, were responsible for ensuring children's well-being and the maintenance of communal traditions.

Resistance to slavery took diverse forms, including cultural resistance, acts of obstruction and sabotage, flight, and physical resistance. The essential point that has emerged from recent scholarship is that slavery involved a process of negotiation and that masters did not exercise a monopoly on power. Negotiations took place over such specific matters as food rations, free time and holidays, funerals, religious ceremonies, and garden plots.

While underscoring slavery's hardships and cruelties, and scrutinizing the power dynamics that sustained the institution, recent scholarship has underscored two crucial facts: that enslaved African Americans succeeded in sustaining a culture independent of their owners; and that, while the enslaved constituted a small proportion of the American population, they shaped many aspects of American culture, including American ideals of freedom. As brutal and destructive as the institution of slavery was, slaves were not defenseless victims. Through families, religion, folklore, and music, as well as through more direct forms of resistance, enslaved African Americans resisted the debilitating effects of slavery and created a vital culture supportive of human dignity. Slave religious and cultural traditions played a particularly important role in helping slaves survive the harshness and misery of life under slavery. Many slaves drew on African customs when they buried their dead. Conjurors adapted and blended African religious rites that made use of herbs and supernatural powers. Slaves also perpetuated a rich tradition of West and Central African parables, proverbs, verbal games, and legends. They also retained in their folklore certain central figures. Cunning tricksters, often represented as tortoises, spiders, or rabbits, outwitted their more powerful enemies.

In the realms of art, dance, folklore, language, music, and religion, slaves created a distinctive culture that blended African and European elements into a new synthesis. During the late eighteenth and early nineteenth centuries, many enslaved African Americans embraced Christianity, but they transformed it to meet their own needs. Slave religious beliefs, a mixture of Christianity and African traditions, provided slaves with the patience and hope necessary to endure slavery. Slave religion also upheld a vision of the spiritual equality of all human beings that strengthened slaves' hopes of eventual deliverance from bondage. Spirituals, like "Go Down, Moses," with its refrain of "let my people go," indicate that slaves identified with the Hebrew people, who had overcome oppression and enslavement. Through folklore, slaves also sustained a sense of separate identity and conveyed valuable lessons to their children. Among the most popular folktales were animal trickster stories, like the Brer Rabbit tales, derived from similar African stories, which told of powerless creatures who achieved their will through wit and guile, not power and authority.

In addition, enslaved African Americans exerted a profound influence on white culture, principally on speech, religion, music, and cuisine. The American language is filled with Africanisms. Such words as *bogus, bug, phony, yam, tote, gumbo, jamboree, jazz,* and *funky* all have African roots. Cuisine, too, is heavily influenced by African practices. Deep-fat frying, gumbos, and fricassees stem from West and Central Africa. American music is particularly dependent on African traditions. Sea chanties and yodeling, as well as spirituals and the use of falsetto, were heavily influenced by African traditions. The frame construction of houses; the "call and response" pattern in sermons; the stress on the holy spirit and an emotional conversion experience—these, too, appear to derive at least partly from African customs. Finally, Africans played a critical role in the production of such crops as rice or sweet potatoes that English had not previously encountered.

But slavery's most enduring legacy was to expand and revitalize American ideals of freedom—and to write them in blood. Slaves played a pivotal role in their own liberation. During the first two years of the Civil War, federal officials refused to enlist black soldiers in the Union Army. But, by early 1863, voluntary enlistments had fallen so sharply that the federal government instituted an unpopular military draft and decided to enroll black troops. Indeed, it was the availability of black troops that allowed President Lincoln to resist demands for a negotiated peace that might have retained slavery in the United States.

Altogether, 186,000 black soldiers served in the Union Army and another 29,000 served in the Navy, accounting for nearly 10 percent of all Union forces and 68,178 of the Union dead or missing. Three-fifths of all black troops were former slaves. The active participation of black troops made it inconceivable that African Americans would remain in slavery after the Civil War. Even though

Americans frequently denied or evaded the reality of black participation in the Civil War, Abraham Lincoln's Gettysburg Address would stand as an indelible reminder that American history was a struggle for liberty and equality.

NOTES

1. John R. McKivigan and Mitchell Snay, eds. *Religion and the Antebellum Debate over Slavery* (Athens: University of Georgia Press, 1998), 11.
2. Ibid., 12.
3. Robert P. Forbes, "Slavery and the Evangelical Enlightenment," in ibid., 68.
4. Garry Wills, *"Negro President": Jefferson and the Slave Power* (Boston: Houghton Mifflin, 2003), 5–7; Leonard Richards, *Slave Power: The Free North and Southern Domination, 1780–1860* (Baton Rouge: Louisiana State University Press, 2000), 9, 56–57, 62, 96, 111, 127, 132, 138; Paul Finkelman, *An Imperfect Union: Slavery, Federalism, and Comity* (Chapel Hill: University of North Carolina Press, 1980), 239; Philip H. Burch Jr., *Elites in American History: The Federalist Years to the Civil War* (New York: Holmes and Meier, 1981), 236–37; Sidney H. Aronson, *Status and Kinship in the Higher Civil Service* (Cambridge: Harvard University Press, 1964), 115; Don E. Fehrenbacher, *The Slaveholding Republic* (New York: Oxford University Press, 2001).
5. Richards, *Slave Power*, 2–27; David Brion Davis, *The Slave Power Conspiracy and the Paranoid Style* (Baton Rouge: Louisiana State University Press, 1970), 7–9, 14–21.
6. John Thornton, *Africa and Africans in the Making of the Atlantic World*, 2nd ed. (New York: Cambridge University Press, 1998), 211–34, 262–71; Michael A. Gomez, *Exchanging Our Country Marks: The Transformation of African Identities in the Colonial and Antebellum South* (Chapel Hill: University of North Carolina Press, 1998), 87, 149–53, 245–51, 262–63, 268.
7. Steven Mintz and Susan Kellogg, *Domestic Revolutions: A Social History of American Family Life* (New York: Free Press, 1988), 70.
8. Deborah Gray White, *Ar'n't I a Woman? Female Slaves in the Plantation South*, rev. ed. (New York: Norton, 1999), 29, 47, 75–76, 120–21, 129; Elizabeth Fox-Genovese, *Within the Plantation Household: Black and White Women of the Old South* (Chapel Hill: University of North Carolina Press, 1988), 49–50, 172–73, 177; Stephen C. Crawford, "Quantified Memory" (Ph.D. diss., University of Chicago, 1980), 162, 169–70; Paul D. Escott, *Slavery Remembered: A Record of Twentieth-Century Slave Narratives* (Chapel Hill: University of North Carolina Press, 1979), 43–48.

ORLANDO PATTERSON

The Ancient and Medieval Origins of Modern Freedom

This essay, by the historical sociologist Orlando Patterson, asks how freedom—personal, civic, and political—became one of the most cherished values in the Western world. Freedom, Patterson argues, is not a universally shared value. Nor is a passion for freedom simply a byproduct of the growth of capitalism. Rather, the ideal of freedom developed during antiquity and through the Middle Ages in direct relationship to slavery and other forms of coerced labor. It was not an accident that classical Greece and Rome, the only ancient societies in which slavery became the dominant labor force, generated an awareness of the value of freedom. The very centrality of slavery in these societies encouraged philosophers, dramatists, and others to reflect on the privileges of freedom and to attempt to rationalize the difference between those who were free and those who were not.

Patterson also stresses the point, a highly significant one, that Western ideas about freedom owe much to Christian theology, and he explores the ways in which various subordinated groups interpreted Christian doctrine. With its emphasis on spiritual freedom, its equation of slavery with sin, and its stress on redemption, early Christianity provided a language for criticizing various forms of coercion.

In this essay, I address two closely related problems in the history of freedom. The first is to understand the presence and pervasiveness of freedom in the early modern West. The second is the problem of continuity—the question of the degree to which the freedom of the early modern world related to or, more strongly, was the product of, the preceding medieval and ancient heritage.

The cultural model and practice of freedom preceded the emergence of capitalism by at least two thousand years and was already deeply and inextricably embedded in both the spiritual and secular domains of Western culture in the sixteenth century, when capitalism began its rapid socio-economic gestation. By "the cultural model and practice of freedom" I mean the following.

First, that a distinct body of ideas and beliefs called freedom can be shown to have existed at any given period of Western history from about the middle of the fifth century BC. Further, these ideas and beliefs have a recognizable subjective coherence, by which I mean that they can be shown to be meaningful and cohere hermeneutically.

What exactly are these ideas, and where did they originate? Here I summarize findings from previous work.[1] Freedom, from its first construction in fifth-century Athens, has always been a tripartite complex of beliefs relating to power. It is the experience and idea of power that gives the belief its meaning and coherence. Freedom is, first, the valorization of liberation or release from the power or control of another agent, usually another person, but also an institution or immaterial force. We are free to the degree that we are no longer under the power of another agent. This is the familiar notion of negative freedom, which some modern philosophers have claimed, prescriptively, to be the only real concept of freedom.[2] Whatever the logical consistency of their claims, the sociohistorical record indicates that two other notions of freedom have always coexisted with this fundamental idea.

Freedom, secondly, has always also meant the power to do what one wants, to fulfill one's desires with the minimum of constraint. For most of Western history, this positive view of freedom included the power to do with another person whatever one pleased, including bringing about their enslavement. Only in the nineteenth century was the qualification added that one was positively free to do what one pleased so long as it did no harm to others or restrained their own freedom.[3]

The third notion of freedom is the idea that one is free to the degree that one shares in the public or communal power of one's society. This is the idea of freedom as participation. It was often expressed as belonging or—in more advanced systems—as citizenship. However expressed, the basic idea is that one is free only to the degree that one has the right to share equally in the public life of one's society should one choose to do so. Equality, or equal claims (and responsibilities) in public life, is the central idea here. It achieved its most powerful embodiment in the idea and practice of democracy—the power of the *demos*—but it is important to note that from its very inception in fifth century Greece the idea also embraced the notion of economic equality. Indeed, for most of the sixth century BC in Athens, the formative struggle for democracy was as much a struggle for economic equality as it was for political equality. Nonetheless, by the time it was finally fashioned in the latter half of the fifth century, the emphasis had shifted to political participation and equality.[4]

It cannot be too strongly emphasized that the Greeks saw these three notions as a tripartite whole focused on the notion of power. Thucydides has left us in no doubt about this, most notably in his account of Pericles' funeral oration.[5] From Greek times, however, an important sociological aspect of this belief system emerged. While all the major classes of society embraced all three notions of freedom, the priority given to one or the other notion varied across classes. Thus, for the Greek ruling class freedom as power and control was the decisive ideal. Freedom as release from another's control was obviously important, but it was simply taken for granted. And while democracy was accepted, it was viewed with great ambivalence or even disdain, as the writings of the aristocratic theorists make clear. For the mass of freeborn Greek citizens, the main notion of freedom was democracy, or power sharing. Belonging to a free state and to an exclusive community that was considered superior to others was the fundamental experience of freedom. Again, there can be no doubt that ordinary Greeks viewed freedom as power favorably: everyone wished to be a slavemaster and to experience the honor and respect—the *arete*—that was the hallmark of the aristocrat. Unlike the elite, ordinary Greeks did not simply take negative freedom for granted. The era of serfdom and debt bondage and the early sixth-century struggle against it was singed into their collective memory and independence was a cherished ideal—so much so that even working for others was considered a serious attenuation of freedom.

There was, third, the large class of freedmen and resident aliens for whom simple negative freedom was the fundamental note of the triad of freedom. Precisely because it had been denied to many in their previous existence as slaves, this notion achieved greater salience. Nonetheless, all sought to experience freedom as power, the more successful becoming slavemasters and businessmen. To this group, however, freedom as power sharing was denied. This does not mean that they did not desire or valorize it. Indeed, the very fact that it was the one thing that they could never hope to achieve made it all the more valuable, and an exceptional few went to great lengths to become citizens who could participate in the democratic process.

The Greeks constructed two other important features of the culture of freedom that was to persist down to modern times. One was a tradition of discourse about its meaning and significance. From very early we find contesting views about what freedom really should mean, in which different thinkers emphasize or condemn one or another element of freedom. By the fourth century this tradition was well developed and informed a good deal of philosophical thinking, most notably that of the Stoics.

The other, equally important aspect of the culture of freedom initiated by the Greeks was the distinction between inner and outer freedom, along with contestation about the relative significance of each. Beginning with Plato, we find a tradition that emphasized inner freedom as superior to the outer, physical freedom of the masses.[6] It is striking, however, that among the Greeks and throughout Western history thereafter, we still find the same tripartite idea when applied to the inner dimension of freedom. Thus Plato simply introjected the outer tripartite notion of freedom to the inner domain, with the same emphasis on freedom as power and control that was typical of his aristocratic class. True freedom, he argued, was escape from and power over the inner slave impulses of one's soul. Others were to follow Plato, but as in the outer world, different groups of thinkers emphasized one or another component of the triad. Cynicism, for example, emphasized inner freedom as pure liberation, in stark and mocking contrast with Plato. Stoicism, which was the most advanced form of thought about inner freedom, also shifted the focus from Plato's aristocratic emphases on control to that of freedom as an inner democracy: perfect freedom was achieved when one's own spirit or soul of reason participated harmoniously with the rationality of world-soul.

How, and under what circumstances, did the Greeks construct this unique tripartite cultural value? I, and others, have argued that the unprecedented existence of large-scale slavery in Greece (and later, Rome) was a necessary condition for this invention.[7] Out of the evil of slave society came the complex, morally fraught idea and experience of freedom. But, although a necessary condition, slave society was by no means sufficient for the construction of freedom. As I have argued elsewhere, it was the combination of large-scale slave society and the specific features of Greek society, including contingencies of its history, that resulted in this outcome. Unfortunately, we do not have the space here to summarize this process.[8]

After the Greek era, there were two other major developments in the history of Western freedom before the Middle Ages. Ancient Roman society inherited much of the intellectual discourse on freedom, mainly via Stoicism, and added relatively little to this aspect of the cultural triad. In purely conceptual terms, the idea of freedom as a tripartite cultural complex remained focused on power. Freedom as the untrammeled exercise of power was, if anything, even more pronounced in the Roman mind. A common view has it that the idea of freedom as belonging and power sharing all but vanished from Rome by the period of the late Republic, but this view has been successfully challenged by recent scholars.[9] While the incipient democracy of the early period and the advanced elite democracy of the third century collapsed during the civil struggles of the late Republic, the idea of participative freedom persisted not only among segments of the elite but also among the Plebs. And it has been shown that the latter expressed their desire for some kind of political influence and recognition in their public behavior, which often took violent turns.

In practical terms, however, the most important development during Roman times was the strong emphasis on negative freedom. Indeed, by the period of the Principate the primary legal definition of freedom was the condition of not being a slave. In this regard, there was a vast expansion of the experience and valorization of freedom in the Roman empire, precisely because slavery was so much more extensive there and the freed population and their descendants such a large (some argue a majority) part of the population. Rome also differed from Greece in the granting of citizenship. Indeed, the manumitted slave of a Roman citizen immediately achieved citizenship. While not democracy in the Greek sense, it must be emphasized that the idea of citizenship does entail some form of power sharing in the broader sense of having claims on, or rights in, the politico-legal community.

It was within the context of imperial Rome that the third decisive development in the pre-medieval history of freedom took place: the birth and rise of Christianity. In its formative, post-crucifixion phase, the primitive church was dominated by freedmen and slaves and, through them, the secular notion of freedom as manumission through redemption. (*Redemption* derives from the Latin *redemptio*, meaning "to be purchased from slavery"). Pauline theology, I and others have argued,[10] simply sacralized the already well-established tradition of freedom as liberation from inner slavery, making it the source for the young religion's theological reconception of the significance of Christ's death. In Pauline Christology, Christ's crucifixion was the price paid to purchase mankind out of its inner enslavement, which originated in the Adamic fall from grace. Freedom was redemption through the blood of Christ. What's more, like Plato and the Stoic thinkers before him, Paul introjected the tripartite secular conception of freedom in its entirety. Thus, he celebrated negative freedom in the letter to the Galatians in a manner that would not be witnessed again until nineteenth-century liberal thought. But he also later emphasized the idea of freedom as power, with the most complete freedom being realized only in the absolute power of God. And, in direct analogy with the Roman freedman's idea of freedom as power through surrender to the absolute freedom of the Emperor in the Imperial cult (dominated by freedmen), Paul's letter to the Romans advocated the idea of true freedom as surrender to the absolute freedom of God. Theologians have long agonized over the differences and possible contradictions between the negative freedom celebrated in Galatians and the austere positive freedom advocated in the book of Romans. However, once we understand how closely Paul modeled his view of freedom on the secular experience of the Roman freedman, the seeming difficulties vanish. Freedom as surrender to the imperial genius in the imperial cult did not entail the loss of men's cherished negative freedom; it was, rather, complementary to the latter and ensured its survival. Similarly, the freedom that came to the Christian through surrender to the absolute power of God—that is, through a form of spiritual reenslavement—did not imply an abandonment of the negative freedom guaranteed by the salvific blood of Christ, as espoused by Paul in Galatians. Rather, this lesser but still important note of the chordal triad was guaranteed by surrender to the absolute freedom of God.

Nor did Paul neglect the third, participatory note of freedom. It was he who also introduced the idea of membership in the church as participative sharing in the body of Christ, symbolically represented in the sacrament that would culminate in the Eucharist. What Paul wrote of the incipient church—forming the basis of the fully developed medieval idea of the *Corpus Christi*—could, in fact, pass as an excellent description of a democratic polity. The church was "one body and one Spirit" in which "members are of one another" (Eph. 4:25). Of the sacrament he asks: "the cup of blessing that we bless, is it not a participation in the blood of Christ? The bread that we break, is it not a participation in the body of Christ?" (1 Cor. 10:16). That the participative feasting on the body and blood of Christ was an aspect of freedom was made clear by Paul when, a few verses later in the same letter, he urged Christians to liberate themselves from their dietary prohibitions and not be intimidated by the religious prohibitions of others: "for why should my freedom be determined by someone else's conscience?" (1 Cor. 10:29).

By incorporating the distinctive triadic notion of freedom, Christianity not only became the first, and only, religion predicated on the notion of freedom but also ensured that freedom would remain a central component of medieval Christendom. It was the primary means by which the ancient intellectual heritage of freedom was transmitted to the Middle Ages and modern world. It also facilitated the institutionalization of the ideology of freedom as an autonomous, self-perpetuating cultural complex.

Let us begin our consideration of the progress of freedom during the Middle Ages by recalling that, although freedom was a cultural triad, different classes tended to emphasize one or other notes of the chord. This simple point will explain a great deal about what is otherwise problematic in the medieval experience and conceptions of freedom. I will begin with a consideration of the experience and meaning of freedom for the vast mass of the population.

Between the end of the fourth century and the fourteenth, the mass of rural Europeans experienced an unrelenting oppression, segregable into three phases. Slavery and serfdom were the two primary modes of domination. The two institutions were very closely related; indeed, they mutually constituted each other. As Ste. Croix has observed, slavery remained the model of ultimate exploitation throughout the Middle Ages.[11] There were three distinct periods of exploitation, each characterized by a different mode of interaction between slavery and serfdom.

It has now been well established that slavery, in varying degrees, persisted in Europe right down to the dawn of modern times. Indeed, the modern plantation system was in good part a direct sociocultural survival from the slave plantations of the late medieval and early modern world.[12] The history of medieval slavery is a complex matter. Before the feudal revolution of the late tenth century, it fell and then rose in various parts of Western Europe. In France it had become nearly extinct during the late seventh and early eight centuries. With the renewed barbarian invasions of the eight century, however, we find it on the rise again throughout the latter half of that century. A similar pattern of decline and rise is found in Spain, where it surged and became endemic after the Muslim conquest. Indeed it has even been argued that for much of the Dark Ages Europe was simply an enormous source of slaves for the Islamic states.[13] We know from the Domesday statistics that it was endemic in England in the eleventh century, with slave proportions of over 20 percent in counties such as Cornwall and Gloucestershire, meaning that they approached the levels of many of the slave states of the American South.[14] And recent studies on Scandinavia show that not only was slave trading a major economic activity but that it fed a large domestic market in addition to markets for northern European slave women in the Black Sea area and Mediterranean.[15]

In the broadest terms, there was a downward trajectory in the enslavement of men from about the middle of the eleventh century, resulting in its absence by about the fifteenth century in a few areas such as England, although it persisted in significant numbers in Scandinavia and went through a revival in Mediterranean lands during the late Middle Ages.[16] Nonetheless, it is critical to understand that, after the waning of these long medieval centuries, the cultural and psychological presence of slavery remained very strong throughout Europe, including places such as England where it had petered out. What is more, as Susan Mosher Stuard has cogently argued, there is an important gender dimension to the story of the decline of slavery in Europe. The story, Stuard argues, is really largely about the ending of male slavery. The enslavement of women persisted in large numbers; indeed, it was on the rise in the great urban households of the Mediterranean during the late Middle Ages. And, in sharp contrast to the changing meaning of the Latin term for slave in the Middle Ages—*servus* eventually morphing into *serf*—the ancient Roman word for a female slave—*ancilla*—"showed remarkable stability of meaning."[17] The result was that, not only was the model of classical slavery—the total ownership of one person by another—maintained throughout the Middle Ages, but the meaning of slavery maintained a "powerful resonance" in European culture, even in those areas where the institution had ceased to be of any significance in the agricultural economy.

Serfdom, the predominant system of labor exploitation during the Middle Ages, coevolved with slavery and, indeed, may even be seen as a recombinant form of it. The period between the late fourth and the late tenth centuries witnessed a transition from the large scale latifundic slavery of late antiquity to what may be called a convergent system of serfdom. Most persons were reduced to a condition of semislavery: former slaves "hutted" up to the status of servile tenants, and formerly free persons were reduced to this and other servile conditions.[18]

During this period the most popular ancient Roman notion of freedom—*libertas*—persisted. A free person was anyone who was not a slave. This persistence of Roman legal thought and language in regard to servitude and freedom served the interests of the rude, ruling groups or big men of the period. Even as more and more persons were reduced to servile status, an increasing number were declared to be manumitted, or free men. The persistence of slavery made this possible. It is tempting to imagine that the mass of subjected people now being called free were simply duped, but there is no reason to believe that this was so. The simple, stark, negative condition of not being a slave—however slight the socioeconomic difference from the condition of real slavery—had great psychological weight throughout the early Middle Ages. At the very least the free man had a modicum of honor, reflected in his honor price, while the slave had none that he could claim.

The radical disruption that swept Western Europe from the eleventh century entailed fundamental changes in the social and political life of great parts of the more advanced areas of the continent.[19] By the end of the eleventh century, central authority had largely broken down on the continent and lordship replaced kingship in what had become collections of localized aristocratic fiefdoms. In many areas, most notably Spain and large areas of what became France, lordship was exercised with brutal force. In Catalonia, military power replaced law in a regime of tyranny that verged on anarchy.[20]

A fundamental change took place in the condition and conception of serfdom and freedom during these centuries. Increasingly, power was exercised directly over the person of the peasant rather than through the lord's proprietary holdings. In this regard, the peasant became more like a slave. More like, but not entirely, for in one other crucial respect the peasant became less and less like a slave, namely, in his sense of belonging to the community. He may have been owned by the lord, and under his complete jurisdiction and power, but there was no longer any sense in which he was an outsider. Indeed, he often went to war with his lord in the defense of their country. This development was reinforced by a parallel development in European slavery. The institution not only slowly declined as a means of production, but changed in character. Increasingly, slaves were outsiders from the east of the continent, so much so that the very word for "slave" changed to reflect the Slavic origin of most of the new entrants. From this period, we find in all the European languages the root term *slav* for "slave."[21]

This linguistic shift meant that all ambiguity was removed from the term "serf," with its origin in the Latin term *servus* (slave). In all this, there was a riot of ironies. As we have already noted, the serf acquired a distinct identity at precisely the moment when, in his relation with his lord, he became more like a slave. But another, even more bitter irony was to emerge in connection with this. Because the serf was now clearly not a slave, he could be considered free in the old Roman sense. Nonetheless, it was clear to everyone that this old Latin meaning of the word *free* applied only to serfs. Among the Lords, as we will see shortly, freedom was alive and well; it was captured not in the Roman term *libertas*, which persisted in its old meaning of "someone who is not a slave," but was a concept unto itself and referred to independence and the capacity to exercise power within one's domain.[22]

The ambiguity was thoroughly exploited by the ruling classes, especially in places like Catalonia, as Paul Freedman has demonstrated.[23] A further complication arose from the fact that not all peasants were serfs in the sense of personally belonging to a lord. A significant proportion of persons lived as tenants on the lord's land and were bound to him as long as they did so. In such cases, the land, rather than the tenant, was considered unfree, although this meant that the tenant was in a condition of servitude. The distinction was in some places referred to as serfs of the blood, *neifty*, and serfs of the estate, or tenurial bondsmen.[24]

The notion of unfree land, and of unfree status being derived from one's tenure on such land is a peculiarly medieval concept, and it created enormous complexity in the conception and reality of freedom during the classic middle centuries of the medieval era. We get a better idea of this complexity if we look more closely at England.

The Domesday records indicate that a substantial proportion of the population was listed as free, including the groups referred to as *villani*, *bodarii* and *cottarii*, the sole reason being that they were not slaves. Between 1086 and 1300 the number of free persons, defined in this classic negative sense, greatly increased, becoming the great majority of the population. At the same time, however, they were not considered *liberi homines*, which denoted a conception of freedom restricted to independent persons, especially lords, who, according to one estimate, made up no more than 14 percent of the population. These two notions of what it meant to be free coexisted right up to the late thirteenth century.

A clear trend can be detected in England, as Jean Scammell shows in her study of the development of knighthood and the gentry in England between 1066 and 1300.[25] The idea of freedom as non-slavery became less and less important as the proportion of real slaves declined. True freedom increasingly came to be extended from the condition of not being owned by another to that of not being under the domination of another. To be sure, the classic Roman idea of freedom as not being owned lingered; there is clear evidence for it in the early thirteenth century, and references have been found as late as 1415, but by then it was on the verge of extinction. Before the end of the twelfth century, knighthood was a function rather than a status; it reflected a person who bore arms, supplied by the lords, who themselves controlled all land and arms. Serf-knights were actually quite common during the tenth and eleventh centuries in Western Europe, and as late as 1166 were still being bought and sold like villeins in England. From this lowly status, two broad categories emerged over the course of the twelfth and thirteenth centuries: knights who had no land but were professional soldiers of the lords, lived as military retainers, and were not servile; and knights who owned their own land. The latter group came to form the original gentry of England, and by the thirteenth century a significant number of them owned both their own land and arms. It was from this group that the principle of taxation with consent emerged, for, as King John and other monarchs were to learn, "taxing without consent of people who had the ability to resist tends to be hazardous."[26] This nascent gentry soon became as class conscious and as acquisitive as the great lords from whom they had bought their independence, and, tracing a pattern of behavior that was as old as Europe, as soon as they acquired their negative freedom—liberation from bondage to their former lords, usually through monetary redemption—they sought to exercise their positive freedom by dominating and exploiting the very serf and peasant classes from which they had come. As Scammell wrote: "Having escaped oppression, the gentry had very quickly themselves become oppressors." When John Ball posed his famous question, "When Adam delved and Eve span, who was then a Gentleman?" this was no romantic harking back to an idealized age. It was a straightforward piece of contemporary sociology, and a pertinent political point.[27]

Accompanying this development were three others. One was the tendency to play down the differences between the many status categories found in the eleventh century, a process no doubt hastened by the newly formed knights-cum-gentry, who found too ill-defined a gradation of statuses too easy a means for the diffusion of liberties and, hence, dilution of the value of their own freedom. The second was to consider serfdom as a condition of unfreedom. And the third was the growing inclination of and effort by the landowning class to abandon the distinction between serfdom based on personal bondage and serfdom based on tenancy on unfree land. By 1266, a clear change in nomenclature had taken place: the remnant of the slave population had largely folded into the category of *villani* and the latter were now regularly listed as unfree.

During the thirteenth century, however, the situation became too complex to speak of Western Europe in general terms. Major demographic, economic and political changes were to take place that interacted in different ways over the continent, with different consequences for the evolution of freedom. We will return to these later. But, at this point, let us pause and take stock of other aspects of the culture of freedom as well as its expression in the other major classes of high medieval Europe.

We have so far considered freedom as a socioeconomic condition and status among the mass of European peasants. Most historians of the Middle Ages tend to refer to this freedom as mere status, as if this was of little significance in the real history of freedom.[28] This is a grossly mistaken view; the status component of freedom has always been central to any experience and idea of freedom among the mass of Western peoples. What scholars have in mind when referring to freedom as mere status are questions concerning the existence of freedom as a broader cultural complex. Was it an ideal cherished as a state of being, an inherent quality of the person—and indeed of personhood—rather than simply a description of their status? Such a view implies some recognition of freedom as a more abstract idea. Put another way, were the chronic struggles between landlords and peasants seen by the latter as something that went beyond mere disputes over land dues and labor services to embrace some notion of a principle that had inherent value, so much so that they would forfeit material gains in its favor?

There is, unfortunately, relatively little data on the state of mind of the peasantry during these long centuries, but much can be inferred from their actions and from the dominant institutions to which they were exposed, and both leave us with little doubt that freedom was a major value among the medieval peasantry. From the earliest periods of the Middle Ages, we find a continuation of the old Roman practice of persons in servile conditions going to great lengths to purchase their freedom, even when such transactions made little sense economically. The case of the purchase of urban freedom by burghers is well known; what is still not sufficiently recognized is the fact that rural communal freedoms were collectively purchased to an even greater degree from as early as the eleventh century. Such collectively won freedom should not lead us to the mistaken traditional view that the medieval experience of freedom was largely a corporate one, for all such corporate liberties had immediate implication for the freedom of the individuals who constituted the group, both at the village and urban level.

However, an even better indication of the individualist nature of the pursuit of freedom among ordinary medieval folks is the alacrity with which they grasped offers of purchase of manumission and the enormous material sacrifice usually incurred in such transactions. Among the best documented cases on record are the manumissions in Senoais, France (corresponding to what is now Yonne) during the thirteenth century. In his careful analyses of these records, Jordan has taken us as close as possible to the motivations and mindset of ordinary Europeans and the emotional intensity of their commitment to freedom.[29] Pressed for cash and constrained by customary practices, especially the system of fixed rents, the ecclesiastical lord of the region came up with a novel, if pernicious, way of solving the community's fiscal problem. Upon discovering that a significant number of his tenants were not fulfilling all their obligations as unfree persons, or *homines de corpore* of the abbey, and in some cases were even denying that they ever were unfree, the abbot required them to purchase their manumission at enormous prices. In the struggle that ensued we learn a great deal about the nature of bondage and manumission, and the degree to which freedom was valued both materially and emotionally. We learn, too, how limited was the option of running away to the towns; as Jordan notes, "these were real people trying to survive in the familiar world they knew."[30] In the end, the peasants paid dearly for their freedom. What they achieved was more than simply emancipation from their lord. The dispute had been resolved only after the intervention of the crown. And what this meant was that the freedmen's status had powerful legal and political recognition, was enforceable in the courts, and entailed "a widely agreed upon set of liberties for free people that were enumerated in a whole range of documents besides manumissions."[31]

A remarkable feature of the behavior of the *emancipati* reveals the deep emotional force of freedom. A large number of them, during their bondage, had been named Felis or Felise, which turned out to be names of debasement, similar to the mocking classical names given to American slaves. And, like American ex-slaves, every single one of the manumitted on which records exist abandoned the despised name for new ones which reflected the dignity of their dearly bought freedom. As Jordan in his explicit comparison with the behavior of black American slaves notes: "it is one way to demonstrate that rustics' concern with heirship transcended mere considerations of property and gave an ardor even to the nonviolent achievements of freedom."[32]

Whenever the opportunity to acquire freedom arose, European peasants grasped at it even when the economic consequences were questionable. Take, first, the case of the landless peasant. A great shroud of ignorance hangs over this group. It was clearly much larger than commonly imagined. In the case of thirteenth-century England, it has been estimated by Hatcher that households renting land directly from landlords constituted perhaps as small as a half of all peasant households and no more than 75 percent, of whom at most 60 percent were unfree. "Household holdings by unfree tenure," he concludes, "may well have constituted little more than a third of total households."[33] Most of the remaining two-thirds of households that were free—either de jure or de facto—would have been landless or subtenants.[34]

Another major indication of the enormous value placed on freedom among the rural masses of Europe is the eagerness with which they engaged in the great land reclamation schemes that took place all over Europe between the eleventh and the thirteenth centuries. This was part of a broader transformation of the European agricultural economy that saw the demise of the early manorial system, a change prompted by a combination of demographic growth, the rise of agricultural prices, increased agricultural efficiency, the monetization of services, and the growth of towns. While peasants hoped to improve their economic situation by participating in this reclamation, there can be little doubt that a primary motivation was the greater freedom they gained in these new settlements. Indeed, although less well known today, the rural counterpart of the famous dictum of urban liberation—*Stadtluft macht frei*—may have been more important to peasants of the twelfth and thirteenth centuries: *Rodung macht frei*, or freedom through land clearance.[35] All over Europe, but especially in the regions that are now Holland, Belgium, northern and eastern Germany, southwestern France, and Switzerland, *Rodungsfreiheit* was the motivation for the great waves of land clearance and resettlements, some culminating in autonomous peasant communities and peasant republics such as Dithmarschen—located between the lower Elbe and northern Frisia— that marked the high point of peasant freedom in the history of the West.

No other aspect of medieval life better expressed the peasants' strong valorization of freedom than their long history of resistance to serfdom. Marc Bloch long ago emphasized the fact that peasant revolts were not merely infrequent aberrations but an entrenched feature of medieval life, the equivalent of strikes in modern capitalism.[36] Resistance, however, was not confined to open revolts. Far more frequent, and in the final analysis, more effective, were the many other forms of resistance, ranging from passive forms of disobedience, such as foot-dragging, to flight and theft.[37] Students of medieval peasant revolts are left in no doubt about the "centrality of serfdom in peasant unrest," their deep resentment of it and wish to abolish it.[38] "The desire for freedom," wrote Hilton, "is continuously present in peasant movements."[39]

An interesting feature of medieval peasant resistance was the way in which they molded tradition to their own ends in their pursuit and justification of freedom. In nearly all revolts throughout Europe peasants invariably insisted on an invented golden past with an ancient liberty that they wished to restore.[40] This sense of a "lost freedom" was a powerful motivating force, driving peasants to regain it at great economic costs.[41] Catalonian peasants regarded their servitude as exemption from "bad custom," which "had become the emblem of personal freedom and self-government for municipalities by the early thirteenth century."[42] They deployed both Christian doctrine and invented history in their epic struggle for freedom.[43]

A variant of this notion of lost liberty was the belief that it had been guaranteed by a direct relation to the crown and that its loss had come about as a result of the intervention of lordly feudal power. Thus the pursuit of freedom was allied to the very traditional reverence for the king, especially in England. Dyer's analysis nicely sums up this belief:

> The widespread and persistent recourse to the plea of 'ancient demesne' by tenants who were not technically eligible for the privilege suggest a general belief in the possibility of recovering primeval freedom. Peasants must have been convinced ... that the king had once been everyone's lord, and that

they could reclaim their freedom through a direct relation with the crown. What at first seems to have been a specific and narrow plea for special privileges could be interpreted as a legally presentable argument, behind which lay hopes of universal liberty.[44]

Dyer's last sentence points to another important feature of freedom consciousness among medieval peasants that comes out powerfully in their revolts. It is the fact that it may well have been the peasants of the Middle Ages who made the first *secular* breakthrough to the idea of freedom as a universal principle, and not the intellectuals, urban merchants, or lords—the Ockhams, Magna Carta barons, or rising burghers—favored by historians of both the right and the left.

Two striking features of medieval peasant revolts strongly support this claim. The first is that they were led and largely supported not by the serfs and lowest orders of society but rather by the most prosperous and technically free peasants. This is true of the great peasant revolts of the fourteenth, fifteenth and early sixteenth centuries that were a major element in the decline and passing of serfdom in Western Europe: the bloody revolt in Maritime Flanders between 1323 and 1328; the widespread revolt of the Jacquerie in France in 1358; the great English rising of 1381; the sustained revolt of the Remences in northern Catalonia between 1462 and 1486; and the highly organized and ideologically driven revolt of the German peasants between 1524 and 1525.[45] As was true of the history of many modern strikes, it was precisely when demographic and changing economic factors improved the bargaining power of the peasants, as occurred during this period, that they were most likely to revolt. Brenner states the issue cogently: "It was the logic of the peasant to try to use his apparently improved bargaining position to get his freedom. It was the logic of the landlord to protect his position by reducing the peasants' freedom. . . . It obviously came down to a question of power, indeed of force."[46]

The second remarkable feature of these revolts is the fact that even though they were led by peasants who were already free and even prosperous, their primary demand was nonetheless the abolition of serfdom and freedom for all. Thus, the rebellion of the peasants of Stellinga in Saxony in 841 was essentially a revolt against the imposition of Frankish feudal rule. The long resistance of the Stedingers during the early thirteenth century was primarily a defense of the freedom and independence they had previously gained in administering their own village affairs and cooperative institutions. The same was true of the peasant communities of Dithmarschen who, unlike the Stedingers, successfully resisted the military assaults of the territorial rulers and preserved their political autonomy until well into the sixteenth century. The revolt of the Flemish peasants from 1323 to 1328, which was originally motivated by outrage against the excessive taxation of the judicial authorities, "soon developed into a universal protest of assertive peasant communities who held much more far-reaching goals."[47] "Peasant enthusiasm for freedom" is clearly demonstrated in the demands of the peasant rebels of 1381. Hilton finds it "remarkable that the demand for it should be first on the list of rebel demands when villeinage was economically and socially a good deal less irksome than it had been in the thirteenth century."[48] In like manner, in "both Catalonia and southwestern Germany, the key conflict was over servitude . . . and its attendant indignities."[49] We fully concur, then, with Hilton's conclusion that "the concept of the freeman, owing no obligations, not even deference to an overlord, is one of the most important if intangible legacies of medieval peasants to the modern world."[50]

Thus far, we have seen that peasants in the Middle Ages had a well developed notion of two of the three elements of freedom identified earlier in our discussion of the ancient world. They had a powerful sense of negative freedom as escape from the often abusive power of their overlords. At the same time, freedom was conceived of in positive terms: it meant a degree of economic security, access to non-servile land and the substitution of money payment for corvee; and it entailed the preservation of "good custom" such as the liberties of access to the commons and, especially in England after the twelfth century, the capacity to enter pleas in common courts. Of course, freedom then (as now, in practice) was always relative. Some had more immunity from the lord's coercive power than others. Indeed, for most freedom required a measure of dependence since this was the price paid for the lord's protection; and without the latter there would be no freedom whatsoever. As Bisson observes, "security of possession" was often what mattered.[51]

And what of the third note of freedom—power sharing, or participatory freedom? Clearly, this was the component of freedom that was least experienced by the mass of peasants during the Middle Ages. It is here, however, that we must be most careful not to commit the error of anachronism. If we define power sharing in modern democratic terms, then clearly no such thing existed in the Middle Ages. Nonetheless, one may reasonably make the claim that notions of communal participation and collective power sharing did exist both as an ideal and in practice among the more prosperous of the peasantry in many parts of Europe, especially Germany, during the Middle Ages.[52]

The village commune was generated mainly by the need to act cooperatively in securing rights to the commons against the lords and in meeting the demands of the three-field agricultural system; such cooperative action was also required in making road repairs, draining swamps, and maintaining communal assets such as wells. In many areas, such cooperative and associative activities evolved between the high and late Middle Ages into the village commune, or "the village community as a body politic" having a legal and administrative identity as formalized in a village charter.[53] Especially in the Verdun region of France and the Moselle and Rhineland regions of Germany, it is no exaggeration to refer to these rural communes as quasi-democratic jurisdictions, since the councils of adult males exercised liberties such as the election of their village assemblies, mayors, and magistrates; the passage of village laws; and the management of village budgets. Remarkably, they sometimes even chose their own priests. The elected village head, who administered the affairs of the village, was a precursor of the modern American city manager. Enfranchised villages emerged especially during the high Middle Ages when landlords had to entice their tenants into not leaving for new settlements.[54]

The important point to remember about these communities is that they were primarily motivated by "a desire on the part of the group's members to come together in order to organize and govern themselves," according to Jeannine Quillet; "their social organization is part of the process of redistributing political power."[55] The fact that the freedom recognized was a collective one made these local village polities no less democratic than their modern counterparts. Indeed, a strong philosophical case could be made for the argument that the general will of the community was more accurately followed in such corporately enfranchised bodies. What's more, such a corporatist, participative conception of democratic freedom was closer to the pristine ancient Greek model of the relation between the individual and the polity than is the modern instrumental liberal view, which sees democracy as electoral restraint on a threatening state and downplays civic participation.

The second point to note, however, is that such a conception of the relation between the individual and the polity is not in any way a denial of individual identities or of the individual experience of freedom. In the final analysis, all social entities are made up of individual agents; and individuality and individual rights can be experienced either in a world conceived as a collective entity, in which the social good is paramount, or as an aggregate of self-interested isolates. We can get some idea of what the localized participative democracy of the medieval village was like by looking at the closest historical counterpart to it surviving in the modern West, the remarkable case of the Swiss canton of

Graubünden (historical Raetia), brilliantly analyzed by Benjamin Barber.[56] Independent in some form since 1291, Graubünden is typical of the highly decentralized local democracy found in Switzerland, exercising far more power than that of the federal government—a near perfect analog of the medieval manor and enfranchised villages and towns that existed within the framework of weak monarchies. In sharp contrast to the antistatist individualism of the Western liberal view of freedom, the conception of freedom that we find surviving here "has been understandable only within the context of community." Freedom is guaranteed not by a bill of rights but by direct participation in local cantonal assemblies, which "lend to citizenship a sense of public virtue and collective responsibility unknown to representative, pluralist democracies."[57]

Raetia emerged as a semiautonomous commune in much the same way that similar enfranchised units did during the high Middle Ages. It began as an effort by the feudal nobility to impose jurisdictional control over a cluster of village communities, which unwittingly initiated the politicization of the peasants. Baber argues that in the course of the long contest between "neighborhood autonomy and feudal hegemony," the peasant achieved a level of political consciousness that permitted him to "explicitly relate *his quest for personal autonomy and collective independence* with the securing of such particular political conditions as the absence of arbitrary external constraints, active political participation in his neighborhood, a dynamic consensus both within and between the communes, and a voice in the institutions that affected his life."[58]

Our consideration of the rural commune leads naturally to the next major source of freedom among the nonaristocratic masses of medieval Europe, namely, the urban communes. The role of towns and cities in the evolution of freedom is well known, indeed too well known, because recent research suggests that it has been exaggerated. The impressive growth of towns between the late tenth and the mid-fourteenth centuries was, in fact, part of the same historical process that generated the growth of rural communes and grew out of the same associational structures—guild confraternities, craft cooperatives, and other cooperative organizations. Similar to the rural communes, the motivation for the towns' development was the desire of lords for trade and commerce in or near their domains, and the yearning for freedom and mobility on the part of the members of fraternities and guilds as well as wandering merchants.

While in a few areas of Europe—most notably northern Italy during the thirteenth century—cities became islands of liberty for the merchants and other guildsmen who dominated them, the historical stereotype of medieval urban centers as fountainheads of European liberty must be sharply qualified. In the first place, the degree to which they attained even collective freedom and autonomy varied considerably over the continent. England stood at one extreme, having the least degree of autonomy, followed by France; at the other extreme were the city states of northern Italy.[59] Even where a fair degree of collective liberty was achieved, it was enjoyed at the grace of the local lord in whom ultimate power remained. The limits of urban collective liberty is well illustrated by an incident that took place in twelfth-century Flanders, which for two centuries had acted like an autonomous state although legally held in fief from both the French and German crowns. In 1127 the local count, William Clito, turned up with his retinue at a fair in Lille, spotted one of his runaway serfs, and ordered him arrested and sent back to the fields. The burgesses came to the defense of the serf, overpowered Clito, and chased him out of town, thereby preserving the principle that *Stadtluft macht frei*. It was a shallow victory: Clito returned with a superior army, forced the town into submission, and ordered it to pay him a huge fine for its insolence. Feudal might trumped urban liberty.[60]

A second important qualification is that the collective liberty of the town was realized in individual terms by only a minority of the privileged in what were highly stratified communities. Hohenberg and Lees states the matter bluntly:

> These were not egalitarian communities. Whatever internal peace and order they achieved came at the cost of systematic repression. Although we associate medieval communes with early advances toward freedom and democracy, they were also citadels of blatant privilege and nit-picking interventionism. Moreover, political inequalities increased over time. Similarly, while the air of the city was held to naturalize the rural stranger, cities were typically xenophobic as well as faction-ridden.[61]

Indeed, the three orders of the broader society—clergy, warrior/leader, and worker—were represented in the medieval towns either directly or through surrogates. The third order itself was highly stratified, different guilds varying widely in prestige and power. And, if it is wondered why it was that more serfs did not flee to the celebrated free air of the city, a brief look at the desperate condition of the urban poor provides a ready answer. Available quantitative data suggest "a lurid picture of golden affluence juxtaposed to abject poverty."[62] Ironically, the very success of the towns led to sharp class divisions within them, sometimes resulting in proto-proletarian revolts and the eventual alliance between the successful merchants and the rural lords from whom their ancestors had bought or wrested their autonomy and liberty.

The importance of towns for our argument is that they were another major site for the valorization and perpetuation of the value of freedom. That the majority of persons did not experience much liberty is beside the point—the fact that the great majority of Americans are not capitalists does not vitiate the claim that America is the quintessential capitalist society and that capitalism is strongly valued and idealized by nearly all Americans. While town residents never completely removed seigneurial power, and in most cases had to contend with only a share of freedom, they nonetheless stood in the midst of the medieval world, alongside their rural counterparts as visible islands of enfranchisement in the ocean of seigneurial domination. And, like the rural communes, towns were living demonstrations of the fact that the lords could not rule by naked force alone, that their own self-interests required them to compromise by granting the carrot that people most wanted and for which they would pay dearly: freedom.

Let us turn, finally, to the most powerful order of medieval society, the aristocrats, and to their notion of liberty. This is the easiest of our tasks, since a great deal has been written on the subject. There can be no doubt now that medieval aristocrats had a highly developed sense of freedom, which bore striking parallels to ancient elite views (though with distinctive medieval coloring) and formed the basis of the early modern elite conception of freedom that was the ideological engine of the agrarian capitalist revolution. I have elsewhere referred to the aristocratic view of freedom as sovereignal liberty. Like all other conceptions of freedom it was tripartite in nature: freedom meant immunity from the power of a superior; the capacity to exercise power within one's domain; and, in regard to levels of political community higher than one's domain, the insistence on some degree of power sharing and representation.

By the twelfth century the free man—the *liber homo*—was one who had a concrete set of negative liberties and positive privileges. He was guaranteed by oath and franchise immunity by the higher authority from interference in his claims to his land and other possessions. In the feudal context, this guarantee was the reciprocal of an oath of loyalty and military support. Such reciprocal dependence was in no way considered a mark of unfreedom or a restraint on individuality, and it ran through the entire vertical hierarchy of lordship from king to minor knight.[63] The Germanic (and feudal) warrior insisted on his freedom from restraint; and the personal character of feudal ties meant that individual claims could be based upon the specific sworn obligation of lord and man to uphold each other's rights (*iura*), notably with respect to person and property. The feudal oath, having defined such obligations, implied that "a man walks freely provided he observes the common law."[64]

The most ancient and fundamental notion in the aristocratic view of liberty was "tenurial immunity."[65] Originally, lordly power and liberty focused on the land over which the lord was allowed to claim ownership. Indeed, during this earlier period, reference was made as frequently to the freedom of the land as to the freedom of the individual. A crucial change eventually emerged—starting in the eleventh century—in which the notion of *dominium*, now identified with lordship, shifted from the things or persons possessed to "the person in whom this power or authority inheres."[66] The idea of freedom thus became focused on the "individual citizen in his proper sphere of life," holding the charter of immunity and his own inviolability.[67] Harding argues that this development marked the shift of the conception of liberty from a concrete set of privileges to a more abstract and individualistic idea. This may have been true for the aristocrats and the intellectuals who wrote for and about them. However, I wholly reject Harding's suggestion that this was the defining or only transition to the notion of freedom as a quality of the individual. As we have seen, the ordinary medieval peasant and his urban counterpart came independently to his critical intellectual transition in the history of freedom.

Like the commoners who emphasized political participation and control as a fundamental aspect of their freedom in the commune, the aristocratic classes all over Europe came to see such power sharing as a fundamental element of the chord of freedom. Of course, this was only relevant and meaningful where there was a hierarchy of communal powers. In those parts of Europe where all forms of broader state authority had effectively collapsed, especially in what are now Catalon and Germany during the eleventh and twelfth centuries, the local manorial power of the lord was the only governmental power, and his *liberalis potestas* meant the free exercise of absolute power over all those who resided within his domain.[68]

Where lordly power was nested in broader political entities the issue of representation and participation inevitably became important aspects of aristocratic liberty. The greater the relative strength of the crown, the more important this aspect of liberty became. Hence, it was precisely in England, with its precocious post-conquest royal power, that representation became salient. Interestingly, feudalism in such contexts, by emphasizing mutual consent, promoted the idea that there were constraints on the power of the sovereign, namely, his sworn obligations to his lordly vassals; and it also suggested the principle that government was based on contract.[69] It is in this context that we must interpret the various charters between king and aristocrats, the most celebrated of which is Magna Carta. It should be made absolutely clear at once that nothing in these struggles over representation and taxation implied any notion of popular sovereignty. The political community was exclusively confined to the king and his aristocratic subjects, and the liberties won were theirs alone. The popular Anglo-American view that Magna Carta began a process that culminated in the revolutionary principle of parliamentary sovereignty is pure historiographic mythology.[70]

Parliaments emerged in nearly all the kingdoms and principalities of Europe from the late thirteenth century. Invariably, these legislative bodies resulted from the needs of the rulers for money, administrative support, and advice. "War," of course, "was the compulsive urgency behind administrative experiment".[71] Inevitably, maintaining a parliament came to be seen by the aristocrats as a right, especially when the process was accompanied by requests for tax revenues.[72] Parliaments were also a means by which kings could keep abreast of the ways in which the liberties they had granted were working in practice.[73] A distinctive feature of the late medieval English parliament was its bicameral nature and the relatively large number of administrative chores it was required to perform. Even so, contrary to Whig historiography, there is no evidence of any ideology of constitutionalism in the late medieval parliament, and certainly nothing approaching parliamentary sovereignty before the seventeenth century. As McKenna baldly put it: "to the question, 'Who ruled medieval England?' the answer still remained: the king."[74] In the unique case of Britain, what triumphed in the end was "administrative convenience" and the advantage it provided to those burdened with it.[75]

While there was little or no continuity in the parliamentary structures and ideologies between the high Middle Ages and what were to emerge much later in Europe, fundamental principles were established which later parliaments and freedom fighters could use both as bases for further demands and as legitimizing points of reference. For Coke in the seventeenth century, as well as for Blackstone and others seeking, in later centuries, continuity in English laws relating to freedom, Magna Carta was transformed into a "sacred text." As Holt cautions, however: "For the modern historian it is a statement of liberties rather than an assertion of liberty; a privilege which was devised mainly in the interests of the aristocracy, and which was applicable at the widest to the 'free man'—to a class which formed a small proportion of the population of thirteenth-century England."[76]

Nonetheless, we should be careful not to be too skeptical in our interpretation of the historical continuity—as distinct from the invented, retrospective continuity—of such achievement of privileges. As Holt himself later goes on to point out: "In the long run the sale of privilege whetted and even created an appetite for liberties. Men came to think that what they obtained by purchase should be theirs by right, *and that what some could buy should be equally available to all.*"⁷⁷

We have seen repeatedly an underlying tendency to transform purchased liberties and privileges into inherent rights among aristocrats, a tendency paralleled among the peasants with their claims of ancient "good custom." We find also a closely related tendency to believe that rights acquired should be available to all, or at least to all members of one's group. Again, this is even more true of peasants than of aristocrats; recall the remarkable insistence on the abolition of serfdom among peasant leaders who were already several generations removed from serfdom, or the call for freedom for all among peasant rebels. A similar tendency could be found in regard to urban dwellers and even to guilds. Confraternities began as exclusive organizations jealous of their "eternal brotherhood"; but from very early we find jurists insisting that their membership should be open and voluntary, "thus affirming in embryonic form the principle freedom of association."⁷⁸ Underlying these two tendencies was the thrust—clearly discernable over the course of medieval history—toward a generalized conception of liberty, one that transcended the particular liberties and privileges over which people fought in specific contexts.

We must now ask what it was that prompted these tendencies. After all, serfs and peasants revolted all over the world, and aristocrats, similarly, struggled with their rulers. Yet, only in the West do we find this extraordinary insistence on the interpretation of such struggles within a distinctive cultural and ideological frame, that frame being the thing called freedom. What was behind this cultural propensity?

The answer is simple and incontrovertible: the religion that dominated the civilization during these long centuries. Christianity was the great intellectual, spiritual and organizational source of the culture of freedom in the Middle Ages, as it was to remain in early modern Europe. It was the institutional repository of ancient views of freedom and, as such, the channel of continuity with the ancient tradition of freedom. But it also influenced the course of freedom in other ways related to the medieval context: in its own organization, and in its political and social relation to the secular world.

It is all too easy to by cynical—and mainly wrong—about the role of Christianity in the medieval history of freedom. There is no doubt that the religion worked, both doctrinally and organizationally, as a close ally of the ruling classes throughout the Middle Ages. Pauline theology, especially the letter to the Romans, and the writings of the church fathers, especially Augustine, were reinterpreted in full support of the hierarchical ordering of medieval society. Even the heavenly society of Augustine—the most powerful influence on medieval doctrinal thought—was an organic hierarchy with different ranks of saints in which "the less rewarded will be linked in perfect peace with the more highly favored." As Van Engen recently observed, churchmen "often turned forms of social domination into spiritual virtues, depicting peasants as people redeemed by their work and their submission to lordship." Power, or rather, powers, were central to this worldview, and the lords who exercised them were implored to exercise their lordly freedom as "ministers of God."[79] What's more, the church's own organizational structure and behavior was a model of the hierarchical distribution of power, both within its ranks and in its secular dealings with its peasants, serfs, and slaves.

But there was another side to all this. In doctrinal terms, it must always be remembered that Christianity was, fundamentally, a religion of freedom. Its core idea was redemption—spiritual freedom—through the salvific blood of Christ. As we have already mentioned, this soteria was the foundation of Paul's introjection of the tripartite secular view of freedom as the exercise of absolute power, the release from power and the participation in power. Medieval churchmen could, and did, argue that the exercise of lordly power was a form of freedom. The ultimate model of such freedom was the power of God, in submission to which the Christian partook of this divine freedom.

Viewed within the broader context of the entire Western history of freedom, there was nothing in the least abhorrent about the idea of lordly power as an element of freedom. It is an idea that would have been readily understood by elite Greeks and Romans;[80] and, although in much disguised form, the notion of freedom as the power to do as one pleases, including power over others, is alive and well today, although the means by which one legitimately does so requires indirect domination through the control of property or powerful corporations.

Medieval churchmen knew very well that lordly freedom, to be anything other than gross domination, had to be placed within the trinitarian structure of the other two notes of the chord of freedom—the negative note of redemption from bondage, and the egalitarian note of participation in a collective body. Here is where the church not so much failed as fudged or fell into internal dispute. Conservative churchmen were fearful of any such secular projection of the other two elements of the freedom trinity. Redemption was to be wholly a spiritual matter; and the equality before God was to be experienced entirely in the corporate body of Christ. Indeed, those who dominated church doctrine for these long centuries were so fearful of the secular implications of these two notes of the chord of freedom that every effort was made to keep Christian doctrine, and the Gospels themselves, from the masses, primarily through the use of Latin.

It did not quite work. At the theological level, there was always a minority of churchmen who rejected the hegemonic view of the Christian doctrine of freedom and insisted on expressing it in its entirety, in both spiritual and secular forms. Among more moderate churchmen, the Christian egalitarian tradition and the component of Pauline doctrine that extolled negative freedom—redemption—in spirit and emancipation from bondage in the temporal domain—both powerfully celebrated in the Letter to the Galatians—was expressed in several ways throughout the Middle Ages.

One was the role of the church in curbing the savagery and oppression that emerged over continental Europe with the collapse of all central authority and the rise of feudal anarchy between the eleventh and twelfth centuries.[81] Using its spiritual authority, the church led a mass movement, the Peace of God, against what J. P. Polly calls the "savage harmony of aristocratic liberty."[82] There was enormous gratitude and enthusiasm among the masses for the church's role in bringing them relief from afflictive lordship exercising absolute freedom unrestrained by any recognition of public order and participation or of the negative rights of others (protecting them from abuse).

Even more important, though less easily documented, was the achievement of moderates in regard to the moral legitimacy of serfdom. Church authorities had no option but to accept the institution; indeed, the church was in many places among the largest owners of serfs or other persons in unfree tenancy. It would be a mistake, however, to conclude from this that serfdom was fully legitimized or considered morally acceptable. While the great leaders of the church—most of whom came from the aristocratic classes—may have fully rationalized serfdom, the situation was quite different among many of the lowly parish priests or the members of the monastic orders. These monasteries were located in rural areas within the heart of the peasantry, and it is they and their attitudes and organizations that were in most direct contact with the peasants and serfs. Many monks were also no more than a generation removed from the peasantry. It is these monks who over the course of the Middle Ages, by their teachings and their own lifestyles, came to sanctify work.[83]

A far more radical Christian tradition existed which both contested the religious legitimization of isolated aristocratic liberty and emphasized the egalitarian teachings of the Gospels. Occasionally, such contestation could be found even among the learned, who, on the whole, supported lordly power and freedom. Philippe Buc has shown that there was a "reformist milieu" in northern France during the twelfth century that strongly contested the legitimization of aristocratic freedom in a "politicized debate, in which influential commentators of the Bible reactivated the negative face of *potestas* and *dominatio*.[84] Potentially radical too was the Church's doctrine of natural law, the "*Ius Naturale*," and its relation to the law of nations, the "*Ius Gentium*," which the church inherited from ancient Roman legal thought, especially Stoicism. Natural law was inherent in human nature and deducible through pure reason. It was rarely achieved, being approximated, instead, by the law of nations.

The history of the church's discourse on natural law was a critical factor in the history of both medieval and modern freedom. It was left to rebel peasants and their leaders, however, to draw out the most radical versions of the Christian gospel of freedom. All students of peasant revolts during the Middle Ages have found that a radical version of Christianity directly informed and inspired their movements.[85] One remarkable document that accompanied the demands of the *Remences* of the dioceses of Old Catalonia in 1450 makes clear not only the centrality of Christian doctrine in the peasants' demand for the abolition of bad custom, but the awareness among them of the doctrine of the *Ius Naturale* and of the radical identification of it with the law of God. The document also very nicely demonstrated how the relation between *Ius Naturale* and *Ius Gentium* could be given a radical interpretation. Freedman writes:

> The notion that the Gospel confers rights of personal liberty on Christian believers . . . would be found elsewhere in late medieval Europe. What was unusual in this record is its response to arguments derived from history that sought to justify seigneurial privileges over a subjected rural population. . . . The prologue begins by contrasting divine grace with human law. Christ's sacrifice freed humanity from servitude and restored to fallen mankind its original liberty. Human beings, by nature free, had been degraded by the law of nations in historical time.[86]

One strongly suspects that the anonymous author was a renegade priest. As Hilton pointed out, a large number of peasant revolts were led by such members of the lesser clergy.[87] Hilton cites a late medieval clause which epitomized the Christian foundation of the ideology of revolt among peasants throughout medieval Europe: "We pray that all bonde men be mad ffre [i.e., made free] for god made all ffre wi his precious blode sheddying."[88]

What all this indicates is that, in spite of the effort of church leaders to keep the Gospel a secret from them, peasants throughout medieval Europe were fully aware of its contents and were disabused of lordly attempts to impose a conservative interpretation of the Gospel on them. How did they gain access to such knowledge? I think medievalists have made far too much of this issue. A debate of several decades continues over the question of whether, as revisionists believe, the religion of the mass of peasants during the Middle Ages was largely a jumble of folk beliefs concerning relics, pilgrims, saints, and either semi-pagan superstitions or safe homilies handed down to them by semiliterate parish priests; or whether, as we have indicated above, and as was traditionally thought, they were knowledgeable about Christian doctrine.[89] Van Engen brilliantly debunks the revisionists as well as scholars such as the Brookes who have been too intimidated by them.[90]

There were two other important ways in which the medieval church powerfully influenced the history of freedom. One was its insistence on and eventual triumph in establishing the principle of the duality of powers—the view that there were two powers, one temporal and the other spiritual; and that they were independent of each other and supreme in their own sphere. Twelfth-century political theory was largely preoccupied with the nature of the relation between these two spheres, or "swords," as they called them.[91] In practice, dualism could be, and was interpreted in different ways. Watts argues that there were two competing models: hierocracy, the claim that the spiritual was dominant and had greater authority; and caesaropapism, the view that the king, as vicar of God, was invested with more power. There was, of course the model of complete equality and independence—dualism—which, as one would expect, rarely operated in practice.[92]

The theory and practice of dual powers was extremely unusual in human history. Indeed, it may have been unique to Christendom, and it had vast implications for the history of freedom in the West. In the first place, it established the principle of divided authority and the idea that there were limits on the power of secular rulers. The church exercised moral and spiritual power, which could be as powerful as great armies, and it did not hesitate to use it when necessary. Second, there inevitably arose conflicts between the secular and spiritual powers, since each deeply believed that it was, or ought to be, superior. The greatest such controversy, of course, was the investiture crisis of the late eleventh and early twelfth centuries.

What is significant is the fact that the church from the very earliest times, expressed its defense of its power in terms of freedom: the *libertas ecclesiae*. It was a conception of freedom that most completely expressed the notion of freedom as absolute power. Because there was no limitation on the absolute freedom of God, and given that the church was founded by Christ, through whom it shared God's absolute freedom, there could be no secular authority that had the right to challenge its liberty.[93] The church's tenacious defense of its liberty had two important consequences for the temporal order. As Tierney and others have pointed out, the church's insistence on its freedom encouraged the development of free institutions in the temporal world.[94] In becoming a separate estate within the medieval kingdoms "with its own rights and privileges," the church offered a model to other estates claiming similar rights and charters of freedom. This was true not only of the nobility but sometimes also the peasants, the most striking example of which was the way in which the investiture crisis immediately encouraged dissent, not only among the German nobility aligned against Henry IV but among the mobilized masses who demanded a new relationship with their lords in what Leyser calls "the first religious mass movement in Europe."[95]

Finally, and most importantly, the church, in defending its freedom and in developing its own ideas about church governance and canonical jurisprudence, created a rich vocabulary of concepts that were eventually adapted by secular thinkers for both radical and conservative ends. Tierney considers this to be the most important contribution of the Church toward the development of modern freedom.[96] Later theorists of divine rights of kings found an abundant harvest of terms in the canon lawyers' many discourses on *plenitudo potestatis* (fullness of power) and *libera potestas* (unlimited power).[97] However, the canonists also explored the constitutional limitations on the pope's exalted power. The idea that there was an "unwritten constitution of the church, the *status ecclesiae*, and the liability of the pope to err" proved potential grist for the mill of later constitutional theorists.[98]

It is important to point out that all aspects of church doctrine, not just the canonists discourses on church governance, were to influence later political thought. As Ernst Kantorowicz brilliantly demonstrated years ago, European political thought, including every idea about freedom worth preserving, began as political theology "hedged in by the general framework of liturgical language and theological thought." Theories of kingship were often no more than secularized Christologies. What's more, this tradition of borrowing wholesale from church discourse did not end with the late Middle Ages. There was a "crypto-theological" quality to almost all European political thought right through to the end of the seventeenth century.[99]

And in no thinker was this tradition of secularized theology more evident than in John Locke, whose writings are generally considered the foundation of the modern liberal doctrine of freedom. The traditional views of Locke as the theorist of agrarian capitalism and the rising bourgeoisie, or of the Glorious Revolution and the newly emerging order, are no longer tenable. What modern analysts have come to recognize is that Locke was a profoundly religious man, and the key to understanding his doctrine of freedom is appreciating where and how it fits into his religious worldview.[100] Locke's doctrine of freedom is, in many ways, the last great political theology of the Middle Ages, even as it stands as one of the greatest founts of modern contractarian theories of freedom.

This reinterpretation of Locke is consistent with the reinterpretation of seventeenth-century British history generally as a period moved primarily by religious forces—theological, intellectual, and sociopolitical.[101] The English Civil War, for example, while profoundly important for the history of liberty, can no longer be seen as the agent of nascent bourgeois capitalists. It was, in all important respects, a religiously inspired revolution that opened the way not for the bourgeoisie—their moment was still over a century away—but for the entrepreneurial section of the British aristocracy, whose push toward a radical restructuring of the British economy was a natural outcome of developments that go back to the late Middle Ages.[102] Agrarian capitalism was the joint product of the British aristocracy, in pursuit of new ways of exercising their sovereignal power and liberty, and of the British masses, whose eager embrace of the widened freedom offered by post-plague Britain resulted in their being hoisted by their own petard. The Reformation, and the emotional, intellectual, and political ferment it unleashed, was the social opening that allowed the British aristocracy to take the lead in fashioning the agrarian capitalism of the eighteenth century.

There was nothing in the conceptions or practices of medieval freedom that prevented its adaptation to the modern capitalist world. A. J. Carlyle demonstrated long ago that there were striking continuities between medieval and modern conceptions of freedom.[103] But what about the practice of liberty? Was there a necessary affinity between capitalism and the atomistic individualism that was associated with it during the heyday of classical liberalism in the nineteenth century? Is there a necessary affinity between capitalism and the atomistic individualism associated with it in the Anglo-American world? The answer is an emphatic no. Capitalism is a promiscuous consort. Any form of freedom can be wedded to it, from the most selfishly atomistic to the communitarian; but it just as easily embraces every vile trick of tyrants, as long as markets remain open and contracts are fulfilled. There is every reason to believe that the impoverished rendition of freedom that reached its apogee during the nineteenth century—and threatens to rear its head again in contemporary America—was an historical contingency, no more required by capitalism than is Chinese communism or Pinochet-style tyranny.

Many modernist theorists explain the rise of modern freedom as a consequence of the development of capitalism. There is, I have argued, no necessary relationship between capitalism and freedom. Freedom emerged in the West over twenty-two hundred years before the seventeenth century. It remained one of the great and pivotal continuities in the civilization. There is nothing in Pericles' detailed specification and celebration of it that the man on the Clapham omnibus or the Boston MBTA would not readily recognize and applaud. A major reason for its continuity, I have argued, was the combination of structural factors that favored its perpetuation and the religion of Christianity, which provided the institutional means by which ancient thought about it was continued but also fashioned and valorized it in numerous ways during the long centuries of the Middle Ages—in its theology and jurisprudential writings, in its teachings, in its organization and in its monumental struggles to preserve its own collective liberty.

We have seen that, in spite of its corporatist structures, there were nonetheless "powerful forces making for the dignity, liberty, and rights of the individual."[104] The individual, to be sure, found himself, his identity, and his purpose not against but with the group; yet he was no less an individualist for that. By the fourteenth century, Europe had moved toward a generalized conception of liberty as a quality of the individual, something that all desire and have a right to. One finds this general concept of a universal liberty in many areas, but nowhere is it more conspicuous than in the liberty poems and fables that were so popular during the high Middle Ages. In numerous manuscripts from the period, for example, we find the ancient moral of the wolf and the bandog—in which the question is posed whether it is better to be a well fed bandog or a free, if hard-pressed wolf—extended to include distichs reflecting an intense idealization, and generalized notion of, freedom. Some six centuries before either Patrick Henry or the African American spiritual, Walter of England, the twelfth-century archbishop of Palermo, issued a collection of fables concerning liberty that became wildly popular all over Western Europe. A common motif was that "Liberty is a resplendent and invaluable thing, by no price can it be divided; servitude generally is called the image of death."[105] And in another:

> A Free beggar is richer than a wealthy serf. The serf does not own either himself or his property, whereas a free man does. Liberty, the eminently sweet good, contains all other goods; if that is not added, I cannot relish the food. Liberty is the food of the soul and its true enjoyment; whoever is rich in that cannot be richer. I shall not sell what is mine for such infamous advantage; who sells his wealth, makes himself poor.[106]

Could there be any more exquisite celebration of the ethos of possessive individualism than these lines from the twelfth century?

NOTES

1 Orlando Patterson, *Slavery and Social Death* (Cambridge: Harvard University Press, 1982); Patterson, *Freedom in the Making of Western Culture* (New York: Basic Books, 1991).
2 Maurice Cranston, *Freedom* (New York: Basic Books, 1967).
3 John Stuart Mill, *On Freedom* (New Haven: Yale University Press, 2003).
4 Robin Osborne, *Demos: The Discovery of Classical Attika* (New York: Cambridge University Press, 1985); Martin Ostwald, *From Popular Sovereignty to Sovereignty of Law* (Berkeley: University of California Press, 1986); Josia Ober, *Mass and Elite in Democratic Athens* (Princeton: Princeton University Press, 1981); Patterson, *Freedom in the Making of Western Culture*, chap. 4.
5 Thucydides, *History of the Peloponnesian War*, trans. Rex Warner (New York: Penguin Books, 1954), 34–65.
6 Plato, *Republic*, trans. H. D. P. Lee (Harmondsworth: Penguin, 1955), 443 c–e, 477d, 486, d–e; Gregory Vlastos, "Slavery in Plato's Thought," in *Slavery in Classical Antiquity*, ed. M. I. Finley (Cambridge: W. Heffer, 1960); Patterson, *Freedom in the Making of Western Culture*, chap. 10.
7 M. I. Finley, "Was Greek Civilization Based on Slave Labor?," in *Economy and Society in Ancient Greece* (London: Chatto and Windus, 1981); Patterson, *Freedom in the Making of Western Culture*, part 2; Kurt Raaflaub, "Democracy, Oligarchy, and the Concept of the 'Free Citizen' in Late Fifth-Century Athens," *Political Theory* 11 (1983): 517–44; Max Pohlenz, *Freedom in Greek Life and Thought* (Dordrecht: D. Riedel, 1966).
8 See Patterson, *Freedom in the Making of Western Culture*.
9 Fergus Millar, "The Political Character of the Classical Roman Republic, 200–151 B.C.," *Journal of Roman Studies* 74 (1984): 1–19; J. A. North, "Democratic Politics in Republican Rome," *Past and Present* 126 (1990): 3–21.
10 Patterson, *Freedom in the Making of Western Culture*, chap. 19.
11 G. E. M. de Ste. Croix, *Class Struggle in the Ancient Greek World* (London: Duckworth, 1981), 259.

12 Charles Verlinden, *The Beginnings of Modern Colonization* (Ithaca: Cornell University Press, 1970); William Phillips, *Slavery from Roman Times to the Early Transatlantic Trade* (Minneapolis: University of Minnesota Press, 1985); Pierre Bonnassie, *From Slavery to Feudalism in South-Western Europe* (Cambridge: Cambridge University Press, 1991); Pierre Dockes, *Medieval Slavery and Liberation*, trans. Arthur Goldhammer (London: Methuen, 1982).

13 Michael McCormick, "New Light on the Dark Ages," *Past and Present* 177 (2002): 17–54.

14 Frederic William Maitland, *The Domesday Book and Beyond* (Cambridge: University Press, 1897).

15 Ruth M. Karras, *Slavery and Society in Medieval Scandinavia* (New Haven: Yale University Press, 1988); Peter Foote and David Wilson, *The Viking Achievement* (London: Sidgwick and Jackson, 1970).

16 Marc Bloch, *Slavery and Serfdom in the Middle Ages* (Berkeley: University of California Press, 1975); Bonnassie, *From Slavery to Feudalism in South-Western Europe*; Karras, *Slavery and Society in Medieval Scandinavia*.

17 Susan M. Stuard, "Ancillary Evidence for the Decline of Medieval Slavery," *Past and Present* 149 (1995): 7.

18 Bloch, *Slavery and Serfdom in the Middle Ages*; Wendy Davies, "On Servile Status in the Early Middle Ages," in *Serfdom and Slavery*, ed. M. L. Bush (London: Longman, 1996), 225–46; Pierre Riche, *Daily Life in the World of Charlemagne*, trans. Jo-Ann McNamara (Philadelphia: University Pennsylvania Press, 1988).

19 Georges Duby, *The Three Orders: Feudal Society Imagined* (Chicago: University of Chicago Press, 1982); Thomas Bisson, "The Feudal Revolution," *Past and Present* 142 (1994): 6–42.

20 Bisson, "Feudal Revolution"; Bisson, *Tormented Voices: Power, Crisis, and Humanity in Rural Catalonia, 1140–1200* (Cambridge: Harvard University Press, 1998); Paul Freedman, *The Origin of Peasant Servitude in Medieval Catalonia* (Cambridge: Cambridge University Press, 1991).

21 M. I. Finley, *Ancient Slavery and Modern Ideology*, ed. Brent Shaw (Princeton: Markus Wiener Publishers, 1998), 124–26, 146–48; Bloch, *Slavery and Serfdom in the Middle Ages*, 124–28.

22 John Hatcher, "English Serfdom and Villeinage: Toward Reassessment," *Past and Present* 90 (1981): 28–29; Davies, "On Servile Status in the Early Middle Ages," 228.

23 Freedman, *Origin of Peasant Servitude in Medieval Catalonia*, 209.

24 M. L. Bush, "Serfdom in Medieval and Modern Europe: A Comparison," in Bush, ed., *Serfdom and Slavery*, 200–201; Harding, "Political Liberty in the Middle Ages"; Jean Scammel, "The Formation of English Social Structure: Freedom, Knights, and Gentry, 1066–1300," *Speculum* 68 (1993): 525–27.

25 Scammel, "Formation of English Social Structure."

26 Ibid.

27 Ibid., 618.

28 Harding, "Political Liberty in the Middle Ages," 423.
29 William Chester Jordan, From Servitude to Freedom: Manumission in the Senonais in the Thirteenth Century (Philadelphia: University of Pennsylvania Press, 1986).
30 Jordan, From Servitude to Freedom, 57.
31 Ibid., 56.
32 Ibid., 96.
33 Hatcher, "English Serfdom and Villeinage," 7.
34 Robert Brenner, "Agrarian Class Structure and Economic Development in Pre-Industrial Europe," in The Brenner Debate: Agrarian Class Structure and Economic Development in Preindustrial Europe, ed. T. H. Aston and C. H. E. Philpin (Cambridge: Cambridge University Press, 1985), 10–63.
35 Werner Rösener, Bauern im Mittelalter (Munich: C. H. Beck, 1985), 227–35.
36 Marc Bloch, French Rural History, trans. J. Sondheimer (Berkeley: University of California Press, 1966), 170.
37 Bush, "Serfdom in Medieval and Modern Europe," 209; Hatcher, "English Serfdom and Villeinage," 32.
38 Freedman, "The German and Catalon Peasant Revolts," American Historical Review 98 (1993): 44.
39 R. H. Hilton, Bond Men Made Free: Medieval Peasant Movements and the English Rising of 1381 (London: Temple Smith, 1973).
40 Ibid., 114.
41 Christopher Dyer, "Memories of Freedom: Attitudes Towards Serfdom in England, 1200–1350," in Bush, ed., Serfdom and Slavery, 280–81.
42 Freedman, Origin of Peasant Servitude in Medieval Catalonia (Cambridge: Cambridge University Press, 1991), 121.
43 Ibid., 191–92.
44 Dyer, "Memories of Freedom," 293–94.
45 Freedman, "German and Catalon Peasant Revolts"; Hilton, Bond Men Made Free.
46 Brenner, "Agrarian Class Structure and Economic Development in Pre-Industrial Europe," 34–35.
47 Ibid., 249–50.
48 R. H. Hilton, "Freedom and Villeinage in England," Past and Present 31 (1965): 14.
49 Freedman, "German and Catalon Peasant Revolts," 53.
50 Hilton, Bond Men Made Free, 173–75.
51 Bisson, Tormented Voices, 47.
52 Rösener, Bauern im Mittelalter, 149.
53 Ibid., 150.
54 Ibid., 155–59.
55 Jeannine Quillet, Le Défenseur de la paix (Paris: Librairie philosophique J. Vrin, 1968), 525.
56 Benjamin Barber, The Death of Communal Liberty (Princeton: Princeton University Press, 1974).

57 Ibid., 11.
58 Ibid., 131.
59 Richard Lachmann, *Capitalists in Spite of Themselves: Elite Conflict and Economic Transitions in Early Modern Europe* (New York: Oxford University Press, 2002), 53–77.
60 R. C. Van Caenegam, "Law and Power in Twelfth-Century Flanders," in *Cultures of Power*, ed. Thomas Bisson (Philadelphia: University of Pennsylvania Press, 1995), 153.
61 Paul Hohenberg and Lynn H. Lees, *The Making of Urban Europe, 1000–1950* (Cambridge: Harvard University Press, 1985), 43.
62 Ibid., 44. See also John H. Munday, "Medieval Urban Liberty" in *The Origins of Modern Freedom in the West*, ed. R. W. Davis (Stanford: Stanford University Press, 1995), 120–27; Stephen Rigby, "Urban 'Oligarchy' in Late Medieval England," in *Towns and Townspeople in the Fifteenth Century*, ed. John A. Thompson (Gloucester: Alan Sutton, 1988), 62–86.
63 Van Caenegem, *Law and Power in Twelfth-Century Flanders*, 163–66.
64 Antony Black, "The Individual and Society" in *The Cambridge History of Medieval Political Thought*, ed. J. H. Burns (Cambridge: Cambridge University Press, 1988), 593.
65 Harding, "Political Liberty in the Middle Ages," 442–43.
66 John Van Engen, "The Christian Middle Ages as an Historiographical Problem," *American Historical Review* 91 (1986): 215–16.
67 Harding, "Political Liberty in the Middle Ages," 442.
68 See, for example, Thomas Bisson, "The Crisis of the Catalonian Franchises (1150–1200)," in *La formacio i esspansio del feudalisme Catala*, ed. Jaume Portella I Comas (Barcelona: Collegi Universitari de Girona, 1986), 163–72.
69 J. P. Canning, "Introduction: Politics, Institutions, and Ideas," in Burns, ed., *Cambridge History of Medieval Political Thought*, 354.
70 G. O. Sayles, *The King's Parliament of England* (New York: Norton, 1974), 1–20.
71 J. C. Holt, *Magna Carta* (Cambridge: Cambridge University Press, 1992), 25.
72 H. G. Koenigsberger, "Parliaments and Estates," in Davis, ed., *Origins of Modern Freedom*, 135–77.
73 Holt, *Magna Carta*, 24.
74 McKenna, "The Myth of Parliamentary Sovereignty in Late-Medieval England," 484.
75 Holt, *Magna Carta*, 28; J. R. Maddicott, "Parliaments and the Constituencies, 1272–1377," in *The English Parliament in the Middle Ages*, ed. R. G. Davies and J. H. Denton (Manchester: Manchester University Press, 1981), 73.
76 Holt, *Magna Carta*, 5.
77 Ibid., 51; emphasis added.
78 Black, "The Individual and Society," 590.
79 St. Augustine, *The City of God* (trans. Gerald G. Walsh and Daniel J. Honan), 20.30, in *The Fathers of the Church* (New York: Fathers of the Church, Inc., 1954), 24:507; Van Engen, "The Christian Middle Ages as an Historiographical Problem."

80 Kurt Raaflaub, "Democracy, Oligarchy, and the Concept of the 'Free Citizen' in Late Fifth Century Athens," *Political Theory* 11 (1983): 517–44.
81 Guy Forquin, *Lordship and Feudalism in the Middle Ages* (Chicago: University of Chicago Press, 1962), 95–96, 170–73; Bisson, "The Crisis of the Catalonian Franchises."
82 J.-P. Poly, *La Provence et la societe feodale* (Paris: Bordas, 1976) cited in Burns, *Cambridge History of Medieval Political Thought*, 187.
83 Van Engen, "The Christian Middle Ages as an Historiographical Problem," 209–11.
84 Philippe, "Principes gentium dominantur eorum: Princely Power Between Legitimacy and Illegitimacy in Twelfth-Century Exegesis," in Bisson, ed., *Cultures of Power*, 311.
85 Hilton, *Bond Men Made Free*, 18, 229; Freedmen, *Origin of Peasant Servitude in Medieval Catalonia*, 191–92; 219–20; Freedman, "German and Catalon Peasant Revolts"; Peter Blickle, *The Revolution of 1525: The German Peasants' War from a New Perspective* (Baltimore: Johns Hopkins University Press, 1981); Janos M. Bak, ed., *German Peasant War of 1525* (London: F. Cass, 1976).
86 Freedman, *Origin of Peasant Servitude in Medieval Catalonia*, 191.
87 Hilton, *Bond Men Made Free*, 124.
88 Ibid., frontispiece.
89 Van Engen, "Christian Middle Ages as an Historiographical Problem," 519–52.
90 Rosalind Brooke and Christopher Brooke, *Popular Religion in the Middle Ages* (London: Thames and Hudson, 1984), esp. chaps. 6–7.
91 J. A. Watt, "Spiritual and Temporal Powers," in J. H. Burns, ed., *Cambridge History of Medieval Political Thought*, chap. 14.
92 Ibid., 422–23.
93 Gerd Tellenbach, *Church, State, and Christian Society at the Time of the Investiture Crisis*, trans. R. F. Bennett (Toronto: University of Toronto Press, 1991), 126–27.
94 Tierney, *Idea of Natural Rights*, 69.
95 Karl Leyser, *Communications and Power in Medieval Europe: The Gregorian Revolt and Beyond* (London: Hambledon Press, 1994), 12–13.
96 Tierney, *Idea of Natural Rights*, 64.
97 Kenneth Pennington, "Law, Legislation, and Government, 1150–1300," in J. H. Burns, ed., *Cambridge History of Medieval Political Thought*, 432–36.
98 Ibid., chap. 15.
99 Ernst Kantorowicz, *The King's Two Bodies: A Study of Medieval Political Theology* (Princeton: Princeton University Press, 1957), 16, 193–94, 235.
100 John Dunn, *The Political Thought of John Dunn* (Cambridge: Cambridge University Press, 1969); Mervyn S. Johnson, *Locke on Freedom: An Incisive Study of the Thought of John Locke* (Austin: Best Print, 1977).
101 J. C. Davis, "Religion and the Struggle for Freedom in the English Revolution," *Historical Journal* 35 (1992): 507–30; J. H. Hexter, "Power Struggle, Parliament

and Liberty in Early Stuart England," *Journal of Modern History* 50 (1978): 1–50; John Coffey, "Puritanism and liberty Revisited: The Case for Toleration in the English Revolution," *Historical Journal* 41 (1998): 961–85.
102 Brenner, "Agrarian Class Structure and Economic Development in Pre-Industrial Europe"; Richard Lachmann, *From Manor to Market: Structural Change in England, 1536–1640* (Madison: University of Wisconsin Press, 1987); Lachmann, "Origins of Capitalism in Western Europe."
103 Carlyle, *Political Liberty*.
104 Ibid., 593.
105 Halvdan Kohnt, "Medieval Liberty Poems," *American Historical Review* 48 (1943): 283; emphasis added.
106 Ibid.; emphasis added.

STANLEY L. ENGERMAN & DAVID ELTIS

Slavery and Evil

Western societies frequently invoke the language of slavery to refer to a wide range of social evils. In the antebellum era, women's rights advocates such as Elizabeth Cady Stanton referred to the patriarchal family as a miniature slave plantation in which each woman was a slave and a slave breeder. In the late nineteenth and early twentieth centuries, trade unionists denounced wage slavery, and today, prostitution is frequently attacked as sexual slavery and sex trafficking.

This essay, by two of the leading economic historians of slavery and the slave trade, explores the challenges of applying the language of slavery to other instances of exploitation and depersonalization. Slavery, they argue, often provides a misleading metaphor that obscures profound differences among various evils. Equally important, the essay asks why slavery itself came to be viewed as a moral problem. While antislavery as an organized movement arose suddenly in the late eighteenth century, it was an outgrowth, the authors argue, of two gradual processes. One involved the narrowing of the category of peoples who could legitimately be enslaved. The other involved the growing sense that even slaves were entitled to minimal forms of humane treatment.

The long fascination with the history of slavery reflects the belief that it represented a unique evil in its absolute control and domination of one individual or group over another. Such controls were legally eliminated in most places in the modern world, even when many other undesirable aspects of human interaction have persisted. Not only is slavery regarded as evil, but it has developed into a term applied to what are regarded as "bad things" in almost any aspect of employer-employee and, indeed, government-citizen relations as well as in such matters as low wages, child labor, bad working conditions, or any distasteful form of labor. Anything regarded as unfavorable is likely to be described as slavery because of the term's connotations. The implication is that, like slavery, these conditions should not be allowed to continue in the contemporary world.

The rise of slavery to the status as the evil has led to a number of philosophical complexities, very well explored by David Brion Davis in his many writings over half a century of examining the "problem of slavery." The semi-conflation of slavery with evil can pose several issues; despite some rhetorical claims, not all evils are cases of slavery. The near ubiquity historically of slavery has meant differences in legal conditions, material treatment, psychological interactions, labor input, and ability to join the slaveholding society. Such variation has meant that compared to free workers, slaves are often fed better, live longer, and have more control over their physical environment. These conditions reflect a paradox of slavery pointed to long ago by H. J. Nieboer—that slave owners will free slaves only when the incomes of all workers, whether slave or free, are at subsistence levels.[1] Indeed, at earlier stages in many societies, where incomes are low and famines are relatively frequent, voluntary slavery of individuals and their family members is a frequent occurrence, a necessary step to allow survival. Several of the great famines, such as those in China and the Soviet Union in the twentieth century, have occurred in free-labor societies; and, while this is not, of course, an argument for slavery, it does point to the fact that major problems for laborers do exist even in the absence of slavery. Freedom may mean freedom to starve, not only freedom to get rich, or freedom to do anything one wants.

The focus on slavery may also mean that some difficult social choices have been overlooked. Thus, it was a practice in many Asian and African societies to solve overpopulation problems by selling people into slavery. This practice was widely censured; yet it should be noted that the Western European solution to problems of overpopulation was, until early modern times, not enslavement but rather infanticide or child exposure. While abandonment was at times part of a ritual wherein the child is taken in by others, this was certainly not always the case. Moreover, even where no slavery exists, government policies can have major impacts on the labor supply and the wage rate, without any apparent direct consent on the part of the working population—even though they do not infringe on free choice among different jobs. Such measures include taxes, restrictions on emigration, vagrancy laws, and reductions in welfare and unemployment benefits. While different from slavery in that there is no tie to specific employment, the desire to increase the labor supply will nevertheless have large implications for human well-being.

The importance of migration for free and slave populations also poses some complications for the equating of slavery and evil. Large-scale slavery generally meant a movement of a population to a new and distant area, where individuals and families could be enslaved and made to work for others. Such a movement was predicated on the willingness of persons in the sending area to sell slaves, and the willingness of those in the receiving area to purchase and use them. In large-scale, New World slave societies, the willingness to accept slaves was based ultimately on a conception of race that permitted this form of intensely discriminatory behavior toward the migrants from Africa at a time when aliens arriving from a wide range of European countries were automatically and unthinkingly accorded free status. Yet, the history of responses to racism points to a lack of easy answers here. Much antislavery thought in the Americas was as racist as proslavery ideology, since a goal of several abolitionist movements was to exclude people of African descent and preserve a homogeneous white society. In a parallel case, Australia ended contract labor not because of concern with the life of the Kanakas (Kanaks) but rather because Australian society wished to maintain a "white Australia." The failure to accept contract labor or slaves may have reduced the numbers enslaved, but it did mean higher populations and lower living standards in the prospective areas of out-migration. Those forced onto vessels and taken to the Caribbean and to what became the United States had progeny that were more nutritionally secure than those who managed to avoid being sent to the Americas. More generally, the relationship between the incidence of slavery and levels of living standards might be direct rather than inverse.

What has been given more attention as part of the discussion about slavery is the various other forms of political coercion, including the right to vote, and the varieties of coerced labor that have long existed. These include formal, legal arrangements such as serfdom, indentured or contract labor, debt bondage, convict labor, and so on, in which, for periods of time, there is control over labor and, in some instances, labor is bought and sold. The limited time of these arrangements is obviously a benefit compared to slavery, but as indentured servants well knew, limited terms gave the owner less of a stake in the future well-being of the servant and could result in poorer treatment of the latter compared to what a slave might experience. And, of course, what some call free labor is termed by others "wage slavery," since without alternative employment opportunities or capital or landholdings, individuals may face somewhat constrained choices.

The ability to single out slavery from other negative aspects of life becomes particularly puzzling when we examine the ending of slavery in Europe, mainly by attrition, around the thirteenth century. Slavery of outsiders continued after this, but the enslavement of other Europeans was no longer possible. Nevertheless, while this implied that Europeans saw each other as in some sense "insiders" on the slavery issue, this did not prevent them from spending the next seven centuries warring with each other (with enormous casualties) and indulging in the full range of murder, rape, and pillage in their relations with each other. While there was some ransoming of prisoners, these were far less frequent than wartime deaths. Widening the definition of insiders to reduce the incidence of slavery did little to guarantee a moral, peaceful subcontinent.

A related issue is the perceived need to equate other evils—those aimed primarily at causing death or providing punishment—with slavery, even when such evils are not fully consistent with slavery as it usually understood. The primary aim of the Nazi Holocaust was quite different from slavery, as judged on economic and social grounds; and the intention of the Soviet gulags was not primarily to exact labor, even though inmates were forced to work. The gulags were quite different from earlier forms of slavery and serfdom either in Russia or in other parts of the world.

At what point did slavery become the apotheosis of evil? And, a question that is clearly related to this, why did slavery happen? As the forgoing suggests, we can see signs of the shift well before abolition became a major issue. Slavery could not exist at all without some implicit agreement, both on the part of society at large and among slaveowners and potential slaveowners, to respect property rights in human beings and categorize certain groups as suited for slavery and others as not. This was essential because voluntary enslavement did not generate enough people to meet the demand for slaves. Very few have ever wanted to be a slave, and thus slavery has always been seen as extremely undesirable at the level of the individual. Perhaps the defining characteristic of abolitionism is the generalization of this personal distaste to the point where it is thought that no one should be a slave. From a broad historical perspective, abolition in the Western world developed very suddenly. Nevertheless, the movement from the particular to the general, marked in Europe by a widening of the category of insider (or a narrowing of "outsidership"), was much more gradual than this suggests. Prisoners taken in conflicts between the core peoples of Western Europe on the one hand and Celts and Viking marauders on the other were much more likely to be killed or enslaved in the tenth century, while at the same time those taken in conflicts *between* western Europeans were more likely to be ransomed and exchanged. By the early sixteenth century, slavery had disappeared altogether from northwestern Europe, and in England and Holland the term "slavery" was usually reserved for something the Spanish and Portuguese did in the Americas, or as synonym for serfdom. The slavery that northwestern Europeans re-embraced in the course of the seventeenth century was generally far away from Europe and was reserved exclusively for sub-Saharan Africans or peoples of sub-Saharan African descent. There were now no Arabs, Asians, and certainly no Europeans—not even "Slavs," whose ubiquity as slaves had earlier ensured that their name would become the general term for slaves in every Western European country. The "Africanization" of slavery constituted a major narrowing of eligibility for enslavement over the millennia.

At the same time, the degradation associated with slave status increased. While there was little essential difference between the Aristotelian conception that certain individuals were born to be slaves and the increasingly exclusive Islamic and European association of Africans with slavery two thousand years later, the racial distinction was of significance. When slavery was just one of many social institutions enshrining subordination, when it was present in some form in almost every society, and when it was largely devoid of racial exclusivity, then it was less likely to have been perceived as exceptional, or, perhaps, immoral. By the late seventeenth century, these three conditions were less true than they had been. Compared to most of the post-Neolithic non-European world, as well as earlier feudal Europe, the extremes of social and economic inequality among Europeans were less in the Europe of the early modern era. Further, slavery had totally disappeared in the northwest of the subcontinent, at least, and the only slaves in the parts of the overseas world controlled by Europeans were of African descent, once the experiment of using East Indian slaves on plantations had been tried and found wanting. Even when Europeans revived indentured servitude under the guise of contract labor in the nineteenth century, the laborers were overwhelmingly Chinese and Indian, not European.

One can detect some unease with slavery even as the European-controlled slave systems spread throughout the Americas. Very soon after the plantation slave systems were set up, all jurisdictions instituted laws designed to ensure minimum treatment, even if they were usually recognized in the breach. There were parallels here with Islamic law going back to the Koran, where manumission of slaves and good treatment were considered virtuous, but no Christian or Islamic tradition suggested that abolishing the institution was a good thing, despite the later claims of western abolitionists. The first aspect of the slave system to come under direct attack, and the first of its practitioners to be cast as morally opprobrious, were the slave trade and slave traders, respectively.

The Portuguese and the British accounted for nearly three-quarters of all Africans carried across the Atlantic. The Portuguese had legislation limiting the number of slaves (or, rather, the human tonnage) carried per vessel as early as 1685, about a century before the better known British Dolben's Act of 1788. They also banned the trade in slaves to Portugal itself in 1761, a decade before the Mansfield case made the legal environment for English holders of slaves in England a little less secure than it had been. Abolition of the slave trade itself emerged first in northern Europe, however, perhaps because the metropolitan economies there were so much larger and more powerful relative to their respective slave colonies than was the case for their counterparts in Portugal (dominated by Brazil) and Spain (then dominated by Cuba). The Danes abolished the trade in 1792, the British and United States, fifteen years later. But, in all cases, action against the slave trade preceded action against slavery itself by some thirty years. In all cases, too, both the slave trade and slavery were flourishing when they were abolished. The only other forms of commerce in western history where this can be said to have been true are perhaps prostitution, alcohol, drugs, and, less certainly, the use of animals for food, though in these cases attempts at suppression have been somewhat less successful than the campaigns against slavery and the slave trade. What all efforts to regulate and forbid human behavior in these areas have drawn on, however, is an enormous moral impulse. And, from the perspective of the early twenty-first century, it is over slavery, or at least legalized chattel slavery, that the moral impulse seems to have achieved its most complete victory. What is also striking is how little scholarly effort has been expended on explaining how and why evil has been redefined over time, and how much academic work assumes that the values that hold today are somehow unchanging and universal. The ancillary to this is that too much effort has been spent creating an image of the past that fits modern values.

The increase in the use of the term "slavery" to describe a victim's plight in any situation of perceived injustice is already striking in the early modern period. A sampling of the index of the Kress-Goldsmith collection of early economic literature, or the collection of Early English published books, shows that by the sixteenth and seventeenth centuries, slavery had come to be used metaphorically as often as it was used to describe actual chattel slavery. In the mid-seventeenth century, royalist Barbadians could claim to be enslaved by Cromwell; and English, Scottish, and Irish prisoners of war sent to the island for a term of years (and often freed before the term was completed) could also claim to have been enslaved. By the nineteenth century, the term was employed to describe working conditions in the factories, the position of women in marriage, and child labor, among other phenomena in need of reform. By the twentieth century, as we have seen, it was used for an even wider range of abuses, including prostitution. More narrowly, one wonders how many of the situations that the modern antislavery society investigates would have been considered chattel slavery by the first abolitionists. But this widening range of applications did not result in any weakening of the term's evil connotations. As institutionalized social subordination continued to decrease, the term's association with evil strengthened and it became even more useful to use rhetorically. The twenty-first century so far suggests that this process is not about to diminish.

Noting the paradox that the societies in history that appear to have made the largest contributions to the ideology of freedom were usually those that relied most heavily on slave labor, Orlando Patterson has argued that the very concept (or more accurately, conceptions) of freedom could not have evolved without the defining influence of the large-scale presence of slavery. The widening recognition of slavery as the ultimate evil in history since the abolitionists began their campaign to eradicate the institution might, however, suggest the opposite association. As halting progress toward the rule of law, recognition of human rights, and political participation for more people occurs, slavery appears more and more as the worst human condition imaginable. One hopes that this will not prevent scholars from evaluating the experience of slaves in history realistically, nor from recognizing the complexity of that experience (including making full room for the agency of slaves), and, above all, avoiding easy answers.

NOTES

1 H. J. Nieboer, *Slavery as an Industrial System: Ethnological Researches*, 2nd rev. ed. (Philadelphia: Free Library of Philadelphia, 1910), 418.

Twin Evils?
Slavery and Homicide
in Early America

> The United States has the highest homicide rate of any advanced industrial country. Within our society, the homicide rate is particularly high in those states where slavery lasted the longest. To what extent, the noted social and cultural historian Randolph Roth asks, is the violent nature of American society a legacy of slavery?
>
> This essay demonstrates that rates of homicide varied starkly during the colonial era by region and historical era. The early colonial period was far more violent than present-day Americans suppose, reflecting the high level of tensions between masters and indentured servants and the significant number of servant women who killed their newborn babies.

New World slave societies were violent. But were they inherently murderous? In retrospect it would seem that they must have been, since every nation in North and South America that was heavily involved in racial slavery, except Cuba, has a comparatively high homicide rate today. So too does every former slave state within the United States. Yet there are some indications that murderousness was not a constant in slave societies. Philip Morgan argues, for example, that murderous violence against slaves may have been less common in the Chesapeake than in the Carolina low country because of differences in the character of work on tobacco and rice plantations and because of the distinctive relationships that cultivation of those crops created among slaves, slaveowners, and nonslaveholding whites.[1] Philip Schwarz finds that homicides decreased among slaves in Virginia during the eighteenth century as demographic forces, cultural change, and oppression forged a strong sense of community among them.[2]

Morgan and Schwarz do not mean to apologize for slavery or to minimize its brutality. By asking how homicide varied among slave societies they are trying to understand slavery historically, as an institution that changed over time and adapted to local circumstances. The moral shorthand that sees all evils as intertwined can sometimes blind observers to the true causes or consequences of particular evils like slavery and homicide.

As it turns out, slavery in British North America was sometimes very homicidal and sometimes less so, especially toward the end of the eighteenth century. Indentured servitude was far more murderous. America was never more homicidal than in the mid-seventeenth century, when indentured servitude reigned supreme. And, while America's homicide crisis in the twentieth and twenty-first centuries is rooted in the nation's history of slavery and racial oppression, the connection between that history and America's contemporary crisis is, like most historical relationships, complicated. America's homicide crisis has more to do with the ways in which the Revolution and the Civil War unsettled class, gender, and race relations, and with the difficulty of ending slavery and racial oppression, than it does with slavery and gender and race relations as they unfolded in the eighteenth century.

Murder rates for European colonists, both children and adults, were high in New England and extraordinarily high in the Chesapeake before 1675.[3] An important cause in New England, and the principal cause in the Chesapeake, was indentured servitude. The "surcharge of necessitous people" in England forced many poor people, especially orphaned children, to seek their fortunes in the New World.[4] Relationships between indentured servants and their owners could be mutually beneficial, if the servants worked hard and if their owners taught them a valuable skill, such as farming or blacksmithing. But masters and mistresses were usually determined to get their money's worth, and if the relationship broke down because of greed, illness, or ill-matched tempers, indentured servants could be subject to abuse, often with fatal results. Neighbors, relatives, and magistrates intervened frequently to protect indentured servants, but intervention could not protect every servant.

Marmaduke Pierce, a tailor in Salem, Massachusetts, lost patience with his young apprentice when the boy became ill. Pierce beat him and refused to feed him a full ration until he returned to work. The boy had suffered a severe head wound that fractured his skull. When neighbors inquired about the injury, the boy said at first that a limb had fallen on him. But when the wound festered and death was certain, he told authorities that his master had hit him with a broom stick and with a "meatyard," or measuring stick.[5] Indentured child servants could also be victims of sadistic abuse. John Walker, who died at age fourteen, was brutalized by his master and mistress, Robert and Susanna Latham of Marshfield, Massachusetts. The inquest found that his entire body "was blackish and blew, and the skine broken in divers places from the middle to the haire of his head," from the whippings they had given him. He had bruises on his arm, hip, and breast, and "three gaules like holes in the hames." The knuckles of one his hands were frozen, as were one of his fingers, both heels, two toes, and the side of his foot. In the days before his death, the Lathams worked John far beyond his strength, even though he was so ill, so that he became incontinent and "did constantly wett his bedd and his cloathes, lying in them, and soe suffered by it, his clothes being frozen on him."[6]

Wherever indentured servitude took root in the New World, children were murdered at an alarming rate. In Maryland, the nondomestic murder rate for European American children was at least 9.5 per 100,000 children under age sixteen per year—six times the rate in New England.[7] The homicide rate for newborn children was also extraordinarily high because of indentured servitude: 50 per 100,000 births in New England and at least 150 to 400 per 100,000 births in Maryland and Virginia. Women servants who gave birth to illegitimate children—sometimes because they had been sexually coerced by their masters—faced whippings, fines, and a year or two of extra service. The pressure to conceal their pregnancies and kill their newborn children was intense.

Adult servants were also subjected to lethal abuse, and some retaliated against their abusers. On a cold evening in Norfolk County, Virginia, Robert Shallicome beat his mistress to death after she struck him for failing to help her start a fire. He claimed that he had hit her only twice, but her wounds betrayed him. He had struck her repeatedly about the head, blackening both eyes and smashing her skull.[8] Sometimes servants murdered their masters or mistresses simply because they stood between them and their freedom. In Spruce Creek, New Hampshire, in 1675, Robert Driver, a Scot, and Nicholas Favor, a Frenchmen, who were indentured to an English fisherman, hacked their master to death with an axe and buried him in a cellar so they could steal his money and finance their flight back to Europe.[9] Such murders helped push the murder rate for adult European colonists to 8 to 10 per 100,000 per year in New England and at least 25 to 30 per 100,000 in the Chesapeake, where a greater portion of the inhabitants were indentured servants.

Indentured servitude was deadly because it placed so much power in the hands of owners and reduced servants to de-facto slaves without giving owners a long-term interest in their health or well-being. It could degenerate into a contest to see who could take the most and give the least over the life of the contract. It made British North America more deadly than England, where indentured servitude never took hold. The rise of slavery and the decline of indentured servitude played important roles in the decline in homicides of white colonists in the late seventeenth century.

In its early years, slavery was relatively murderous. In New England, murder rates for African children and adults were as high in the late seventeenth and early eighteenth centuries as the rates for Europeans had been in the heyday of indentured servitude.[10] Much of that violence fell on children. The murder of illegitimate mulatto newborns by white mothers comprised a fifth of all black neonaticides, but the balance were committed by black or mulatto women, nearly all enslaved. The high rate of neonaticide stemmed from New England slaveowners' attitudes toward enslaved women of childbearing age. Because there were few plantations in New England, female slaves worked almost exclusively as domestic servants and were expected to devote themselves to their owners' families. Many New England owners refused to sanction slave marriages and routinely sold slaves who were pregnant or likely to become pregnant, as well as the children of such slaves, because they did not want to lose "the attention and labor of servants preoccupied with their own families."[11] Enslaved women, fearful that they or their babies would be sold, restricted their fertility as best they could, and many of them chose to do away with their newborns rather than endure the ordeal of separation.

The circumstances of African American mothers who committed neonaticide were almost always identical. Like Grace, the slave of a merchant in Boston,[12] or Rose, the slave of a Boston baker,[13] or Jane, the slave of a shipping magnate in Portsmouth, New Hampshire,[14] most neonaticidal mothers had good positions and lived in towns where they could socialize with other African Americans. They had a lot to lose if they were sold for having children that their owners did not want. Elizabeth Colson, a freed mulatto woman, could not find work because she had given birth to an illegitimate child and had compounded her problems by stealing. She abandoned her child and moved to another town for a fresh start. When a second illegitimate child arrived, she abandoned it too. When she conceived a third child out of wedlock in 1726, she did not hesitate to treat it similarly: she gave birth to the baby in a swamp and murdered it.[15]

African American infants and older children were also likely to be murdered. A few were murdered by parents who were depressed or had lost all hope for a better life. Pegg, owned by a mariner in Swansey, Massachusetts, carried her two children to the Great River one morning and drowned them.[16] Most often, however, black children were murdered by nonrelatives. Because enslaved parents worked long hours and lacked custody of their children, they could not shield them from abuse or random violence. Nimrod, an enslaved boy, was beaten to death by his master, John Ambler, a farmer in Dover, New Hampshire. Ambler was a brutal man who mistreated his wife and family. He had beaten Nimrod repeatedly in the months before his death and had deprived him of food and water in an effort to "correct" his behavior. On the fatal day, Ambler beat Nimrod so badly that blood covered the stump where he had been tied. Neighbors, alarmed by Nimrod's cries, ran to the scene to restrain Ambler, but they arrived too late. The beating was so brutal that Ambler's whipping stick penetrated Nimrod's back and broke off.[17] Dilla Cosada, an Indian woman from Edgartown, Massachusetts, beat a black infant in her care to death.[18] Cato, an enslaved boy in Boston, was shot dead in the street when an enslaved man went on a murderous rampage, firing at every man, woman, and child who came within range.[19] Yet another child lost his life when a drunken sailor on a slave ship anchored at Middletown, Connecticut, seized the boy, saying "He would have a Servant of his own," and leapt into the river, where both drowned.[20]

By the mid-eighteenth century, however, murder rates for black children had declined in New England. The black birth rate had risen, and a greater proportion of black women were able to form families and raise children, which lessened the pressures that led to murder. Family formation was still restricted, so child murder rates were twice those of whites at the end of the eighteenth century. But they were comparable to those of poor whites and were, by contemporary standards, extraordinarily low.[21]

The early years of New England's slave regime were also fairly murderous for African adults. The cause was straightforward: brutal, unprovoked violence by slaveowners.[22] Fatal beatings had more to do with racial hatred and impatience with "out of country" Africans than with discipline. Neighbors in Suffield, Massachusetts, had witnessed farmer Joseph Lawton's brutal treatment of his servant, Congo, a recent arrival from Africa. They had seen Lawton's temper flare when he told Congo to fetch a rope to tie up a hog and Congo hesitated because he did not understand. When they had not seen Congo for a while they became suspicious and asked Lawton if he had come to some harm. Lawton did not confess, but by way of reply he asked his neighbors, "Why is it any hurt to kill him? Has he got any soul?" Congo's body surfaced in a brook the following spring. His skull had been crushed.[23]

Africans, free and enslaved, were also subject to lethal assaults from non-slaveholders determined to dominate a people they considered inferior. In 1721, London, a free laborer, exchanged friendly barbs with William Ripp, a white laborer, as they unloaded a boat in Newbury, Massachusetts. "In jest," Ripp called London a "Black Rogue." London told Ripp, "He was No more [a] black Rogue than himself." Ripp and London took their "Jocose Speeches . . . in good part," but another white boatman, Ralph Wheeler, did not. Wheeler asked London "how he dar'd to Speak Such words to a White Man?" London told Wheeler "to mind his Own Business," and Wheeler struck him with a club, killing him.[24]

Whites also ganged up on disobedient blacks. In 1741, three white men in Roxbury, Massachusetts, took the law into their own hands when they suspected a slave had stolen money from them. They tied the slave to a tree and beat him to death as they tried to force a confession.[25] In Boston in 1746, Jonathan Simpson Jr. ran into the street crying for help. He had tried to whip his father's slave, Bristol, and Bristol had drawn a knife and threatened to "Stab or kill any person that shd: offer to lay Hold on him." Simpson returned with three watchmen, who strangled Bristol in their effort to subdue him.[26]

In the late seventeenth and early eighteenth centuries, blacks also killed blacks. Joseph Hanno, a free man, murdered his wife Nancy in Boston in 1720. They had quarreled over the degree to which they were willing to accommodate themselves to white society. Joseph, born in Africa, had been raised a Christian. He rewarded his owners' ministry with devotion and service and was proud of his faith, but his wife's refusal to attend services irked him. He had never considered murder "till she told me, that she had a liev talk with the Devil, as talk with any of GODS Ministers." When asked by a minister who visited him in jail if he understood the principles of Christianity, Joseph replied without irony, "Yes, Sir, I have a Great deal of Knowledge. No body of my Colour, in Old England or New, has so much." "I wish you were less Puffed up with it," the minister replied.[27]

Abuse, racial prejudice, and cultural conflict claimed the lives of many Africans, enslaved and free, in early New England. What is remarkable, however, is that murders of blacks almost disappeared after 1750. The murder rate for black adults, like the murder rate for black children, was remarkably low—only 1 to 2 per 100,000 per year in the entire African population. Although the rate for white adults in New England was lower still, this was a rate that any modern nation could envy. Among blacks in New England during this period there was almost no record of abuse, cultural conflict, domestic discord, or anything else that could lead to lethal violence.

The patterns are nearly identical in the Chesapeake and in the Shenandoah Valley. The surviving records show a steady, gradual decline in the rate at which African adults were murdered by Africans and a steeper decline in the rate at which African adults were murdered by Europeans.[28] Murders of slaves by masters did not disappear, but the rate dropped by two-thirds in the 1730s and 1740s, the same decades that such murders disappeared in New England.[29] The decline in murders of African adults by Africans reflected a decline in all types of homicidal violence among blacks: murders of family members, murders of unrelated slaves in the same household, and murders of other unrelated slaves and free blacks.[30] By the late eighteenth century, their murder rate was lower than that for Virginia whites.

How might we explain the simultaneous decline in the eighteenth century in lethal violence against blacks in New England and Virginia? Similar forces may have been at work. As enslaved Africans adjusted to life in New World and European colonists accepted the humanity (if not the equality) of Africans, slaveowners adopted a paternalistic ethos toward the enslaved and developed personal relationships with their bondservants, and lethal discipline declined or disappeared. The work routines involved in tobacco production, mixed farming, domestic service, seafaring, and small-scale manufacturing required close contact and cooperation between slave laborers and their masters, mistresses, or overseers.[31] In such circumstances, personal relationships could develop between owners and slaves that, however strained, inhibited violence and allowed the economic logic of slavery to prevail. The destruction of a slave meant the destruction of a sizeable investment, so murdering one's slave made little sense.

It is more difficult to explain the decline in non-household murders of blacks by whites. By mid-century, European colonists in New England extended nearly the same consideration to Africans as they did to one another. They considered homicide unthinkable. New England's European colonists did not extend such consideration to Native Americans. They murdered them at an alarming rate through the 1790s. But, by mid-century, they perceived blacks as members of their communities—and worthy ones for the most part, if memorial notices for African neighbors, servants, and coworkers can be trusted. Prejudice, discrimination, and everyday violence persisted, but in ways that did not brutalize most blacks or block efforts during and after the Revolution to abolish slavery and grant blacks basic civil rights.

The reasons for the decline in non-household murders of blacks by whites in Virginia may have been less benign. Slaveowners who dominated Virginia's courts punished whites who damaged or destroyed their property. They imposed civil or criminal penalties on whites who used violence against other people's slaves without sufficient cause. Whites had reason to consider the consequences of losing their tempers and taking the law into their own hands.

The decline in homicides of blacks by blacks in Virginia, which Philip Schwarz first observed, was in his opinion a consequence of social and cultural change. "Ethnic quarrels and differing experiences" had led Africans and African Americans to "quarrel regularly" during the early 1700s. But, in the mid- and late 1700s, as "immigration declined and then stopped, plantation sizes increased, the proportion of blacks in the population grew," families formed, kinship networks appeared, and bonds among neighbors intensified. Divisions among slaves diminished as their common identity as an oppressed people came to the fore. These forces, in Schwarz's opinion, militated against lethal violence.[32]

Solidarity among blacks may have been even more intense in New England because blacks were so few and so highly concentrated in ports or maritime counties. A third of New Hampshire's blacks lived in Portsmouth, a third to a half of Massachusetts' in Boston, nearly half of Connecticut's in New London or Fairfield county, and three-fourths of Rhode Island's in Providence or Newport.[33] Cultural prohibitions against homicide may also have been stronger in New England, as they were for working class whites. Native American women who married African American men noted that they were less violent than Native American men,[34] a fact borne out by homicide statistics. The rate of spouse murder was seventeen times higher among Native Americans than among African Americans. Black Yankees revealed the same sense of humor, irony, and self-deprecation that white working-class Yankees did. They were suspicious of those who put on airs or who thought themselves more godly than others, and they defended themselves with wit.[35] To this day, African Americans are less likely to commit murder and be murdered in New England than anywhere else in the United States, just as European Americans are.

That does not mean, however, that slaves in New England or Virginia passively accepted their plight. Indeed, as soon as murders of slaves by owners and overseers declined in the 1720s and 1730s, slaves started murdering their masters, mistresses, and members of their families, and in a few instances neighbors or strangers. Part of that increase stemmed from the increased proportion of blacks in the population, but most represented a real increase in homicide. Slaves used clubs, knives, hatchets, and poison to retaliate against whites.[36] In 1729, in Prince George County, Maryland, a slave murdered his mistress and two of her children and fled with his master's guns. When a white posse tracked him down, he tried to kill his master, shooting him through the hand. That same year, a slave in Baltimore shot and killed his master outright.[37] In 1731 in Wallingford, Connecticut, Hannah, a slave of a prominent family, attacked her master's niece and a neighbor with a knife, killing the latter.[38] In Virginia in 1737, an enslaved woman murdered her mistress with a broad axe in Nansemond County, and an enslaved man killed his master and another white man in Orange County.[39]

Such murders were fatalistic. None of the murderers fled, and few tried to hide their crimes. They wanted revenge, regardless of consequences. Like most

Twin Evils?   81

slaves who resisted in the mid-eighteenth century, these murderers had yet to embrace a wider vision of African American identity or of the struggle for freedom. They were focused on immediate problems: harsh discipline, poor working conditions, mistreatment of family members, and insults from neighbors or strangers. But the surge in homicides was in a sense political: these slaves decided to strike back against their oppressors. Why such a movement emerged simultaneously in New England and Virginia is uncertain. It may have been a truly intercolonial movement, if homicides in Pennsylvania, New York, New Jersey, and Maryland fit the same pattern.[40]

One indication that these homicides may have been political is that they declined as the revolutionary crisis unfolded in the 1760s and early 1770s. The promise of the Revolution, the possibility that rebellion, flight, manumission, or emancipation might make them free, may have made desperate, homicidal acts less attractive; and the exciting prospect of extraordinary political change may have diverted everyone's attention from the sort of day-to-day problems that would ordinarily spark violence. Where abolition became a reality, as it did in New England in the 1780s and 1790s, homicides of whites by blacks largely disappeared. Where dreams of emancipation lived on in the South, as they did in Virginia in the same decades, the rate at which blacks murdered whites remained low. Whites murdered each other at higher rates during the Revolutionary crisis, but every murder rate involving blacks fell further as optimism and revolutionary solidarity spread through the black community and as antislavery whites adopted more humane attitudes toward blacks.

Finally, the rise of racial slavery contributed to a sudden decline in homicides among whites in the late seventeenth century. The white homicide rate fell abruptly in New England, from 8 to 10 per 100,000 adults per year to 1 to 2 per 100,000; and, in the Chesapeake, it fell from at least 25 to 30 per 100,000 to 10 per 100,000. Moreover, the rates remained low until the Revolution. The decline of indentured servitude, which lessened class antagonism among whites, played an important role in this decline, as did the return of political stability and the rise of British patriotism after the Glorious Revolution, which put an end to political violence and strengthened fellow-feeling among British colonists. But the rise of racial slavery, together with the disastrous Indian wars of 1675–76, played the most important role in decreasing the white homicide rate by making race the most important divide in colonial society and unifying white colonists. It is ironic to think that a successful white supremacist campaign might lower the homicide rate among white supremacists, but that is what happened in the late seventeenth century.

What, then, was the relationship between slavery and homicide in early

America? Blaming slavery for America's high homicide rate today places America's homicide problem far back in history, in the colonists' decision to establish slavery in North America. But slavery was not the most homicidal labor system in American history, and it became less homicidal during the eighteenth century. And the societies slavery created in the eighteenth century were not the most homicidal in American history, because of the premium they placed on solidarity among blacks and whites.

That is not an excuse for slavery, of course. Where the Revolution brought freedom to African Americans and hope to all Americans, as it did in the New England in the early nineteenth century, the homicide rate fell to its lowest level in the nation's history, for blacks and whites. But where the Revolution failed to fulfill its promise, as it did in Virginia in the early nineteenth century, the homicide rate rose. African Americans who had expected freedom, nonslaveholding whites who had expected greater equality among whites, and slaveholders who had expected continued deference from their inferiors took out their frustrations on each other. The shock of Nat Turner's rebellion nearly put a stop to homicidal behavior in Virginia in the 1830s: whites and blacks dared not kill within or across racial lines. But that shock was short-lived, and Virginia's homicide rate rebounded in the 1840s, as the contradiction between the promise of the Revolution and the reality of life in the slave South persisted.

America's homicide problem became national in the mid-nineteenth century, as the nation divided over slavery and race. The homicide problem became worse for blacks than for whites in the late nineteenth and early twentieth centuries, when white supremacists regained the upper hand and terrorized and oppressed blacks everywhere. America's contemporary homicide problem is not rooted in freedom or in slavery per se, but in the difficulties the nation experienced in getting rid of slavery and creating a free society. That is why the legacy of racial slavery has been terribly homicidal, for blacks and whites.

NOTES

The author would like to thank Jim Stewart for his comments on this paper. He would also like to thank the Harry Frank Guggenheim Foundation, the National Endowment for the Humanities, the National Science Foundation, and the College of Humanities and the Criminal Justice Research Center at Ohio State University for their support.

1 Philip D. Morgan, *Slave Counterpoint: Black Culture in the Eighteenth-Century Chesapeake and Lowcountry* (Chapel Hill: Omohundro Institute of Early American History and Culture, University of North Carolina Press, 1998), 662–63, 257–317.

2 Philip D. Schwarz, *Twice Condemned: Slaves and the Criminal Laws of Virginia, 1705–1865* (Baton Rouge: Louisiana State University Press, 1988), 64–65.

3 The sources and methods used to estimate homicide rates in New England are discussed in Randolph Roth, "Child Murder in New England," *Social Science History* 25 (2001) 101–47, and Roth, "Homicide and Neonaticide in Early Modern Europe, 1549–800: The Need for a Quantitative Synthesis," *Crime, Histories, and Societies* 5 (2001), 33–67. The rates for Virginia and Maryland are based on early histories, newspapers, and examinations of homicide suspects by county and provincial courts. The records studied include W. H. Browne, et al., ed., *Archives of Maryland* (Baltimore: Maryland Historical Society, 1883–972), 4, 10, 41, 49, 53–54, 57, 65–67; C. C. Hall, *Narratives of Early Maryland, 1633–1684* (New York: Barnes and Noble, 1910); Peter Charles Hoffer and William B. Scott, *Criminal Proceedings in Colonial Virginia* (Athens: University of Georgia Press, 1984); H. R. McIlwaine, ed., *Minutes of the Council and General Court of Colonial Virginia, 1622–632, 1670–676, with Notes and Excerpts from Original Council and General Court Records, into 1683, Now Lost* (Richmond: Virginia State Library, 1924); J. Smith, *The Complete Works of Captain John Smith*, ed. P. L. Barbour, 3 vols. (Chapel Hill: University of North Carolina Press, 1986); *Maryland Provincial Court Judgments*, 1682–707; *Virginia Gazette*, 1736–780; *Maryland Gazette*, 1749–755. The order books and/or wills and deeds books for the following Virginia counties were also studied: Amelia, 1735–800; Augusta, 1745–800; Botetourt, 1770–800; Charles City, 1655–65, 1677–79, 1688–95; Lancaster, 1652–800; Middlesex, 1679–725, 1745–82, 1784–97, 1799–800; Spotsylvania, 1724–65, 1768–98; Surry, 1662–718, 1741–76, 1782, 1786–800; Sussex, 1754–800; Westmoreland, 1663–64, 1671–73, 1677–88, 1698–710; and York, 1657–62.

A complete survey of sources and methods will appear in my forthcoming book, *American Homicide*, and in the Historical Violence Database (http://www.sociology.osu.edu/cjrc/hvd), a collaborative effort to gather data on the history of violent crime and violent death.

4 A. E. Smith, *Colonists in Bondage: White Servitude and Convict Labor in America, 1607–776* (Chapel Hill: University of North Carolina Press, 1947), 147–51, 67–86, 165–67. Some poor children were kidnapped outright and sold as indentured servants in the New World. See also James Horn, *Adapting to a New World: English Society in the Seventeenth-Century Chesapeake* (Chapel Hill: Institute of Early American History and Culture, University of North Carolina Press, 1994), 266–76.

5 J. Noble, *Records of the Court of Assistants of the Colony of the Massachusetts Bay*, 3 vols. (Boston: County of Suffolk, 1901–928), vol. 2, pt. 1: 86, 89; and J. Winthrop, *The Journal of John Winthrop, 1630–649*, ed. R. S. Dunn, J. Savage, and L. Yeandle (Cambridge: The Belknap Press of Harvard University Press, 1996), 310–1, 528–30.

6 N.B. Shurtleff, ed., *Records of the Colony of New Plymouth in New England*, 10 vols., (Boston: W. White, 1855–861), 3:70–72, 73, 82, 143. See also the cases in Noble, *Records of the Court of Assistants of the Colony of Massachusetts Bay*, 1:11; N. B. Lacy, *Records*

of the Court of Assistants of Connecticut, 1665–701, 2 vols., M.A. thesis, Yale University (1937), 1:193–94; and in Connecticut Superior Court records, 9: 157, 169; Connecticut Public Records, 7:433; and *Boston Newsletter*, December 7, 1732.

7 For examples of murdered child servants in the Chesapeake, see Lower Norfolk County [Virginia] Wills & Deeds, D: 1656–666: 335b; Archives of Maryland, 54: 390–; 57: 59–65; 4: 254–55, 260; 41: 81–82; and Provincial Court Judgments [Maryland] (1692–93), 4: 340–42.

8 Lower Norfolk County (Virginia) Wills & Deeds, D: 1656–666: 398b.

9 Otis G. Hammond, ed., New Hampshire Court Records 1640–692, Court Papers 1652–668, in New Hampshire State Papers Series, 40 (Concord: State of New Hampshire, 1943), 318, 329, 337; New Hampshire Court Papers, 1674–77, 3: 7, 297, in New Hampshire State Archives; Suffolk Files 1349, 1363, Massachusetts State Archives; M. Halsey Thomas, ed., *The Diary of Samuel Sewall, 1674–729* (New York: Farrar, Straus and Giroux, 1973), 10; and "The Diaries of John Hull, Mint-master and Treasurer of the Colony of Mass Bay," *Transactions of the American Antiquarian Society* 3 (1857): 239–40.

10 Homicide rates for blacks in New England were 12 per 100,000 persons per year for adults and 20 per 100,000 persons per year for newborns, infants, and children (1670–709).

11 William D. Piersen, *Black Yankees: The Development of an Afro-American Subculture* (Amherst: University of Massachusetts Press, 1988), 19; Edgar J. McManus, *Black Bondage in the North* (Syracuse: Syracuse University Press, 1973), 37–38; Lorenzo Johnston Greene, *The Negro In Colonial New England, 1620–776* (New York: Columbia University Press, 1942), 213–6.

12 Massachusetts Superior Court of Judicature, 1:51–52; Cotton Mather, *Pillars of Salt* (Boston: B. Green, and J. Allen, 1699), 99–102; Thomas, *Diary of Samuel Sewall*, 1:310; Cotton Mather, *Magnalia Christi Americana* (Hartford: S. Andrus, 1820), 2:362; Massachusetts Archives, 60:279; and D. A. Hearn, *Legal Executions in New England: A Comprehensive Reference, 1623–960* (Jefferson, N.C.: McFarland, 1999), 103.

13 Massachusetts Superior Court of Judicature, v. 1700–714: 12; Suffolk file 162532.

14 New Hampshire Supreme Judicial Court minutes, August 1742; and New Hampshire Provincial Case Files, 22312. See also the case of Dorcas, Connecticut Superior Court records, 10: 139–41.

15 Massachusetts Superior Court of Judicature records, v. 1725–29: 111; Suffolk file 20195; *New England Weekly Journal*, May 29 and June 19, 1727; and Hearn (1999), 122.

16 Massachusetts Superior Court of Judicature, 1760–62: 271–72; and Suffolk files 81201 and 82379.

17 New Hampshire Superior Court of Judicature minutes, Box 1; and New Hampshire Provincial Case file, 18708. See also the murder of an enslaved boy by his master, John Sloss, in Fairfield, Connecticut, in 1705. Lacy (1937), 2: 606–7. See further the murder of Zeno, an enslaved child, by her master, Nicholas Lechmere, in New Lon-

don, Connecticut, in 1761. Connecticut Superior Court Records, 10: 279; New London County Superior Court Files, Papers by Subject: Inquests, c. 1711–870, A-M, Box 134, RG-3.
18 Suffolk file 144565.
19 Suffolk file 100142; *Boston Newsletter*, March 26 and September 3 and 17, 1747; *Boston Gazette*, March 24 and October 20, 1747; *Boston Post Boy*, October 19, 1747; and Hearn (1999), 138. See also the murder of Jack by Mingo in Fairfield, Connecticut. Lacy (1937), 1: 298.
20 *Connecticut Gazette*, July 9, 1763.
21 The rate was 2 per 100,000 persons per year for black children and 0.5 per 100,000 for white children.
22 See for example the murder of Andrew in Dartmouth, Massachusetts in 1711, Massachusetts Superior Court of Judicature Records, 1700–714: 265; and the murder of Fortin in Sandwich, Massachusetts, in 1719, Massachusetts Superior Court of Judicature Records, 1715–721: 25–26, and Suffolk Files 13190, Massachusetts State Archives.
23 Massachusetts Superior Court of Judicature Records, 1715–721: 248; and Suffolk files 12068, Massachusetts State Archives.
24 Massachusetts Superior Court of Judicature Records, 1721–25: 34; and Suffolk files 15551, Massachusetts State Archives. See also the murder of Cuffee by William Hamilton, Massachusetts Superior Court of Judicature Records, 1733–36: 286–77; *Boston Gazette*, September 8 and November 11, 1735.
25 *Boston Gazette*, July 20, 1741; *Boston Newsletter*, July 23, 1741.
26 Suffolk file 61453.
27 Massachusetts Superior Court of Judicature records, 1715–721: 355–56; Suffolk files 14687, 15099, 15186; *Boston Newsletter*, May 29, 1721; and Cotton Mather, *Tremenda. The Dreadful Sound with which the Wicked are to be Thunderstruck* (Boston: printed by B. Green for B. Gray and J. Edwards, 1721), 31–40.
28 The surviving records for the Chesapeake and the Shenandoah Valley of Virginia are not as complete or diverse before the 1780s, so it is impossible to estimate directly the number of homicides that drew public notice during most of the eighteenth century. Few inquests or case files have survived, nor have many diaries, local histories, or newspapers. It is possible, however, to trace homicides that led to the examination of homicide suspects in county courts or to payments to slaveowners for fugitive slaves who died trying to escape justice, some of whom were killed by the authorities and some of whom had themselves committed murder. The records of examination courts and claims courts do not include information on homicide victims killed by unknown persons or whose killers escaped, and they probably understate the number of slaves murdered by slaves of the same owner. Owners had no financial incentive to report such murders, because they had no one to sue for the wrongful death of the murdered slave and because they would receive only partial compensation if the murderer were executed, because the government discounted

slaves who had committed crimes. Still, Virginia's examination courts and claims courts heard a wider range of homicide cases than courts in other colonies, so they offer a substantial, although incomplete record of homicides.

29 In Virginia, the examination rate for whites accused of murdering blacks fell from 10.1 per 100,000 adults per year (1690–729) to 3.4 (1730–75).

30 In Virginia, the examination rate for blacks accused of murdering blacks fell from 5.5 per 100,000 adults per year (1690–729) to 2.2 (1730–775).

31 Piersen, Black Yankees, 3–61; Morgan, Slave Counterpoint, 257–300, 662–63.

32 Schwarz, Twice Condemned, 64–65. On these cultural and social changes, see Allan Kulikoff, Tobacco and Slaves: the Development of Southern Cultures in the Chesapeake, 1680–800 (Chapel Hill: Institute of Early American History and Culture, University of North Carolina Press, 1986); Douglas R. Egerton, Gabriel's Rebellion: The Virginia Slave Conspiracies Of 1800 And 1802 (Chapel Hill: University of North Carolina Press, 1993); and James Sidbury, Ploughshares into Swords: Race, Rebellion, and Identity in Gabriel's Virginia, 1730–810 (New York: Cambridge University Press, 1997).

33 Piersen, Black Yankees, 14–22.

34 Ibid., 19–20.

35 Ibid., 74–86, 96–40.

36 See the murder of Jemima Beacher in Wallingford, Connecticut in 1731, Connecticut Superior Court records, 9: 11; and Connecticut Superior Court files, Drawer 325; the murder of Tabitha Sandford in Mendon, Massachusetts, in 1745, Massachusetts Superior Court of Judicature records, 1740–46: 218; Suffolk files 61062, 61173; and Boston Newsletter, September 20, 1745; and the murder of John Codman in Charlestown, Massachusetts, in 1755, Massachusetts Superior Court of Judicature records, 1755–56: 123–24; Suffolk files 174038; Boston Gazette, July 7 and Aug. 11, 1755; Boston Newsletter, August 21, 1755. See also Massachusetts Superior Court of Judicature records, 1763–64: 193; Suffolk files 145054; Boston Gazette, June 13, October 24, and December 12, 1763; and Boston Evening Post, June 13 and December 5, 1763.

37 Boston Newsletter, May 12, 1729.

38 Connecticut Superior Court records, 9: 11; and Connecticut Superior Court files, Drawer 325.

39 Virginia Gazette, February 4 and 25, and June 10, 1737. For additional cases in New England, see Connecticut Superior Court records, 11: 23; and Connecticut Superior Court files, Box 171; Massachusetts Superior Court of Judicature records (1755–56): 251; Suffolk file 75651, 137014; Boston Gazette, August 11, 1755; Connecticut Gazette, August 16, 1755; and Boston Newsletter, July 1 and August 5, 1756; Massachusetts Gazette, September 5 and 19, 1754; Massachusetts Superior Court of Judicature records, 1740–46: 218; Suffolk files 61062, 61173; Boston Newsletter, September 20, October 3 and 24, 1745; Boston Post Boy, October 28, 1745; Connecticut Superior Court records, 12: 246; Connecticut Superior Court files, Box 10; Massachusetts Superior Court of Judicature records (1750–51): 180; Suffolk files, 67676; Boston Gazette, January 22, March 5, 9, April 16, and May 21, 1751; Proceedings of the Massachusetts Historical

Society (March 1883): 122–46; Massachusetts Superior Court of Judicature records, 1755–56: 123–24; Suffolk files 147038, 147042, 147043; *Connecticut Gazette*, July 12 and September 27, 1755; *Boston Gazette*, July 7 and August 11, 1755; and *Boston Newsletter*, August 21, 1755; Massachusetts Superior Court of Judicature records, 1763–64: 193; Suffolk files 84646, 145054; *Boston Gazette*, June 13, October 24, December 12, 1763; and *Boston Evening Post*, June 13 and December 5, 1763; Connecticut Superior Court Records, 18: 115–18; Massachusetts Superior Court of Judicature records, 1767–68: 124; Suffolk files 87278, 87368, 88563, 100902, 100906, 101112, 173044; *Boston Newsletter*, November 13, 1766; *New London Gazette*, December 5, 1766. For additional homicides in Maryland and Virginia, see Ellefson (1963: 308n255), December 6 and 13, 1753; *Virginia Gazette*, June 15 and July 20, 1769; *Massachusetts Gazette*, December 6 and 13, 1753; and *Connecticut Journal*, June 13, 1770.

40 See, for instance, the homicides reported in *Boston Gazette*, April 9, 1739, January 9, 1753; and *Boston Newsletter*, July 9, 1741.

IRA BERLIN

The Transformation of Slavery in the United States, 1800-1863

Far from being a static, unchanging institution, American slavery underwent far-reaching transformations between the seventeenth and mid-nineteenth centuries. In this essay, the prize-winning authority on American slavery Ira Berlin explores a series of revolutions that drastically altered the institution of slavery and the experience of blacks in bondage.

At the time that Thomas Jefferson was born in 1743, most slaves were born in Africa, few were Christian, and very few were engaged in raising cotton. Slavery was largely confined to eastern areas near the Atlantic Ocean and to the lowland regions of the Carolinas and Georgia. The slave population was not yet able to reproduce its numbers naturally. By the time of Jefferson's death in 1826, however, a majority of slaves had been born in the New World; most were Christian; a growing number lived in the "black belt" of Alabama, Mississippi, and Louisiana; and the largest number were cultivating cotton using the gang system of labor. Meanwhile, the slave population was expanding rapidly through natural reproduction.

The current renascence in the history of slavery in the United States has focused attention on the period prior to the American Revolution, emphasizing slavery's *longue durée* and connecting slavery's history to that of the larger Atlantic. The new scholarship of slavery redressed both a chronological and conceptual imbalance that made the study of U.S. slavery an appendage to the history of the American Civil War. In the process, however, it has revealed the weaknesses in slavery's antebellum historiography. Almost without exception, the great studies of nineteenth-century slavery presumed a fixed, unchanging character for their subject. "The rigid and static nature of ante-bellum slavery, 1830–1860," wrote Kenneth Stampp in his classic study *The Peculiar Institution*, "makes it possible to examine it institutionally with only slight regard for chronology."[1] Eugene Genovese, in his *Roll, Jordan, Roll*, another foundational text, and almost all other scholars—even those critical of Stampp and Genovese—have followed Stampp's lead.[2] Yet, if the new history of slavery reveals anything, it indicates that slavery changed in the nineteenth century and that the velocity of that change accelerated as the Civil War neared. On the eve of the great conflict, slavery was a radically different institution than it was following the American Revolution or even following Thomas Jefferson's election in 1800.

When the first shots on Fort Sumter signaled the beginning of the end for chattel bondage in the United States, slave life was defined by three characteristics: cotton cultivation, black-belt residence, and Afro-Christianity. The majority of southern slaves spent most of their work-a-day lives in the cotton fields. The most productive of these cotton fields were in the black belt, a broadband of rich, loamy soil that stretched from upcountry Georgia to the Mississippi River, where it turned north and followed the great River between New Orleans and Little Rock. Moreover, whether they resided in the black belt or not, the most prominent institution within the slave community was the African-Christian church. Although the character of African American slavery on the eve of the Civil War could be described in many ways, few would deny these as antebellum slavery's signal markers.

None of these markers were in place in 1800. At the turn of the century, few slaves grew cotton, hardly any resided in the black belt, and the overwhelming majority evinced no interest in Christianity. In short, between 1800 and 1860, slave life was transformed. Tobacco and rice growers became cotton cultivators; residents of the seaboard became residents of the interior; and men and women committed to a variety of African faiths from animism to Islam embraced Christianity.

Little in the present scholarship explains this change. A new history is needed that begins with an appreciation that the nineteenth century was not a period of slavery's static maturity but a time of dramatic change. I would like to extend the recent studies of slave life in the seventeenth and eighteenth centuries to the nineteenth century by briefly exploring three of the most dramatic changes in the nature of American slavery: the Cotton Revolution, the Great Migration from the upper to the lower South, and the advent of African-American Christianity in the slave quarters.

THE COTTON REVOLUTION

In 1800, the largest portion of American slaves grew tobacco in the Chesapeake and rice in the lowlands of Carolina and Georgia. Only a small minority of slaves—most of whom resided in the South Carolina sea islands—cultivated a long-staple cotton (that is, a variety with a long fiber). But already a new, short-staple cotton that could be grown just about anywhere in the South had begun to spread through the uplands. Technical problems of separating the fibers from the sticky green seeds had been solved by a host of tinkerers, the most prominent of whom was Eli Whitney. In the next half century, short-staple cotton raced across the continent, as slaveholding planters—following behind U.S. diplomatic initiatives (the purchase of Louisiana by Thomas Jefferson and the seizure of Florida by James Monroe) and military actions (the victory of Andrew Jackson at Horseshoe Bend and the destruction of the Negro Fort)—expanded their regime. Planters cleared European competitors from the North American continent; evicted Native Americans and pushed them across the Mississippi River; and ousted small farmers and drovers and relegated them to the hills and swamps, leaving themselves in control of the best lands. Cotton production skyrocketed. In 1800, the South produced less than 100,000 bales of cotton; sixty years later, production stood at over four million bales. On the eve of the Civil War, some three million slaves—slightly less than three-quarters of the American slave population—were directly involved in the production of cotton.

The Cotton Revolution transformed the lives of slaves because it required a different labor discipline and industrial regimen than the ones used in the production of tobacco or rice. Whereas tobacco had generally been cultivated on small plots, or "quarters," by squads of slaves often laboring independently or alongside white supervisors, and rice had been grown and processed on large estates by the task often under the direction of black drivers, cotton planters organized their slaves in large gangs under the direction of white overseers. The Cotton Revolution had enormous consequences for the way slaves worked and for the work regimen itself. It affected the occupational structure of the plantation, the division of labor, the slaves' economy, and the mobility of the slave population, all of which, in turn, reflected on the social relations between slaves, their owners, nonslaveholding whites and blacks, and among slaves themselves. No one has explained how the social relations of cotton production transformed the slaves' domestic life, their sacred world, and their general outlook, or *mentalité*.

THE SECOND GREAT MIGRATION

The Cotton Revolution initiated a second Great Migration. It uprooted nearly *one million* slaves—almost twice the number transported to mainland North America from Africa—from their seaboard communities and sent them across the lower South. In 1800, more than 80 percent of the slave population resided between the Delaware and Savannah rivers in Maryland, Virginia, and North and South Carolina. By the beginning of the Civil War, only a third of the slave population still lived in the upper South. Instead, most found their home in a new region called the black belt.

The movement of some one million slaves from the seaboard to the black belt deeply disrupted the civilization that black people had established in the aftermath of their forced exodus from Africa. In the almost two centuries of settlement along the seaboard, African and African American slaves had created complex communities, linked together by ties of kinship and friendship and resting upon a foundation of shared values and beliefs. Those communities became increasing self-contained with the closing of the slave trade, which had ended in the lower South by constitutional mandate in 1808 and a generation earlier in the upper South. The westward movement of plantation culture—whether it was driven by individual planters who accompanied their slaves or by professional slave traders who speculated in human flesh—tore that society asunder.

Changes founded on the seaboard resonated in the interior. Generally, it was the young who were the first to be sent west, as frontier planters needed both the muscle of young men and women to clear the land and their reproductive capacity to assure a steadily expanding labor force. On the frontier, slaves—many of them children by any reasonable standard—reconstructed African American life from the memories of the older seaboard civilization, much as their ancestors had earlier refashioned their lives on the western side of the Atlantic from memories of Africa.

The impact of the second Great Migration cannot be exaggerated. In the lower South, families and communities had to be reconstituted, leadership reasserted, and culture—those common ways of thinking and acting—refashioned in new circumstances, so that a new generation, which would know its parent's homeland only through dim recollections, could be tutored in the ways of the old country. In numerous ways, the memory of Virginia and Carolina—kept alive by the continued influx of newcomers to the west—became as important for black people in the nineteenth-century black belt as the memory of Africa had been for black people in the seventeenth- and eighteenth-century seaboard.

The forcible extraction of thousands of African Americans from the seaboard states also reshaped the lives of those left behind. Molding hopes and expectations to the relentless reality of deportation, those who lived under the ever-present threat of sale "down the river" also reformulated African

American life. Among the new truths was the sad fact that many could not expect to see their children grow to maturity. During the nineteenth century, more than a third of the children in the upper South were separated from their parents by the process of sale to the interior. Parents, too, were separated from each other, for husbands and wives might be sold at anytime. If African American society on the frontier was a culture of youth, slave society on the seaboard was weighted toward the aged and was often bereft of children, just as it was sundered by the separation of spouses and siblings. Few slaves could expect to nurture their children to maturity, see their grandchildren grow up, and succor their own parents in their last years. In short, the transformation of slavery played havoc with African American family and community life in both the new frontier and the old settlements in ways that need to be fully explored.

AFRO-CHRISTIANITY

The combined effects of the Cotton Revolution and the Great Migration from the upper to the lower South transformed life within the quarter. No aspect of slave life from the family to the structure of leadership remained unchanged. But perhaps none changed more than the slaves' religious life. A people who had defiantly rejected Christianity for more than two centuries suddenly embraced Jesus Christ.

Parts of the story are well known. Prior to American independence, most slaves knew little of Christianity, and most slaveholders were indifferent—or antagonistic—to their slaves imbibing the teaching of Jesus. A series of evangelical awakenings that accompanied the American Revolution and continued into the nineteenth century changed that radically. To the evangelicals, nothing more fully validated the power of God's grace than the conversion of the lowly slave. But the egalitarianism of the evangelical revivals waned in the late eighteenth century and was all but extinguished among slaveholders by the first decade of the nineteenth century.

The advent of African American Christianity thus drew from new sources. For a variety of reasons, some slaveholders encouraged slave conversion, not so much as Christian egalitarians seeking a unity in Christ but as Christian stewards bringing their God to heathens and as slaveholding paternalists bringing their civilization to savages. That the promise of a better life in the afterworld might make for greater subordination in the slave quarter only made the new missionary spirit more compelling, at least to some members of the slaveowning class, and they built plantation chapels, invited itinerants to preach to their slaves, and—taking up the paternalist role directly—led their slaves in prayer.

For their part, slaves were increasingly receptive to Christianity. For some, it meant the surety of a day away from the fields or a chance to win the slaveowner's confidence. But it also was an opportunity to practice a religion that, by the story of Moses, promised liberation from earthly bondage and that, by the story of Jesus, promised eternal redemption and divine justice, by which the wicked would be punished. During the nineteenth century, tens of thousands of slaves converted to Christianity and many thousands more were born into a faith that their eighteenth-century forebears knew not or had consciously rejected. Why they did so remains an open question, although recent work has provided a number of clues.[3] What is clear is that the creation of African American Christianity was as much the creation of a new faith as it was the expansion of the white man's religion for the brothers and sisters who gathered together in hush harbors.

The Cotton Revolution, the second Great Migration, and the advent of African American Christianity were not the only changes in black life during the nineteenth century. With them came changes in the standing of free people of color, the nature of slave law, and the contents of racial ideologies. But these three major components are enough to suggest how dramatically black life was transformed between the Revolution of 1800 and the Revolution of 1861.

NOTES

1 Kenneth M. Stampp, *The Peculiar Institution: Slavery in the Ante-Bellum South* (New York: Knopf, 1956).
2 Alternative views of slavery include Ira Berlin, *Generations of Captivity: A History of African-American Slaves* (Cambridge: Harvard University Press, 2004) and *Many Thousands Gone: The First Two Centuries of Slavery in North America* (Cambridge: Harvard University Press, 2000); David Brion Davis, *Inhuman Bondage: The Rise and Fall of Slavery in the New World* (New York: Oxford University Press, 2006); Peter Kolchin, *American Slavery, 1619–1877* (New York: Hill & Wang, 1994).
3 Janet Duitsman Cornelius, *Slave Missions and the Black Church in the Antebellum South* (Columbia: University of South Carolina Press, 1999); Albert J. Raboteau, *Slave Religion: The "Invisible Institution" in the Antebellum South*, updated ed. (New York: Oxford University Press, 2004); John B. Boles, ed., *Masters & Slaves in the House of the Lord: Race and Religion in the American South, 1740–1870* (Lexington: University Press of Kentucky, 1988); Paul Finkelman, ed., *Religion and Slavery* (New York: Garland, 1989).

PAUL FINKELMAN

The Significance and Persistence of Proslavery Thought

Slavery, an institution that traces its origins to prehistoric times, evolved for many centuries without much criticism. Apart from a few scattered critiques, slavery was regarded as a basic fact of life, an accommodation to humankind's fallen state. Beginning in the mid-eighteenth century, however, slavery aroused growing moral qualms. In this essay, Paul Finkelman, one of the nation's leading legal historians, examines how the South's intellectual elite defended slavery. Carefully disentangling the various proslavery arguments, he shows that defenders of slavery drew upon history, theology, economics, and science to justify the institution. Ultimately, however, proslavery arguments rested on a single factor, race.

After 1830, white southerners stopped referring to slavery as a necessary evil. They argued, instead, that it was a beneficial institution that created a hierarchical society superior to the leveling democracy of the North. By the late 1840s, a new and more explicitly racist rationale for slavery had emerged.

As David Brion Davis taught us nearly four decades ago, for most of human history slavery was an accepted system of labor management and an accepted status for human beings.[1] Slavery was not defended in any great detail, because it was so rarely attacked. Shortly before the American Revolution, however, slavery came under attack from religious groups, especially Quakers and Methodists. After the Revolution, the ideology of the new nation further challenged slavery.

These changes in American culture led southerners, beginning with the Second Continental Congress, to offer public defenses of slavery. The very fact that the southern master class had to defend its ownership of human beings underscores the "peculiar" nature of American slavery. Masters in earlier times and in other places felt no need to explain to anyone why they held slaves. In most cultures, and at most times, ruling classes accepted that others in society would be treated as inferiors and might be enslaved or oppressed without any moral issues arising. Romans saw nothing peculiar about slavery and therefore saw no need to defend it. For Rome, and for most of the ancient world, as Moses Finley noted, "Ideological openness was facilitated by the nakedness of the oppression and exploitation: no 'false consciousness' was necessary or possible."[2]

In the classical world, early modern Europe, the Islamic world, much of pre-Columbian America, and throughout Asia and Africa, the legitimacy of slavery often rested on notions of warfare. Under accepted rules of war, enemies captured in battle could be summarily killed. Those whose lives were spared were, in effect, "socially" or legally "dead" and thus might be enslaved.[3] This also held true for civilians captured in cities, especially if those cities had previously refused to surrender to the ultimately successful army. Thus, throughout these slaveholding societies, people from all walks of life might find themselves in some form of bondage if they ended up on the losing side of a military conflict. Such people might also regain their liberty through a reversal of military fortune or through a ransom.

Before the 1500s, and the European settlement of the Americas, slavery was only marginally based on race or ethnicity. Often, slaves were from another ethnic group—Greeks enslaved captured Persians; Romans enslaved captured Carthaginians; but, by the same token, Persians enslaved Greeks, and Carthaginians enslaved Romans. Although most classical slaves were "barbarians" from other cultures, members of the same ethnic and racial groups also enslaved each other. As Moses Finley observed, "There were Greek slaves in Greece, Italian slaves in Rome."[4] Similarly, there were Chinese slaves in China, Egyptian slaves in Egypt, Hebrew slaves in ancient Israel, Babylonian slaves in Babylonia, and Russian slaves in Russia. Africans enslaved not only Africans of different ethnic groups but also members of their own communities. Europeans enslaved each other throughout ancient times and well into the modern period.[5] The nature of slavery was further complicated by the possibility of manumission, through which slaves became free. Because slavery was not tied to race, manumission was easier, and, in the ancient world and throughout much of Africa, once free, former slaves—or at least their children or grandchildren—were often indistinguishable from other free persons. In other words, an individual in the ancient world, Africa, much of Asia, the Islamic world, and early modern Europe might conceivably be a free person, a slave, a free person again, and perhaps even a slaveowner or slave trader, all within one lifetime.

Most strikingly, nowhere in the world before the sixteenth century was enslavement ever confined to a single race or ethnic group. In most premodern societies, enslavement could be the fate of anyone, at any time.[6] The historian Carl Degler notes that "[t]here was a time in antiquity when anyone, regardless of nation, religion, or race, might be a slave."[7] Alan Watson has shown that most legal records of Roman slavery bear on the enslavement of elite slaves, who were often from the same class and race as their masters.[8] This serves to remind us that it was only in the New World, and particularly in what became the United States, that race became centrally connected to slavery. Indeed, the most striking aspect of Roman slavery, in comparison with slavery in the United States, was the extent to which enslavement had nothing to do with race.[9] Enslavement could happen to anyone.

The biblical story of Joseph demonstrates the possibility in the ancient world that anyone could become a slave, and also that it was not implausible to believe that someone could rise from enslavement to the highest level of political power. Joseph began his life as the spoiled, favorite son of a wealthy Hebrew patriarch. He was sold into slavery by his jealous brothers, dropping dramatically in his social status. Later, he gained favor in the eyes of Pharaoh and was elevated to the highest office in Egypt. He functioned as the Pharaoh's right-hand man, even though he was both a former slave and a foreigner. Whether the story of Joseph is accurate or not—or whether it happened at all—is irrelevant. The point here is that no one doubted it could have happened, despite the fact that Joseph was a Hebrew and a slave living in Egypt.[10]

It is of course quite impossible to imagine an African American slave gaining his freedom and, like Joseph, becoming an advisor to a political leader at any time before the Civil War. Unlike "[f]reedmen in the New World," who "carried an external sign of their slave origin in their skin colour, even after many generations," slaves in the ancient world who became free "simply melted into the total population within one or at the most two generations."[11] In Rome, "tens of thousands of freedmen's sons" rose "into a world remote from that of the masses."[12]

In the years immediately following the Revolution, slaveowners began to offer defenses of slavery. For the first time, a defense of slavery seemed necessary.[13] Before the Revolution, there was no necessity to defend slavery per se. It was simply one more level of social status in the British Empire; slavery fit perfectly well into a society built on hierarchy. But, with hierarchy under attack, American masters had to develop some explanation for why they continued to hold slaves. During the Revolution, the British intellectual Samuel Johnson asked, "How is it that we hear the loudest *yelps* for liberty among the drivers of negroes?"[14] The move toward abolition in the North suggested that some Americans agreed with the implications of Johnson's question. The onus was now on the slaveowners of the new nation to answer Johnson.

Fittingly, perhaps, as well as ironically, the most important early defense of the institution came from a person most remembered for his articulation of the rights of man and the fundamental importance of liberty: Thomas Jefferson. Equally ironic was the defense of slavery that developed at the Philadelphia Convention in 1787, which drafted a national constitution for a "free people."

In the Declaration of Independence, Jefferson had set out, unintentionally perhaps, the argument for abolition: "We hold these Truths to be self-evident, that all Men are created equal, that they are endowed by their Creator with certain unalienable Rights, that among these are Life, Liberty, and the Pursuit of Happiness." This language threatened the legitimacy of slavery, for at least some Americans saw these words as universally applicable to all people rather than as a political theory designed solely for themselves. Thus, the Revolution set the stage for a defense of slavery.

A few years after drafting the Declaration, Jefferson developed the outlines of a number of important proslavery arguments that countered his assertions of equality. In his *Notes on the State of Virginia*, the author used arguments based on history, science, political theory, practical necessity, and, most of all race to justify the continued enslavement of Africans.

Jefferson argued that blacks were inherently inferior to whites in their mental abilities and their moral virtues. He would not speculate on whether blacks were "originally a distinct race, or made distinct by time and circumstances," but, whatever the cause, he asserted that they were "inferior to the whites in . . . body and mind."[15] He claimed that he had never found a black who "had uttered a thought above the level of plain narration; never seen an elementary trait of painting or sculpture." He found "no poetry" among blacks. Jefferson conceded that blacks were brave, but this, he said, was due to "a want of forethought, which prevents their seeing a danger till it be present."[16] He offered pseudoscientific theories of race, speculating that blackness might come "from the colour of the blood" or that blacks might breed with the "Oranootan."[17] He posited, without offering any proof, that black men preferred white women as their sexual partners but that their sexuality, like everything else about blacks, was less human and more animalistic. "They are more ardent after their female," he wrote in *Notes on the State of Virginia*, "but love seems with them to be more an eager desire, than a tender delicate mixture of sentiment and sensation. Their griefs are transient."[18] Indeed, he found that

In general, their existence appears to participate more of sensation than reflection. To this must be ascribed their disposition to sleep when abstracted from their diversions, and unemployed in labour. An animal whose body is at rest, and who does not reflect, must be disposed to sleep of course. Comparing them by their faculties of memory, reason, and imagination, it appears to me, that in memory they are equal to the whites; in reason much inferior, as I think one could scarcely be found capable of tracing and comprehending the investigations of Euclid; and that in imagination they are dull, tasteless, and anomalous.[19]

Initiating a historical argument that would become a mainstay of proslavery thought, Jefferson noted that ancient Rome had also been a slaveholding society. He observed, however, that many Roman slaves achieved great accomplishments because "they were of the race of whites"; American slaves, on the other hand, could never achieve such distinction because they were not white.

Jefferson feared race war and its opposite, interracial love and marriage; and these fears, combined with the necessity of brute labor, led to an early and important defense of slavery. In it, Jefferson set out four proslavery themes. First, since antiquity, he wrote, slavery had been an accepted social and economic institution in all of the great nations of the world, including Rome and Greece. Second, ending slavery would lead to chaos and the destruction of civilized society. Third, the southern economy depended on slave labor, and there really was no viable alternative to this labor. And, fourth, blacks, he proffered, were genetically inferior to whites while at the same time innately predisposed to sexually immorality; they were, in essence, a dangerous class that had to be controlled at all times. Slavery was obviously the most effective, most efficient, and most profitable way to control the Africans and their descendants living in the United States.

Proslavery thought evolved after Jefferson in a variety of ways. Many modern scholars have focused on the theoretical defenses of slavery, linking it to attacks on capitalism and market economies. Some have used proslavery thinkers to defend their own modern arguments about societies and economic development. Although such arguments are intellectually interesting, they have ignored what was the central focus of slavery: race. Even proslavery theorists like George Fitzhugh, who are known for their sophisticated analysis of society, ultimately tied their arguments to race.

Between 1820 and 1861, southerners developed a variety of defenses of slavery that were rooted in traditional academic, professional, and political categories commonly understood by most educated Americans. This defense also responded, in kind, to attacks on slavery. Southerners turned to theology, history, political theory, law, science, and economics to defend the central institution of their society. They expressed their views in almost every conceivable form, including sermons and speeches, delivered orally and then published; popular essays and learned articles on the Bible, history, and philosophy; economic analyses of labor, management, and production; books and articles in scientific and medical journals on all manner of subjects, from anthropology to zoology; contemporary descriptions of Haiti and other places where slavery had been abolished; legal treatises and judicial opinions; and novels, short stories, poems, and book reviews.

The common themes of this literature included arguments on black inferiority; the notion that slavery is both universal and natural in all societies; and the idea that southern slavery is the most humane system of slavery ever devised because it protects and nurtures the slaves, who are inferior beings in need of care and supervision.

All of these arguments could not fit into a single, coherent defense of slavery. Some were mutually exclusive. For example, the largest single body of proslavery literature is based on religious defenses of slavery. Such defenses appealed to the overwhelmingly Protestant, often evangelical, southern population. They were also aimed at the South's Protestant counterparts in the North and in Great Britain. But these religious defenses of slavery were often incompatible with the proslavery arguments based on science, medicine, and anthropology, which attracted some of the sharpest minds of the South.

One important debate illustrates this conflict between religion and science. Southern ministers and their allies argued that all humans were the descendants of Adam and Eve and existed as a result of a single creation, as described in the Bible. These ministers claimed that blacks were the descendants of Noah's son Ham and Noah's grandson Canaan. After the flood, according to the biblical story, Noah cursed Canaan, and proslavery ministers claimed that the biblical "curse of Canaan" meant that Canaan and all his descendants became black.[20]

Mid-nineteenth century scientists argued that this biblical literalism was nonsense. They rejected the whole notion of monogenesis, asserting that blacks had in fact been separately created. Some of these scientists argued that blacks were a separate species of beings, somewhere on the evolutionary scale between the great apes and humans. These scientists asserted that blacks had a different anatomy than whites and were even susceptible to different diseases.

Many in the overwhelmingly Protestant and evangelical South rejected the scientific arguments and stuck to their biblical defense. This forced them, however, into a debate over the Bible with northern ministers, who had their own biblical arguments on the immorality of slavery. In the North, at least, and in much of the rest of the world, the antislavery biblical argument neutralized or defeated the proslavery biblical argument in the struggle for public opinion outside of the South. The antislavery forces focused on the Golden Rule—"Do unto others as you would have them do unto you"—to make the persuasive point that slavery was antithetical to the spirit of Christianity. The result was that by fighting the intellectual debate over slavery on biblical grounds, the South was in fact fighting the antislavery forces on their strongest ground.

Ironically, opponents of slavery had few scientific arguments of their own; in terms of convincing outsiders, therefore, the scientific arguments may have been the strongest in the South's intellectual arsenal.[21] Yet many of the most prominent southerners refused to use these arguments because they were in conflict with scripture.

Some proslavery theorists tried to please both the scientists and the clergy, accepting the idea of a single creation but searching the Bible for an explanation of the origin of the races. Some claimed that when God cursed Cain for killing Abel, he made Cain black. This theory, however, was relatively weak because it did not explain the existence of other races. Some southerners argued that the different races emerged when God transformed the builders of the Tower of Babel. The most common explanation for the existence of blacks was, again, the story of Noah and the curse of Canaan. Dr. Samuel Cartwright of New Orleans was perhaps the most creative of all. He argued that blacks and all other nonwhites were among the "other creatures" that God placed in the Garden of Eden before the creations of Adam. Cartwright suggested that the biblical story of Eve and the Tree of Knowledge had involved not a serpent but rather a "negro gardener" who handed Eve the apple.[22]

Beyond the disputes between the scientists and clergy, important proslavery thinkers differed substantially among themselves about other issues. Many proslavery theorists, such as Thomas Jefferson and George Fitzhugh, had a strong animus towards capitalism, industrial society, urbanization, and market economies. These southern leaders extolled the virtues of an agrarian, noncapitalist society. On the other hand, the fiercely proslavery James D. B. DeBow, editor of *De Bow's Commercial Review of the South and Western States*, was a forceful advocate of southern industrialization. Similarly, those who advocated that "Cotton is King," such as Senator James Henry Hammond, implicitly endorsed the importance and power of world markets.

The defense of slavery that allowed it to coexist with American democracy relied on numerous theories and factual assertions based on a wide variety of perspectives, philosophies, and principles. This defense also responded, in kind, to attacks on slavery. Southerners turned to theology, history, political theory, law, science, statistics, census data, and economics to defend the central institution of their society. They used sermons, speeches, essays, scientific articles, short stories, novels, poems, and book reviews not merely to defend slavery from its opponents but to aggressively argue that the institution was a blessing, a benefit, a "positive good" for the masters, the slaves, the nonslaveholding whites, and, indeed, for the entire society.

Ultimately, the defense rested on six interrelated prongs: history, religion, economics, political and constitutional arguments, social necessity, and science and medicine. Tied to all of these defenses, and woven throughout them, were arguments and discussions of race. Law, literature, theology, and all other disciplines and arts were applied to these defenses.

The *historical defense* was based on the argument that slavery was a central institution in all great societies, and that democracy, higher learning, and even civilization itself all relied on slavery. The proponents of this view noted that the great classical philosophers, especially Plato and Aristotle, assumed that slavery was an integral part of any great society. Southerners pointed to the accomplishments of the Grecian democracy and the grandeur of the Roman Republic to make the point that truly great cultures and societies not only accepted slavery but depended on it. These southerners noted that slavery allowed the leaders of a society to avoid manual labor and gave them time to devote to affairs of state. Thus, classical support for slavery dovetailed with the notion, advanced by many southerners, that slavery was a prerequisite to maintaining a ruling elite within a democratic society. As the historian David Brion Davis noted of Aristotle, "Living in a society that increasingly dissociated culture and public service from the slightest taint of manual labor," he (Aristotle) "saw slavery as a necessary means of supplying the wants of life."[23] Southern whites heartily agreed with such observations.

The logic of this argument was illustrated, in the mind of southerners, by the contributions to national life made by the great planter-politicians such as George Washington, George Mason, Thomas Jefferson, and General Charles Cotesworth Pinckney. In the antebellum era, this sort of contribution continued with leaders such as Andrew Jackson, James Polk, John C. Calhoun, and Henry Clay. These men could devote their lives to public service because they had slaves to provide for their economic needs and their domestic comforts, just as the great slaveholding citizens of Greece and Rome were afforded the opportunity to devote their lives to the common good.

Southerners often turned to the ancient world to justify their modern institution. In looking at the ancient world, they found support from some of the most important thinkers in Western culture. Plato, for example, opposed the enslavement of fellow Greeks, and in *The Republic*, he rejected the enslavement of citizens as punishment for crimes. Significantly, however, Plato and other Greek philosophers took for granted the enslavement of non-Greeks—barbarians—and, in fact, "had come to believe that the inferiority of barbarians could be seen in their willingness to submit to despotic and absolutist rulers."[24] Barbarians were in effect a "slavish people" who were unfit for self-government and naturally suited for bondage. This meant that in their own countries they would be perpetually ruled by tyrants, and also that, if manumitted in Greece, they could not possibly govern themselves. Similarly, Aristotle "built his entire argument" for slavery "around Plato's theory of natural inferiority."[25] Indeed, he believed that Greeks should find a different race of people to serve as their slaves.[26]

Southern defenders of democracy and slavery, such as Thomas Jefferson, instinctively understood this concept. The Greek ideas of natural slavishness converged perfectly with southern notions of slavery. One need only substitute "black" or "African" for "barbarian," to see how easily southerners could recognize that the great thinkers of Ancient Greece were truly their allies. An important illustration of this comes from *An Inquiry Into the Law of Negro Slavery*, written by Thomas R. R. Cobb, a cofounder of the first law school in Georgia. In this treatise, Cobb quoted Plato, Euripides, Juvenal, and other classical writers to teach his readers that slavery, especially Negro slavery, was accepted by the greatest minds of Western culture. Tying race to history, Cobb insisted that at an "early day" the "negro was commonly used as a slave at Rome." Implicitly comparing the South to the Roman Republic, he noted that "For her footmen and couriers" the Roman "wife "preferred always the negroes" and that "Negroes, being generally slaves of luxury, commanded a very high price." Similarly, Cobb averred that in Ancient Israel "many" of the slaves "were Africans of negro extraction" and that "Among the Egyptians . . . there were numbers of negro slaves." Making similar claims for Assyria and Alexander the Great's empire, he concluded "the negro was a favorite among slaves" in the ancient world.[27] Although there is no historical support for these ideas, Cobb's assertions went unchallenged by most readers, who had little knowledge of or access to serious works of ancient history. Cobb's historical claims, however, factually inaccurate though they were, illustrate well the way in which southerners used (or misused) history to support the idea of slavery in general and of racially based slavery in particular.

The holiness of ancient Israel was the starting place for the *religious defense* of slavery. Most of the biblical Patriarchs, beginning with Abraham, were slaveowners. In testing Job, God allowed all of his slaves to be taken from him, and in rewarding Job for his piety, God made sure that Job had more slaves than before. Leviticus set out elaborate laws for governing slaves, but nowhere did the texts even implicitly condemn slavery. On the contrary, the law of the Old Testament *assumed* the existence of slavery, and merely attempted to regulate it. A minor example of this illustrates the point in a way that southern slaveowners surely will have understood. Leviticus declared that, "And whosoever lieth carnally with a woman, that is a bondmaid, betrothed to an husband, and not at all redeemed, nor freedom given her; she shall be scourged, they shall not be put to death, because she was not free."[28] Sexual relations with another man's slave woman, even if she were married, would not lead to a punishment, the text says, because the slave's marriage was not recognized by the law in the same way that a free person's marriage was. This passage also assumed, without comment or explanation, that male masters were free to have sex with their female slaves. If God ordained slavery in the Old Testament—and even explained how to deal with sex between slave women and free men—then how, southerners asked, could there be any moral taint from owning slaves?

Proslavery theorists were equally at home turning to the New Testament for their support of slavery. Paul's "Letter to Philemon" explicitly endorsed the return of fugitive slaves. The Corinthian letters proclaimed that slaves should be satisfied with their lot: "For he that is called in the Lord, *being a servant*, is the Lord's freeman; likewise he that was called, *being* free, is Christ's servant."[29] Southern ministers defended slavery with countless sermons on these and other texts. They were certain that the Bible, both the Old and the New Testament, supported their system of bondage.

While noting that the Bible supported slavery, they also urged masters to apply Christian principles to their treatment of slaves. Ministers argued for moderate punishment, sufficient food, decent housing, and even giving slaves leisure time, including an observance of the Sabbath that precluded work.

From the beginning of slavery in the Anglo-American world, one defense of bondage had been that it allowed for the conversion of pagans. This continued after the slave trade had ended. The *Duties of Christian Masters*, published by the

Baptist State Convention of Alabama, exhorted masters to care for the souls as well as the bodies of slaves. The author advised that "short portions of Divine truth should be read and explained, and their particular application to them urged with kindness and faithfulness. Let the master exercise his judgment, that his servants may be benefited by his wise arrangements for their spiritual well-being."[30]

The religious arguments for slavery tied in with racist assumptions held by whites. Southern ministers accepted the idea that only through enslavement could a Christian morality be imposed on blacks. While supporting slavery, ministers also encouraged masters to respect slave marriages when at all possible, and, of course, to avoid sexual exploitation of slaves. Their argument was a strong one: if southern slavery was humane and generous, and rooted in Christianity, then it could easily be justified to the entire world as an institution beneficial not only to the master class but to the slaves themselves. Southern masters, in other words, could do well by doing good.

Finally, southern religious leaders offered a biblical defense of black enslavement. As noted above, slaveowners turned to the story of Noah to explain the origins of blacks and to legitimize slavery. After the flood, Noah was "drunk and uncovered himself inside his tent." His son Ham "saw his father's nakedness, and told his two brothers outside." When Noah awoke he cursed Ham's son, Canaan, declaring "Accursed be Canaan. He shall be his brothers' meanest slave." He then blessed his other sons, declaring "may Canaan be his slave."[31] Slaveowners argued that part of the "curse of Ham" was the transformance of Canaan into a black man. Hence, the Bible taught that slavery was legitimate and that race justified slavery. Southern ministers retold and explained this biblical story throughout the antebellum period.

Throughout the antebellum period, numerous defenders of slavery stressed its importance to the *American economy*. In urging the admission of Kansas as a slave state, Senator James Henry Hammond of South Carolina argued that "the strength of a nation depends in a great measure upon its wealth," which, he said, was created by exports. He estimated that about two-thirds of America's exports were either produced by slave labor, as in the case of raw cotton, or were manufactured goods tied to slavery, as in the case of cotton cloth. In addition, Hammond noted that much of the North's industrial production was based on the cotton, tobacco, and hemp that the South produced. Furthermore, he noted that much of England's economy was tied to southern production.

Equating attacks on slavery with attacks on the productions of slave labor, Hammond was emphatic: "No, sir, you dare not make war on cotton. No power on earth dares make war upon it. Cotton is king."[32]

Like the American system of government itself, the *legal defense* of slavery had both a state component and a federal component. It also had a theoretical component. Legal theorists, such as Thomas R. R. Cobb, offered arguments based on property, history, and the needs of a stable society to defend the existing slave system and to show what laws were necessary to preserve it. Proslavery legal theorists like Cobb argued that blacks were inferior to whites and thus that there had to be special laws and special punishments for both free blacks and slaves. If blacks were inherently a criminal element, as proslavery theorists maintained, then the law had to be harsh and strict in keeping such people in their place.

State judges provided decisions, analyses, and precedents designed to protect slavery. Some of the case law was directed at protecting slave property *within* the South. For example, in *State v. Hale* the North Carolina Supreme Court upheld the prosecution of a white man for beating a slave owned by someone else.[33] The court noted that such offenses were "usually committed by men of dissolute habits, hanging loose upon society, who, being repelled from association with well disposed citizens, take refuge in the company of slaves, whom they deprave by their example, embolden by their familiarity, and then beat, under the expectation that a slave dare not resent a blow from a white man."

Decisions such as *State v. Hale* protected the property interest of a master in a slave but permitted the punishment of whites who harmed slaves. At the same time, in cases such as *State v. Mann* the courts affirmed the rights of masters to treat a slave however they wished, as long as they did not murder him or her.[34] The purpose of slavery, according to the legal systems of the southern states, was to benefit the master. As North Carolina's chief justice, Thomas Ruffin asserted: "The end is the profit of the master, his security and the public safety; the subject, one doomed in his own person and his posterity, to live without knowledge and without the capacity to make anything his own, and to toil that another may reap the fruits." Because of this, "the power of the master must be absolute to render the submission of the slave perfect." The majesty of the law, and the power of the courts, secured to the master the authority to coerce the slave. The legal system defended slavery, affirming that the courts could not "allow the right of the master to be brought into discussion in the courts of justice. The slave, to remain a slave, must be made sensible that there is no appeal from his master; that his power is in no instance usurped; but is conferred by the laws of man at least, if not by the law of God."[35]

At the federal level, the master class turned to the United States Constitution for the protection of slavery. Under the Constitution, masters could regain their fugitive slaves and rely on the national government to protect their property interest in their slaves. Neither slaves nor free blacks could hope for any legal protection from the U.S. Constitution. In Dred Scott v. Sandford, Chief Justice Roger B. Taney constitutionalized this theory while nationalizing southern concepts of race.[36] Taney found that, under the Constitution, blacks "had no rights which the white man was bound to respect."[37] Applying a rigorous, although not necessarily accurate argument based on the intentions of the Constitution's framers, the chief justice found that "neither the class of persons who had been imported as slaves, nor their descendants, whether they had become free or not, were then acknowledged as a part of the people, nor intended to be included in the general words used in that memorable instrument."[38]

Scientists, physicians, and anthropologists offered their own defenses of slavery. Some of these defenses were implicit. Northern scholars, such as Samuel G. Morton of Philadelphia, argued that blacks were a separate species from whites and biologically and intellectually inferior to them. Morton did not talk about slavery but limited his discussions to "science" as he understood it. He made no direct comments about slavery but was, of course, fully aware that others would use his scientific "discoveries" to support slavery.

More directly concerned with slavery were two southern physicians, Samuel Cartwright of New Orleans and Josiah C. Nott of Mobile, Alabama. Both were significant figures in the medical communities of the antebellum South. They contributed numerous articles to southern medical journals on subjects that had nothing to do with slavery. Nott was an expert on yellow fever, and posited the theory, which proved to be correct, that the disease was transmitted to humans through an intermediate host. Dr. Walter Reed would later use Nott's theories to solve the mystery of the spread of both yellow fever and malaria.

Nott and Cartwright also wrote extensively on the connections between science, race, and slavery. Cartwright was well known as a "Negro" doctor, someone who specialized in treating slaves. Masters throughout Louisiana, as well as other parts of the deep South, brought their slaves to him for care. Cartwright thus observed slaves and reached what he believed to be scientific discoveries about blacks.

The southern doctor argued that blacks and whites had significant anatomical differences and that blacks were suited for slavery. He wrote that a black had more nerve endings than a white person but that, "the brain being ten per cent less in volume and weight, he [i.e., the black] is, from necessity, more under the influence of his instincts and *animality*, than other races of men and less under the influence of his reflective faculties."[39] This, Cartwright believed, made blacks more suited to slavery than were members of other races. Cartwright also believed that blacks suffered from diseases that whites could not catch. He identified "Dysaethesia Aethiopica" as an illness that caused slaves to misbehave, as if by compulsion. Another disease, "Drapetomania," affected the minds of slaves, "causing negroes to runaway."

Cartwright's scientific observations led him to defend slavery because, in his mind, slavery protected the inferior (black) race, which he believed could not survive in a state of freedom. Dr. Josiah Nott was equally certain of the justice of slavery, but he rejected Cartwright's acceptance of blacks as merely an inferior group within the human family. Nott, instead, concluded that blacks were a separate species from whites, having been created by God solely to be slaves for whites.[40] For Nott, black inferiority was "a fixed law of nature," and thus slavery was not only logical but moral.[41]

The South also turned to a *cultural defense* of slavery. Using short stories, novels, book reviews, and poems, southerners offered a romantic, fictionalized portrayal of slavery to counter growing northern hostility. Sometimes the literature was explicitly political. William J. Grayson's "The Hireling and the Slave," for example, a fifty-page poem, compared the lot of the slave to that of the hired worker in a free market. The message was clear: a slave was protected from the cruelties of the market while the free worker was not. Other literary works included reviews of *Uncle Tom's Cabin* as well as stories and novels modeled on Stowe's masterpiece but written to provide a sympathetic view of slavery.

The *political argument* in favor of slavery proceeded from the assumption that any attack on slavery would lead to a civil war and that the American political and constitutional system was based implicitly on the understanding that slavery was sacrosanct. In addition, proslavery theorists argued that slavery ultimately made democracy work. Such theorists as Senator James Henry Hammond and George Fitzhugh claimed that the greatest threat to democracy came from class warfare, which destabilized the economy and threatened a peaceful and harmonious implementation of the laws. Other proslavery theorists asserted that slavery eliminated this problem by elevating all free people to the status of "citizen" and removing the lowest classes of society—what Hammond called "the mudsill"—from the political process.[42] Those who would most threaten economic stability and political harmony—the lower classes—were not allowed to undermine democratic society because they were not allowed to participate in it. Thus, the rights of life, liberty, and happiness proclaimed in the Declaration of Independence could be universally applied to white Americans precisely because they were not applied to blacks.

A subset of the political defense of slavery involved southern responses to the Declaration of Independence. Some southerners categorically rejected the entire ideology of the Declaration of Independence. In 1826, John Randolph of Roanoke proclaimed that the Declaration was " 'a most pernicious falsehood.' "[43] Edmund Ruffin, one of the South's earliest secessionists, thought the Declaration was a dangerous document. John C. Calhoun, according to contemporary sources, "labeled the idea of equality a 'false doctrine,' only 'hypothetically true,' [something] that had been 'inserted' in the Declaration of Independence 'without any necessity.' "[44] James Hammond sneered at the "fine sounding and sentimental" language of the Declaration.[45]

In 1854, George Fitzhugh provided an elaborate proslavery attack on the Declaration. Fitzhugh believed that the United States was founded on "abstractions" that had been "professed falsely."[46] He candidly proposed that "men are not born physically, morally or intellectually equal" and that, contrary to the ideology of the Declaration, "their natural inequalities beget inequalities of rights." All blacks, Fitzhugh believed, were born "weak in mind or body,"[47] and because of this, "nature has made them slaves; all that law and government can do, is to regulate, modify and mitigate their slavery." He argued that, on historical grounds, " 'life and liberty' are not 'inalienable'; they have been sold in all countries, and in all ages, and must be sold so long as human nature lasts." Slavery, in Fitzhugh's mind, was not peculiar but rather fundamental to society. He believed that the North, not the South, had a peculiar institution—freedom. It was thus the purpose of the government "to restrict, control and punish man 'in the pursuit of happiness.' " The preamble to the Declaration, according to Fitzhugh, was "verbose, newborn, false, and unmeaning." The body of the document was "exuberantly false, and arborescently fallacious."[48] Fitzhugh and other proslavery theorists perceived that all men were not created equal and that inequality was a common, natural, and universal phenomenon. Rejecting the Declaration and its theories of equality, many southerners instead developed their own proslavery arguments, ultimately holding that slavery was a positive good for the slave and the master.[49]

Numerous southerners continued to endorse the Declaration but denied that it could affect slavery. Some southerners took a high road by arguing that the Declaration, like its Virginia counterpart, applied only to citizens or political communities. Slaves were naturally excluded from these categories.[50] One Virginia Congressman argued that "no ingenuity" could "torture the Declaration of Independence into having the remotest allusion to the institution of domestic slavery."[51] Alexander Stephens, the future vice president of the Confederacy, believed the framers had established "the first great principles of self-government by the governing race."[52]

The key for Stephens, and other southern supporters of the Declaration, was race. Race made it possible for slaveowners to accept the credo of America because they could reject its application to their own slaves. Thus, one Louisiana slaveowner affirmed that all men were created "free and equal as the Declaration of Independence holds they are."[53] He then added: "But all men, niggers, and monkeys *aint*."[54]

While Calhoun, Fitzhugh, and other white southerners rejected the Declaration because it undermined slavery, other masters "frequently made the Fourth of July a holiday for their slaves."[55] Slaves at a barbecue to celebrate the signing of the Declaration of Independence may seem ironic, but for many masters it was not. Masters considered slavery a benefit provided to blacks, who were, in their eyes, racially inferior. American independence could thus be celebrated with slaves because it was independence from Britain that allowed American slaveowners to develop the political and legal system that perpetuated and strengthened slavery—an institution that they claimed was a positive good for slaves and masters alike.

In the end, the key to the proslavery argument was *race*. It served as the basis for all other defenses of slavery. Indeed, it might be said that the racial argument was the "mudsill" of proslavery theory, just as James Hammond had sought to proclaim that slavery was the mudsill of southern society. Ultimately, all of the defenses of slavery came back to race. This was necessary for two reasons. First, in the end only race could counter the obvious point that slavery contradicted the egalitarian and free-labor basis of American society. Second, if race was not the ultimate basis of slavery, then all of the arguments in favor of slavery might be applied to poor whites or immigrant whites in addition to their traditional African American target.

The racial defense of slavery was based on two interrelated arguments. First, that blacks were inferior to whites and were indeed better off as slaves; and, second, that if freed, people of African ancestry could not survive in the United States or live in peace with whites. The racial argument was tied to all other arguments defending slavery because, for Americans, "race has always been the central reality of slavery."[56]

Because slavery in the United States was "black slavery," the study of slavery remains current and vital, and "even a 'purely historical' study of an institution now dead for more than a century cannot escape being caught up in the urgency of contemporary black-white tensions."[57] Ultimately, southerners turned to history, religion, and science to defend the concept of race as a justification for slavery. Using science, the Bible, or both, southerners strove mightily to demonstrate why blacks were "inferior" to whites. Even after slavery ended, many of these arguments remained, being used to defend segregation, racism, and inequality. To this day, remnants of proslavery thought can be found in our public discourse as well as in Americans' private conversations.

NOTES

1 David Brion Davis, *The Problem of Slavery In Western Civilization* (Ithaca: Cornell University Press, 1966).
2 Moses I. Finley, *Ancient Slavery and Modern Ideology* (New York: Viking Press, 1980), 117.
3 On the concept of social death, see Orlando Patterson, *Slavery and Social Death* (Cambridge: Harvard University Press, 1982).
4 Finley, *Ancient Slavery*, 118.
5 In the 1940s, Germans enslaved their fellow countrymen (as well as Russians, Poles, and other Europeans). Those sent to German industries as slaves or to German slave labor camps (as opposed to death camps like Auschwitz) were often physically indistinguishable from those who commanded their labor. Under German theories of race, however, those enslaved were designated as members of different races or as politically corrupted.
6 For example, see Patterson, *Slavery and Social Death*.
7 Carl N. Degler, "The Irony of American Negro Slavery," in *Perspectives and Irony in American Negro Slavery*, ed. Harry P. Owens (Jackson: University of Mississippi Press, 1976), 19.
8 Alan Watson, "Seventeenth Century Jurists, Roman Law, and Slavery," in *Slavery and the Law*, ed. Paul Finkelman (Madison: Madison House, 1997), 367–78.
9 Moses Finley argues that "racism" was a factor in ancient slavery, "despite the absence of the skin-colour stigma; despite the variety of peoples who made up the

ancient slave populations; despite the frequency of manumission and its peculiar consequences." Thus it was "commonplace in Roman Republican speeches that Jews, Syrians, Lydians, Medes, indeed all Asiatics are 'born to slavery.' " Finley, *Ancient Slavery*, 118, 119.

10 *Genesis*, chaps. 37, 39–41.
11 Finley, *Ancient Slavery*, 97–98.
12 This was also a result in Africa, where "slaves could often anticipate the gradual assimilation of their descendants into the social mainstream." James Oakes, *Slavery and Freedom: An Interpretation of the Old South* (New York: Random House, 1990), 32.
13 There were some defenses of slavery in the Americas before the Revolution, made in response to attacks on slavery; see, for example, John Saffin, *A Brief and Candid Answer to a Late Printed Sheet, Entitled, 'The Selling of Joseph'* (Boston, 1701). This phenomenon is discussed in Davis, *Problem of Slavery in Western Culture*, 344–48. See also John Wood Sweet, *Bodies Politic: Negotiating Race In the American North, 1730–1830* (Baltimore: Johns Hopkins University Press, 2003), 59–64.
14 Quoted in Donald L. Robinson, *Slavery in the Structure of American Politics, 1765–1820* (New York: Harcourt Brace, 1971), 80.
15 Thomas Jefferson, *Notes on the State of Virginia*, ed. William Peden (Chapel Hill: University of North Carolina Press, 1954), 138–43.
16 Ibid., 142–43.
17 Ibid., 138, 139.
18 Ibid., 139.
19 Ibid., 162, 138. On Jefferson as a scientist, see Silvio A. Bedini, *Thomas Jefferson: Statesman of Science* (New York: Macmillan, 1990), esp. 89–124.
20 "And he [Noah] said: Cursed be Canaan; a servant of servants he shall be unto his brethren.
"And he said, Blessed be the Lord God of Shem; and Canaan shall be his servant.
"God shall enlarge Japheth, and he shall dwell in the tents of Shem; and Canaan shall be his servant." Gen. 9:25–27.
21 See, for example, William R. Stanton, *The Leopard's Spots: Scientific Attitudes Toward Race in America, 1815–1860* (Chicago: University of Chicago Press, 1960); Josiah Nott, *Types of Mankind* (Philadelphia: Lippincott, 1854); and various articles in Paul Finkelman, ed., *Articles on American Slavery*, vol. 16, *Religion and Slavery* (New York: Garland, 1989).
22 Samuel Cartwright, "The Unity of the Human Race Disproved by the Hebrew Bible," *DeBow's Review* 29 (1860): 130.
23 Davis, *Problem of Slavery in Western Culture*, 70.
24 Ibid., 66–67.
25 Ibid., 70.
26 Ibid., 72.
27 Thomas R. R. Cobb, *An Inquiry into the Law of Negro Slavery in the United States of America*,

To Which is Prefixed An Historical Sketch of Slavery (Philadelphia: T. & J. W. Johnson; Savannah: W. Thorne Williams, 1858), xl, lxxxi, lxvi, lxxxiii, lxvii.

28 Lev. 19:20. See also *The Jerusalem Bible: Reader's Edition* (Garden City, N.Y.: Doubleday, 1966), 128.

29 1 Cor. 7:22. The alternative, modern translation is more blunt. "A slave, when he is called in the Lord, becomes the Lord's freeman; and a freeman called in the Lord becomes Christ's slave." *New Jerusalem Bible*, 1 Cor. 7:22.

30 Rev. A. T. Holmes, "The Duties of Christian Masters," reprinted in *Duties of Masters to Servants*, ed. Holland N. McTyeire (Charleston, S.C.: Southern Baptist Publication Society, 1851), 149.

31 Gen. 9:18–25.

32 James Henry Hammond, *Congressional Globe*, 35th Cong., 1st sess., Mar. 6, 1858, 61.

33 State v. Hale, 2 Hawks (N.C.) 582 (1823).

34 2 Dev. L. Rep. (N.C.) 263 (1829).

35 State v. Mann, 13 N.C., 266, 267.

36 Dred Scott v. Sandford, 60 U.S. (19 How.) 393 (1857).

37 Ibid., 407.

38 Ibid.

39 Quoted in William Sumner Jenkins, *Pro-Slavery Thought in the Old South* (Chapel Hill: University of North Carolina Press, 1935), 250–51.

40 Reginald Horsman, *Josiah Nott of Mobile: Southerner, Physician, Racial Theorist* (Baton Rouge: Louisiana State University Press, 1987), 82.

41 Ibid., 125.

42 James Henry Hammond, "Speech on Admissions of Kansas," U.S. Senate, Mar. 4, 1858, *Congressional Globe*, 35 Cong., no. sess., 961–62.

43 Quoted in Jenkins, *Pro-Slavery Thought in the Old South*, 60.

44 John W. Blassingame, ed., *The Frederick Douglass Papers*, series 1, *Speech, Debates, and Interviews*, 1847–54 (New Haven: Yale University Press, 1982), 488, n. 15.

45 Quoted in Harvey Wish, *George Fitzhugh: Propagandist of the Old South* (Baton Rouge: Louisiana State University Press, 1943), 96.

46 George Fitzhugh, *Sociology for the South, or the Failure of Free Society* (Richmond, Va., 1854), 177; quotation in the rest of this paragraph are from pages 177–78, 179, 180, 182.

47 Ibid. 178. Fitzhugh believed that some whites, too, were born "weak in mind" and that they could therefore be legitimately enslaved.

48 Ibid. 182.

49 See generally Jenkins, *Proslavery Thought in the Old South*; Eugene D. Genovese, *The World the Slaveholders Made* (New York: Pantheon, 1969).

50 Jenkins, *Proslavery Thought in the Old South*, 156–57. In Hudgins v. Wrights, Virginia's highest court applied this analysis to similar language in the state's Declaration of Rights; see 11 Va. (1 Hen. & M.) 134 (1806).

51 Quoted in James Oakes, *The Ruling Race: A History of American Slaveholders* (New York: Knopf, 1982), 143.
52 Ibid.
53 Ibid.
54 Ibid.
55 Ibid., 142.
56 David Brion Davis, "Slavery and the American Mind," in Owens, ed., *Perspectives and Irony in American Slavery*, 59.
57 Finley, *Ancient Slavery*, 11.

ROBERT E. BONNER

Confederate Racialism and the Anticipation of Nazi Evil

Adolf Hitler admired the Confederacy, arguing that it anticipated his goal of creating a society that rested on racial hierarchy and slave labor. In this essay, Robert Bonner, a leading historian of the American South, explores the degree to which white southern leaders did regard the Confederacy as a "racial state" in which social hierarchy rested on differences among human races. For the most part, Confederate officials were reluctant to invoke scientific racism to legitimize their new republic. Two notable exceptions were Vice President Alexander Stephens and Henry Hotze, a Confederate editor and agent in England who sought to link the Confederate bid for independence with the anthropological racism that was gaining support among Europeans seeking justification for imperial expansion over nonwhite peoples in Africa and Asia.

In the 1930s, Confederate nostalgia became a global sensation, thanks in large part to *Gone with the Wind*'s international success. Among the Lost Cause enthusiasts of these years was the Nazi leader Adolph Hitler, who offered one of the most intriguing tributes ever extended to the South's vanquished civilization. According to the German Führer, the Union victory of 1865 had come with enormous consequences, even if it had defied "all historical logic and sound sense." "The beginnings of a great new social order based on the principle of slavery and inequality were destroyed by that war," Hitler grumbled, "and with them the embryo of a future truly great America." Had the Confederacy prevailed, "a real *Herren*-class" (master class) would have been created that would have "swept away all falsities of liberty and equality."[1]

If Hitler's off-handed association of the Nazis with the southern Confederacy still resonates in popular culture, few scholars have considered the validity of such a pairing in historical terms. We have little sense of how ideological currents from the 1860s South might have anticipated the most notorious of the twentieth century's racist regimes, not least because Confederate racialism itself has received remarkably little attention. Neither Civil War scholars nor students of comparative Western racism have charted the patterns of racial thought produced by southern Confederates during the 1860s.[2] As a result, we are left with only the most general sense of how the experience of the wartime white South can either be connected to or compared with that most spectacular of all forms of modern evil—the Nazi atrocities witnessed two generations after Appomattox.[3]

Within published Confederate propaganda, there were two instances in particular that can help to situate the wartime South in this larger history of western racial thought and practice. Alexander Stephen's "Cornerstone Speech" of 1861 belongs in a class by itself, since this represented the most sustained attempt to legitimize the new Confederate government by linking it to scientifically verifiable differences between human races. Elsewhere, Confederates were more cautious when it came to scientific racism, with the result that Confederate racialism was less robust than the southern anti-black racism of the 1850s, the Negrophobia practiced by the Democratic party in the Civil War North, or even the new ethnological interest in "northern" and "southern" races that dominated the most important Confederate journals during the opening years of war. Besides Stephens, the most interesting Confederate racialist was the editor Henry Hotze, who linked the southern bid for national independence with the anthropological racism then captivating the imagination of Western Europe. In pursuing his propaganda work within Europe, Hotze went farther than any other Confederate in discerning those strands of Western thought that would continue to intensify during the last third of the nineteenth century and reach their acme during the first half of the twentieth century.

Hitler's praise for Confederates' "great new social order" was at odds with the prevailing Lost Cause position, which held that the South had fought to preserve a traditional society against the onslaught of Yankee innovation. Yet, in what became the most infamous of all wartime speeches, Confederate Vice President Alexander Stephens presented the southern rebellion as a forward-looking enterprise that, at least in intellectual terms, was intent on building a race-conscious future destined to gain universal acceptance. In an address subsequently dubbed the "Cornerstone Speech," Stephens committed himself and his government to racial hierarchy with surprising frankness. Explaining the new Confederate constitution to a Savannah audience in the spring of 1861, he explained that the new southern government was based on the exact opposite ideas from those embodied in Jefferson's Declaration of Independence. "Its foundations are laid, its corner-stone rests upon the great truth that the negro is not equal to the white man," Stephens boasted, insisting that this new government would be the "first in the history of the world, based upon this great physical, philosophical, and moral truth."[4]

While Confederates did move toward establishing a more powerful central state in the 1860s, they did so to conduct a modern war rather than to establish the sort of far-reaching policies toward racial "inferiors" that would be enacted by the Nuremberg laws in 1935. The main responsibility for subjugating African Americans remained with private masters and those local officials who had long been charged with governing free blacks. The administration of Jefferson Davis was relatively content to leave this division of responsibility in place, though late in the war, the central government did consider how black slaves might be enlisted in the southern armies. In the realm of ideas, the Richmond government played an even more modest role, never encouraging a counterpart to those efforts undertaken by the Union's (admittedly private) Loyal Publication Society. The sort of propaganda ministry characteristic of the Third Reich would have been unthinkable. When racial themes did appear it was through an extensive, if uncoordinated, series of pamphlets, in the pages of the daily press, and in journals like *DeBow's Review* and *Southern Literary Messenger*, two publications that represented the most regular Confederate attempts to situate the southern struggle within larger contexts. It is to this diffuse realm of propaganda that one must turn in establishing the place of Confederate racial ideology within the country's broader national dialogue.

The "Cornerstone Speech" sparked a backlash that discouraged later Confederate propagandists from broadcasting their country's commitment to racial principles with the boldness and clarity Stephens had dared. This decline says far more about the shifting values of the 1860s than about the southern quest for a slave republic. In nearly every aspect of wartime policy, Confederate officials demonstrated their commitment to the permanent supremacy of those with white skin.[5] But the fact remains that overt invocations of southern racialism were more tepid during the war than might have been expected; the very few original contributions to racial theory had already appeared once the conflict entered its second year.[6] Popular overviews of the Confederate cause usually touched upon black inferiority before moving on to other concerns, blending the racialism developed during the antebellum years with new arguments about the legality of secession, the history of northern ingratitude, and the dependence of the new country on God's will. Thomas MacMahon's *Cause and Contrast*, a self-conscious compendium of the Confederate cause that appeared early in 1862, opened with a lengthy explanation of how the "physiologically and psychologically degraded" African was "of an inferior species of the human race." But MacMahon (himself a newcomer to the South) went on in far greater depth to detail the "cruel sectional war" conducted by the Puritanical Yankees upon a new country whose struggle for its own freedom was more important than its subjugation of others.[7]

A perceptible decline in racial theorizing was evident within Confederate journals of opinion. James DeBow captured a prevailing sense of editorial caution when he urged contributors in 1861: "Let us [do] away with all abstract reasonings and go to the work in developing the great political and industrial future which is before the South." To this he added that "the negro, except in his relation to these, is clearly used up."[8] *De Bow's Review* during the war largely relinquished what had been an obsessive interest in black inferiority during the late 1850s. There was no wartime equivalent of the nine consecutive investigations of black depravity that were offered by W. W. Wright during 1859 and 1860.[9] In fact, the only sustained topic concerning the nature and origin of Africans Americans published in the wartime *De Bow's* concerned Dr. Samuel Cartwright's fanciful claim, made in 1860, that the serpent who had tempted Eve had in fact been a "negro gardener." A series of esoteric replies contested this claim largely on scriptural grounds,[10] leaving Cartwright himself to move his own attention from racial theory to the political ramifications of disunion.[11]

Racial hierarchy hardly disappeared as a theme in Confederate nationalism, even if there was an unmistakable shift in tone and emphasis. The scientific racism that slaveholders such as Cartwright, Josiah Nott, and George Sawyer developed in the 1850s gave way to a broadly held concern for Christian stewardship and mission infused with scriptural sanctions of good mastery.[12] The decline of "hard" racism within the wartime South better fit the new circumstances of the 1860s, as did the upsurge of racial propaganda among the Copperhead Democrats in the North. Denying the common humanity of blacks was a powerful means for northern opponents of Lincoln to attack the president, especially after he issued the Emancipation Proclamation. But for Confederates, overt racism risked alienating an international audience that seemed far more willing to sympathize with a nationalist uprising or a battle for constitutional principles than with a war to establish a hierarchy of races. While the old Democratic alliance of North and South had sustained itself by emphasizing a unifying commitment to white supremacy, those who sought southern political independence turned to other arguments. The beneficial effects of an ever-expanding system of Christian slavery became a major theme, as did appeals to protecting domestic dependents, an appeal crucial in eliciting the support of white, nonslaveholding men who filled Confederate armies.

As attention to the significance of white and black skin declined within

Confederate journals, they shifted their emphasis to a starkly different sort of racial theorizing. In 1860, the Alabama lawyer William Falconer became the first to extend the old literary device of Puritans and Cavalier of the English Civil War backward to the Norman Conquest of the Anglo-Saxons in 1066 and forward to the American Civil War. His initial exploration of this theme was followed by a steady string of essays in *De Bow's Review* and the *Southern Literary Messenger* that presented the current North American conflict as the third episode in an ancestral blood strife nearly eight centuries old. There was a brief vogue among the Confederate intelligentsia for this "ethnological" explanation of sectional tensions that identified the new country's racial identity as much a consequence of their southern blood as of their white skin.[13]

Confederate publicists who glorified their own "Norman" race presented southern slaveholders as a "*Herren* class" akin to those fighting masters that Hitler would look back fondly upon during the 1930s. The same capacity for governance that made "Southrons" the natural masters of black slaves made them the appropriate guardians of the future of their own autocratic republic, if not that of the entire North American continent. The starkly reactionary streak that typified proponents of "Cavalier" rule gradually lessened the appeal of such arguments for the wider Confederate public, however. By 1863, a series of political and religious objections to the dichotomy between Norman Cavaliers and Saxon Puritans thus emerged within Confederate discourse. "We—not the Pantheistic despots of New England but we of the South" were "the Puritans in this controversy, if any Puritans in it there be," the Rev. William Hall wrote in 1864. The editors of the Richmond *Enquirer* went even further in denouncing such ethnology, writing that "All this talk about race is dubious and suspicious," especially given the "political bias which usually actuates those who profess to examine it."

Confederate discussions of racialism were influenced by the larger context of world opinion. Stephens's exaltation of the place of the Confederacy in Western government had this global context in mind, as did the broader trend of moving from black depravity to the nobility of Cavalier blood.[14] The international dimension of racial theorizing was particular evident in the case of Henry Hotze, whose editorship of the weekly London *Index* was heavily subsidized by the Confederate government. Hotze's wartime writings come closest to a body of racial ideas representing an official Confederate position, even though it is clear that Hotze never took orders on what to publish from Richmond—or from anyone else, for that matter.

Hotze had good credentials to be the Confederacy's most significant racial propagandist, having already distinguished himself as the first English translator of Comte de Gobineau's *Essay on the Inequality of the Races*, a work that would later present a doctrine of Aryan supremacy central to Nazi ideology. As an associate of the leading members of the "American School" of racist ethnology, Hotze was clearly prepared to make the most of the transitional period in European attitudes toward race that marked the 1860s. As David Brion Davis has remarked: "For reasons that have not yet been fully explained, most of the Western world [at this time] began accepting racist theories that had earlier lacked the sanction of science and that had generally been limited to the United States." In contrast to the timidity and caution of most Confederate racialists, Hotze's European experience gave him a mixture of hope and trepidation for the future. These were clear both in his frequent dispatches to his Richmond superiors and in his public writings for the *Index*.[15]

Hotze's foray into racist anthropology was hardly the most important aspect of his propaganda work, even though he included his own belief in the "degrees of progressive difference" between racial groups starting with the very first issue of the *Index*. His open commitment to white racial supremacy represented a marked shift. The South's first propaganda efforts in Europe had tended to disassociate the Confederacy from slavery and race even more starkly than did writers within the wartime South. The influential Liverpool propagandist James Spence even predicted that upon gaining their independence, white southerners would commit themselves to ridding their new country of the "foul blot" of bondage. By 1863, the London anthropologist James Hunt offered a nearly opposite tactic, successfully urging Hotze to recognize how the overt racialism of his new Anthropological Society might bolster Confederate fortunes. Hotze was intrigued by this development, and responded in 1863 and 1864 by contributing money to the new Anthropological group, by publicizing its meetings in the *Index*, and by reaching beyond England to encourage the dissemination of scientific racism as far away as Italy. In doing so, Hotze saw glimmers of hope that Europeans were moving beyond their refusal to dispense with what Hotze called the world's "most dangerous idea," which he explained—in terms evocative both of Alexander Stephens and of the later Nazi period—was simply "the dogma of the equality of man."

Hotze's work on behalf of racialism in Europe did not succeed in assuring Confederate independence, of course, though the cause of racist anthropology and southern white supremacy long survived the fall of the Richmond government.[16] After American emancipation was complete, the intertwining of government policy and racial dominance made scientific claims about human difference newly relevant, with the result that there was an outburst in racial theorizing of the same order that had accompanied the end of West Indian slavery a generation earlier.[17] In the late Victorian period, the notion of a "race state" became increasingly important to whites in the United States and to European proponents of imperialism and anti-Semitism. Viewed from century's end, Hotze's vision seemed ahead of its time, even if from the perspective of the 1930s his advocacy of racial governance would have seemed underdeveloped, if not quaint.

Hitler and other subsequent admirers of the Confederacy realized that what mattered were the actions that white southerners had taken, not the words that they committed to paper in the 1860s. The corpus of Confederate writings would have been, even if they were more fully developed, less important in providing twentieth-century racists a "usable past" than the simple fact that this slaveholders' republic had launched an armed revolt to preserve a system of African American bondage. Nazis leaders like Hitler knew that this attempt was relevant and that it was proof that white Americans' race-consciousness might be rekindled.

In the same passage in which the Führer mused plaintively about the outcome of the Civil War, Hitler identified elements in American society of the 1930s that perhaps bore greater relevance to his own vision for the Aryan future. Just as Hitler saw that it "was not the Southern States, but the American people themselves who were conquered" during the Civil War, so he saw nothing particularly sectional about the "sound fighting spirit" displayed by America's white supremacist middle class during his own day. He took care to distinguish the race-consciousness of the American people from the United States government that was, in his opinion, degenerate and mongrelized. As he explained, those "scholars who have studied immigration and gained an insight, by means of intelligence tests, into the inequality of races" provided a source of hope that the racial cause that Confederates pursued sixty year earlier might be reestablished in the New World.[18]

Progressive-era racialists practicing pseudoscience may not have tugged at Hitler's heartstrings as powerfully as did those long-dead gray ghosts of the Confederacy. But it was this group's version of evil that he had in mind as he boldly imagined a future in which National Socialism was "destined to liberate the American people from their ruling clique and give them back the means of becoming a great nation." Functionaries of the eugenics movement seemed, even in Hitler's mind, to have anticipated the Nazi project more fully than had Confederate ideologues, whose hesitancy seemed to outweigh their confidence, except perhaps in the case of Hotze.

Hitler's appreciation for modern American eugenicists exemplifies the tendency of evil to emerge not just during moments of self-proclaimed heroism and the passions of conquest, but in the context of banality and numbing indifference to human dignity. The pairing testifies to a less noted aspect of proponents of evil who, whether in the Third Reich or elsewhere, have rarely been satisfied with yearnings for past failures or even the most romantic lost causes. For those who perpetrated Nazi atrocities, historical legacies might have provided rhetorical flourishes. But what ultimately counted was the quest for power over good, realized through the most modern and effective means available. These were meant to be implemented not for the sake of nostalgia but for both the near and the distant future.

NOTES

1 Hitler quoted in Hermann Rauschning, *The Voice of Destruction* (New York: Putnam's, 1940), 68–69. For a broader context of Hitler's remarks, see John Haag, "Gone with the Wind in Nazi Germany," *Georgia Historical Quarterly* 73 (1989): 278–304; and Johnpeter Horst Grill and Robert L. Jenkins, "The Nazis and the American South in the 1930s: A Mirror Image?," *Journal of Southern History* 58 (1992): 667–94.

2 George Fredrickson looks at a single Confederate text, the "Cornerstone speech" of Alexander Stephens, in his *The Black Image in the White Mind: The Debate on African-American Character and Destiny, 1817–1914* (New York: Harper and Row, 1971), while he omits the Confederacy altogether in his most recent book *Racism: A Short History* (Princeton: Princeton University Press, 2002). Nor is the Confederacy mentioned in Ivan Hannaford, *Race: A History of an Idea in the West* (Baltimore: Johns Hopkins University Press, 1996). Scholars tend to compare Nazi atrocities more regularly to the slave trade or to slavery more generally than to the Civil War South, as in Laurence Thomas, *Vessels of Evil: American Slavery and the Holocaust* (Philadelphia: Temple University Press 1993).

3 David Brion Davis emphasizes the need for both "connected" and "comparative" approaches in "Looking at Slavery from Broader Perspectives," *American Historical Review* 105 (2002): 452–66.

4 "Alexander Stephens's Cornerstone Speech," in *Southern Pamphlets on Secession*, ed. Jon Wakelyn (Chapel Hill: University of North Carolina Press, 1996).

5 This was true even of the schemes of Confederate emancipation in 1865, which were offered as a means of maintaining white control over the end of slavery at a time when the end of that institution seemed to be irreversible.

6 The two most explicit Confederate publications devoted to race were James Warley Miles, *The Relation Between the Races at the South* (Charleston: Evans & Cogswell, 1861) and Joseph C. Addington, *Reds, Whites and Blacks, or, the Colors, Dispersion, Language, Sphere and Unity of the Human Race . . .* (Raleigh: Strother & Marcom, 1862).

7 Thomas W. MacMahon, *Cause and Contrast: An Essay on the American Crisis* (Richmond: West and Johnson, 1862), ix–x, 37–63.

8 DeBow, editorial note before Rev. B. Mays, "Thomas Jefferson and the Divine Lega-

tion," *De Bow's Review* 31 (May-June 1861); DeBow had earlier suggested that abstract answers to the "mooted question of the races of men" were interesting though not terribly important in justifying slavery; see his editorial introduction to Samuel Cartwright, "Unity of the Human Race Disproved by the Hebrew Bible," *De Bow's Review* 29 (August 1860), 129.

9 Wright's articles, listed in chronological order, were: "The Coolie Trade, or the Encomienda System of the Nineteenth Century," *De Bow's Review* 27 (September 1859); "Free Negroes in Haiti," *De Bow's Review* 27 (November 1859); "Free Negroes in Jamaica," *De Bow's Review* 28 (January 1860); "British West Indies," *De Bow's Review* 28 (February 1860); "Free Negro Rule," *De Bow's Review* 28 (April 1860); "Free Negroes in the Northern States," *De Bow's Review* 28 (May 1860); "Relations of the Negro Race to Civilization," *De Bow's Review* 28 (June 1860); "Amalgamation," *De Bow's Review* 29 (July 1860); "Cotton and Negroes," *De Bow's Review* (August 1860).

10 Cartwright's position was laid out in "Unity of the Human Race Disproved by the Hebrew Bible," *De Bow's Review* 29 (August 1860), and "Nacash, Canaan and the Negro Identical," *De Bow's Review* 29 (October 1860). The three subsequent responses were: Rev. W. D. Skull, "Dr. Cartwright on the Negro Race," *De Bow's Review* 29 (December 1860); Rev. B. B. Mays, "The Serpent, the Ape, and the Negro," *De Bow's Review* 31 (December 1861); Mays, "Dr. Cartwright on the Negro, Reviewed," *De Bow's Review* 32 (January-February 1862), continued in *De Bow's Review* 32 (March and April, 1862), and concluded in *De Bow's Review* 32 (May-August 1862).

11 Cartwright, "Negro Freedom Impossible," *De Bow's Review* 30 (May 1861) was followed by "The Existing Crisis," *De Bow's Review* 32 (January and February 1862) and "Abolitionism, A Curse to the North and a Blessing to the South," *De Bow's Review* 32 (March-April, 1862). Cartwright died in 1863, at the age of 70.

12 For the clergy's role in guiding Confederate understandings of slavery see Drew Faust, *The Creation of Confederate Nationalism: Identity and Ideology in the Slaveholding South* (Baton Rouge: Louisiana State University Press, 1989).

13 Material in this and the following paragraph is documented in Robert E. Bonner, "Roundheaded Cavaliers?: The Context and Limits of a Confederate Racial Project," *Civil War History* (March 2002). James McPherson offers a contrasting interpretation of what he terms "ethnic nationalism" in *Is Blood Thicker than Water?: Dilemmas of Nationalism in the Modern World* (New York: Vintage, 1998).

14 Paul Kramer charts the relationship between racial theorizing and diplomacy, albeit at a different historical moment, in "Empires, Exceptions, and Anglo-Saxons: Race and Rule between the British and United States Empires, 1880–1910," *Journal of American History* 88 (2002): 1315–53.

15 For a more thorough discussion of Hotze's wartime racialism (and for citations from his writings mentioned in this essay), see Robert E. Bonner, "Slavery, Confederate Diplomacy, and the Racialist Mission of Henry Hotze," *Civil War History* 51 (September 2005). Hotze is mentioned in both Davis, *Slavery and Human Progress* and in several passages of R. J. M. Blackett, *Divided Hearts: Britain and the American Civil War*

(Baton Rouge: Louisiana State University Press, 2001). Hotze's translation of Gobineau, and their dispute over American slavery, is discussed in Michael D. Biddiss, *Father of Racist Ideology: The Social and Political Thought of Count Gobineau* (New York: Weybright and Talley, 1970).

16 Beginning with the January 19, 1865, issue, the *Index* ran a header note for several issues that lamented not only the diplomatic betrayal of England, but "the perplexity, to the European mind, of the unsolved and unprecedented problems involved in the management and education of four millions of the African race, intermingled with a population of the highest Caucasian type."

17 Among those suggesting a connection between West Indian emancipation and a more robust ordering of racial distinctions are Thomas Holt "The Empire of the Mind," in *Region, Race, and Reconstruction: Essays in Honor of C. Vann Woodward*, ed. J. Morgan Kousser and James M. McPherson (New York: Oxford University Press, 1982); Seymour Drescher, "The Ending of the Slave Trade and the Evolution of European Scientific Racism," *Social Science History* 14 (1990): 415–50.

18 Stefan Kuhl, *The Nazi Connection: Eugenics, American Racism, and German National Socialism* (New York: Oxford University Press, 1994).

The Antislavery Impulse

STEVEN MINTZ

Introduction

The history of the antislavery movement is far more than a simple tale of the forces of righteousness battling the evil of slavery. It is a story that forces us to ask a number of difficult questions about moral perception, psychological motives, public perception, and the efficacy and social consequences of reform. Why were a small group of people able to perceive a moral evil that others had remained blind to for hundreds of years? Why did the abolitionist movement evoke vociferous opposition not only from slaveholders but from northern mobs led by "gentlemen of property and standing"? Did the abolitionist movement—especially its polarizing rhetoric and tendency to view slavery as a personal moral failure of individual slaveholders rather than a structural and economic problem—accelerate or impede the emancipation of slaves? It also leads us to explore the extent to which white abolitionists overcame racial prejudice and promoted racial equality, the degree to which their agitation was responsible for the Civil War and emancipation, and, equally important, whether the abolitionists' assumptions—especially their commitment to individual economic striving and Christian self-help—contributed to the abandonment of former slaves following Reconstruction.

It was during the colonial era that slavery, an institution that had existed since prehistoric times, began to be viewed as a sin, a violation of fundamental human rights, and as an obstacle to economic progress. In English North America, there were isolated critiques of slavery in the late seventeenth and early eighteenth century. The first known attack was a 1688 petition signed by four Quakers in Germantown, Pennsylvania, who stressed that all human beings, regardless of race, shared an immortal soul. In 1700, three years after he publicly apologized for his role as one of the Salem witchcraft judges, Samuel Sewall, a leading Boston merchant, published *The Selling of Joseph*, which questioned the biblical rationalizations used to justify slavery.[1]

The first organized opposition to slavery emerged among the Quakers during the Seven Years' War, when a minority of Quakers argued that slavery violated the sect's commitment to the equality of all human beings, that it rested on force and violence, split families, and encouraged sloth, indolence, and display among slaveholders. For a growing number of Quakers, the war resulted in intense soul-searching and a quest for self-purification. Slavery seemed to be at odds with the sect's ideal of a sanctified community living in conformity with the law of love.[2] The American Revolution intensified qualms over slavery, by underscoring the glaring contradiction between the American revolutionaries' ideals of liberty and the base reality of slavery, which was legally permissible in each of the thirteen colonies. Following the American Revolution, antislavery evangelicals such as the Baptist David Barrow, the Methodist James O'Kelly, the Presbyterian David Rice, and the Congregationalist Samuel Hopkins, believing in the importance of revelation and the premise that all human beings were capable of salvation, argued that slavery was a temptation to sin and a barrier to Christian simplicity. By the end of the eighteenth century, slavery, which had once been considered an inevitable part of a hierarchical social order, was increasingly viewed as a source of sin, violence, and economic inefficiency.[3] Contributing to the growing unease over slavery were mounting protests by the enslaved themselves. During and after the American Revolution, enslaved African Americans challenged the legitimacy of slavery through petitions and court cases.[4] In the Haitian Revolution, which erupted in Saint Domingue in 1791, the enslaved embraced the revolutionary ideals of liberty and equality.[5]

By the early nineteenth century, separate streams of antislavery thought, religious, secular, philosophical, legal, literary, and moral, had begun to converge. These included the Quaker emphasis on an inner light shared by all human beings and the sect's growing perception of slavery as a form of violence; the Enlightenment preoccupations with natural rights; the evangelicals' millennialist expectations and emphasis on redemption; the republican ideology's association of arbitrary authority with corruption; and Scottish moral sense philosophy's stress on human benevolence. Meanwhile, Adam Smith and other early political economists viewed slavery as economically inefficient and argued that slavery instilled a contempt for labor, a love of luxury, and a lust for domination. Deprived of traditional justifications and rationalizations of slavery, the only excuses for enslavement were based on notions of racial incapacity, a conception of slavery as a form of Christian trusteeship, and an unbending commitment to property rights.[6]

Initially, many opponents of slavery thought of themselves as moral conservatives persons seeking—like earlier opponents of profanity, Sabbath-breaking, and the drinking of hard liquor—to convince Americans to conform to the moral government of God. But, in challenging slavery, abolitionists attacked a vital national interest, the lynchpin of the nation's economy and the key to its system of racial control. Further, in attacking slavery, the abolitionists inspired attacks on other examples of inequality, exploitation, and the abuse of power, forcing a reconsideration of family relations, women's roles, and conceptions of masculinity and femininity. Far from being neurotic firebrands, radical abolitionists proved to be powerful agents of modernization, activists who challenged traditional values such as the notion of maintaining separate spheres for women and men and who promoted a new set of values emphasizing contract and consent.[7] Even some of their most visionary ideas, such as their call for world peace, proved less utopian than many imagined, as new notions of international law were promoted in international conferences and codified in the decades following the Civil War.[8]

Several issues have dominated recent discussions of antislavery. The first is why slavery, an institution that had been accepted as an inevitable part of the social order for thousands of years in most parts of the world, came to be viewed in the late eighteenth century as a moral evil. Religious, economic, ideological, political, and social forces contributed to a profound shift in moral sensibilities and the emergence of the first mass movements to abolish slavery. Religion lay at the heart of opposition to slavery. In its earliest phases, antislavery thought proved particularly attractive to pietistic churches that sought to create a community of believers free of sin. The evangelical revivals of the late eighteenth and early nineteenth centuries, and the new ideas about human agency, the nature of sin and redemption, and the prospects for the millennium that the revivalists promoted, helped to disseminate antislavery ideas. Antislavery was religiously rooted in a new way of thinking about sin, not as a metaphysical abstraction, but as a concrete example of injustice.[9] At the same time, faced with the fact that divine scripture seemed to sanction slavery, a number of influential abolitionist theologians developed the notion of a new dispensation, under which God had inaugurated a new age of history governed by higher set of moral principles.[10]

The Revolution itself helped transform slavery into a moral problem. Grounded on the principles of liberty, equality, and inalienable rights, the Revolution precipitated a crisis of conscience among many slaveholders and led every colony to stop participating in the African slave trade. Slavery represented a violation of republican principles, since absolute power over another human being, according to this view, inevitably breeds corruption. Following the Revolution, every northern state abolished slavery or adopted a gradual emancipation plan. Every southern state except South Carolina ended the slave trade; most made it easier for slaveowners to emancipate slaves; and one, Delaware, made it illegal to sell slaves out of state.[11]

Antislavery was also related to the economic transformations associated with the early stages of the Industrial Revolution. The growth of antislavery sentiment coincided with the demise of household manufacturing, indentured servitude, and the craft system of production and with the expansion of wage labor, factory discipline, and a market economy. Antislavery reinforced and legitimated wage labor, even as it served as a catalyst for radical criticism of many forms of exploitation, including the subjugation of women. On the one hand, antislavery arose as part of a broader shift in attitudes toward labor incentives and labor discipline. It sought to replace overt forms of physical restraint with internalized forms of self-discipline. On the other hand, the abolitionist critique of slavery was instrumental in awakening the public to analogues to slavery, including flogging, impressment, indentured servitude, and imprisonment for debt.[12]

Abolitionist movements were confined largely to four societies, Britain, the United States, and, to a lesser extent, France and Brazil. Why was it that the two societies that stood at the forefront of the Industrial Revolution produced the strongest movements against slavery? Early in the twentieth century, Charles Beard linked abolition to the growing hegemony of northeastern commercial and industrial interests, but this argument failed to demonstrate specific links between abolitionists and the interests of a rising entrepreneurial class. In recent years, scholars have focused on the ideological links between antislavery and a shifting economic order. Some abolitionists staunchly promoted the virtues of a free-labor society. Viewing slavery as a relic of barbarism, these abolitionists repudiated economic paternalism and instead advocated economic individualism and free competition in an open marketplace. Others, however, were uneasy about the new forms of exploitation that accompanied the early nineteenth-century market revolution. Antislavery petitions were signed by many skilled artisans, who associated slavery with aristocratic values and monopolistic power, as well as by many factory workers, eager to dissociate wage labor from connotations of servility. If the antislavery movement helped to legitimate the wage-labor system as less oppressively authoritarian than slavery, it also provided a language of exploitation that was essential in criticizing the abuses of the new industrial order.[13]

Accompanying examinations of the origins of antislavery thought has been a debate over whether the American Revolution produced a moment of intellectual and cultural fluidity when slavery might have been placed on the road to extinction. Although the issue remains hotly contested, a growing consensus has concluded that the answer is "no." Even in the North, slavery was not as insignificant or as easily abolished as previously assumed. Slavery was an important symbol of prestige; slave labor freed professionals and artisans to perform other tasks; and the slave workforce was the driving force behind the highly profitable production of provisions for the West Indian sugar colonies. Slave prices remained high in the northern states until the institution was abolished or gradual emancipation laws were enacted.[14]

If, on the one hand, the Revolution underscored the contradiction of slavery in a land dedicated to freedom and equality, it also was a struggle waged, in part, in defense of property rights. These included not only the right to dispose of land and goods and to trade freely without government interference but also the right to own human property. A preoccupation with property rights was evident in the gradual emancipation schemes adopted in all of the northern states except Vermont and Massachusetts. These statutes granted freedom only to those African Americans born after the laws' enactment and, only then, following a term of service lasting until their mid-twenties. In effect, slaves were required to pay for their own emancipation. Yet, even after gradual emancipation plans were adopted, many of their provisions were ignored or evaded. Birthdates were altered; free blacks were steered away from many towns and subjected to special taxes. Free blacks were forced to occupy a netherworld between slavery and freedom.[15]

Yet another issue that has evoked a great deal of contention involves continuity and discontinuity in the history of antislavery. In the past, there was a tendency to draw a stark contrast between the immediatist movement that arose in the early 1830s and the earlier, elite-led, cautious, gradualistic movement that arose in the wake of the Revolution. Changes there were, especially in tactics, but recent scholarship has also identified important continuities in personnel, language, and arguments.[16]

Postrevolutionary antislavery societies, such as New York's Manumission Society and the Pennsylvania Abolition Society, drew support not only from an upper-class elite (including many slaveholders) but also from small shopkeepers and skilled artisans. Although they did not support immediate, uncompensated emancipation, they did lobby for gradual emancipation laws and worked through the courts to free individual slaves, protect free blacks from kidnappers, prosecute cruel slaveowners, and enforce laws against the slave trade. With the rise of the colonization movement following the War of 1812, early opponents of slavery were forced to confine their efforts to protecting free blacks from kidnapping, assisting fugitive slaves, and enforcing provisions of gradual emancipation statutes. Even before the founding of The Liberator in 1831 and of the New England Anti-Slavery Society in 1832, however, more radical condemnations of slavery and of colonization appeared within the North's rapidly growing free-black communities. Free blacks helped persuade William

Lloyd Garrison to abandon colonization by convincing him that it was a ploy that reinforced northern racism while doing nothing to end slavery.[17]

The shift toward immediatism reflected a number of influences. Along with the influence of northern free blacks and of the evangelical revivals of the Second Great Awakening, there was the example of the temperance movement in producing a national organization and popular support; the mounting white hostility toward free blacks, apparent in mob attacks on black communities; and, above all, the success of British abolitionists in mobilizing millions of men and women of diverse classes and religions to petition Parliament for the abolition of slavery. Lacking an all-powerful parliament capable of abolishing slavery, facing hostile mobs and a national government dominated by southern slaveholders, northern abolitionists sought to dramatize the evil of slavery through lectures, pamphlets, court cases, petitions, and vivid firsthand testimony by fugitive slaves. Through a confrontational strategy of public agitation, a commitment to inclusion and mass action, including direct appeals to women, the radical, romantic movement of the 1830s sought to abolish slavery and promote racial equality. Yet, for all the differences in means and ends, there were important links between postrevolutionary antislavery and the abolitionist movement of the 1830s. Many leading white abolitionists served apprenticeships in the colonization movement. Their strident denunciations of slavery echoed not only the arguments of the British Quaker Elizabeth Heyrick's *Immediate, Not Gradual Emancipation* (1824) but also those of earlier radical critics of slavery such as the Baptist minister David Barrow of Kentucky, the English-born minister George Bourne of Virginia, and the Irish immigrant and repentant slaver Thomas Branagan. Evolution, not transformation, characterized the history of antislavery.[18]

In addition to debates over the roots and evolution of antislavery, there has been growing interest in abolition as a social movement. Many individual abolitionists found in antislavery a surrogate religion that provided them with a missionary-like vocation. Like later Civil Rights activists, abolitionists formed networks that shared a common ideological perspective and sense of mission. Organized around dominant personalities (such as William Lloyd Garrison, Lewis Tappan, and Gerrit Smith), these social circles provided members with an emotional, financial, and intellectual base of support that sustained their reform activities over the years. Many of the disputes that raged among abolitionists—over religion, politics, violence, women's roles, and tactics—pitted one network against another.[19]

A more inclusive approach to abolition has revealed the central role of African Americans and women, black and white, in the movement. Much recent scholarship has focused on abolition's biracial character and the degree to which white abolitionists were able to overcome their society's racism. According to Samuel Cornish, "the worst feature of abolitionism ... [is its] prejudice against color."[20] Yet, at least a few white abolitionists were able to rise above the prejudices of their time. In the face of violence, revilement, and contempt, some black and white abolitionists achieved a degree of intimacy and trust that would be unusual even today. If racial paternalism characterized the attitudes of some white abolitionists, a few, like Gerrit Smith and John Brown, argued that whites needed to acquire a "black heart."[21]

Like later radical social movements, abolitionism breached the public-private divide. Some abolitionist marriages challenged Victorian notions of separate spheres and placed unusual emphasis on mutual affection. Prizing individuality, a number of leading abolitionist women kept their maiden names and rejected marriage vows that would have required them to obey their husbands.[22]

Women's rights was abolition's most radical outgrowth. A transatlantic movement involving editors, writers, lecturers, and reformers from England, France, the German states, Hungary, Ireland, Poland, and Scotland, as well as the United States, women's rights grew out of Owenite and Saint-Simonian socialism in Europe in the 1820s and 1830s.[23] In the United States, the temperance and antislavery movements gave women unprecedented opportunities to collect petitions, engage in boycotts, lobby politicians, and found and manage organizations, but they also underscored the restrictions under which women reformers suffered. Women were confined to separate female auxiliaries, barred from decision-making roles in national organizations, and forbidden to speak to "promiscuous" audiences that included men. Female abolitionists turned to women's rights not only because they encountered limitations within the antislavery movement but also because they could find motivation in the potent metaphor of slavery itself, which suggested that every family was a miniature slave plantation and every woman a slave and a slave breeder.[24]

The election in 1840 of Abby Kelley to the business committee of the American Anti-Slavery Society precipitated a division within the abolitionist ranks. The Garrisonians seized control of the society and proceeded to elect seven women as delegates to the World's Anti-Slavery Convention in London, where they were humiliated by being denied their seats and forced to watch from a special, roped-off section in the convention hall. Eight years later, Lucretia Mott, one of the delegates, and Elizabeth Cady Stanton, whose husband had been a delegate, organized the first convention in history dedicated to women's rights, in Seneca Falls, New York. Inspired by the abolition of slavery in the

French empire in 1848, the delegates echoed the words of the Declaration of Independence, insisting that "the history of mankind is a history of repeated injuries and usurpations on the part of man toward woman, having in direct object the establishment of an absolute tyranny over her." The delegates demanded equality of rights, including the right to vote. But assaults against the slavery of sex provoked not only resistance but ridicule and scorn. Unlike any other movement for expanded voting rights, women's suffrage generated opposition from groups of women. In many states, when women finally received the right to vote, suffrage was adopted for reasons that had little to do with sexual equality.[25]

Of all the issues that antislavery has raised, the most fiercely contested involves abolition's responsibility for the Civil War and emancipation and for the nation's ultimate retreat from Reconstruction. It is clear that the antislavery movement helped transform an otherwise dormant issue into a moral problem. Political abolitionists focused the nation's attention on the question of whether slavery would be allowed to expand into the western territories.[26] Abolitionism helped shape the response of the white South's political leadership. In the face of abolitionist attacks, southern leaders abandoned their earlier defensiveness about slavery as a necessary evil and announced that slavery was a positive good. John Brown's raid on the federal arsenal at Harpers Ferry, Virginia, succeeded in convincing many white southerners that antislavery northerners would resort to race war to abolish slavery.[27] Some abolitionists struggled against discriminatory laws and customs in the North. In four states, they succeeded in obtaining the vote for black men. In Wisconsin and Connecticut, free soilers fought for black suffrage. In Ohio and Indiana, they also fought against black laws. In Massachusetts, they succeeded in overturning segregated railcars and fought against segregated schools.[28] During the Civil War, many abolitionists pressed to make emancipation a war aim, and when the war was over, the descendants of abolitionists were at the forefront of efforts to establish black colleges and to end lynching and were among the founders of the National Association for the Advancement of Colored People.[29] Still, given the fact that former slaves and their descendants were relegated to a century of Jim Crow discrimination in the South and to policies of exclusion and separation in the North, one must ask whether abolitionists might have contributed to a better outcome.

NOTES

1 David Brion Davis, *The Problem of Slavery in Western Culture* (Ithaca: Cornell University Press, 1966), 342–48.

2 Ibid., 303; Davis, *The Problem of Slavery in the Age of Revolution* (Ithaca: Cornell University Press, 1975), 44–45.

3 Davis, *Problem of Slavery in the Age of Revolution*, 255–342.

4 Sylvia R. Frey, *Water from the Rock: Black Resistance in a Revolutionary Age* (Princeton: Princeton University Press, 1991); Loren Schweninger, ed., *The Southern Debate over Slavery: Petitions to Southern Legislatures, 1778–1864* (Urbana: University of Illinois Press, 2001).

5 Laurent Dubois, *Avengers of the New World: The Story of the Haitian Revolution* (Cambridge: Belknap Press of Harvard University Press, 2004); David P. Geggus, *Haitian Revolutionary Studies* (Bloomington: Indiana University Press, 2002); Geggus, ed., *The Impact of the Haitian Revolution in the Atlantic World* (Columbia: University of South Carolina Press, 2001).

6 David Brion Davis, *Problem of Slavery in the Age of Revolution*; Davis, Constructing Race: A Reflection," *William and Mary Quarterly*, 3rd ser., 54 (1997): 7–18; Bruce Dain, *A Hideous Monster of the Mind: American Race Theory in the Early Republic* (Cambridge: Harvard University Press, 2002); Paul Finkelman, *Slavery and the Founders: Race and Liberty in the Age of Jefferson*, 2nd ed. (Armonk, N.Y.: M.E. Sharpe, 2001).

7 Amy Dru Stanley, *From Bondage to Contract: Wage Labor, Marriage, And The Market In The Age Of Slave Emancipation* (Cambridge: Cambridge University Press, 1998).

8 Steven Mintz, *Moralists & Modernizers: America's Pre-Civil War Reformers* (Baltimore: Johns Hopkins University Press, 1995), 118.

9 Ibid., 28; James D. Essig, *The Bonds of Wickedness: American Evangelicals Against Slavery, 1770–1808* (Philadelphia: Temple University Press, 1982); Douglas M. Strong, *Perfectionist Politics: Abolitionism and the Religious Tensions of American Democracy* (Syracuse, N.Y.: Syracuse University Press. 1999).

10 David Brion Davis, *Antebellum American Culture* (Lexington, Mass.: D.C. Heath, 1979), 348.

11 Arthur Zilversmit, *The First Emancipation: The Abolition of Slavery in the North* (Chicago: University of Chicago Press, 1967); Patricia Bradley, *Slavery, Propaganda, and the American Revolution* (Jackson: University Press of Mississippi, 1998).

12 Thomas Bender, ed., *The Antislavery Debate: Capitalism and Abolitionism as a Problem in Historical Interpretation* (Berkeley: University of California Press, 1992); Myra C. Glenn, *Campaigns Against Corporal Punishment: Prisoners, Sailors, Women, and Children In Antebellum America* (Albany: State University of New York Press, 1984).

13 David Brion Davis, "Reflections on Abolitionism and Ideological Hegemony," *American Historical Review* 92 (1987): 797–812; Mintz, *Moralists & Modernizers*, 127; Philip Gould, *Barbaric Traffic: Commerce and Antislavery in the Eighteenth-Century Atlantic World* (Cambridge: Harvard University Press, 2003).

14 Davis, *Problem of Slavery in the Age of Revolution*, 285–342; Gary Nash and Jean R. Soderlund, *Freedom By Degrees: Emancipation in Pennsylvania And Its Aftermath* (New York: Oxford University Press, 1991); Shane White, *Somewhat More Independent: The End of Slavery in New York City, 1770–1810* (Athens: University of Georgia Press, 1991).

15 Joanne Pope Melish, *Disowning Slavery: Gradual Emancipation and "Race" in New England, 1780–1860* (Ithaca: Cornell University Press, 1998); Robert William Fogel and Stanley Engerman, "Philanthropy at Bargain Prices: Notes on the Economics of Gradual Emancipation," *Journal of Legal Studies* 3 (1974): 377–401.

16 Richard S. Newman, *The Transformation of American Abolitionism: Fighting Slavery in the Early Republic* (Chapel Hill: University of North Carolina Press, 2002); Paul Finkelman, ed., *His Soul Goes Marching On: Responses to John Brown and the Harpers Ferry Raid* (Charlottesville: University Press of Virginia, 1995).

17 James Oliver Horton and Lois E. Horton, *In Hope of Liberty: Culture, Community, and Protest among Northern Free Blacks, 1700–1860* (New York: Oxford University Press, 1998); Patrick Rael, *Black Identity & Black Protest in the Antebellum North* (Chapel Hill: University of North Carolina Press, 2002).

18 David Brion Davis, "The Emergence of Immediatism in British and American Antislavery Thought," *Mississippi Valley Historical Review* 49 (1962): 209–30.

19 Lawrence J. Friedman, *Gregarious Saints: Self and Community in American Abolitionism, 1830–1870* (Cambridge: Cambridge University Press, 1982).

20 Samuel Cornish quoted in Michael R. Greco, "The Legacy of Failure: Abolitionism and Racism," *Reviews in American History* 3 (1975): 325.

21 John Stauffer, *The Black Hearts of Men: Radical Abolitionists and the Transformation of Race* (Cambridge: Harvard University Press, 2002); Paul Goodman, *Of One Blood: Abolitionism and the Origins of Racial Equality* (Berkeley: University of California Press, 1998).

22 Chris Dixon, *Perfecting the Family: Antislavery Marriages in Nineteenth-Century America* (Amherst: University of Massachusetts Press, 1997).

23 Bonnie S. Anderson, *Joyous Greetings: The First International Women's Movement, 1830–1860* (New York: Oxford University Press, 2000).

24 Julie Roy Jeffrey, *The Great Silent Army of Abolitionism: Ordinary Women in the Antislavery Movement* (Chapel Hill: University of North Carolina Press, 1998); Karen Sanchez-Eppler, *Touching Liberty: Abolition, Feminism, and the Politics of the Body* (Berkeley: University of California Press, 1993); Gerda Lerner, *The Grimké Sisters from South Carolina: Pioneers for Women's Rights and Abolition*, rev. and expanded ed. (Chapel Hill: University of North Carolina Press, 2004); Joelle Million, *Woman's Voice, Woman's Place: Lucy Stone and the Birth of the Woman's Rights Movement* (Westport, Conn.: Praeger, 2003); Geoffrey C. Ward, *Not for Ourselves Alone: The Story of Elizabeth Cady Stanton and Susan B. Anthony* (New York: Knopf, 1999); Sylvia D. Hoffert, *When Hens Crow: The Women's Rights Movement in Antebellum America* (Bloomington: Indiana University Press, 1995).

25 Lerner, *The Grimké Sisters from South Carolina*; Ward, *Not for Ourselves Alone*; Hoffert, *When Hens Crow*.

26 Frederick J. Blue, *No Taint of Compromise: Crusaders in Antislavery Politics* (Baton Rouge: Louisiana State University Press, 2005); Jonathan H. Earle, *Jacksonian Antislavery &*

the Politics of Free Soil, 1824–1854 (Chapel Hill: University of North Carolina Press, 2004).

27 David S. Reynolds, John Brown, Abolitionist (New York: Knopf, 2005); Zoe Trodd and John Stauffer, Meteor of War: The John Brown Story (Maplecrest, N.Y.: Brandywine, 2004).

28 Richard H. Sewell, "Politics and Principle," Reviews in American History 1 (1973): 533.

29 James M. McPherson, The Abolitionist Legacy: From Reconstruction to the NAACP, 2nd ed. (Princeton: Princeton University Press, 1995).

WILLIAM CASEY KING

Icarus Unbound
Ambition and Sin in
Anglo-American
Culture, 1560-1776

Opposition to slavery was rooted in part in a momentous shift in Christian attitudes toward sin. For centuries, slavery received religious sanction from the Christian notion of original sin. Fallen man's natural sinfulness condemned humanity to accept the natural order, despite its many inequities. Slavery, according to this view, was one of God's punishments for humanity's corrupt nature.

In this essay, the cultural historian William Casey King traces changes in the definition and meaning of sin between the mid-sixteenth and the late eighteenth centuries, focusing on shifting ideas about ambition. Vigorously condemned as a particularly pernicious form of sinfulness in sixteenth- and early seventeenth-century England, ambition began to be viewed more positively later in the seventeenth century. As a drive for self-improvement and achievement came to be regarded as admirable, subjection to authority began to be viewed much more negatively than in past.

"Men are qualified for civil liberty," wrote Edmund Burke, "in exact proportion to their disposition to put moral chains on their own appetites."[1] American historians have spent considerable energy untangling the "moral chains" of political thought throughout the origins and evolution of the American republic. Notions like virtue, honor, and fame have been teased from the sources, proffered as the essential correctives to the appetites inherent in man's nature and as fundamental to American national character.[2] The maladies, however, the evils against which they were directed, are given considerably less attention. But recognizing and understanding a society's perception of vice, or sin, can be as illuminating as comprehending its notion of virtue.

This point was made clear more than thirty years ago when David Brion Davis articulated one of the central tenets of his *Problem of Slavery in Western*

Culture. Professor Davis wrote, "The essence of both sin and slavery was a denial of self-sovereignty, a negation of the natural ability to will that which was just and lawful. All men were condemned by Adam's sin to sweat for their bread.... The point is that men could not fully perceive the moral contradictions of slavery until a major religious transformation had changed their ideas of sin and spiritual freedom."[3]

Despite Professor Davis' emphasis on this profound cultural and religious shift, relatively little scholarly attention has focused on untangling the divergent strains of sin, its specific definition and subsequent recasting. My intention is to consider ambition in the context of Professor Davis' argument.

Twenty-first-century Americans have a certain ambivalence toward ambition. Ambition can inspire, but it can also destroy. We see it as potentially corrupting, but nonetheless as our daily goad. As we detest laziness, we laud ambition, but not an excess of it. We praise ambitious students but loathe ambitious politicians. Ambition provides direction, but it can misdirect us. Exactly what constitutes misdirected or excessive ambition is often ill defined. We are told that our reach should exceed its grasp. But, like Icarus, it is only after the too ambitious have fallen from the sky that they are retrospectively seen as having flown too close to the sun.

Fraught with paradox, burdened with contradiction, ambition is nevertheless a strong component of American national character, intrinsic to the American mythos. It is defined as "an ardent desire for rank, fame or power; desire to achieve a particular end ... desire for activity or exertion."[4] But dictionary definitions seem to fall short of capturing its import. From rags to riches, enslaved to liberator, log house to White House, ghetto to C.E.O., ambition drives the American dream. This is, of course, provided that the ends conform to a carefully circumscribed notion of what it means to dream and to whom certain dreams are allowed.

Nonetheless, we promulgate ambition internationally through our cultural exports, celebrate it in self-help business books, market it in "motivational" seminars, chant its promise in pithy maxims like prayers. It is the "giant within,"[5] "that which makes us go,"[6] "the fuel of all achievement,"[7] greed's more comely cousin, the hope to each endeavor, the carrot at the end of a stick that only exists by some failure of our own will or determination.

But in sixteenth- and early seventeenth-century England, ambition was considered a pernicious and dangerous vice, everything from a cause of madness to an impetus to original sin. Let us start with a definition.[8] The 1570 *Homily Against Disobedience and Wilful Rebellion*, required reading from the English pulpits, defines *ambition* as "the unlawful and restless desire in men to be of higher estate than God hath given or appointed unto them." The Homily identifies Satan as the chief embodiment and champion of ambition. It also identifies ambition as one of the major causes of human rebellion. "The restless ambitious having once determined by one means or other to achieve their intended purposes, when they can not by lawful and peacable meanes clime so high as they do desire, they attempt the same by force and violence."[9]

In Robert Burton's *Anatomy of Melancholy*, ambition is described as "a proud covetousness, or a dry thirst of honour, a great torture of the mind, composed of envy, pride, and covetousness, a gallant madness . . . a canker of the soul, an hidden plague . . . a secret poison, the father of livor [envy], and mother of hypocricy, the moth of holiness, and cause of madness, crucifying and disquieting all that it takes hold of."[10]

In addition to these maladies, ambition had a specific religious import. Ambition and sin were virtually synonymous. This fundamental point is made in the definitive prescriptive source on all human behavior: the Bible. The Bible was the *basso ostinato* of everyday life, present at every significant ritual from birth until death, supplying everything from the reasons for a good harvest to the language of mourning. Historians of ideas are sometimes accused of privileging words or documents of the elite at the expense of the vox populi; the public voice is at times more difficult to hear. But a vernacular Bible, in a largely literate, profoundly biblical culture such as that of sixteenth- and seventeenth-century England allows us a unique source.[11] In it are the clues to the cultural logic not only of elite man but also of every man.

Before turning to the Bible in search of ambition, we must ask, which Bible was used by the majority of subjects in Anglo America? The Geneva Bible was the dominant biblical translation from the mid- to late sixteenth century until the mid-, and perhaps the end, of the seventeenth century in both England and the American colonies. The Geneva represented a revolution in vernacular bibles. Harry Stout calls it the "first popular reformation document."[12] While vernacular bibles precede the Geneva, the Geneva was smaller in size—quarto—and moderately priced. It quickly became the "family Bible" in England and Scotland. While its popularity was discouraged by ecclesiastical authorities after the publication of the King James in 1611, it continued to be the "people's choice" for three-quarters of a century, published in no less than 160 editions.[13]

A more careful look at the Geneva reveals that it may, in fact, be viewed as two distinct books. The first is the actual English translation of the Greek, Hebrew, and Aramaic. The second is the commentary, running some 300,000 words, integrated throughout chapter and verse. I would argue that this marginalia be given its due as a separate Calvinist text, the most widely read and extensively distributed political treatise of the early modern era.[14]

There are some sixty references to ambition in the margin notes of the Geneva Bible. Ambition is associated with "pride," "cruelty of the wicked," "malice," "vaine glorie," "greedy desire to reign," and the catch-all "cruelty and all kind of vice".[15] "But it is the first margin note that is the most important for the purposes of my argument. It appears in the Book of Genesis 3:6, as sin slithers its way into the Divine Order at the moment when Eve and Adam first sample the fruit of knowledge. Adam's motivation for this usurpation of divine prerogative is explained in the note. He ate the apple "not so much to please his wife, as moved by ambition at her persuasion." The note makes clear that this act is not done out of pride (although the two are connected), as some earlier interpretations assert. Ambition was the impetus for original sin.

This point is later reiterated in Genesis 3:22, as God reproaches Adam before casting him from paradise. The verse reads, "And the Lord God said, Beholde, the man is become as one of us, to knowe good and evil." The note tells us that "by this derision he reproacheth Adam's miserie, whereinto he was fallen by ambition." Adam's fall—original sin, the gravest offense—is ascribed to the vice of ambition.

But by the mid- to late seventeenth century, "ambition as sin" virtually disappeared from religious discourse. Of obvious relevance was the publication in 1611 of the King James, what was to become the authorized version of the Bible. In the King James there were only seven references to ambition. Ambition, then, becomes less "evil" if only by sheer quantity alone. This is partially due to the fact that almost all references to ambition in the Geneva are made within the margin notes. The King James eliminated these notes, although certain King James Bibles were published with the King James text and the Geneva notes (in Holland in 1642 and in England in 1649, 1679, 1708, and 1715).[16] But gradually the King James took hold without margin notes or significant references to ambition. John Milton sees Adam's fall not due to ambition, as in the Geneva commentary, but rather to uxoriousness.[17] On the other side of the Atlantic, Cotton Mather, in the first American Bible, the Biblia Americana, interprets Adam's fall as a process of inevitable maturation. To Mather, prelapsarian man was in a state much like that of a child. As a child desires knowledge as a normal part of the process of growing up, so too did Adam.[18]

This change reflected larger trends within society. During the seventeenth century, social fluidity was becoming a more accepted facet of Anglo-American life and culture. Lawrence Stone labeled 1540–1640 in England as "the century of mobility."[19] He further discussed the "seismic upheaval of unprecedented magnitude" occasioned by the profound changes owing to this mobility. Vertical mobility became common, and perhaps even more striking was the growth of the upper classes that, according to Stone, "trebled at a period when the total population barely doubled. The number of peers rose from 60 to 160; of baronets and knights from 500 to 1,400 of squires perhaps 800 to 3000 or armigerous gentry from perhaps 500 to around 15,000."[20]

It seems reasonable to assume that as ambition becomes more accepted, those strata of society that resist change become more vulnerable to criticism. Of course, the two most static places in the social hierarchy were those traditionally considered as existing outside the social order: the very top and the very bottom, or the King and the slave. The changing notion of sin made possible not only antislavery thought, but also antimonarchical stirrings. Once ambition was no longer synonymous with sin, and was even celebrated within certain circles, men could perceive the moral contradictions of both subjection to King and subjugation of slave. Once ambition was accepted, the existence of Kings and slaves seemed, in the words of Professor Davis, "to threaten the moral security provided by a system of values that harmonized individual desires with socially defined goals and sanctions."[21] Regicide and antislavery are, in fact, two sides of the same coin.

While this connection seems to make logical sense, does it make good historical sense? We have obvious evidence of regicide in the fate of Charles I in 1649, but if antimonarchical thought and antislavery are intimately linked, why is it that the first criticisms of the institution of slavery do not appear until the late seventeenth century?[22] If the relationship was strong, why was there no critique of slavery from English Puritans?

In fact, some evidence suggests just such a connection. In a biblical commentary of 1657, under the index note "slavery grievous," the English Puritan minister John Trapp uses a commentary on Nehemiah—"behold we are servants this day"—as a springboard for a critique of slavery. He writes that slavery is "here bewailed as a singular unhappinesse." He then cites Turkish slavery as evidence for the grievousness of slavery.[23]

Of course, slavery was a distant fact to most English men and women in the mid-seventeenth century. The English participation in the slave trade would not become vigorous until the latter half of the seventeenth century. This was spurred, first, with the formation of the Company of Royal Adventurers Trading to Africa in 1663 (later called the Royal Africa Company), and, more significantly, with the opening of the trade to private commercial ventures in 1698, at which time, in the words of Professor Davis, "the African coast swarmed with independent traders."[24] The total slave population in the West Indies is estimated at 1,500 in 1650 and as rising to some 115,000 in 1700.[25] The fact that there are not more contemporaneous critiques of the institution is not surprising. The fact that there are any at all is much more striking.

In addition to criticisms of actual bondage, there was a dramatic and fulsome criticism of slavery occasioned by the "tyrannical" policies of Charles I, but it was grounded in a more fundamental critique of hereditary entitlement. John Milton, in his 1649 *Tenure of King and Magistrates, proving it is lawful to call to account a wicked King and . . . put him to death*, defended regicide explicitly and ambition implicitly: "to say" that "the King hath as good [a] right to his crown and dignitie, as any man to his inheritance, is to make the subject no better than the King's slave, his chattell, or his possession that may be bought or sould."[26] Milton's words would seem to signal a general acceptance of ambition in regard to regicide and rebellion. But dominant conceptions die hard. Over one hundred years later, it would become clear that the notion of ambition as sin had not entirely disappeared from the Anglo-American cultural system. Loyal English subjects would identify ambition as the cause of colonial rebellion, with all its damning implications.

In 1776, at the very nadir of revolutionary fortunes, loyalists in British-occupied Long Island staged a two-act play titled *The Battle of Brooklyn*. As rebellion at this point was open and much blood had been shed, a work written about the revolution inevitably expressed a certain poignancy. But the "Battle of Brooklyn" was written not as a tragedy but as a farce. Farce, while often treated as a genre not worthy of scholarly study, dismissed as appealing to the lowest or basest elements, is elevated in our search for meaning outside the traditional "elite" sources. Laughter is predicated on the assumption of a group recognition of the absurd. As farce is drama written for the masses, we can recognize an echo of the vox populi in the dramatists' efforts to get a laugh. In this case there is the "group recognition" of what was driving George Washington specifically, and the leaders of the American Revolution by extension, to an act of rebellion. In a soliloquy reminiscent of Macbeth's murdered sleep, George Washington laments his decision to bring ruin to his "native country." "Oh!" he begins, "Could I congratulate myself, on finding my lost peace of mind!—on the restoration of my honor!" What is Washington's tragic flaw? "Oh cursed *ambition*!" he cries, "What have I sacrificed to thee?"[27]

Earlier religious connotations within the popular perceptions are echoed as well in a well-known loyalist ballad. The ballad was titled *Adam's Fall: The Trip to Cambridge*, and was sung to the tune of "Yankee Doodle." It lampooned Washington's assumption at the head of the rebel army. This ballad implies that

Washington, "clothed in power and breeches," like Adam, falls from God's grace by his act of irreconcilable disobedience to George III.[28] If Adam ate the fruit because he was moved by ambition, what was Washington's "fruit"? Loyalist minister Jonathan Boucher, almost perfectly paraphrasing the Geneva marginalia, answers this question, denouncing independence as the "forbidden and accursed fruit."[29]

The colonists, too, were acutely aware of the charges of ambition and attempted to guard against them. Republican governments require disinterest, the antithesis of ambition. In the 1775 *Declaration of the Causes and Necessity of Taking Up Arms*, they proclaim that they "have not raised armies with ambitious designs of separating from Great-Britain, and establishing independent state."[30] Franklin's "natural man," the simplicity of Jeffersonian architecture, Washington's invocation of Cincinnatus, a figure from antiquity identified as a model of "anti-ambition," were all attempts to identify the project of independence not as a desire to have a higher station but as a step toward establishing a more perfect union.[31]

Other revolutionaries, like Thomas Paine, would reject loyalist definitions of sin and denounce more profound evils—monarchy and slavery—for which independence was the only reasonable recourse. Paine wrote in *Common Sense*, "For as in Adam all sinned, and as in the first electors all men obeyed; as in the one all mankind were subjected to Satan, and in the other to Sovereignty; as our innocence was lost in the first, and our authority in the last; and as both disable us from reassuming some former state and privilege, it unanswerably follows that original sin and hereditary succession are parallels." Paine went on to directly link monarchy and slavery: "The nearer any government approaches to a republic, the less business there is for a king . . . and it is easy to see that when republican virtue fails [and there is need for a king], slavery ensues. Why is the constitution of England sickly but because monarchy hath poisoned the republic, the crown hath engrossed the common?"[32]

If ambition is sin, and sin itself is redefined, it would be reasonable to expect a redefinition of ambition as well. Evidence suggests just such an ideological transformation. John Adams wrote: "Ambition in a Republic is a great Virtue, for it is nothing more than a Desire to Serve the Public, to promote the Happiness of the People, to increase the Wealth, the Grandeur, and the Prosperity of the Community. Thus Ambition is but another Name for public Virtue, and public Spirit."[33] Ambition had been transformed from a manifestation of original sin to "another name for public Virtue."

Thus far I have discussed ambition, sin, antislavery and antimonarchy both in the seventeenth century and during the Revolution. What of regicide?

Winthrop Jordan has described the American Revolution in exactly those terms. "One can propose," Jordan wrote, "that in 1776 George III was killed in his American provinces vicariously but very effectively."[34]

Loyalists and rebels waged war not only over the meaning of good government but also over the meaning of sin itself. King and slave in the new American Republic, founded on ambition, bespoke a social absolutism that ambition despised. It is important to recall that the founders like Jefferson and Washington who hated monarchy and owned slaves considered slavery an inefficient vestige of an old economic model, one that progress would soon efface. Slavery, they assumed, would soon die a natural death.

But in the nineteenth century, with monarchy gone, slavery was very much alive. Sin and slavery became synonymous, and redemption could be won only with the renunciation of absolutisms' other half, the enslaved. In the early republic a new "social mentalité" emerged, reflected in a burgeoning national success literature.[35] The new literature stressed the virtue of individual industry, vigor and frugality, an ambition that would be rewarded not with damnation but with success. While ambition was once a sin, the absence of it in individuals and the negation of it in the system of slavery became far more sinful. It is only when we accept the centrality of David Brion Davis' argument regarding the changing ideas of sin and spiritual freedom, and understand ambition's relationship to sin, that we can fully understand the spirit of antislavery, born in the age of Revolution, consolidated in the age of Emancipation.

NOTES

1 *The Works of Edmund Burke* (Waltham, Mass.: Little, Brown, 1866), 2:51.
2 The most well known example is Douglass Adair, *Fame and the Founding Fathers* (New York: Norton, 1974). A more recent work is Joanne B. Freeman, *Affairs of Honor: National Politics in the New Republic* (New Haven: Yale University Press, 2001).
3 David Brion Davis, *The Problem of Slavery in Western Culture* (Ithaca: Cornell University Press, 1966), 292.
4 *Merriam-Webster's Collegiate Dictionary*, 11th ed., s.v. "Ambition" (Springfield, Mass.: Merriam-Webster, 2003).
5 Anthony Robbins, *Awaken the Giant Within: How to Take Immediate Control of Your Mental, Emotional, Physical and Financial Destiny* (New York: Free Press, 1992).
6 James Champy and Nitin Nohria, *The Arc of Ambition: Defining the Leadership Journey* (Cambridge: Perseus Books, 2000).
7 Joseph Epstein, *Ambition: The Secret Passion* (New York: E. P. Dutton, 1980).
8 Ronald B. Bond, ed., *Certain Sermons or Homilies (1547) and A Homily against Disobedience and Wilful Rebellion*, (Toronto: University of Toronto Press, 1987), 236.

9   Ibid.
10 Robert Burton, *The Anatomy of Melancholy*, ed. Floyd Dell and Paul Jordan Smith (New York: Tudor Publishing Company, 1927), 243.
11 Kenneth A. Lockridge, *Literacy in Colonial New England* (New York: Norton, 1974); Richard Vann, "Literacy in Seventeenth-Century England: Some Hearth-tax Evidence," *Journal of Interdisciplinary History* 5 (1974): 292; David Cressy, "Literacy in Pre-industrial England," *Societas* 4:3 (Summer 1974): 234–40; Cressy, "Levels of Illiteracy in England, 1530–1730," *Historical Journal* 20 (1977): 5–10.
12 Ibid., 22.
13 Lewis Lupton, *A History of the Geneva Bible*, 7 vols. (London: Fauconberg Press, 1966); Charles Eason, *The Geneva Bible: Notes on Its Production and Distribution* (Dublin: Eason & Sons, 1937).
14 Maurice S. Betteridge, "The Bitter Notes: The Geneva Bible and Its Annotations, *Sixteenth Century Journal* 14 (1983): 41–62; Dan G. Danner, "The Contribution of the Geneva Bible of 1560 to the English Protestant Tradition," *Sixteenth Century Journal* 12 (1981): 5–18; Richard L. Greaves, "Traditionalism and the Seeds of Revolution in the Social Principles of the Geneva Bible," *Sixteenth Century Journal* 7 (1976): 94–109; Greaves, "Concepts of Political Obedience in Late Tudor England: Conflicting Perspectives, *Journal of British Studies* 22 (1982): 23–34.
15 The Geneva, as well as other early English Bibles, is now available on CD-Rom. *The English Bible* (London: Chadwyck-Healey, 1996).
16 S. L. Greenslade, ed., *Cambridge History of the Bible*, (Cambridge: Cambridge University Press, 1963), vol. 3: 361.
17 John Milton, *Paradise Lost: a Poem in Twelve Books*, 2nd ed. (London, 1750).
18 Cotton Mather, "Biblia Americana," unpublished manuscript, Massachusetts Historical Society. The "Biblia" is unpaginated but follows the traditional Old Testament chapter-and-verse arrangement. The Historical Society manuscript is considered the first American Bible. It is primarily a biblical commentary.
19 Lawrence Stone, "Social Mobility in England, 1500–1700," *Past and Present* 33 (1966): 16–55; Stone, "The Inflation of Honors 1558–1641," *Past and Present* 14 (1958): 45–70.
20 Stone, "Social Mobility," 16.
21 Davis, *Problem of Slavery in Western Culture*, 292.
22 The regicides themselves did not see their actions as ambitious, but as an unfortunate and greatly regretted last recourse. There is evidence, however, of a contemporary counter-narrative, one that decried the usurpation of legitimate authority, one that saw regicide as an act of ambition with all its homiletic and Genevan biblical connotations. For evidence of this, see David Underdown, *A Freeborn People: Politics and Nation in Seventeenth-Century England* (New York: Clarendon Press, 1996), esp. Chapter 5; and for an explicit charge of ambition, see John Crouch, *Man in the Moon*, April 23 to April 30, 1649, no. 3, 18.

23 John Trapp, *A Commentary or Exposition upon the books of Ezra, Nehemiah, Ester, Job and Psalms*, (London, 1657). The commentary quoted refers to Nehemiah 9:36.
24 Davis, *Problem of Slavery in Western Culture*, 131.
25 Keith Wrightson, *Earthly Necessities: Economic Lives in Early Modern Britain* (New Haven: Yale University Press, 2000), 238–39.
26 John Milton, *The Tenure of Kings and Magistrates* . . , 2nd ed. (London: Mathew Simmons, 1649), 12. For more context, see Robert Zaller, "The Figure of Tyrant in English Revolutionary Thought," *Journal of the History of Ideas* 54 (1993): 603.
27 *The Battle of Brooklyn* (New York: J. Rivington, 1776), 25.
28 "Adams Fall: The Trip to Cambridge," in *The Spirit of Seventy-Six: The Story of The American Revolution as Told By its Participants*, ed. Henry Steele Commager and Richard B. Morris (Edison, N.J.: Castle Books, 2002), 144.
29 Jonathan Boucher, *A View of the Causes and Consequences: in Thirteen Discourses, Preached in North America between the Years 1763 and 1775: With An Historical Preface* (London, 1797), 349.
30 http://speaker.house.,gov/library/texts/colonial/takearms.asp.
31 For a discussion of Cincinnatus and other classical models during the American Revolution, see Carl J. Richard, *The Founders and the Classics: Greece, Rome, and the American Enlightenment* (Cambridge: Harvard University Press, 1994). Garry Wills also addresses Washington and Cincinnatus, and, in addition, ties Jeffersonian architecture to Republican virtue. See Garry Wills, *Cincinnatus: George Washington and the Enlightenment* (Garden City, N.Y.: Doubleday, 1984).
32 Thomas Paine, "Of Monarchy and Heredity," lines 14–23, in *Common Sense*, http://www.bartleby.com.
33 John Adams to Unknown, April 27, 1777, in Paul H. Smith et al., eds., *Letters of Delegates to Congress, 1774–1789* (Washington, D.C., Library of Congress, 1976).
34 Winthrop Jordan, "Familial Politics: Thomas Paine and the Killing of the King, 1776," *The Journal of American History* 60 (1973): 294.
35 Steven Watts, *The Republic Reborn, War and the Making of Liberal America, 1790–1820* (Baltimore: Johns Hopkins University Press, 1987), esp. section II.

PETER HINKS

Timothy Dwight, Congregationalism, and Early Antislavery

During the late eighteenth century, Yale College was a center of elite antislavery thought. In this essay, Peter Hinks, a leading authority on antislavery, explores the nature of American elite attitudes toward slavery, emancipation, and race by critically examining the ideas of Yale president Timothy Dwight. Challenging those who argue that Dwight was not an authentic enemy of slavery, Hinks contends that earlier scholars have misread Dwight's writings and failed to grasp his religion. Dwight was heavily influenced by the New Divinity, a religious theology that emphasized divine sovereignty and human accountability and that provided the foundation for antislavery in many parts of New England. Highly moralistic, proponents of the New Divinity were contemptuous of American society's growing commercialism and materialism, epitomized by slavery. It is no accident that the Connecticut-born abolitionist John Brown, who viewed slavery as a sin that could be purged only with blood, was a product of the New Divinity.

In 1794, in his epic poem, "Greenfield Hill," a paean to the republican virtues embodied in the village life of rural Connecticut, Timothy Dwight vociferated against slavery:

Thus slavery's blast bids sense and virtue die;
Thus lower'd to dust the sons of Afric lie.
. . .
O thou chief curse, since curses here began;
First guilt, first woe, first infamy of man;
. . .
O slavery! Laurel of the infernal mind,
Proud Satan's triumph over lost mankind![1]

Six years later, in 1801, Dwight chided an arrogant Virginia for its democratic pretensions, warning the state of the just wrath of its enslaved:

> Proceed great state—thy arts renew,
> With double zeal thy course pursue,
> Call on thy sister states t' obey,
> And boldly grasp at sovereign sway
> Then pause—remember ere too late,
> The tale of St. Domingo's fate,
> Though Gabriel dies, a host remain
> Oppress'd with slavery's galling chain,
> And soon or late the hour will come,
> Mark'd with Virginia's dreadful doom.[2]

In 1810, in *The Charitable Blessed*, a sermon preached in New Haven, Dwight described with guilt how "Our parents and ancestors have brought their parents, or ancestors, in the course of a most iniquitous traffic, from their native country; and made them slaves." "Happily for us," he continued, that traffic is abolished. "Under the influence of overwhelming conviction, we have made the descendants of these abused people free."[3]

And in 1812, Dwight heralded as a sign of divine favor "the final termination of that disgrace to the nature of mankind, that insult to Heaven, the African Slave Trade."[4] As late as 1815, he wrote in one of the many letters contained in his *Travels in New England and New York* that "the white population of this country is universally free. This I trust, will ere long be true of the black population. In 1810, near two hundred thousand of these people had been emancipated, or born in a state of freedom. The number is annually increasing. The disposition to emancipate slaves, and the conviction that they ought to be emancipated, are gaining ground; and there is no reason to doubt that they will spread wherever slaves are holden."[5] Dwight, an early supporter of the Connecticut Abolition Society, considered slavery an abomination and emancipation a proper and felicitous event.

Yet, over the last two decades, Dwight has acquired a reputation as not only a supporter of slavery but a pivotal voice in the early formulation of the proslavery argument. This surprising transformation is largely the result of critiques by two compelling historians, the late James Essig and Larry Tise. James Essig in his book, *The Bonds of Wickedness: American Evangelicals Against Slavery, 1770–1808*, belittles and questions the convictions and activism of Dwight and other clerical antislavery figures who were members of the Connecticut Society for the Promotion of Freedom.[6] Indeed, Essig argues that, rather than being an active agent for black freedom and uplift, the Connecticut Society was intended primarily to establish the Congregational elite's leadership over a current secular issue as well as to facilitate connections between this religious elite and the professional elite to whom the clerics were apparently losing prestige and relevance. Dwight looms large in Essig's argument as an important member of that Society who was actually very lukewarm as an antislavery advocate. Larry Tise argues in *Proslavery: A History of the Defense of Slavery in America, 1701–1840* that Dwight was in fact a primary architect of a conservative counterrevolution that followed upon the election of Jefferson and the decline of the Federalists after 1800.[7] Rejecting the egalitarian and democratic values of the Revolution and dreading the force of faction, France, Catholicism, the Illuminati, and secularism on the young nation, Dwight and other of his Federalist/Congregational associates such as Jedidiah Morse articulated a new conservative and authoritarian philosophy and sought, through the pulpit, classroom, publishing, voluntary associations, and journalism to implement it outside of an electoral politics that were now corrupted and tyrannized by the mobocratic Jeffersonian Republicans.

One of the most indicative flags, claims Tise, of this transformation was Dwight's growing ease with slavery that culminated, by the mid-1810s, in his apparent full embrace of the institution in his work *Remarks on the Review of Inchiquin's Letters*. There, Dwight wrote in a footnote: "The Southern Planter, who receives slaves from his parent by inheritance, certainly deserves no censure for holding them. He has no agency in procuring them: and the law does not permit him to set them free. If he treats them with humanity, and faithfully endeavors to Christianize them, he fulfills his duty, so long as his present situation continues." As Tise pronounced, "nothing reveals the cracks—indeed, the chasms—that time had wrought in the fabric of the Revolutionary ideology any more clearly than Dwight's changing attitude toward slavery." But of even greater weight for Essig and Tice in highlighting this emerging acceptance of slavery was Dwight's *Greenfield Hill*. Both historians largely concur on this significance of the epic poem and where in the poem it was revealed.

Their reading of this key component of purported evidence, however, as well as that of *Inchiquin*, is deeply flawed. Both historians focus on a specific section of *Greenfield Hill* as evidence of Dwight's growing ease with, or at best ambivalence over, the institution of slavery:

But hark! What voice so gaily fills the wind?
Of care oblivious, whose that laughing mind?
'Tis yon poor black, who ceases now his song,
And whistling, drives the cumbrous wain along.

He never, dragg'd, with groans, the galling chain;
Nor hung, suspended, on th' infernal crane;
No dim, white spots deform his face, or hand,
Memorials hellish of the marking brand!

. . .

Here law, from vengeful rage, the slave defends,
And here the gospel peace on earth extends.

. . .

He toils, 'tis true; but shares his master's toil;
With him, he feeds the herd, and trims the soil;
Helps to sustain the house, with clothes, and food,
And takes his portion of the common good:
Lost liberty his sole, peculiar ill,
And fix'd submission to another's will.[8]

Tise and Essig concur that Dwight in this passage is laboring to show both the good and the evil in slavery. Tise has written: "For the first time Dwight conjoined attributes of both evil and good in his description of slavery, a constant juxtaposition that characterized American discussions of slavery from the 1790s until the rise of abolitionism." Essig, with a slightly different twist, agrees: "After struggling to make slavery conform to a vision of rural felicity, Dwight admitted that servitude impaired the black's moral and intellectual faculties, reducing him to a status below that of whites."[9] Both authors, however, completely fail to recognize in this key section that what Dwight is praising here is not at all the relative benignity of slavery in Connecticut but rather the fact that moral benevolence and influence had developed to such a high degree in the state that they can alter the character of an institution that is by definition ungodly and depraved, whether existing in St. Domingue or Connecticut. Yet Dwight, it seems clear, is concerned to contrast the relative benignity of Connecticut slavery to that of the British West Indies. Unfortunately, both Tise and Essig fail to quote six decisive lines that follow immediately after "Lost liberty his sole peculiar ill, / And fix'd submission to another's will."

Ill, ah, how great! Without that cheering sun,
The world is chang'd to one wide, frigid zone;
The mind, a chill'd exotic, cannot grow,
Nor leaf with vigour, nor with promise blow;
Pale, sickly, shrunk, it strives in vain to rise,
Scarce lives, while living, and untimely dies.[10]

The very first word, "Ill," is evidently intended to refer back to the "peculiar ill," now identified as an ill "how great!," neither incidental nor trivial. Life is deformed and stunted without liberty, "that cheering sun." The ensuing lines summarize how slavery crushes the natural human impulse to mature and improve. Indeed, the next twenty-five lines afford more detail to this summary and show how the individual is corrupted unavoidably by slavery:

See fresh to life the Afric infant spring,
And plume its powers, and spread its little wing!
Firm is its frame, and vigorous is its mind,
Too young to think, and yet to misery blind.
But soon he sees himself to slavery born;
Soon meets the voice of power, the eye of scorn;
Sighs for the blessings of his peers, in vain;
Condition'd as a brute, tho' form'd a man.
. . .
Thus, shut from honour's paths, he turns to shame,
And filches the small good, he cannot claim.
To sour, and stupid, sinks his active mind;
Finds joys in drink, he cannot elsewhere find;
Rule disobeys; of half his labor cheats;
In some safe cot, the pilfer'd turkey eats;
. . .
Sees from himself his sole redress must flow,
And makes revenge the balsam of his woe.
. . .
Thus slavery's blast bids sense and virtue die;
Thus lower'd to dust the sons of Afric lie.[11]

What both Tise and Essig fail to appreciate is that Dwight in fact intended to trick readers with the earlier, bucolic characterization, to rhapsodize them with the state's mellifluous assumptions about slavery's benignity, the more readily to smack them with its frank reality. Dwight actually had direct experience with slavery throughout his life, and his remarkably incisive portrayal of the institution's baleful psychological effects issued from these personal observations.[12] Along with witnessing slavery in late colonial Northampton and New Haven, Dwight had an opportunity to observe it closely while serving as the resident minister from 1780–94 of Greenfield Hill, a parish of the town of Fairfield, Connecticut, which in 1774 had 315 slaves, representing 7 percent of its total population. While in Greenfield Hill, Dwight in fact purchased "a negro woman," Naomi, and contracted to release her after several years when her labor would have refunded his original expense for her. As he stressed in the contract, "I never intended her for a slave."[13] *Greenfield Hill* did not strive to illuminate both the "evil and good" in slavery in Connecticut. Wherever it existed, slavery was an evil, and no society could approach godliness until it was extirpated.

Yet slavery had been mollified in Connecticut. Why? Because,

> For here mild manners good to all impart,
> And stamp with infamy th' unfeeling heart;
> . . .
> Here law, from vengeful rage, the slave defends,
> And here the gospel peace on earth extends.[14]

Even though slavery stained it, Connecticut remained for Dwight the paradigm of republican virtue and simplicity, and the relative mildness of slavery there testified to the force of the state's moral character. In Connecticut,

> Where Freedom walks erect, with manly port,
> And all the blessings to his side resort,
> In every hamlet, Learning builds her schools,
> And beggars, children gain her arts, and rules;
> And mild Simplicity o'er manners reigns,
> And blameless morals Purity sustains.[15]

What Dwight was asserting first of all in *Greenfield Hill* was the moral and republican preeminence of Connecticut, in particular as it compared to England but also as it stood in relation to other monarchial and class-ridden nations in Europe—and even to the American South. Dwight saw in Connecticut America's fullest realization of the Puritan ideal of small, covenanted communities concerted in a classless republicanism, where devoutness, Christian mutualism, and an agrarian simplicity prevailed, the whole serving as exemplar for the young nation. What finally deepened the moral preeminence of Connecticut was not its particular adaptation of slavery but rather its capacity to extirpate the institution and draw closer to godliness by forging a just, interracial society. This understanding of slavery as iniquity equally informed a section from Dwight's *Remarks on the Review of Inchiquin's Letters*, a passage from which (wherein Dwight states that planters who receive slaves by inheritance deserve no censure so long as they treat them "with humanity") Tise has nevertheless excerpted to highlight the author's apparent transformation to proslavery by the time of the work's publication in 1815.[16] Dwight's broader intent in *Remarks* was to counter various British authors who had recently ridiculed and defamed Americans and their national institutions. The passage cited here was embedded in a section dedicated to exposing British hypocrisy in condemning Americans for their use of slavery while ignoring Britain's own crucial role in furthering the institution in the Atlantic world in the eighteenth century and their own vastly more brutal West Indian slavery. The above passage, which was only a footnote, was offered in no way to sanction American slavery. Dwight made this very clear several pages later when he wrote: "I hope, Sir, we shall never more hear any comparisons made between your slaveholders and ours. Stigmatize both as severely as you please: but let your journalists, and your travellers, when they are branding ours with infamy, remember *Hodge* and *Huggins* [two notorious West Indian slaveholders]."[17]

In the following paragraph, Dwight also praised the African Institution, led by Thomas Clarkson, "for their noble effort in behalf of these abused people. The hand of God be with them, and make their way prosperous."[18] Nothing Dwight had written in the passage regarding the Southern Planter reveals any transformation whatsoever in long-held assumptions about slavery or about how gradual emancipation was to be implemented, especially in the more problematic South. Those holding slaves in the South, Dwight held, must continue to do so until the state provides for a lawful, careful, and benevolent emancipation. Masters were obligated to treat the enslaved with humanity and Christianize them "so long as his present situation continues." This concluding phrase is critical and points to Dwight's resolve that "his [i.e., the slave's] present situation" will not continue and that emancipation was sweeping irrepressibly across the nation.

Correcting these misreadings of Dwight is important: in late summer 2001, an uproar was created at Yale University and in the national press after several Yale graduate students published a scathing indictment of Yale's apparent historic connivance with slavery and theories of black inferiority and of Timothy Dwight's prominent role in these crimes.[19] Their flagrant misrepresentations of Dwight were in large part drawn from Larry Tise's *Proslavery*. Yet there are other reasons for us to discern the true orientation of Dwight on slavery and race. Despite James Essig's charge of a glib and inactive clerical antislavery in Connecticut, the roots of antislavery in America were planted in religion and in New England, and their dynamic taproot was in the Connecticut-led New Divinity movement of Samuel Hopkins, Levi Hart, and Jonathan Edwards Jr. The New Divinity movement sought to rejuvenate and innovate upon the strict Calvinist theology of Jonathan Edwards and did so principally with Hopkins' novel doctrine of disinterested benevolence. This doctrine was a stern upholding of the sanctified individual dead to self-interest and will, who sought only to alleviate human suffering and oppression caused by sinning.[20] The doctrine led the three men to conclude in 1775 that slavery was a deep, grave sin, an affront to the essential unity and fellowship of humankind as ordained by God. As Hart wrote, these afflictions were "God's common way to punish communities in a manner answerable to the nature of their crime." They postulated a guilt suffered by the whole community for the sins of any individual who was involved with slavery. While more mainstream, moderate Calvinists scoffed at this New Divinity from the backwoods, the New Divinity evaluation of slavery would undergird the Connecticut Abolition Society, formed in 1790, to which many more moderate men including Ezra Stiles, James Dana, and Simeon Baldwin, would belong. Numerous members of the Society assisted African American children and adults in litigating freedom suits and cases involving kidnapping or and illegal enslavement.

In 1794, New Divinity leaders of the Society spearheaded the drive to abolish slavery altogether in the state, the furthest any northern state in this era pushed toward total abolition, an effort for which Dwight likely contributed *Greenfield Hill*.[21] Dwight would prove not only an important descendant of theirs but a significant innovator of the doctrine of disinterested benevolence. The reform activity of Dwight's that historians usually highlight is that focused on immorality, social disorder, and irreligion. This particular orientation was embodied in Dwight's involvement with the creation of the American Board of Commissioners for Foreign Missions.[22] Yet, far less noted was Dwight's application of this fervor for associational activity to the pursuit of interracial fellowship and racial justice. Dwight adapted the doctrine of disinterested benevolence—or "charity," as he more commonly phrased it—to accord with his growing faith in the value of voluntaristic reform as the proper method for addressing not only disorder, immorality, and irreligion in American society but also social exclusion and suffering.

Rather than pursuing some dark, authoritarian scheme, as has been claimed by Tise and others in connection with his involvement in missionary and moral reform associations, Dwight pursued publicly the original Christian mutualism animating the covenanted communities of Puritan Connecticut, now upheld as a vision for the nation as a whole.

This understanding of charity as fundamental to community included as a significant corollary a powerful mandate to black inclusion and interracial fellowship.[23] As Dwight wrote in 1810, "To give them liberty, and stop here, is to entail upon them a curse." Dwight, like many other elite white New Haveners, by 1810 was deeply troubled by the course that the growing body of the town's free blacks seemed to be following. In 1811, he observed that: "Their vices are of all kinds, usually intended by the phrase 'low vice.' Uneducated to principles of morality, or to habits of industry and economy, they labour only to acquire the means of expense, and expend, only to gratify gross and vulgar appetite. Accordingly, many of them are thieves, liars, profane, drunkards, sabbath-breakers, quarrelsome, idle, and prodigal."[24] Slavery had apparently done its job well in schooling them in such, and Dwight was never sparing in condemning free blacks for their vices. Yet Dwight never used this recognition to propose their quarantining, their removal, or their innate inferiority as a growing body of elite and ordinary whites would do as the 1810s unfolded. Instead, Dwight was forthright in explaining their predicament in the same sermon cited above: "We complain of their vice. Who in such circumstances would not be vicious?" While in 1811 Dwight highlighted a number of black men and women who had contributed to civic life and conducted themselves with decorum, most of the town's free blacks had been damaged by the experience of enslavement, he argued, and then "turned out in to the world, in circumstances, fitted to make them only nuisances to society." He then continued decisively: ". . . these people are thus in a great measure unable to provide for themselves, and to regulate their own conduct." In the sermon, Dwight emphasized that they are not "weaker, or worse, by nature, than we are; but because they are destitute of the advantages, which, under God, raise us above their miserable level." As emancipation unfolded, the white community had a duty to deliver precisely those "advantages" to the aggrieved.[25]

Dwight asserted that whites had a responsibility to blacks, that the elevation of blacks in American society was to be nurtured and applauded, and that the future of whites and blacks in America was inextricably bound together. He argued that whites had incurred a debt to blacks:

> when we introduced these unhappy people into this country, we charged ourselves with the whole care of their temporal and eternal interests; and became responsible to God for the manner, in which we should perform this duty. It is in vain to alledge, that *our ancestors* brought them hither, and not we. . . . This debt, particularly, we are bound to discharge: and, when the righteous Judge of the Universe comes to reckon with his servants, he will rigidly exact the payment at our hands."[26]

This debt demands charity, admonished Dwight, but not in the form of passive almsgiving. Charity for Dwight was an active cohering force, "a free willing outpouring of the heart," a caritas that recognized both the guilt and fellowship binding all members of the community together—black and white. Such an affectional force was a fundamental component binding together the covenanted communities that Dwight described in *Greenfield Hill*. In the *Charitable Blessed*, Dwight highlighted such racially directed charity in a local school organized for black girls by several young white women from prominent families: "I feel a peculiar interest in that, which has been established for *the benefit of the female children of the blacks*. This unfortunate race of people are in a situation, which peculiarly demands the efforts of charity, and demands them from us."[27]

This organized and loving outreach of members of the community to other members was a tame version of Hopkins's disinterested benevolence, where the sanctified individual is willing to be damned for the alleviation of suffering and the glory of God. Yet its stress on the need of the faithful to recognize fellowship and assist with "their suffering fellow-creatures" as a "prelude" to the selfless benevolence of heaven had its roots in Hopkins' doctrine. It also highlighted the growing importance of the voluntary reform association for figures such as Dwight for sustaining and extending their evangelically driven faith and charity.[28]

Dwight's support of this charitable endeavor should not be overlooked. One of Dwight's biographers recalled how,

> [w]hen three young ladies . . . boldly started a school in New Haven to teach negro children how to read, the civil authorities frowned upon the project as having dangerous possibilities. But the local guardians of the public welfare dared not prosecute the defiant daughters of three of Connecticut's foremost citizens, as happened some twenty years later in the case of Prudence Crandall. The ladies, adamant in the conviction that teaching negroes to read the Bible was a religious duty, persisted in their effort. President Dwight took their side, publicly commending their "dignified superiority to ordinary prejudices." . . . [H]e raised a "considerable fund" for the school, by lecturing, and the good work continued for many years."[29]

In 1831, the launching in New Haven of a much larger school for blacks, the Negro Training College, was one of the first key projects that the new abolitionists undertook to establish their dedication to black uplift and equality. It, too, encountered keen local opposition but this time found no support from notable Yale professors and administrators, and this absence was instrumental to the failure of the proposal. Prudence Crandall's academy for black women in Canterbury lacked a strong supporting voice like Dwight's in 1833 and was soon routed from the town by the enraged citizenry. Connecticut offered little encouragement for organized black improvement in the antebellum years. Yet, Timothy Dwight did not hesitate to endorse this "noble example" in the heart of his beloved New Haven. Dwight perceived in this school, and in the interracial charity it embodied, the essential benevolence necessary to promote the progressive elevation and inclusion of African Americans and, thereby, to prove yet again the regenerative force of a godly and congregational Connecticut, a state in which the evils of human bondage and racial prejudice were surmountable so long as it remained constant to its original faith and benevolence.

Dwight's faith, nurtured on the millennial hopes of Congregationalism, pursued the evangelization of the world, a universal Christian unity that would usher in Christ's thousand-year reign on earth. His vision, shared by many other reformers in Jeffersonian America, was vital to the formation of key reform societies dedicated to achieving this Christian uniformity and thus striking against the perceived irreligion of Jeffersonian Republicans. These reformers also sought to curtail various personal and social practices that they believed had removed the individual's awareness of his or her utter dependence on God and faith. While the reform societies that Dwight and others organized were certainly intended to rally Americans to a particular religious vision and to influence the behavior of both the righteous and the wayward, they were by no means the coercive weapons of social control that Clifford Griffin has famously characterized them as; nor were they intended to perpetuate racism and slavery, as Larry Tise has suggested.[30] Indeed, overlooked by these critics and others is the degree to which Dwight's understanding of the fundamental unity of all humankind through God enabled him to propound a view of racial inclusion and fellowship that undercut rapidly rising theories of essential racial separateness and inequality, especially by the 1810s. Dwight was closer to the abolitionists of the 1830s than we have been inclined to recognize: he is actually an important transitional figure between the New Divinity-influenced abolitionists of New England in the late eighteenth century and the more radical and confrontational immediatists of the 1830s.

The black freedom that finally came to Connecticut was imperfect and incomplete and would require much more financial and institutional support than that of a small school for black children. Timothy Dwight's understanding of the relationship of blacks and whites was not in the ascendancy in the 1810s. Largely lacking access to education and capital, and confronted with a persistent and constraining racism, most African Americans would find it near impossible to achieve substantive economic and social advance, and many of the state's whites responded by increasingly doubting blacks' capacities and prospects. By the late 1810s, anti-black thought in Connecticut and the North was becoming more strident; by 1817, the new American Colonization Society focused on demanding the removal of free blacks from the country because they were designated a people degraded and unassimilable. By 1820, a number of formerly prominent members of the Connecticut Abolition Society would join the local auxiliary of the American Colonization Society (ACS) and express hope that the black freedom and interracial fellowship, articulated so eloquently by Hart, Edwards, and Dwight, had dissipated.

The freedom that did come, imperfect as it was, had profound significance. By 1820, the vast majority of African Americans in Connecticut and the North were free, and their ardent voices would have momentous consequences for the struggle against slavery and racism and for the mounting divide between North and South. Emancipation in the North remained the first and largest state-sponsored emancipation in the Atlantic World until those undertaken in the emerging republics of Latin America in the 1820s. In 1817, as the ACS was being created, Timothy Dwight died, never having uttered a word in support of its vision of black unassimilability and removal. Instead, he had spoken against the proliferation of invidious racial distinctions and had asserted the fundamental equality and unity existing among all members of God's human creation and the need to administer to those damaged by a sinfulness to which the benevolent were directly connected.[31] A few years before his death, Dwight warmly summarized this irenic Christian vision for Connecticut, the nation, and beyond: "The stranger will every where find a home; and the wanderer, an asylum. The heart of charity will no longer be icy; nor her hand shut: nor will the cry of suffering ever plead in vain."[32]

NOTES

1 Timothy Dwight, *Greenfield Hill: A Poem, in Seven Parts* (New York: Childs and Swaine, 1794), 38.
2 "Triumph of Democracy," *New England Palladium*, January, 6, 1801, as reprinted in *Amazing Grace: An Anthology of Poetry About Slavery 1660–1810*, ed. James G. Basker (New Haven: Yale University Press, 2002).
3 Timothy Dwight, "The Charitable Blessed," a sermon delivered in the First Church in New Haven, August 8, 1810 (New Haven, 1810), 20.
4 Timothy Dwight, *A Discourse, in Two Parts, Delivered August 20, 1812, on the National Fast* (New York, 1812), 4.
5 Timothy Dwight, *Travels in New England and New York*, ed. Barbara Miller Solomon, 4 vols. (Cambridge: Belknap Press, 1969), 4.
6 James D. Essig, *The Bonds of Wickedness: American Evangelicals Against Slavery, 1770–1808* (Philadelphia: Temple University Press, 1982), 100–103.
7 Larry Tise, *Proslavery: A History of the Defense of Slavery in America, 1701–1840* (Athens: University of Georgia Press, 1987), 204–27.

8 Dwight, *Greenfield Hill*, 36–37.
9 Tise, *Proslavery*, 211; Essig, *Bonds of Wickedness*, 101.
10 Dwight, *Greenfield Hill*, 37.
11 Dwight, *Greenfield Hill*, 37–38.
12 Unfortunately, Dwight's biographers have all but completely overlooked the impress of slavery on his life experience and on his theological and moral systems. See Charles E. Cunningham, *Timothy Dwight 1752–1817: A Biography* (New York: Macmillan, 1942); John R. Fitzmier, *New England's Moral Legislator: Timothy Dwight, 1752–1817* (Bloomington: Indiana University Press, 1998); Kenneth Silverman, *Timothy Dwight* (New York: Twayne, 1969); Colin Wells, *The Devil & Doctor Dwight: Satire & Theology in the Early American Republic* (Chapel Hill: University of North Carolina Press, 2002). However, John Saillant has written a very insightful treatment of Dwight's thought on race and slavery in post-Revolutionary America: see *Black, White, and "The Charitable Blessed": Race and Philanthropy in the American Early Republic* (Indianapolis: Indiana University Center on Philanthropy, 1993).
13 "Contract, 1788," in Dwight Family Papers, group 187, record unit I, box l, folder 1, Manuscripts & Archives, Sterling Memorial Library, Yale University, New Haven.
14 Dwight, *Greenfield Hill*, 37.
15 Dwight, *Greenfield Hill*, 36.
16 [Timothy Dwight], *Remarks on the Views of Inchiquin's Letters, Published in the Quarterly Review; Addressed to the Right Honourable George Canning, Esquire* (Boston, 1815), 81 (note).
17 [Dwight], *Remarks on the Views of Inchiquin's Letters*, 86.
18 [Dwight], *Remarks on the Views of Inchiquin's Letters*, 86.
19 Anthony Dugdale, J. J. Fueser, and J. Celso de Castro Alves, *Yale. Slavery and Abolition* (New Haven: The Amistad Committee, 2001), 12–14. See also www.yaleslavery.org.
20 Joseph A. Conforti, *Samuel Hopkins and the New Divinity Movement: Calvinism, the Congregational Ministry, and Reform in New England Between the Great Awakenings* (Grand Rapids, Mich.: Eerdmans, 1981), 109–41.
21 Peter P. Hinks, "'It is at the extremest risque if we still hold fast the accursed thing': Connecticut's Abolition Bill of 1794, the New Divinity, and Antislavery in the Late Eighteenth Century Atlantic World," in *Prophets of Protest: Reconsiderations of American Abolitionism*, ed. Timothy McCarthy and John Stauffer (New York: New Press, 2006).
22 Tise, *Proslavery*, 212–19.
23 See also John Saillant's relevant discussions in *Black, White, and "The Charitable Blessed"* and in *Black Puritan, Black Republican: The Life and Thought of Lemuel Haynes, 1753–1833* (New York: Oxford University Press, 2003), 135–43.
24 Timothy Dwight, "A Statistical Account of the City of New Haven," in *Voices of the New Republic: Connecticut Towns 1800–1832*, ed. Christopher P. Bickford, 2 vols. (New Haven: The Connecticut Academy of Arts and Sciences, 2003), 1:325.
25 Dwight, "The Charitable Blessed," 23.

26 Ibid., 22–23.
27 Ibid., 20, 23.
28 David W. Kling has an astute discussion of this development in *A Field of Divine Wonders: The New Divinity and Village Revivals in Northwestern Connecticut, 1792–1822* (University Park: Pennsylvania State University Press, 1993), 45–57.
29 Cunningham, *Timothy Dwight*, 336.
30 Clifford S. Griffin, *Their Brothers' Keepers: Moral Stewardship in the United States, 1800–1865* (New Brunswick: Rutgers University Press, 1960).
31 In a probing essay, David Brion Davis argues that an immediate theological descendant of Dwight, the Rev. Leonard Bacon of New Haven's First Church, reached diametrically opposed conclusions regarding black assimilability by the early 1820s. See Davis, "Reconsidering the Colonization Movement: Leonard Bacon and the Problem of Evil," *Intellectual History Newsletter* 14 (1992): 3–16.
32 Timothy Dwight, "Sermon, Delivered in Boston, Sept. 16, 1813 Before the American Board of Commissioners for Foreign Missions" (Boston, 1813), 17.

DAVID WALDSTREICHER

Benjamin Franklin, Religion, and Early Antislavery

In November 1789, six months before his death at the age of 84, Benjamin Franklin denounced slavery as "an atrocious debasement of human nature." In the weeks before his death, he signed, as president of the Pennsylvania Society for Promoting the Abolition of Slavery, a petition to Congress against the slave trade and slavery. He also published a satire of proslavery arguments in a letter to the *Federal Gazette*, which appeared to justify the enslavement of Christians by the so-called "Barbary Pirates" in North Africa.

Franklin, the only one of the nation's founders to serve as president of an antislavery society, is often upheld as one of the new nation's pioneering abolitionists, but David Waldstreicher argues that the Pennsylvanian's antislavery reputation is exaggerated. Franklin in fact owned slaves for nearly fifty years, from 1735 to 1781. As a printer, he profited from publishing notices of slave auctions and advertisements for the return of runaway slaves; in fact, fugitive slaves were brought to his printing shop so that they could be returned to their owners. During the imperial crisis of the 1760s and early 1770s, Franklin blamed Britain for imposing slavery on the colonies, downplayed slavery's economic significance, and disparaged slaves as "sullen, malicious, revengeful, and cruel in the highest Degree." During the Revolution, he complained about slaves who escaped to the British army. Only at the very end of his life did he take an unambiguous stand against slavery.

According to a scholarly consensus, Benjamin Franklin converted to antislavery gradually, between 1750 and the 1770s, after exposure to Quakers at home and *philosophes* abroad.[1] This interpretation makes it all the more surprising that a younger Franklin enjoyed close proximity to, and personal relationships with, British North America's important public critics of slavery. Samuel Sewall was a member of Old South, his father's church. Cotton Mather, to whom Ben delivered candles from his father's shop, made the reform of slavery a significant agenda in his refashioning of godly paternalism. Young

Ben participated enthusiastically in the attacks on ministerial authority launched by James Franklin and the *New England Courant*, a campaign in which Sewall and Mather figured as key targets. Franklin's first employer in Philadelphia, after he ran away from his brother-master's beatings, was Samuel Keimer, the printer and former French Prophet (a religious sect) who proposed to open a school for African children in 1722. During the late 1720s and 1730s Franklin printed for Ralph Sandiford and Benjamin Lay, the first two significant antislavery dissenters in the Quaker meeting. All of these figures associated with the blacks they hoped to uplift. And all four based their criticisms of slavery on God's law and on a pious reformed Christian identity.

Most of the literature rightly stresses the ways in which certain strains of Protestantism advanced antislavery thinking in the eighteenth century. What then in Franklin's life can explain his rejection of a theologically inspired antislavery so available to him? The spectacle of religious controversy and fanaticism, so rife in his Anglo America and so damaging to the careers of his first employers in the printing trade, provided a crucial rationale for keeping antislavery at a distance. Franklin early on decided that religious disputation would fail him as a path to advancement. Economic interest meshed with a new, pluralist approach to religion in keeping antislavery at bay.

When Franklin worked for Samuel Keimer, the two at first "liv'd on a pretty good familiar Footing and agreed tolerably well." They took mutual pleasure in arguing about anything and everything; Keimer developed so high an opinion of Franklin's skills that he proposed they extend their employment relation from printing to prophesying—to start a new sect in which Keimer would "preach the Doctrines" and Franklin "confound all Opponents."[2]

Franklin drew amusement and profit from humoring Keimer. He agreed to his unattractive doctrines (including not shaving and keeping the sabbath) only on the condition that the master follow his journeyman's vegetarian practice. In the *Autobiography*, Franklin stresses how he saved some money by creating a two-man vegetarian cooperative with his boss, but there was more to this episode. Franklin introduces the episode by reminding us (he had mentioned it before) that he had been a devotee of "my Master" Thomas Tryon's *The Way to Health, Long Life and Happiness* (1683), an influential ethical tract that advocated dietary moderation and avoidance of all animal flesh. In his brother's house he had followed a similar scheme in order to avoid meals with James and the other workers. In doing so he gained a critical distance from his brother's oversight, extra money for books, and time to read and write.

In recreating this moment, however, Franklin avers that *before* setting up his vegetarian scheme with Keimer, he had actually given up the practice, on his return voyage to Philadelphia after a visit home.

> I believe I have omitted mentioning that in my first Voyage from Boston, being becalm'd off Block Island, our People set about catching Cod and hawl'd up a great many. Hitherto I had stuck to my Resolution of not eating animal Food; and on this Occasion, I consider'd with my Master Tryon, the taking every Fish as a kind of unprovok'd Murder, since none of them had or ever could do us any Injury that might justify the Slaughter. All this seem'd very reasonable. But I had formerly been a great Lover of Fish, and when this came hot out of the Frying Pan, it smelt admirably well. I balanc'd some time between Principle and Inclination: till I recollected, that when the Fish were opened, I saw smaller Fish taken out of their Stomachs: Then thought I, if you eat one another, I don't see why we mayn't eat you. . . . So convenient a thing it is to be a *reasonable Creature*, since it enables one to find or make a Reason for every thing one has a mind to do.[3]

What were the implications of such a change of heart—or mind? It is worth noting that Franklin does not say that Tryon was *wrong*, only that it was useful to rationalize his way out of his Tryon-inspired regimen. With regard to Keimer, it meant that he could treat his employer as another fish in a predatory sea. And indeed, Franklin soon tells us that Keimer himself failed to keep his part of the bargain. He invited Franklin and two female friends to a breakfast of roast pig, and "ate it all up before we came."[4] A would-be follower of Mosaic laws, Keimer is exposed by Franklin as a swine who gobbled swine.

There was more at stake, clearly, than dinner. But so there had been for Tryon as well. Tryon himself had once been an apprentice "who worked eighteen hour days to earn extra money so that he might buy books and hire himself tutors." Tryon's vegetarianism was grounded in a rejection of colonial trade—he had made and sold beaver hats in London and Barbados—and in a conviction that flesh eating was inherently violent and ungodly. "The Tyranny of Man over his fellow-Creatures" violated the golden rule. In *The Way to Health* Tryon included not only recipes but impromptu speeches by cows, sheep, birds, and horses, against their oppression by their masters—men. In other works he applied this religiously based logic to man's oppression of other men, becoming one of the earliest and most widely read critics of slavery. The year after publishing *The Way to Health* he brought the critique of ecology and slavery together in a persuasive demonstration of the British colonies' military-sugar-skins complex.[5]

As an enthusiast of Tryon in the 1710s and 1720s, Franklin could hardly have been unaware of Tryon's bracing critique of slavery. Tryon's egalitarianism probably made his vegetarianism appealing in the first place for this youngest son and ambitious apprentice. Franklin could also relish in the slave's accusation that West Indian planters' invocations of Christianity, like those of Boston's authorities, served as a mask for their power, while not having to face up to any incendiary call for revolt. For, despite his devastating critique of the system, Tryon carefully called for Christian treatment by owners, predicting obedience in return by the slaves.

Tryon's advice, in short, was for masters, not servants; though hardly less radical for that, it had limited use for the eighteen-year-old journeyman. Franklin must have been aware that slaveholders like Boston's John Saffin had already defended themselves against antislavery critiques by pointing out that Africans enslaved each other—that in their own tropical pond they were big fish who ate little fish. The fish in question in Philadelphia—Keimer, and the master class—eat each other, as well as us; why can't we "eat" them when we get a chance? Why couldn't he employ their tricks? This is not to say that Franklin quickly, or ever, threw off ethics to embrace a nihilistic relativism. Rather, he was preparing for a major change—to leave, for the second time, the employ of an elder who he felt took advantage of him. Any doctrinal constraints, any filial remonstrance, did an injustice to his position. Religious critiques of slavery did not permit of the possibility of running away—or of servants becoming masters.

Keimer detected his journeyman's rebellious spirit and responded much as Cotton Mather had. He accused his former employee of impiety. Franklin turned the tables, though, mocking Keimer's quasi-Quakerism and trumping him when his serialization of a cutting-edge London encyclopedia, beginning with the letter "A," failed to excise an article on "abortion." In perhaps the best known section of the *Autobiography*, Franklin describes this period, from 1729 into the early 1730s, as a time when he set in place the personal habits and the interpersonal "Interests" that would make him a successful printer. Within a short time, his writing as well as printing ability won him influential patrons and customers.

Franklin expanded his market activities in order to pay off his debt. He also acquired his first African American slaves and servants, as part of a household of his own.[6] And he continued to find that his perspective on things sacred had to be honed—very, very carefully. In pluralist, Quaker-dominated Pennsylvania, religion was not an easy commodity in which to speculate, and yet most public matters had ecclesiastical, if not theological, implications. In April

1730, for example, Franklin's "Letter of a Drum" ridiculed ministers who believed in witchcraft and spirit possession; he followed it up in the next issue of the Gazette with an equally anonymous defense of the satire, of true religion, and of the printer, whose willingness to print this reply showed his true receptiveness to religiosity. In July, when Franklin printed several essays on the origins of Christianity from a London newspaper, he heard that several divines were outraged and invited them to please reply at the same length as the original essays. The next spring, after he printed an ad from a sea captain who refused boardings by "black gowns" and other pests, he had to defend his press as not anti-clergy but rather open to all. His first, landmark defense of freedom of the press, and his market rationale for understanding its workings, was, in other words, a plea that, notwithstanding persistent rumors, he was not irreligious. For Franklin at twenty-four, this was more of the same. His inability to break with his brother and still remain in Boston had been shaped by his "indiscreet Disputations [about] Religion" which "ma[d]e me pointed at with Horror by good People, as an Infidel or Atheist." [7]

No strong adherent to a sect, and no atheist, could have made the *Pennsylvania Gazette* please its various constituencies; the publisher had to remain open, and liberal; to provide a space for religious controversy without taking it, or its awe-inspiring implications, too seriously. He understandably remained extremely sensitive to accusations of imbalance or partisanship on the topic of religion—so much so that when a new Presbyterian preacher, Samuel Hemphill—(the first minister to keep Franklin in a pew for successive Sundays)—came under attack in 1735 for insufficient orthodoxy, Franklin, uncharacteristically enough, identified strongly with the charismatic young preacher and mistook a parish war among Presbyterians for a full-scale assault on liberty. In his second pamphlet on the subject, Franklin pulled out all the stops and accused the clergy of being enemies of "truth and Liberty." He contrasted true "Christian liberty," a "Privilege common to Mankind," to a clergy "too fond of Power," who seemed most interested in "enslaving people's minds." "Nothing, in all Probability, can prevent our being a flourishing and happy People, but our suffering the Clergy to get upon our Backs, and ride us, as they do their Horses, where they please." [8]

For Franklin in 1735, religious establishments and religious doctrines endanger personal freedom and public liberty. Clerics threaten to *enslave* those who obey them. Cooler heads should prevail, and when they do, colonists join the mainstream of human and British liberty. In Franklin's emerging vision of a pluralist colony, guided by the tolerance of its Quaker business and political leaders, there is no place for moral absolutes of the kind he associated with Presbyterian orthodoxies. It is bad for business and bad for him.

Franklin deserves credit for his consistency. He did not merely become the Quakers' pet printer, for he actually kept his press open to the Quaker dissidents who were the first major antislavery writers. To understand the choices Franklin was making, we need to consider the substance and the logic of the dissidents' attack on slavery.

In March 1729, at a time when Franklin was mocking Keimer in the pages of their rival William Bradford's *Weekly Mercury*, a Quaker merchant named Ralph Sandiford came to him with an antislavery manuscript. A cautious Franklin agreed to publish it for the author, though without the printer's name on the title page; Sandiford would have to purchase and give away most of the copies. Like Thomas Tryon and most early opponents of slavery, Sandiford had seen the New World version of the institution at first hand in the Bahamas and in South Carolina. He had moved to Philadelphia but in the late 1720s found slavery on his doorstep, in the form of an increased number of sales occurring literally right down the street from his shop, especially after the assembly lowered the duty on slaves imported from £10 to 20 shillings.[9]

Like Samuel Sewall, whom he cited, Sandiford defined slavery as an immoral and wicked kind of trade. He countered the argument that it had biblical sanction. He went further, though, and suggested that the church everywhere—and perhaps especially its ministers—was threatened by this iniquity. He took a page from Tryon, as well, describing the immorality of oppressing any beasts of burden. He even identified and updated a particularly North American version of Tryon's slavery-military-colonialism complex: when South Carolinians sold captured Indians into slavery, they encouraged Indians, and Spanish, to do the same, provoking new colonial wars. The entire skin trade, and the exploitation of the Indians, appeared to Sandiford as part and parcel of the same colonial reliance on exploitation: "we go to the very Indies for fans and Umbrella's, which are for the same Service to us; for which the very Indians upbraid us, for Robbing the Creatures of their natural Covering, and yet cover ourselves with borrowed Hair, which is unnatural, which shews the great Degeneracy & Fall of Man from his first Creation." Sandiford defined Africans as a captured nation who had not "forfeited their Country and Liberty" and whose captivity was not being redeemed in any way, as the oft-cited biblical precedents for slavery clearly required.[10]

Although Sandiford begged his readers not to mind that his sentiments had not been approved by the Quaker yearly meeting, he was banished from the sect for publishing without the meeting's approval. He died a broken man at the age of forty, in 1733. By that time, he had been befriended by another refugee Quaker merchant, Benjamin Lay, who bought copies of Sandiford's book from Franklin and continued to distribute them gratis.

Lay defined himself as a direct disciple of Sewall, Tryon, and Sandiford himself. A sailor who settled in Bermuda as a merchant, he earned the hostility of his fellow white islanders for attempts to ameliorate slavery. Emigrating to Pennsylvania in 1731, he hoped to find a more sympathetic audience there, but discovered instead that slaveholding was on the rise among Quakers, as in the colony as a whole. Lay would prove to be a twenty-five year thorn in the side of the Quaker majority. He took Tryon's injunctions so seriously as to embrace vegetarianism, refuse to eat with slaveholders, and refrain from wearing any garments that were the product of slave labor. During the 1730s he sought a mutually supportive relationship with the animal world, raising vegetables and flax, keeping bees, and occasionally living in a cave and engaging in at least one very public fast. He received admiring visitors, including Franklin and the governor of Pennsylvania, and for more than a decade sought new ways to demonstrate his conviction that slavery was "the Mother of all Sins."[11]

Lay might be called the first modern abolitionist, not only because of his religiously based view that slavery was a sin but also because of the way he insisted that slavery leached evil throughout the entire community. Believing so, he testified regularly in Quaker meetings and churches—and was often forcibly removed from them. During the 1730s and 1740s, he developed more and more dramatic ways of making his point that slavery exemplified and combined all the deadly sins. On one occasion, he publicly destroyed his wife's fine china, as a symbol of the violence wrought by sugary treats. In the most famous episode, Lay stood up in the Burlington, New Jersey, regional yearly meeting of 1738 to denounce slaveholding among Quakers as not only a violation of the golden rule but as the ultimate warlike act. Friends might as well renounce their pacifism and put on armor, he exclaimed, opening his overcoat to reveal his military garb below. He then took out a sword and stated that slaveowners committed a sin as grievous as murder—and thrust his weapon into a Bible that hid a bladder of red pokeberry juice, spattering himself and those who shared his bench with the ersatz blood.[12]

As his guerilla theater suggests, Lay sought to make slavery a personal matter. His other recorded protests include a pseudo-kidnapping, in which he detained the child of a neighboring slaveowner, asking the worried parent if he did not suppose that his slaves' parents or grandparents had once felt that way. On one cold winter day he stood outside a meeting house with one bare foot in the snow, comparing his self-imposed plight to the daily shiverings of parishoners' underclothed slaves. Slaves, as Cotton Mather had insisted, were members of the family. Even if servants were part of the natural order of things (Lay and Sandiford, like Tryon before them, explicitly distanced themselves from any attempt to delegitimate all relations of mastery and servitude), ungodly dealings with servants, like disrespect for parents, siblings or spouses, could be the most mortal of sins. As a result, in the colonies, the more genuinely authoritarian and powerful the church, apparently, the more theoretical protection afforded the slave.[13]

It is clear that Franklin and Lay had an interesting relationship. Franklin assembled and printed the latter's 1737 collection of testimonies and reflections, *All Slave-keepers That Keep the Innocent in Bondage* (though again without the printer's own name on the title page), and reported Lay's more spectacular doings with some respect in the pages of the *Pennsylvania Gazette*. Lay seems to have visited Franklin's shop regularly when he ventured from his country home in Abingdon, to purchase paper, ink, legal forms, and books to give away. He also subscribed to the newspaper. Deborah Franklin admired him enough to keep an engraved portrait of the man her husband called the "Pythagorean-Cynical-Christian Philosopher" displayed in their home—a print in which Lay conspicuously displays a copy of "Trion on Happiness."[14]

Sandiford and Lay, like Franklin, attacked vanity, inhumane waste, and the pretensions of ministers. Franklin's early appreciation of Tryon, his own battles with religious authorities, and his appreciation for Quaker sobriety and egalitarianism made him receptive to the two authors' religiously based criticisms of the entire social order. They probably knew what they were doing when they approached the young printer for help. As the Hemphill affair shows, Franklin could get genuinely excited about the contemporary indictment of religious authority as a form of "slavery." He might even have sympathized with attacks on religious hypocrites who sought moral authority in the community but were just as guilty of holding slaves.

And yet, during these same years Franklin, as owner of the *Pennsylvania Gazette* and a general store, began to profit from slavery and the trade in slaves in multiple ways, and it is then that he began to own slaves for the first time. Precisely because of his predisposition to agree with critiques of slavery, Franklin needed a rationale for his keeping a sympathetic distance. He found it, first, in religious pluralism, his commitment to freedom of the press for which suited his desire to expand his market beyond any one denomination. This pluralism, which took God seriously but withheld the powers of divine judgment and church discipline, ignored one crucial aspect of the emerging antislavery argument from faith. Slaves, in the vision of Mather, Sewall, Tryon, Sandiford, and Lay, were not only members of the human family but also members of a society of families whose government was subject to church as well as state.

By printing Lay and Sandiford but not following their ministries, Franklin enacted his carefully considered religious pluralism as well as his work ethic. When he did begin to publicly criticize slavery in writings of the 1750s and 1760s, it would be on economic and racism-based, not religious, grounds, subordinated to arguments for colonial autonomy from imperial regulations.[15]

What are the implications here for our understanding, not just of Franklin, but of religion and antislavery? It has been tempting for some of late to invoke Weber's thesis of secularization to explain the rise of rationalistic, even liberal critiques of unfreedoms such as slavery. In this light, Franklin represents the search for purifying vocations, thus laying the groundwork for modern capitalism and eventually for cosmopolitan secular reforms that took the languages of the Enlightenment and the American Revolution, more than that of the Bible, as inspirations. The problem with this view is that it dismisses a very important half-century of history—the years that compose most of Franklin's life, in fact. In the not-so short run of the early to mid-eighteenth century, the secular, ecumenical, human-centered approach worked rather differently, helping Franklin to run from its very real alternative—a decidedly evangelical kind of antislavery—as if from the plague. Weber's neglect of the persistence of enthusiastic religion as a cultural and political force (like his neglect of slavery's importance in the rise and growth of capitalism) means that the German thinker's thesis about the "protestant ethic and the spirit of capitalism" needs a more thorough revision, especially if it is to be of any use in understanding the rise and decline of New World slavery.[16]

Rather than enabling people to envision and sympathize with the distant other, such as slaves, capitalism, shorn of religion first—and, I would argue, most lastingly—made it easier to ignore the other next door, or within one's own household, or, most certainly, abroad.[17] If there is one thing that is striking about the criticisms of slavery offered by Mather, Sewall, and Lay, it is the critics' concern with actual, local people. These authors and activists saw slaves not as distant, abstract moral equals in an empire but rather as members of a family and, often, of a congregation. By contrast, when Franklin spoke publicly of local people and household relations in this period, it is in a very different voice—the very voice of market rationality, in which people and their labor are equated with their capacities for producing wealth. Whether one finds that perspective egalitarian and liberating or soulless and oppressive, there is one aspect to it that has not received nearly enough scholarly attention. In its original context, the Franklinian, or Protestant, work ethic conflated the labor- and capital-saving actions of the self-owning freeman in the marketplace with the labors and properties of the laborers *owned*—the members of the family who had been bought and sold and reduced to commodities.[18]

In this light, more Marxist than Weberian, it is all the more significant that much of the emergent critique of slavery that Franklin knew so well and so intimately—at least in the case of the colonial travelers Tryon, Sandiford and Lay—was also a critique of merchant capitalism undertaken by those who had seen it in the metropolis, the Caribbean, and North America. Sandiford and Lay addressed the problem directly by spectacularly giving away goods and refusing products of the West Indies like sugar. As a group, Quakers ultimately accepted these criticisms of the capitalism-slavery complex and, in a remarkable development, required each other to reject personal involvement in slavery.

Franklin made a different choice. Instead of following through on the implications of everyone's soul being savable, he explored the merchant capitalist reality that everyone's time was becoming money. Everyone could be bought and sold. The underside of Franklin's so-called Protestant ethic, then, was the increasing reality, in his Boston, Philadelphia, and Atlantic world, of the slave and the servant as fungible, money-making commodities. This was pluralism, relativism, and cosmopolitanism with a vengeance.[19] Who could understand it better than an apprentice who had been exploited in his own family? A man whose reforming masters had denied the salience of their critiques of power to their own power in the household that was also the workplace? Better to embrace public life, and a less unitary religious culture, that would not inquire so insistently—or, perhaps, inconsistently—into affairs in the home.

Capitalism's characteristic separation of public and private, when coupled with its proponents' assumptions about progress, blinded Anglo Americans to the other closer to home, including slaves, long before it encouraged leisured regard for more distant others. Given the recent confidence in progress evinced by our most prominent historians of the early American republic, and their equation of antislavery with tradition-breaking capitalism and with the American Revolution, all of which is personified in this literature by Benjamin Franklin, it is all the more important to heed David Brion Davis' warnings about "generational chauvinism" and to look at slavery and American development "from broader perspectives."[20] We must also remain open, as Davis has been, to religious, to Weberian, and to Marxist perspectives if we are to understand the spirit of capitalism and the spirit of antislavery.

NOTES

1. Claude-Ann Lopez, "Franklin and Slavery: A Sea Change," in her *My Life with Benjamin Franklin* (New Haven: Yale University Press, 2000), 196–204.
2. *The Autobiography of Benjamin Franklin* (New Haven: Yale University Press, 1964), 88.
3. Ibid., 87–88.
4. Ibid., 88–89.
5. Michael V. DePorte, "Introduction" to Thomas Tryon, *A Treatise of Dreams and Visions . . . [and] a Discourse of the Causes, Nature and Cure of Phrensie, Madness or Distraction* [1689], Augustan Reprint Society, vol. 160 (Los Angeles, 1973), i–ii; Thomas Tryon, *The Way to Health, Long Life, and Happiness*, 2nd ed. (London, 1691), 367, 368–82; Tryon, *Friendly Advice to the Gentlemen-Planters of the East and West Indies. In Three Parts* (London, 1684), 75–222; Tryon, *Tryon's Letters, Upon Several Occasions* (London, 1700), 183–85, 198–200; Tryon, *Friendly Advice*, in *Caribbeana: An Anthology of the English Literature of the West Indies*, ed. Thomas Crise (Chicago: University of Chicago Press, 1999), 53, 64, 66 76. For Tryon's importance in early antislavery see David Brion Davis, *The Problem of Slavery in Western Culture* (Ithaca: Cornell University Press, 1966), 371–74; Wylie Sypher, *Guinea's Captive Kings: British Antislavery Literature of the Eighteenth Century* (Chapel Hill: University of North Carolina Press, 1942), 67–68; Alden T. Vaughan, *Roots of American Racism: Essays on the Colonial Experience* (New York: Oxford University Press, 1995), 74–76; Dickson D. Bruce Jr., *The Origins of African American Literature, 1680–1815* (Charlottesville: University of Virginia Press, 2001), 22–25, 73, 100; Philippe Rosenberg, "Thomas Tryon and the Seventeenth-Century Dimensions of Antislavery," *William and Mary Quarterly* 61 (2004): 609–42.
6. Bills from E. Warner and Charles Moore, volume 66, folios 46a and 71a, Benjamin Franklin Papers, American Philosophical Society, Philadelphia, Penn.
7. J. A. Leo LeMay ed., *Franklin: Writings* (New York: Library of America, 1987), 145–51; LeMay, *The Canon of Benjamin Franklin* (Newark: University of Delaware Press, 1987), 42–46; *Philadelphia Gazette* [hereafter, PG], July 30, 1730, in *The Papers of Benjamin Franklin* [hereafter PBF], ed. Leonard W. Labaree, et al. (New Haven: Yale University Press, 1959–), 1:187; "Apology for Printers," PG, June 10, 1731, in PBF, 1:194–99; see also Benjamin Franklin, "Witch Trial at Mount Holly," PG, October 22, 1730, in PBF, 1:182–83; Franklin, *Autobiography*, 71.
8. Franklin, "Dialogue Between Two Presbyterians," PG, April 10, 1735; Franklin, *Some Observations on the Proceedings Against the Rev. Mr. Hemphill; with a Vindication of his Sermons* (Philadelphia, 1735); Franklin, *A Letter to a Friend in the Country . . .* (Philadelphia, 1735), all in PBF, 2:27, 37–65, 66–67, 71, 84.
9. Ralph Sandiford, *A Brief Examination of the Practice of the Times* (Philadelphia, 1729); PG, December 22, January 26, 1731; Roberts Vaux, *Memoirs of the Lives of Benjamin Lay and*

Ralph Sandiford (Philadelphia: Solomon Conrad, 1815), 59–73; Thomas E. Drake, *Quakers and Slavery in America* (New Haven: Yale University Press, 1950), 39–40; Davis, *Problem of Slavery in Western Culture*, 320–31.

10 Sandiford, *Brief Examination*, 9, 13, 17–20, 22, 24–25, 38, 41.
11 Benjamin Lay, *All Slave-keepers That Keep the Innocent in Bondage* (Philadelphia, 1737), 106; Vaux, *Memoirs of the Lives*, 17, 20, 24, 32; Drake, *Quakers and Slavery*, 43–44.
12 Ledger A and B, Benjamin Franklin Papers, American Philosophical Society; PG, August 10, 1738; March 25, 1742, in PBF, 2:357; Vaux, *Memoirs*, 28, 32; Davis, *Problem of Slavery in Western Culture*, 321–24; Drake, *Quakers and Slavery*, 43–46; Jean R. Soderlund, *Quakers and Slavery: A Divided Spirit* (Princeton: Princeton University Press, 1985), 16.
13 Winthrop D. Jordan, *White Over Black: American Attitudes Toward the Negro, 1550–1812* (Chapel Hill: University of North Carolina Press, 1967), 210.
14 PG, August 10, November 2, 1738, March 25, 1742; Ledger D, Franklin Papers.
15 I consider these developments in "Capitalism, Slavery, and Benjamin Franklin's American Revolution," in *The Early American Economy: New Directions*, ed. Cathy D. Matson (University Park: Pennsylvania State University Press, 2006), 183–217, and in *Runaway America: Benjamin Franklin, Slavery, and the American Revolution* (New York: Hill and Wang, 2004).
16 Max Weber, *The Protestant Ethic and the Spirit of Capitalism*, trans. Talcott Parsons (New York: Scribner's, 1930), 48–55, 65, 71, 1224, 180; Thomas L. Haskell, "Capitalism and the Origins of the Humanitarian Sensibility," in *The Antislavery Debate*, ed. Thomas Bender (Berkeley: University of California Press, 1992), 107–60.
17 My understanding of the process of distancing the close other is indebted to Robert John Ackermann, *Heterogeneities: Race, Gender, Class, Nation, and State* (Amherst: University of Massachusetts Press, 1996), 9–30.
18 Haskell misses this because he assumes, even as he too invokes Franklin, that slavery was a distant phenomenon in reformers' Anglo America. It was not.
19 David Waldstreicher, "Reading the Runaways: Self-fashioning, Print Culture, and Confidence in Slavery in the Eighteenth-Century Mid-Atlantic," *William and Mary Quarterly*, 3rd ser., 56 (1999): 243–72.
20 Gordon S. Wood, *The Radicalism of the American Revolution* (New York: Knopf, 1991); Joyce Appleby, *Inheriting the Revolution* (Cambridge: Belknap Press, 2000); Joseph J. Ellis, *Founding Brothers: The Revolutionary Generation* (New York: Knopf, 2001); David Brion Davis, "Free At Last: The Enduring Legacy of the South's Civil War Victory," *New York Times*, April 26, 2001; Davis, "Introduction," *The Boisterous Sea of Liberty: A Documentary History of America from Discovery Through the Civil War*, ed. Davis and Steven Mintz (New York: Oxford University Press, 1998), 2; David Brion Davis, "Looking at Slavery from Broader Perspectives," *American Historical Review* 105 (2000): 452–67.

JONATHAN A. GLICKSTEIN

The Specter of White Chattelization
William Goodell's Abolitionist Thought

In colonial America, wage labor, not slave labor, was the "peculiar institution." As late as 1800, wage labor was a rarity, but by 1860, perhaps 40 percent of northern workers labored in exchange for wages. In antebellum America, skilled and unskilled workers, eager to free wage labor from its earlier association with servile dependence, expressed disdain for the "nonproducing" classes of society and celebrated physical labor as the true source of society's wealth. A number of leading labor leaders vociferously criticized exploitative, oppressive, and "unrepublican" working conditions that threatened to reduce manual laborers to the status of wage slaves.

In this essay, Jonathan Glickstein, a leading authority on the rise of free labor in pre–Civil War America, examines the thought of William Goodell, an important yet neglected abolitionist. One of the organizers of the American Anti-Slavery Society and of the Liberty Party, which advocated civil rights for blacks as well as the abolition of slavery, Goodell was a principal advocate for the idea that the Constitution was an antislavery document. In the 1830s, Goodell combined his critique of slavery with condemnation of the North's economic system, insisting that an unholy alliance of southern slaveholders and northern manufacturers and financiers threatened to reduce white workers to the status of chattel. After 1840, however, Goodell gradually retreated from this radical critique of northern capitalism and instead came to view slavery as wholly different from other forms of labor exploitation.

To what extent did pernicious moral values and social practices in the free-labor North have strictly indigenous causes? To what degree, in particular, were more powerful northerners responsible for the growing prominence of such values and practices? Alternatively, how much did the root causes of the North's moral and social ills lie not in the free states at all but rather to the south, in the corrupting influence of slave labor and the slaveholding elite? No abolitionist of the 1830s wrestled more fully with these questions—with the ambiguity of evil and its sources—than did the New York reformer William Goodell (1792–1878).

Many, if not most, radical abolitionists in the 1830s believed that the affinity of interests between northern and southern elites had eventuated in a concerted partnership to protect and extend black slavery. Goodell, however, was among a minority of abolitionists who went still further: he publicly accused capitalists and other wealthy "idlers" in the free states of actually conspiring with the southern slavocracy to chattelize northern white workers. At the height of the elite-led antiabolition mob violence of the 1830s, Goodell warned "the laboring people of the North, that the Anti-Abolition Aristocracy are ready to join in the Southern project of enslaving them."[1]

Goodell entered the 1830s primed to believe the worst of northern "aristocrats." In the previous decade, working as a reform journalist in Providence and Boston before moving to New York City, he manifested a marked antipathy to materialist values and such forms of capitalist exploitation as the payment of starvation wages to urban seamstresses. Paul Goodman has most recently emphasized the plebeian and Calvinist religious roots of Goodell's "moral economy" sensibility: his birth into poverty in rural New York; the evangelical faith of the Connecticut grandmother who raised him for a time; his subsequent immersion in the Second Great Awakening; and his series of financial reverses as a small merchant.[2] All were among the factors that, by the late 1820s, had instilled in Goodell a pronounced hostility to the "market revolution." It was this animus that in the next decade situated him in the left wing of the radical antislavery movement: during the 1830s, he came to regard the antiabolitionism of the North's "gentlemen of property and standing" as the strongest legitimation yet of his preexisting populist and anticapitalist antipathies.[3]

In embracing the new crusade of radical abolitionism, Goodell, along with many of his cohorts, began an intellectual process of externalizing, or "southernizing," the source of moral and social evil in the free states. In 1839, for example, he proclaimed that "labor is despised at the south, and therefore is becoming to be despised at the north."[4] But because Goodell's antipathy for elite northerners was also more long-standing and intense than that of nearly all other abolitionists, he did not, at least during the 1830s, dismiss them as secondary members of the national slavepower—as mere dupes and tools of the southern slavocracy. For Goodell, more than for other abolitionists of the period, the externalization of the sources of northern corruption could only go so far. Thus he followed the above remark with the claim that "the idlers of the south, live upon the unrequited toil of the laborer, and the idlers of the north are forward to emulate, as far as possible, their example."

Goodell's anticapitalist white-chattelization warnings of the 1830s accordingly represented a working-out (consciously or otherwise) of a quite distinctive position. The spirit of slavery emanating from the South exerted so contagious a national influence—and might eventuate in the chattelization of northern whites—precisely because it stimulated the instinctive, preexisting propensity to oppress that also resided in the hearts of northern men of privilege and power. Put another way, southern black chattel slavery threatened to metastasize into northern white chattel slavery exactly because the most powerful of passions among all exploitative elites—in the free as well as the slave states—was the thirst for total domination, together with the love of idleness that total domination facilitated. Inspired by their counterparts in the South, the North's "lordly supervisors of the *American laboring poor*" would choose the purest, most clear-cut ways to "trample upon the laboring classes" and "grind the faces of the poor."[5]

Goodell's assumptions that some men thirsted for power and that power had an intoxicating effect on those who acquired it were not unique. Prominent abolitionists commonly insisted that human beings were too depraved or vulnerable to sin to be entrusted with the kind of power possessed by slaveholders. In fact, many of these abolitionists held that it was the blasphemous, God-like dominance that slaveholders enjoyed, and not profit-maximizing imperatives, that accounted for the resilience of southern slavery. William Lloyd Garrison spoke for such abolitionists when he asserted that "the master-passion in the bosom of the slaveholder is not gain, but the possession of absolute power, unlimited sovereignty."[6]

Goodell accepted the antislavery orthodoxy proclaiming the economic superiority of free labor. He insisted that "slaves have no interests in common with their masters," and because it "must be carried on by the cheapest and most bungling utensils," slave cultivation "finally impoverishes the planter."[7] Goodell agreed with many other abolitionists that slaveholders' perverse love of dominance overruled their best economic interests, and that they would have reaped higher profits by converting their workforce into free laborers. What set Goodell apart from most of his abolitionist cohorts was his extension of the same reasoning to capitalists and other "aristocrats" in the free states. Driven by their own extra-economic thirst for dominance, the North's antiabolitionist "gentlemen of property and standing" were eager to impose the same evil of chattel servitude on their own laboring population. Goodell's demonization of northern capitalists surpassed that of other abolitionists precisely because it rested on the conclusion that northern capitalists, in seeking to emulate the South's slaveholding elite, were similarly willing to injure themselves economically by enslaving their work force.

During the 1830s, Goodell developed a position on northern evils and inequities that might be characterized as left-evangelical abolitionist. This perspective reflected Goodell's beliefs from his pre-abolitionist days that the exploitation of child laborers and factory operatives by the north's "nobility" was markedly increasing. On the other hand, the extirpation of southern slavery and its lethal contempt for labor remained for Goodell vitally important for the removal of northern social evils. Indeed, only the abolition of these contaminants would prevent the northern evils from assuming a yet more perversely oppressive form. Supporting the spread of the abolitionist message to northern manufacturing regions, Goodell advised "the laboring classes, especially the operatives in the manufactories, . . . to *beware* how they sanction the doctrine of unrequited labor." Otherwise, "the aristocracy that grinds the colored man will soon break over the distinction of color."[8]

When Goodell warned of the chattelization of white workers in the free states, he was not only resting such warnings on the belief that "the capitalists of the North" were falling "more and more in love with the beauties" of slave labor.[9] Goodell was also speaking to the demoralization and complicity of workers in their own enslavement. Here, too, despite the atypical nature of his chattelization theme, Goodell was drawing on assumptions more widely shared among abolitionists of the 1830s. For Garrison, James G. Birney, Gerrit Smith, and others, the proslavery servility of the antiabolitionist, working-class pockets in the free states was an ominous starting point for the subjugation of the North's entire laboring population.[10]

From early on, Garrison and other abolitionists had rejected as specious and offensive the various "wage slavery" arguments advanced either by the South's proslavery conservatives or by northern workingmen's party and other labor radicals. Goodell shared the labor radicals' critical perspective on such economic disparities, but he rejected the wage slavery critique by insisting that chattel slavery was a greater, more crushing evil than northern free-labor exploitation and poverty. The moment that "the heavier oppressions of slavery are removed, the way will be prepared to remove more effectually the lighter burdens that press on the free."[11]

However, Goodell's and other abolitionists' rejection of the wage-slavery critique remained more equivocal than historians have generally believed precisely owing to the abolitionist conviction that this critique could so demoralize and enfeeble northern workers as to have a paradoxically self-fulfilling effect. From Goodell's perspective, the worst-case scenario remained the chattelization of northern workers. But, during the 1830s, he also described an intermediate condition that resembled wage slavery: "Patronize and sustain the papers that oppose the immediate emancipation of the slaves. They cannot fail to inculcate, directly or indirectly, the doctrine that laborers are 'better off' in slavery than in freedom. And whenever this doctrine obtains ascendancy, there will be nothing to prevent laborers of all colors from being enslaved."[12]

Garrison similarly argued in 1836 that the unholy alliance between predatory southern and northern elites aimed to create a northern laboring population whose continued possession of its self-ownership and other nominal freedoms did not preclude its economic and intellectual degradation. Garrison verged on endorsing Goodell's accusation that northern "aristocrats" ideally aspired to chattelize workers in the free states, even if the latter's enfeeblement stopped at something resembling wage slavery.[13] But a basic question remains: why did not more abolitionists, despite their hostility to elite proslavery northerners during the 1830s, and growing demoralization of northern workers, also endorse or come close to endorsing the stronger chattelization accusation leveled by Goodell?

Many, if not most, abolitionists likely believed that elite northerners' strict economic self-interest rendered them inimical to the extremity of enslaving northern white workers. Powerful northerners like Massachusetts textile magnate Nathan Appleton enjoyed varied ties with the southern slavocracy, but did not aspire to turn back the clock in northern workshops and factories in strict emulation of southern unfree practices.[14] In contrast to Goodell's apocalyptic slavepower conspiracy thinking, most abolitionists' distaste for the proslavery northern elite appears to have been qualified by the conviction that even these "aristocrats" accepted the northern system of wage labor incentives and individual autonomy as an economic and ethical advance over southern slave labor.

To put these points differently, nearly all abolitionists, including Goodell, embraced Adam Smith's claims regarding the economic shortcomings of slave labor. But where Goodell evidently concluded that northern capitalists, driven by their thirst for power, were willing to damage themselves economically by chattelizing their workers, the majority of his cohorts thought otherwise. Either they attached greater importance to narrow profit-maximizing considerations as a motivator of the northern elite, or they retained a higher opinion of the elite's overall values.

The variations and nuances in abolitionist commentary of the 1830s, including the extreme anticapitalist perspective of Goodell, suggest several generalizations.[15] First, the abolitionist agreement that southern slave labor was inefficient and evil failed to generate an equally broad abolitionist consensus extolling the northern social order. Second, abolitionists on the left—those most critical of northern social arrangements—were the abolitionists most likely to entertain the threat of employers seeking to enslave their workers.[16] In taking seriously the threat of northern workers' chattelization, left-abolitionists, and especially Goodell, differed markedly from the Joshua Leavitts and other abolitionists to their right, who insisted on the equity and health of the northern capitalist order.

At the same time, left-abolitionists such as Goodell distinguished themselves from the contemporary nonabolitionist co-occupiers of the left. Such northern proponents of the wage-slavery critique as the radical Democrat Orestes Brownson agreed with Goodell about the growing prevalence of capitalist oppression in the free states. But they believed that factory owners and other employers had no aspirations whatsoever to convert their "proletaries" into chattel slaves.[17] For Brownson and company, northern capitalists fully appreciated that they could appropriate a greater portion of the fruits of their workers' labor through the more impersonal coercions of the "free" market.[18]

In resisting Goodell's tendency to characterize northern capitalists as a would-be slavocracy, conservative reformers exemplified what would become the central thrust of abolitionist thought in the 1840s and 1850s.[19] Events in these decades, such as the waning of elite antiabolitionist violence and the intensifying northern nationalism of the 1850s, tended to soften Goodell's own criticisms of northern "aristocrats" and capital-labor arrangements in the free states. Goodell joined other abolitionists in blaming the South for northern moral corruption and social ills—a process that began in the 1830s. Absent from Goodell's post-1840 writings are the white-chattelization warnings that had targeted capitalists and other "aristocrats" in the free states as fully co-equal members of the slavepower.[20]

By 1860 Goodell was giving all of his support to a different scenario of future white chattelization in the free states, a scenario whose primary dynamic was the ongoing mulattoization of southern slavery. Whereas Goodell's earlier scenario had featured northern "aristocrats" who would disregard the existing racialized basis for chattel slavery, the 1850s scenario elided these northern actors. It more exclusively located the chattelization threat in the southern slavocracy and its proclivity for exploiting a process that was biologically obliterating slavery's racialized basis.[21]

William Goodell's anticapitalist white-chattelization warnings of the 1830s, marked by their demonization of the practices, values, and aspirations of northern "aristocrats," represented a recessive strain of abolitionist thought. In the manner that he held slavery and the southern slavocracy only partially responsible for the existence of evil and oppression, and for the threat to freedom itself in the North, Goodell carved out a distinctive abolitionist position during this period. Yet, Goodell's warnings remained an extreme version of abolitionists' common insistence on the contingent nature—indeed, the apocalyptic fragility—of America's free institutions. In this respect Goodell not only spoke for many other abolitionists but also notably anticipated Lincoln's articulation of the "house divided" theme. The relationship between free labor and slave labor, Goodell proclaimed in 1835, was inherently unstable: they "cannot much longer co-exist" in the United States. And free labor's victory over slavery, Goodell warned, was by no means assured: "One must prevail to the destruction of the other. The laborers at the south will be free, or the laborers at the north will lose their freedom."[22] Goodell's anticapitalist white-chattelization warnings of the 1830s represented an extreme variant of abolitionism's general rebuke to American complacency.[23]

NOTES

1 Goodell, in one of the many newspapers he edited, *The Friend of Man* (Utica, N.Y.), August 25, 1836
2 Paul Goodman, *Of One Blood: Abolitionism and the Origins of Racial Equality* (Berkeley: University of California Press, 1998), 69–75.
3 Like other moral reformers who raged against intemperance, Goodell refused to absolve the free laboring poor of all responsibility for their plight. The antipathy that he shared with the early labor movement for capitalist exploitation and inordinate wealth (most particularly the consumerism and financial machinations of the urban propertied classes) did not completely override his Calvinist inclination to conceptualize other social evils, including poverty, in terms of the sufferer's moral weakness and corruption; Goodman, *Of One Blood*, 75; Meyer Leon Perkal, "William Goodell: A Life of Reform" (Ph.D. diss., City University of New York, 1972), 50–51.
4 *Anti-Slavery Lecturer* (Utica, N.Y.: New York Anti-Slavery Society), Lecture V and Lecture VII, May and July 1839; see also Lecture VIII, reprinted in *The Liberator* (Boston), October 18, 1839.
5 "W. G.," "What They Would Do If They Could. Addressed to the Free Laborers of the United States," *The Emancipator* (New York), December 1835; W. G., "Solution of a Puzzle. Why Do the Aristocracy Encourage Mobs?" *Emancipator*, July 21, 1836; see also Goodman, *Of One Blood*, 139–40.
6 "To Peleg Sprague," *Liberator*, March 1, 1850; Ronald G. Walters, *The Antislavery Appeal: American Abolitionism after 1830* (Baltimore: Johns Hopkins University Press, 1976), 71–72.

7 Lecture V; see also Lecture VII.
8 "A Seasonable Hint," *Emancipator*, January 28, 1834; see also Goodell's remarks in "Working Men," *Friend of Man*, January 19, 1837.
9 Anonymous abolitionist, "Important to the Workers," in *Human Rights*, reprinted in *Emancipator*, July 18, 1839.
10 "Anti-Slavery Anniversaries," *The Philanthropist* (Cincinnati), June 10, 1836.
11 "Working Men," January 19, 1837. For Goodell's criticism of the arguments, whether southern or northern in origin, that "insultingly" referred to northern free laborers as " 'white slaves,' " see Lecture IV, *Anti-Slavery Lecturer*, April 1839; W. G., "What They Would Do If They Could." Goodell's rejection of the wage slavery argument as insulting to northern laborers cannot be separated from his disposition to view individual character failings as the root cause of social evils. Abolitionists, including Goodell, were inclined to exempt only chattel slaves from all personal responsibility for their moral and intellectual condition.
12 W. G., "What They Would Do If They Could."
13 "Lyman Beecher," *Liberator*, July 30, 1836.
14 James L. Huston, *Securing the Fruits of Labor: The American Concept of Wealth Distribution, 1765–1900* (Baton Rouge: Louisiana State University Press, 1998), 187–88, 313–14.
15 During the 1830s Goodell occasionally moderated his expressed antagonism toward northern capitalists; see his "An Appeal in Behalf of the American Anti-Slavery Society—Addressed to the People of the City of New-York"; *Emancipator*, August 26, 1834.
16 A partial list of left-abolitionists, approaching Goodell in their demonization of the North's capitalist "aristocracy," would include Gerrit Smith, Nathaniel P. Rogers, Adin Ballou, Parker Pillsbury, William I. Bowditch, and Garrison in the middle and late 1830s.
17 Orestes A. Brownson, "The Laboring Classes," *Boston Quarterly Review* 3 (July 1840): 368–73; (Oct. 1840): 461–68.
18 Jonathan A. Glickstein, *American Exceptionalism, American Anxiety: Wages, Competition, and Degraded Labor in the Antebellum United States* (Charlottesville: University of Virginia Press, 2002), 80–83. Southern proslavery proponents of the wage slavery critique argued similarly; see George Fitzhugh, *Cannibals All! or, Slaves without Masters*, ed. C. Vann Woodward (Cambridge: Belknap Press, 1960 [orig. 1857]), 223.
19 For a contrary view that regards antagonism to market-capitalist forces and outcomes in the North as characteristic of mainstream abolitionist thought, see James L. Huston, "Abolitionists, Political Economists, and Capitalism," *Journal of the Early Republic* 20 (2000): 487–521.
20 This is not to claim either that Goodell's antagonism toward the northern "aristocracy" completely receded in the 1840s and early 1850s, or that his southernization of the sources of northern ills followed an unbroken path. Such claims would be belied by Goodell's populist political activity and writing during this period.

21 "The American Oligarchy—Wherein Lies Its Strength?" *The Principia* (New York), ed. Goodell, April 7–July 21, 1860.
22 W. G., "What They Would Do If They Could."
23 For a more comprehensive version of this essay, see Glickstein, "The Chattelization of Northern Whites: An Evolving Abolitionist Warning," *American Nineteenth Century History* 4 (2003).

MARGARET M. R. KELLOW

The Oriental Imaginary Constructions of Female Bondage in Women's Antislavery Discourse

Northern women made up much of the grassroots support of the abolitionist movement. Largely unaware of the fact that slaves could be found in every one of the original northern states up until the Revolution, many women looked elsewhere to understand slavery's true evil, especially to the Islamic world. As Margaret M. R. Kellow demonstrates in the following essay, when many abolitionist women imagined what slavery was like, they immediately thought of the enslavement of white women by the North African "Barbary pirates." For many of these women, it was sexual abuse that gave a sense of urgency to the moral problem.

North African slavery, although far smaller in scale than New World slavery, was not insignificant in size. A recent study by the historian Robert C. Davis entitled *Christian Slaves, Muslim Masters* estimates that North African pirates captured and enslaved more than a million Europeans between 1530 and 1780. Seized from ships or abducted in raids along the coast of France, Italy, Portugal, and Spain, and as far north as England and Iceland, European captives toiled in galleys, quarries, construction, and clearing trees. Many female captives were forced to become concubines for Muslim masters in what is now Morocco, Tunisia, Algeria and Libya. Among the captives were 130 Americans taken from ships in the Mediterranean between 1785 and 1793. Images of white women forced into sexual slavery made it easier for some female abolitionists to break through the psychological barriers that had inhibited empathy with enslaved African Americans and to appreciate slavery's horrors.

How can we account for the passion with which some American women embraced abolition, especially those who lived in New England, far away from the unnumbered oppressions of plantation slavery? For some white female abolitionists, the same political and legal concerns over slavery that spurred their male counterparts provided sufficient motivation. Others, however, felt themselves called to take up the cause of the slave by the plight of their "sisters in bondage." For the latter, their understanding of the particular evils inherent in the enslavement of women mandated their involvement. Writing in the 1842 antislavery annual *The Liberty Bell*, the Boston matron Eliza Lee Follen observed:

> Is it not natural and right that women should feel most for the sufferings and degradation of their own sex? And are not women the greatest sufferers from slavery? . . . Weak and trembling, she stands before her tyrant, utterly defenceless, entirely subjected to his power, crushed soul and body, the willing or the unwilling victim of his brutal will. Doubtless the men in slavery suffer much, but what pure mind would not prefer the hard work, the cruel lashes, all that a man can endure, to the hideous catalogue of miseries, to which the female slaves are often doomed?[1]

Follen's comment revealed a well-defined image of the essence of female bondage, one to which no true woman could be indifferent. In her mind, the monstrous evil inherent in the enslavement of women did not lie in the denial of personal autonomy in a political sense. In contrast to abolitionist attacks on the enslavement of black men, Follen's analysis did not wrestle with the ontological contradiction inherent in the humanity of the slave. Nor did she draw attention to the labor regime of the plantation South, which saw enslaved women performing harsh field labor undistinguished from that of male workers. Follen does not even mention the repeated fragmentation of slave families, although this issue concerned many white female abolitionists. For Follen, and for many white female abolitionists, the evil at the heart of the enslavement of women involved a sexual crime. This paper seeks to identify some of the sources of this perception and to explain why this particular image of female bondage played such a prominent role in the discourse of white female antislavery.

Angelina Grimké observed that "none but those who know from experience what it is to live in a land of bondage can form any idea of what is endured by those whose eyes are open enough to feel for these miserable creatures."[2] In her view, one had to see slavery to understand what it meant. This being so, how and from what sources did women in New England and the other northern states construct their images of female enslavement by the antebellum period? How did these women who would form the "Great Silent Army of Abolitionism" conceptualize what it meant for a woman to be a slave?[3] Three potential sources present themselves: New England women could have drawn on (1) their knowledge or awareness of the bondage of African Americans that had existed previously in their own society; (2) accounts of New World slavery in the American South or the West Indies; or (3) accounts and stories of enslavement emanating from the Muslim Mediterranean.

Had New England women wished to explore the question of female enslavement in the 1820s, evidence concerning the experience of women in bondage in their own society would not have been difficult to uncover. Slavery had a long history in New England, and communities of African Americans existed in virtually every northern city of any size. Yet, as Joanne Pope Melish has demonstrated, a willful amnesia blinkered the minds of white New Englanders where slavery was concerned.[4]

In the mental landscape of many white New England women, slavery existed only in other places, places far away in both geographic and moral terms. Melish's observation holds true even for prominent abolitionists such as Lydia Maria Child. Child employed an African American woman as a domestic on at least one occasion and most certainly encountered Boston's black community from time to time in her antislavery work and in other contexts.[5] Yet neither her published work, including her celebrated *Appeal in Favor of that Class of Americans Called Africans*, nor her personal correspondence conveys a sense of the process by which African Americans had come to be in Massachusetts in the first place. Like so many of her fellow New Englanders, Child's determination to construct Massachusetts and New England as a bastion of liberty in opposition to a slavery-infested South blinded her to the legacies of slavery in her own community.[6] Rooted in this vantage point, white New England women were unable to draw on the experience of their own communities to understand what enslavement might have meant for the African American women in their midst.

Although they ignored the evidence that slavery had existed in their own communities, white northern women clearly knew that slavery flourished in many parts of the "New" World: in the American South, the West Indies, and in South America. These places, however, lay far beyond the personal experience of most people. Travel to these destinations was for the most part the prerogative of elites, few of whom were disposed to be critical of slavery in anything more than a perfunctory sense. For example, Rev. Convers Francis of Watertown, Massachusetts, visited Baltimore in the fall of 1827 and opined to his diary that slavery assumes no very odious or unpleasant appearance. The slaves are generally house-servants, and appear cheerful, happy, and much attached to the families in which they live. However, slavery no doubt assumes its mildest forms in the city; on the plantations, in the country, we should doubtless see more of the evils, which it must necessarily bring in its train.

It cannot be too much regretted that such a thing as slavery exists; but so far as concerns the actual situation of slaves at the South, I think New England prejudices have been violent and unreasonable.[7]

In the early national period, observers with political or commercial interests in the South had little reason to embark on searching explorations of slave life. For those unwilling to search out abolitionist literature, accounts of life in the South or in the West Indies were not hard to come by, but few of these had much to say specifically about the nature of female bondage.[8]

If slavery in the Americas failed to provide adequate representations of female bondage, a rich reservoir of images of the enslavement of women arose from the Muslim Mediterranean. While New Englanders firmly repressed their own history as it related to slavery, and while national political tensions encouraged sanitized images of the slave South, representations of Middle Eastern slavery remained relatively unproblematic. These images entered American culture readily, owing to their literary, political, and religious pedigrees. Once there, they did much to shape the ways in which those American women who had not personally observed the enslavement of women configured female bondage.

Oriental imagery, by which is meant Western representations of the East in writings for other Westerners, had been entering Western European and, by extension, American culture for at least a century before the early national period. Over the course of the eighteenth century, publications such as *The Arabian Nights* portrayed the Orient as an exotic and fabulous locale.[9] The East and, in particular, the harem, with its female inmates, became a useful position for framing political and social critiques of European manners and customs. Montesquieu's *Persian Letters* (1721), Mozart's *The Abduction from the Seraglio* (1781), and Susanna Rowson's *Slaves in Algiers* (1794) are but a few of the artistic representations of the Orient that satirized contemporary European and American mores at the same time that they familiarized Europeans and Americans with the supposed circumstances and dynamics of life in an Oriental harem. Significantly, the political critiques implicit in many of these works were often articulated by female characters. This strategy defused and masked the criticisms, shielding their authors from authoritarian and repressive regimes, but it also gendered the victims of despotic regimes as female.[10]

If representations of women enslaved in the seraglio were largely satiric and parodic in eighteenth-century Europe, the emergence of romanticism by the early nineteenth century invoked the harem as a very different place. Instead of a site from which to critique western society, the East and the harem became, in the work of Byron and others, a place where the constraints and conventions of bourgeois society and morality did not obtain. As rationalism, sensibility, and, especially, evangelical self-discipline gained ascendancy in European and American polite society, the "mysterious East," and in particular the harem, became a convenient locus onto which unruly passions such as cruelty and sensuality could be displaced.[11] As a consequence of these two developments, American authors such as Rowson, Royall Tyler, and Washington Irving wielded a fully-articulated, but at the same time highly ambivalent, cultural tool when they invoked harem imagery to satirize and critique aspects of American society in the early national period. No matter how the harem came to be regarded, however, each invocation of this mythic locus and its denizens emphasized the identification of female bondage with sexual exploitation.[12]

The American experience in the early national period underscored these literary and cultural evocations of oriental imagery. Encounters with the Barbary pirates resulted in the capture and eventual rescue of a number of American sailors by the early nineteenth century, giving rise, among other things, to a genre of antislavery literature.[13] In this literature, female captives figured prominently, although in fact no American woman was ever captured by the Corsairs.[14] Yet, because images of white Americans in slavery arising from this episode became linked to a national triumph, such imagery could circulate freely in American society in the early national period.

The almost certainly fictional tale of a British woman who had been captured illustrates these themes effectively. *The History of the Captivity and Sufferings of Mrs. Maria Martin, who was six years a slave in Algiers: Two of which she was confined in a Dark and Dismal Dungeon, Loaded with Irons, for refusing to comply with the Brutal Request of a Turkish Officer* first appeared in the United States in 1807 and was reprinted at least eleven times in various editions by 1818. Martin, the twenty-one-year-old wife of a British captain, claimed to have been captured when the vessel on which she was travelling to Minorca was shipwrecked. She detailed her experience of being appraised and sold in a slave market. After three years as a slave in the household of the Grand Vizier of the city, her master approached her one evening with an interpreter who

... informed me that his master pretended to harbour an unusual degree of love for me, and through fear of being betrayed and punished agreeable to the laws of the country, should he attempt by forcible means to gratify a lustful passion, he had commanded him [i.e. the interpreter] to solicit my compliance, and to inform me that if I would willingly consent to indulge him in what he should request, he would extend to me the same liberty which his wives (or concubines) enjoyed!

When Martin refused the Grand Vizier's advances, "he became now like a madman, drawing his dirk, he threatened me with instant death, unless I would immediately comply with his request; but finding that I still persisted in my determination, he left me, swearing that my obstinacy should yet cost me my life!"

After two years in chains, the efforts of the British consul secured Martin's release. Accounts such as Martin's underscored the impact of the emergence of the *roman du sérail* ("romance of the harem") as a literary genre, one that persisted long after the depredations of the Corsairs had been terminated by treaty in 1815. More important, such accounts propagated images of the sexual exploitation of enslaved women.[15]

These representations received heightened attention during the 1820s, as Americans focused on the Greek struggle for independence from the Ottoman Empire. Americans repeatedly configured the struggle in gendered terms. Specific events of the Greek revolt underscored the identification of Greece with female vulnerability. Fitz-Greene Halleck's poem "Marco Bozzaris" (1827), a popular recitation piece in antebellum America, captured the essence of this depiction.

> At midnight, in his guarded tent,
>   The Turk was dreaming of the hour
> When Greece, her knee in suppliance bent,
>   Should tremble at his power.[16]

In 1822, the Greek island of Chios, known to Americans as Scio, was sacked by a Turkish commander. Samuel Gridley Howe's *Historical Sketch of the Greek Revolution*, published in 1828, included eyewitness accounts of the massacre, although the details were widely known well before this time. Howe observed that "[t]he only exception made during the massacre, was in the favour of the women and boys, who were preserved to be sold as slaves. Many of the former were running to and fro half frantic, with torn garments, and dishevelled hair;

pressing their trembling infants to their breasts, and seeking death as a preservation from the greater calamities that awaited them."

Howe claimed that thousands of women and children had been abducted by the Turks and added in a note that "the fate of these captives ... is known to the world; the open exposal in the slave markets of the beautiful women and children of Scio, in the presence of the Ambassadors of all the European Courts at Constantinople, could not pass unnoticed."[17] Similarly, the account of a Greek woman, one Sophia Mazro, who survived the battle in which Byron had died, disclosed that following the Greek defeat, her "daughters were given to understand that their fate was determined upon—that they were to be sent with many of their Christian female companions to some distant part of the Grand Seignior's [Turkish ruler's] dominions, there to be disposed of as slaves, to the highest bidders!"[18] In American minds, the Greek Revolt tied notions of political tyranny to sexual despoliation inextricably, and despotism to voluptuousness and indolence explicitly, thereby effecting key linkages. All despots were slaveholders, and all slaveholders were sexual predators.

So, by the late 1820s the combination of literary and actual interfaces with the Orient, primarily the Muslim Mediterranean, had served to elide slavery and the sexual exploitation of women in the imagination of many white Americans. Slavery became yoked to decadence, luxury, and vice. This linkage was important for two reasons. On the one hand, repeated representations of women enslaved in Oriental harems provided a reservoir of images from which women could draw to visualize what slavery might entail for a woman. Well before New England women encountered antislavery in a formal sense, the ambient culture had equipped them with a whole suite of images of female bondage. Initially there was no consistent argument embedded in these images. They were just readily available in cultural forms directed to women. Eventually, however, oriental imagery depicting women enslaved in harems would be used deliberately to persuade women to embrace antislavery. Owing to the prevalence of this imagery in antebellum culture as a whole, the first of these processes would greatly facilitate the second.

Gift books, annuals and children's literature from the period—the cultural forms directed to and sometimes produced by women—frequently contained Oriental tales, including romances, adventures, and poetry. In the 1820s, especially, these texts frequently celebrated noble Greeks who resisted Turkish tyrants and repeatedly made reference to women incarcerated in harems. Here the picture of female enslavement that emerged proved all the more powerful for being unattached to abolitionism. For example, *The Atlantic Souvenir: A*

Christmas and New Year's Offering 1826 opened with "The Eve of St. John," which related the story of a young Greek couple separated by a despotic Turkish ruler. On their island, Turkish domination guaranteed that "the possession of beauty leads only to its slavery and pollution," and the ruler seizes the young woman for himself. When lover and tyrant confront each other, the young woman steps in to save her beloved, claiming "I had rather be polluted by the gaze of a voluptuous tyrant, than this peaceful home of my father should be stained with blood." In a gesture easily recognizable to bourgeois northern women, her response mobilized prevailing gender conventions. This portrayal of a pure, self-sacrificing, domestic woman facilitated identification between the reader and the heroine. This same volume also contained a travelogue about Athens and a poem celebrating the Greek struggle entitled "Freedom."[19]

Similarly, the *Forget Me Not; A Christmas and New Year's Present*, which appeared in 1828, contained three different Oriental items. In "The Euthanasia: A Tale of Modern Greece," readers enjoyed the following description of a lovely young woman's history: "her mother, a Georgian, [was] stolen or strayed from the establishment [i.e., the harem] of Mourad Ali, once pasha of the Morea, and famous for the most delicate taste in horses and women. . . ." "The Zanteote Lovers" told of a young Greek man who barely escaped execution because he refused to answer to the name of "slave." Another story entitled "The Houri" described a young shah who inadvertently killed the woman he loved. Thereafter "he avoided the pleasures of the chase, the banquet and the harem," becoming indifferent to "the beautiful females, Circassians, Georgians, and Franks, who thronged his court, and who tasked their talents and charms to the utmost to find favour in the eyes of the shah."[20] *The Beauties of the Muses; or Select and Entertaining Tales, Prose and Verse* of 1829 included two Oriental tales, both of which implied a widespread traffic in women. In "Achmet and Selima" the heroine is captured by an "Algerine Corsair" who presented her "to the bashaw [pasha], who was so smitten with her charms, that he resolved to present her to the dey. The dey on receiving her, was not less astonished at her beauty, and looked upon her as the ornament of his seraglio."[21] For those seeking more serious reading, *The Moral and Religious Souvenir*, published in Boston in 1828, compared the impact of Christianity and Islam on women and concluded the following: "As the religion of Mahomet extended and established itself in Asia, it sealed forever the domestic slavery and relative degradation of women . . ." These and many other similar items were reinforced by missionary and travel narratives from the Middle East as well.

Oriental representations were not only literary. Political speeches invoked the same imagery. Sereno Edwards Dwight warned a Boston audience in 1824 that Greece had been "subjected to a slavery, which in all the odious features of brutality and cruelty, of rapacity and pollution, lack[ed] a parallel in the annals of this world." The Greeks had risen even though they "perfectly understood . . . that they put in jeopardy . . . the purity of their wives and daughters." "If Greece should fall," he predicted, "her wives and her daughters will glut the slave-market, until no more purchasers can be found."[22] Gregory T. Bedell, put the following image of the Greek struggle before his Philadelphia congregation in 1824: "the young and delicate females, whom the very savage of the forest would almost have respected, were given to the immediate brutal lust of their invaders, or sold in the public market, to be separated from their desolated homes . . . [and] abandoned to the will of men, more savage that the tyger who kills his prey for food.[23]

A published letter of the Rev. Jonas King averred that among the victims of the Greek conflict, "the beautiful woman seeks death, . . . rather than be left to fall into the hands of a brutal Turk, . . . to drag out a wretched life in a Mussulman haram . . ."[24] These vivid depictions of enslaved women, repeated in countless published addresses and broadsides, all conveyed the same message: bondage for women meant sexual violation.

Even lighter entertainment underscored the message. Notes from the Boston Theater in Federal Street from 1796 to 1797 indicate that a number of Oriental-themed plays appeared on its playbill, including Isaac Bickerstaffe's *The Sultan; or a Peep into the Seraglio* and Sir George Collier's *Selina and Azor, A Persian Tale*.[25] Rowson's *Slaves in Algiers* continued to be performed into the 1820s. Mordecai Noah's *The Grecian Captive, or the Fall of Athens*, published in New York in 1822, reworked a French melodrama. At the climax of the play, the heroine Zelia is seized by Achmet, a Turk, who proclaims "No entreaties, thou fair piece of mischief. In me thou wilt find no fawning, love-sick slave—no soft-sighing swain, but a soldier, rough and untamed—the foe of Greece and all thy hated race."[26] Plays, like public addresses and political speeches, animated Oriental imagery and kept evocations of brutalized and dishonored women vivid and accessible throughout this period.

Thus, Oriental imagery abounded in American culture in the early national and antebellum periods, constituting an extensive repertoire of stock figures, many of which might resonate with American slavery. As one early abolitionist observed, "a planter with his hundred wenches about him is in some respects at least like the Sultan in his seraglio."[27] White American women could draw readily from this cultural repertoire in order to envision the nature of female enslavement. Moreover, by the late 1820s, any mention of Turks or Algerines conjured up allusions of vice and debauchery. Not surprisingly, antislavery activists eagerly seized the polemic potential of this discourse. They consciously deployed explicitly Oriental imagery and other allusive representations in order to mobilize support among women for immediate abolition.

Elizabeth Chandler's pioneering role in antislavery in the early phase of immediate abolitionism has been widely acknowledged. As the author of a column entitled "The Ladies Repository" in one of the first abolitionist newspapers, *The Genius of Universal Emancipation*, Chandler attempted to inspire sympathy for the female slave in the hearts of her women readers. Her approach envisaged forging a sympathetic bond between the reader and the female slave and she described this process as "Mental Metempsychosis." "Could we but persuade those with whom we plead in behalf of the slave," she wrote in 1831, "to imagine themselves for a few moments in his very circumstances, to enter into his feelings, comprehend all his wretchedness, transform themselves mentally into his very self, they would not surely long withhold their compassion."[28] Although in this instance she spoke of the slave as male, Chandler focused much of her writing on the plight of enslaved women. She realized that the real and fictional experiences of white women captive in the Islamic world could serve as a template for the identification she attempted to foster. White women who had read Byron or *Maria Martin* and who lived in the towns and cities whose names commemorated the Greek struggle for independence could draw on this imagery to envisage what it would be like to be a slave. In this imaginative world, the consequences of female enslavement were invariably sexual. For antislavery women, as Karen Sanchez-Eppler has indicated, sexual abuse was a particularly heinous aspect of slavery. More important, in the mental world of American women who for two generations had repeatedly encountered Oriental imagery, sexual abuse approached the *sum total* of female enslavement.[29]

One can see Chandler attempting to facilitate this kind of sympathetic identification in a column she produced a few months earlier. "Slave Market in Constantinople" quoted at length from the account of a traveler in the Middle East. Chandler put before her readers a description of "this horrid place, where perhaps the loveliest women in the world are bought and sold, like cattle, in[s]pected by every scoundrel who wears a turban . . ." Ignoring the implications of several negative allusions to African women in the slave market, Chandler's extract focused on "the poor Greek women . . . huddled together. I saw seven or eight in one cell, stretched on the floor, some dressed in the vestiges of former finery; some of them were from Scio, others from Ipsara; they had nothing in common but despair! All of them looked pale and sickly, and all of them appeared to be pining after the homes they were never more to see again, and the friends they were to meet no more." But the centrepiece of the account was the fate of a young Greek girl, whose experience recapitulated exactly the conventional assumptions about the sexual depravity of Oriental societies.

> I saw one poor girl of about fifteen brought forward to exhibit her gate [sic] and figure to an old Turk. He twisted her elbows: he pulled her ankles, felt her ears, examined her mouth and then her neck, all this while the slave-merchant was extolling her shape and features and protesting she was only turned of thirteen, that she neither snored nor started in her sleep, in every respect she was warranted. I loitered about the bazaar until I saw this bargain brought to a conclusion; the girl was bought for 280 dollars.[30]

Chandler recognized that this image of violated white womanhood had enormous power to persuade and to mobilize support for antislavery among northern women.

Other abolitionists soon followed her lead. An 1834 convention in Concord, New Hampshire, debated the propriety of the formation of female antislavery societies. The elision of enslavement and sexual exploitation effected by Oriental imagery in the configuration of female bondage was quite apparent in the discussion.[31] A woman, the delegates argued, "would be more than unfeminine if she could overlook the situation of many of her sex in the southern states. Can she see the marriage relation unregarded, all the nicer sensibilities of her sex annihilated, and all the licentiousness incident to slavery, and not feel and act for her injured and oppressed sisters?" At the same convention, William Lloyd Garrison described slavery as "a system of lewdness."[32] A Vermont society warned "that the system of slavery annihilates the marriage relation among the inslaved [sic], and exposes to pollution more than half a million of American females."[33] Citing abolitionist author George Bourne, the same convention heard the following observation by two prominent Virginian women: "We are called wives, and as such are recognized in law; but we are little more than superintendents of a colored seraglio."[34] Two years later, Nathaniel P. Rogers addressed another convention in Concord and reminded his audience that ". . . Algerine bondage, Turkish bondage, West Indian bondage fall as far in the rear of ours, as their mastery does in its professions of Liberty and Justice. . . . An escape from our slavery into the deepest dungeon in Algiers, would amount to deliverance and emancipation."[35]

Antislavery women made use of these allusions as well. The Anti-Slavery

Convention of American Women held in New York in the spring of 1837 drafted *An Appeal to the Women of the Nominally Free States* that warned that in the South, African American women could be "torn from their husbands, and forcibly plundered of their virtue." This *Appeal* went on to speculate, "Can northern men go down to the well watered plains of the South to make their fortunes, without bowing themselves in the house of Rimmon and drinking of the waters of that river of pollution which rolls over the plain of Sodam [sic] and Gomorrah?"[36]

Perhaps the most direct evidence of the power of Oriental imagery came in a pamphlet entitled *Why Work for the Slave? Addressed to the Treasurers and Collectors in the anti-slavery cent-a-week societies,* published in 1838. As Julie Roy Jeffrey points out, cent-a-week societies were almost entirely the province of antislavery women.[37] After citing a number of examples of the outrages inherent in slavery, the author, Nathaniel Southard, suggested the following to his readers: "We may enter into the feelings of a slave by reading the story of Maria Martin, an American woman [sic] enslaved in Algiers. In 1800, she embarked for Cadiz, and when almost there, was seized, carried to Algiers." Southard felt sure that, having entered into sympathetic identification with a white woman supposedly imprisoned and threatened with sexual exploitation in an Oriental setting, American women would be willing to work for the deliverance of women enslaved in the American South.

Invoking the discourse of Orientalism served to sexualize slavery and give it a moral immediacy. This immediacy moved slavery out of the realm of political/legal debates over the status of African American individuals and framed it in terms of sin, depravity, and victimized womanhood. The image of enslaved women as unwilling victims in sexual bondage presented antislavery women with a fundamental challenge and provoked an especially strong response. As such, it constituted a critical juncture in the development of abolitionist discourse, particularly as it related to women.

NOTES

1 Eliza Lee Follen, *The Liberty Bell,* ed. Maria Weston Chapman (Boston, 1842), 7–8.
2 Angelina Grimké, Diary, April 1829, as quoted in Jean Fagan Yellin, *Women & Sisters: The Antislavery Feminists in American Culture* (New Haven: Yale University Press, 1989), 30.
3 See Julie Roy Jeffrey, *The Great Silent Army of Abolitionism: Ordinary Women in the Antislavery Movement* (Chapel Hill: University of North Carolina Press, 1998).

4 See, for example, Starksborough and Lincoln Anti-Slavery Society, *Address of the Starksborough and Lincoln Anti-Slavery Society, to the Public* . . . (Middlebury, Vt.: Knapp & Jewett, 1835), 3 (American Antiquarian Society, Worcester, Mass.; hereafter AAS).

5 For Lydia Maria Child's employment of an African American domestic, see LMC to Lucretia Child (sister-in-law), September 27, 1829, in *The Collected Correspondence of Lydia Maria Child, 1817–1880*, ed. Milton Meltzer and Patricia G. Holland (Millwood, N.Y.: Kraus Microforms, 1980).

6 See for example Lydia Maria Child, *An Appeal in Favor of that Class of Americans Called Africans* (New York: John S. Taylor, 1836), 105–22, in which Child's discussion of American politics since the Revolution is framed entirely in terms of conflicts between the South and "free" states.

7 Francis's observations were later published in his sister Lydia Maria Child's magazine for children. See "F" [Convers Francis Jr.], "Extracts from a Journal," *The Juvenile Miscellany* 3 (November 1827), 227–36; cf. Guy R. Woodall, ed. "Journal of Convers Francis, II," in *Studies in the American Renaissance, 1982*, ed. Joel Myerson (Charlottesville: University Press of Virginia), 227–84.

8 Accounts of travel in the south frequently mentioned slaves, but the slaves referred to were usually male and when enslaved women were mentioned little was said about distinctive aspects of their experience. See, for example, William Bartram, *Travels through North and South Carolina, Georgia, East and West Florida* . . . (London, 1792), which mentions slaves (some of whom may have been Indians) numerous times but says nothing about the particular experience of enslaved women.

9 *The Arabian Nights* had been translated into French at the end of the seventeenth century and was available in English soon afterwards. Six American editions had appeared by 1800 and many more followed. For an early, but useful, survey of this literature, see Martha Pike Conant, *The Oriental Tale in England in the Eighteenth Century* (New York: Columbia University Press, 1908; repr. Octagon Books, 1966).

10 See for example the character Blonde's part in a duet from Act Two of Mozart's *Abduction from the Seraglio*. As Blonde's master attempts to extort sexual favors from her, she sings "A heart born in freedom / Never allows itself to be treated slavishly; / It remains, even when freedom is lost, / inwardly proud, and laughs at the world." The liberatory and egalitarian import of the lyrics is underscored by the fact that it is a serving woman who sings them. Moreover, the score pitches her part in the register usually reserved for the "leading lady" in operatic productions. The opera offers pointed political criticism of the oppressive conditions obtaining in the Austrian Empire of the day. See Ronnie Apter, "Introduction," *Entführung aus dem Serail (Abduction from the Seraglio)*, trans. Mark Herman and Ronnie Apter (n.p.: 1981), ix–xi. See also Montesquieu, *Persian Letters*, trans. C. J. Betts (New York: Penguin Classics, 1973 [French orig., 1721]) and Susanna Rowson, *Slaves in Algiers* (1794; reprint, Acton, Mass.: Copley, 2000).

11 Edward Said has documented the emergence of Orientalism as a major cultural development in Western Europe by the beginning of the nineteenth century. The East

fascinated Romantic thinkers, who rejected the rationalism of the Enlightenment for the esoteric mysteries of the Orient. In the Romantic imagination, as Byron's *Don Juan* makes plain, the Orient represented a place where Western/Christian standards of conduct did not apply. Lastly, Said demonstrates that Napoleon's foray into Egypt in 1797 laid the groundwork for academic Orientalism, which formalized the construction of the Orient as mysterious, foreign, and "Other." In his discussion of the manner in which the Orient has been constructed in the minds of Westerners, Said makes the following observation: "In the system of knowledge about the Orient, the Orient is less a place than a *topos*, a set of references, a congeries of characteristics, that seems to have its origin in a quotation, or a fragment of a text, or a citation from someone's work on the Orient, or some bit of previous imagining, or an amalgam of all these." Edward W. Said, *Orientalism* (New York: Vintage Books, 1979), 177.

12 See Rowson, op. cit., Royall Tyler, *The Algerine Captive* (London, 1797) and Washington Irving, *Salmagundi* (New York: D. Longworth, 1807–1808).

13 For American encounters with the Barbary pirates, see David A. Carson, "Jefferson, Congress, and the Question of the Tripolitan War," *Virginia Magazine of History and Biography* 94:4 (October 1986): 409–24; Peter Earle, *Corsairs of Malta and Barbary* (London: Sidgwick and Jackson, 1970), 261–62; and Gary E. Wilson, "American Hostages in Moslem Nations, 1784–1796: The Public Response," *Journal of the Early Republic* 2 (1982): 123–41. For antislavery uses of this genre, see Lofti Ben Rejeb, "America's Captive Freemen in North Africa: The Comparative Method in Abolitionist Persuasion," *Slavery and Abolition* 9 (May 1988): 57–71; and Benilde Montgomery, "White Captives, African Slaves: A Drama of Abolition," *Eighteenth Century Studies* 27 (1994): 615–30. For an additional discussion of America's literary encounters with the Orient, see Robert J. Allison, *The Crescent Obscured: The United States and the Muslim World, 1776–1815* (New York: Oxford University Press, 1995), 35–85.

14 The accounts of the Barbary captives also added to an already-established genre in American literature, that of the Indian captivity narrative, in which, as June Namias points out, captivity for European women always encompassed at least the potential for sexual violation. See Namias, *White Captives: Gender and Ethnicity on the American Frontier* (Chapel Hill: University of North Carolina Press, 1993), 85–99. For an almost certainly fictional example of this genre, see *The History of the Captivity and Sufferings of Mrs. Maria Martin, who was six years a slave in Algiers: Two of which she was confined in a Dark and Dismal Dungeon, Loaded with Irons, for refusing to comply with the Brutal Request of a Turkish Officer*, which appeared first in 1807 and was reprinted at least eleven times in various editions by 1818. See also Allison, *The Crescent Obscured*, 35–85.

15 See Maria Martin, *History of the Captivity and Sufferings of Mrs. Maria Martin . . . To which is appended A History of Algiers* (Boston: W. Crary, 1807), 64, 65. No British editions of Martin's account have come to light, and this raises some question about its authenticity. Nevertheless, whether fact or fiction, its wide distribution in the United States attests to its "fit" with prevailing cultural assumptions about the behavior of "Algerines" and "Turks" toward white women. These reservations about the authenticity

of Martin's account are shared by Robert J. Allison. See Allison, *The Crescent Obscured*, 79–80.

16 Re: American responses to the Greek Revolt, see Stephen A. Larrabee, *Hellas Observed: The American Experience of Greece, 1775–1865* (New York: New York University Press, 1957). American interest in the Greek struggle for independence is particularly in evidence in Genesee, Allegany, and Onondaga counties in upstate New York (note, for example, the towns and villages of Byron, Corfu, Ionia, Minoa, Mycenae and Navarino), and in Kent and Washtenaw counties in southern Michigan (Ionia, Ypsilanti, Corinth, and Sparta). It is worth pointing out that the towns of the "Greek Corridor" of upstate New York and southern Michigan would be extremely fertile ground for antislavery in the wake of the Greek struggle for independence. See Lawrence S. Kaplan, "The Monroe Doctrine and the Truman Doctrine: the Case of Greece," *Journal of the Early Republic* 13 (1993): 9. Quotation from Halleck, "Marco Bozzaris," *A Library of the World's Best Literature: Ancient and Modern* (New York: The International Society, 1897), 17:6862.

17 Sophia Mazro, *Turkish Barbarity.: An Affecting narrative of the unparalleled sufferings of Mrs. Sophia Mazro, a Greek lady of Missolonghi* . . . (Providence, RI: G. C. Jennings, 1828), 11. (AAS).

18 Samuel G[ridley] Howe, *An Historical Sketch of the Greek Revolution*, (New York: White, Gallagher and White, 1828), 101 and 103.

19 *The Atlantic Souvenir: A Christmas and New Year's Offering 1826* (Philadelphia: Carey & Lea, 1826). Quotations at pages 2 and 34 respectively (AAS).

20 Quotations from *Forget Me Not; A Christmas and New Year's Present*, ed. Frederic Shoberl (Philadelphia: Carey, Lea and Carey, 1828), 109 and 165 respectively (AAS).

21 Quotation from "Achmet and Selima,"*The Beauties of the Muses; or Select and Entertaining Tales, Prose and Verse, From recent works of Merit, by Eminent Authors* (New York: George G. Sickles, [1829]), 79 (AAS).

22 Sereno Edwards Dwight, *The Greek Revolution, an Address delivered in Park St. Church, Boston on Thursday, 1 April [1824] and repeated at the Request of the Greek Committee in the Old South Church* . . . (Boston: Crocker & Brewster, 1824), 10, 16, and 20 (AAS).

23 Gregory T. Bedell, *The Cause of the Greeks, a sermon preached in St. Andrew's Church Philadelphia, January 18, 1824, on the occasion of a collection for the Greek Fund* (Philadelphia, 1824), 29 (AAS).

24 Quoted in [Anonymous], *To the Friends of Humanity* [1827?] (AAS).

25 See John Alden, "A Season in Federal Street: J. B. Williamson and the Boston Theater, 1796–1797," *Proceedings of the American Antiquarian Society* 65 (1955), 9–74.

26 Mordecai M. Noah, *The Grecian Captive, or the Fall of Athens* (New York: E. M. Murden, 1822), Act III, 45 (AAS). Kent G. Gallagher makes reference to a number of other similarly themed plays that were performed during this period, including James Ellison's *The American Captive* (1812), Maria Pinckney's *Young Carolinians, or Americans in Algiers* (1818), and John Howard Payne's *Ali Pasha* (1822). Gallagher, *The Foreigner in Early American Drama: A Study in Attitudes* (The Hague: Mouton, 1966), 154–71.

27 Jonathan Edwards Jr., *The Injustice and Impolicy of the Slave-Trade and of the Slavery of the Africans* (New Haven, 1791), 11.

28 Elizabeth Chandler, "The Ladies Repository," *The Genius of Universal Emancipation*, February 1, 1831, 171.

29 For an acknowledgement of Chandler's role in fostering female antislavery, see Hersh, *The Slavery of Sex*, 7–10, and Jean Fagan Yellin, *Women and Sisters*, 12–14. See Karen Sanchez-Eppler, *Touching Liberty: Abolition, Feminism, and the Politics of the Body* (Berkeley: University of California Press, 1993), 22.

30 [Richard Robert Madden,] "Slave Market in Constantinople," *Genius of Universal Emancipation*, August 1830, vol. 1, 3rd series, no. 5. Extract from Richard Robert Madden, *Travels in Turkey, Egypt, Nubia and Palestine in 1824, 1825, 1826 and 1827* (London: H. Colburn, 1829; Philadelphia: Carey and Lea, 1830).

31 This should not in any way be taken to suggest that enslaved African American women were not subject to widespread sexual abuse, nor that sexual abuse does not constitute a profound assault on a woman's selfhood, but rather that the nature of the problems they faced were both more varied and more complex than an exclusive focus on sexual exploitation would suggest. For a perceptive rendering of an actual African American woman's experience in this regard, see Melton A. McLaurin, *Celia: A Slave* (Athens. University of Georgia Press, 1991). McLaurin's work details the experience of a young girl who was raped and repeatedly impregnated by her elderly master until she finally murdered him in Missouri in 1855. Interestingly, Celia's subsequent conviction and execution were reported in *The Liberator* (October 19, 1855), but the report indicated that she had acted without any apparent motive.

32 *Proceedings of the N. H. [sic] Anti-Slavery Convention, held in Concord, on the 11 & 12 November 1834.* (Concord, N.H.: Eastman, Webster, 1834), 9, 13 (AAS).

33 Starksborough and Lincoln Anti-Slavery Society, *Address*, 13 (AAS).

34 Ibid, 15. Quotation is from George Bourne, *Picture of Slavery in the United States of America* (Middletown, Conn.: Edwin Hunt, 1834), 92 (AAS).

35 *An Address delivered before the Concord [NH] Female Antislavery Society, at its annual meeting, 25 Dec. 1837* by Nathaniel P. Rogers, (Concord, N.H.: William White, printer, 1838), 7 (AAS).

36 *An Appeal to the Women of the Nominally Free States, Issued by an Anti-Slavery Convention of American Women* (New York: William S. Dorr, 1837), 13, 14 (AAS).

37 Jeffrey, *Great Silent Army of Abolitionism*, 85.

PAULA KANE

The Supernatural and Slavery
Catholics, Power, and Oppression

Early nineteenth-century America was a deeply religious society, but historians still know surprisingly little about the links between religious belief and attitudes toward slavery. In this pioneering essay, the religious historian Paula Kane explores antebellum Catholic attitudes toward slavery and antislavery. Although Pope Gregory XVI denounced the slave trade in 1839 and criticized Christians who treated Negroes as "mere animals," Kane concludes that American Catholics tended to support slavery as long as slaves were afforded access to religious instruction and the sacraments.

Catholics resisted abolition partly because antebellum reform was spearheaded by an aggressively anti-Catholic Protestant moral elite. In addition, many working-class Irish Catholics feared competition from African American workers and associated antislavery with hated British colonizers. An underappreciated contributor to Catholic resistance to abolition lay in the mid-nineteenth century Church's heightened emphasis on the supernatural, which contributed to an antimodern, antiliberal outlook hostile toward liberal individualism and utilized miracle stories to support the status quo, including the institution of slavery.

Theodore Parker expressed a sentiment shared by many antebellum Americans in remarking that "the Catholic clergy are on the side of slavery . . . They love slavery itself; it is an institution thoroughly congenial to them . . ."[1] The opinions of anti-Catholics on the one hand and of prominent Catholic clergy and laymen on the other are well-known, but Catholics have typically been represented in slavery's history only by official papal documents about the slave trade.[2] If there is a "gap" in American antislavery studies, it is the lack of comprehensive treatment of the position of American Catholics on slavery.

Little has been done to characterize the sentiments of ordinary American Catholics about the "peculiar institution" and their participation in it.[3]

If papal opinion is considered the paramount source of Catholic opinion, then American Catholics were disloyal. They remained participants in slavery even though Gregory XVI had condemned the slave trade in an apostolic letter of 1839 titled "*In supremo apostolatus fastigio*."[4] In that document the pope rebuked any Christians who treated Negroes "as if they were not men, but mere animals, howsoever reduced to slavery."[5] He did not define slavery as intrinsically evil or opposed to natural law, however, nor did his words have an immediate impact on American practices. In fact, the U.S. *Catholic Miscellany* published an unsigned editorial that defended the position of American bishops John Ireland and Francis Kenrick in support of the status quo on the grounds that the pope was not referring to American-style "domestic" slavery: "We apprehend there is a vast difference between the Slave-Trade and Domestic slavery. At least our own laws make the distinction—punishing the one and sanctioning the other. It is absurd then to conclude, that because the Apostolical Letter condemns the piratical Slave-Trade, it is also aimed against Domestic Servitude."[6]

Differences with the Vatican were one issue facing the Catholic community, as were tensions with Protestants, who implicated Catholics in the slave question and its regional dynamics as early as the 1830s: northern Protestants feared an alliance between Roman Catholics and southern interests represented by the "slave power." In that decade American Catholic leaders had already taken pains to reassure non-Catholics that their theology would never "be tinctured with the fanaticism of abolition."[7] This policy remained so consistent that "not one prominent American Catholic urged immediate abolition before the Civil War."[8] By claiming to expose the affinities between Romanism and bondage, Protestant abolitionists and moral reformers used inflammatory rhetoric to warn citizens that the United States was about to become a victim of popish conspiracies whose goal was the destruction of the Protestant moral elite and the expansion of slavery. Where many Americans saw only the degeneracy of Romanism and understood its affinity to slavery as a "parallel despotic system,"[9] American abolitionists and antislavery groups went further and took steps to isolate themselves from the slave system as the premier evil of the nineteenth century. The most radical among them, the Garrisonians, renounced the federal Constitution, indicted organized religion, and even attacked the portions of the Bible that did not agree with their principles, in their sweeping condemnation of slavery as sin that was social as well as personal. In the radical abolitionist crusade to shun all American institutions with any connection to slavery, individual conscience became the supreme source for judging good and evil.

Despite Protestant anxieties, the number of Catholic slaveholders was not extensive since few Catholics were members of the master planter class. Moreover, outside of Maryland and parts of Kentucky, Louisiana, and Missouri, the Catholic population of the antebellum South was itself negligible.[10] Recent historical accounts have focused more upon the Irish Catholics of New York City who supported slaveholding interests through an alliance between the Democratic machine at Tammany Hall and the proslavery Catholic establishment represented by Archbishop John Hughes, but much work remains to be done to establish the percentages of Catholic small-scale farmers and slaveholders and thus to illuminate the spectrum of Catholic agrarianism prior to the Civil War.[11] Throughout Europe the Church's history and loyal constituency was linked to rural areas and peasant identity. Given the lack of a peasantry in the United States, the closest thing to the idea of a Christendom rooted in the soil was the southern plantation economy. Yet Catholics never became a significant presence in the southern states. Although there was a sixfold increase in the southern Catholic population between 1870 and 1970, by 1970 still only 4 percent of southerners were Catholic.[12] Nationwide, in 1860 Catholics comprised only about 14 percent of the population.[13]

Catholics did own slaves, however, and in several celebrated instances, such as the 1838 decision of the Maryland Jesuits, sold their slaves to affirm their moral convictions.[14] Since the Jesuit's sale took place a year before the pope issued "In supremo," the action was not in response to Vatican pressure. This was not a pure moral victory, however, since although the Maryland Jesuit provincial stated that his goal was to prevent the breakup of slave families, another consideration in the sale was to avoid Protestant buyers who would fail to educate slaves in the Catholic faith.[15] In some aspects of religious practice such as worship services, Catholics had proved to be more racially integrated than Protestants who had evolved the custom of segregated congregations. Of the African American Catholic communities that emerged in New Orleans, Mobile, Savannah, St. Louis, Baltimore, and Washington, D.C., some did establish separate black parishes.[16] Two black Catholic sisterhoods were also founded in the antebellum era. The apparent harmony between black and white Catholics, however, eroded in the era of Jim Crow when most bishops sanctioned segregation, denying blacks access to Catholic schools, hospitals, and orphanages.[17]

By the terms of the Church's official position, antebellum Catholics were committed to the impossible principle of defending the sanctity of private property, including slaves, and profits derived therefrom, and yet at the same time, of protecting each human soul. Hence, Catholics could tolerate slavery without promoting it, as long as they insisted that masters recognize slave marriages and provide their slaves with catechesis and access to the sacraments. In short, as of 1839 the Vatican had condemned the sale of human beings but not their status as property once purchased, as long as the spiritual needs of the enslaved were met. In this regard, Catholics mirrored the ambivalent legal status of slaves in the antebellum South, a status that vacillated between property and personhood.[18] Catholics also shared, but for different theological and historical reasons, the aversion of southern planters to industrial capitalism, thus preparing them to similarly favor the ideology of plantation life.

The Catholic recourse to devotions and supernatural power fortified an antimodern outlook that accepted slavery (especially within an agrarian context) as part of the naturalness of social hierarchy. Further, in the nineteenth century an increasing emphasis by Catholics upon supernaturalism in the form of events like Marian visions and stigmata, and renewed attention to devotional practices, especially those invoking the passion, blood, and heart of Jesus Christ, subtly articulated the Church's antimodern agenda and perhaps represented an unconscious evasion of the material reality of slavery by white Catholics. Devotions forged a privatized piety, dependent upon bonds between humans and the saints sustained by prayer and the performance of certain rituals. The very privacy of such acts also served to avoid offending or alarming Protestants, whose curiosity about Catholicism, nevertheless, reached new peaks in the mid-1800s.

A regard for intense expressions of piety was not limited to antebellum Catholics, however. At the same time that devotions were on the rise among Catholics, Protestants and abolitionists developed a strong martyrological tradition, especially in the decades 1830–60. Jesus became their concentrated substitute for the Catholic cult of saints. The figure of the crucified Christ, not surprisingly, became central to abolitionists' identification with suffering and produced a cult of abolition martyrs. The branded hand of Jonathan Walker, a white man who helped slaves escape in the 1840s, became the most celebrated visual image of white martyrdom on behalf of Africans.[19] The Passion of Christ was even evoked to describe the nation itself: in his speech to the U.S. Senate about the provisions of the Compromise of 1850, Senator Henry Clay compared the savior's "five wounds" to the suffering of the American body politic. President Zachary Taylor's failure, according to Clay, was to treat but one wound and "leave the other four to bleed more profusely than ever," by the sole admission of California (as a free state).[20]

The history of popular religious practices can help explain why even though no Catholic would describe slavery as a positive good, few worked to overthrow the "dreadful institution." A combination of sociological and theological factors contributed to Catholic acceptance of slavery, among which I shall consider five aspects. First, the socioreligious position of Catholics as a minority in the United States, and especially in the South, made them unlikely defenders of the slave. In antebellum America, Catholics were a diverse community made up of immigrant groups with separate cultural and linguistic ties to Europe and to a medieval religious tradition that was despised and rejected by Protestants, at least until the late nineteenth century when a series of Gothic Revivals transcended denominational boundaries.

Second, Catholic behavior on the slavery issue as well as every other social and moral question was guided by the Catholic Church's opposition to liberal individualism, which it associated with Protestants and atheists. Catholic antiliberalism hindered Catholic identification with an emerging liberal platform in the United States as well, whose planks included emancipation of slaves and laissez-faire capitalism. The leading role of the Irish-Catholic working class of New York City in the Draft Riots of 1863 revealed the potential violence underlying their fear of losing economic advantages and "white-skin privileges" to emancipated blacks.[21] To prevent such violent outbursts, Catholics of elite and working-class status were encouraged to reject revolutionary means of social change as they had done in Europe following the 1830 and 1848 revolutions, and were led to picture the Church as "patient, long-suffering, gentle," "when she has not the legislative power in her hands."[22] After slave emancipation, however, American Catholic leaders showed themselves capable of a quick reversal as they immediately endorsed racial equality in print, even if not always in practice.

A third consideration that inhibited Catholic abolitionist sentiment in the United States was partisan politics. After 1854, many Catholics associated antislavery politics with the anti-Catholic Republican Party; they therefore opted instead for the Democratic Party, which mingled its pro-immigrant sentiments with proslavery.

Divisions among Catholics provided a fourth deterrent to their ability to respond as a united bloc on the slavery debate, or, indeed, most any other antebellum political issue. Despite Protestant fantasies of a Roman monolith, American Catholics were neither centralized nor united. Universal papal authority would not become a force until after Vatican I (1870); nor did the American bishops, mostly southern, draft policy statements for the nation's Catholics before the Third Plenary Council of Baltimore in 1884. Modern histories of the Draft Riots give the impression that Archbishop Hughes of New York wielded influence equal to that of Archbishop Gibbons of Baltimore during the Gilded Age, but the former's authority was much less extensive. Further, a priest shortage left many geographic regions of the nation without adequate clergy, which meant that many Catholics did not have regular habits of attending Mass and receiving the sacraments. Devotional practices seemingly filled the gap. Contests between clergy and laity, between bishops and clergy, and between men and women, as well as differences between sectional and ethnic groups, separated white Catholics from each other, quite apart from distinctions of race. In Louisiana, for instance, some Creole Catholics joined the Know-Nothing movement to protest the Irish who were moving into their region and imposing "foreign" religious norms.[23]

A fifth area where new Catholic immigrants and their predecessors could form common bonds was around the power conferred by whiteness.[24] Before the arrival of large numbers of Irish and German immigrants in the 1840s, Catholics "were even more confined to the South than slavery was."[25] But as Catholic immigrants became concentrated in the urban North, their identification with whiteness became an important social phenomenon. Irish Catholics learned in America, as Theodore Allen, Noel Ignatiev, David Roediger, and Alexander Saxton have demonstrated convincingly, that investing in anti-black racism confirmed their social status as "white" and guaranteed certain economic and employment advantages.[26] But, as Allen has concluded, "Irish-Americans were not the originators of white supremacy; they adapted to and were adopted into an already 'white' American social order."[27]

As the largest segment of American Catholics, Irish immigrants freely displayed racist prejudices. Archbishop Hughes played a major role in steering the New York Irish away from abolitionism, despite the racial egalitarian sentiments he had once expressed in a poem titled "The Slave."[28] The inchoate racism of the Irish coalesced at mid-century, when Irish immigrants refused the appeal of the Irish patriot Daniel O'Connell to defend Ireland by uniting with the abolitionists in recollection of their long struggle against British domination.[29] Irish Americans chose other strategies instead: to oppose antislavery as a demonstration of their American patriotism, hence rejecting O'Connell's views as unwanted "foreign" influences, or to profess their Catholic faith by rejecting a Protestant cause.[30] In the following decade the conflict took to the streets when Irish-American workingmen and poor rioted in New York City to oppose their conscription into the Union army "to save Negroes."[31] In addition to the racism and economic anxieties of Catholics, the Church's assumptions about the fixed nature of social, gender, and racial hierarchy, combined with the static character of Catholic theology, made it difficult for Catholics to imagine a nation based upon racial equality or upon an evolutionary notion of morality that admitted the error of previous positions.

In the most recent consideration of Catholics and the slavery debate, John McGreevy surveys Catholic opinion as expressed by several Catholic elites: the lay convert Orestes Brownson, and three bishops: Hughes of New York, Kenrick of Philadelphia, and Martin Spalding of Louisville. Each of the bishops published speeches or tracts that defended slavery, indicating that sectional loyalty was not a determining factor. The Vermonter Brownson's opinions on slavery, as on most issues, seem to reflect his fears of too much democracy—and not enough. Brownson vacillated maddeningly through the years between the poles of ultramontanism and liberalism, but he eventually did endorse antislavery, particularly to protest the "appalling" Dred Scott decision of 1857, which was written by a distinguished Maryland Catholic, Chief Justice Roger Taney, a former slaveholder.[32] Five months after Dred Scott was handed down, Taney disclosed his rationale for the decision in a private response to a letter and pamphlet sent him by a northern minister: "Every intelligent person whose life has been passed in a slave holding State," he wrote, "... will see that a general and sudden emancipation would be absolute ruin to the negroes, as well as to the white population," for slaves "are for the most part weak, credulous, and easily misled by stronger minds."[33] No lay Catholic version of Garrison's "come-outerism" could be expected to emerge from Taney's paternalism, and Brownson's outspoken criticism of Dred Scott gained little support in America. Except for Claude Maistre, the lone abolitionist priest in New Orleans, few public outcries against slavery came from priests either.[34]

Why were lay American Catholics detached from movements opposing slavery? As noted above, advocates of bottom-up histories of slavery, labor, and race have suggested that Catholic immigrants, predominantly Irish and German, were striving to join a system of white privilege that was already in place. From a top-down perspective, religious historians describe Catholic strategy between the 1830s and 1850s in an alternative way, as one of self-preservation, whereby bishops as a group "concentrated on private behavior rather than social ethics." Because American bishops rigidly separated private and publics spheres, any public criticism of slavery by them became "unthinkable."[35] No guidance could be expected from the Vatican, either, since Propaganda Fide, the administrative unit responsible for such matters, acted almost entirely as a reactive body, responding only to complaints that it received rather than formulating policy.[36]

The private character of most Catholic piety also discouraged antislavery activism; and it can be most clearly seen in the practice of devotions. Devotions implied a Christian worldview that "presupposed the existence of social relationships between faithful Catholics and supernatural beings, and provided a means of interacting with them."[37] Since the French Revolution, the Catholic Church had relied upon the populist appeal of the saints, miracles, processions, and pilgrimages to maintain its appeal among the working classes and to preserve its institutional authority against the growing tide of criticism of "throne and altar" politics.[38] European Catholics deployed devotionalism as proof of the existence of supernatural power against forms of political and intellectual liberalism and radicalism that were challenging the authority of the Catholic Church. In this sense, supernaturalism was serving an antimodern ideology. Throughout most of the nineteenth century, American Catholics often found devotions, practiced at home, more satisfying and available than the sacraments. As a result, they emphasized the relevance of signs and wonders for the current age. They tended to believe in miracles as rebukes against sin and proofs of God's intervention in the world. Miracles and their testimonies not only challenged the Common Sense philosophic tradition associated with Protestantism (and antislavery); they refreshed the faith of Catholics and led to new conversions. The notion of a "household of faith" conjoining the living and the dead was comforting to Catholics. It converged with the family-centered norms that governed contemporary Protestant piety; and it conveniently separated domestic and political spheres.

Each factor in Catholics' disengagement from the politics of slavery enlarges our understanding of their position: Catholics dreaded being labeled as fanatics, they feared anti-Catholicism, and they were affected (adversely) by the reactive nature of the Vatican bureaucracy. An additional factor—consideration of what Catholics actually did when they practiced their faith by an emphasis upon miracles, saints, and devotional bonds—projects an image of the Catholic community as apolitical and conformist in public life while deeply countercultural in private. The relationship of Catholics to slavery demonstrates how religious ideas interact with and are affected by material forces. In this case, the violence of human bondage contrasted starkly and horribly with the Christian belief in the human being as an *imago Dei*. The supernaturalism that would saturate popular Catholicism after the mid-1800s would continue to captivate the faithful: miracles (and their antithesis, demonic forces) enabled Catholics to lay claim to an autonomous, impenetrable realm of experience that endured despite (and against) the forces of rationalization, mechanization, and depersonalization—a realm that augured a religious solution to the ailments of modernity and tended to justify preservation of the status quo, even slavery. Catholics looked to the devotional world and to the supernatural realm to answer their fears about overcoming the bondage of original sin and to await the ultimate victory of God over Satan, yet, at the same time, they seemed blind to the sinful bondage of Africans in their midst.

NOTES

1 John T. McGreevy, *Catholicism and American Freedom: A History* (New York: Norton, 2002), 63.
2 See Joel S. Panzer, *The Popes and Slavery* (New York: Alba House, 1996).
3 The most recent work to explore the topic is McGreevy, *Catholicism and American Freedom*, chap. 2. Among the few books devoted to the subject is the documentary anthology by Kenneth J. Zanca, *American Catholics and Slavery: 1789–1866* (Lanham, Md.: University Press of America, 1994). Useful for its archival documentation and its conclusions is the essay by R. Emmett Curran, "Rome, The American Church, and Slavery," in *Building the Church in America*, ed. Joe Linck and Ray Kupke (Washington, D.C.: Catholic University Press, 1999). An early account is Madeleine Hook Rice, *American Catholic Opinion in the Slavery Controversy* (New York: Columbia University Press, 1944). Regional and state studies include Randall Miller and John Wakelyn, eds., *Catholics in the Old South* (Macon, GA: Mercer University Press, 1983; Stafford Poole and Douglas J. Slawson, *Church and Slave in Perry County, Missouri, 1818–1865* (Lewiston, N.Y.: E. Mellen Press, 1986); and Roger Baudier, *The Catholic Church in Louisiana* (New Orleans: printed by H. W. Hyatt, 1939).

A separate, growing bibliography exists on black Catholics, including Cyprian Davis and Jamie Phelps, eds. *'Stamped with the Image of God': African Americans as God's Image in Black* (Maryknoll, N.Y.: Orbis, 2003); William Kelly, ed., *Black Catholic Theology: A Sourcebook* (New York: McGraw-Hill, 2000); Cyprian Davis, *Black Catholics in the United States* (New York: Crossroad, 1990); Stephen J. Ochs, *Desegregating the Altar: The Josephites and the Struggle for Black Catholic Priests, 1871–1960* (Baton Rouge: Louisiana State University Press, 1993); William A. Osborne, *The Segregated Covenant: Race Relations and American Catholics* (New York: Harper & Row, 1967.)
4 Nicholas Atkin and Frank Tallett, *Priests, Prelates, People: A History of European Catholicism since 1750* (New York: Oxford University Press, 2003), 192–93.
5 Quoted in Chester Gillis, *Roman Catholicism in America* (New York: Columbia University Press, 1999), 59.
6 "Unsigned Editorial, 'The Catholic Church, Domestic Slavery, and the Slave Trade,' *United States Catholic Miscellany*, December 9, 1843," in Steven M. Avella and Elizabeth McKeown, eds., *Public Voices: Catholics in the American Context* (Maryknoll, N.Y.: Orbis, 1999), 39.

7 Ibid., 39.
8 McGreevy, *Catholicism and American Freedom*, 51.
9 Ibid., 57.
10 After slave emancipation in 1863, a priest wrote to the *Catholic Telegraph* (Cincinnati) to suggest that slavery explained the demographic scarcity of southern Catholics: "When the slave power predominates, religion is nominal." "It appears to us, therefore, that slavery is not friendly to the propagation of the Catholic Faith—or to its charity and fervor when it happens to be professed." Rev. Edward Purcell, "The Church and Slavery," April 8, 1864, in Avella and McKeown, eds., *Public Voices*, 44.
11 On the Irish Catholic dimension, see Theodore W. Allen, *Invention of the White Race*, vol. 1, *Racial Oppression and Social Control* (New York: Verso, 1994), 186.
12 Randall M. Miller, "Roman Catholic Church (in the South)," *Encyclopedia of Religion in the South*, ed. Samuel S. Hill (Macon, Ga.: Mercer University Press, 1984), 653. Miller notes further that in the twentieth century the largest increase in Catholic membership was due to converts who married Catholics.
13 Kenneth J. Zanca, "Slavery and American Catholics," *Encyclopedia of American Catholic History* (hereafter EACH), Michael Glazier and Thomas J. Shelley, eds. (Collegeville, Minn.: Liturgical Press, 1997), 1320.
14 In 1838 the Jesuit provincial of the Maryland province sold more than 270 slaves to two Louisiana planters, 49 of them to Senator Henry Johnson. Curran, "Rome, the American Church, and Slavery," 39; Zanca, "Slavery and American Catholics," EACH, 1323. The Jesuits reasoned that it would be a poor example for them to be slaveowners, and that they should select a buyer who would be able to attend to the slaves' religious needs. The profits from the sale were to generate only "Capital which fructifies." "Bill of Sale for Negroes of the Maryland Mission, 1835," in Avella and McKeown, *Public Voices*, 38. See also Thomas Murphy, *Jesuit Slaveholding in Maryland, 1717–1838* (New York: Routledge, 2001).
15 McGreevy, *Catholicism and American Freedom*, 50. Curran depicts a more complicated scenario, in which Jesuits who opposed the sale warned slaves to protect their families by hiding from the sheriff to avoid the likelihood of being separated: "Rome, the American Church, and Slavery," 39.
16 Gillis, *Roman Catholicism in America*, 59.
17 Miller, "Roman Catholic Church (in the South)," 655. Miller ascribes the "southernness" of Catholics in that region to the Church's emphasis upon "personal salvation through the sacraments rather than ethical responsibility." 657.
18 See Amy Dru Stanley, *From Bondage to Contract: Wage Labor, Marriage, and the Market in the Age of Emancipation* (Cambridge: Cambridge University Press, 1998).
19 Marcus Wood, *Blind Memory: Visual representations of Slavery in England and America 1780–1865* (New York: Routledge, 2000), 248–49.
20 I thank Iver Bernstein for the Henry Clay citation.
21 Iver Bernstein, *The New York City Draft Riots: Their Significance for American Society and*

Politics in the Age of the Civil War (New York: Oxford University Press, 1990), 113; Allen, Invention of the White Race, 192.
22 Purcell, "The Church and Slavery," in Avella and McKeown, Public Voices, 44.
23 Miller, "Roman Catholic Church (in the South)," 652.
24 The study of "whiteness" has been a recent successful growth field in history. Several founding texts governing my interpretation include David Roediger, The Wages of Whiteness: Race and the Making of the American Working Class (London: Verso, 1991); Allen, Invention of the White Race, and Alexander Saxton, The Rise and Fall of the White Republic (London: Verso, 1990).
25 Curran, "Rome, the American Church, and Slavery," 32.
26 Noel Ignatiev, How the Irish Became White (New York: Routledge, 1995); Roediger, Wages of Whiteness, and Saxton, Rise and Fall of the White Republic. German immigrants were more diverse in their outlooks and allegiances than were the Irish.
27 The text of O'Connell's address of 1842 is reprinted from The Liberator in appendix L of Allen, Invention of the White Race, 229–30. Allen's account of the creation of a coalition in the Democratic Party between Irish immigrants and southern slaveholders and their Tammany Hall supporters is the most helpful explanation of why the Irish, oppressed by Protestants in Ireland, rejected abolitionism in America and stood with the Protestant slaveholders: see p. 199
28 The poem is reprinted in Allen, Invention of the White Race, 226–28.
29 On Daniel O'Connell's attacks on American slaveholders, see Allen, Invention of the White Race, 170–99.
30 Ibid., 82.
31 On the July, 1863, riots, see Iver Bernstein, New York City Draft Riots.
32 "Roger Brooke Taney," EACH, 1364–66.
33 "Roger Brooke Taney, Chief Justice, U.S. Supreme Court, to Rev. Samuel Nott of Wareham, Massachusetts, 19 August 1857," quoted in Avella and McKeown, Public Voices, 41–43.
34 Stephen J. Ochs, A Black Patriot and a White Priest: André Cailloux and Claude Paschal Maistre in Civil War New Orleans (Baton Rouge: Louisiana State University Press, 1990.)
35 Curran, "Rome, the American Church, and Slavery," 40; 47.
36 Ibid., 41
37 Ann Taves, The Household of Faith: Roman Catholic Devotions in Mid-Nineteenth Century America (Notre Dame, Ind.: University of Notre Dame Press, 1986), 47.
38 Hugh McLeod, Religion and the People of Western Europe, 2nd ed. (Oxford: Oxford University Press, 1997), 62.

CATHERINE CLINTON

Souls of Darkness
Dominance and
Submission in the
Narratives of
Frederick Douglass
and Harriet Jacobs

Slavery in the antebellum South differed in a number of significant respects from slavery elsewhere in the Americas. One important difference was demographic: Compared to plantations in the West Indies or Brazil, those in the South had far fewer slaves. Another key difference was relational: absentee ownership was much less common, and interactions between slaves and masters were more intimate and personal. A third major difference was psychological. It appears that a significant number of southern masters sought to convince enslaved African Americans of the legitimacy of slavery and to encourage a sense of psychological dependence and even gratitude. Thus, one of the gravest challenges for many of the enslaved was to sustain a core of self-respect.

In this essay, the noted southern historian Catherine Clinton explores how two prominent slaves, one male and one female, succeeded in overcoming the pressure to submit to a slaveowner's authority and managed to preserve a sense of personal independence. For Frederick Douglass, learning to read and write was as important as physical self-assertion in resisting the damage that slavery might inflict on his manhood. For Harriet Jacobs, a young woman's vulnerability to sexual exploitation was among slavery's worst evils. She managed to repel her master's sexual advances, but at the cost of bearing another white man's child. She found it much less degrading to give herself voluntarily than to be forced to submit to her owner. Even if her options were narrowly circumscribed, she succeeded in preserving a sense of agency and integrity.

For the past several decades, scholars of American slavery have explored a myriad of evils associated with human bondage, from the banal to the brutal, from the subtle to the sensational. Even more recently, American historians have begun to highlight the posttraumatic aspects of the system suffered by African Americans trapped within bondage, and some have launched a battle cry for reparations.[1] Whatever the outcome of these escalating arguments, debates about the evils of slavery will be on the agenda for American historians for decades to come.

The study of evil presents a booming enterprise, in part owing to the flourishing of holocaust studies. Samantha Powers's *"A Problem from Hell:" America and the Age of Genocide* won several prizes in 2002. Anne Applebaum's magisterial *Gulag* widened and deepened our understanding of forced labor and extermination within the Soviet Union, while Peter Balakian's *The Burning Tigris* trained its sights on genocide in Armenia and Turkey, and Daniel Bergner's *In the Land of Magic Soldiers* highlighted ongoing brutalities in Sierre Leone—to name but three of the most compelling contributions to this literature in 2003. Studies of the Khmer Rouge in Cambodia, tribal wars in Rwanda, as well as chronicles of Bosnian atrocities continue to fill bookshelves, side-by-side with the steady stream of works on Nazi Germany.

Within all these gripping volumes—memoirs, policy studies, historical analyses—writers probe the nature of evil. In two of the most powerful personal narratives of slave experience published in nineteenth-century America, those of Frederick Douglass and Harriet Jacobs, this question of evil is given extraordinary interrogation. The power of the individual is on prominent display in these compelling memoirs of survival.

Unlike the majority of the over one hundred published narratives of the period, both Douglass and Jacobs concentrate on questions of "will." Both are preoccupied with issues of "submission" as well—Douglass focusing on this bone of contention for asserting manhood, and Jacobs refining this issue as it relates to womanhood. Even free women struggled over issues of subjugation within antebellum culture, and Jacobs powerfully contextualizes her choices. Both narrators explore the problem of exerting free will, of asserting humanity while boxed into a rigid grid of dominance and submission.

Breaking the will of the subjugated is a key preoccupation of mastery within the Old South. As Kenneth Greenberg illuminated in *Honor and Slavery*, masters went to extraordinary lengths to maintain dominance. In one incident, a slave is accused of wrongdoing and taken to the woods, stripped and tied to a tree, then severely beaten. This is an exercise in mastery, as the master "would require the poor slave to confess the truth, and then deny it, and then back again, and so on, beating him from truth to lie, and from a lie to the truth, over and over again."[2] The goal of the master was to destroy his human property's ties with natural law and common sense, and to replace them with the slaveholder's will—the only reality in the slaveholder's universe.

Douglass carefully outlined the initiation of this process in his 1845 narrative, highlighting the damage done to those born enslaved: "Frequently, before the child has reached its twelfth month, its mother is taken from it, and hired out on some farm a considerable distance off, and the child is placed under the care of an old woman, too old for field labor. For what this separation is done, I do not know, unless it be to hinder the development of the child's affection toward its mother, and to blunt and destroy the natural affection of the mother for the child."[3] Thus Douglass demonstrated that the first stroke of cruelty within slavery was to attempt to eradicate natural bonds between parent and child.

This practice was echoed within Jacobs's narrative. She complained about the death of her father and her inability to attend his funeral or even to mourn: "the dead body of my father was lying within a mile of me. What cared my owners for that? He was merely a piece of property. Moreover, they thought he had spoiled his children by teaching them to feel they were human beings. This was blasphemous doctrine for a slave to teach, presumptuous in him, and dangerous to the masters."[4] From a young age, enslaved children were exposed to slavery's brutalities, brutalities that scarred and shaped the souls of all black folks in antebellum America.

Denied by his father, robbed of his only remaining parent by his mother's death, from a very young age Douglass was left unprotected.[5] He described the whipping of his Aunt Hester: "I was so terrified and horror-stricken at the sight, that I hid myself and a closet and dared not venture out till long after the bloody transaction was over. I expected it would be my turn next. I had never seen anything like it before."[6] As Douglass grew older, worse scenes would follow. The murder of a fellow slave, Denby, struck terror. This hapless victim was given two warning shots, and then a third took his life: "His mangled body sank out of sight, and blood and brains marked the water where he had stood. A thrill of horror flashed through every soul upon the plantation, excepting Mr. Gore [the assassin]."[7]

Facing this nightmare of infinite savagery, many turned to religion—praying for a better life in the next world. Douglass believed slave spirituals projected a hopeless quality, as much as any sense of redemption: "If anyone wishes to be impressed with the soul-killing effects of slavery, let him go tot Colonel Lloyd's plantation, and, on allowance day, place himself in the deep pine woods, and there let him, in silence, analyze the sounds that shall pass through the chambers of his soul."[8] The roots of Douglass's resistance ran deep. He claimed that "from my earliest recollection, I date the entertainment of a deep conviction that slavery would not always be able to hold me within its foul embrace."[9] This framed his discussion of leaving the plantation for Baltimore, which "opened the gateway to all my subsequent prosperity. I have ever regarded it as the first plain manifestation of that kind providence which has ever since attended me and marked my life with so many favors." Further, Douglass believed this was destiny at work, and "I should be false to the earliest sentiments of my soul, if I suppressed the opinion. I prefer to be true to myself, even at the hazard of incurring the ridicule of others."[10]

When his owner, Mr. Auld, forbade his wife to teach Douglass to read, this became Douglass's obsession: "What he [Auld] most dreaded, that I most desired. What he most loved, that I most hated. That which to him was a great evil, to be carefully shunned, was to me a great good, to be diligently sought; and the argument which he so warmly urged, against my learning to read, only served to inspire me with a desire and determination to learn. In learning to read, I owe almost as much to the bitterest opposition of my master, as to the kindly aid of my mistress."[11]

Thus Douglass highlighted the enslaved individual's only path to fulfilling human potential: resistance. Once awakened to slavery's true nature, the enslaved person must battle subjugation at any cost. Douglass proclaimed: "I have only one life to lose. I had as well be killed running as die standing."[12] His consciousness became fully formed by his opposition to slavery.

The majority of enslaved African Americans did not seize freedom by taking to the road as fugitives. Many determined to fight the slave power to try to save their own souls. In Douglass's case, this was a veritable battle royal, a struggle that propelled him toward personal liberation. Douglass was handed over to a "slavebreaker" named Covey. Covey was sent recalcitrant young slaves—free of charge for up to a year—so that he would return them to owners submissive and pliant.[13]

Douglass's first experience as a field hand in 1833 was a low point in his life: "I was made to drink the bitterest dregs of slavery, that time was during the first six months of my stay with Mr. Covey . . . my natural elasticity was crushed . . . the dark night of slavery closed in upon me; and behold a man transformed into a brute!"[14] Yet, again, Douglass's inborn insubordination saved him. Douglass's bloody encounter with Covey signified a permanent transition, one that Kenneth Greenberg has suggested was a duel.[15] The two fought in hand-to-hand combat for nearly two hours, and Douglass himself confessed that "this battle with Mr. Covey was the turning point in my career as a slave. It rekindled the few expiring embers of freedom, and revived within me a sense of my own manhood. It recalled the departed self-confidence, and inspired me again with a determination to be free."[16]

Although it did not signal his material freedom, it symbolized his spiritual release. Douglass revealed that "I now resolved that, however long I might remain a slave in form, the day had passed forever when I could be a slave in fact."[17] It was many more years before Douglass would assume the status of free black in the North. He declared with satisfaction: "I was now my own master. It was a happy moment, the rapture of which can be understood only by those who have been slaves."[18] However, this sense of "being his own master" underscores subtle differences between Douglass's sense of freedom and Harriet Jacobs's struggles for autonomy.

Jacobs, as noted, testified to slavery's horrors and provided compelling personal details. The particular evil explored in her memoir was alluded to in Douglass's narrative: "The slaveholder, in cases not a few, sustains to his slaves the double relation of master and father."[19] The sexual exploitation of slaves was not restricted to female slaves, but it was most commonly manifested by slaveholding males forcing enslaved women to submit to their sexual demands. Jacobs wrote openly about her predatory owner, and with great pathos: "I now entered my fifteenth year—a sad epoch in the life of a slave girl. My master began to whisper foul words in my ear . . ."[20] Her master reported that she was "his property" and should be " subject to his will in all things." She reported that her " soul revolted against the mean tyranny. But where could I turn for protection?"[21] She knew her mistress would only feel jealousy and rage, unable to empathize with what this poor young slave girl was suffering. Further, her master "met me at every turn, reminding me that I belonged to him, and swearing by heaven that he would compel me to submit to him."[22]

Jacobs reported that her master was the father of eleven slave children, but his paternity was only alluded to in whispers among the enslaved community."[23] She suggested that "even the little child, who is accustomed to wait on her mistress and her children, will learn, before she is twelve years old, why it is that her mistress hates such and such a one among the slaves."[24] Jacobs wanted to tell her grandmother about her master's designs on her, but her owner threatened to kill her if she did. At the same time, he tried to keep peace on the homefront, proclaiming his innocence to appease his wife. In the glare of the neighborhood, he intended to "conceal his crimes," because "some outward show of decency" was necessary.[25]

Behind this thinly veiled masquerade, her master continued his relentless, brutish pursuit. When Jacobs refused to be alone with him, he held a razor to her throat to convince her to change her mind.[26] He pleaded with her in vain:

"Poor foolish girl! You don't know what is for your own good. I would cherish you. I would make a lady of you."[27] Jacobs vowed she would rather be sold than to become his concubine, but evasion was proving more and more challenging.

It is important to remember that Harriet's master clearly had dominance over her and could take her by force. Yet Jacobs was forced to participate in an elaborate cat-and-mouse game, one that illustrates the seamier side of slavery. Her owner insisted that she give herself to him. The more he reached out, the more she withdrew. He maintained his resolve, building her a cabin for assignations—as Jacobs became more and more desperate. A sympathetic young white man in the neighborhood became her confidante and eventually her lover. Jacobs explained that "it seems less degrading to give one's self, than to submit to compulsion."[28] She poignantly acknowledged that women had few choices and slave women even fewer.

When Jacobs announced her impending motherhood, both her black grandmother and her white master reacted in horror. She gave birth to two children by her white suitor. Jacobs's gamble that her master might sell her to her children's father failed. She also gave up her dream that her children might be purchased and emancipated. She escaped from her master, hid in her grandmother's house for several years, then made her way north to freedom—and finally secured her children's freedom.

Although literary and historical scholars continue to debate the details of Jacobs's narrative, there can be no denying that she condemned the sexual dynamics of enslavement with her elaborate and detailed account of its "atmosphere of hell."[29] Her precise and penetrating depictions of these base yet commonplace practices were eye-opening. For the slaveholders of the South, it was deeply troubling to have the lascivious, exploitative side of slavery exposed. For the abolitionists of the North, it was confirmation of the horrors they dared not imagine.

Moving beyond the simple moral divide between good and bad, Jacobs renders an acidic portrait of genuine evil. Jacobs's master is not just interested in the end results of sexual conquest, he contrives to extract submission. His campaign of corruption fails, as Jacobs repels his advances. Her portrayal of slavery's inner workings shows the human spirit defying the dictates of evil. Although she was forced to choose an "immoral" path to avoid concubinage with her master, she understood the empowerment of choice. Thwarting her master's will propelled her along her own pathway to freedom. Like Douglass before her, Jacobs felt her soul " roused to eternal wakefulness."[30] With this awakening, Jacobs could seek enlightenment, and eventual freedom. She might have been boxed into a confined space, trapped within the South while a fugitive from slavery, but her soul was working its way toward the light, unleashed from slavery's twin evils of submission and domination.

The narratives of Douglass and Jacobs revealed not only the fundamental flaws of a system based on duress; they also showcased raw human conflict. The battle of wills between slaveholders and the humans they struggled to enthrall was filled with unspoken as well as overtly expressed horrors. Both Douglass and Jacobs wanted their readers to comprehend the subterranean fissures that slavery might inflict: not just the stripping of the body—but of the self. They demonstrated the way the human spirit navigated the shoals of cruelty and coercion. They plumbed the depths of evil. Despite their long, hard ordeal of slavery, these souls emerged from darkness, and their stories taught their contemporaries and ours the harder truths of slavery's wrongs.

NOTES

1 See, for example, the plenary lecture by Nell Irvin Painter delivered at the Southern Association for Women Historians Conference, Athens, Georgia, June 6, 2003.
2 Kenneth Greenberg, *Honor and Slavery* (Princeton: Princeton University Press, 1996), 41.
3 Frederick Douglass, "Narrative of the Life of Frederick Douglass," in *The Civitas Anthology of African American Slave Narratives*, ed. William L. Andrews and Henry Louis Gates Jr. (Washington, D.C.: Civitas, 1999), 117.
4 Harriet Jacobs, "Incidents in the Life of a Slave Girl, Written by Herself," in Andrews and Gates, eds., *Civitas Anthology*, 474.
5 Douglass, "Narrative," 133.
6 Ibid., 121.
7 Ibid., 130.
8 Ibid., 124–25.
9 Ibid., 135.
10 Ibid., 135.
11 Ibid., 137.
12 Ibid., 155.
13 Ibid., 151–52.
14 Ibid., 154.
15 Greenberg, *Honor and Slavery*, 35–37.
16 Douglass, "Narrative," 160.
17 Ibid.
18 Ibid., 186.
19 Ibid., 118.
20 Jacobs, "Incidents," 489.
21 Ibid., 490.

22 Ibid.
23 Ibid., 496.
24 Ibid., 490.
25 Ibid., 491.
26 Ibid., 493–94.
27 Ibid., 496.
28 Ibid., 514.
29 Ibid., 301.
30 Douglass, "Narrative," 140–41.

Imagining Emancipation

III

JOHN STAUFFER

Introduction

When northern reformers thought about emancipation, they imagined a nation free from sin and people living in perfect freedom. Slavery was "the dark underside of the American Dream, the great exception to our pretensions of perfection," as David Brion Davis recently noted.[1] Such millennial beliefs increased in the 1840s and 1850s, despite the growing belligerence of the southern states, resulting in a surge of optimism among reformers.[2] Although Herman Melville is generally not known for his cheerful optimism, he captured Americans' millennial faith in his 1850 novel, *White-Jacket*. Melville urged Americans to reject the "maxims of the Past" and "prove a teacher to posterity, instead of being the pupil of by-gone generations." America, he stated, was the new Israel:

> Escaped from the house of bondage, Israel of old did not follow after the ways of the Egyptians. To her was given an express dispensation; to her were given new things under the sun. And we Americans are the peculiar, chosen people—the Israel of our time; we bear the mark of the liberties of the world. . . . God has predestinated, mankind expects, great things from our race; and great things we feel in our souls. The rest of the nations must soon be in our rear. We are the pioneers of the world; the advance-guard, sent on through the wilderness of untried things, to break a new path in the New World that is ours. In our youth is our strength; in our inexperience, our wisdom.[3]

The American people would pave the way to a new "dispensation," and the nation itself, rather than an individual messiah, would be the catalyst for this transformation.

Although Melville soon became disillusioned with the tendency to reject all limits and boundaries in quest of the new age, many if not most reformers remained optimistic throughout the 1850s. In 1855 Walt Whitman articulated a new dispensation, boundless in form and content, that was defined by America and took the form of free verse. In 1858 the editors of *Harper's New Monthly Magazine*, one of the nation's most popular periodicals, effusively described America's providential role and characterized American identity as inseparable from God's will. America's "intellect and activity," its "reliance on political institutions," its "faith in means and men," were "human instrumentalities" of God's will for the nation. "We believe that the deepest feeling of the American heart springs from a conviction that Providence has presided over the colonization and progress of this country," the editors wrote." "Providence has its purpose in our national growth and will fulfill its far-reaching scheme" of a new age. Although "a few men ordinarily determine public opinion," those few "never create a deep, genuine, wide-spread, public feeling." Such a feeling sprang from God, where "down in the depths of the heart," He gave birth to the spirit of America's mission. "Our traditions, ancestry, circumstances" spring "from God." Slavery might be tearing the nation apart, but God would ensure a solution, either through moral suasion and peaceful means or through an apocalyptic battle against Satan. Either way, a new day was at hand.[4]

One of the most popular books in the nineteenth century ends on this very note of millennial optimism; and it points to two possible paths to the new age—one peaceful (or postmillennial), the other apocalyptic (or premillennial). Harriet Beecher Stowe's *Uncle Tom's Cabin* (1852) not only helped crystallize antislavery feeling in the North; it shaped and reflected America's millennial mission. In the last few pages of the novel, Stowe sketches out two possible solutions to the persistence of America's sin. One instructs people to "listen to their own heart," which leads down the peaceful path: "An atmosphere of sympathetic influence encircles every human being; and the man or woman who feels strongly, healthily and justly, on the great interests of humanity, is a constant benefactor to the human race. See, then, to your sympathies in this matter! Are they in harmony with the sympathies of Christ? or are they swayed and perverted by the sophistries of worldly policy?" In addition to such sympathetic identification, people can pray for "heathens" at home and abroad and for the "distressed Christians" of the South. And they can offer to repair the damage done to blacks: "Does not every American Christian owe to the African race some effort at reparation for the wrongs that the American nation has brought upon them?" Stowe was an early proponent of reparations to blacks for the nation's sins.[5]

But if Americans forsook sympathy, prayer, and reparations, and continued to indulge in "the sophistries of worldly policy," then the path to the millennium would be volcanic: "This is an age of the world when nations are trembling and convulsed. A mighty influence is abroad, surging and heaving the world, as with an earthquake. And is America safe? Every nation that carries in its bosom great and unredressed injustice has in it the elements of this last convulsion."[6] Here Stowe is self-consciously using the language of apocalypse. Her use of "earthquake" signified the violent overthrow of all evil, a usage she was familiar with, as Ernest Tuveson noted. In Babylon's final days, the nations are "trembling and convulsed." And the Reformation was widely referred to as the "earthquake" par excellence.[7]

Americans also invoked the symbol of "earthquake" to characterize the economic depressions of 1837 through the mid-1840s and in the 1850s. Such convulsions signified the beginning of the end. Stowe's brother Henry Ward Beecher described the Panic of 1837 in terms of an apocalyptic earthquake: in its wake, he said, Americans "wandered like bereaved citizens among the ruins of an earthquake, mourning for children, for houses crushed, and property ruined forever." Whether the earthquake was economic, social, or political, it was a marker of the apocalypse.[8]

Stowe ends her book by instructing her readers to "read the signs of the times!" "A day of grace is yet held out to us," she concludes. It will come through "repentance, justice and mercy." Or it will come through the eternal law, which says that "injustice and cruelty shall bring on nations the wrath of Almighty God!"[9]

Much as there are two paths to the millennium, Stowe also describes two different visions of it. The first vision, which was comparatively rare in America and underdeveloped in the novel, is of an *interracial* promised land. She refers to middle-class blacks living peaceably in Cincinnati, "to show the capability of the race, even without any very particular assistance or encouragement." Such examples of success existed "in all states of the Union" and occurred "in the face of every disadvantage and discouragement." Yet her interracial utopia *depended* upon black uplift and self-help. For Stowe, "respectability" was a prerequisite of equality.[10]

The other, dominant vision of the new age, in the novel and in the 1850s North, was a homogenous white one. For Stowe and most white reformers, the purging of the nation's sin came with colonization. Stowe's black characters emigrate to Africa at the end of the novel; and she instructs her readers to promote colonization: "assist them [blacks] in their passage to those shores, where they may put in practice the lessons they have learned in America."[11] This vision of cleansing the nation's sin through colonization was closely linked to the very efforts to end all evil. Imagining the nation as a new Israel led Americans to conceive of blacks as "the Great American Problem," according to Davis. "The road would be clear," the millennium would be at hand, were it not for the presence of blacks. Such thinking was at the heart of the efforts of colonization. "Hence the victims of the great sin of slavery became, in this ghastly psychological inversion, the embodiment of sin."[12]

Black abolitionists also defined America in millennial terms. Until the Dred Scott decision of 1857, which declared that blacks "had no rights which the white man was bound to respect," they remained optimistic about emancipation and the fulfillment of the nation's ideals.[13] Their optimism persisted even during a period in which they experienced a dramatic loss of basic rights and a revived interest in black colonization on the part of white reformers. In the wake of the Fugitive Slave Act of 1850, there was a surge of emigration; though no precise figures exist, somewhere around 15,000 to 20,000 fugitives fled to Canada in the decade before the Civil War.[14] Those who remained were much more militant in their efforts to resist a slave republic, and their vision of the millennium came with apocalyptic violence. The rescues of the fugitives Shadrach (Frederick Wilkins) in Boston and William (knows as "Jerry") Henry in Syracuse illustrated to black and white radicals the effectiveness of militancy in defying the government in the name of democratic principle.[15]

The optimism of black abolitionists in the 1850s is reflected in their writings. The decade witnessed an African American literary renaissance, according to William Andrews, as activists entered public discourse and fought to realize their visions of emancipation.[16] And the endings of their narratives convey their millennial hopes for their country. Austin Steward ends his 1856 narrative, *Twenty-Two Years a Slave and Forty Years a Freeman*, "hoping that nothing in our past history will serve to becloud the bright future beginning to dawn on the prospects of our disfranchised and oppressed countrymen."[17] Josiah Henson, who Stowe said was the historical parallel to her fictional Uncle Tom, ends his 1849 narrative cherishing his "religious hopes" for the future and believing that his example of piety will benefit "not only the present, but many future generations of my race."[18] Frederick Douglass's 1855 autobiography, *My Bondage and My Freedom*, differs dramatically from his 1845 *Narrative*, which ends with a mocking parody of a southern hymn. *My Bondage*, by contrast, ends with Douglass emphasizing his faith in a new world: "Old as the everlasting hills; immovable as the throne of God; and certain as the purposes of eternal power, against all hindrances, and against all delays, and despite all the mutations of human instrumentalities, it is the faith of my soul, that this anti-slavery cause will triumph."[19] William Cooper Nell ends his 1855 history of African Americans in similar language: "So sure as night precedes day, war ends in peace, and winter wakes spring, just so sure will the persevering efforts of Freedom's army be crowned with victory's perennial laurels!"[20]

Such visions about the end ultimately reflected beliefs about one's own end, as St. Augustine observed, and about the larger meaning of history and progress. When people set their memories in a narrative that has a beginning and an end, it is a way of making sense of their lives and showing that time has a goal or purpose. Once the millennium becomes imaginable as imminent, it also tends to become immanent.[21] These endings illustrate how reformers dispensed with linear chronology and experienced an eschatological leap, a sharp break from the sins of the past. Even though slavery was expanding and the sins and sophistries of the world were increasing, they imagined a glorious future at hand. They conceived of the project of emancipation as apocalyptic, acted on it, and experienced an ecstasy of liberation and release, as though the burden of sin and its attendant hierarchies had been lifted at last.[22]

It is no wonder, then, that when the war came, reformers defined it in apocalyptic terms.[23] On April 14, 1861, as the Confederates declared victory at Fort Sumter, Henry Ward Beecher gave a sermon likening America to the ancient Israelites. He instructed his large congregation to heed God's trumpet, which had just sounded: "Now our turn has come. Right before us lies the Red Sea of war." Walk through it, he instructed, toward the "bright future."[24]

Frederick Douglass likened the war to Revelations 12, where Michael and his angels battled against Satan. When the guns shook Fort Sumter, he sang out "God be praised! that it has come at last."[25] For months he had been despondent over the Lincoln administration's response to secession, and had planned a trip to Haiti as a site of possible emigration, which he cancelled when the war came.

The "apocalyptic trumpet sounded its clearest note" in Julia Ward Howe's "Battle Hymn of the Republic" (1862), as Tuveson noted. The images and symbols of prophesy in Howe's poem respond directly to biblical theories that were available to her and convey "a message about the precise place and point of the war in the" road to salvation. "Clearly, the war [was] a major part of the 'reaping' of the accumulated evils of the long reign of the Beast." Reformers both black and white were thrilled to be part of the generation that God had called upon to fulfill the prophesies and realize the new age.[26]

Understandably, the Emancipation Proclamation appeared to black and white reformers as an instantaneous deliverance from evil.[27] Although the Proclamation liberated only those slaves in the rebel states, reformers treated it as a revolutionary document and a sacred text. For Douglass, it turned the war into a "contest of civilization against barbarism" rather than a struggle for territory, as he put it. It acquired for him "a life and power far beyond its letter" and restored the Declaration to its rightful place at the center of the nation's laws. Henceforth, he said, January 1 and July 4 would rank as the twin birthdays of liberty.[28]

Throughout the North the celebratory speeches on New Years Day 1863 captured the sense of a new dispensation. In Boston a jubilee concert was held at the Music Hall, with most of the literati of New England in attendance. A few blocks away, at the Tremont Temple, thousands of abolitionists (mostly black) kept vigil with speeches and prayers while waiting for the official announcement. When the Proclamation finally came across the wires late in the evening, the Temple erupted with cries of joy, and then everyone spontaneously sang the millennialist tune, "Blow ye the trumpet, blow." Douglass declared the moment to be a sharp break from the sins of the past: "We have had a period of darkness, but are now having the dawn of light, and are met today to celebrate it."[29]

In Washington, D.C., the black preacher Henry M. Turner described the effect of the Proclamation as it was read to crowds that lined Pennsylvania Avenue:

> Men squealed, women fainted, dogs barked, white and colored people shook hands, songs were sung.... Every face had a smile and even the dumb animals seemed to realize that some extraordinary event had taken place.... Rumor said that the very thought of being set at liberty and having no more auction blocks, no more separation of parents and children, was so heart-gladdening that scores of colored people literally fell dead with joy. It was indeed a time of times and a half time. Nothing like it will ever be seen again in this life.[30]

Further south, at Camp Saxton, South Carolina, Charlotte Forten Grimké recorded in her journal that January 1, 1863, was "the most glorious day this nation has yet seen, I think."[31] Thomas Wentworth Higginson attended the formal celebration with Grimké and described how two black women and a black man suddenly arose from behind the platform and began singing, "as if by an impulse that could no more be repressed than the morning note of the song-sparrow":

> My Country, 'tis of thee,
> Sweet land of liberty,
> Of thee I sing!

"I never saw anything so electric," Higginson noted; "it made all other words cheap; it seemed the choked voice of a race at last unloosed."[32]

These outbursts and expressions of joy suggest that for countless men and women, New Years Day 1863 represented a moment when national and scriptural prophesies were being fulfilled. The line between heaven and earth, present and future time, seemed suddenly to vanish.

The Confederacy responded to the Emancipation Proclamation with scorn and ridicule. Jefferson Davis issued a southern version of the Proclamation, consistent with Confederate ideals. On January 5, 1863, he published an "Address to the People of the Free States by the President of the Southern Confederacy," which declared all free blacks in the Confederacy to be "forever" *slaves*. He also stipulated that blacks captured by the Confederacy in *free* states would become slaves, "so that the respective normal condition of the white and black races may be ultimately placed on a permanent basis."[33] Davis and other Confederates followed a long tradition in Western culture, dating back to Aristotle, in believing that some people were born to rule and others to do the basic work of society.

These responses to emancipation, in both the North and the South, also illustrate the problem of freedom. With emancipation, African Americans saw in one divine event the end of all doubt and disappointment, as W. E. B. Du Bois shrewdly noted. Slavery was "the sum of all villainies, the cause of all sorrow, the root of all prejudice; Emancipation was the key to a promised land of sweeter beauty than ever stretched before the eyes of wearied Israelites. In song and exhortation swelled one refrain—Liberty."[34] Freedom came suddenly, fearfully, as if in a dream. But the dream soon turned into a nightmare: it was as though the apocalypse had come but the new age was nowhere in sight. White reformers experienced a similar disillusionment. After Armageddon, millennial hopes petered out and reformers alternated between "disillusionment and frantic activism," as James Moorhead summarized.[35] And Southerners responded to Emancipation much as Jefferson Davis did: they redeemed themselves by retaliating against blacks. By envisioning an end of all evil, reformers sowed the seeds of future evils, bearing all-too-tempting fruits.

NOTES

1 David Brion Davis, *Challenging the Boundaries of Slavery* (Cambridge: Harvard University Press, 2003), 32.
2 On the surge of optimism among reformers, see Ernest Lee Tuveson, *Redeemer Nation: The Idea of America's Millennial Role* (Chicago: University of Chicago Press, 1968), 191.

3 Herman Melville, *White-Jacket; or, The World in a Man-of-War* (1850; reprint, Evanston and Chicago: Northwestern University Press and The Newberry Library, 1970), 150–51.

4 "Editor's Table: Providence in American History," *Harper's New Monthly Magazine* 17:101 (October 1858): 694.

5 Harriet Beecher Stowe, *Uncle Tom's Cabin, or Life Among the Lowly* (1852; reprint, New York: Penguin Books, 1986), 624–25 [chap. 55].

6 Ibid., 629.

7 Tuveson, *Redeemer Nation*, 191.

8 Henry Ward Beecher, quoted from John Stauffer, *The Black Hearts of Men: Radical Abolitionists and the Transformation of Race* (Cambridge: Harvard University Press, 2002), 115.

9 Stowe, *Uncle Tom's Cabin*, 629.

10 Ibid., 627, 628. See also James Brewer Stewart, "The Emergence of Racial Modernity and the Rise of the White North, 1790–1840," *Journal of the Early Republic* 18 (Summer 1998): 181–217.

11 Ibid., 626.

12 Davis, *Challenging the Boundaries of Slavery*, 32–33.

13 Paul Finkelman, ed., *Dred Scott v. Sandford: A Brief History with Documents* (Boston: Bedford Books, 1997), 61.

14 Fred Landon, "The Negro Migration to Canada after the Passing of the Fugitive Slave Act," *Journal of Negro History* 5:1 (January 1920): 22; C. Peter Ripley, ed., *The Black Abolitionist Papers*, vol. II: *Canada, 1830–1865* (Chapel Hill: University of North Carolina Press, 1986), 10, 28. Robin W. Winks, " 'A Sacred Animosity': Abolitionism in Canada," *The Antislavery Vanguard: New Essays on the Abolitionists*, ed. Martin Duberman (Princeton: Princeton University Press, 1965), 304–12; William H. and Jane H. Pease, *Black Utopia: Negro Communal Experiments in America* (Madison: State Historical Society of Wisconsin, 1963).

15 Some historians identify the man as Jerry "McHenry," following Samuel Joseph May's postbellum recollections of the "Jerry rescue"; but abolitionist newspapers from the 1850s refer to him as William (or Jerry) Henry. See Samuel Joseph May, *Some Recollections of Our Antislavery Conflict* (1869; reprint, New York: Arno Press, 1968), 373–84. On historians who use "Henry" and draw from contemporaneous sources, see Benjamin Quarles, *Black Abolitionists* (New York: Oxford University Press, 1969), 209–11; Stanley W. Campbell, *The Slave Catchers: Enforcement of the Fugitive Slave Law, 1850–1860* (1968; reprint, New York: W. W. Norton, 1972), 154–57; Gary Collison, *Shadrach Minkins: From Fugitive Slave to Citizen* (Cambridge: Harvard University Press, 1999), 198; Stauffer, *The Black Hearts of Men*, 174.

16 William L. Andrews, *To Tell a Free Story: The First Century of Afro-American Autobiography, 1760–1865* (Urbana: University of Illinois Press, 1986), 169.

17 Austin Steward, *Twenty-Two Years a Slave and Forty Years a Freeman* (1857; reprint, Reading, Mass.: Addison-Wesley, 1969), 204.

18 Josiah Henson, *The Life of Josiah Henson, Formerly a Slave, Now an Inhabitant of Canada, as Narrated by Himself* (Boston: Arthur D. Phelps, 1849), 76.
19 Frederick Douglass, *My Bondage and My Freedom* (1855; reprint, New York: The Modern Library, 2003), 292.
20 William Cooper Nell, *The Colored Patriots of the American Revolution, with Sketches of Several Distinguished Colored Persons . . . , with an Introduction by Harriet Beecher Stowe* (Boston: Robert F. Wallcut, 1855), 381.
21 Frank Kermode, *The Sense of an Ending: Studies in the Theory of Fiction with a New Epilogue* (1966; reprint, New York: Oxford University Press, 2000), 186; James H. Moorhead, *World Without End: Mainstream American Protestant Visions of the Last Things, 1880–1925* (Bloomington: Indiana University Press, 1999), xii.
22 Stauffer, *Black Hearts of Men*, 34–35.
23 See David Brion Davis, "The Emancipation Moment," in Gabor S. Boritt, ed., *Lincoln, the War President* (New York: Oxford University Press, 1992), 65–88.
24 Henry Ward Beecher, "The Battle Set in Array," in Conrad Cherry, ed., *God's New Israel: Religious Interpretations of American Destiny* (1971; reprint, Chapel Hill: University of North Carolina Press, 1998), 172, 183.
25 Frederick Douglass, "The Fall of Sumter," *Douglass' Monthly*, May 1861, in Philip S. Foner, ed., *The Life and Writings of Frederick Douglass*, vol. III: *The Civil War, 1861–1865* (New York: International Publishers, 1950), 89; Douglass, "The American Apocalypse: An Address Delivered . . . on June 16, 1861," in John Blassingame, ed., *The Frederick Douglass Papers*, series 1, vol. 3 (New Haven: Yale University Press, 1985), 437. See also David W. Blight, *Frederick Douglass' Civil War: Keeping Faith in Jubilee* (Baton Rouge: Louisiana State University Press, 1989), 1–25, 101–21.
26 Tuveson, *Redeemer Nation*, 197, 199, 200.
27 Davis, "Emancipation Moment," 72.
28 Douglass, "The Proclamation and a Negro Army: An Address Delivered in New York, on February 6, 1863," in Blassingame, ed., *The Frederick Douglass Papers*, 1:3, 551, 552, 563–64; Douglass, *Life and Times of Frederick Douglass, Written by Himself* (1892; reprint, New York: Collier Books, 1962), 354–55 (quoted). See also Blight, *Frederick Douglass' Civil War*, 101–21.
29 Benjamin Quarles, *The Negro in the Civil War* (1953; reprint, New York: Da Capo Press, 1989), 170–74, quotation from 173; Douglass, "Emancipation and the Dawn of Light: An Address . . . on January 1, 1863," in Blassingame, ed., *Frederick Douglass Papers*, 1:3, 547. "Blow ye the trumpet blow" had been John Brown's favorite song. See Stephen B. Oates, *To Purge this Land with Blood: A Biography of John Brown* (1970; reprint, Amherst: University of Massachusetts Press, 1984), 16, 49–50, 194, 358.
30 Henry M. Turner, quoted from Dorothy Sterling, ed., *Speak Out in Thunder Tones: Letters and Other Writings by Black Northerners, 1787–1865* (1973; reprint, New York: Da Capo Press, 1973), 315–17.
31 Brenda Stevenson, ed., *The Journals of Charlotte Forten Grimké* (New York: Oxford University Press, 1988), 428.

32 Thomas Wentworth Higginson, *Army Life in a Black Regiment* (1869; reprint, New York: Norton, 1984), 60. Higginson describes the same incident in slightly different form in his private journal. See Christopher Looby, ed., *The Complete Civil War Journal and Selected Letters of Thomas Wentworth Higginson* (Chicago: University of Chicago Press, 2000), 76–77.
33 Jefferson Davis, quoted from Quarles, *The Negro Civil War*, 180.
34 W. E. B. Du Bois, *The Souls of Black Folk* (1903; reprint, New York: Penguin Books, 1989), 7.
35 James H. Moorhead, *American Apocalypse: Yankee Protestants and the Civil War, 1860–1869* (New Haven: Yale University Press, 1978), 243.

IVER BERNSTEIN

Political Evil and the Body Politic in Mid-Nineteenth-Century America

What is the relationship between the body politic and individual bodies? In early modern England, Thomas Hobbes in *Leviathan* (1651) depicted the body politic as a metaphor of a body that was at once human and national. The king constituted the head and individual Britons made up the remaining body parts. The United States from the post-Revolutionary period to the late 1840s saw the body politic in similar terms, replacing the king with representatives of democratic law and government. The constituent elements of the body politic were autonomous individuals endowed with the capacity for reason and rational thinking. Individuals were distinct from the body politic; they were part of it, but did not constitute it. As Iver Bernstein phrases it, "to create an autonomous self" was "an act of separation; to create a national government was an act of joinder."

But by the 1850s, there was a profound shift in the relationship between the body and the body politic. Americans increasingly became a *synecdoche* for the body politic. They stood for, and represented, their nation. This new individual commitment to the nation-state reflected a "dramatic shift in consciousness," as Bernstein shows. The new meaning of the body politic not only erased the distinction between the state and the individual, fusing the many into the one; it taught Americans to see individual and national sin as inseparable. As a result, slaveowning became, in the minds of Republicans, a cancer on the nation's body. In fact from 1854 until his election, Lincoln repeatedly used the cancer metaphor. For Jefferson Davis, the new Southern Confederacy constituted "men of one flesh, one bone, one interest, one purpose, and of identity of domestic institutions." The invasion of Union troops was like an open wound on the new nation's flesh, affecting all citizens.

The logic of fusing the human body with the body politic demanded that people sacrifice self for nation. Now everyone could imagine gaining the immortal status of martyr. Ironically, though, annihilation of the self, which was one of

Americans' deepest fears in the 1850s, was also a precondition for this martyrdom: "the sufferer needed to embrace such annihilation, as martyrdom could not be seized in an act of personal aggrandizement. It could only be granted by the sacred community after a heroic death." Such martyrdom had the potential to create a more inclusive nation-state: now, even social outsiders, from blacks and women to other "stigmatized" individuals, could, through martyrdom, become part of the sacred community. It was also predicated on a vision of demonic evil breathtaking in its power. The result was a harvest of death almost beyond imagining.

In the Congressional debate over the crisis of Union in 1850, Senator Henry Clay referred to the issues at hand as "five wounds," "open and bleeding," which only his Compromise could permanently heal.[1] "Now, what is the plan of the President? I will describe it by a simile, in a manner which cannot be misunderstood. Here are five wounds—one, two, three, four, five—bleeding and threatening the well being, if not the existence of the body politic. What is the plan of the President? Is it to heal all these wounds? No such thing. It is only to heal one of the five, and to leave the other four to bleed more profusely than ever, by the sole admission of California, even if it should produce death itself. I have said that five wounds are open and bleeding. What are they?" "First," Clay went on, "there is California; there are the territories, second; there is the question of the boundary of Texas[,] the third; there is the fugitive slave bill[,] the fourth; and there is the question of the slave trade in the District of Columbia[,] fifth. The President, instead of proposing a plan of comprehending all the diseases of the country, looks only at one. . . . After the observations which I addressed to the Senate a week ago, I did hope and trust there would have been a reciprocation from the other end of the avenue, as to the desire to heal, not one wound only, which being healed alone would exasperate and aggravate instead of harmonizing the country, but to heal them all." "Unless some such measure will prevail," Clay concluded, "the wounds of the country . . . will flow in still greater quantities, with still greater danger to the Republic."[2]

Clay's audience seized on his metaphor of the "five wounds"—the image served as a framing device not only for Clay's comments and perspective but also for an ongoing discussion. In his "Anti-Compromise Speech" delivered several weeks later, Thomas Hart Benton knew of "no distress in the country, no misery, no strife, no distraction, none of those five gaping wounds of which the Senator from Kentucky made enumeration on the five fingers of his left hand, and for the healing of which, all together and all at once, and not one at a time, like the little Doctor Taylor, he has provided this capacious plaster in the shape of five old bills tacked together."[3] A New York newspaper editor compared Clay's Compromise with Benton's position, "While the one naturally leads to a rational, friendly, and just compromise of the great questions of the day, . . . the other has no tendency but to prolong the agitation, to keep the wounds of the body politic still bleeding, and to jeopardize the integrity of this great confederacy."[4]

The following summer, Samuel A. Cartwright, the Louisiana physician and proslavery ideologue, contested Clay's notion of the Compromise as a cure for the nation's "five wounds": instead, claimed Cartwright, "two bleeding wounds" persisted, the denial of the South's "equality" and the forcing of the South into submission, resulting from the perversion of the "political compact" by an "unbridled majority." Clay could not stanch those wounds, nor could the "sovereign people," who lacked the "requisite knowledge of the anatomy of the body politic." Slavery, Cartwright explained, was "not a blot or excrescence" on the body politic. Rather, destroying it would kill off "the organism uniting all the parts of this confederacy into a grand, wonderful and progressive whole": the reason was that "the African is not constituted in mind or body, in the skin or under the skin, like the white man."[5] A year later, the black nationalist Martin Robison Delany, who may well have seen himself joining a conversation about the body politic, contended in his treatise on "the destiny of the colored people of the United States" that northern free blacks, like southern slaves, "are ruled and governed without representation, existing as mere nonentities among the citizens, and excrescences on the body politic."[6] As late as 1858, a correspondent of the New York *Tribune* described the Kansas slavery crisis in Clay's terms: "No delusion of words, no quackery of form, no emollient of ingenuity, will soothe or heal this bleeding wound, which gapes more widely and ghastly than the five which Mr. Clay held up with so much effect to the pitying gaze of an excited country only seven years ago . . . Therefore, it is useless to try plasters when surgery alone will serve."[7]

RE-MYSTIFYING THE POLITY

The concept of the body politic, as detailed in Clay's "Five Wounds" speech and the ensuing discussion, became a central part of political debate in the 1850s. Why did such a conversation take place and why was there an increasing appearance of bodily metaphors in the years leading up to the Civil War? This was highly charged language designed for times of emergency. Such metaphors signaled an eruption of conflicts and concerns outside the rule and adjudication of law. Indeed, to talk of the body politic was to speak to a crisis of law in which the very survival of the polity and the individual was at stake.

What exactly was the crisis of law and the threat to the polity and individual in the mid-nineteenth century? After the flurry of the first twelve amendments between 1791 and 1804, the Constitution was not again amended until the passage of the Thirteenth Amendment abolishing black chattel slavery in 1865. By the 1840s, the founding document had not been altered for decades, and the sacred text's preservation, "as it was," was considered by most Americans to be necessary for the preservation of popular liberties.

But the crisis and the threat went deeper still, and involved not only constitutional stasis but also what might be called a twofold problem of attachment: of individuals to the government, and of individuals to each other. One can hardly grasp the full dimensions of the "crisis of Union" in the 1850s without understanding that beneath that crisis—and any consideration of "Union"— lurked a problem of how to achieve meaningful and lasting attachment in a liberal regime and society in which reason, contract, and the material interest of autonomous individuals were understood to be the constitutive elements of public order. The political evil or "disease" that Henry Clay and his respondents attempted to isolate was rooted in this problem of achieving attachment or intimacy under such conditions. The growing talk of the "body politic" in the 1850s was an attempt to address this problem and was part of a historic shift in consciousness toward a modern nationalism that, by the time of the Civil War, merged the state and the individual in a way that would have shocked most Americans thirty years before. The historian David M. Potter suggested the centrality of such concerns when he observed that "the nineteenth-century conjunction of nationalism and liberalism was by no means inevitable," and that "to regard it as inevitable is to lose the larger meaning of the Civil War."[8]

The conversation about the body politic in the 1850s needs to be understood as a rich and revealing point of entry into this puzzle of how an older conception of liberal individualism was transformed into a modern commitment to the nation-state. When placed in this context, that conversation illuminates a historic shift in consciousness, an alteration of the very paradigm of political culture. The conversation supplies a crucial perspective to our understanding of the coming of the Civil War, and of individuals who would fight and die for their respective nations.

How this new kind of attachment or merger of individuals into new northern and southern nations would be achieved by 1861 was, as we shall see, no small problem. Liberty, generations of American and European political thinkers had long determined, was the unshackling of the individual from the despotism of the state and its powers to oppress and corrupt. To create a self, one might say, was an act of separation; to create a national government was an act of joinder. The two, self and nation, were incommensurables, competing truths. Individual liberty could be accomplished, many Americans continued to assume through the 1830s, but only at the expense of attachment to the nation. Indeed, the great achievement of the Americans' Constitution and Union, based on reason, contract, and individual interest, was, from this perspective, its success in demystifying authority. Americans, it seemed, had figured out how to do away with Old World states and their tyrannical tendency to consolidate individuals into larger political wholes in ways that overrode their autonomy. All the more striking, then, the resort to the consolidating logic of the "body politic" in the 1850s, during that decade's political crises. Antislavery North and proslavery South, and their presidents Abraham Lincoln and Jefferson Davis, would each find ways to transcend the paradox of individual and nation, indeed, to merge individuals into nation-states. Both would re-mystify the polity. But they would work their unifying legerdemain through strikingly different styles of rhetoric and action and with vastly different implications for the democratic possibilities of the northern and southern nations they were conceiving.

1830S CONTEXTS: LIBERAL ORTHODOXY, LINCOLN'S LYCEUM SPEECH

The triumph of liberal conceptions of contract in American state and society by the mid-nineteenth-century was a major historical accomplishment. In England, dating back to early modern times, the mystification of authority had been a defining element of a monarchical political culture. The legal fiction of the "king's two bodies" had allowed that, even with the death of the king in his physical body, he survived in his "mystical body," in which capacity "the king is esteemed to be immortal, invisible, not subject to death, infirmity, nonage, etc."[9] The metaphor had at least two contradictory implications for politics. It at once had the potential to limit the power of a living king and of the monarchy *and* to arrogate for a living king limitless power and endow the monarchy with stability and permanence. The fiction of a body politic conjured a political community set apart from the arbitrary personal rule of any particular king. As such, it offered the possibility of subordinating the person of the ruler to law. This was the implication of the metaphor that the English Parliament seized upon during the seventeenth century to hold the king to account.[10] The creation of the United States, with its Constitution, one could say, was a culmination of this development; one is reminded of Thomas Paine's famous response to the question, "Where . . . is the King of America?" in *Common Sense*: "in America THE LAW IS KING."[11] Hence, the metaphor of the body politic became vestigial in a world of modern American legalism that, as one historian has observed, "clearly distinguishes occupant from office, subordinates person to law, and addresses the contractual relations of separate, single individuals."[12]

By the 1830s the metaphor had been driven far to the margins of the political culture. By then a liberal outlook that celebrated the contractual relations of single, separate, and rational individuals had come to dominate American conceptions not only of polity but also of society. The most insistent and systematic endorsements of such a perspective came from the free-trade political economists who wrote the standard college texts of the day and had the ear of many of era's leading jurists and political figures.[13] Henry C. Carey (before his conversion to protectionist nationalism in the late 1840s), Francis Lieber, John McVickar, John Adams Dix, and Francis Wayland are some of the economic writers who come to mind, but no one was more relentlessly committed to stripping away the mystifications of Old World power and building a polity solely on the material interest of autonomous individuals than the aging British émigré and South Carolina College professor Thomas Cooper.[14] Cooper's insistence that self-interest was the only form of attachment that could bind citizens to the government or to each other furnished a powerful justification for South Carolina's nullification of Congress's 1828 "tariff of abominations." His encouragement of South Carolinians to "calculate the value of the union" sent shockwaves of anxiety through the country's political culture.[15]

It is well known that President Andrew Jackson won the political struggle with Cooper and the nullifiers in 1832–33 and kept South Carolina in the Union. Harriet Martineau may only have exaggerated a little when she said of the treasonous South Carolinians that "the vision of the scaffold was before other men's eyes, and must have been before their own."[16] But if South Carolina lost the immediate political battle with the government in Washington, it won the ideological war. The version of liberalism that guided the Democratic administrations and Congresses following Jackson had a distinctly South Carolinian cast, evident in intensely Anglophobic and antiabolitionist policies (the British emancipation of West Indian slavery had occurred in 1833) and in a rigidly laissez-faire conception of free trade, culminating in the reduced duties of the Walker tariff of 1846. A gathering political orthodoxy of the 1830s and 1840s regarded the "individual" as "economic man" pursuing his material self-interest across a world theater and bonding with other such individuals through contract and consent. Such "economic men," taken together, were understood to be the parts that made up a cosmopolitan political and economic whole, and that whole was regarded as exactly the sum of the parts, so defined. In a new global political dispensation, to be inaugurated by the United States, warlike and tyrannical Old World states would wither away and Americans and those who united with them would demonstrate, in Thomas Jefferson's words, "the degree of freedom and self-government" that "a society may venture to leave its individual members."[17] The separation and diffusion of autonomous individuals across space defined this outlook: such decentralization was the hedge against the aggrandizement of Old World states, so threatening to individual liberty. But the antebellum political economists hammered these Jeffersonian views of state, society, and the individual into a formalized and spiritualized creed that the third president would have found unfamiliar. Free trade, Francis Lieber drilled his students at South Carolina College, was "nothing but the natural state of things, like free communion"; indeed, it was like "free breathing," and only became a "separate subject" when it was invaded; it was "the gospel of peace and good will, carried out in the world of exchange."[18]

Indeed, the free-trade liberals' gospel of an ever-widening "harmony of interests" should come with a surgeon general's warning for the unwary historian. It was a profoundly ideological and politicized construction, shaped in the red heat of the era's arguments over the significance of the Haitian Revolution and British emancipation. At the level of world politics, the vision of a peaceable and expanding American Union created by freely contracting polities could serve to justify egregious American acts of territorial aggrandizement in the name of protecting vulnerable states on the American periphery against British imperialism, mercantilism and abolition.[19] At the level of household politics, the free-trade vision's emphasis on individual separation and autonomy in the public sphere contrasted jarringly with violent efforts at home to "consolidate" slaves and other household dependents into the civic personality and will of the master. The free-trade orthodoxy of the 1830s and 1840s, with its strong South Carolinian accent, was not only about tariff policy but also about the validation of a certain form of political attachment based on reason and material interest and the steadfast invalidation of other forms based on passion, violence, sexual desire across the color line, and religious community. Allowing these alternative forms of attachment to infect public life would have revolutionary implications, so the argument went, and lead to what were perceived as the twin monstrosities of black rule and economic ruin à la Haiti or Jamaica.[20]

One can go further and suggest that part of the American liberals' frantic fear of the wrong kinds of attachment producing the wrong kinds of New World nations amounted to an admission of just how vulnerable the American Union was to the challenge of such competing forms of nationality—a covert concession of the problem of attachment at the core of an American regime predicated on reason, contract, and individual interest. Indeed, if one goes back to Adam Smith, whom the political economists of the mid-nineteenth century revered, it is worth noting that his "theory of moral sentiments" represented an implicit acknowledgement that that "interest" alone would not produce enduring ties among autonomous individuals. Smith conceded the difficulty of achieving attachment, let alone intimacy, between two persons: at best, one could hope for "two sentiments" in "correspondence with one another, . . . sufficient for the harmony of society. Though they will never be unisons, they may be concords, and this is all that is wanted or required."[21] By elevating Smithian "interest" to political dogma, the free traders inherited the problem of attachment—of binding individuals to the government and to each other—that bedeviled that Enlightenment outlook.

Nonetheless, the proponents of liberal orthodoxy had succeeded in relegating alternative forms of attachment to the margins of the political culture by the1830s. They had, it could be said, demystified the polity and proclaimed the triumph of reason, contract, and material self-interest as the only way to bind individuals to the government or to each other.

Still, as marginalized as the body politic metaphor may have become by the 1830s, it was not and never could be wholly excised from the political culture The metaphor had a long and episodic history, exploding into usage at moments of political and legal uncertainty and social anxiety. For instance, at the height of the controversy over the admission of Missouri as a slave state in 1821, James Madison wrote a parable of North and South, "Jonathan Bull and Mary Bull." Jonathan and Mary were married, but Mary, "when a child, had unfortunately received from a certain African dye a stain on her left arm, which had made it perfectly black, and withal somewhat weaker than the other arm." Though Mary was pleasing in all other regards, Jonathan "looked at the black arm, and forgot all the rest": "if the color could not be taken out, either tear off the skin from the flesh, or cut off the limb," he would sue for divorce and "there should be an end of all connexion between them and their estates."[22]

Abraham Lincoln's 1838 address to the Young Men's Lyceum of Springfield,

Illinois, was a response to a similar moment of perceived breakdown in law, a nationwide outbreak of mob violence. The speech must be read as a response to the problem of attachment that a republic of reason, contract, and individual autonomy exposed but could not, at least on its own terms, satisfyingly resolve. The opposite of contract, the English political philosopher John Locke observed, was slavery, and although Lincoln and his audience were not chattel slaves, there was a sense in which they were dispossessed: that is, not fully represented by a constitutional contract they did not create and could not change, indeed, to which they had not formally consented and which did not acknowledge their emotional selves. As a covert insurgency of the dispossessed, and in its exploration of bodily sacrifice during war, the Lyceum Address anticipated the conversation about the body politic of the 1850s.

In the speech's remarkable "psychological" section, Lincoln wondered whether the passionate Americans of his day could develop an attachment to the political institutions of the Union. He saw an experiential divide between the Founders and himself and his contemporaries. They were able to realize a complete selfhood in the rational act of creating American law and government *and* in the emotional one of sacrificing life, liberty, and sacred honor for the Declaration of Independence. He and his generation would not be able to act on the Declaration's invitation to sacrifice life for liberty without destroying law, government, and Union.[23] His generation would be hindered by passion: only "reason—cold, calculating, unimpassioned reason"—and reverence for law would aid them in their task of preserving American institutions.[24]

Yet, for all of its insistence on redoubled devotion to lawful obedience and reason, Lincoln's Lyceum Address was, at least covertly, a brief for the position, once advanced by Edmund Burke in the context of the French Revolution, that authority based on reason and contractualism alone could not command the affections of the people. Lincoln referred to the scarred bodies of the Revolutionary war veterans—"limbs mangled"—as a kind of living, familial connection to both the nation's founding and its political institutions. But by 1838, with the founding generation dying out, "*those* histories are gone."[25] Bloody personal sacrifice in the name of liberty, Lincoln was suggesting, would be the only way to engage the individual's visceral loyalties and reinvigorate law and political institutions. The vivid political community of the Founders, the one created by their fight for liberty and symbolized by their war wounds, had died with their bodies. Lincoln implied that the challenge for his generation was to create a body politic, a vital political community that did not fade out, but endured in fame and in memory.

Elijah Lovejoy, the Alton, Illinois, antislavery editor murdered in the act of defending his constitutional right of free speech, had to have been on Lincoln's mind, if barely acknowledged in his speech.[26] Lovejoy's murder eleven weeks earlier was certainly the occasion for the speech. Mobs had destroyed three printing presses that Lovejoy had tried to set up in Alton. The editor's willingness to expose himself to their fury in order to set up a fourth, and his calm, self-sacrificing death in the face of extreme danger, inspired many in the northern antislavery movement. Some were moved to activism; others proclaimed Lovejoy a martyr.[27] A Groton, Connecticut, meeting to commemorate the editor resolved that "our brother's blood" urges us "manfully to defend the cause of suffering, oppressed humanity, if need be, unto death."[28] Perhaps most important was the sense of moral and political breakthrough that antislavery northerners felt after the murder: Wendell Phillips recalled: "I can never forget the quick, sharp agony of that hour which brought us news of Lovejoy's death.... The gun fired at Lovejoy was like that of Sumter—it scattered a world of dreams."[29]

In 1838, Lincoln was hardly ready to proclaim himself as an antislavery activist, let alone recognize Lovejoy as a martyr—the speech, one could say, was a scarcely concealed effort to keep the ghost of Lovejoy at bay. But Lovejoy had by his actions hinted at a way out of the dilemma Lincoln posed at the Lyceum, that of surmounting the incommensurability of the Constitution's commitment to law and the Declaration's to liberty.[30] In death, Lovejoy showed how the example of one individual willingly sacrificing self in the name of law and liberty could forge new forms of political community. Indeed, in the resolutions of the many northern protest meetings, one could discern something more: a perception of the murder and the outrage it provoked as a "decisive moment" of qualitative change that could transcend unresponsive law, challenge "demonic power," and usher in a sacred community so compelling that people would die for it.[31] Here, at least potentially, was a solution for Lincoln's problem of political attachment.

Lincoln was furtively imagining a version of self and political community other than the one grounded solely in reason, contract, and material interest and enshrined by liberal orthodoxy. The speech was an explicit turning away from the stage of global political economy and external challenges to the Union and toward a world of internal threats within the Union and the individual psyche. Destruction would not "come from abroad," said Lincoln; if such "be our lot, we must ourselves be its author and finisher."[32] His image of a body politic constituted by the martyred bodies of war heroes was a move from a polity of separate, autonomous individuals to one in which sacrifice could transform destructive passions into the stuff of attachment, both to other selves and to the state. A nation so conceived might engage the fervent ambition of individuals like Lincoln himself and, in so doing, survive.

But Lincoln's tone in 1838 was one of suppressed longing; his rhetorical maneuvers were cloaked. When the metaphor of the body politic erupted into Congressional debate during another moment of political and legal crisis, in 1850, its dominant messages likewise were those of reason and lawful constraint; implications of passion, law-breaking, or martyrdom, while present, were still veiled. It would take the rhetorical virtuosity of figures such as Frederick Douglass, Harriet Beecher Stowe, and a mature Lincoln, as well as the pressure of the more desperate struggles for national and individual survival in the 1850s, to make those meanings explicit.

CLAY'S "FIVE WOUNDS"

It is hard not to be struck by the confidence of Clay's pronouncement on the Senate floor in May 1850, and not only because the legislator was facing down a sitting president, Zachary Taylor. Clay was offering himself, in rhetorical terms, as a kind of physician of the body politic, whose analogy of "five wounds" could frame how Americans understood the tangle of issues roiling the Congress and lead them to a safe political and constitutional solution that would keep the Union and Americans' project of popular self-government intact. His use of the image of the body politic was like the surgeon's elaborate routine of donning mask, gown, and gloves and scrubbing in before proceeding with a delicate and dangerous operation. The metaphor allowed Clay to handle the potentially septic "private" matter of slavery without unduly invading the dominion of the slaveowning paterfamilias and the "protected" status of slaves and other dependents therein, and to do so without compromising the rationality of the public, political sphere for which he spoke in his capacity as a U.S. senator.[33] He was confident that he could mobilize the conventions of neoclassical oratory to play a dramatic but highly sensitive role: he sought to contain within the domain of *talk* the controversies over the status of fugitive slaves and the demands of Texas and the admission of California as a free state, all of which had the potential to spark revolutionary *action* in the form of insurgencies that might yield independent nationality.

Clay's use of the metaphor of the body politic, then, was part of a bold effort to open up, examine, and renegotiate the political contract of the Union, but to do so within tightly scripted constraints, under the trusteeship of select leaders, without unleashing the destabilizing and more fully democratic possibilities of mobilizing those who were not considered to be full parties to that contract. The elderly former president James Madison congratulated Clay after his 1833 speech on the tariff that helped seal that year's historic compromise, "I need not repeat what is said by all, on the ability and advantages with which the Subject was handled. It has certainly had the effect of an Anodyne on the feverish excitement under which the public mind was laboring; & a relapse may happily not ensue."[34] It was this realm of "anodyne," as Madison put it, the soothing treatment of the body politic, that promised political stability and fell short of constitutional amendment or radical transformation, which Clay captured so convincingly for many antebellum Americans.

THE CONVERSATION TRANSFORMED

By the mid-1850s, such legal fictions as the "body politic" no longer provided a way to contain conflict and win assent. The very term was becoming one of fierce contest. Slavery, Francis Blair Jr. said during the Lecompton crisis, was a "cancer on the face, which, unless removed, would eat into the vitals of the Republic." Not slavery but sectionalism, Jefferson Davis countered, was the true "epidemic" of the body politic.[35] In 1854, Senator Sam Houston caught the new mood of skepticism. "The physic works," he said of Stephen A. Douglas's effort to heal the crises of nation and slavery through the Kansas-Nebraska Act. "It works badly," he went on. "It works upward."[36]

Blair's reference to cancer in 1858 is worth flagging and considering alongside Abraham Lincoln's use of that metaphor four years earlier. In his first thoroughgoing antislavery speech at Peoria, delivered after the passage of Kansas-Nebraska, Lincoln said, "I particularly object to the NEW position which the avowed principle of this Nebraska law gives to slavery in the body politic." Referring to the absence of the words "slave" or "slavery" in the federal constitution, and to the clause putting off the prohibition of the African slave trade for twenty years, he observed, "The thing is hid away . . . just as an afflicted man hides away a wen or a cancer, which he dares not cut out at once, lest he bleed to death; with the promise, nevertheless, that the cutting may begin at the end of a given time."[37]

The cancer metaphor was new in Lincoln's oratory in October 1854; he would resort to it repeatedly thereafter.[38] It announced a shift away from Clay's confident "therapeutic" statesmanship, which assumed that the ills of the body politic could be readily managed by timely intervention. Here was the language of social and political alarm, signaling a diminished optimism about the ability of the physician of the body politic to master evils and restore the community to health. Cancer had special rhetorical appeal: in an era in which disease was often understood in general philosophical terms, as a moral imbalance that altered the state of being of the whole person (Koch's discoveries regarding the specificity of "germs" would not come until the 1880s), cancer was seen as a specific material growth. To invoke cancer was to consider an evil that had intransigent physical presence and a distinctive logic, an evil that one could not be readily talked or reasoned out of. Indeed, in a body politic corrupted by cancer, all were potentially tainted, even the physician of the polity. The image of the cancerous body politic was so toxic as to shadow forth the destruction of the political community and the rational "statesman" who might heal its conflicts.[39]

DOUGLASS AND RYNDERS AT THE BROADWAY TABERNACLE

Just days before Clay delivered his "Five Wounds" speech, the abolitionist and former slave Frederick Douglass confronted the gang leader Isaiah Rynders at a meeting of the American Anti-Slavery Society in New York City. Their encounter revealed a world where healing metaphors were unavailable or irrelevant, violence was in the air, and political community and self were in real peril. Douglass was fighting for his life, in a literal, physical as well as social and political sense.

Race baiting the abolitionists and rabble rousing the party faithful, the editor James Gordon Bennett had called for a show of the Democratic masses' loyalty to "Constitution and Union," to the South, and to slavery. The perfect storm was in the making: William Lloyd Garrison was at the podium; Rynders, poised to wage proxy war for slavery, was in the wings; and Rynders' Irish b'hoys and abolitionist women and men, black and white, packed the house. With national crisis as backdrop, here was a convocation of outcasts, all finding their claims to self-government and full membership in the national political contract subject to derision. Garrison was hardly interested in deliberative talk in the manner of Clay, and Rynders' *"forte,"* as one editorial put it, was "not in words."[40] One "Dr. Grant," a small-time scientific racist, declaimed that blacks were animals, "anything else but a human being," and that abolitionists' attempt at "amalgamation" was "monstrous in the extreme."[41]

Amid the ensuing uproar, Douglass rose in self-defense. He did so with Rynders standing "at his elbow," a framing device both white and patriarchal, as it were, warranting that if Douglass "spoke disrespectfully of the South, or Washington or Patrick Henry, or of the President, then he would knock him down."[42] The frameworks for interpreting the occasion shifted beneath

Douglass's feet: was this "Garrison's nigger minstrels," as one headline had it, or was this "Yaller Gals," a minstrel show with Rynders the interlocutor?[43] Was it a race scientist's examination table, a mock slave auction, or an incipient lynch mob? Each view conspired to drum Douglass out of the body politic—strip him naked, lavish dehumanizing attention on his body, and symbolically divest him of property in himself and any claims to masculine self-government and membership in the political community.

Drawing up to his full height and using his own body as a kind of exhibit, Douglass launched into an examination of American race relations and nationality. "It would be quite discreditable for so large an assembly as this if it could be disturbed by a monkey . . . I invite you to the examination and ask the audience to be a judge whether I am a man." Rynders interjected: "You are not a black man—you are a half-brother: you are only half a Negro."

> F. DOUGLASS: He is correct. I am, indeed, only half a Negro and am half a white man—a half-brother to Mr. RYNDERS. (Loud laughter.) Now here I would call for your special attention: stick a pin here—make a mark there. I was not bred among abolitionists but among slaveholders. . . . Yes, the son of a slaveholder stands before you by an adored mother—a mother as dearly beloved as if she had been white as snow. . . . To whom do the remarks apply which are made in relation to amalgamation in this country? Not to the North but to the South. The whole country south of Mason's and Dixon's line is given up to amalgamation. . . . if a black woman was to lift up her hand in defense of her virtue, the southerner would be permitted by the law to strike her dead. (Sensation.)
>
> Captain RYNDERS: There is no such law in the South.
>
> F. DOUGLASS. Yes, in Virginia. If a black should raise the hand to strike a white man, the white man may strike the black dead. We are not only an enslaved, but we are a slandered people. . . . Yes, I am a fugitive. I glory in the name.[44]

Douglass had succeeded in reading himself back into the body politic, using his body as a means of establishing his possible biological connection to Rynders as brother, to Rynders' Virginian slaveowning father, and, using Rynders' own logic, to the patrimony of the Constitution, the Union, and the South—of "Washington or Patrick Henry"—that Bennett and Rynders had invoked. He displayed his superior knowledge of law; he also demonstrated that what Rynders understood as the rule of law, reason, and political virtue was, in the context of southern slavery, nothing more than the rule of men in its most corrupt form—that is to say, white masculine sexual passion run amuck.

In Douglass's scheme, black womanhood supplanted the discredited white paterfamilias and his laws as a standard of virtue. Douglass, as the guardian of black true womanhood in the debate with Rynders, became a model of the patriarch who could protect his dependents.

But all of these moves, inventive as they were, in a sense accepted the terms of the confrontation as Grant and Rynders had set them: Douglass was put in the position of saying "me, too": I am not an animal, I, too, am a man, a member of the American political family, a son of the Founders, a paterfamilias, and, by extension, a person of intellect and reason. But after rebutting Grant by detailing the persistence of blacks and mulattos in the American population, and noting the contributions of blacks to American wars and industry, Douglass presented his most imaginative stroke:

I don't care if I am a monkey; I have eyes; therefore God has given me to see. I have a head to think therefore I have a right to think as long as I have a language to speak and a heart to feel; and as long as God enables me, I will exercise my thoughts, my tongue, and all my powers, on behalf of freedom and justice for every man. (Cheers.)"[45]

A seeing, thinking, feeling monkey has more insight into what being an American is than you do, Douglass was saying and, in effect, had proven to Rynders. Now, in this ironic way, Douglass set forth the character of the "bodily Douglass" and invited his audience to peer behind it to see the Douglass of carefully constructed logic and practical common sense. Put otherwise, he transformed the defective body and toxic identity served up to him into a framing device for generating good growth for self and community. He did not name the Declaration in his final pledge of allegiance to freedom and equality, but he might as well have. Douglass and others were assailed, observed the poet-abolitionist John Greenleaf Whittier, because they were "practical believers in the doctrine of the Declaration of Independence."[46] Douglass was, in short, an innovator of an antislavery body politic that featured new forms of attachment, of self, and of nationality.

Rynders was no less innovative, and it is useful to set his performance and outlook alongside other efforts to define a proslavery body politic, looking backward to the furor over Lovejoy in 1837–38 and forward to southern secession in 1860–61. At a meeting at Boston's Faneuil Hall, the commonwealth's attorney general, James Trecothick Austin, sought to justify the actions of the antiabolitionist mob that had killed Lovejoy and destroyed his printing presses, but in so doing, he offered a conception of law, political community, and self that went a considerable way toward explaining the rationales of Bennett and Rynders in 1850 and of southern secessionists in 1860–61.

Are you not aware, Austin asked his audience in December 1837, that there were times when your fathers "found it inevitable that they should take the law into their own hands,—extreme cases, in which indeed there was no law reaching to their condition but the original and immutable law of self-preservation, and necessary self-defense?"

> Satisfy a people that their lives are in danger, by the instrumentality of the press, injudiciously and intemperately operating on the minds of slaves; give them reason to fear the breaking out of a servile war, in which their wives and daughters are to be the victims of that brutal ferocity that knows how to aid horrors to death, and if you can keep such a people calm, and tranquil, and quiet, obedient to the restraints of any law that can be made, or to any power that can enforce it, you must first beat out of them every vestige of humanity, and make them more abject than slavery itself.[47]

For Austin, the "self" that was being preserved in these moments of release of male passion was that of the white paterfamilias protecting patriarchal prerogatives over household dependents. But such passionate masculine "self-preservation" could also yield a kind of community. Amid mounting insurrection against federal legal authority and the euphoria of national independence, the soon-to-be-inaugurated president of the Confederacy, Jefferson Davis, proclaimed to a Montgomery, Alabama, crowd in February 1861, "Now we are brethren not in name merely, but in fact—men of one flesh, one bone, one interest, one purpose and of identity of domestic institutions."[48] This rhetorical baptism of the new slave republic was a rite of purification: it hoped to accomplish what Rynders' mob had sought at the Broadway Tabernacle, the perfect realization of a deathless body politic of white brethren and the erasure of white women and enslaved blacks from public life.[49]

The ideological work needed to create that moment at Montgomery had gone on in the preceding months. John Townsend, a South Carolina slaveowner and president of the "Edisto Island Vigilant Association," made the case for the "doom of slavery in the Union [and] its safety out of it" in an address delivered on the eve of Lincoln's election and published in pamphlet form. The most revealing part of this crisis-time literary production was the appendix on the Texas slave insurrection scare of summer 1860. A letter from a white Texan reprinted by Townsend sounded the ultimate alarm for white southerners:

"Our houses, &c., were not only to be burned and our citizens murdered, but the young women and little girls were to be saved to become the wives or concubines of these fiends of hell."[50] The arid arguments of John C. Calhoun, arraigning northern antislavery forces as violators of law and southern interest, certainly took the southern republic-in-the-making a considerable way toward independence. But it required special challenges to patriarchal rule to move white southerners of all social stripes to participate in a gigantic civil insurrection and bind themselves to a new nation. Austin had suggested a solution to the problem of political attachment, and Davis brought it to fruition. It was nonetheless the peculiar gift of polemicists such as Townsend to understand the sort of hysteria that could bind "white brethren" together.

MARTYRDOM

A willingness to rely on white patriarchal prerogative to resolve national crisis formed the core of Stephen A. Douglas's defense of the Kansas-Nebraska Act in winter and spring 1854; Lincoln's broadside against Douglas's views, presented at Peoria in that fall, attacked Douglas on just that particular. Lincoln's increasing resort to intimations of his own sacrificial death was part of an effort to use the Declaration of Independence to dismantle Douglas's patriarchal perspective and, at the same time, to address the problem of political attachment. The challenge was to champion the principles of the Declaration without inviting the release of passions that would destroy law and Union. Douglas would repeatedly argue that to invoke the Declaration was to invite black men to consort with white daughters and undermine the authority of the white head of household.[51] That authority was, for Douglas, the basis for the racial and patriarchal solidarity that was the key to political attachment and the survival of the nation. Lincoln's solution was not to reject personal power outright as a source of political attachment, but to give the Declaration a specific human face—his own.

The rhetorical problem was how to inspire Americans to love the Declaration and its universal truths, which had been effectively attacked as abstractions and generalities or dismissed as a "self-evident lie"?[52] And how to do this without displacing the primacy of the Constitution and the Fathers' Republic? The idea of martyrdom had a kind of secret life in the rhetoric of politicians of the Whig stripe in the period before the mid-1850s. It appeared *sotto voce*, as subtext, in Henry Clay's "Five Wounds" speech: the "Five Wounds" were the stigmata of Christ on the cross, and throbbing beneath the persona of doctor Clay is that of the self-sacrificing, Christ-like Clay who routinely commented that he would not outlive the Union.[53] The image of the martyr could also erupt, almost unbidden, in the unlikely context of the end of a dry Lincoln address on the subtreasury, delivered in Springfield almost two years after the Lyceum appearance. If the country lost its liberty, succumbing to President Martin Van Buren's "evil spirit," "a great volcano . . . belching forth the lava of political corruption," Lincoln would still be able to proclaim "not that I was the *last* to desert, but that I *never* deserted her."[54] The implication in both instances was that the speaker would suffer and sooner die than allow the enemies of liberty to overthrow law. A way to fuse law and liberty was suggested, though the cause of liberty was not directly tied to the Declaration of Independence.[55] A charismatic, bodily appeal was introduced, albeit slyly, into otherwise rational address.

In Lincoln's rhetoric, the 1854 Kansas-Nebraska crisis and the Peoria speech represented a turning point. Now intimations of martyrdom were linked directly to the Declaration. Law, reason, and deliberative talk remained Lincoln's controlling themes. But if the principles of the Declaration could not be carried through such means, he clearly authorized a cleansing of the body politic through bloody self-sacrifice: "Our republican robe is soiled, and trailed in the dust. Let us repurify it. Let us turn and wash it white, in the spirit, *if not the blood*, of the Revolution. Let us turn slavery from its claims of 'moral right,' back upon its existing legal rights, and its arguments of 'necessity.' Let us return it to the position our fathers gave it; and there let it rest in peace. Let us re-adopt the Declaration of Independence, and with it, the practices, and policy, which harmonize with it."[56]

Four years later, in the famous debate with Stephen A. Douglas, Lincoln spoke of the possibility of his own martyrdom even more vividly as he urged listeners skeptical of the Declaration to "return to the fountain whose waters spring close by the blood of the Revolution": "You may do anything with me you choose, if you will but heed these sacred principles. You may not only defeat me for the Senate, but you may take me and put me to death."[57] At Cooper Union in February, 1860, presidential candidate Lincoln's closing words, "LET US HAVE FAITH THAT RIGHT MAKES MIGHT, AND IN THAT FAITH, LET US, TO THE END, DARE TO DO OUR DUTY AS WE UNDERSTAND IT" were likely understood by his audience in the context of blood sacrifice for the principles of the Declaration.[58] Indeed, in the months after John Brown's raid on Harpers Ferry, with politicians toting weapons on the floor of the United States Congress, thoughts of physical danger were widely shared among antislavery activists. President-elect Lincoln, standing in Independence Hall, the Founders' temple of liberty, on Washington's Birthday, 1861, and aware of an actual plot against his life, said "If this country cannot be saved without giving up that principle [of freedom and equality in the Declaration], I was about to say I would rather be assassinated on this spot than to surrender it."[59]

The publication of Harriet Beecher Stowe's *Uncle Tom's Cabin* in 1852 was an important watershed in the shift from Henry Clay's implicit references to Christ's Five Wounds to Lincoln's and other northerners' willingness to offer up their own bodies as a sacrifice to preserve constitutional union in the name of liberty and equality. In Anglo-American political culture, appropriating the actual body of Christ was not something that everyone could do. Invoking or identifying with Christ the King was different from actually becoming Christ, this last something jealously guarded against by the churches.[60] Stowe's Uncle Tom was not just Christ-like: Tom was imagined as a nineteenth-century Christ, as James M. McPherson has observed, his death "parallel" to Christ's crucifixion.[61] The character of Tom was an effort to embody the real divine presence and create a mystical body the martyrdom of which could transcend or transform law (both the Constitution of reason and the Fugitive Slave Act of 1850) and regenerate the nation.[62] Uncle Tom's martyrdom had accomplished what Elijah Lovejoy's only intimated, the creation of a broad community of committed and self-sacrificing antislavery women and men.[63] Christian self-sacrifice, long a dominant theme in women's reform, was now enshrined as a potent element in northern political culture, despite efforts of Douglas and others to dislodge it.[64]

The mid-nineteenth-century conversation about the body politic accordingly revealed shared premises and some crucial points of difference. By the 1850s there was tremendous anxiety, north and south, about issues Lincoln had raised in his Lyceum Address: could passionate Americans find a place for themselves in the republic of reason formed by the Constitution? Would they fail in their historic task of perpetuating American political institutions? Could they negotiate the different emphases of the Declaration of Independence and the Constitution? And what would be the fate of insurgencies driven by alternative conceptions of attachment, nationality, and self? The rhetorical device of the body politic had offered mid-nineteenth-century Americans imaginative means to address these issues, if not necessarily to resolve them. Constitutional and political contract among consenting individuals and separation of powers remained the dominant paradigm of political culture, but the body politic offered a way to personalize power and collapse these separations in order to imagine a political community that could survive and grow, command the allegiance, even love, of the people, and transform law and the self. Indeed, the greatest attraction of the body politic for individual Americans was its promise of immortality.⁶⁵ A deathless political community and the immortality it made possible offered a way to both compensate for and redress the stymied and incomplete sense of political selfhood that Lincoln reported in the Lyceum speech.

But by 1860–61, southerners and northerners were defining the body politic very differently. The fiction of the king's two bodies traced its lineage back to Christ's two bodies, but the two fictions, the king's and Christ's, were fundamentally different. The king, as the historian Michael Paul Rogin observed, "augmented his human body with a royal body; he aggrandized his mortal person with the immortal body politic." Christ's kingship instead "served transcendent vision, not personal identity. The proof lay in his sacrifice."⁶⁶

Rynders, Austin, Townsend, and Davis, to be sure, understood white southern men's acts of defending home, property, and dependents as acts of bodily sacrifice. But the slave republic of white brethren that Davis called into being and celebrated in February 1861 calls to mind a kingly taking, not a giving. Each white paterfamilias projected his control of household dependents out into the body politic. The promise of individual immortality in the southern body politic came from the social and political permanence that whiteness promised: the threat posed by the great southern bugbear of miscegenation must be understood in this context. The Confederate republic was created by acts of aggrandizement—a ruthless purging of abolitionists, northerners, outsiders of all kinds, from the South, especially in the wake of John Brown's raid, as well as the imposing of drastic limits on the rights of free blacks.⁶⁷ In a sense, the white southerners' rhetoric of invasion—the threat of Yankee and antislavery Goths and vandals sweeping down on their homesteads—was disingenuous.⁶⁸ Threatened, in fact, was not only white male control of homesteads but also the control of public life, national destiny, and memory based on such domestic control. White southern men were quick to accuse their enemies of rape: indeed, by the eve of the war, they could not conceive of power without rape. So thoroughly intertwined was rape with their own social practice and sense of self, they could hardly imagine another group or nation possessing power without exercising it in that way.

Lincoln's version of the body politic represented a giving, not a taking. One put oneself in a position of mortal risk to defend law and liberty against demonic evil and facilitate the rise of the sacred national community. As Lincoln put it in 1854, "If we do this, we shall not only have saved the Union; but we shall have so saved it, as to make, and to keep it, forever worthy of the saving. We shall have so saved it, that the succeeding millions of free happy people, the world over, shall rise up, and call us blessed, to the latest generations."[69] But one could only claim the immortal status of martyr through a sacrificial death. Only through such a death had Christ given "birth to the community and was [he] taken back into it."[70] The heroic possibilities of the act were available to the social and political outcast. "I am nothing," said Lincoln in 1858. "*But do not destroy that immortal emblem of Humanity—the Declaration of American Independence.*"[71] Annihilation of the self, the deepest fear of the 1850s, was actually a precondition for this martyrdom; the sufferer needed to *embrace* such annihilation, as martyrdom could not be seized in an act of personal aggrandizement. It could only be granted by the sacred community after a heroic death. Here, then, was a form of citizenship open to African Americans, women, and other stigmatized or indelibly wounded individuals, those whose "defective" bodies disqualified them from citizenship in the republic of reason. Moreover, martyrdom had a charismatic quality, a potential for inspiring love of nation, which Frederick Douglass's ironic reversals at the Broadway Tabernacle, for all of their inventive genius, did not. Lincoln's conception of martyrdom was, in short, full of democratic and nation-building possibility. And Lincoln, we know, would give the last full measure of devotion to a nation dedicated to law, liberty, and equality.

Martyrdom did become a major theme of Confederate national culture. In May 1861, James Jackson was killed defending the Confederate "Stars and Bars" against the Union colonel Elmer Ellsworth's efforts to tear it down and haul it away. (Jackson had the temerity to hoist from the roof of his Alexandria, Virginia, inn a flag so large that it could be seen from the White House; he killed Ellsworth before he was himself fatally shot.) Jackson was hailed from Richmond to New Orleans as "The First Martyr in the Cause of Southern Independence."[72] It is worth underscoring that, in spring 1861, southerners could not point to a long martyrology in the way that antislavery northerners could—Elijah Lovejoy, Charles Sumner (who survived the brutal attack of South Carolina Representative Preston Brooks on the floor of the U.S. Senate in 1856 but whose near-martyrdom was hailed throughout the North), and, of course, John Brown.[73] Antebellum white southerners nonetheless celebrated powerful examples of heroic sacrifice—the shedding of southern patriots' blood in the American Revolution, the deaths of southern soldiers in the Mexican War, which many believed demanded a compensatory recognition of the right to slave property in the territories acquired by that sacrifice.[74]

But, at a deeper level, white southerners were both wary of martyrs and, at the same time, fascinated by them.[75] It seems significant in this context that

James Jackson advertised his southern loyalties in the months before the war by exhibiting "Black Republican Trophies" that included a pike that John Brown had purportedly wielded at Harpers Ferry and even a "piece of flesh" he claimed was "a part of the ear of John Brown, Jr."—he boasted of "lively conversations with 'old Brown' after his capture."[76] Jackson's preoccupation with John Brown calls to mind that of Lincoln's assassin John Wilkes Booth, who loathed Brown's vision of racial equality at the same time that he admired his courage and conviction and envied the surpassing power of his martyrdom.[77] The martyr's blood baptized a body politic predicated on an unflinching embrace of the status of outsider and a thoroughgoing transformation of nation and self. So profound a transformation could be abided by neither Jefferson Davis nor the Confederate brethren he rallied in February 1861, for whom the prerogatives of mastery trumped transcendent vision. In this sense, Davis's call to "baptize in blood the principles for which our fathers bled in the Revolution" invoked a rebirth that was not a rebirth, in the same way that the creation of the Confederacy was a revolution that was not a revolution.[78]

In the end, the pre-war conversation about the body politic, in both its northern and southern variants, represented a move toward a shift in consciousness, and not its full realization. The metaphorical efforts to merge individual and nation during the 1850s were attempts to personalize polity and society, to create a nation by synecdoche, to leap across the chasm separating the individual from the nation and somehow incorporate the latter in the former. In the most excruciating of ironies, the intimate and enduring attachment to other human beings that those who used the metaphor so deeply craved could only be accomplished by the war's vast sacrificial slaughter of human beings.

NOTES

I thank the participants at the Conference on "Race, Freedom, and Bondage," Yale University; the Graduate History Workshop at Rutgers University; the Politics, Ethics and Society Workshop at Washington University; and Ira Berlin, Howard Brick, Catherine Clinton, David Brion Davis, Wayne Fields, Eric Foner, William Forbath, Robert Forbes, Margaret Garb, Paula Kane, David Konig, Jan Lewis, James Livingston, Larry May, Steven Mintz, Linda Nicholson, Peter Onuf, and John Stauffer for their insights and suggestions.

1 *Congressional Globe*, 31st Congress, 1st sess., Appendix Pt. I, 615 (May 21, 1850).
2 Ibid.
3 Ibid., 676–77 (June 10, 1850).

4 New York Herald, April 19, 1850.
5 Samuel A. Cartwright, "How to Save the Republic, and the Position of the South in the Union," De Bow's Review, 11 (August 1851), 188.
6 Martin Robison Delany, The Condition, Elevation, Emigration, and Destiny of the Colored People of the United States, Politically Considered (Philadelphia: The Author, 1852), 14.
7 New York Daily Tribune, January 5, 1858.
8 David M. Potter, "The Civil War in the History of the Modern World: A Comparative View," in The South and the Sectional Conflict (Baton Rouge: Louisiana State University Press, 1968), 296–97.
9 See Edward Coke, Calvin's Case (7 Co. Rep. 18, 1608) quoted in David T. Konig, "Legal Fictions and the Rule(s) of Law: The Jeffersonian Critique of Common-Law Adjudication," in The Many Legalities of Early America, ed. Christopher L. Tomlins and Bruce H. Mann (Chapel Hill: University of North Carolina Press, 2001), 100. The starting point for all discussion of the body politic is Ernst H. Kantorowicz, The King's Two Bodies. A Study in Mediaeval Political Theology (Princeton: Princeton University Press, 1957).
10 Edmund S. Morgan, Inventing the People: The Rise of Popular Sovereignty in England and America (New York: Norton, 1988), 82–83.
11 Thomas Paine, Common Sense (1776; reprint, London: Pelican, 1976), 98.
12 Michael Paul Rogin, "The King's Two Bodies: Lincoln, Wilson, Nixon, and Presidential Self-Sacrifice," in Ronald Reagan The Movie and Other Episodes in Political Demonology (Berkeley: University of California Press, 1987), 81.
13 A good source regarding Francis Lieber's influence and range of political associates is Frank Freidel, Francis Lieber: Nineteenth-Century Liberal (Baton Route: State University of Louisiana Press, 1947), esp. 165, 225, and 251–52.
14 For a survey of the thought of the antebellum political economists, see Joseph Dorfman, The Economic Mind in American Civilization (New York: Viking, 1946), vols. 1 and 2; Paul K. Conkin, Prophets of Prosperity: America's First Political Economists (Bloomington: Indiana University Press, 1980), and for its treatment of Henry C. Carey and Friedrich List, Bernard Semmel, The Liberal Ideal and the Demons of Empire: Theories of Imperialism from Adam Smith to Lenin (Baltimore: Johns Hopkins University Press, 1993); for biographical treatments, see Freidel, Francis Lieber, John Brett Langstaff, The Enterprising Life: John McVickar, 1787–1868 (New York: St. Martin's, 1961), and esp. Dumas Malone, The Public Life of Thomas Cooper, 1783–1839 (New Haven: Yale University Press, 1926); for key works in the articulation of the antebellum free trade outlook, Thomas Cooper, Lectures on the Elements of Political Economy (Columbia, S.C.: printed by D. E. Sweeny, 1926); Henry C. Carey, Essay on the Rate of Wages (Philadelphia: Carey, Lea, 1835), The Harmony of Nature, as Exhibited in the Laws Which Regulate the Increase of Population and the Means of Subsistence . . . (Philadelphia: Carey, Lea, 1836); Principles of Political Economy (Philadelphia: Carey, Lea, 1837–1840), and, after his

conversion to protection, *The Past, The Present, and The Future* (Philadelphia: Carey & Hart, 1848), and *The Slave Trade, Domestic and Foreign: Why It Exists, and How It May Be Extinguished* (Philadelphia: A. Hart, 1853); Francis Wayland, *The Elements of Political Economy* (New York: Leavitt, Lord, 1837); Francis Lieber, *Manual of Political Ethics*, 2 vols. (Boston: Little, Brown, 1838–1839), *Essays on Property and Labour as Connected with Natural Law and the Constitution of Society* (New York: Harper & Bros., 1841), and 'Free Trade and Other Things. A Philosophical Tutti Frutti," *De Bow's Review*, XV (1853), 53–65; John Adams Dix, "The Rise, Nature and Objects of the Science of Political Economy," *Northern Light* (April 1841).

15 Malone, *Public Life of Thomas Cooper*, 307–36.

16 Harriet Martineau, "The Brewing of the American Storm," *Macmillan's Magazine* 6 (June 1862): 97–107, and esp. 101.

17 Thomas Jefferson to Joseph Priestley, June 19, 1802, quoted in Robert W. Tucker and David C. Hendrickson, *Empire of Liberty: The Statecraft of Thomas Jefferson* (New York: Oxford University Press, 1990), 11.

18 Francis Lieber, *Some Truths Worth Remembering, Given, as a Recapitulation, in a Farewell Lecture to the Class of Political Economy of 1849* ("Published by the Class" [1849?]), Francis Lieber Papers, Huntington Library, San Marino, Calif.; Lieber, 'Free Trade and Other Things," 54.

19 See Peter Onuf and Nicholas Onuf, *Federal Union, Modern World: The Law of Nations in an Age of Revolutions, 1776–1814* (Madison: Madison House, 1993), on the cosmopolitan vision of world peace at the center of Jeffersonian understandings of international law and political economy; for a reference to the plan of peace of Henry IV of France in the context of 1840s free trade liberalism, see James Buchanan, "Speech of Mr. Buchanan, of Pennsylvania, in Senate, June 8, 1844 . . . in favor of the treaty for the annexation," *Cong. Globe*, 28th Cong., 1st sess., Appendix, 721.

20 On the South Carolinian perspective on British emancipation of slavery in the West Indies, see Joe Bassette Wilkins Jr., "Window on Freedom: The South's Response to the Emancipation of the Slaves in the British West Indies, 1833–1861" (Ph.D. diss., University of South Carolina, 1977); David Brion Davis, *Challenging the Boundaries of Slavery* (Cambridge: Harvard University Press, 2003), 79–89; for the perspective of antebellum political economists on British emancipation, see esp. Henry C. Carey, *The Slave Trade*.

21 Adam Smith, *The Theory of Moral Sentiments* (Amherst, N.Y.: Prometheus Books, 2000), 23; also, Sheldon S. Wolin, *Politics and Vision: Continuity and Innovation in Western Political Thought* (Boston: Little, Brown, 1960), 350.

22 "Jonathan Bull and Mary Bull," in James Madison, *Letters and Other Writings of James Madison, Fourth President of the United States* (Philadelphia: J. B. Lippincott, 1865), 3:249–56.

23 Roy Basler, ed., *The Collected Works of Abraham Lincoln* (New Brunswick: Rutgers University Press, 1953–55), 1:112.

24 Ibid., 115.
25 Ibid.
26 See the reference, in passing, to the "vicious portion of population" that "gather in bands" to "throw printing presses into rivers, shoot editors," ibid., 111.
27 The American Anti-Slavery Society formally adopted Lovejoy as a martyr. Merton Dillon, *Elijah P. Lovejoy, Abolitionist Editor* (Urbana: University of Illinois Press, 1964) 177. See, too, the account of the "large and respectable meeting of the citizens of color" in New York City to protest the Lovejoy murder ("the blood of the marutred Lovejoy calls upon us, an oppressed people, to become more united in sentiment and effort"), reported in *The Liberator*, December 29, 1837. At the end of a memorial service for Lovejoy, John Brown stood up and swore that from that moment he would "consecrate" his life to "the destruction of slavery." John Stauffer, *The Black Hearts of Men: Radical Abolitionists and the Transformation of Race* (Cambridge: Harvard University Press, 2002), 118–19.
28 *Liberator*, December 29, 1837.
29 Phillips quoted in Dillon, *Elijah P. Lovejoy*, 178. An abolitionist plan to transport Lovejoy's body from Alton to Maine for burial, in a kind of 1,800-mile funeral, was scotched—a fascinating anticipation of the martyred Lincoln's funeral train from Washington to Springfield. Ibid., 177–78.
30 The issue of the conflict of law and liberty in American political culture was also posed incisively by the American Freedmen's Inquiry Commission during the Civil War, in an effort to explain why the United States, at the vanguard "with the foremost and freest nations in asserting the principles of liberty and human rights," lagged behind Europe "on the subject of negro emancipation": "The chief reason is, that a regard for law conflicted with a regard for liberty." "Final Report of the American Freedmen's Inquiry Commission," *War of the Rebellion*, III–IV, 360.
31 The phrases "decisive moment" of change and "demonic power" are Paul Tillich's. I rely heavily on David Brion Davis's discussion of the Tillich's concept of *kairos* as a window onto how British antislavery victories were conceived as "eschatological leap[s]." David Brion Davis, *Slavery and Human Progress* (New York: Oxford University Press, 1984), 128–29.
32 Basler, ed., *Collected Works of Abraham Lincoln*, 1:109.
33 Of course, it was the contention of many of slavery's defenders—fiercely contested by northern antislavery critics—that the slaveowning family did protect slaves as cared-for "dependents" and not degrade and exploit them as chattel property.
34 "James Madison to Henry Clay, Montpelier, Va., April 2, 1833," in *The Papers of Henry Clay*, ed. Robert Seager II, et al. (Lexington: University Press of Kentucky), 8:635.
35 *Cong. Globe*, 35th Cong., 1st sess. (1857–58), 293–94. "Remarks of Jefferson Davis in reference to the Kansas Message, Feb. 8, 1858," in *Jefferson Davis Constitutionalist: His Letters, Papers, and Speeches*, ed. Dunbar Rowland (1923; reprint, AMS Press, 1973) 3:173–74.

36 *Cong. Globe*, 33rd Cong., 1st sess., 619.
37 Basler, ed., *Collected Works*, 2:274.
38 See, for example, the reference to "a wen or cancer upon your person" in Lincoln's speech at Alton during the Lincoln Douglas debates of 1858. Basler, ed., *Collected Works*, 3:313. He also used the image of a tumor at the Soldier's Home, in Washington, D.C., in 1862. It came up in the context of remarks about slavery as something that had grown up inside and now permeated the Union, north and south. See Don E. Fehrenbacher and Virginia Fehrenbacher, eds., *Recollected Words of Abraham Lincoln* (Stanford: Stanford University Press, 1996), 367–68. Lincoln's words were recalled years later by Elbert S. Porter, clergyman and editor of a religious newspaper.
39 See especially the discussion of changing conceptions of disease (and the timing of those changes) in Charles E. Rosenberg, *The Cholera Years: The United States in 1832, 1849, and 1866* (Chicago: University of Chicago Press, 1962).

For an extended analysis of Lincoln's use of the cancer metaphor and the place of cancer within mid-nineteenth-century understandings of disease, see Iver Bernstein, "Abraham Lincoln's Body and Body Politic: Two Puzzles in Mid-Nineteenth-Century American Political Language and Culture," in *The Lincoln Forum: Rediscovering Abraham Lincoln*, ed. John Y. Simon and Harold Holzer (New York: Fordham University Press, 2002), 135–59.
40 *The New-Englander*, reprinted in *National Anti-Slavery Standard*, May 30, 1850.
41 *Philadelphia Public Ledger*, May 8, 1850.
42 *New York Herald*, May 8, 1850.
43 *New York Sunday Era*, as reprinted in *The Liberator*, May 31, 1850.
44 *New York Herald*, May 8, 1850.
45 Ibid.
46 Letter from John G. Whittier to William Lloyd Garrison, Amesbury, May 13, 1850, reprinted in *The Liberator*, May 17, 1850.
47 "Speech of Mr. Austin," in *The Liberator*, December 15, 1837.
48 Lynda Lasswell Crist and Mary Seaton Dix, eds., *The Papers of Jefferson Davis* (Baton Rouge: Louisiana State University Press, 1992), 7:46.
49 See the discussion in Stephanie McCurry, " 'The Soldier's Wife': White Women, the State, and the Politics of Protection in the Confederacy," in *Women and the Unstable State in Nineteenth Century America*, ed. Alison M. Parker and Stephanie Cole (College Station: Texas A&M University Press, 2000), 15.
50 See appendix on "The Abolition Plot in Texas," in [John Townsend], *The Doom of Slavery in the Union: Its Safety Out of It* (Charleston, S.C.: printed by Evans & Cogswell, 1860), 36.
51 See, for example, Basler, ed., *Collected Works*, 3:56.
52 John Pettit had advanced the argument that the Declaration's statement that "all men are created equal" was a "self-evident lie," contradicting what Americans knew about their society from social observation, common sense, at the Indiana Constitutional Convention in late 1850. But it was his repetition of that phrase and viewpoint

in the U.S. Senate debate over Kansas-Nebraska in 1854 that drew the national attention and the ire of antislavery figures such as Lincoln and Frederick Douglass. *Cong. Globe*, 33rd Cong., 1st sess., Appendix, 214 (John Pettit, Speech on "Nebraska and Kansas," February 20, 1854).

53 The political symbolism of the "Five Wounds" in European political culture dated back to early modern times. Peasant rebels in Germany (1524–25) and in England (1536) took up the "Banner of the Five Wounds."

54 Basler, ed., *Collected Works*, 1:178.

55 See George B. Forgie, *Patricide in the House Divided: A Psychological Interpretation of Lincoln and His Age* (New York: Norton, 1979), 83–87.

56 Basler, ed., *Collected Works*, 2:276. Italics added.

57 Ibid., 2:547.

58 Ibid. 3:550. Italics added.

59 Ibid, 4:240.

60 Paul Kleber Monod, *The Power of Kings: Monarchy and Religion in Europe, 1589–1715* (New Haven: Yale University Press, 1999), 145–46.

61 James M. McPherson, "Tom on the Cross," in *Drawn With The Sword: Reflections on the American Civil War* (New York: Oxford University Press, 1996), 35.

62 On Tom's embodiment of the real presence, and Stowe's "gesture of respect," through Tom, toward the Catholic Virgin, see Andrew Delbanco, *The Puritan Ordeal* (Cambridge: Harvard University Press, 1989), 237. Joan Hedrick calls *Uncle Tom's Cabin* the "Protestant equivalent of a Roman Catholic mass, a dramatic re-enactment of the Crucifixion. Tom's body, given for others, was to be the bread and wine of a social revolution that would bring the kingdom of heaven." Joan Hedrick, *Harriet Beecher Stowe* (New York: Oxford University Press, 1995), 215.

63 The anti–Kansas-Nebraska petition of over three thousand Protestant clergy from New England that was delivered to the Senate in March, 1854, was both organized by Harriet Beecher Stowe and inspired by her. Albert J. Von Frank, *The Trials of Anthony Burns: Freedom and Slavery in Emerson's Boston* (Cambridge: Harvard University Press, 1999), 14–15.

64 Harriet Beecher Stowe's sister Catherine Beecher, of course, played a crucial role in conceiving of Christian sacrifice as strategy for women's self-development and the perpetuation of American political institutions. See especially, Catherine E. Beecher, *Treatise on Domestic Economy for the Use of Young Ladies at Home and at School* (Boston: Marsh, Capen, 1843) and *The Duty of American Women to Their Country* (New York: Harper & Bros., 1845).

65 See Paul W. Kahn, *Legitimacy and History: Self-Government in American Constitutional Theory* (New Haven: Yale University Press, 1993) and Robert Bruce, "The Riddle of Death," in *The Lincoln Enigma* (New York: Oxford University Press, 2001), 130–45.

66 Michael Paul Rogin, "The King's Two Bodies," 85.

67 For an example of the purging of outsiders after John Brown's raid on Harper's Ferry, see William W. Freehling's account of the tarring and feathering of Irish

stonecutter James Powers in Columbia, South Carolina, in *The Road to Disunion: Secessionists at Bay, 1776–1854* (New York: Oxford University Press, 1990), 100–101; on southern mob attacks on northern teachers, church members, and others, after the Brown raid, see McPherson, *Battle Cry of Freedom*, 212–13. The movements to reopen the African slave trade and enslave domestic free blacks in the late antebellum South were important parts of this process.

68 James M. McPherson, *What They Fought For: 1861–1865* (Baton Rouge: State University of Louisiana Press, 1994), 19–21; McCurry, "'A Soldier's Wife," 17–20.

69 Basler, ed., *Collected Works*, 2:276.

70 Rogin, "The King's Two Bodies," 84.

71 Basler, ed., *Collected Works*, 2:547.

72 *Life of James W. Jackson, The Alexandria Hero, the Slayer of Ellsworth; the First Martyr in the Cause of Southern Independence* (Richmond: n.p., 1862); *Savannah Daily Morning News*, May 28, 1861; "Jackson Our First Martyr," in *Southern Field & Fireside* 3 (June 1, 1861), 1; "To the Memory of the Lamented Jackson," *Richmond Enquirer*, June 13, 1861; *New Orleans Daily Picayune*, June 6, 1861. Also, Robert E. Bonner, *Colors and Blood: Flag Passions of The Confederate South* (Princeton: Princeton University Press, 2002), 68–75. Ellsworth, for his part, became a Union martyr.

73 Harriet Martineau, *The Martyr Age of the United States* (Boston: Weeks, Jordan, 1839); also, see the incoming correspondence for late May and June 1856 in The Papers of Charles Sumner, Houghton Library, Harvard University. See S. D. Porter to Charles Sumner, Rochester, N.Y., May 24, 1856, for one of many invocations of Tertullian's assertion that "the blood of the martyr is the seed of the church" after the beating of Sumner. Blake Leyerle, "Blood is Seed," *Journal of Religion* 81 (2001): 26–48, discusses the rich significance of Tertullian's remark in its early Christian context. Sumner's near-martyrdom was understood by some commentators as the direct result of Sumner's naming of the Southern practice of rape (the "rape of a virgin territory") in the "Crime Against Kansas" speech.

74 See, especially, Iveson L. Brookes, *A Defence of the South Against the Reproaches and Incroachments of the North: In Which Slavery is Shown to be an Institution of God Intended to Form the Basis of the Best Social State and the Only Safeguard to the Permanence of a Republican Government* (Hamburg, S.C., 1850), 10.

75 One of many instances in the 1850s of Southern suspicion of martyrdom was the case of Anderson Jennings, a Kentucky slaveowner whose fugitive-hunting efforts in Ohio gained him notoriety in the Oberlin-Wellington Rescue and ensuing trials of 1858–59. Jennings was arrested on kidnapping charges and spent over a week in a Lorain, Ohio, county jail. He then returned to Kentucky and attempted to parlay the publicity into a run for the Kentucky Legislature. His candidacy went nowhere. One newspaper emphasized that Jennings's proslavery credentials were no better than any of the other candidates and "we shall suggest to the other candidates that to get even with Mr. Jennings they ought to start out after some runaway and get them-

selves made Martyrs of." Nat Brandt, *The Town That Started the Civil War* (Syracuse: Syracuse University Press, 1990), 223.

76 James Jackson quoted in W. Burns Jones Jr., "The Marshall House Incident, *Northern Virginia Heritage* 10 (February 1988), 5.

77 See Booth's letter to the *National Intelligencer*, April 14, 1865, and the insightful analysis of it, in Zoe Trodd and John Stauffer, eds., *Meteor of War: The John Brown Story* (Maplecrest, N.Y.: Brandywine Press, 2004), 251–55.

78 Crist and Dix, eds., *Papers of Jefferson Davis*, 7:46.

SHARON HARTMAN STROM

Labor, Race, and Colonization
Imagining a Post-Slavery World in the Americas

The movement to colonize African Americans in Africa had considerable popular appeal in the United States. Most American statesmen who believed that slavery was a sin endorsed colonization as the solution to the national evil. Colonization, like political parties, appealed to different types of people. One category of colonizationists was whites who hated blacks and shuddered at the thought of living with them as citizens. But another category included whites and blacks who believed that American prejudice was so rampant and entrenched that blacks could find freedom and the possibility of equality only outside the national geography. In fact the most powerful opponents of colonization were proslavery advocates in the deep South. They viewed colonization as a "Trojan Horse designed to undermine and slowly destroy slavery," according to David Brion Davis, and they effectively "killed any prospects for the federal funding that would have been essential" for colonization to succeed. In some respects colonizationists were *more* realistic in their vision of emancipation than the immediate abolitionists, whose understanding of freedom depended upon their millennialist faith in a sharp break from linear chronology and in an impending new dispensation, or world without sin.[1]

During the Missouri crisis of 1819, James Madison wondered how "slavery as a national evil is to be abolished"? Colonization was his answer. Since slavery was a national sin, abolition should be a "national expense," he wrote. It was an affordable expense: "it is the peculiar fortune, or, rather a providential blessing of the U.S. to possess a resource commensurate to this great object, without taxes on the people, or even an increase of the public debt." Madison was referring to the huge supply of public lands. He accurately estimated the number of slaves in the United States to be about 1.5 million, with an average market price of about $400 per slave, amounting to a total redemption cost of $600 million.

Such an expenditure could be paid for by selling 200 million acres of public land at $3 per acre; or 300 million acres at $2 per acre—"a quantity which, tho' great in itself, is perhaps not a third part of the disposable territory belonging to the U.S. . . . And to what object so good so great & so glorious, could that peculiar fund of wealth be appropriated?" Madison further estimated that the sale of public land would keep pace with slave redemptions, which "must be gradual." Before the Civil War, immediate abolitionists could not begin to articulate with such empirical precision the costs of emancipation.[2]

Many northerners and possibly most Republicans in the 1850s and 1860s also viewed colonization as a "responsible solution" to the problem of slavery and the threat of amalgamation, as Sharon Hartman Strom argues. Much like James Madison, Republicans saw colonization as a practical program that fit within their broader agenda of national reform. Colonization could purify the nation by excluding blacks, preserve the ideal of free white labor, and accommodate imperial visions. It was no more grand than other national reform projects. After all, within fifteen years of the party's emergence, Republicans destroyed hundreds of millions of dollars of property, inaugurated a national income tax and conscription, displaced countless numbers of Indians, and helped establish the transcontinental railroad. As Strom notes, "centrist Republicans abandoned the idea of colonization reluctantly, if at all."

In the years between the Mexican-American War and end of the second Grant administration, when the formal (and informal) boundaries of the United States were in flux and slavery was abolished, the discussion of who should be a citizen in an as yet undefined geographical space constituted a national project. As public commentators looked southward to Mexico and beyond, their assessment of the virtue of acquiring new U.S. territory included the evaluation of "foreign" populations in relation to a national standard of "whiteness."[3] There were perplexing questions about how manifest destiny (or "manifest national piracy," in the words of Frederick Douglass) should proceed.[4] The language of this discourse referred to bodies, borders, ethnicities and the civic danger to the body politic posed by the imagined pollution of racial amalgamation.

At the same time, a competing but sometimes complementary discourse of economic imperialism envisioned the exploitation of labor and natural resources in ways that required capital and labor to flow freely, unconstrained by national or ethnographic boundaries. Benedict Anderson has described these constructions of the body politic as a transcendent nationalism that "thinks in terms of historical destines" or a racism that "dreams of eternal contaminations, transmitted . . . through an endless sequence of loathsome copulations."[5] The Missouri Representative Frank Blair summed up the critical question in 1859: what was to be the "destiny of the races of this continent" in a world without the ownership of African American men and women but open to the free-wheeling accumulation of other kinds of property?

In the first two years of the first Lincoln administration, leaders of the border states had extraordinary influence. Lincoln advocated policies designed to please border state free soilers, policies often drafted in collaboration with former Democrats Francis P. Blair and his sons, Montgomery and Frank. Lincoln believed that these policies were critical both to winning the Civil War and to his political survival. They consisted of (1) gradual emancipation (Lincoln suggested in his message to Congress of December 1862 that slavery could be gradually phased out as late as 1900), (2) compensation to loyal slaveholders, and (3) the migration of freed blacks to sites somewhere else in the Americas through a government-financed program of colonization.[6]

Republicans thought the emigration of free blacks from the United States to the Caribbean basin was not only a critical element in their chances for political success but a responsible solution to the perceived horrors of racial amalgamation. This was a political party that contemplated the dissolution of millions of dollars worth of property, and one that saw the federal government as an active force in Indian removal, banking and monetary policy, internal improvements, and foreign affairs. A grand government-endorsed plan for colonization did not seem so far-fetched. Centrist Republicans abandoned the idea of colonization reluctantly, if at all.[7]

Moreover, Civil War–era foreign policy, as it refined earlier notions of manifest destiny in the western hemisphere, incorporated colonization as a strategy of U.S. expansionism. Plans to open up, conquer, and profit from countries in the Caribbean basin thus became entwined with what Thomas Schoonover has described as "social *and* economic imperialism," that is, "a policy that aims to resolve internal social problems through the resort to external policy."[8] Colonization provided a rationale for an economically vibrant Americas, but one that defined ex-slaves as regimented workers without full rights and demonstrated the "crucial linkage between ideas and practices of citizenship, race, and labor" in "the evolution of a capitalist system and . . . liberal ideology."[9]

Colonization as national policy emerged from the antebellum free-soil politics of the border states. Free soilers believed that their region was the heart and soul of the country, an egalitarian frontier for (white) mechanics, farmers, and self-made men; a place where the ultimate destiny of slavery would be determined through economic development uncontaminated by plantation slavery.[10] Ports, canals, bridges, telegraphs, mail systems, homesteading, colleges, and railroads were all suitable government enterprises; they also required liquid capital, a flexible labor force, and an end to sectionalism. Lincoln described the development of east-to-west improvements in 1857 as "growing larger and larger, building up new countries with a rapidity never before seen in the history of the world." "Steam, telegraphs, and intelligence" were not just inventions of the modern age but a major ingredient in welding the "variety of climate and productions" of the United States into "the home of one national family." Frank Blair depicted the "magnificent national [rail]road" as a "great Aorta in our system, scattering the currents of life throughout the body."[11]

Where would be the boundaries of this national family, this body? During the Mexican-American War, with U.S. troops poised on the outskirts of Mexico City, cries of "All Mexico" resounded in the jingoist press. But Mexico differed from the borderlands north of the Rio Grande. It could not be considered, even by the United States, to be empty or without a history. Its large populations of Indios, Catholic Latinos, and *mestizos* might contaminate white Yankee "blood" and culture. Free soilers also feared that the slavocracy might triumph in an annexed Mexico and Cuba.[12]

No one was more important in creating and representing free-soil policies than the border-state Blairs, as well known a political dynasty in the United States as the Adams clan of Massachusetts.[13] A personal confidante of President Andrew Jackson, Francis P. Blair occupied a townhouse across the street from the White House and retreated in the summer to a splendid country "farm" staffed by slaves in Silver Spring, Maryland. He was the founder of the powerful Washington newspaper, the *Globe*, and, until 1841, had recorded the speeches and debates of Congress in the *Congressional Globe* under government contract. Blair's defection from the Democrats to the Republicans in 1856 was an important factor in securing the new party's legitimacy; he was chairman of the nominating convention in 1860 and helped make Lincoln president.

A lawyer of St. Louis who specialized in railroads and real estate, Montgomery Blair joined his father in 1853 in Washington, D.C., where he argued for the freedom of St. Louis plaintiffs Dred and Harriet Scott before the Supreme Court. The Court's rejection of the Scotts' claims and of Montgomery's arguments for their freedom in the territories became a major rallying point of free-soil rhetoric after 1857. Montgomery Blair became Lincoln's first postmaster general.[14]

Frank Blair was the family's aspirant for higher political office, and the young and dashing redhead seemed to be well on his way, perhaps even to the presidency, when he was elected to Congress from St. Louis as a free-soil Democrat in 1856. Frank gave widely distributed public addresses in which he formulated solutions to ending slavery that might prevent civil war. He advocated the removal of free blacks from the United States combined with gradual, compensated emancipation and also promoted a more aggressive foreign and economic policy throughout the Americas. Meanwhile Lincoln's arch rival, Democratic Stephen Douglas, found approval from many whites for his assertion that free blacks were not even citizens let alone future voters. Those who suggested otherwise were portrayed as political subversives of the white republic.[15]

Lincoln and other moderates were vulnerable to such attacks. Lincoln deplored the Dred Scott decision, not just because it threatened to extend slavery into the territories but because of Justice Roger Taney's assertion that persons of African descent were not included in the fundamental rights and protections of the Constitution. As a result, the Illinoisan was open to the charge that he promoted full civil rights for blacks and would tolerate amalgamation. He made repeated claims that he was "not nor ever [had] been in favor of making voters or jurors of negroes, nor of qualifying them to hold office, nor to intermarry with white people." He suggested that whites—and free blacks—would be better off if blacks left the United States. But he also insisted that the constitutional rights of life, liberty, and property could not be denied on the basis of ethnicity or race.[16]

Interest in the Americas as a site for African American colonization, coupled with entrepreneurial schemes, was growing, especially after gold was discovered in California in 1848. Enterprising capitalists patched together routes across Central America to shorten travel from east to west, and visions of isthmian railroads and canals soon followed. U.S. official diplomacy in Central and South America, despite the posturing of the Monroe Doctrine, had been remarkably ineffective in the first half of the nineteenth century. Great Britain dominated the region, encouraging its Conservatives to reject both liberal political ideas and Yankee invaders. Confused as to who was in power or could stay in power, individual Americans, often posing as diplomatic representatives and business investors at the same time, attempted to make deals with factional political leaders in Central America for trade agreements, land and mine titles, transportation routes, and liberal immigration policies, sometimes with intimations of annexation.[17]

One of the most important of these deal-makers was E. George Squier, who arrived in Central America in 1849 as U.S. *chargé d'affaires*. Squier epitomized the economic and political thrust of U.S. imperialism. Not only a diplomat, he was also a railroad promoter, political essayist, novelist, and prominent ethnographer. His work on Indian burial mounds of the upper Mississippi Valley was solicited by Albert Gallatin as the first publication of the Smithsonian Institute, and Squier was considered by many Europeans to be a legitimate heir to the legacy of Alexander von Humboldt. Although his research was used by the polygenists of the American School to argue for separate creations and the biological inferiority of nonwhites, Squier did not commit himself to their views entirely. He hoped to prove instead that North and South American indigenous peoples were part of a common, and noble, ancient culture. Like most ethnographers of the time, however, he held that climate, race, and culture were indisputably linked and that Africans were at the bottom of the ethnographic ladder. Race and climate were the chief predictors of any civilization's success, with inferior races inhabiting the torrid zones and superior ones creating great civilizations in temperate regions.[18] For more than ten years, he used his scientific reputation to promote a Honduran Inter-Oceanic Railway across the isthmus from the Bay of Honduras to the Bay of Fonseca.[19]

While Squier the ethnographer was anxious to prove that racial interbreeding was a disaster, Squier the railroad promoter was in search of a viable labor force to build a trans-isthmus railroad in Central America. He was well aware of the labor forces recruited by British logging interests in Central America; those considered to be the best workers were West Indians, often of mixed race.[20] Squier saw "Caribs"—his artful term for Central Americans of mixed African and Indio descent—as an ideal labor force for building his railroad. "Intelligent, faithful, inured to the climate, and moreover, expert in the use of the axe, and with some knowledge of the building of roads and bridges, they must prove of the greatest service in the future development of the vast resources of that country [Honduras], and of the utmost importance in the construction of the proposed railway between the seas."[21] Squier assaulted the U.S. public consciousness in the 1850s through magazine articles, lectures, travelogues, scientific treatises, and a novel, all of which provided a set of ready-made arguments for those who sought to combine the colonization of ex-slaves, the mobilization of labor forces of color, and economic expansion into Central America.[22]

Squier, Lincoln, and Blair were familiar with the ideas of Robert Walker, a transplanted Pennsylvanian who had invested heavily in land in Texas and who served in Polk's cabinet as secretary of the Treasury in 1846. An unmitigated expansionist who suggested acquiring not only Texas but Canada and Mexico, Walker was committed, both in his personal finances and in his public pronouncements, to railroads, mines, and expanding U.S. trade. By 1852 he had grandiose plans for an isthmian canal or railroad, and, as Squier cast around for investors in his Honduran Inter-Oceanic Railway (HIOR) in 1853, Walker contributed $1,000 and became a major partner.[23] Persuaded to become the territorial governor of Kansas in 1857, Walker opposed the proslavery Lecompton constitution and became a free-soil hero.

Walker was among the first politicians to argue that the supposed propensity of persons of African descent for the tropics might be used to remove U.S. blacks entirely from North America and send them southward. He had warned in a widely circulated 1844 "Letter Relative to the Annexation of Texas," published in the Blairs' Washington Globe and as a pamphlet, that declining agricultural productivity in the slaveholding states would lead to emancipation in the upper South and flood the Midwest with free blacks. Walker used newly collected (and wildly incorrect) statistics from the Census of 1840 to prove that free African Americans in the northern states had exceptionally high rates of crime, indigence, mental illness, and physical deformity. The only solution to avoiding the burden of free blacks was to open new plantation sites in Texas and drain off the African population. Most blacks would drift southward toward their "natural" climate, and with vast possibilities for expansion into Mexico and Central and South America, the United States might use African Americans to extend U.S. influence throughout the hemisphere.[24]

In 1856, when the Republican Party was about to choose a presidential nominee, Abraham Lincoln speculated that Salmon P. Chase, William Henry Seward, John C. Fremont, and Frank Blair might all be on the list of potential candidates.[25] While Lincoln occasionally referred to colonization, Blair made it a linchpin of his political rhetoric, using it to cast himself as a moderate who would end slavery and solve the race problem at the same time. Blair "is no believer," said one authorized biography, "in the unholy and disgusting tenets advocated by abolition fanaticism but advocates the gradual abolition of slavery in the Union and the colonization of the slaves emancipated in Central America, . . . [whose] climate appears to be happily adapted to their constitutional idiosyncrasies."[26] Viewed as a progressive on the race question in 1858 (to the amusement of Frederick Douglass), perhaps no one was as surprised as Frank Blair to learn that his emphatic endorsement of the removal of free blacks would make him an arch conservative ten years later.[27]

But Lincoln also endorsed colonization as a preventative to amalgamation; it was one of the visionary federal policies Republicans could offer the nation: "A separation of the races is the only perfect preventive of amalgamation," said Lincoln, "and if white and black people never get together in Kansas, they will never mix blood in Kansas." "Separation, if ever effected at all, must be effected by colonization; and no political party, as such, is now doing anything directly for colonization. . . . The enterprise is a difficult one; but when there is a will there is a way; and what colonization needs most is a hearty will."[28] Lincoln conferred with Blair in Missouri in 1857 and depicted Blair in his 1858 debates with Douglas and in the presidential campaign of 1860 as a courageous thinker whose ideas might solve the slavery issue without destroying the principles of the Constitution.[29]

Robert Walker and E. George Squier's hopes for launching capitalist investment projects in Central America—along with their assumptions that blacks belonged in the tropics—provided a concrete plan for putting the free-soil moderates' colonization ideas into motion. In the mid-1850s, Squier pressed his friends, who included the *North American Review* editor Charles Eliot Norton and the Rhode Island senator Henry Bowen Anthony, with requests to circulate the Honduran Inter-Oceanic Railway's prospectus and to buy more of its stock. One investor reported in 1856 that John C. Fremont, "whom the Republicans will probably nominate for President told a friend of mine . . . that the U.S. should possess our route if they had to pay 20 millions for it."[30] Frank Blair underlined passages in the HIOR prospectus describing the Honduran government's concessions of land to immigrants and the glories of the country's natural resources.[31] He gave speeches in Boston, Cincinnati, and before the House of Representatives in 1858 and 1859 linking colonization, commerce, and the penetration of Central America.[32]

Blair sought to make colonization palatable to several critical interest groups. He disavowed "filibustering," or the taking of territory south of the border by armed aggression. Instead, diplomacy, the enlargement of trade, and the extension of liberal values would accomplish what the filibusterers had failed to achieve through force. Blair hoped to persuade abolitionists and African American leaders that colonization was in the best interests of free blacks. The latter, he said, would not only thrive in the tropics, they and they alone would "reclaim the vast level plains and pampas, the tierra caliente of the continent." He promised that any colonization policy would proceed "with ample guarantees" of the "personal and political rights" of freed colored persons of the United States; no already-free persons would be compelled to leave the country against their will (a policy the Blairs would later rescind).[33]

Blair also incorporated free-soil rhetoric aimed at Midwestern and border-state whites. Colonization would further the economic interests of ordinary white men because it would prevent free blacks from lowering their wages. Most important, it would prevent the amalgamation that had been encouraged by slavery. If race mixing were to continue after slavery, the result would be "a mongrel race, inferior to either of the original types.... Nothing can save us from pollution but a complete separation."[34]

Blair stressed that investment in commerce and transportation systems in Central America were critical to U.S. interests, and that agreements with Central American governments to establish such systems, along with the importation of adequate labor supplies, could lead to U.S. dominance in the southern hemisphere. He depicted Squier's original but ill-fated deal with the Liberal government of Honduras as a magnificent but lost opportunity to expand "our national greatness [and] ... to control ... the continent and the oceans that washed its shores."[35]

Far from admitting to the difficulties of transporting a huge population of African Americans, Blair saw colonization as a continuation of the vast movement of peoples of the world begun by the importation of African slaves, the relocation of Native Americans, the westward movement of Yankee pioneers, and the migration of hundreds of thousands of European immigrants.[36] Persons of African descent from the United States were already part of a capitalist economy, most were Protestants, and their experiences under slavery would make them efficient workers in an economic hierarchy managed by U.S. business interests: in Blair's words, "Can any doubt that the American-born and American-instructed African, carrying with him the intelligence, the industry, the progressive impulse, acquired by all engaged in the agriculture of this country, would fail to carry success with them to their new abodes?"[37]

If these policies were pursued, the result was to be "our India," a western-hemisphere version of the British empire, in which colonial subjects, mainly persons of color, would be bound to the regime in Washington through common culture, economic trade, and egalitarian political institutions. Mexico would be buffered to the south by U.S. colonies, and the end result would be "a grand confederacy of American republics," the erasure of British and Spanish influence in the region, and the end of "ever-recurring revolutions ... by which ... commerce has been depressed and destroyed."[38] To return to the dichotomy of nationalism posed by Benedict Anderson, it could be said that Blair managed to combine a timeless fear of "contamination" with an expanding economic imperialism set in real time.

Once Lincoln took office in 1861, he and the Blairs moved to implement the federal funding of colonization and arrangements with other countries to receive ex-slaves. Lincoln instructed Seward to pursue negotiations with governments south of Texas, and Montgomery Blair initiated talks with Mexico to secure the Yucatan. Francis Blair Sr. advised Lincoln to issue a government contract to the Chiriqui Improvement Company, which promised to mine coal deposits in Panama and to transport African Americans there. The Missouri Republican Henry T. Blow, whose family had once owned and then freed Dred Scott after Scott lost his case in the Supreme Court, stood by in Venezuela to execute the wishes of the president. Elisha O. Crosby, who had become familiar with Central America while a representative of the Pacific Mail Steamship Company, was dispatched by Lincoln to Guatemala to secure ports on the Atlantic to Union shipping and to confer with President Rafael Carrera about the prospects of colonization.[39] He would later describe this mission as one "conceived by old Francis P. Blair" and endorsed by the Radical Republicans Benjamin Wade and Charles Sumner as well: "It was thought, by such an arrangement . . . that a very large surplus of the black population of the South could be disposed of and that many Southern men were disposed to relinquish their slaves, either voluntarily or for moderate compensation."[40]

In his State of the Union messages of 1861 and 1862, Lincoln devoted considerable space to the links between gradual emancipation and colonization. A House Committee on Emancipation and Colonization, with Frank Blair playing a leading role, recommended in July 1862 that the Congress appropriate the staggering sum of $20 million for the purposes of colonization and linked its success to compensated emancipation in the border states. The spring and summer of 1862 saw a flurry of legislation in Congress to provide federal subsidies to the loyal states for compensation, and to allocate more modest funds—$600,000 in all—for colonization.[41] An emigration agent assigned to investigate the practicalities of colonization painted a rosy picture of such in a December "Report on Colonization and Emigration" to the secretary of the Interior.[42] The cabinet officials Edward Bates and Montgomery Blair argued for the forced deportation of slave contraband coming into Union lines; Lincoln rejected the idea and continued to hope that African American leaders would endorse voluntary emigration.[43]

The president met with five leading "colored men" in a famous encounter at the White House in August 1862. His words were, essentially, Blair's: "The place I am thinking about having for a [colored people's] colony is in Central America. . . . Unlike Liberia it is on a great line of travel—it is a highway. The country is a very excellent one for any people, and with great natural resources and advantages, and especially because of the similarity of climate with your native land—and thus being suited to your physical condition."[44] Lincoln's gestures were promptly rebuffed at an angry meeting of African American leaders a few days later in Washington.[45]

Lincoln's colonization project would soon collapse. The president was far too pressed by the continuing catastrophe of Civil War to insist on colonization as a necessity of Republican policy. Nor would he contemplate the forced expulsion of African Americans. Seward, who had grave doubts about diminishing the labor force of the United States by as much as one-seventh, argued that African American labor would be needed in the South for the foreseeable future.[46]

Attempts to make arrangements with governments in the Americas for African American immigration, with the exception of the disastrous Haitian experiment of 1862–63, were futile.[47] Central American governments were anxious to promote the immigration of white Europeans, not ex-slaves, and also feared that the United States might use blacks, as Frank Blair had suggested, to foster U.S. political influence and Protestantism in their countries. The claims that capitalist promoters such as Squier had made of vast riches and easy opportunities for development in Central America were vastly inflated; there were no coal deposits in Chiquiri, and building a railroad across Honduras proved to be impossibly expensive.

Most tellingly, as African Americans emancipated themselves and imagined their own future, colonization was not a part of their plan—nor of their ex-masters'. While resigning themselves to a semblance of emancipation, southern plantation owners were desperate to keep blacks in the South as a near-captive labor force; African Americans continued to push for land of their own.[48] Frederick Douglass stated the case with typical clarity: "this talk of the expatriation of the slaves . . . is not more shocking than it is unwise. . . . To say that negroes shall not live in the Southern States is like saying that the lands of the South shall be no longer cultivated. . . . Who wants to take their places in the cotton field, in the rice swamp, and sugar fields, which they have tilled for ages? The whole scheme of colonization would be too absurd for discussion, but that the madness of the moment has drowned the voice of common sense as well as common justice."[49]

Plans for the Honduran Inter-Oceanic Railway, like those of the colonization of ex-slaves, never came to fruition. But the discussions of race, labor, capital, and citizenship that took place in the 1850s and 1860s would provide the rationalization for outside intervention and investment in the Caribbean Basin for decades to come, including the creation of Panama and the building of a U.S.-financed canal. Emphasizing the "universality of work and the worker, alongside . . . notions of the 'peculiarity' of the African,"[50] racial hierarchies governed these enterprises and the sense of American entitlement to their labor value for decades to come.

NOTES

1 David Brion Davis, *Challenging the Boundaries of Slavery* (Cambridge: Harvard University Press, 2003), 66–69; quotation from p. 68.
2 James Madison to Robert J. Evans, June 15, 1819, quoted in *Racial Thought in America*, vol. I, *From the Puritans to Abraham Lincoln*, ed. Louis Ruchames (Amherst: University of Massachusetts Press, 1969), 285–86.
3 On "whiteness," see Alexander Saxton, *The Rise and Fall of the White Republic: Class Politics and Mass Culture in Nineteenth-Century America* (London: Verso, 1990), and David R. Roediger, *The Wages of Whiteness: Race and the Making of the American Working Class* (London: Verso, 1991).
4 "Santo Domingo: An Address Delivered in St. Louis, Missouri, on 13 January 1873," in *The Frederick Douglass Papers*, ed. John Blassingame (New Haven: Yale University Press. 1991), 4:344.
5 Benedict Anderson, *Imagined Communities: Reflections on the Origin and Spread of Nationalism* (London: Verso, 1983), 136. The question of boundaries and populations is "Janus-faced," as Homi K. Bhabha has observed: see his "Introduction: Narrating the Nation," in *Nation and Narration*, ed. Homi K. Bhabha (London: Routledge, 1990), 4.
6 "Annual Message to Congress, Dec. 1, 1862," in *The Collected Works of Abraham Lincoln*, ed. Roy P. Basler (New Brunswick: Rutgers University Press, 1953), 5:528.
7 Allan Nevins, *The War for the Union* (New York: Scribner's, 1960), 2:10. William W. Freehling contends that colonization was not an impossible idea in " 'Absurd' Issues and the Causes of the Civil War: Colonization as a Test Case," part of his *Reintegration of American History: Slavery and the Civil War* (New York: Oxford University Press, 1994). For the continued problematic of colonization in the Lincoln administration, see also David Herbert Donald, *Lincoln* (New York: Simon and Schuster, 1995).
8 *The United States in Central America, 1860–1911* (Durham: Duke University Press, 1991), 3 and 7. Also see Bernard Semmel, *Imperialism and Social Reform* (Cambridge: Cambridge University Press, 1960).
9 Frederick Cooper, Thomas C. Holt, and Rebecca J. Scott, *Beyond Slavery: Explorations of Race, Labor and Citizenship in Postemancipation Societies* (Chapel Hill: University of North Carolina Press, 2000), 19.
10 Montgomery Blair, Frank P. Blair, O. D. Filley, et. al., "Address to the Democracy of Missouri" (n.p., 1850), Library of Congress, Washington, D.C. On free-soil politics, see Eric Foner, *Free Soil, Free Labor, Free Men: The Ideology of the Republican Party Before the Civil War* (New York: Oxford University Press, 1970), Eugene H. Berwanger, *The Frontier against Slavery: Western Anti-Negro Prejudice and the Slavery Extension Controversy* (Urbana: University of Illinois Press, 1967), James A. Rawley, *Race and Politics: "Bleeding Kansas" and the Coming of the Civil War* (Philadelphia: J.B. Lippincott, 1969), and Richard H. Sewell, *Ballots for Freedom: Antislavery Politics in the United States 1837–1860* (New York: Oxford University Press, 1976).
11 "Speech to the Jury in the Rock Island Bridge Case, Chicago, Illinois, September 22,

1857," Basler, ed., *Collected Works of Abraham Lincoln*, 2:527; "Annual Message to Congress," December 1, 1862, ibid., 6:527, Frank P. Blair Jr., "The Destiny of the Races of this Continent," an address delivered in Boston on January 27, 1859 (Washington, D.C.: Buell and Blanchard, 1858), 12.

12 Robert E. May, *The Southern Dream of a Caribbean Empire* (Baton Rouge: Louisiana State University Press, 1973). John C. Calhoun had hoped to annex Mexico to extend slavery southward, but in the face of a militant free-soil coalition agreed that "the greatest misfortunes of Spanish America are to be traced to the fatal error of placing these colored races on an equality with the white race." Calhoun is quoted by Frederick Merk with the collaboration of Lois Bannister Merk, *Manifest Destiny and Mission in American History: A Reinterpretation* (New York: Knopf, 1963), 162. See also Reginald Horsman, *Race and Manifest Destiny: The Origins of Racial Anglo-Saxonism* (Cambridge: Harvard University Press, 1981), 247; Thomas R. Hitela, *Manifest Design: Anxious Aggrandizement in Late Jacksonian America* (Ithaca: Cornell University Press, 1985), 134; Walter La Feber, *The American Age: United States Policy at Home and Abroad Since 1750* (New York: Norton, 1989), 137–38.

13 On the Blairs, see William Ernest Smith, *The Francis Preston Blair Family in Politics* (New York: Macmillan, 1933), 2 vols.; Leonard B. Wurthman Jr., "Frank Blair: Lincoln's Congressional Spokesman," *Missouri Historical Review* 64 (1970): 263–88; Elbert R. Smith, *Francis Preston Blair* (New York: Free Press, 1980); and William Parrish, *Frank Blair, Lincoln's Conservative* (Columbia: University of Missouri Press, 1998).

14 Vincent C. Hopkins, *Dred Scott's Case* (New York: Atheneum, 1967), and Kenneth Stampp, *America in 1857: A Nation on the Brink* (New York: Oxford, 1990), 68–109.

15 As Larry Kincaid has observed, the growing antipathy to slavery in the 1850s seemed to lead to a kind of "two steps forward, one step back" historical process. "Two Steps Forward, One Step Back: Racial Attitudes During the Civil War and Reconstruction," in *The Great Fear: Race in the Mind of America*, ed. Gary B. Nash and Richard Weiss (New York: Holt, Rinehart and Winston, 1970), 45–70.

16 Abraham Lincoln, "Fourth Lincoln-Douglas Debate, Charleston, Illinois, September 18, 1858," in Basler, ed., *Collected Works of Abraham Lincoln*, 3:145–46; and "Speech on the Dred Scott Decision at Springfield, June 26, 1857," ibid., 2:409.

17 Joseph B. Lockey, "Diplomatic Futility," *Hispanic American Historical Review* 10 (1930): 265– 294. See also Robert R. Russel, *Improvement of Communication with the Pacific Coast as an Issue in American Politics 1783–1864* (Cedar Rapids, Ia.: Torch Press, 1948), 202–18; Thomas M. Leonard, *Central America and the United States: The Search for Stability* (Athens: University of Georgia Press, 1991), 15–33; Michael L. Conniff, *Panama and the United States: The Forced Alliance* (Athens: University of Georgia Press, 1992), 24–40; and May, *Southern Dream of a Caribbean Empire*, 77–110. For the political crosscurrents of the time in Central America, see Frederick Stirton Weaver, *Inside the Volcano: The History and Political Economy of Central America* (Boulder, Colo.: Westview Press, 1994), 35–66.

18 On nineteenth-century scientific ideas about race, see William Stanton, *The Leopard's*

Spots: Scientific Attitudes toward Race in America 1815–1859 (Chicago: University of Chicago Press, 1960); George M. Fredrickson, The Black Image in the White Mind: The Debate on Afro-American Character and Destiny (New York: Harper, 1971), 71–96; and Stephan Jay Gould, "American Polygeny and Craniometry Before Darwin: Blacks and Indians as Separate, Inferior Species," in The "Racial" Economy of Science: Toward a Democratic Future, ed. Sandra Harding (Bloomington: Indiana University Press, 1993), 84–116; Nancy Stephan, The Idea of Race in Science: Great Britain, 1800–1960 (Hamden, Conn.: Archon Books, 1992).

19 On Squier, see Charles Lee Stansifer, "The Central American Career of E. George Squier" (Ph.D. diss., Tulane University, 1959) and "E. George Squier and the Honduras Interoceanic Railroad Project," Hispanic American Historical Review 46 (1966): 1–27; Delmer G. Ross, Visionaries and Swindlers: The Development of the Railways of Honduras (Mobile: Institute for Research in Latin America, 1975); Micheal D. Olien, "E.G. Squier and the Miskito: Anthropological Scholarship and Political Propaganda," Ethnohistory 32 (1985): 111–33; and Sharon Hartman Strom, "E.G. Squier y el Ferrocarril Oceánico Hondureño: Centro America en la Imaginación Norteamericana," Yaxkin 14 (October 1996): 127–37.

20 For a helpful discussion of these workers, see Coniff, Panama and the United States, 26–27; Martin A. Klein, "Slavery, the International Labour Market and the Emancipation of Slaves in the Nineteenth Century," Slavery and Abolition 15 (1994): 212.

21 E. G. Squier, The States of Central America (New York: Harper & Bros., 1858), 232. Squier's approval of the Caribs was shared by other travel writers in Central America. See Thomas Young, Narrative of a Residence on the Mosquito Shore (London: Smith, Elder, 1847), 122–34; and William V. Wells, Explorations and Adventures in Honduras (New York: Harper & Bros., 1857), 350. On the Caribs, see Rebecca B. Bateman, "Africans and Indians: A Comparative Study of the Black Carib and Black Seminole," Ethnohistory 37 (1990): 1–24.

22 Of particular importance here were Squier's lengthy informational and editorial articles in the U.S. Magazine and Democratic Review between 1852 and 1858. Blair was probably most influenced by Squier's "The Nicaraguan Question," U.S. Magazine and Democratic Review 41 (February 1858): 115–23.

23 On Robert Walker's business activities, see Stansifer, "E. George Squier and the Honduras Interoceanic Railroad Project," 3; and James P. Shenton, Robert John Walker: A Politician from Jackson to Lincoln (New York: Columbia University Press, 1961).

24 The text of Walker's "Letter Relative to the Annexation of Texas" is reprinted in full and discussed in Frederick S. Merk with Lois Bannister Merk, Fruits of Propaganda in the Tyler Administration (Cambridge: Harvard University Press, 1971), 95–120, and 221–51. See also Hitela, Manifest Design, 10–54.

25 Abraham Lincoln to Lyman Trumball, June 7, 1856, in Basler, ed., Collected Works, 2:342.

26 As quoted in Smith, Frances Preston Blair Family, 1:402.

27 On Douglass's reaction, see "The Political Response to Slavery's Aggressions: Addresses Delivered in Syracuse, New York, on 28 May 1856," in Blassingame, ed., *Frederick Douglass Papers*, 3:141–42.
28 June 26, 1857, in Basler, ed., *Collected Works*, 2:408–9.
29 See, for example, ibid., 3:256 and 314, and 4:11. A helpful discussion of the range of opinion endorsing colonization at this time can be found in Richard H. Sewell, *Ballots for Freedom: Antislavery Politics in the United States, 1837–1860* (New York: Oxford University Press, 1976), 316–27.
30 See, for example, letters from Norton to Squier of June 20, 1856, and March 21 and April 12, 1861, reel 4, E. G. Squier Papers, Library of Congress. The Fremont reference was made by HIOR board member Henry B. Stanton in a letter to E. G. Squier, June 15, 1856, box 4, Squier Papers, Huntington Library, San Marino, California.
31 A copy of the "Charter of the Honduras Interoceanic Railway," with "Hon. F. P. Blair, House of Representatives" written across the top, is in the Blair Papers, reel 13, Library of Congress.
32 Smith, *Frances Preston Blair Family*, 2:462–63.
33 As Hans Trefousse observes, Blair's ideas on colonization were not necessarily at odds with those of the Radical Republicans, many of whom agreed that Blacks belonged in the tropics. See Trefousse, *The Radical Republicans: Lincoln's Vanguard for Racial Justice* (New York: Knopf, 1969), 29–32.
34 F. P. Blair Jr., "Destiny of the Races of this Continent," 23.
35 Blair, "On the Acquisition of Territory in Central and South America, to be Colonized with Free Blacks, and Held as a Dependency by the United States," an address to Congress, January 14, 1858 (Washington, D.C.: Buell and Blanchard, 1858), 14.
36 The prospectus for the HIOR in Frank Blair's papers is followed by an unidentified newspaper editorial on "The Removal of Slavery," which insisted the "transporting [of] the entire slave population to the West Indies" was not insurmountable. Blair Papers, reel 13.
37 "Destiny of the Races of This Continent," 4 and 16. See also "Emancipation and Colonization," Report No. 148, 37th Congress, 2nd sess., House of Representatives, 24; Elizabeth Blair Lee, *Wartime Washington: The Civil War Letters* (Urbana: University of Illinois Press, 1991), 91.
38 "Emancipation and Colonization," 25.
39 For the diplomatic correspondence related to these negotiations, see *Diplomatic Correspondence and Foreign Relations of the United States* (Washington, D.C.: 1862), 202, 227, 236, 634, 704, 712, 880–910, and (1863), 63, 461, 582, 620, 634, 647.
40 *Memoirs of Elisha Oscar Crosby: Reminiscences of California and Guatemala from 1849 to 1864* (Los Angeles: Huntington Library Press, 1945), 87; Trefousse, *The Radical Republicans*, 301, Allan G. Bouge, *The Earnest Men: Republicans of the Civil War Senate* (Ithaca: Cornell University Press, 1981), 156–59. Charles Sumner had recuperated at the Blair estate in Silver Spring after his caning by Preston Brooks. Sumner voted to approve funds for colonization in 1862 but also referred to colonization as a "delusion." See Beverly

Wilson Palmer, ed., *The Selected Letters of Charles Sumner* (Boston: Northeastern University Press, 1990), 2:129, and 329; and David Herbert Donald, *Charles Sumner and the Rights of Man* (New York: Knopf, 1970), 443.

41 The $600,000 appropriation was substantial and demonstrated serious commitment to the cause. U.S. Department of Commerce, Bureau of the Census, *Historical Statistics of the United States, Colonial Times to 1970* (Washington, D.C.: GPO, 1975), 1114.

42 For summaries of these efforts, see Walter L. Fleming, "Deportation and Colonization: an Attempted Solution to the Race Problem," in *Studies in Southern History and Politics* (New York: Columbia University Press, 1914), 3–30; and Warren A. Beck, "Lincoln and Negro Colonization in Central America," *Abraham Lincoln Quarterly* 6 (September 1950): 162–83.

43 This debate was recorded by Edward Bates in his diary and is discussed by Marvin R. Cain, *Lincoln's Attorney General Edward Bates of Missouri* (Columbia: University of Missouri Press), 219–22.

44 "Address on Colonization to a Deputation of Negroes, August 14, 1862," in Basler, ed., *Collected Works*, 5:373.

45 James T. Holly and J. Dennis Harris, *Black Separatism and the Caribbean, 1860*, ed. Howard H. Bell (Ann Arbor: University of Michigan Press); and James Redpath, *A Guide to Hayti* (Westport: Negro Universities Press, 1970).

46 John M. Taylor, *William Henry Seward: Lincoln's Right Hand* (New York: HarperCollins, 1991), 191. G. S. Boritt suggests that "Permanent territorial acquisition was perhaps not an unavoidable corollary of black colonization; the losing of population, one seventh of the census of 1860, was," in Boritt, *Lincoln and the Economics of the American Dream* (Memphis: Memphis State University Press, 1978), 259.

47 On American colonization efforts in Mexico and Central America, see William J. Griffith, "Attitudes toward Foreign Colonization: The Evolution of Nineteenth-Century Guatemalan Immigration Policy," *Middle American Research Institute*, pub. 23, no. 4 (New Orleans: Tulane University, 1972), 73–110; and Thomas Schoonover, "Misconstrued Mission: Expansionism and Black Colonization in Mexico and Central America During the Civil War," *Pacific Historical Review* (1980): 607–20.

48 Gerald David Jaynes, *Branches without Roots: Genesis of the Black Working Class in the American South 1862–1882* (New York: Oxford University Press, 1986); and Klein, "Slavery, the International Market and the Emancipation of Slaves in the Nineteenth Century," 197–220.

49 "The Black Man's Future in the Southern States: An Address Delivered in Boston, Massachusetts, on 5 February 1862," in Blassingame, ed., *Frederick Douglass Papers*, 3:506.

50 Cooper et al., *Beyond Slavery*, 11.

EDWARD J. BALLEISEN

Bankruptcy and Bondage
The Ambiguities of
Economic Freedom in
the Civil War Era

In 1867, two years after the Thirteenth Amendment made involuntary servitude a crime (except for convicted criminals), the Republican Congress passed the nation's third Bankruptcy Act. Proponents of bankruptcy law saw themselves as reformers, as Edward Balleisen notes. The act provided economic protection to insolvent debtors and the hope of rebirth. But there was also a moral component to the act. Bankruptcy reformers used metaphors of bondage to characterize insolvency, and they drew on the language of liberation to convey what it meant to receive protection from debtors. For the vast majority of middle-class Americans, bankruptcy, like bondage, was a sin, a blemish on an individual's character and a collective stain on the fabric of the nation. Protection from creditors was thus a source of moral as well as economic redemption, much as emancipation redeemed the sin of slavery. And the limits of emancipation related to attitudes toward bankruptcy: the curtailment of black rights was part of the larger tension and hand-wringing about the nature of competition in a capitalist society after the Civil War.

Although bankruptcy reformers championed economic autonomy, they viewed debt as more enshackling than wage labor and worried about allowing too many employers in the field of American capitalism. They sought to limit the number of employers in two ways: (1) by encouraging middle-class white men without access to capital or particular commercial expertise to become respectable employees rather than debt-ridden employers; and (2) by using race as a crucial factor in the selection process for land grants. Full-fledged economic redemption was possible among white bankrupts, and theoretically even for slaves. But in the eyes of postbellum northern reformers, neither emancipated slaves nor whites who aspired to proprietorship but lacked familial connections, capital, and entrepreneurial talent deserved immediate grants of economic independence. Indeed, for most middle-class whites, ex-slaves threatened the freedom of white capitalists; despite emancipation, they were still perceived as being tainted with sin.

In the aftermath of the Civil War, the United States Congress adopted two very different emancipations. The far more momentous and well-known was the Thirteenth Amendment, which confirmed the self-ownership of roughly four million former slaves. But two years later, Republicans also enacted the 1867 Bankruptcy Act, which, its supporters proclaimed, would free a class of oppressed debtors from unfeeling and rapacious creditors. Like the abolition of American slavery, the creation of a national bankruptcy system grew out of several decades of sermonizing and politicking for change. And, like abolitionists and many other middle-class antebellum reformers, such as temperance activists, proponents of a federal bankruptcy law consistently couched their arguments in the paired motifs of enslavement and liberation. To their nineteenth-century champions, insolvent debtors had conveyed their "privileges as . . . freem[e]n and sold [their] bod[ies] and mind[s] into perpetual bondage," while court-mandated bankruptcy discharges would "strike off the fetters and set the bondmen free."[1]

Historians of nineteenth-century American reform have not paid much attention to the period's endeavors to revamp the treatment of insolvency, and one can see why. Proponents of bankruptcy reform lacked the organizational sophistication and popular participation of the era's major reform movements. For the most part, their endeavors did not find expression in specially focused publications or organizations.[2] Nonetheless, efforts to reform the handling of insolvency overlapped with other reform movements, and especially those pursued by the northern middle class. Advocates of bankruptcy reform tended to embrace other antebellum reform movements, such as temperance and, in the North, abolitionism; leading activists of those other movements tended to accept the arguments and proposals put forth by bankruptcy reformers; and proponents of bankruptcy reform emulated the rhetorical strategies of other reformers, especially by conceptualizing the injustices faced by insolvent debtors as a kind of slavery and by linking efforts at moral suasion with attempts to reshape the law.[3]

The debates surrounding nineteenth-century bankruptcy reform highlight the limitations of America's eventual abolition of slavery, and especially the unwillingness of so many diehard abolitionists to support thoroughgoing land redistribution as a crucial element of emancipation. A focus on reformers' approaches to bankruptcy reveals a fundamental tension in their thinking about economic freedom. As their stress on the provision of bankruptcy discharges indicates, reformers lauded the personal economic independence associated with the self-direction of proprietorship. But they also worried about a perceived surfeit of independent actors in the nineteenth-century American marketplace, which they viewed as a consequence of too-ready access to credit and a cause of the county's high rates of business failure.[4] To the extent that these latter concerns reflected more general anxieties within the northern reform ethos, they offer some additional clues to reformers' postbellum reluctance to push for land grants to former slaves.

In several respects, the periodic nineteenth-century campaigns for a national bankruptcy law highlight the racial and class dimensions of Republican and abolitionist antipathy to land reform. When bankruptcy reformers pleaded for federal relief to bankrupts, they invariably embraced not only the position that insolvent Americans deserved legal releases from their outstanding financial obligations, but also the proposition that their appropriate status was as self-employed proprietors. From the 1820s through the 1860s, supportive newspaper editors, bankrupts, and congressional advocates all argued for the enactment of a federal bankruptcy law as a mechanism of commercial resurrection—a means for beaten down white men to regain their rightful place as self-employed, enterprising citizens. The proponents of bankruptcy reform repeatedly invoked comparisons between failed white business owners and emancipated slaves. Some of these comparisons in the Civil War era simply implored Congress to offer the same justice to bankrupts as it had already furnished to "the poor African." But in many cases they took on a more invidious tone, as when a St. Louis bankrupt urged in 1866 that the "bondage" of failed white businessmen—persons who were "educated, refined, and generous"—was "far more galling" than that experienced "by the colored man." This line of argument, which dated back to the 1840s, portrayed formerly self-employed whites as possessing capabilities far beyond those of former slaves and as deserving far better treatment at the hands of the federal government.[5]

Such assessments of white bankrupts' status left their imprint on the bankruptcy statute that eventually cleared Congress and gained Andrew Johnson's signature in March 1867. The Bankruptcy Act of that year incorporated a pivotal innovation that promised to give many failed proprietors a basic capital stake in addition to a release from indebtedness—something that freed slaves and some of their Radical Republican allies sought largely in vain. Unlike the previous federal bankruptcy statute, the 1867 law specifically incorporated the homestead exemptions of the individual states. As a result, in the majority of states that prohibited creditors from taking a debtors' home and surrounding acreage, debtors could apply for bankruptcy relief secure in the knowledge that they would retain a core set of assets. With this provision, advocates of bankruptcy legislation hoped to provide momentum to the "fresh starts" provided by bankruptcy certificates, which would mean far more if they were complemented by a base of capital. "The debtor," Iowa Representative John Kasson insisted, "cannot make his first start in the recovery of his property and the comfort of his family unless he has a shelter for his wife and children."[6]

Nineteenth-century supporters of bankruptcy proposals further articulated a clear expectation that releases from debt would enable bankrupts quickly to "travel the road to a new commercial life." The kind of insolvent proprietors conjured up by advocates of bankruptcy legislation were the losers of "large fortunes," individuals who were among "the most intelligent [and] active . . . men of the country." For such enterprising and well-connected businessmen, bankruptcy discharges would clear the way for new infusions of capital and credit, usually from relatives or close business associates.[7]

Thus the tangible meanings that northern reformers often gave to bankruptcy discharges diverged starkly from the ones they gave to slave emancipation. When responding to the demands of a group of social and political insiders, most bankruptcy reformers conjured up images of formerly insolvent businessmen who would quickly return to positions of proprietorship. After getting free from the shackles of debt, bankrupts could expect to keep their homes, might even get to hold onto a sum that would facilitate future business ventures, and often could look forward to fresh access to additional commercial credit. By contrast, even radical whites often assumed that newly freed slaves would receive only the freedom to choose between employers; their emancipation would lead, at least in the short run, only to the market for free labor.[8]

So far the comparison between bankruptcy reform and the eventual dynamics of abolition fits rather comfortably into prevailing explanations for northern opposition to the freed people's demands for forty acres and a mule. Northern Republicans and even many abolitionists viewed the provision of land to former slaves as inconsistent with free labor ideology. Ignoring both the sacrifices of generations of African-Americans and the role of their uncompensated labor in building up the southern economy, Republicans viewed land reform as an unjust gift of economic resources that would impede the freed people's sense of personal responsibility; they further worried that land confiscations and redistribution risked political and legal assaults on the property claims of northern businesses, especially northern workers.[9] The priority that northern reformers placed on returning white bankrupts to the ranks of business owners only makes their distaste for southern land redistribution all the more telling.

Nineteenth-century bankruptcy reformers, however, did not solely direct their efforts toward the goal of releasing shackled bankrupts from the bondage of debt. Bankruptcy reform had another side as well, one that sought to regulate behavior in the marketplace and to smooth out economic fluctuations by restricting the extension of credit to would be entrepreneurs. Indeed, those individuals who wished to reconfigure legal and social approaches to insolvency increasingly manifested an ambivalence about the value of economic independence; and that ambivalence suggests an additional barrier to post–Civil War land reform.

Throughout the early and mid-nineteenth century, the most constant advocates of a federal bankruptcy system were a group of commercial moralists—a cluster of northeastern businessmen, ministers, writers, and lawyers that included Arthur and Lewis Tappan, Henry Ward Beecher, the prolific fiction writer and temperance activist T. S. Arthur, and the Supreme Court justice Joseph Story. The moralists sought to influence informal codes of commercial behavior and to reshape bankruptcy law, most tangibly through the adoption of a permanent federal bankruptcy system that would police their vision of appropriate commercial conduct.

Commercial moralists and their political allies readily embraced court-mandated discharges for insolvent Americans who gave up their property for the benefit of their creditors. But alongside their strident pleas for creditors to remove their boots from the necks of insolvent proprietors were calls for debtors to abide by a set of precepts about commercial conduct: avoid plunging into speculative ventures that might place their creditors at risk; inform creditors immediately when business reversals made insolvency a distinct possibility; and avoid special favors or payments to any select group of creditors, such as family members or close business associates. And, just as the commercial moralists envisaged the use of federal power to compel the removal of creditors' boots, they advocated a federal bankruptcy system that would pin down debtors who violated the principles of mercantile behavior that they held dear. Their efforts were reflected in the short-lived 1841 Bankruptcy Act, which both barred discharges to individuals who concealed property or made preferential payments in the midst of business failure, and gave creditors the ability to force delinquent and evasive debtors into bankruptcy proceedings.[10]

Northern reformers additionally tended to view the discharge mechanisms of a federal bankruptcy law as a way to reign in capitalist excesses. When creditors placed too much confidence in their ability to collect debts through the courts, bankruptcy reformers argued, they far too readily extended loans or sold on credit. A proper bankruptcy code would shift the psychology of credit transactions. The inexperienced or speculatively inclined would find it more difficult to attract capital, as would the financially troubled. By curbing flows of credit, a permanent bankruptcy law would smooth out business fluctuations, imparting a more measured tone to the American economy.[11]

Even more significant for this comparison of bankruptcy reform and emancipation, the moralists tended to see a link between ease of entry into the American marketplace and high rates of bankruptcy. By the 1840s and 1850s, some commercial moralists became so impressed by the risks associated with independent business ventures that they began to espouse a new ideology of economic independence, one predicated on salaried wage work rather than economic self-direction. Wishing to shape attitudes and career strategies, these business reformers pointed to the frequency of bankruptcy as a warning to young men to resist the temptation to chase after self-employment. On occasion, the purveyors of these ideas went so far as to characterize independent proprietorship as itself potentially a form of slavery, since inexperienced and undercapitalized businessmen so often became enthralled to their creditors and to the anxieties created by pecuniary distress even before they became insolvent. For the short story writer E. M. Gibson, writing in *Ballou's Magazine* in 1855, the harried merchant constituted "a mere cipher in the sum of business relations—the veriest slave of every one he owes, and of those from whom he wished to borrow." Instead of an honorable place in republican society, this kind of a proprietor found only "a miserable, truckling, precarious, dependent existence" that compared unfavorably to the lot of a "day laborer, hand-cartmen, hod-carrier, or . . . plantation negro."[12]

To social commentators who found this way of thinking compelling, the ostensible horrors of mercantile "servitude" suggested a corresponding deliverance, though not one to be found in debt releases that would unleash new commercial schemes. Instead, emancipation lay with the acceptance of such steady, white-collar positions as clerks, bookkeepers, or agents, which enabled prudent employees to steer clear of crippling debt while still maintaining a respectable standard of living. As one of E. M. Gibson's fictional characters explained while rebuffing a close friend's suggestion that he give up his clerkship to join a mercantile venture, "the moment I relinquish my salary and go round begging for credit, I shall lose the glorious feeling of independence that I now enjoy." From this perspective, the key reform necessitated by bankruptcy was a shift in individual aspirations and values and a reconceptualization of economic freedom. The goal here was to convince middle-class Americans that true autonomy lay with a market-based form of economic security, especially if individuals lacked the experience and capital to insulate themselves from the financial crises that so frequently plagued the nation's mercantile and manufacturing enterprises.[13]

All of these concerns shaped Civil War–era congressional debates over bankruptcy. The 1867 Bankruptcy Act, the nation's third experiment with a federal bankruptcy system, thoroughly incorporated the regulatory impulses of commercial moralism. Its chief advocates viewed the bankruptcy bill as creating a permanent system of national commercial law.[14] This statute, like the Bankruptcy Act of 1841, contained measures that gave substantial power to creditors and penalized commercial behavior that deviated from the requirements of moralists. Some supporters viewed it as a vehicle to slow down the furious pace of America's credit system, making it more difficult for inexperienced, poorly capitalized individuals to gain access to credit and the status of proprietorship. In its restraining features, the 1867 Bankruptcy Law reflected apprehensions about the virtues of self-employment in an expansive, rapidly industrializing society.

America's Reconstruction-era bankruptcy system accommodated several regulatory impulses. The 1867 legislation made a failing debtor's special treatment to unsecured creditors (such as family and friends) a bar to a bankruptcy discharge, and proclaimed that preferential payments on the eve of a business suspension had no legal force. These stipulations reflected the longstanding concern about the widespread culture of preference within the credit system, which often enabled capital-poor individuals to acquire sufficient credit to begin mercantile careers on their own account. Republicans such as New York Representative Roscoe Conkling hoped that by restricting the ability of "men without substance or stability of their own" to borrow money, and thus amass a "fictitious capital," a federal bankruptcy system would help to stabilize the country's economy. The resulting higher barriers to entry for all businesses would lower rates of failure and lessen the severity of financial crises.[15]

Incorporation of involuntary bankruptcy extended the 1867 Bankruptcy Law's measures of restraint. As with earlier federal bankruptcy statutes, the postbellum legislation permitted creditors to initiate bankruptcy proceedings against debtors if they violated the basic precepts laid out by the commercial moralists, such as transferring property in order to frustrate the efforts of creditors to collect through the courts, or giving preferences in anticipation of insolvency. Unlike previous federal bankruptcy legislation, the 1867 Act did not restrict the subjects of involuntary petitions to merchants, brokers, and bankers. So long as creditors could claim debts of $100 or greater against particular individuals or businesses, and so long as they alleged one of several "acts of bankruptcy," they could haul those persons or firms into federal bankruptcy court. Reformers repeatedly depicted these provisions as efforts to "secure honor and integrity in the commercial relations of this country"— and, in the process, to curb recklessness and speculation by the nation's businessmen.[16]

Civil War–era supporters of bankruptcy legislation made analogous arguments about the long-term impact that bankruptcy discharges would have on America's credit system. Echoing earlier bankruptcy debates, proponents of a national bankruptcy law in the 1860s contended that such legislation would exert a calming effect on the American economy. *The Independent*, a New York antislavery newspaper, voiced its strong endorsement of a bankruptcy statute partly in order to "release thousands of men from a cruel and useless bondage" but also as "an Act of National Morality" that would "become a regulative element in business," encouraging a "salutary retrenchment of credit." Expressing great concern over the "demoralization" caused by "abuse" of credit, the newspaper confidently predicted that "a judicious Bankrupt Act would . . . tend to make sellers cautious of the terms upon which they put property into other men's hands." In Congress, the Massachusetts senator and Radical Republican Henry Wilson offered similar reasoning in support of incorporating homestead exemptions into the pending bankruptcy bill. "Nine-tenths of the credits in this country are injurious and demoralizing to the people of this country," Wilson proclaimed in February 1867. By reducing potential creditors' expectations that they would be able to collect on unpaid debts, the existence of homestead exemptions would make creditors pay closer attention to "the integrity and personal character of the person[s] to whom [they] give . . . credit." Although the individuals who received bankruptcy certificates would have newfound opportunities to pursue entrepreneurial schemes, champions of bankruptcy reform remained confident that creditors in general would scrutinize potential debtors more closely and would be far less likely to provide the credit that might launch unseaworthy commercial vessels onto the seas of trade.[17]

The postbellum Republican position on bankruptcy policy, then, suggested a more general nervousness about having too many independent economic actors in the American marketplace. Civil War–era bankruptcy reformers wished, as the New York Republican Roscoe Conkling declared during his 1863 speech, to "allow . . . the unfortunate and the prostrate to rise up." At the same time, Republicans spied "defects and deficiencies in our legal and commercial policy which . . . demand restraints [on] excessive and morbid enterprise."[18] This fundamental tension in thinking about economic freedom had long characterized middle-class reform initiatives in the United States. Reformers across a broad swath of movements, including temperance and abolitionism, viewed individual liberation as a fundamental aim, and understood liberation partly in economic terms. But generally such liberation was to occur within an ethic of disciplined self-control, mediated by governmental restraints and tempered by concerns for social and economic stability. And, in the eyes of at least some middle-class northerners, an individual's economic "autonomy" depended not on the freedom to pursue dreams of economic self-direction but rather on freedom from the dependencies that the pursuit of such dreams often entailed.

This tension within nineteenth-century reform suggests a further dimension to the class-based worldview that guided white proponents of emancipation as they considered the question of how the national government should define the contours of economic freedom for former black slaves. In the two decades leading up to the Civil War, northern reformers manifested increasing skepticism about the advantages of independent proprietorship, especially for individuals who lacked the requisite experience, social connections, and capital. This skepticism extended not only to wage earners but also to aspiring business owners, whose tenuous enterprises, reformers believed, threatened the stability of American commerce. To both of these groups, the message from commercial moralists increasingly was not so much to forego aspirations of self-employment as to temper them and to adopt patience in their pursuit. Such anxieties about excessive self-direction in the marketplace heightened doubts about the wisdom of using federal power to advance the freed persons' deep aspirations for farms that they could call their own, making it easier for northern reformers to accept a policy of emancipation that came without title to land.

NOTES

1 *The Expediency of a Uniform Bankrupt Law* (New York: n.p., 1840), 13; Speech of Sen. Oliver H. Smith, May 15, 1840, *Appendix to the Congressional Globe*, 26th Cong., 1st sess., 836. For broader discussions of antebellum conceptualizations of "debt slavery," see Edward Balleisen, *Navigating Failure: Bankruptcy and Commercial Society in Antebellum America* (Chapel Hill: University of North Carolina Press, 2001), 165–67; and Scott Sandage, *Born Losers: A History of Failure in America* (Cambridge: Harvard University Press, 2005), 190–99.

2 The Boston Prison Discipline Society did make a priority of opposing imprisonment for debt, but the abolition of that legal institution constituted only one facet of the broader impulse to reconstruct the handling of personal and business insolvency.
3 Antebellum reformers who embraced the calls for revamping the way that Americans handled bankruptcy included Arthur and Lewis Tappan, the Philadelphia minister and writer Henry Boardman, and the editors of the New York City abolitionist newspaper *The Colored American*.
4 Nineteenth-century observers repeatedly estimated that over 90% of American mercantile concerns eventually ended in bankruptcy. See Balleisen, *Navigating Failure*, 3–7.
5 On Civil War–era comparisons between bankrupts and slaves, see Sandage, *Born Losers*, 199–218; for a discussion of analogous comparisons in antebellum debates over bankruptcy, see Balleisen, *Navigating Failure*, 166–67.
6 "An Act to Establish a Uniform System of Bankruptcy throughout the United States," *United States Statutes at Large* (Washington, D.C.: GPO, 1937–), 14:522–23, sect. 14; Speech of Representative Kasson, March 27, 1866, *Congressional Globe*, March 27, 1866, 39th Cong., 1st sess., 1686. See also the speech of Senator Doolittle, February 1, 1867, *Congr. Globe*, 39th Cong., 2nd sess., 951.
7 Speech of Representative Jenckes, June 1, 1864, *Congr. Globe*, 37th Cong., 1st sess., 238. For close parallels in the debates surrounding the 1841 Bankruptcy Act, see Speeches of Representatives Milton Brown and Fessenden, August 12, 11, 1841, *Appendix to the Congressional Globe*, 27th. Cong., 1st sess., 482, 271.
8 James H. Morehead, *American Apocalypse: Yankee Protestants and the Civil War, 1860–1869* (New Haven: Yale University Press, 1978), 121–25, 194–96.
9 Leading accounts of abolitionist views of land reform include: Richard Curry, "The Abolitionists and Reconstruction: A Critical Appraisal," *Journal of Southern History* 34 (1968): 527–45; Eric Foner, *Politics and Ideology in the Age of the Civil War* (New York: Oxford University Press, 1980), 97–149; Richard H. Abbott, *Cotton and Capital: Boston Businessmen and Antislavery Reform, 1854–1868* (Amherst: University of Massachusetts Press, 1991), 138–215.
10 Balleisen, *Navigating Failure*, 69–108.
11 Joseph Hopkinson, "Lecture on Commercial Integrity," *Hunt's Merchants' Magazine* 1 (1839): 378; *Expediency of a Uniform Bankrupt Law*, 15–17; J. N. Bellows, "The Morals of Trade: Number 5," *Hunt's Merchants' Magazine* 6 (1842): 453; "The Late Bankrupt Law of the United States," *Pennsylvania Law Journal* 3 (1844): 13.
12 E. M. Gibson, "Going into Business," *Ballou's Magazine* 1 (1855): 37–41.
13 Gibson, "Going into Business." See also *Shinning It: A Tale of the Tape-Cutter; or, The Mechanic Turned Merchant* (New York: M. Y. Beach, 1844); T. S. Arthur, "Marrying a Merchant," *Godey's Lady Book* 25 (1842): 160–66; "The Value of a Clerkship in New York," *Hunt's Merchants' Magazine* 20 (1849): 570; A Counting-House Man [author], *Herbert Tracy; or, The Trials of Mercantile Life and the Morality of Trade* (New York: J. C.

Riker, 1851); Freeman Hunt, *Worth and Wealth: A Collection of Maxims, Morals and Miscellanies for Merchants and Men of Business* (New York: Stringer & Townsend, 1856), 315–17.

14 Speech of Senator Stewart, February 4, 1867, *Congr. Globe*, 39th Cong., 2nd sess., 980. This expectation eventually proved incorrect, as Congress repealed the Bankruptcy Act in 1878.

15 Speech of Representative Conkling, January 8, 1863, *Congr. Globe*, 37th Cong., 2nd sess., 223.

16 On the regulatory provisions of the 1867 legislation, see "An Act to Establish a Uniform System of Bankruptcy," 517–41, and especially sections 26, 30, 31, 35, and 39. The quotation is from Edwin James, "Letter to the Editor," *New York Times*, February 4, 1865.

17 *The Independent*, December 24, 1863; speech of Senator Wilson, February 4, 1867, *Congr. Globe*, 39th Cong., 1st sess., 980. For similar sentiments concerning the impact of a federal bankruptcy law on the supply of credit, see the speech of Representative Lovejoy, January 7, 1863, 37th Cong., 2nd sess., 224.

18 Speech of Representative Conkling, January 8, 1863.

LAURA L. MITCHELL

More Meteor than Martyr
The Legacy of John Brown

Ralph Waldo Emerson did as much as anyone to immortalize John Brown's murderous and treasonous actions and generate widespread sympathy for Brown among white northerners. On November 8, 1859, one week after Brown was sentenced to die for raiding the federal arsenal at Harpers Ferry, Virginia, in the hopes of freeing the slaves, Emerson rescued Brown from a barrage of attacks on all sides—from Democrats and southerners to Republicans—and helped turn the tide toward sympathy and respect for Brown. Emerson was in a position to influence such a change. He was "widely regarded as America's leading intellectual," according to David Reynolds, and in the fees he received as a popular lecturer, he was second only to Wendell Phillips. He did not frequently weigh in on the social issues of the day, but when he did, "it was with the power, the overwhelmingness, of an avalanche," as Walt Whitman noted. Emerson had previously immortalized the town of Lexington, Massachusetts, saying that it was here that "the shot heard round the world" was fired. Now, one month before Brown died, he provided another unforgettable characterization, this one of John Brown: "the new saint awaiting his martyrdom . . . will make the gallows glorious like the cross." If Brown himself "manufactured martyrdom," he received a lot of help from people like Emerson.[1]

Emerson's remarks may have influenced Lincoln. On December 1, 1859, one month after Emerson's statement on Brown and the day before Brown was hung, Lincoln referred to Brown with surprising respect, even though, as a Republican candidate for president, it was crucial that he distance himself from Brown and his treasonous raid. Lincoln acknowledged that "John Brown has shown great courage, rare unselfishness, as even" Governor Henry Wise of Virginia "testifies." A few days later, while vigorously denouncing Brown's violent actions, Lincoln identified with him by saying that Brown "agreed with us in thinking slavery wrong."[2]

Four years later, in August 1864, Lincoln felt so inspired by Brown's raid on Harpers Ferry that he sought, in effect, to emulate it. In the midst of civil war, he could now endorse rather than shun principled and violent actions. He requested an urgent meeting with Frederick Douglass, who had already declared Brown to be "THE man of this nineteenth century" and considered Brown's friendship "among the highest privileges of my life." Lincoln was dejected about his gloomy prospects for reelection and worried that if he failed to be re-elected, there would be a negotiated peace with slavery still intact. And so he proposed to Douglass a plan that resembled John Brown's efforts to invade the South and free the slaves. He wanted Douglass to organize a band of black scouts "to go into the rebel states, beyond the lines of our armies, and carry the news of emancipation, and urge the slaves to come within our boundaries," as Douglass recalled. Douglass was amazed by Lincoln's John Brown plan, for although he considered Brown a hero and martyr (as did almost every other African American) and knew that Brown stood apart from virtually every other white man in his ability to befriend and identify with blacks and make their cause his own, he also knew that Lincoln was no radical and in 1860 had denounced Brown's militant actions. Douglass eagerly accepted Lincoln's proposal and began preparing for the invasion, until Sherman's victory at Atlanta all but clinched Lincoln's prospects for reelection and rendered the plan unnecessary. After his meeting with Lincoln, Douglass saw the president in a new light. His John Brown plan "showed a deeper moral conviction against slavery than I had ever seen before in anything spoken or written by him," Douglass noted.[3]

If Brown was treated as a fanatic, madman, and pariah at the time of his capture in October 1859, by the summer of 1861 he was "a mascot of sorts for the Union army," as Franny Nudelman notes. Time and again, Union soldiers commemorated his martyrdom by singing "John Brown's Body," which became a favorite Union song throughout the war:

John Brown's body lies a-mouldering in the grave,
His soul is marching on.
Glory, glory hallelujah!
His soul is marching on.
He's gone to be a soldier in the army of the Lord,
His soul is marching on.
John Brown's knapsack is strapped upon his back,
His soul is marching on!
His pet lambs will meet him on the way,
They go marching on!
They will hang Jeff Davis to a sour apple tree,
As they march along!
Now, three rousing Cheers for the Union,
As we are marching on!

Hundreds of thousands of Union soldiers regularly chanted these lines to inspire them, and give them courage and comfort, as they prepared for battle and possible death.[4]

John Brown's actions at Harpers Ferry also inspired Julia Ward Howe to change the lyrics (though not the music) of "John Brown's Body," and create in 1862 "The Battle Hymn of the Republic," one of the great war songs in the nation's history, which likened the war to Armageddon. And John Brown's actions inspired Sojourner Truth to write a song, also to the tune of "John Brown's Body," for the "first Michigan Regiment of colored troops," as they marched to battle.[5]

John Brown's actions at Harpers Ferry, Emerson's words at Concord, and the song that immortalized Brown for the masses were understandable responses to a culture of violence. In times of peace, Brown never achieved the status of hero in mainstream American culture. According to Laura Mitchell, he was "martyr to some" but a "motivator to few." But in a culture of war, Brown's militant means provided inspiration and motivation to millions. Such endorsement can be seen most clearly in African American writings from Frederick Douglass through Malcolm X. Black writers have generally characterized their America as a culture of violence—racial violence in particular—and have rarely wavered in championing Brown and endorsing his use of violence, much as they have rarely criticized violent efforts among slaves to gain freedom. Numerous other Americans have also treated Brown as a hero during what they perceived to be a culture of war. During the Vietnam war, the Weather Underground offered a tribute to Brown by titling their journal *Osawatomie*, after the sobriquet Brown received while fighting in Kansas. In mainstream culture, Brown's status as a hero has risen during wartime and receded in times of peace. But many radicals and others occupying the social margins have felt that America is *always* a culture at war; for them, John Brown has been a beacon of truth and constant source of inspiration.

Historians have been trying to make sense of John Brown for almost 150 years. Who was he? A perpetually failing businessman or a victim of economic forces beyond his control? A dedicated family man or a restless wanderer who abandoned his wife and younger children for months and even years at a time? A noble abolitionist or a cold-blooded murderer? A madman or a martyr? Ultimately, the effort to create a clearer picture of John Brown may be futile. The complexity of his beliefs, ambitions, and actions, however well documented, is almost dizzying, or, at any rate, defies attempts to paint a coherent portrait of the man who played a significant role on the road to the Civil War.[6]

What is clear about John Brown is that he sought to confront the evil of slavery and to destroy it. His plan in October 1859 was to raid the federal arsenal at Harpers Ferry and distribute the weapons to slaves so that they could, in effect, free themselves. Although Brown did not put in place a network to notify the slaves of his attack, he seems to have fully expected them to hear of the raid once it occurred and to flock to Harpers Ferry to take up arms. For numerous reasons, Brown's raid failed. But, even in failure, John Brown transfixed the populace and helped propel the nation to war.[7]

Northerners and southerners predictably had differing interpretations of the events of late 1859. But, although opinions about Brown varied by region and within each region, the image of Brown as a martyr to his cause was central to all. The South uniformly condemned the raid, rejoiced over Brown's execution, and insisted that the North follow suit. Southerners viewed Brown as the North's martyr and as proof that cooperation with the North was futile. Southern editors, focusing on the abolitionists, rather than on more moderate northerners, told their readers that a majority of the North supported Brown as a martyr and a hero, not held him in contempt as a robber and murderer.[8]

Northern reactions, however, were varied, and no monolithic praise or denunciation of Brown and his raid emerged. Abolitionists, always a small percentage of the population, hailed him as a saint. But many in the North, most notably Abraham Lincoln, concluded that although Brown's goal to end slavery was laudable, his means were indefensible. Still other northerners dismissed Brown as a treasonous lunatic.[9]

The variety of opinion about Brown arises in part because, although his death certainly made him a martyr, his status as such was ambivalent. Martyrs derive their power not only from the manner of their deaths or the justice of their causes, but also from the moral suasion of their actions. Most in the North concluded along with the South that Brown was neither an admirable example of Christian behavior nor a moral leader. With the exception of the abolitionists, many northerners rejected Brown and were not inspired by his example to work actively for the eradication of slavery. In the end, Brown's raid and his death likely did more to further alienate the South from the North than to encourage the North to wage war against slavery.

Although most northerners rejected Brown and his raid, Brown generally appears in the historical record as an inspirational hero-martyr. This is due in part to the abolitionists' hagiography of Brown. One particularly compelling analysis of Brown as martyr is Paul Finkelman's "Manufacturing Martyrdom:

The Antislavery Response to John Brown's Raid." Finkelman details how abolitionists elevated Brown to a martyr's status and how Brown himself used the last month of his life to cultivate this image. Although abolitionists, including those who backed Brown's raid, initially distanced themselves from Brown, they "soon realized that John Brown was potentially the most significant martyr to the cause since Elijah P. Lovejoy." Even before Brown's sentencing, opponents of slavery saw glory in his execution and seized upon the day as a publicity opportunity. In speeches and meetings before large crowds, Finkelman observes, abolitionists began "Brown's canonization" in concert with Brown's own "carefully cultivated" martyrdom in prison and in the courtroom.[10]

Finkelman also points out the ways in which the South contributed to Brown's sanctification. By forcing Brown to stand trial immediately after he was captured, wounded and without benefit of his own attorney, the State of Virginia added to the halo that northern abolitionists had bestowed on Brown. Lying on a pallet in the courtroom, Brown looked every bit the victim of the South. At the same time, Virginia officials allowed Brown to correspond and conduct interviews, giving him the opportunity "to write hundreds of letters, justifying his crusade to the North and to the world" and thus inadvertently furthering a negative image of the South by means of Brown's own words. The fame he gained from his verbal raid from prison was one reason Brown could confidently write to his brother Jeremiah: "I am worth inconceivably more to hang than for any other purpose."[11]

And John Brown was right: his was a purposeful death. Even before his execution, abolitionists began publishing speeches, books, and memorabilia to establish him as a human sacrifice on the altar of freedom. Abolitionists recounted numerous "holy" moments in Brown's life and death, such as the tale of Brown kissing a slave child on the way to his execution. The versions vary, but each contains roughly the same elements: Brown, having refused the ministrations of a proslavery pastor, instead seeks solace from slaves, either in the form of a slave child or a slave mother and her children. He kisses a slave child tenderly, either at the jail or at the gallows. The story, first published in the New York Tribune, does have some basis in fact, but, as Finkelman points out, its embellished retelling quickly became more fiction than reality.[12]

Two of the most famous versions of the story appear in poetry: John Greenleaf Whittier's *Brown of Osawatomie* and Lydia Maria Child's *The Hero's Heart*. Both poets depict Brown as a loving patriarch and as the embodiment of Christian sacrifice. Whittier, describing Brown's last moments on earth, wrote:

More Meteor than Martyr 291

> Then the bold, blue eye grew tender,
> And the old, harsh face grew mild,
> As he stooped between the jeering ranks
> And kissed the negro's child!

Whittier dwells particularly on the redemptive power of Brown's kiss and sees in it the halo of martyrdom:

> That kiss, from all its guilty means,
> Redeemed the good intent,
> And round the grisly fighter's hair
> The Martyr's aureole bent!

For Whittier, Brown's kiss rights all wrongs; the power of his kiss seems equal to, and perhaps is the metaphoric opposite of, Judas's kiss of betrayal. Whittier then implored the reader to focus on the sacrifice of Brown's death rather than the violence of his life:

> Not the raid of midnight terror,
> But the thought which underlies;
> Not the outlaw's pride of daring,
> But the Christian sacrifice.[13]

Similarly, Lydia Maria Child painted Brown as a representative of Christian sacrifice in her poem *The Hero's Heart*:

> The old man met not friendly eye,
> When last he looked on earth and sky;
> But one small child, with timid air,
> Was gazing on his silver hair.
>
> As that dark brow to his upturned,
> The tender heart within him yearned;
> And, fondly stooping o'er her face,
> He kissed her, for her injured race.

As with Whittier's depiction of the same act, Child imbues Brown's kiss with power to redeem an entire group of people. Like Christ, Brown has the power to save. And, as Child rhapsodized, Christ approved:

> But Jesus smiled the sight to see,
> And said, "He did it unto me"![14]

Thus enhanced for effect, Finkelman argues, the story "helped guarantee Brown's status as a martyr, especially as it was well suited to the sentimental tendencies of Victorian Americans."[15] Furthermore, as Seymour Drescher has written, abolitionists characterized Brown as a Christ figure on the way to the Golgotha of slavery: Brown left his jail cell, bid farewell to his compatriots, and kissed the slave child in a Christ-like manner. He then mounted his coffin for the ride to the gallows, just as Christ had carried his own cross. Once at the gallows, he refused a signal from the executioner; Christ had refused the wine and gall. And Brown died slowly, not as slowly as one who is crucified; but his pulse beat for 35 minutes after he was hung. This chain of events puts Brown—executed on a Friday, no less—on his own Via Dolorosa with readily identifiable Stations of the Cross.[16]

This story about Brown's final hours, as arresting today as it was in 1859, is an intensely dramatic image of Brown as a martyred hero. In this context, it is not surprising that Henry David Thoreau declared that future generations would honor Brown, or that Henry Highland Garnet confidently predicted that December 2 would live on in the hearts of men. The Civil War itself also seems to vindicate the abolitionists' terminology. In retrospect, Brown's personal sacrifice appears to presage the nation's four-year-long human sacrifice. And Brown seems to be a prophet whose prophecy came true: the issue of slavery was, as he wrote in his final statement, settled by blood.[17]

But despite Thoreau's and Garnet's predictions, Brown never really attained the status of hero in mainstream American culture that his martyrdom may have promised. Although some of Brown's admirers formed (and continue to maintain) societies in the man's honor, Brown has never enjoyed the broad and enduring respect and recognition given to other American notables. Everyone knows the Fourth of July; no one knows the Second of December. Federal holidays commemorate the lives of Washington and Lincoln; in October, the calendar pauses for Columbus, not John Brown. Children are still taught the song *John Brown's Body*, but the *Battle Hymn of the Republic*, which Julia Ward Howe composed to the tune of *John Brown's Body* after she heard Union soldiers singing the song, is arguably the more famous of the two lyrics.[18]

There are several reasons why Brown, although martyr to some, was motivator to few. One is the question of Brown's sanity. Brown was routinely characterized as insane at the time of the raid, and historians continue to look for clues to his mental state in the late 1850s. Immediately after the raid, abolitionists as well as leading Republicans dismissed Brown as insane, and members of his family petitioned the court with evidence of a family history of mental illness in an attempt to spare Brown the death penalty. Some suggested that Brown's experiences in Kansas, especially the loss of his son, had left him in mental torment. Leonard Bacon, a leading northern clergyman and an editor of the *Independent*, called Brown's brain "diseased." Importantly, at the same time that many of Brown's critics dismissed the raid as the result of mental imbalance, they granted that his cause was just.[19]

In addition, many northerners saw Brown as an arrogant, even treasonous, man who presumed too much about his own moral authority. Clearly, Brown had little regard for the formal or informal rules of civil society. Capable of violence, he had also written a Provisional Constitution for a new territory to be populated by freed slaves. Perhaps the best summation of northern opinion about Brown can be found in Abraham Lincoln's Cooper Union address in February 1860. In his now famous speech, Lincoln condemned Brown and made clear his and the Republican Party's intention to squash insurrection. While not condemning Brown's commitment to end slavery, Lincoln characterized Brown as a danger to the nation because of his belief that he was ordained by God to avenge the sin of slavery outside of the political process. As the historian Bertram Wyatt-Brown explains, some saw Brown "as a sectional Judas Iscariot, the betrayer of long-standing political and moral compromises. Moderates on both sides of the great division hoped to diminish his stature, whether as either Satan's envoy or God's archangel." Northern clergymen, including those who wished for an end to slavery, echoed this view. Richard Carwardine, in his landmark study on the politics of antebellum evangelicals, writes that "[m]any northern clergy of impeccable antislavery credentials took the view that the raid had been foolhardy and wrong."[20]

Brown also fell short of being a moral exemplar because of the moral ambiguity of violence as a means to a defensible end. Many of Brown's most ardent defenders were pacifists and non-resistants who either rejected Brown's violence or accepted his methods only with great difficulty. This was especially true because of the timing of Brown's raid. By late 1859, the political process in Kansas seemed to be working and a peaceful end to slavery seemed like a possibility.[21] Eventually, many of Brown's pacifist supporters did condone his methods, but in so doing, they embraced him only as an imperfect tool of divine justice, like a plague. For William Lloyd Garrison, writes historian George Fredrickson, John Brown was "an instrument of divine judgment—like fire or pestilence.[22]

For all of these reasons, the image of Brown as a heroic martyr was less powerful in the North than the abolitionists manufacturing his martyrdom may have hoped. Although most northerners agreed with Brown that slavery was wrong, few could say that his raid at Harpers Ferry was "good" or even feasible. They could conclude only that he had wanted to do something good and that he had failed. And, in late 1859, with the political process appearing to work in Kansas, the true Christian was called to persevere patiently in that process. Ultimately, northerners embraced Brown reluctantly and half-heartedly.

But that does not imply that Brown's life and death had no impact. The raid on Harpers Ferry and the resulting executions, while not galvanizing the North to behave violently, nonetheless introduced violence as a possible means for ending slavery. Like the beating of Charles Sumner in the Senate, Harpers Ferry helped create an atmosphere in which violence was a part of the controversy over slavery. As Paul Finkelman puts it, Brown "prepared the antislavery movement for the shift from an age of Christian love and peace to one of Christian visions of an apocalypse and Old Testament notions of a vengeful God."[23]

The historian Peter Knupfer makes a similar case, arguing persuasively that war was not a foregone conclusion in late 1859. The fact that slaves had not joined Brown's raid was evidence to some northerners that no irrepressible conflict existed. Knupfer also points to northerners who argued against Brown's execution in order to "deprive abolitionists of a martyr." But the calls for mercy for John Brown were not heeded, North or South. Citing George Fredrickson, Knupfer concludes that the reaction to Brown's raid "signaled a growing approval of strong, decisive, and violent action." As for southerners, Knupfer contends, the raid "affirmed . . . not that disunion and war were inevitable but that a Republican victory would mean disunion and war."[24]

Perhaps with this in mind, the poet Longfellow wrote in his diary that December 2 was "a great day" in American history, "the date of a new Revolution—quite as much needed as the old one." Lydia Maria Child also saw the events of late 1859 as foreshadowing a new revolution. And Herman Melville, in his poem "The Portent," struck a similar theme, calling Brown "The meteor of war."[25] Despite the swiftness with which Brown was apprehended, tried, and executed, Brown was still, as Melville put it, a meteor. For the South, he was a white Nat Turner. As a martyr, he legitimated his own death, and, as meteor, he signaled a growing acceptance of violence and death as a means of resolving political conflict.

NOTES

1 David S. Reynolds, *John Brown, Abolitionist: The Man Who Killed Slavery, Sparked the Civil War, and Seeded Civil Rights* (New York: Knopf, 2005), 363–67, quotations from 364–66.

2 Roy Basler, ed., *The Collected Works of Abraham Lincoln* (New Brunswick: Rutgers University Press, 1953), 3:496, 502.
3 John Stauffer, "Across the Great Divide: The Friendship between Lincoln and Frederick Douglass required from both a change of heart," *Time Magazine: Special Issue*, July 4, 2005, 65; Douglass, quoted in John Stauffer, *The Black Hearts of Men: Radical Abolitionists and the Transformation of Race* (Cambridge: Harvard University Press, 2002), 251.
4 Franny Nudelman, *John Brown's Body: Slavery, Violence, and the Culture of War* (Chapel Hill: University of North Carolina Press, 2004), 14–15.
5 Ernest Lee Tuveson, *Redeemer Nation: The Idea of America's Millennial Role* (Chicago: University of Chicago Press, 1968), 197–202.
6 The best current overview of John Brown's life and the impact of the Harpers Ferry raid is Paul Finkelman, ed., *His Soul Goes Marching On: Responses to John Brown and the Harpers Ferry Raid* (Charlottesville: University of Virginia Press, 1995). Two enduring biographies of Brown are Stephen Oates, *To Purge This Land with Blood*, 2nd ed. (Amherst: University of Massachusetts Press, 1984); and Richard O. Boyer, *The Legend of John Brown* (New York: Knopf, 1973). The image of John Brown among women is explored in Wendy Haman Venet, " 'Cry Aloud and Spare Not': Northern Antislavery Women and John Brown's Raid," in Finkelman, ed., *His Soul Goes Marching On*, 98–115.
7 Brown's raid is generally seen as a failure, and most argue that given Brown's poor planning, he could not reasonably have expected slaves to hear of the raid and respond quickly. For example, see Paul Finkelman, "Manufacturing Martyrdom: The Antislavery Response to John Brown's Raid," in Finkelman, ed., *His Soul Goes Marching On*, 41–66; and Oates, *To Purge This Land*, 287. In contrast to this view, John Stauffer has argued that slaves and free blacks around Harpers Ferry did have information about the raid and assisted in several ways. Stauffer, *The Black Hearts of Men*, 256–57. Whether he succeeded or failed, Brown still had achieved fame (or infamy) throughout the nation.
8 Peter Knupfer, "Crisis in Conservatism: Northern Unionism and the Harpers Ferry Raid," in Finkelman, ed., *His Soul Goes Marching On*, 123. For a brief overview of reactions in northern and southern newspapers to Brown's raid and trial, see Edward Stone, ed., *Incident at Harper's Ferry* (Englewood Cliffs, N.J.: Prentice-Hall, 1956), 154–81.
9 See especially the following in Finkelman, ed., *His Soul Goes Marching On*: Finkelman, "Manufacturing Martyrdom"; Daniel C. Littlefield, "Blacks, John Brown, and a Theory of Manhood," 67–97; Wendy Haman Venet, " 'Cry Aloud and Spare Not': Northern Antislavery Women and John Brown's Raid," 98–115; and Seymour Drescher, "Servile Insurrection and John Brown's Body in Europe," 253–95.
10 For a thorough treatment of the Secret Six, see Jeffery Rossbach, *Ambivalent Conspirators* (Philadelphia: University of Pennsylvania, 1982).
11 Finkelman, "Manufacturing Martyrdom," 43.

12. Images of Brown, including one by Currier and Ives, were sold to raise money for Mary Brown and her family, as were poems and books; see ibid., 44–47, 51, 53.
13. John Greenleaf Whittier, "Brown of Osawatomie," in *Echoes of Harper's Ferry*, ed. James Redpath (1860; reprint, Arno Press, 1969), 303–4.
14. Lydia Maria Child, "The Hero's Heart," in Redpath, ed., *Echoes*, 348.
15. Finkelman, "Manufacturing Martyrdom," 52.
16. For Drescher's findings about the European reaction to Brown, see Drescher, "Servile Insurrection." For a succinct recounting of Brown's final hour, see Charles Joyner, "Guilty of the Holiest Crime: The Passion of John Brown," in Finkelman, ed., *His Soul Goes Marching On*, 296–98.
17. Henry David Thoreau, "Lecture Delivered October 30 and November 1, 1859," in Redpath, ed., *Echoes of Harper's Ferry*, 42. Garnet is quoted in Littlefield, "Blacks, John Brown, and a Theory," 67.
18. For Julia Ward Howe and Battle Hymn of the Republic, see Venet, "'Cry Aloud and Spare Not,'" 99.
19. Recent evidence indicates that Brown may have suffered from a mood disorder, perhaps manic-depression. See Robert E. McGlone, "John Brown, Henry Wise, and the Politics of Insanity," in Finkelman, ed., *His Soul Goes Marching On*, 213–52. Leonard Bacon is cited in Richard Carwardine, *Evangelicals and Politics in Antebellum America* (New Haven: Yale University Press, 1993), 284, n. 19. For Brown's family's attempt to spare Brown's life using an insanity defense, see Oates, *To Purge This Land*, 329–32.
20. Wyatt-Brown in Soul, "'Volcano beneath a Mountain of Snow': John Brown and the Problem of Interpretation," in Finkelman, ed., *His Soul Goes Marching On*, 11–12; Carwardine, *Evangelicals and Politics*, 283–84. See also Knupfer, "Crisis in Conservatism," 135–37 and Joyner, "'Guilty of Holiest Crime,'" 315, 317. Northern newspapers reinforce this impression. See Stone, ed., *Incident at Harper's Ferry*, 154–83.
21. Oates, *To Purge This Land*, 217, 257. Wendy Hyman Venet writes that Lydia Maria Child "deplored" Brown's timing; see Venet, "'Cry Aloud and Spare Not,'" 106.
22. George M. Fredrickson, *The Inner Civil War: Northern Intellectuals and the Crisis of the Union* (New York: Harper and Row, 1965), 41–43. For the reactions of Lydia Maria Child and other female abolitionists, see Venet, "'Cry Aloud,'" 100–103.
23. Wyatt-Brown "'Volcano beneath a Mountain of Snow,'" 24, 31; Finkelman, "Manufacturing Martyrdom," 59–60.
24. Knupfer, "Crisis in Conservatism," 119, 125, 140, 142.
25. Longfellow quoted in Stone, ed., *Incident at Harper's Ferry*, 198. For Child, see Venet, "'Cry Aloud'," 106. Melville's poem appears in Stone, ed., *Incident*, 199.

RICHARD WIGHTMAN FOX

Performing Emancipation

Richard Wightman Fox describes with great verve the ritualized performance of emancipation at Henry Ward Beecher's Plymouth Church in Brooklyn, New York. By raising money for a light-skinned slave named Sarah, congregants could "feel themselves to be imitators of Christ as well as antislavery emancipators." And while they helped liberate Sarah from slavery, they also found deliverance from their own bondage to sin.

As Fox shows, there were strict limits on the nature and form of such performances of emancipation. The slave in question had to meet three criteria: she needed to be in the midst of an escape attempt, willing to risk everything for freedom; she needed to be a "Christian girl"; and she needed to be beautiful, which for Beecher meant a light-skinned black. In rescuing light-skinned female slaves, Beecher's performance of emancipation "mirrored" southern slave auctions, which similarly placed far greater value on light-skinned female slaves

THE "FREEDOM RING." MR. BEECHER PLEADING FOR MONEY TO SET A SLAVE CHILD FREE.

On February 5, 1860, nine-year-old "Pinky" was "redeemed" at Plymouth Church for $800. Beecher later said of her that "she was too fair and beautiful a child for her own good." From Thomas W. Knox, The Life and Work of Henry Ward Beecher (Philadelphia, 1887), p. 159.

than on dark-skinned ones. And by selecting a light-skinned, Christian woman, his congregation, when looking into her face, could see themselves and their own purity, threatened by southern corruption. In Beecher's noble-hearted efforts to emancipate slaves, he accommodated prevailing understandings of race, gender, political economy, and religion. His performances of slave emancipation expose the limits to freedom and the dark side of the American soul.

One of Harriet Beecher Stowe's many memorable characters in Uncle Tom's Cabin (1852) is Ohio state senator John Bird. Like many northerners, he has gone on record in support of the Fugitive Slave Act of 1850, despite its unsavory requirement that citizens help turn runaway slaves over to the law. Public duties are not always pleasant, he tells his wife Mary, who promptly chastises him for his insufferably "political" distinction between the public and the private. If he were ever to meet a runaway slave face to face, she says, he would spontaneously do the right thing in spite of his rigid political reasoning. Naturally their argument is interrupted by commotion on the back porch: runaway slave Eliza Harris and her son Harry, fresh from their miraculous escape across the ice-clogged Ohio River, have arrived in search of solace. Mary's prediction, of course, comes true. Quickly John dispatches his principles and joins the campaign to protect Eliza.[1]

In Stowe's apt phrase, drawn from the Catholic theology of the Eucharist, John Bird has been transformed by "the magic of the real presence of distress." In her visible suffering, Eliza becomes the outward sign of an inward social evil—slavery—the moral degradation of which (Stowe notes throughout her novel) is often hidden from view by compromising politicians and economic interest-seekers, north and south. The goal of her novelistic preaching is to awaken readers to the evil disclosed in the obvious sufferings of slaves—the beatings, the family separations, the enforced ignorance and illiteracy (preventing slaves from reading the Bible and thus having a chance at becoming true Protestant Christians)—but also in the less highly publicized practice that threatened a young female slave such as Eliza: purchase for sexual exploitation. In Uncle Tom's Cabin Stowe's characters Cassy and Emmeline had already succumbed to sexual slavery; the fleeing Eliza ran the immediate risk of falling into it, despite her marriage and her child.[2]

Mrs. Stowe grasped that even indirect reference to sexual bondage (in Uncle Tom's Cabin she had her characters speak of it, and described the sale of a teen-aged victim, but she did not portray it) possessed tremendous power to mobilize northern opinion against slavery. She had watched as her younger brother Henry Ward Beecher had taken a leading part in the 1848 campaign to purchase the freedom of the Edmondson sisters. In the concluding chapter of *Uncle Tom's Cabin* Stowe cited the "Edmundson" [sic] sisters as proof that her characters Cassy and Emmeline were drawn from real life. An examination of Henry's involvement in the Edmondson's "redemption," and of one later slave purchase that he organized, helps illuminate the ways in which many evangelical northerners brought to mind the evil of slavery in the 1840s and 1850s. They saw it as an unconscionable evil in its deprivation of liberty, but they took it as a Satanic evil in its assault upon the virtue of black women, especially of those black women who looked virtually white.

From a twenty-first century standpoint, the efforts of antislavery evangelists such as Harriet Beecher Stowe and Henry Ward Beecher may well appear fatally compromised by prejudicial presuppositions of their own, including gross stereotypes of African Americans and insidious distinctions between light-skinned and dark-skinned blacks. But a social evil as deeply entrenched as American slavery could probably only be uprooted in mid-nineteenth-century America by a broad coalition, one that joined a tiny band of radical abolitionists (some of whom, like Angelina and Sarah Grimké, Theodore Weld, William Lloyd Garrison, Gerrit Smith, Wendell Phillips, and Parker Pillsbury, to name a few, had moved beyond the conventional conception of inherent racial or gender differences) to a large cohort of cultural moderates (including the Beechers) for whom racial and gender typing formed part of the order of things. A Henry Ward Beecher carried enormous personal influence into the antislavery cause, and that cause became the abolitionist's pressing priority after he got wind of the fugitive-slave provisions of the Compromise of 1850. Naturally, he brought his entire social worldview into the battle with him. Emancipation for African Americans depended on the militant activity of black and white abolitionists, but it also relied on the efforts of mainstream leaders such as Beecher, who maintained rigid views of black-white differences—including black-white differences within the slave population.

On October 23, 1848, Beecher appeared as a featured speaker at a Broadway Tabernacle "Liberation Meeting" called by a Methodist committee to raise $2,000 for the redemption of the two Edmondson sisters, captured at sea in an escape attempt organized by their father. At the meeting, a collection was taken up and, as the baskets were passed, a group of young men promised to make up whatever deficiency might remain. "They seemed to feel," wrote one observer, "that one young libertine at the South would pay half the price himself, to possess half such 'property.' " The northerners apparently imagined themselves locked in battle with southern dandies over the fate of two beautiful women. Battling licentiousness as well as slavery, they concurred with their southern rivals about one thing: the Edmondson sisters' beauty.[3]

The young northerners' desire to protect the sisters from the depredations of southern men may have been sparked by the passionate conclusion of Beecher's speech. His remarks were framed as a series of beliefs that governed his approach to slave redemption. At the outset he contended that slave purchase could never become a general strategy for putting an end to slavery. Like other moderates, he did not mind the idea of compensating slaveowners, but he believed that "the money is not to be had. It does not exist in all the coffers of the North for such a purpose."

Only special cases merited the extraordinary expedient of a northern fundraiser. Three elements in the Edmondsons' case made a financial rescue mandatory and urgent. First, the Edmondsons had been rounded up while in the midst of an escape attempt. Their willingness to risk everything for liberty obligated anyone who cherished freedom to subscribe to the redemption campaign. Slaves who accepted their fate, by contrast, deserved not "one cent" toward their purchase. Second, the Edmondsons were "Christian girls." Beecher barraged the Tabernacle audience with that phrase. "A sale by human flesh dealers of Christian girls! I love to repeat that epithet, Christian girls! The Edmondson girls does very well, but Christian girls! Christian slaves!! It seemed to me as I first uttered these words as if I could hear a scoffing, jeering fiend of hell echo them with a grin of derision."

Finally, the sisters merited redemption for a reason that, according to Beecher, went to "the interior of slavery." He said that no words could express the horror that this third reason aroused in him—"as if all words were spirits which hover around one and mock his desire to speak." Southerners were buying the beauty as well as the brawn of slaves, their souls as well as their bodies. Slave marketers carefully calibrated the spirit and appearance of slaves and gave those characteristics commercial value. "Here at the north, to be of comely presence is considered a blessing; there at the South, so much money is made of it in the market." It was bad enough that "a slave will bring all the more for being such a fine looking man." But

> if the slave chances to be a woman, she will sell much higher on the stand because she is handsome. That which excites among us the profoundest respect, goes there to augment her value—not as a wife, not as a sister, but for purposes from the bare idea of which the virtuous soul revolts. In the slave-girl, beauty, refinement, is not a matter of respect, but of profit. And

suppose you add thrift, skill, intelligence. Here, at the North, we take all this as so much added to the man; but there the more there is of thrift, of skill, of intelligence, of enterprise, the higher their price in the market.

The deepest "interior" of the slave system concerned women, not men; at the core lay not merely the alienation of a person's self-control but the reduction of beauty to commerce, a perversion that produced female sexual slavery.[4]

A second slave purchase engineered by Beecher in 1856 allowed him once again to expose what struck him as the darkest evil of the slave system and to spotlight, by contrast, what he considered the moral heart of northern culture: its protection and veneration of women. On a bright Sunday morning in June 1856, Beecher surprised the three thousand worshippers at Plymouth Church in Brooklyn by interrupting the service just before the final hymn. He stepped to the edge of the platform and recounted the story of a young slave woman who had recently been sold by her white father to a slave trader in Virginia. The father, according to Beecher, had wished her to be sent "far south," "for what purposes you can imagine when you see her." The congregation strained for a glimpse of the woman, who was sitting in a front pew. Like Eliza, who suddenly appeared in Senator Bird's home, this young slave woman's surprise appearance in Plymouth Church confronted Beecher's congregants with "the real presence of distress." And she permitted Beecher to put a face on the interior evil of slavery without having to speak of it directly—a near impossibility for him, as he had said at the Broadway Tabernacle in 1848, since in a case of this kind "all words were spirits which hover around one and mock his desire to speak."[5]

Beecher continued his story: the slave trader proved good-hearted, and "moved by compassion" he offered Sarah "the opportunity to purchase her freedom." He raised $200 himself and then let the woman go to Washington to try to raise the rest. She had gotten $500 but still needed $500 to meet the $1200 purchase price. Beecher had been approached (by whom he didn't say) about supplying the remainder. He had agreed to try, but only if the woman came to New York and appeared in his church. The trader had allowed her to go to Brooklyn, but she was honor-bound to go back to slavery in Richmond if she couldn't collect the $500.[6]

Having finished his story, Beecher looked down into the front pew, saying "Come up here, Sarah, and let us all see you." "The slave rose in her seat," the *Times* reported, "a tall, fine looking woman, with barely enough of tinge in her complexion and wave in her hair to betray her colored blood, and hardly an eye in the immense audience but was wet with sympathetic tears, as she, trembling, and completely overcome with emotion, stumbled up the pulpit stairs." The *Independent*'s account concurred on the young woman's color: "The white blood of her father might be traced in her regular features and high, thoughtful brow, while her complexion and wavy hair betrayed her slave mother." Beecher pointed at Sarah and noted ironically, "this is a marketable commodity." He harped on the additional value represented, in the south, by her light skin. Women like her were "put into the scales and silver heaped up as an equivalent for them." "I reverence woman," he went on. "For the sake of the love I bore my mother [who had died when Beecher was a small child], I hold her sacred, even in the lowest position, and will use every means in my power for her uplifting. What will you do now? May she read her liberty in your eyes? Shall she go out free? Christ stretched forth his hand and the sick were restored to health; will you stretch forth your hands and give that without which life is of little worth? Let the plate be passed, and we will see."

A frenzy of giving ensued. "Every purse was in requisition," said the *Independent*. "They gave, and then returned and gave again," wrote the *Times*. "Ladies took rings from their fingers . . . A gentleman from Missouri, a slave-owner, who happened to be present, gave twenty dollars. A prominent Wall Street 'operator' who also happened to be present, gave a fifty dollar bill. One lady took a diamond cross from her dress, and put it into the money box." To cap off the delirious proceedings, Lewis Tappan rose from his pew and told Beecher that he and a few other gentleman would make up any remaining deficit. "Then she was free!" exalted the *Independent*. "And when Mr. Beecher told her [Sarah] so, and announced it to the congregation, there was an involuntary burst of applause."[7]

Late-nineteenth- and twentieth-century accounts of the Plymouth Church fund-raiser of 1856 have labeled it a "slave purchase," "slave redemption," or "slave auction." In a talk at a Plymouth Church meeting some time before his death in 1887, Beecher himself recollected that "I was accustomed, from time to time, to buy slaves here; and it was thrown up that this was one of the best slave-auction places anywhere to be found—that better prices were obtained for slaves that were put up for sale here than for any others." But of course Sarah was not purchased, redeemed, or auctioned by the church, which merely gathered a portion (five-twelfths) of her fixed purchase price by "passing the plates." Sarah actually purchased herself, and that event took place whenever she gave the outstanding balance to her slave-trader owner and he signed away his control. What Beecher's recollection discloses is the possibility that slave traders may have targeted northern antislavery churches when they wished to receive top dollar for certain fair-skinned slave women.[8]

But the idea that Plymouth Church redeemed her indicates an important truth about the fund-raiser. In retrospect, we can see the event as a ritualized performance of emancipation in which Sarah, Beecher, his congregation, and the newspaper reporters all collaborated. They all got to witness what they took to be the exact moment of a human being's liberation from slavery. "Then she was free!," cried the *Independent*. It didn't matter that this wasn't the moment of her legal freedom. It was the moment that joined her impending legal freedom to shared yearnings for full spiritual deliverance. As the pastor of a Manhattan Church had realized when the Edmondson sisters attended his Sunday service after their emancipation, all of the worshippers now shared the same condition: civilly free yet still "slaves to sin and to Satan." The sisters, as "redeemed captives from temporal bondage," could stand as "an emblem and an illustration" of his text for the day, Isaiah 35:10: "The ransomed of the Lord shall return and come to Zion with songs, and everlasting joy upon their heads: they shall obtain joy and gladness, and sighing and sorrow shall flee away." Ongoing cravings for spiritual liberty magnified the celebration of newly enacted civil liberty.[9]

In his remarks from the platform Beecher tied Sarah's condition to that of the man with the withered hand whom Jesus had healed. (He shrewdly chose this text to disarm anyone who might be squeamish about conducting such business on the Sabbath; Jesus, he pointed out, had irked the Pharisees by picking the Sabbath for the healing of the withered hand.) Beecher gave to his audience, not to himself, the power to do as Jesus had done. "I cannot say to her 'Stretch forth thy hand and be free,' " the *Times* had him telling the congregation, "but I can say to you 'Stretch forth your hands and make her free.' " The audience members could feel themselves to be imitators of Christ as well as antislavery emancipators. At the same time, like the Manhattan congregation sharing their service with the Edmondson sisters in 1848, they could experience the hope of deliverance from slavery to sin.

Sarah, meanwhile, liberated herself by locating a preacher and a congregation with whom she could share her power to emancipate and her need for emancipation. Sarah's owner had given her the power to free herself by collecting a sum of money. Taking that power to Plymouth Church, she joined Beecher in giving the congregation the power to liberate her: she bestowed that power by dramatizing her dependence upon them. As she sank sobbing into the chair on the platform beside Beecher, the congregation paid eagerly for the privilege of joining its longstanding commitment to freedom (civil and spiritual) to its spontaneous compassion for Sarah. (Had they been forewarned that a fund-raiser of some kind would occur on that June morning, or did they always bring piles of cash and jewels to church? Did Beecher get a prior promise from Lewis Tappan to cover any shortfall, or was everyone aware of the slave-redemption ritual in which one noble soul would always step up to cover the deficiency? Did conscience-stricken slaveowners like the man from Missouri always show up for services at Plymouth Church, or were they invited to Brooklyn for this particular event?)

The Plymouth fund-raiser for Sarah required a substantial suspension of disbelief on the part of Beecher and his congregation. Beecher was forthright, according to the *Times*, about the speed with which he had brought the case to the congregation. "I could not spend time to go round among you individually to state the case," he told them just before asking Sarah to mount the platform. "And there was need of haste, for the time was limited, and so I thought it best that she should come here among us today, and I would tell you the story and we would see if we could lend her a helping hand." Afterwards rumors flew that Plymouth Church had been scammed by Sarah and the slave trader. Beecher biographer Paxton Hibben wrote in 1927 that Beecher made no effort to verify the facts. In Hibben's view he needed some good press in June 1856 to counteract the bad publicity sparked by the "Beecher Bibles"—the twenty-five Sharp's rifles sent by his church to support the free-Kansas forces. Beecher, according to Hibben, wished to retreat from his new and unwelcome reputation as a radical abolitionist, so he grabbed the expedient of a sentimental slave purchase to reaffirm his moderate antislavery stance.[10]

But Hibben supplies no documentary evidence to back his linkage of the Beecher Bibles to the Beecher slave redemption. Beecher already had plenty of reason to act precipitously in Sarah's case. An exhaustive investigation would certainly delay and perhaps jeopardize the rescue of a young woman from sexual slavery. By taking Sarah's story at face value, Beecher was acting impulsively; but if he was going to err it was going to be on the side of protecting "woman," whom he "reverenced." Her story fulfilled the three conditions he had laid down in 1848 for redeeming a female slave: she was trapped in sexual bondage, she had demonstrated her desire for freedom by fleeing, and she was a Christian (at least according to the *Times* story—neither the *Times* nor the *Independent* reported Beecher making that point from the stage). Beecher's Plymouth congregation went along eagerly. They had no more need of proof than he did. It sufficed that their cash and jewels targeted a likely manifestation of the interior evil of slavery.[11]

In his postbellum recollection of the Plymouth slave purchases, Beecher said that he was criticized at the time by "some [who] thought there was an inconsistency in it." He did not specify what the inconsistency was, but he may have been referring to the common abolitionist complaint that it made no sense to condemn southern slave traders for putting a price on a human soul and then proceed to pay that price. That act could be seen as legitimizing the slave system both in principle and in practice: in principle, by conceding the right of one person to own another; and in practice, by inuring Americans to slave marketing. Obviously, Beecher rejected both parts of that argument. In his later recollection he tried to answer the practical objection: his slave auctions did not normalize slave selling; they "arouse[d] men's feelings against the abomination of slavery, which I hated with an unutterable hatred, and which I still hate in memory as much as then I hated it in substance and in fact." As to principle, Beecher implicitly argued that some abolitionists' focus on the pure logic of the situation blocked them from reacting humanely during emergencies. Their rigidity, he might have said, resembled that of Senator Bird in *Uncle Tom's Cabin*. The urgent rescue through purchase of a woman at risk of sexual slavery no more endorsed her former owner's right to own slaves than Senator Bird's concealing of Eliza amounted to a general attack on the institution of the law. Ethical decisions could not always be rendered in strict obedience to abstract principles.[12]

A more compelling accusation of inconsistency in Beecher's position concerns his apparent limitation of special rescue campaigns to light-skinned female slaves and their children. (His later recollection refers to his having redeemed "living men and women," but I have found no evidence of his having raised funds for the purchase of adult male slaves. "Living men" may refer to male children, like Ellen Mitchell's "brown-haired boy" redeemed at Plymouth Church in 1859.) His slave purchases mirrored southern slave trading not because they involved paying a price for a human soul—Beecher's money-gathering led to a slave's freedom, after all—but because they affirmed that light-complected female slaves were of greater value than their darker sisters. In a sense, they were "fancies" for Beecher, just as they were for their southern owners or traders.[13]

Beecher did not register, much less answer, this objection to his slave purchases. As he had made clear in December 1848, young slaves like the Edmondson sisters constituted a "race" apart from those slaves of darker skin with whom they shared a legal status. Had anyone confronted Beecher with the charge that he was giving up the game, at the very moment of emancipation, by reintroducing southern-style distinctions of color among African Americans, he would have responded, I suspect, in two ways. First, he would have denied introducing differences of rank or color among blacks. In his view, fair-skinned slaves did not belong to the same cultural group as their dark-skinned neighbors, despite their common bondage. The two groups could not be compared, only contrasted. Second, he would have conceded that (a) some light-skinned slaves, by slothfully embracing their life of sin, had voluntarily reentered the "ostracized class" of "colored people"; and (b) some dark-skinned slaves might, against all odds, embark upon the path of civilized striving that Sarah and the Edmondson sisters had already traveled.[14]

In the long run, thought Beecher, progress on the long track of civilization was available to all. "There is a moral force in developed intellect," he said in 1848, "which none can resist; and if colored men and women become educated and wise, there is nothing on earth that can prevent them from standing alongside of any other race or community. Let them become of value in society, and they will take their just place. Every effort they make, therefore, to rise by instruction and other legitimate methods, ought to be encouraged by every philanthropist and Christian. We ought to prepare them to rise, so that in time they shall be benefactors and teachers to others." Beecher made the same point again in 1866 in his famous "Cleveland" letter explaining why he supported a "go-slow" approach to Reconstruction. Former slaves would eventually rise, but only by navigating the same gauntlet of obstacles that had faced every other rising group in history.

> Civilization is growth. None can escape that forty years in the wilderness who travel from the Egypt of ignorance to the promised land of civilization. The freedmen must take their march. I have full faith in the results. If they have the stamina to undergo the hardships which every uncivilized people has undergone in their upward progress, they will in due time take their place among us. That place cannot be bought, nor bequeathed, nor gained by sleight-of-hand. It will come to sobriety, virtue, industry and frugality.[15]

The same Christian evangelical perspective that had pushed Beecher urgently into the antislavery movement before the war allowed him to counsel patience after emancipation. After the passage of the Thirteenth Amendment, the moral emergency, in his eyes, was over: women could no longer be legally subjected to sexual slavery. Christian instruction could now devote itself to the slow cultivation of "sobriety, virtue, industry and frugality." Beecher and his fellow Christian moderates could readily adopt the long view—cultural equality would be achieved some day—because they believed that spiritual equality, the free gift of God, was available now. God had already taken care of the most basic need of all human beings, black and white.

Here we can see how Beecher's religious beliefs subtly permeated his views of race, gender, culture, and political economy. God's gift of spiritual freedom permitted patience in the face of injustice and inequality even as it galvanized believers to resist unconscionable evils such as sexual slavery. From Beecher's standpoint the slave purchases helped launch a grand rebellion against sin: southern sins of the spirit and flesh (sloth as well as fornication, on the part of slaves and slaveowners alike) and northern sins of the spirit, especially greed (the profits to be made trading with the south) and complacency (particularly complacency about collaboration with southern sins of the flesh and spirit). The slave women Beecher helped emancipate could stand symbolically at one and the same time for the sinfulness of slavery, the virtue of full womanhood, the striving for self-realization in a free economy, and the yearning for spiritual deliverance.[16]

NOTES

1 Harriet Beecher Stowe, *Uncle Tom's Cabin* (1852; New York: Norton, 1994), 77.
2 Stowe, *Uncle Tom's Cabin*, 77.
3 J. C. H., "Communications," *The North Star*, November 10, 1848 [available online from "Nineteenth-Century African-American Newspapers," *www.accessible.com.ezp1 .harvard.edu*, item #12998].
4 "Meeting at the Tabernacle," *The Christian Contributor* (Utica, N.Y.), November 8, 1848, 145 (excerpt reprinted in *The North Star*, November 17, 1848 [online at "Nineteenth-Century African-American Newspapers," item #13058]). "The Edmonson [sic] Sisters," *Independent*, December 21, 1848, p. 9, reports on a follow-up meeting held at the Broadway Tabernacle on December 7 to raise money for the young women's education. Beecher spoke again, telling the Edmondson sisters (seated this time in the hall) "Do not measure yourselves by the rank you hold among the colored people around you . . . they are a race by themselves." The Edmondson sisters had demonstrated their readiness for "literary education," as the *Independent*'s writer noted, by their "sprightly and intelligent" bearing and (in the words of the speaker following Beecher) by "their pious devotional behavior" as committed Methodists.
5 The *True Wesleyan*, quoted in the *Christian Contributor*'s account of the 1848 Tabernacle Meeting, shows that not all mid-century religious voices shared Beecher's inhibition about calling things by their names: "the [Edmondson] girls were about to be sold," wrote the *True Wesleyan*, "beyond all doubt for prostitution."
6 This account of the 1856 slave redemption at Plymouth Church draws on two contemporary reports, "An Affecting Incident at Mr. Beecher's Church," *New York Times*, June 3, 1856, 3, and "Dean" [Edna Dean Proctor], "A Slave Made Free in Plymouth Church," *Independent*, June 5, 1856, 184. The *Independent* (which by this time employed Beecher as a "special contributor") and the *New York Times* accounts differ on some small points, but for simplicity of presentation I have included only points on which they agree. In an accompanying editorial (quite possibly written by Beecher) "A Slave Ransomed in Plymouth Church" (180), the *Independent* summed up the event and

added a Cinderella twist (nasty sisters): "a woman with an intelligent face, a commanding mien, and a noble heart—but a slave, daily down-trodden in her father's house, suffering continual indignities and rebuffs from sisters more legitimate but less accomplished than herself—sent by her own father to the auction-block, and sold for money under the hammer of the auctioneer—such an one comes into a church, makes a mute plea before a company of strangers for her ransom from slavery, receives as a spontaneous offering the generous purchase of her liberty."

7 The *Times* and *Independent* reports differ on one major issue: whether the generous slave trader decided only after buying Sarah to help her purchase her freedom (implied by the *Times*), or bought her preemptively to prevent her father from selling her "south" and to allow her to raise the funds for her emancipation (implied by the *Independent*).

8 Beecher quoted in William C. Beecher and Samuel Scoville, *A Biography of Henry Ward Beecher* (New York: Charles L. Webster: 1888), 294. The only true "auctions" that took place at Plymouth Church were the annual auctions for pews. See Beecher's impassioned defense of those auctions in "Plymouth Church (The Rev. Henry Ward Beecher's) in Brooklyn," *New York Times*, January 28, 1859, 4–5. Beecher put on at least two other slave-purchase fund-raisers at Plymouth Church. The first was in 1859, at the conclusion of one of his regular Wednesday evening lectures. On the spot the congregation raised $300 toward the $1,000 purchase price of Virginia slave Ellen Mitchell and her five children (she had already collected $500 in Philadelphia). Beecher asked Mitchell, accompanied by one of her children, to stand up and be recognized. "She rose," wrote the *New York Times*, "as white, as free apparently from all taint of negro blood, in hue or hair or speech or manner, as any member of that congregation! And her little brown-haired boy was as sweet a child as any mother fondles in New-York." "A Touching Scene," *New York Times*, March 31, 1859, 4. (Details of her story were reported in "A White Woman and her Children Held in Slavery," *New York Times*, March 22, 1859, 5.)

The second occasion was in 1860, when "Pink" or "Pinky," a nine-year-old girl—in Beecher's later comment "too fair and beautiful a child for her own good"—was "redeemed" at the conclusion of Beecher's morning sermon on February 5. (Beecher quoted in Beecher and Scoville, *A Biography*, 296). The *Times* reported that Pink had "in her veins only one-sixteenth part African blood (although that was more than enough to make her a slave)." As in 1856, Plymouth Church guaranteed fulfillment of the entire purchase price ($800) when (as the *Times* wrote) "a lady in the audience sent word to the pastor that she would make up the deficiency, if any should be found. This announcement was received with an irrepressible demonstration of applause." "An Interesting Scene at Plymouth Church—Purchase of a Slave by the Congregation," *New York Times*, February 6, 1860, 8. See also "Ransom of a Slave-Girl at Plymouth church, Brooklyn," *Independent*, February 9, 1860, 3.

9 "Dean," "A Slave Made Free in Plymouth Church," *Independent*, June 5, 1856, 184; "The Edmonson Sisters," *Independent*, December 21, 1848, 9.

10 Paxton Hibben, *Henry Ward Beecher: An American Portrait* (New York: George H. Doran, 1927), 160–61. A month after the Plymouth Church service, the *Independent* tried to refute the charge that Beecher and his congregation had been bilked by Sarah and the slave trader, whom the paper identified as Frederick Sheffer of Virginia. "Public Opinion in Slave States," July 3, 1856, 209. The *National Era* (Washington, D.C.), August 7, 1856, p. 126, said the "Pro-Slavery press" was spreading "the base falsehood" that Sarah and Sheffer had bilked Beecher and his congregation. "She is now in Washington, a *free woman*, and employed as a domestic in one of the most respectable families in the city." The *New York Times* published a letter on August 9, 1865, p. 4, purportedly written by Sheffer, who rejected rumors that Sarah had "returned to me." He denied having had anything to do "with her going to new-York," or with "her coming away from there." He confirmed receipt of the outstanding balance and his signing of the "emancipation papers in the usual way." According to him, Sarah "is living in Washington City with a widow lady, and is learning to read and write." In "A Perverted Sympathy," August 28, 1856, p. 273, the *Independent* went back over the facts of the case and reasserted the truth of Beecher's version.

11 Paxton Hibben contended that Beecher-style slave purchases were common in the evangelical churches, and that Beecher got the idea from his Brooklyn Congregational colleague Richard Storrs. Hibben, *Henry Ward Beecher*, 160. We need a full-scale study of the slave-purchase phenomenon, one that would combine Beecher-style slave redemption with a wide spectrum of other "ransomings," including those of Frederick Douglass, Anthony Burns, and the slave preachers redeemed by white ministers. The prolific antislavery church press (including weeklies such as *The Christian Contributor* [1846–1849] and the *Independent* [1848–1865], both available at the American Antiquarian Society, Worcester, Mass.) will be an essential component of such a study, since they would presumably have taken pride in documenting all instances of redemption.

12 Beecher and Scoville, *A Biography*, 294, 296. Aileen Kraditor discusses the debate over the 1847 purchase of Frederick Douglass in *Means and Ends in American Abolitionism: Garrison and His Critics on Strategy and Tactics, 1834–1850* (New York: Pantheon, 1969), 220–21. Garrison himself supported the purchase of Douglass, on grounds similar to those I impute to Beecher in the case of Sarah in 1856. Other Garrisonians, like Henry C. Wright, opposed the Douglass purchase. As early as 1839 Gerrit Smith had taken the Beecher-Garrison position that purchasing the legal freedom of a particular slave did not contravene the abolitionist principle that slaveholders deserved no compensation for their chattel property. (Kraditor, *Means and Ends*, 234, n. 103.)

13 Beecher and Scoville, *A Biography*, 294.

14 "The Edmonson Sisters," *Independent*, December 21, 1848, 9.

15 Ibid.; Beecher ["Cleveland Letter"] to Charles G. Halpine, et al., August 30, 1866, reprinted in the *Independent*, September 6, 1866, 8.

16 A fuller treatment of Beecher's slave redemptions would put them in the context of

his thinking about gender and political economy as well as race and color. On Beecher's approach to gender, which owed a great deal to his oldest sister Catharine's debates with the Grimké sisters in the 1830s, see his speech to the Women's Rights meeting at the Cooper Institute, New York City, on February 2, 1860, three days before his purchase of "Pink" at Plymouth Church. There he distanced himself from Catharine's traditionalism by arguing that women should receive "the same legal and civil rights that man now enjoys" (including the vote), and be encouraged to participate in all public affairs and activities. Women should pursue their gifts wherever they led. "When God gave the gift He gave the right and no law ought to be allowed to interfere with her." This was a matter of equal rights but also (in keeping with Catharine's position) of seeding the public domain with woman's purity. "Man thinks from the physical and passionate standpoint, that gives him power. Woman thinks from affection, that gives her purity . . . For woman to change her nature, would spoil all." "The Women's Rights Meeting," *New York Times*, February 3, 1860, 8.

On Beecher's zeal for the competitive economic marketplace as a molder of men, see Jonathan A. Glickstein, " 'Poverty Is Not Slavery': American Abolitionists and the Competitive Labor Market," in *Antislavery Reconsidered: New Perspectives on the Abolitionists*, ed. Lewis Perry and Michael Fellman (Baton Rouge: Louisiana State University Press, 1979), 205–6. Beecher was very articulate about the deprivations suffered by free black men in the north, but he wavered between blaming those deprivations on the cultural failings of blacks themselves and the intolerance of their white neighbors. See his *Freedom and War* (Boston: Ticknor and Fields, 1863), 11–24.

IV

Post-Emancipation America

JOHN STAUFFER

Introduction

In his 1899 story, "The Man That Corrupted Hadleyburg," Mark Twain exposes the "banality of evil" long before Hannah Arendt gave currency to the phrase to describe Nazi war crimes.[1] The story is a wonderful and intricate parable about what happens to a community that devotes itself to the ideal of perfection and freedom from sin. It is also a brilliant critique of romantic reform and religious liberalism, and a warning for the twentieth century.[2]

For three generations, or some sixty years, the town of Hadleyburg had been a model town and beacon of truth; it was "the most honest and upright town in all the region about." Hadleyburg was "so proud of" its upright ways, "and so anxious to insure its perpetuation, that it began to teach the principles of honest dealing to its babies in the cradle." It sought to banish not only sin but temptation: "throughout the formative years temptations were kept out of the way of the young people, so that their honesty could have every chance to harden and solidify, and become a part of their very bone." Honesty and righteousness became the "staple of their culture." The neighboring towns became jealous, and called Hadleyburg's pride "vanity," but acknowledged that "Hadleyburg was in reality an incorruptible town."[3]

Of course Hadleyburg is neither incorruptible nor free from sin and deception, and in a society of such moral supremacy, righteousness is ripe for a fall. The tempter, the man who corrupts Hadleyburg, is Satan. He goes by the mundane name of Howard L. Stephenson, and appears in the guise of a gambler, foreigner, wanderer, tempter, and "mysterious big stranger." Formally he is cast as an impersonal rather than personal figure ("the man *that* corrupted" rather than "the man *who*"). Stephenson focuses on Hadleyburg because he had been "offended" while passing through on a previous visit, and the townspeople were ignorant of their offense; they felt so "sufficient" and autonomous that they "cared not a rap for strangers or their opinions." Stephenson "was a bitter man and revengeful," and when he decided to corrupt a place, he did it on a large scale. "He contrived many plans, and all of them were good, but none of them was quite sweeping enough. At last he had a fortunate idea, and when it fell into his brain it lit up his whole head with an evil joy." His plan was to tempt the "Nineteen" leading citizens of Hadleyburg and publicly expose their greed, hypocrisy, and lies. He felt confident that the "Nineteeners" would fall for his temptation, for he knew that "the weakest of all weak things is a virtue which has not been tested in the fire."[4]

Stephenson's "fortunate idea" leads to Hadleyburg's fortunate fall. Fortunate, because Hadleyburg's sterling reputation is a sham—it only *appears* honest and incorruptible. People *perceive* themselves as honest because they have been trained to be honest from birth and have had little experience with temptation. But genuine honesty needs to be tested in the fires of temptation, as Mary Richards, a townswoman, realizes. She and her husband Edward, a poor banker and a "Nineteener," are the first in Hadleyburg to be tempted by Stephenson. He arrives at their home one evening, and leaves a large sack of gold coins worth $40,000, with a note explaining that the money is to be given to the good Samaritan in Hadleyburg who had once given Stephenson $20 in a time of need. But as Mary and Edward know, the only person in Hadleyburg generous enough to give a stranger $20 recently died. They are tempted to keep the money, and although they don't, their temptation causes them enormous guilt and anxiety. As Mary tells her husband:

> it's been one everlasting training and training and training in honesty—honesty shielded, from the very cradle, against every possible temptation, and so it's *artificial* honesty, and weak as water when temptation comes, as we have seen this night. . . . I—Edward, it is my belief that this town's honesty is as rotten as mine is; as rotten as yours is. It is a mean town, a hard, stingy town, and hasn't a virtue in the world but this honesty it is so celebrated for and so conceited about; and so help me, I do believe that if ever the day comes that its honesty falls under great temptation, its grand reputation will go to ruin like a house of cards.

For Twain, the wages of innocence is hell.[5]

Judgment day comes on a Friday. It occurs at a town-hall meeting, presided over by the Reverend Burgess, an outcast minister because he had once been accused (falsely) of evil. At this meeting, according to Stephenson's instructions, the man who purportedly gave him the money will be identified and receive the gold. Stephenson has already tempted each Nineteener; each of them has been encouraged to lie at this meeting, to pretend that *he* alone was the man who had once given Stephenson money, so that he will receive the $40,000 in gold. People come from far and wide to witness the event, for Hadleyburg is "world-celebrated" for its honesty and righteousness. Instead of bearing witness to Truth, all of the Nineteeners play into Stephenson's hand, lying to try to receive the gold. They disgrace themselves and become "Symbols" of corruption, hypocrisy, and greed. And they sin for nought, for the gold coins are only "gilded disks of lead," much as the Gilded Age, the name Twain gave to the era, was corrupt at its core."[6]

Of the "Nineteen," Richards alone is saved from disgrace, even though he is as guilty of lying as the rest. He retains the appearance of purity because Burgess saves him from exposure. As a result, the townspeople elect him "sole Guardian and Symbol" of the "Hadleyburg Tradition, with power and right to stand up and look the whole sarcastic world in the face." Satan believes in Richards' façade of innocence, and sends him checks totaling almost $40,000, along with an explanatory note: "I am a disappointed man. Your honesty is beyond the reach of temptation. . . . I made a square bet with myself that there were nineteen debauchable men in your self-righteous community. I have lost. Take the whole pot, you are entitled to it."[7]

Flush with fame and fortune, Edward and Mary Richards lack the fortitude to confess their sin of lying, and again succumb to guilt and anxiety. Stephenson's note "seems written with fire—it burns so," Edward tells his wife, and then he throws it "in the fire." For a few days their consciences quieted down: "the old couple were learning to reconcile themselves to the sin which they had committed. But they were to learn, now, that a sin takes on new and real terrors when there seems a chance that it is going to be found out." Instead of learning from the past, they continue to hide their sin. As a result, they become paranoid and imagine conspiratorial plots against them. Their fears of exposure make them sick and delirious. They try to absolve themselves by destroying Stephenson's checks: "They came from Satan," Edward says. During his feverish "gabblings," he experiences a moment of honest lucidity: "I saw the hellbrand on them [the checks], and I knew they were sent to betray me to sin." Just before he dies, he confesses: "I was clean—artificially—like the rest; and like the rest I fell when temptation came. I signed a lie, and claimed the miserable sack" of gold.[8]

The town, now "stripped of the last rag of its ancient glory," mourned deeply. It changed its name to try to forget its past; and it altered its motto, which "for many generations had graced the town's official seal," from "LEAD US NOT INTO TEMPTATION" to "LEAD US INTO TEMPTATION." Out of evil, goodness comes; by embracing temptation, Hadleyburg becomes "an honest town once more, and the man will have to rise early that catches it napping again."[9]

"The Man That Corrupted Hadleyburg" reveals many things about the relation between evil and national identity. It shows how the perfectionist impulse, coupled with the attempt to ignore collective sin, can lead society into self-righteousness and jingoistic smugness. Such an impulse precipitates conspiratorial thinking and a "paranoid style" that has long plagued America. And the story shows how people will go to great lengths to deny or distort the existence of evil. W. E. B. Du Bois echoed this sentiment in his history of Reconstruction by referring to the blindness of American historians: "One is astonished in the study of history at the recurrence of the idea that evil must be forgotten, distorted, skimmed over." The problem with this philosophy, he added, "is that history loses its value as an incentive and example; it paints perfect men and noble nations, but it does not tell the truth."[10] It is a statement that could as easily apply to Hadleyburg. In fact, Twain suggests the link between national identity and evil by repeatedly referring to Hadleyburg's Nineteen self-righteous leading citizens as "Symbols"—they are symbols of national corruption.[11]

One of the morals of Twain's (and Du Bois') narratives was to acknowledge the permanence of evil. To be human is to sin, and to forget that, to deny that, is to live a lie. This is why Twain emphasized the need for *experiencing* temptation, why Hadleyburg altered its motto and began to *confront* temptation, so that people could learn how to behave in a sin-filled world without succumbing to every temptation. By experiencing temptation, Hadleyburg ends up honest, its citizens no longer denying sin. It is an appropriate ending for *fin-de-siècle* America, for Twain sought to explore, artistically and socially, how society might "find 'salvation' in an apparently unsalvageable world."[12]

As a realist writer, Twain continually grappled with sin, and in this sense he anticipated the Christian realism of Reinhold Niebuhr. Like Twain, Niebuhr understood the importance of experiencing temptation and confronting sin: "The children of light must be armed with the wisdom of the children of darkness but remain free from their malice," the theologian wrote. The virtuous must not be ignorant of evil. "They must know the power of self-interest in human society without giving it moral justification." The one character in Twain's story who fits Niebuhr's characterization of a virtuous citizen, Barclay Goodson, also understands the power of evil. Goodson was not only the most generous citizen of Hadleyburg; he saw the lie in believing that one could be perfect, and tried to expose it. Like Niebuhr, he was tough-minded, calling the people of Hadleyburg "narrow, self-righteous, and stingy." He was hated for it but "didn't care." His knowledge of evil stemmed from the fact that he was not born in Hadleyburg, was a "foreigner" to the town, and was thus not trained from the cradle to avoid temptation and deny sin. Significantly, he is the only character who Satan is afraid of. In fact it is only after Goodson dies that Satan comes to Hadleyburg to operate his scheme: "Heaven took Goodson; then I knew I was safe, and I set my trap and baited it," Stephenson says. To avoid temptation, and pretend ignorance from sin, is to court the devil.[13]

"The Man That Corrupted Hadleyburg," like most of Twain's work, responded to the widespread tendency after the Civil War to deny or distort the existence of evil. Such casual attitudes toward evil can be seen most clearly in collective memories of the Civil War. After Reconstruction, the North and South reconciled their differences, and by the turn of the century, northern and southern whites looked back on the conflict in terms that avoided ethical responsibility; neither side was good or evil, winner or loser, according to David Blight. It was a stark contrast from the outset of secession, when each side fought for or against slavery, believed itself to be in the right, and invoked God's aid against the other, as Lincoln famously said. Although "each side fought to defend a distinct vision of the good society," as Eric Foner put it, "each vision was destroyed by the very struggle to preserve it." Reconciliation erased the moral certitude of both sides. By the turn of the century, whites ignored the cause of slavery, either as a positive good or as the sum of all evil, and explained the conflict in terms of *amoral* economic forces. By distorting and ignoring conceptions of evil, the reconciliation of the North and South fueled the rise of white supremacy, which greatly overshadowed the vision of emancipation and civil rights for blacks. As Blight aptly put it, "the inexorable drive for reunion both used and trumped race."[14]

With the rise of white supremacy and segregation, the idea of "whiteness" became a fundamental tenet of morality, a form of secular perfectionism. "Are we not coming more and more, day by day, to making the statement 'I am white,' the one fundamental tenet of our practical morality?" Du Bois asked in "The Souls of White Folk," first published in 1910. No one, he concluded, "ever took himself and his own *perfectness* with such disconcerting seriousness as the modern white man." For such perfectionists, the devil was always "black," and Du Bois suggested that despite legal freedom, citizenship, and suffrage, blacks were no better at the turn of the century than they had been in 1857, when Chief Justice Roger Taney issued his famous opinion in the *Dred Scott* case: "a White Man is always right and a Black Man has no rights which a white man is bound to respect."[15]

The color of the devil revealed a lot about Americans' conceptions of evil. When the devil was black he was denied democracy in the Land of Democracy, and whites sought to punish or avoid him: the "righteousness of the indignation" against him "sweeps the world," Du Bois noted. But when the devil was white, he was virtually indistinguishable from any other white; he fit right in or was even likeable. In Twain's story, the devil is a likeable character; as readers, we root for him, *want* him to corrupt the town, and cheer as the smug and vain Nineteeners (except the Richardses) receive their comeuppance. And Satan looks no different from the other whites. Stephenson is only once referred to as Satan, when Richards, in his feverish but honest "gabblings," acknowledges that Stephenson's checks "came from Satan." Evil was banal when white, more horrifying than ever when dark.[16]

The banality of evil can also be seen in the ways in which white ministers and other moral reformers distorted or ignored the conditions of the poor white, whose ranks burgeoned in the Gilded Age. Henry Ward Beecher justified the unprecedented and widening disparity between rich and poor by linking poverty to personal sin: "looking comprehensively through city and town and village and country, the general truth will stand, that no man in this land suffers from poverty unless it be more than his fault—unless it be his sin." What is shocking about this statement is not that Beecher (and other moralists) ignored certain passages of the Bible and emphasized others—they had always been doing that. Rather, it was the degree of their moral shift. While abolitionists and women's rights reformers in the antebellum era used scripture to demand racial and gender equality, now moralists revised scripture to link all wealth with virtue and poverty with sin. The Reverend William Morris, Episcopal bishop of Massachusetts, frankly dispensed with the lessons of "history, experience," and "the Bible," which collectively distrusted "the effect of material wealth on morality," and asserted that "in the long run, it is only to the man of morality that wealth comes." Probably the most famous sermon between 1873 and 1924, purportedly delivered more than six thousand times, was the Baptist minister Russell Conwell's "Acres of Diamonds," which argued that it was a Christian duty to get rich. Such twinning of wealth with Christ's example was a majority view among ministers from the 1870s through the 1920s.[17]

The most pervasive manifestation of the banality of evil in post-Reconstruction America was the acceptance of war as an apt metaphor of life itself. While moralists agreed that "war is hell," the ultimate evil, they eagerly defined society as a state of war (or hell), though without the same amount of bloodshed, thus suggesting that hell, like war, was a positive good. The dwindling of peace activists and nonresisters after the Civil War indicates the pervasiveness of such attitudes; by the eve of World War I, Protestant support for the war was "not only almost unanimous but also almost unquestioning," according to Donald Meyer. War became "an ideological benchmark" for assessing the efficiency and success of society. The values of laissez-faire economics and social Darwinism adhered to this ideology: the one embraced ruthless competition as a social and moral good; and the other perceived nature itself not as source of Divinity, as Emerson and other antebellum reformers had believed, but as a battleground. Moralists now argued that society should mimic Darwin's conception of nature, which was war, and allow the weak to die out so as to ensure the advance of civilization.[18]

Even reform organizations that did not subscribe to laissez-faire capitalism or social Darwinism embraced the war metaphor, transforming martial ideology into a positive good. The Salvation Army, which started in England by William and Catherine Booth in 1878 to "save" the poor, perfected a military technique and soon spread throughout the United States. It was organized as "the Army of the Lord," with corps commanders and officers who established "Slum Brigades" in war zones. Soldiers were sworn in and required to wear uniforms that united the symbols of Christ with those of the military. The Army's motto, "Blood and Fire," signified a battlefield as well as "the blood of Jesus and the fire of the Holy Ghost." It was inscribed across a yellow star that betokened military rank and the "fiery baptism of the Holy Ghost." Soldiers had to obey their officers and abstain from drink, tobacco, and worldly amusements; and officers could not marry without the consent of their district commander, and their spouses had to be willing to cooperate with them in the work of the Lord. By 1900, the Army's aptly named organ, *The War Cry*, boasted a circulation of over 51 million copies a year, printed in fourteen languages. In the United States alone, the Salvation Army had over 700 corps with over 20,000 privates commanded by nearly 3,000 officers, which held 11,000 weekly meetings attended by over 2 million people. Although the ostensible concern of the Army was to save people from sin, it devoted most of its time to improving the conditions of the poor. In this sense, the Army's embrace of the war metaphor made sense: it saw firsthand the costs of economic war, and it functioned like the Red Cross, treating the war's casualties.[19]

The military metaphor was primarily perpetrated by elites who were immune to the ravages of laissez-faire capitalism. Although William James was no social Darwinist, he famously endorsed the war metaphor in his call for a "Moral Equivalent of War (1910), which applied martial virtues to society. For James, "the horrors" of war were what made life fascinating: "War is the *strong* life; it is life *in extremis*; . . . Militarism is the great preserver of our ideals of hardihood, and human life with no use for hardihood would be contemptible." While Russell Conwell linked wealth to morality, James and the Salvation Army twinned war with morality. As James put it, "martial virtues must be the enduring cement" of morality. But James differed from the Salvation Army in that he wrote from the perspective of the victor. How many hungry and homeless people thought their lives were "fascinating" because of the horrors of they endured? And how many impoverished men believed that "militarism," as played out in the economy, preserved their "ideals of hardihood?" Very few.[20]

It was a short step from acknowledging evil to accepting it, mimicking it, or treating it as banal. For James and other pragmatists and reformers, the lesson of the Civil War was that "moral certainty" was something one "should sacrifice a little of in exchange for order" and the prevention of bloodshed. James knew that the war stemmed from the evil of slavery, but by the turn of the century he refused to identify evil in such absolute terms, leading him to endorse a moral equivalent of evil (or war). As a result of the pragmatic turn, the price of liberal reform in the United States from the 1880s through World War I was "the removal of the issue of race from the table," as Louis Menand has noted.[21]

Metaphors of war encouraged actual warfare, especially against a "savage" or racialized other. By the turn of the century, the working class was filled primarily by immigrants from eastern Europe. They were seen as nonwhite, and the labor organizers that came from their ranks were called savages or anarchists. David Perry, the president of the National Association of Manufacturers, equated strikers with savagery in his 1903 assessment of manufacturing conditions: "Organized labor knows but one law, and that is the law of physical force—the law of the Huns and Vandals, the law of the savage." Two years after the Pullman Strike of 1894, Marshall Kirkman published *The Science of Railways*, in which he characterized strikes as a form of mutiny or desertion. "The force that operates a railway is like an army. It is methodically organized and drilled. It has its commanders, its rank and file." Thus, "insubordination among railway men is as great an offense as insubordination in an army," and "a country thus cursed is in as great a danger as if its soldiers were traitorous."[22]

Metaphors of war also led white Americans to seek imperial conquest over "savages" in Cuba and the Philippines in order to establish themselves among "the great fighting races," especially the British. "On a certain level Americans were becoming cosmopolitan," notes Nell Painter. Elite white men celebrated transatlantic friendships, English spelling, and especially a quest for empire. They also saw human history defined not by individuals or nations but by "races" with certain traits. Such logic meant that the "the United States must rule the Philippines out of duty" to the "dark" races who needed to be civilized. Senator Albert Beveridge described such logic in these terms: God did not "prepare the English-speaking and Teutonic peoples for a thousand years" for merely "vain and idle self-contemplation." "No!" he continued, "he has made us the master organizers to establish [a rational] system where chaos reigns. He has given us the spirit of progress to overwhelm the forces of reaction throughout the earth. He has made us adepts in government that we may administer government among the savage and senile peoples of the earth." In a similar vein, Theodore Roosevelt likened Filipinos to Indians; both were backward races that needed to be either exterminated or civilized. The myth of Progress demanded that the Philippines be conquered.[23]

What drew these politicians, businessmen, intellectuals, and moralists to the military metaphor was partly the purported efficiency of war as an organizing principle. But they also affirmed hierarchy and applied the ideology of slavery to industrial life, drawing rigid distinctions between commanders and subordinates. A large number of postbellum leaders had served in the war, and they viewed it as an apt model for organizing and managing people. Former officers became heads of state, corporate, and clerical organizations; and the war taught them to understand dissent, resistance, and the dismantling of hierarchy as savage anarchy. Thus, while the war ended slavery, its organizing principle emulated the rigid hierarchies of power that were characteristic of slavery. Using the Civil War as an organizing principle also required massive amounts of historical distortion. While military organizations tolerated neither dissent nor much free speech, democracies depended upon public debate and the consent of the governed. And the Civil War was anything but "efficient," except in killing people; it was marked by colossal amounts of waste and destruction.[24]

The tendency to deny or distort evil was only one side of Gilded Age morality. The other side was the displacement of God from the affairs of the world. For people brought up on millennialist faith, God's glory reigned during the Civil War: He trampled out the vintage where the grapes of wrath were stored; He unleashed, like lightning, His terrible swift sword; and He sounded forth the trumpet that would never call retreat. Millions of northerners sung these words. The war brought Judgment Day, the sifting out of the hearts of men. In its wake, Truth was supposed to reign, God would march on, and a jubilant, glorious new age would prevail. But the Gilded Age looked nothing like this. Sin continued to run rampant, and Americans responded by ignoring God's presence or denying sin (or both), in order to maintain their faith in progress and justify the costs of war. They experienced, in other words, a profound crisis of faith. Andrew Delbanco summarized this shift by saying that "before the war, Americans spoke of Providence. After it, they spoke of luck," dismissing God from the stage. But ministers and "success mythologists" continued to assume that God affected the affairs of the world. By maintaining their faith in Providential progress, believers either denied luck, or were sorely tempted to distort evil.[25]

The displacement of God from the affairs of the world began with the shift in soldiers' attitudes during the war. As the historian Gerald Linderman has shown, northern and southern soldiers believed at the beginning of the war that with faith in God, coupled with courage, they would survive and conquer the enemy. But as the war dragged on, soldiers became disillusioned and no longer believed that God could protect them. They increasingly felt like objects rather than actors in events; and by war's end, many had become fatalists or replaced Providence with chance. In the last year of the war, soldiers on both sides felt sure they would die in battle, that their time had come. As a result, they reenlisted in order to obtain an *immediate* thirty-day furlough, so that they could see loved ones and snatch a few more moments of life and happiness before returning to battle and death.[26]

After the war, writers increasingly began to secularize religious language rather than dispense with religious tropes altogether. Utopian ideals were no longer linked to Christ's reign on earth but rather to economic transformations modeled on military-style organization. The two most popular postbellum novels, Edward Bellamy's *Looking Backward* (1888) and Upton Sinclair's *The Jungle* (1906) were analogs to Stowe's *Uncle Tom's Cabin* in their influence. Both books articulate a future utopia, much as Stowe does, except that God is nowhere present.[27]

In *Looking Backward* Bellamy described a utopian future so compelling that his novel spawned a new political party, the National Party. His utopia is a quasi-socialist society built around the efficient workings of an "Army of Industry." It emerges without protest or conflict, betraying Bellamy's faith in "the progress that shall be made, ever onward and ever upward, till the race shall achieve its ineffable destiny." This "destiny" was white, however; and it depended on the tenets of social Darwinism, which endorsed the status quo in order for society to move ever upward. Through his mouthpiece, Dr. Leete, Bellamy rhapsodizes over the virtues of natural selection: "For the first time in human history the principle of sexual selection, with its tendency to preserve and transmit the better types of the race, and let the inferior types drop out, has unhindered operation." He viewed labor activists as misguided reformers impeding progress. The efficient and "natural" consolidation of industry led inevitably to an end of competition and a socialist promised land.[28]

While *Looking Backward* focused on the utopian future, *The Jungle* detailed horrible conditions in the present, specifically the meat-packing industry. Sinclair self-consciously sought to emulate Stowe's success: "In many respects I had 'Uncle Tom's Cabin' in mind as a model of what I wished to do," he wrote. Like Stowe, he prophesied at the novel's end an apocalyptic war and the realization of his utopia, except in wholly secularized form. The Beef Trust replaces slavery, and Socialism takes the place of Christ's reign. Sinclair called socialism "the new religion of humanity—or you might say it was the fulfillment of the old religion, since it implied but the literal application of all the teachings of Christ." But for Sinclair, one need not believe in Christ for this change to occur. His goal was to change the hearts of readers and convert them to socialism, not Christianity. The middle classes read it as a consumerist critique against the meat industry and were not interested in labor conditions. As a result, while the novel did nothing to combat working conditions, it mobilized public opinion and helped pass the Food and Drug Act of 1906. Sinclair thought he had failed in his purpose: "I aimed at the public's heart, and by accident I hit it in the stomach."[29]

Mark Twain, who was perhaps the most famous man in America by 1900 owing to his popularity as a writer, continually subverted antebellum conceptions of God and spirituality. Huck Finn hates being "sivilized" and rejects Christian morality entirely. Three pages into *Adventures of Huckleberry Finn* (1885), Twain shocks his sentimental readers when his hero, Huck Finn, tells Miss Watson that he *wants* to go to hell. Huck repeats this wish in the novel's moral climax, when he tears up the letter he wrote to Miss Watson, revealing the whereabouts of his fugitive friend Jim, by saying: "All right, then, I'll *go* to hell." With God absent, and Providential moralists distorting the nature of God's America, hell could be reconceptualized as a virtuous place.[30]

In 1901 Twain drew attention to the nation's backsliding by revising Julia Ward Howe's "Battle Hymn of the Republic". He brings it "up to date" by justifying war on secular grounds. War is no longer apocalyptic or a battle for righteousness and truth; it is about greed and lust:

Mine eyes have seen the orgy of the launching of
    the Sword;
He is searching out the hoardings where the
    stranger's wealth is stored;

> He hath loosed his fateful lightnings, and with
> woe and death has scored;
> His lust is marching on.

This kind of satirical rendering of a religious hymn, which makes God irrelevant and parodies religious language, would have been unthinkable among antebellum writers.[31]

With so many people having needlessly died in the war, irony became an acceptable, even desirable, way to represent reality. Irony reflected the abridgement of hope and certainty in a world that could no longer depend on God. And it exploded myths about war as glorious, honorable, and divinely sanctioned. Herman Melville's line from his war poem, "Shiloh," foreshadowed the shattering of such sentiments: "what like a bullet can undeceive." It is no coincidence that Melville and Hawthorne, the two great ironists of the 1840s and 1850s, were also opposed to war and the moral certainties on which it was based. Yet, despite Melville's quarrel with God, he never *abandoned* God in the way post-Reconstruction writers did. In this sense, his worldview remained anchored to the antebellum era.[32]

The displacement of God from worldly affairs was not limited to liberal whites. Frederick Douglass, who had been a millennial nationalist from the 1850s through Reconstruction, abandoned his faith in God as immanent or indwelling by the 1880s. A heaven on earth increasingly seemed to him a dangerous illusion; and he no longer believed that God could change the world or affect the laws of nature. In his third autobiography, he castigated blacks for believing that they could procure "help from the Almighty." By remaining true to their faith, blacks were "false to fact" and thus to history, he argued. Material facts and the laws of nature now trumped "all the prayers of Christendom."[33]

Liberal clergy also secularized Providence. They experienced a loss of faith in eschatology and post-millennialist thought. Particularly during the period from 1880 to 1925, visions of a world without *sin* were replaced by beliefs in a "world without *end*." While postmillennialism was not entirely rejected, "it eroded into something more amorphous," notes James Moorhead: "a decisively this-worldly hope for limitless spiritual improvement and temporal progress." Much as writers and intellectuals secularized religious language in their art, mainstream ministers reduced the Second Coming "to a metaphor of perpetual improvement" whereby progress was a goal unto itself, adhering to the new science of bureaucratic rationality and efficiency. Given the declension that had occurred since the Civil War, liberal reformers' faith in linear progress required them either to cling to illusions of righteousness in the face of corruption or accept temptation and sin. Not coincidentally, these are the options that define the opening and ending of Twain's "Hadleyburg." They were the two faces of progress among liberal whites from 1880–1925.[34]

Liberals looked a lot like the citizens of Twain's Hadleyburg. This was especially true after World War I. Following a war that was supposed to make the world safe for democracy, they guiltily remembered their enthusiasm for it and vowed not only to resist the temptation of war in the future; they believed "temptation itself had to be eradicated," as Donald Meyer notes. In a 1931 poll of 19,000 ministers, over half (10,000) said that they "could not and would not, as individuals, sanction any future war." It was a stark reversal from their acceptance of righteous violence on the eve of World War I. Stamping out temptation meant supporting only those policies that were consistent with absolute peace. But such absolutist positions required a willful ignorance of state-sanctioned slavery that was spreading throughout Europe. And there were other moral dilemmas that liberals could not resolve. In the 1930s, Reinhold Niebuhr led the way in developing "neo-orthodoxy," so named for the renewed focus on the permanence of sin in the world. Neo-orthodox ministers affirmed the centrality of revelation and God's transcendence while acknowledging the limits of religion as a social force. "The War convinced me that religion can be effective only if it *resists* the embraces of civilization," Niebuhr wrote in 1928. The religious faithful had to be tough, practical, and willing to accept sordid means to achieve good ends in the world. They could not rely on their faith to reform society, for Christianity had no "positive prescriptions" for society; only people did. The love and goodwill of Christ would not change the world. As Richard Fox summarized, neo-orthodoxy had a "devastating impact" on liberal ideals.[35]

The other blow to liberal ideals came from conservative evangelicals, who are often defined under the rubric of "Fundamentalists." They were more clear-eyed in their perception of society, in the sense that they had no faith in secular progress and were obsessed with sin. There were three broad groups of religious conservatives: Pentacostalists, who spoke in tongues; Fundamentalists, who took their name from a series of books called *The Fundamentals* (1910–15) that affirmed orthodox doctrine and lashed out at religious liberals; and other evangelicals who did not identify themselves as part of the first two groups. What they agreed upon theologically was the importance of a born-again experience; bearing witness to Christ; *sola scriptura* (believing that the Bible is the only source of authority); and a premillennial vision of the future. In their social vision they "regarded the current age as hopelessly corrupt and incapable of redemption until the Second Coming," according to Moorhead. The most that one could do was to accept Christ as one's savior and await the new dispensation. They accepted traditional understandings of sin, which led to traditional white values: blacks, alcohol, foreigners, and independent women were all icons of evil.[36]

Not every premillennialist in the early twenties was a Nativist, racist, and misogynist. Pentecostalism had emerged in 1906–8 as an interracial movement through the influence of the black preacher William J. Seymour at the Azusa Street revivals; but Pentecostalism was "only momentarily integrated," and people quickly began to organize in segregated churches. The rise of premillennialism and orthodoxy in the 1920s coincided with the rise of Nativism and the reemergence of the Ku Klux Klan, which targeted Catholics and Jews as well as blacks. Such cultural fears were mainstream beliefs; and in the immediate wake of World War I, Prohibition and immigration restriction assumed Nativist overtones. Although the number of recorded lynchings would decline during the 1920s, there was a huge spike from 36 in 1917, to 76 in 1919. The social tensions of the era—the rise of divorce; the emergence of enfranchised women; the "Great Migration" of blacks; and the cultural effects of Darwinism—added fuel to the fires of Fundamentalist-Liberal culture wars. The two sides generally agreed on one thing, though: that blacks embodied sin and needed to be controlled or ignored.[37]

When Du Bois asked the question, "How does it feel to be a problem?" in *The Souls of Black Folk* (1903), he was responding to these distortions of evil by whites. He sought to reclaim for blacks a soul that was not corrupted by whites. His solution was racial equality and integration. The "end" of his striving was "to be a co-worker in the kingdom of culture, to escape both death and isolation, to husband and use his best powers and his latent genius." To be both black and American required a dialectical tension that kept the divided self in harmony and rejected both assimilation and separatism: "He would not Africanize America, for America has too much to teach the world and Africa. He would not bleach his Negro soul in a flood of white Americanism, for he knows that Negro blood has a message for the world. He simply wishes to make it possible for a man to be both a Negro and an American, without being cursed and spit upon by his fellows, without having the doors of Opportunity closed roughly in his face." Reconciling this divided self required a new conception of history and progress, one that moved beyond the experience of slavery and the problems it brought for freedom. It also required a change in the white heart, so that blacks could enjoy the same rights, and "move arm in arm with Balzac and Dumas." Being thus "wed with Truth," blacks would be able to transcend the color line and live "above the Veil."[38]

Such a vision was profoundly optimistic for its time. It was tantamount to a cultural and political revolution, a secular millennium, and can be seen as one aspect of religious liberalism. It was also limited to the "Talented Tenth" of college-educated blacks ("Talented Hundredth" would have been more accurate), who would help lift the race. To insist on equality could be dangerous unless one spoke from a position of power, as Du Bois did with his Harvard education, access to money, and light skin. As the twentieth century deepened in tragedy, Du Bois lost hope and became increasingly bitter about America.[39]

There were more practical and realistic responses to white distortions of evil. Bishop Henry Turner and his followers in the A.M.E. Church advocated emigration as a means to self-realization, as did Marcus Garvey and his United Negro Improvement Association. Others, like Booker T. Washington, sought patient and gradual reform by urging southern blacks to lift themselves through hard work, practical education, and self-improvement without outwardly challenging white supremacy. A few radical sectarians in the North, like Father Divine and his Peace Mission, believed that a new dispensation had already occurred. "Heaven [was] now on earth"; God Himself celebrated at the feast of Holy Communion; and true faith brought freedom from sin and a oneness with Christ. Father Divine's perfectionism liberated people from the burden of the past and bore striking similarities with New Thought (many congregants had also experimented with Christian Science). He influenced whites as well as blacks, and his message of peace even reached the White House; President Eisenhower quoted Father Divine's slogan, "Peace, it's Wonderful." Black Pentecostalists and other premillennialists also envisioned a sharp break from the downward spiral of history. But social change was out of their hands, they believed; God would decide when Judgment Day came.[40]

What unites these diverse worldviews is that they all offered hope in a white world that viewed blacks as devils and treated them with pity at best and at worst lynched them or reenslaved them in the new prison system. Without hope of some kind—whether from integration, emigration, gradualism, or millennialism—it was all too easy to succumb to the psychology of slavery, succinctly captured by Frederick Douglass: "The thought of only being a creature of the *present* and the *past* troubled me, and I longed to have a *future*—a future with hope in it. To be shut up entirely to the past and present is abhorrent to the human mind; it is to the soul—whose life and happiness is unceasing progress—what the prison is to the body; a blight and mildew, a hell of horror." A life without progress, "shut up entirely to the past and present," was tantamount to "hell," an internalization of white attitudes.[41]

Out of evil, goodness came. Ironically the evil of war brought blacks freedom, rights, and power. During the Civil War, World War II, and the Cold War especially, as Philip Klinkner and Rogers Smith have argued, policy-makers believed that America's survival depended upon the economic and military mobilization of blacks. The enemy seemed to threaten whites' freedom, not just black's, prompting leaders to ally themselves with blacks and endorse inclusiveness and egalitarian ideals. Additionally, a sustained protest movement among blacks pressured leaders to effect new policies in accord with egalitarian ideals.[42]

The effect of World War I on race relations was limited for two main reasons: American leaders did not view Germany as a paramount threat to white Americans; and American involvement in the war was too brief for policy-makers to see blacks' role as crucial to America's success. As a result, egalitarian policies never got off the ground. Nevertheless, the war was suffused with the rhetoric of democratic principles; and it showed blacks that war could serve as the catalyst for achieving racial equality. Even radical activists such as Du Bois endorsed America's entry into the war. And there were some positive results. Black veterans returned from the war with a newfound sense of pride and confidence after being treated with respect while stationed in France. Their confidence and insistence on better treatment fueled the Great Migration. To be sure, a major impetus of the Great Migration was economic. Blacks could make a lot more money in the industrial cities of the North and West than staying in the South. But they also went North because of greater degrees of freedom and respect. A researcher at Tuskegee Institute explained the causes of the Great Migration this way: "The treatment accorded the Negro always stood second, when not first, among the reasons given by Negroes for leaving the South." While Harlem became a haven for blacks during the twenties, hopes for a broad-based social transformation were quickly snuffed out. The economic crisis of 1919, coupled with white fears of black empowerment, exploded into the "Red Summer," the name James Weldon Johnson gave to the epidemic of racial violence.[43]

World War II and the cold war transformed race relations in America. They made civil rights an important part of American identity for the first time since the Civil War era, and eroded the moral, intellectual, and artistic claims for white supremacy. Nazism and the Holocaust "made blatant racism of all kinds morally disreputable," George Fredrickson has noted. Communism replaced Nazism as America's enemy, and among whites, it soon vied with blacks as the embodiment of all evil. The call for civil rights intensified, and African Americans had unprecedented leverage in arguing for basic rights. America's self-consciousness about its democratic image proliferated in the 1950s and 1960s: "Our failure to live up to the pledges of our Declaration of Independence and our Constitution embarrasses our friends and heartens our enemies," Secretary of State Dean Rusk declared in 1963: "The Communists clearly regard racial discrimination in the United States as one of the their most valuable assets." Civil rights had become a matter of foreign policy, crucial to the war on communism and the survival of the nation.[44]

For ministers and other moralists, the positive effects of evil made it increasingly difficult to sustain any single ideological position, from pacifism and righteous violence to socialism and capitalism. There were times to preach the gospel of love and peace, and times to embrace the evil of war in order to achieve justice. World War II brought the flowering of neo-orthodox religious beliefs, with its leader, Reinhold Niebuhr, gracing the cover of *Time Magazine* in 1948. Reformers began to realize that life was tragic, filled with flaws, limits, and contradictions. You could not depend on any fixed doctrine or system of belief. Abandoning cherished beliefs and shifting perspectives led to enormous anxiety. But it was a mistake, as both Niebuhr and Twain recognized, to try to eradicate temptation and evil in order to check anxiety.[45]

In 1963, at the height of the cold war, James Baldwin reached a conclusion similar to that of Twain and Niebuhr about the importance of accepting temptation and repudiating fixed doctrines. Most whites likened the "Russian menace" to blacks, Baldwin noted: both were evil. But whites did not want to confront evil because it threatened their sense of security. This was why white Americans ignored "reality" when they "regard[ed] a Negro." Reality meant living with anxiety, temptation, and fear. It meant acknowledging "the fact that life is tragic," a view that Twain and Niebuhr also shared. "Life is tragic," Baldwin continued, "simply because the earth turns and the sun inexorably rises and sets, and one day, for each of us, the sun will go down for the last, last time." To face life was to accept the fact of death and the limitations of beliefs and doctrines: "It seems to me that one ought to rejoice in the *fact* of death—ought to decide, indeed, to *earn* ones' death by confronting with passion the conundrum of life. . . . But white Americans do not believe in death, and this is why the darkness of my skin so intimidates them." Death was the great leveler, making everyone equal. But white Americans ignored death, much as they denied racial equality and distorted evil.[46]

In 1963 Baldwin hoped that a transcendent notion of "love" would solve America's race problem. He wrote during the reemergence of religious liberalism, especially in black culture. "Love takes off the masks that we fear we cannot live without and know we cannot live within." Love involved daring, growth, anxiety. But he was not wedded to this belief. He ends his book by invoking its title, a biblical prophecy sung by slaves: *"God gave Noah the rainbow sign, No more water, the fire next time!"* The evil of racism, if ignored or left unchecked, would come back to haunt the nation in different forms. Baldwin understood, as did Twain, Du Bois, and Niebuhr, that evil became banal when people viewed it as static and unchanging.[47]

NOTES

1 Hannah Arendt, *Eichmann in Jerusalem: A Report on the Banality of Evil* (New York: Viking Press, 1963). Arendt's book first appeared as a series of essays in *The New Yorker*.
2 None of the criticism of "The Man Who Corrupted Hadleyburg" places it in the broader religious and cultural tradition. In my analysis of the story, I have relied on the following: Clinton S. Burhans, Jr., "The Sober Affirmation of Mark Twain's Hadleyburg," *American Literature* 34 (1962): 375–84; Leslie F. Chard II, "Mark Twain's 'Hadleyburg' and Fredonia, New York," *American Quarterly* 16 (1964): 595–601; Cynthia Ozick, "Mark Twain and the Jews," *Commentary* 99 (May 1, 1995): 56–63; Peter Messent, "Carnival in Mark Twain's 'Stirring Times in Austria' and 'The Man That Corrupted Hadleyburg,'" *Studies in Short Fiction* 35 (1998): 217–233; Gary Scharnhorst, "Paradise Revisited: Twain's 'The Man That Corrupted Hadleyburg,'" *Studies in Short Fiction* 18 (1981): 59–64; Henry B. Rule, "The Role of Satan in 'The Man That Corrupted Hadleyburg,'" *Studies in Short Fiction* 6 (1969): 619–29; Thomas Werge, "Mark Twain and the Fall of Adam," *Mark Twain Journal* 15 (1970): 5–13; Stanley Brodwin, "Mark Twain's Masks of Satan: The Final Phase," in *On Mark Twain: The Best from American Literature*, ed. Louis J. Budd and Edwin H. Cady (Durham: Duke University Press, 1987), 149–70.
3 Mark Twain, "The Man That Corrupted Hadleyburg," *Collected Tales, Sketches, Speeches, and Essays, 1891–1910* (New York: Library of America), 390.
4 Ibid., 390, 391, 426.
5 Ibid., 400. Twain is thus revising Paul's statement in Romans 6:23: "For the wages of sin is death."
6 Twain, "The Man That Corrupted Hadleyburg," 402, 421, 422, 427.
7 Ibid., 425, 433.
8 Ibid., 433, 434, 436, 437.
9 Ibid., 437–38.
10 W. E. B. Du Bois, "The Propagation of History" [from *Black Reconstruction*], *Writings* (New York: Library of America, 1986), 1040; Twain, "The Man That Corrupted Hadleyburg," 430. On conspiratorial thinking and the "paranoid style," see Richard

Hofstadter, *The Paranoid Style in American Politics and Other Essays* (New York: Knopf, 1965); and David Brion Davis, *The Slave Power Conspiracy and the Paranoid Style* (Baton Rouge: Louisiana State University Press, 1969). See also David W. Blight, "W.E.B. Du Bois and the Struggle for American Memory," in his *Beyond the Battlefield: Race, Memory, and the American Civil War* (Amherst: University of Massachusetts Press, 2002), 223–257.

11 There is a rich context for "Nineteen" symbolizing national corruption that Twain was almost certainly familiar with. He wrote the story in Vienna, and was appalled with the corruption and anti-Semitism in Austria. There were nineteen states in the Austrian parliament, and much like the nineteen leading citizens of Hadleyburg, they hated each other and furiously competed. Even more significantly, "Nineteen" also figures in the Bible as a symbol of evil: nineteen of David's servants are missing when he needs them (2 Kings 2:30); and in the nineteenth year of his reign, King Nebuchadnez'zar (also Nebuchadrez'zar) of Babylon burns the house of the Lord and all the houses in Jerusalem. And Twain knew his Bible. As a young boy in Hannibal, he regularly attended the Presbyterian church. Hannibal was also something of a "burned-over district," having been scorched by spiritual fires when Twain lived there. It was a center of Campbellites, a millennialist group headed by Alexander Campbell that resembled William Miller's premillennialist sect. Millerites were also active in Hannibal. In fact, on his last visit to Hannibal, Twain recalled how Millerites "donned their ascension robes and awaited the end, on October 22, 1844, and he pointed out the place where they gathered." See Ernest Lee Tuveson, *Redeemer Nation: The Idea of America's Millennial Role* (Chicago: University of Chicago Press, 1968), 216 (quoted); Ozick, "Mark Twain and the Jews," 3–5.

12 Brodwin, "Mark Twain's Masks of Satan," 150.

13 Twain, "The Man That Corrupted Hadleyburg," 394, 395, 426; *The Essential Reinhold Niebuhr: Selected Essays and Addresses*, ed. Robert McAfee Brown (New Haven: Yale University Press, 1986), 181.

14 David W. Blight, *Race and Reunion: The Civil War in American Memory* (Cambridge: Harvard University Press, 2001), quotation from p. 2; Abraham Lincoln, ["Second Inaugural"], *Great Speeches* (New York: Dover, 1991); Eric Foner, *Politics and Ideology in the Age of the Civil War* (New York: Oxford University Press, 1980), 33.

15 Du Bois, "The Souls of White Folk," *Writings*, 926, 927, 933.

16 Du Bois, "The Souls of White Folk," *Writings*, 926–27; Twain, "The Man That Corrupted Hadleyburg," 436.

17 *God's New Israel: Religious Interpretations of American Destiny, New and Updated Edition*, ed. Conrad Cherry (Chapel Hill: University of North Carolina Press, 1998), quotation from Beecher on p. 219, from Lawrence on p. 250; Henry F. May, *Protestant Churches and Industrial America* (New York: Harper & Row, 1967), 69; William Leach, *Land of Desire: Merchants, Power, and the Rise of a New American Culture* (New York: Pantheon, 1993), 192.

18 Donald Meyer, *The Protestant Search for Political Realism, 1919–1941*, 2nd ed. (Middle-

town: Wesleyan University Press, 1988), 350; Richard Slotkin, *Gunfighter Nation: The Myth of the Frontier in Twentieth-Century America* (New York: Athenaeum, 1992), 88–122, quotation from p. 88; Richard Hofstadter, *Social Darwinism in American Thought* (1944; reprint, Boston: Beacon Press, 1992), chaps. 1–2, 5, 9–10; Carl N. Degler, *In Search of Human Nature: The Decline and Revival of Darwinism in American Social Thought* (New York: Oxford University Press, 1991), 3–31; George M. Fredrickson, *The Inner Civil War: Northern Intellectuals and the Crisis of the Union* (1965; reprint, Urbana: University of Illinois Press, 1993), 166–238; T. Jackson Lears, *No Place of Grace: Antimodernism and the Transformation of American Culture, 1880–1920* (New York: Pantheon, 1981), 97–140.

19 Charles A. Briggs, "The Salvation Army," *North American Review* 159:457 (December 1894): 697–710, quotation from p. 700; Aaron Abell, *The Urban Impact on American Protestantism, 1865–1900* (Cambridge: Harvard University Press, 1943). See also Lillian Taiz, "Applying the Devil's Works in a Holy Cause: Working-Class Popular Culture and the Salvation Army in the United States, 1879–1900," *Religion and American Culture* 7 (1997): 195–223; Herman Ausubel, "General Booth's Scheme of Social Salvation," *American Historical Review* 56 (1951): 519–25; Norman H. Murdoch, "Female Ministry in the Thought and Work of Catherine Booth," *Church History* 53 (1984): 348–62; Debra Campbell, "A Catholic Salvation Army: David Goldstein, Pioneer Lay Evangelist," *Church History* 52 (1983): 322–32; C. C. Carstens, "The Salvation Army—A Criticism," *Annals of the American Academy of Political and Social Science* 30 (1907): 117–28; Clark C. Spence, "The Landless Man and the Manless Land," *The Western Historical Quarterly* 16 (1985): 397–412.

20 William James, "The Moral Equivalent of War," in *The Essential Writings*, ed. Bruce W. Wilshire (Albany, N.Y.: State University of New York Press, 1984), 349–61, quotations from 350, 353, 358; Fredrickson, *Inner Civil War*, 217–38.

21 Louis Menand, *The Metaphysical Club: A Story of Ideas in America* (New York: Farrar, Straus and Giroux, 2001), 337–76, quotation from p. 374; Menand, "John Brown's Body," *Raritan* 22 (2002): 59.

22 Slotkin, *Gunfighter Nation*, Perry quotation from p. 91, Kirkman quotation from p. 90.

23 Ibid., 106–22, quotation from p. 106, Beveridge quotation from p. 108; Nell Irvin Painter, *Standing at Armageddon: The United States, 1877–1919* (New York: Norton, 1987), 142.

24 Slotkin, *Gunfighter Nation*, 89–92; Alan Trachtenberg, *Reading American Photographs: Images as History, Mathew Brady to Walker Evans* (New York: Hill and Wang, 1989), 90–111; Robert H. Wiebe, *The Search for Order, 1877–1920* (New York: Hill and Wang, 1967), 11–43, 76–110, 133–63; Alan Trachtenberg, *The Incorporation of America: Culture and Society in the Gilded Age* (New York: Hill and Wang, 1982), 38–100.

25 Andrew Delbanco, *The Death of Satan: How Americans Have Lost the Sense of Evil* (New York: Farrar, Straus and Giroux, 1995), 138; Jackson Lears, *Something for Nothing: Luck in America* (New York: Viking, 2003), 156–57.

26 Gerald F. Linderman, *Embattled Courage: The Experience of Combat in the American Civil War* (New York: Free Press, 1987), 1–6, 216–97.

27 Ernest Lee Tuveson, *Millennium and Utopia: A Study in the Background of the Idea of Progress* (1949; reprint, New York: Harper & Row, Publishers, 1964), ix–xi; Krishan Kumar, "Utopia and Anti-Utopia in the Twentieth Century," *Utopia: The Search for the Ideal Society in the Western World*, ed. Roland Schaer, Gregory Claeys, and Lyman Tower Sargent (New York: New York Public Library/Oxford University Press, 2000), 251–53.

28 Edward Bellamy, *Looking Backward, 2000–1887* (New York: Penguin, 1986), 36, 191. See also Richard Slotkin, *The Fatal Environment: The Myth of the Frontier in the Age of Industrialization, 1800–1890* (Middletown: Wesleyan University Press, 1985), 516–17; John L. Thomas, *Alternative America: Henry George, Edward Bellamy, Henry Demarest Lloyd and the Adversary Tradition* (Cambridge: Harvard University Press, 1963), 237–67.

29 Upton Sinclair, *The Jungle: A Norton Critical Edition*, ed. Clare Virginia Eby (New York: Norton, 2003), 299, 350, 351, quotations on p. 350 and p. 351 from Sinclair, "What Life Means to Me" (1906); Morris Dickstein, *A Mirror in the Roadway: Literature and the Real World* (Princeton: Princeton University Press, 2005), 41–50.

30 Mark Twain, *Adventures of Huckleberry Finn: A Norton Critical Edition*, ed. Thomas Cooley (New York: Norton, 1999), 13, 15, quotation from p. 223.

31 Twain, "Battle Hymn of the Republic (Brought Down to Date)," in *Collected Tales, Sketches, Speeches, and Essays*, 474–75.

32 Herman Melville, *Battle-Pieces and Aspects of the War* (1866; reprint, New York: Da Capo Press, 1995), 63.

33 Frederick Douglass, *Life and Times of Frederick Douglass* (New York: Collier Books, 1962), 479, 480. See also John Stauffer, "Frederick Douglass and the Aesthetics of Freedom," *Raritan* 25 (2005): 131–36; David W. Blight, *Frederick Douglass' Civil War: Keeping Faith in Jubilee* (Baton Rouge: Louisiana State University Press, 1989), 1–25.

34 James H. Moorhead, *World Without End: Mainstream American Protestant Visions of the Last Things, 1880–1925* (Bloomington: Indiana University Press, 1999), xii.

35 Meyer, *Protestant Search for Political Realism*, 217–306, 349–403, quotations from pp. 220 (Niebuhr) 296, 351; Richard Wightman Fox, "Experience and Explanation in Twentieth-Century American Religious History," *New Directions in American Religious History*, ed. Harry S. Stout and D. G. Hart (New York: Oxford University Press, 1997), 394–413, quotation from p. 402; Moorhead, *World Without End*, 191–96; Sydney E. Ahlstrom, *A Religious History of the American People* (New Haven: Yale University Press, 1972), 877–948.

36 Moorhead, *World Without End*, 170–96, quotation from p. 171; George M. Marsden, *Fundamentalism and American Culture: The Shaping of Twentieth-Century Evangelicalism, 1870–1925* (New York: Oxford University Press, 1980), 141–70, 199–228; Peter J. Boyer, "The Big Tent: Billy Graham, Franklin Graham, and the Transformation of American Evangelicalism," *The New Yorker*, August 22, 2005, 42–55.

37 Ahlstrom, *Religious History*, 805–24, 842–56, 1058–61, quotation from p. 1059;

Michael Barkun, *Religion and the Racist Right: The Origins of the Christian Identity Movement* (Chapel Hill: University of North Carolina Press), 17–46; Adam Fairclough, *Better Day Coming: Blacks and Equality, 1890–2000* (New York: Penguin, 2001), 87–109; Orlando Patterson, *Rituals of Blood: Consequences of Slavery in Two American Centuries* (Washington, D.C.: Civitas/Counterpoint, 1998), 176–81.

38 Du Bois, *The Souls of Black Folk* (1903; reprint, New York: Penguin, 1989), 3, 5, 90; David Levering Lewis, *W.E.B. Du Bois: Biography of a Race, 1868–1919* (New York: Henry Holt, 1993), 277–283.

39 Du Bois, *Souls of Black Folk*, 87; Lewis, *Du Bois*, 289–290; Ralph E. Luker, *The Social Gospel in Black and White: American Racial Reform, 1885–1912* (Chapel Hill: University of North Carolina Press, 1991), 1–6, 212–217.

40 Ahlstrom, *Religious History*, 1055–72, quotation from p. 1062; Fairclough, *Better Day Coming*, 41–65, 111–31; Gayraud S. Wilmore, *Black Religion and Black Radicalism: An Interpretation of the Religious History of Afro-American People*, 2nd ed. (Maryknoll, N.Y.: Orbis Books, 1993), 122–29, 135–66.

41 Frederick Douglass, *My Bondage and My Freedom* [1855], ed. John Stauffer (New York: Modern Library, 2003), 156.

42 Philip A. Klinkner, with Rogers Smith, *The Unsteady March: The Rise and Decline of Racial Equality in America* (Chicago: University of Chicago Press, 1999), 3–4

43 Ibid., 106–35; Fairclough, *Better Day Coming*, 87–109, quotation from p. 102.

44 George M. Fredrickson, *Racism: A Short History* (Princeton: Princeton University Press, 2002), 132; Klinkner, with Smith, *Unsteady March*, 161–287, quotations from pp. 224, 269; Fairclough, *Better Day Coming*, 203–248; Thomas Borstelmann, *The Cold War and the Color Line: American Race Relations in the Global Era* (Cambridge: Harvard University Press, 2001), 45–134.

45 Meyer, *Protestant Search for Political Realism*, xiii–xix, 292–297, 404–13; Richard Fox, *Reinhold Niebuhr: A Biography* (New York: Pantheon, 1985), 193–275.

46 James Baldwin, *The Fire Next Time* (1963; reprint, New York: Vintage, 1993), 82–106, quotations from pp. 91, 92.

47 Ibid., 95, 105–06.

MICHAEL FELLMAN

The Transferability of Otherness
American Expansionists Greet the Filipinos, 1898-1902

With the imperial urge to conquer the Philippines in 1898, American statesmen and the military drew on stereotypes of racial outsiders. In the minds of many Americans, Filipinos were lazy and dirty barbarians who needed to be civilized. "When it came to conquest, such images of Otherness were a continuous and powerful ideological resource," as the esteemed historian Michael Fellman emphasizes. Some commentators explicitly linked Filipinos to the North American Indians, and most of the leading American officers applied the strategies they had learned fighting Indians to the Philippines. The result was that American views toward Filipinos took two forms: "benevolent assimilation" or extermination. Richard Henry Pratt's belief about Native Americans—"kill the Indian and save the man"—applied to Filipinos as well. But the benevolent side of this dialectic of racial Otherness took a back seat to the policy of extermination. Guerrilla warfare and strategies of terror became the rule with American soldiers. And terror begat more terror. Filipinos, like the Indians before them, used terror; thy sought to annihilate the invader while ruthlessly disciplining their own people. But Americans were familiar with terrorism, for terror is how they had dealt with the "lesser races" for centuries.

Although the United States conquered a far-distant colony for the first time in the Philippines in 1898, Americans were far from uninitiated in colonial warfare when they reached across the Pacific Ocean to seize territory. For nearly three hundred years, ever since Europeans first showed up to settle the vast North American continent, they had fought what amounted to a protracted war against the Indians who had been there for 12,000 years: the last open battle with the Indians—a massacre in fact—at Wounded Knee, was fought in 1890. So it should be considered no surprise that when it came time to conquer another nonwhite race only eight years later, the template of Indian warfare was laid onto the Filipinos. In his 1901 essay, "Philippine Ethnology," published in the widely read middle-class journal, Harper's Weekly, Frank D. Millet made the connection clearly when he asserted that, "our North American Indians so thoroughly interpret to us this type of humanity, [that we may find] that some of our present hostiles are blood-relations to the poor foes of the centuries earlier of the Pilgrims and the Puritans."[1]

For their part, three centuries earlier, defining the Indians whose land they were colonizing, New Englanders applied what their culture had taught them about the Irish, onto whose territory their countryman had long since expanded. Observing Indian funeral customs, including face painting with lead and soot, William Wood noted almost casually that the ceremonies were accompanied with 'Irish-like howlings." Roger Williams, that most enlightened of Puritans, whose cultural benevolence extended to opposition to enslaving the Indians, warned without any apparent irony that such oppression would encourage them to remain enemies, "or turn wild Irish themselves."[2]

When it came to conquest, such images of Otherness were a continuous and powerful ideological resource. Filipinos, like Indians before them and the Irish before them were idle, lazy, dirty, licentious and heathen barbarians in the eyes of their invading dominators. Back in the sixteenth century, for example, Sir Henry Sidney, lord deputy of Ireland from 1565 to 1579, and a moderate Protestant, wrote in his report for 1567 about ruling the province of Munster, "Swerlie there was never people that lived in more miserie than they doe, nor as it should seme of wourse mynds, for matrimonie emongs them is no more regarded in effect than conjunction betwene unreasonable beastes, perjurie, robberie and murder counted alloweable, finallie I cannot finde that they make anny conscience of synn and doubtless I doubte whether they christen ther children or no, for neither finde I place where it should be don, nor any person able to enstruct them in the rules of a Christian, or if they were taught I cannot see they make any accompte of the woorlde to com."

Such a culturally miserable people deserved to be conquered by civilized Christians and then ruled with an iron rod. And so was northern Ireland overwhelmed, the Irish displaced and their land planted with colonies of what the invaders believed to be culturally far more evolved English farmers. Sir John Perrott, who served under Sidney as lord president in Munster, insisted about his means of rulership in 1573, "there ys noi waye better than to make those wyld people . . . to feare, so they be kepte in servile feare," an opinion seconded by William Fitzwilliam, a less ferocious man than Perrott, who acknowledged that "nothing but feare and force can teach duty and obedience [to this] rebellious people."[3]

When, in 1649, it was the turn of the senior Puritan, Oliver Cromwell, to conquer more unruly Irish barbarians, he willingly slaughtered 2,800 civilians in Drogheda, and 1,500 more in Wexford, acting with a brutality he never applied to Royalist enclaves in England itself. Far from feeling remorseful, after the second massacre he wrote that he had acted as God's righteous minister, smiting His enemies. "God, by an unexpected providence, in His righteous justice brought a just judgment upon them, causing them to become a prey to soldiers who in their piracies had made preys of so many families, and with their bloods to answer the cruelties which they had exercized upon the lives of divers poor Protestants."[4] Cromwell felt deep human ties with his suffering people, English Protestants, who were locked in mortal combat with the heathen, barbarian Other. In America, his crusading brothers, the American Puritans, and English settlers more generally, were well prepared even before first contact to deal with the Indians as they had the Irish. Of course much the same could be said about the Spanish conquerors in the New World: there was nothing so exceptional about the English variant of European chauvinism when they set out to conquer strange new lands, but it was the English version that taught American settlers how to think.

Although one can analyze a thousand battles and countless smaller but still lethal collisions during the centuries it took white settlers to expand from coast to coast, it is noteworthy that during the American Civil War, a truly national bloodletting, white soldiers, if they abused white civilians in every other way, did not slaughter them, and took white combatants prisoner rather than shooting them when they surrendered. Confederates did not apply such rules to captured black soldiers, however, treatment that African American soldiers returned in kind. Similarly, before and after the Civil War, during their protracted expansion onto Indian lands, white soldiers and civilians alike not infrequently slaughtered civilians of another alien race—treatment never meted out to racial kin, even those who sinned through disunionism.

One cold December morning in 1866, Captain William J. Fetterman's company of eighty-one officers and men rode after the Sioux enemy near Fort Kearney, Nebraska. They were ambushed and annihilated, and the Indians then mutilated the troopers' bodies in gory fashion. Immediately after the massacre (when American troops were killed, it was called a massacre, though not when Indians were the victims), General William T. Sherman, commander in the West, wrote to Ulysses S. Grant, army Commander-in-Chief, "we must act with vindictive earnestness against the Sioux, even to their extermination, men, women and children. Nothing else will reach the root of this case." For one unguarded moment Sherman blurted out genocidal desire, something he had never expressed toward white enemies, even while he was ravaging Georgia and the Carolinas during the Civil War. However, he was far from alone when he lusted for revenge. Two years before Sherman articulated his wish, a Colorado regiment of 700 men had surprised and destroyed a peaceful band of Cheyenne at Sand Creek, killing at least 28 men and 105 women and children. They then mutilated the corpses, gathering fingers and ears to take back to Denver as trophies, several soldiers cutting out the genitals of women and stretching them over their saddlebows and hats.[5]

Such episodes had continued, off and on, for countless years as white settlers pushed westward across the continent. But in the thirty years it took to thoroughly suppress the Plains Indians in post–Civil War America, army strategy did not amount merely to slaughter, nor was genocide the goal. Militarily, the plan, first fully formulated in 1868, and refined in practice over the remainder of the century, was to herd nomadic Indians into concentration areas, where they would be fed and protected by the American government as the railroads pushed westward through their lands, bringing buffalo hunters and settlers, rebuilding the West into a Progressive and Civilized part of the United States. Those Indians who refused this solution and went off the concentration areas to hunt and raid were enemies entering what amounted to free-fire zones, fair game for the military to hunt down, return to the reservations, or kill.

So long as bands of Indians resisted staying in their places, the violent portion of this concentration policy amounted to unstoppable if sporadic warfare, including exterminationist episodes when those proved expedient. It must be stressed, however, that the other half of the dialectic of white Indian policy was assimilation. Here, reformers, often in conflict with the military, urged a peaceful program that would suppress Indian forms of family life, community organization, and religion—replacing them with Christian nuclear families. Reformers placed special emphasis on retraining Indian children, if necessary taking them away from their parents by force to send them to boarding schools, where they would compel them to speak English only, and to learn to mind their p's and q's. In time, communal land was to be privatized in the hands of these newly minted White Indians. Thus were nomadic, hunter-warrior societies to be assimilated into Christian, capitalist Anglo-Saxon America. As Richard Henry Pratt, the leading Indian educator, founder of the Carlisle Indian School in Pennsylvania, proudly declared, the aim was to "kill the Indian and save the man."[6]

Because most of the leading American officers commanding the Philippines War had spent their careers fighting Indians, it was not surprising that they applied the analogy of Indian warfare to new and distant hostile peoples they wanted to dominate. Furthermore, when, after losing a disastrous conventional military struggle, the Filipino nationalists resorted to guerrilla warfare, much like the strategy that Indians employed, combat grew increasingly savage. At this juncture, Colonel Jacob Smith, for one, told reporters in Manila that dealing with these "natives" was "worse than fighting Indians," and that without waiting for direction from higher brass, he had naturally adopted tactics that he had learned fighting America's own "savages." Restraints off, terror became the general policy for both sides, with the far better armed and organized Americans colonizers capable of using force more lethally, particularly as they believed themselves culturally licensed to subdue this repellant inferior race. For Vice President Theodore Roosevelt, the Philippines was only a "jumble of savage tribes" that he likened to Apaches, while General Charles King asserted that "the Filipino" was "utterly without conscience and as full of treachery as our Arizona Apache," who finally had been subdued in 1886, after decades of ferocious small-scale battle.[7]

It was not that the Filipinos, nor the Indians before them, were passive victims to American armed hegemony. They too used terror, aimed at disciplining their own people with ruthless control as well as killing the invaders; and American soldiers replied with equal or greater brutality. Once it became a matter of revenge for enemy savagery, the cycle of retributive slaughter and other forms of terror rolled on and on.

The conquest of the Philippines, a spin-off from the destruction of the doddering Spanish empire in the Spanish-American War of 1898, started not in the name of military conquest and economic domination but rather in the spirit of the peaceful pole of American expansionist ideology—assimilationist idealism. Americans intended to bring proper Christianity and universal libertarian ideals to a poor oppressed people for their own good rather than for selfish American ends. On December 21, 1898, President William McKinley set the high moral tone of the war that was to come in his proclamation accompanying the dispatch of the first sizable contingent of troops to a land the United States had just purchased for $20,000,000 by signing the Treaty of Paris with the defeated Spanish government. "It should be the earnest and paramount aim of the military administration to win the confidence, respect, and affection of the inhabitants of the Philippines by assuring them in every possible way that full measure of individual rights and liberties which is the heritage of a free people, and by proving to them that the mission of the United States is one of *benevolent assimilation*, substituting the mild sway of justice and right for arbitrary rule."[8] Given their history of liberty for all, Americans colonizers would be unlike those nasty European imperialists: they would bring freedom rather than tyranny.

The lead implementer of American policy in the Philippines was Commissioner William Howard Taft, former governor of Ohio, whose performance as the civil governor of the Philippines was one of the main reasons Theodore Roosevelt chose him as his successor in 1908. Taft formulated his position most clearly in February 1902, in his testimony before a Senate committee investigating the American-Philippine War, still dragging on after four brutal years. A self-confessed optimist when it came to his time in Manila, Taft generally presented an upbeat picture of the happy submission of the Filipino people to American rule. In kindly paternalist style he was reputed to have called them his "little brown brothers." Yet Taft was no Pollyanna: he saw the negative side of the American occupation as well as hope for the future. Indeed, he had written to Secretary of State Elihu Root in 1901, "the severity with which the inhabitants have been treated would not look well if a complete history of it were written out."[9] But that was not the message he wanted to share with his fellow Americans back home.

As did McKinley, Taft generally expressed the warmest version of imperialism, though his kindliness only partially masked a darker version of the Filipino "character." With considerable sophistication, understanding that the powerful are free to project images upon the lowly upon which they then can act, Taft portrayed what other Americans made of Filipinos, especially their reputed "treachery"—apparent welcome of Americans masking extreme hostility. "It is said that this is an oriental people . . . that loves siestas; that seized every occasion to have a joyful gathering, and therefore that we, blind optimists, have been misled" by their appearances, Taft analyzed. "Well, of course, if you assume that the individual with whom you are dealing has none of the elements of human nature with which you are acquainted, is a different animal, is engaged in every thought in deceiving somebody, no matter how ignorant he may be, no matter how simple in appearance, you can reach any conclusion you desire in construing those evidences of . . . [hospitality and kindness] . . . that we have every day." Rather, Taft argued that to act fairly,

American colonizers must remember that the average Filipino "is moved by similar considerations to those which move other men." If "violent crimes, ambush, assassination" are more common than in European countries, "it is also true that kindness" reduces violence against Americans if used regularly, rather than "abrupt and unconciliatory" methods.[10]

Taft believed that the "terrorism of the guerrilla campaign," had distorted the normally peaceful character of the Filipinos, for it was "indispensable" to such warfare that they had to practice "murder and assassination" of their own people as well as Americans. Taft seemed here to be arguing from social determinism. "War, of course, provokes cruelty in everyone," he said. There was, however, something—a sort of innate racial characteristic—in this culturally backward people that rendered them particularly open to conversion into horrific warriors. "The uneducated Filipino is a docile person, but left to the natural ferocity which war and hostility of that sort provokes, he becomes very cruel," Taft concluded. The guerrillas are "ignorant, uneducated and cruel men, for the uneducated native, I am sorry to say, is cruel to animals and as little regard for human life."[11] Here was Taft's negative version of the docile and cheerful "native."

In response to the provocations of a ruthless guerrilla war, Taft reassured the committee, and, beyond them, the American public, that in comparison to other wars against "inferior races," Americans used "more compassion and more restraint and more generosity" than had any previous colonial power. And yet Taft conceded that when they saw evidence of Filipino cruelty in finding the mutilated bodies of their dead comrades, "it is not to be wondered at that . . . small bodies of American soldiers . . . should possibly at times have yielded in their outraged feelings . . . and resorted to [brutal] methods [including torture] which under the circumstances they regarded as more or less justified." From his office in Manila, he had heard many allusions to torture, though he had never tracked them down. "Of course it was no duty of mine. That was a military responsibility," Taft said, passing the buck. Yet he would not condemn American torture of Filipinos outright. Imagine that a soldier finds his "Bunkie" dead in the field and mutilated. Revenge would be a normal response. "You must understand that a soldier has human nature and that things are done which a commanding officer would not approve and yet cannot be prevented because of the outrage of feelings. That is the explanation of a great many things."[12]

This almost honest and probably unplanned admission of American atrocities caused a considerable reaction in the press. But in the balance of his testimony, Taft reverted optimistically to the civilizing mission he believed he had been leading. He was certain that the alternative of granting independence to the Filipinos would bring chaos and absolutism while driving out capital and development. Rather, through enlightened occupation, no matter how long it might take, "it is in my judgment the duty of the United States to continue a government there which shall teach those people individual liberty, which shall lift them to the point of civilization of which I believe they are capable, and which shall make them rise to call the name of the United States blessed." Here was a "problem worthy of solution"; and who better to do the job than Americans, a people ever ready to experiment in good will. Armed intervention, though the United States did not necessarily have to undertake it for American reasons, "is the best possible thing for the Filipino people . . . Probably the United States is only taking its burden of civilized peoples in helping out uncivilized peoples." However reluctant he might have been to get engaged out there initially, Taft concluded that "going as far as I have gone now, and feeling the missionary spirit as I think I may say I have it," Americans had no choice but to stay the course and expand the blessings of liberty to this hitherto uncivilized Asian people.[13] Taft served as the American point man earnestly taking up the white man's burden assigned his nation by the British propagandist, Rudyard Kipling, in his poem, "The United States and the Philippines Islands, 1899," published in *McClure's Magazine* precisely at the moment when the Treaty of Paris had hung in the balance in the Senate.[14]

Whatever the ideological nuances with which leaders like Taft presented the war back home, men in the field set the actual terms of combat. Their attitudes and their behavior as they experienced terrifying combat—which in guerrilla warfare means nasty ambushes and raids by small groups of men on both sides—expressed actual American beliefs enacted through concrete actions. Much about their behavior came out in the testimony of junior officers and enlisted men at the Senate hearings. And in the songs they sang, the opinions they expressed in their letters, one can uncover widely shared attitudes toward the enemy and the war they were conducting, as their belief system was subjected to the coruscating pressures of combat on the other side of the earth.

As in every war, to defuse shared anxieties and to express solidarity while on the march, men adapted old songs to new situations, songs that rapidly spread in the army. Through this collective folk art, the soldiers indicated their awareness of the hostility of the Filipinos, the dreadful nature of guerrilla war and of everyday life in fetid jungles and on bleak mountainsides. They also expressed their contempt for leaders who used grand abstractions in order to justify the war and made rosy predictions about a quick victory. To the tune of "Son of a Gamboleer," foot soldiers sang:

I'm only a common soldier in the blasted
Philippines.
They say I've got brown brothers here,
But I dunno know what it means.
I like the word fraternity, but still
I draw the line.
He may be a brother of Big Bill Taft,
But he ain't no brother of mine!

So much for Taft's sense of Mission and his cheery optimism. In this song, the men indicated that the enemy was an Enemy; brotherhood was reserved for the band of soldiers with whom the individual enlisted man was fighting. Their other best friend was their rifle—in this case the weapons were Krags. The soldiers wanted to destroy an enemy they detested and return to their normal lives back home as quickly as possible. That was their sense of mission. Thus, to the tune of "Tramp, Tramp, Tramp, the Boys are Marching," soldiers joined in singing:

Damn, damn, damn the Filipinos
Cut-throat khakiac ladrones!
Underneath the starry flag
Civilize them with a Krag
And return us to our beloved home.[15]

Whatever else motivated soldiers, virulent racism was perhaps the most unifying belief. While senior officers most often referred to Filipinos as Indians, and while some men did as well, the usual names for the enemies were "niggers" or "gugus." As one soldier pointed out to his parents, "Almost without exception, soldiers, and also many officers, refer to the natives as 'niggers.'" Niggers, Indians, and Filipinos could be melded into one image, and the soldiers were well aware of traditional army attitudes toward Indians, which had easy racial transferability to this new scene of expansionist colonial war. As one Kansas volunteer put it, "the country won't be pacified until the niggers are killed off like the Indians."[16]

For accuracy of reportage, letters from the front are hardly to be trusted, but even when one makes allowances for the distorting braggadocio of embattled young men wishing to appear powerful to the folks back home, they revealed much about attitudes toward the enemy. Letters depicted events in an intellectual and ideological context that soldiers believed their families shared and admired. With considerable exaggeration, a Washington state volunteer reported that in the wake of his regiment after one battle "there were 1008 dead niggers, and a great many wounded. We burned all their houses. I don't know how many men, women and children the Tennessee boys did kill. They wouldn't take any prisoners . . . At the best, this is a very rich country; and we want it. My way of getting it would be to put a regiment into a skirmish line, and blow every nigger into nigger heaven." Whether or not the Tennessee regiment involved in the battle really shot every Filipino civilian, this Washington volunteer certainly expressed genocidal desires, as did another soldier who wrote, "the boys say there is no cruelty too severe for these brainless monkeys." [17]

Quite often, the young soldiers called their fighting style "Gugu hunts." Better than going off on one's own to shoot game, hunting could deepen group solidarity among one's comrades and heighten the meanings of the sport for each member. One volunteer from Washington reported on the sense of collective blood lust that accompanied one such hunt: "Our fighting blood was up, and we wanted to kill 'niggers.' This shooting of human beings is a 'hot game,' and beats rabbit hunting all to pieces. We charged them and such a slaughter you never saw. We killed them like rabbits; hundreds, yes thousands of them. Every one was crazy." Such a tall-tale rendition of whatever might have been an actual event nevertheless indicated something authentic about the Gugu hunt. Another soldier stepped back slightly from his similar report of martial blood and individualized his responses when he concluded, "I am probably growing hard-hearted, for I am in my glory when I can sight my gun on some dark skin and pull the trigger." [18]

If that soldier had some moral doubts about becoming the killer of these strange and alien enemies, Minnesota volunteer George Osborn seemed to suffer from none when he described a skirmish in which "we just shot the niggers like a hunter would rabbits." Although perhaps not writing home exactly what transpired, this account sounds closer to the language that soldiers were likely to have used on the field of battle. "The Capt yelled out 'Remember the name of the fighting Sixth' and Lieut Nesbitt says 'Give em hell boys' . . . and as the Col had told us to take no prisoners *we did not* . . . we just shot niggers every which way and at last we had to use our bayonets and in about 3 min after we drew our steel the niggers began to run . . . in all the fight we took 1 prisoner who 'died' before we got back to [the base]. And when we got back . . . we had a good chicken dinner . . . and I tell you it was good." [19]

Especially considering that this dangerous guerrilla enemy was the current representation of a long line of despised races, it should not be surprising that, in the field, embattled American soldiers resorted to extreme measures when attempting to suppress them. This colonial war was characterized by torture, burning of villages and towns, sometimes killing many civilians at the same time, shooting prisoners, and creating concentration camps and burned out free-fire zones. The testimony of many junior officers and enlisted men at the 1902 Senate hearings, even when read skeptically for bias and exaggeration, demonstrated the widespread pattern of such actions, which were not aberrations, as the administration and army wanted to suggest they were, but standard operating procedure, if rarely stemming from direct orders from the top down. Commanders gave their subordinates considerable latitude, and the enlisted men also pushed for intense action against an enemy they both feared and despised.

The "water cure" was the most common and most talked about form of torture, in fact becoming emblematic of the conduct of the whole war in the eyes those Americans who opposed it. In the press, in their letters back home and in conversations with journalists, and at the Senate hearing when they had their day in "court," many soldiers testified, often in graphic detail, to the use of the water cure by the American army.

For example, Charles Riley described the torture of the *presidente* of the town of Igbaras, a place of about two or three thousand people, in front of two companies of about eighty American soldiers, under the command of two Captains. At the head of the stairs in the town hall was a raised, galvanized water cistern holding about one hundred barrels of rainwater. Four or five soldiers stripped the presidente to the waist, tied his hands behind him, threw him to the floor, wedged open his mouth with a stick or a bayonet and placed him under the tank. "The faucet was opened and a stream of water was forced down . . . his throat; his throat was held so he could not prevent swallowing . . . so that he had to allow the water to run into his stomach." This lasted somewhere between five and fifteen minutes. Then one of the soldiers stomped him with his foot, or punched him, so that the water spurted out in gushes two or three feet high, "like an artesian well." The presidente then gave some information and agreed to lead the Americans into the hills to find the local militia. Once outside, asked for more information, he refused, whereupon the same men threw him on the ground and started over, this time with water poured from a five-gallon jerry can. At this point Dr. Lyons, a contract surgeon attached to the regiment, intervened. He took out two syringes, putting one up the presidente's nose and another in his mouth. "Then the doctor ordered some salt, and a handful . . . was thrown into the water." Finally, after being pumped full of water and pounded in the stomach again, the man gave in, and, with a mounted company, went off after the Filipino soldiers. Before leaving the next morning, the Americans burned down the town.[20]

Several units, including the "Gordon Scouts" of the Eighteenth Infantry, had regularly designated "water details." A number of witnesses before the Senate committee said they knew of hundreds of cases, sometimes a dozen in one day in one locale. They believed that the water cure was a well-established fact of the American expeditionary force, at least in the latter stages of the war and in particularly difficult provinces. In several departments, the local Judge Advocate ran the water cure procedures. At his court-martial in 1900, Captain Cornelius M. Brownell admitted that under his command water cure was used "several times on different natives," always proving a useful means of eliciting valuable information. Far from apologizing for his conduct, he asserted that he had made "humane" use of this method, insuring that the water detail "were chosen with a view to having only intelligent, careful and humane men perform the operation." Furthermore, many others knew of what he was doing and in fact used the same procedure. "There was no secrecy about it; every officer and every man, both in my regiment and of every other regiment with which I served, knew when it was given, and I was never criticized by any officer . . . for administering it."[21]

Rumors swirled back from the Philippines that in addition to using torture and burning towns and villages, it was understood procedure to take no prisoners. Official army records noted, as several senators emphasized during the hearings that few Filipinos were taken captive. Between November 1, 1899, and September 1, 1900, American losses were 268 killed and 750 wounded, while Filipino casualties for the same time were 3,227 killed and 694 wounded. Several senators wanted to know why the number of killed relative to wounded was "in such immensely greater disproportion than the records" of any other known war. One senior American general replied that the Americans shot straighter, and that the Filipinos did not know how to sight their guns, which meant that American troops could charge to within fifteen feet of them without being hit. Also, the Filipinos could easily haul their wounded into the dense bamboo thickets for hiding.[22]

Although not offering a complete explanation of this highly unusual killed-to-wounded ratio, Corporal Richard J. O'Brien indicated a plausible way in which the order to take no prisoners might be given without any officer directly implicating himself in what he knew to be an illegal command. Asked whether there were any orders given before American soldiers shot down two elderly men carrying flags of truce as well as at least two women with their babies when his company had marched into the town of La Nog one morning, O'Brien replied "No, sir. In regard to that order being issued, we would go along in Indian file, the word would pass along 'take no prisoners.' Nobody would know where it emanated from." O'Brien stated that not finding such an order unusual, he did not bother to ask who issued it. Later, he heard Sergeant Conway report to the company commander "that he had killed two more niggers." As for the typicality of such incidents, he said "some officers were more humane than others; every officer had a law to himself." This particular officer, Captain McDonald, "was generally known as a 'nigger hater.'"[23]

During the last two years of the war, in order to clear out the worst guerrilla areas, the American army resorted to constructing concentration camps in which to sequester the civilians among whom the guerrillas moved. The American press noted this development with considerable alarm, as such camps imitated the policy of "Butcher Weyler" in Cuba that had done so much to arouse the American populace to invade that island for humanitarian purposes in 1898. Colonel Arthur L. Wagner, Assistant Adjutant General of the army had just toured several such camps before he told the senators about them. They were meant to be as civilized as they could be, Wagner said. In one of the camps, about 8,000 people had been gathered in an area about two miles by one mile. People were assembled according to their own barrios, sanitary conditions were carefully inspected and the streets were "scrupulously neat." The people "seemed to be surprisingly contented." It was true that there was a "dead line drawn in a perimeter drawn 300 to 800 yards out from the camp," but otherwise people had "perfect liberty" within. And really the camp was necessary to cleanse the province of cruel warfare. "I do not see how we could have stamped out the trouble otherwise . . . the island was practically in the possession of a blind giant: strong, but unable to see where to strike." Model concentration camps provided evidence that the war was being conducted "as humanely as any war that was ever waged."[24]

Other reports suggested that the camps were far from the ideal Wagner that presented. One senator read into the record the anonymous letter from a West Point graduate who had paid a visit to one camp. This officer had wound eight miles up a "slimy, winding bayou" in a navy tug, until it reached "a piece of spongy ground about 20 feet above the sea level . . . this little spot of black sogginess is a reconcentrado pen," replete with "corpse-carcass stench" and fetid sewer odors. "I found 30 cases of smallpox and fresh ones of an average of 5 a day, which practically have to be turned out to die. At nightfall crowds of huge vampire bats softly swirl on their orgies over the dead . . . It seems way out of the world . . . like suburb of hell." In fact, however lurid this picture appears to be, the most careful modern study suggests that a very high mortality rate due to poor sanitation, disease, and demoralization was characteristic of these camps.²⁵ In the countryside as well as in these camps, the army produced an ecological disaster that led to hundreds of thousands of deaths from disease among homeless, malnourished Filipinos.

Such an overseas adventure aroused the contempt of a vocal minority of Americans who could not accept this version of the exportation of American benevolence. Finley Peter Dunne, perhaps the most biting satirist of his day, was one of the most cutting anti-imperialists. Writing in the uneducated but cunning stage Irish-American voice of the Chicago barkeeper, Mr. Dooley, Dunne listened closely to the paternalism, racism, and underlying menace of the supporters of the war, about which Mr. Dooley observed:

> Whin we plant . . . the starry banner iv Freedom in th' Ph'lipeens . . . an' give th' sacred blessin' iv liberty to the poor, downtrodden people iv thim unfortunate isles,—dam thim!—we'll larn thim a lesson. . . . We say to thim: 'Naygurs,' we say, 'poor dissolute, uncovered wretches,' says we, 'whin th' crool hand iv Spain forged man'cles f'r ye'er limbs . . . who was it crossed th' say an' sthruck off the' comealongs? We did . . . an' now, ye mis'rable, childish-minded apes, we propose f'r to larn ye th' uses iv liberty . . . an' when ye've become edycated an' have all th' blessings iv civilization that we don't want, that'll count ye one. We can't give ye any votes, because we haven't more thin enough to go round now; but we'll treat you the way a father shud treat his childher if we have to break ivry bone in ye'er bodies. So come to our arms.²⁶

In a parallel if more high-toned fashion, William James, who wrote to Charles Francis Adams in 1902, "God damn the U. S. for its vile conduct in the Philippines," proclaimed that he was certain that American intervention would only kill Filipino national life: "we can destroy their old ideals, but we can't give them ours." Talking of educating and eventually liberating them was only "sniveling . . . loathsome cant." Writing in the *Boston Evening Transcript* in 1899, James declared in white hot anger that the United States had come upon "an intensely living and concrete situation," and had blown it apart with "bald and hollow abstractions" about good government, waving the American flag while assuming the "unfitness" of the Filipinos for self-government. "Such bald abstractions as Reason and the Rights of Man, spelt with capitals" were now being used in "stark-naked abstract" ways to kill Filipinos. "Could there be a more damning indictment of that whole bloated idol termed 'modern civilization' than this amounts to? Civilization is, then, the big, hollow, resounding, corrupting, sophisticating, confusing torrent of mere brutal momentum and irrationality that brings forth fruit like this?"[27]

Thus did Americans greet the Filipinos, knowing beforehand how to deal with lesser races. Thus had the English colonizers greeted the Indians long before that, and before them the Irish. Thus no doubt had the civilizing Romans greeted the Britons, painted blue, shaking spears and howling to uncivilized gods at the Roman legions marching in to conquer yet another savage land. This ancient chain of unbeing was deeply embedded in American cultural structure, there to be used against the next racial enemy in the Philippines. And the next in Latin America, in Vietnam, and now in Iraq. And in the future, if need be, in Iran, North Korea, and elsewhere, wherever ennobled civilizing forces meet opponents they know in their ideological bones to be the Godless and Barbarian Other.

NOTES

1 *Harper's Weekly*, May 13, 1901, quoted in Richard Slotkin, *Gunfighter Nation: The Myth of the Frontier in Twentieth-Century America* (New York: Athenaeum, 1992), 110.
2 Both quotations are from Alden T. Vaughan, *New England Frontier: Puritans and Indians* (Boston: Little, Brown, 1965), 42–43, 208. Vaughan points out that, should enslavement go ahead, Williams had requested an Indian captive to serve him.
3 All these quotes are from Nicholas Canny's seminal essay, "The Ideology of English Colonization: From Ireland to America," *Past & Present*, 3rd series, 30 (1973): 575–98, at 585 and 593. Also see Canny, *Making Irish British, 1580–1650* (New York: Barnes & Noble, 1976). The English made much the same analysis of the savage and demonic Scots when it came to dominating them. See Arthur H. Williamson, "Scots, Indians and Empire: The Scottish Politics of Civilization, 1519–1606," *Past & Present* 150 (1996): 46–83.
4 Quoted in Charles Firth, *Oliver Cromwell, and the Rule of the Puritans in England* (1900; reprint, Oxford University Press, 1956), 256.
5 Sherman quoted in Michael Fellman, *Citizen Sherman* (New York: Random House, 1995), 264. For the Fetterman and Sand Creek slaughters, see Fellman, *Inside War: The Guerrilla Conflict in Missouri During the American Civil War* (New York: Oxford University Press, 1989), 213, and Richard White, *"It's Your Misfortune and None of My Own:" A History of the American West* (Norman: University of Oklahoma Press, 1991), 90.
6 White, *"It's Your Misfortune,"* 109–13; Robert M. Utley, *Frontier Regulars: The United States Army and the Indian, 1866–1891* (New York: Macmillan, 1973), 133.
7 Smith quoted in Stuart Creighton Miller, *"Benevolent Assimilation:" The American Conquest of the Philippines, 1899–1903* (New Haven: Yale University Press, 1982), 95; King quoted in Mark D. Van Ells, "Assuming the White Man's Burden: The Seizure of the Philippines, 1898–1902," *Philippine Studies* 43 (1994), 612; Roosevelt quoted in Slotkin, *Gunfighter Nation*, 106.

8 Quoted in Miller, "Benevolent Assimilation," frontispiece, emphasis added.
9 Quoted in Andrew J. Birtle, "The U. S. Army's Pacification of Marinduque, Philippine Islands, April 1900–April 1901," The Journal of Military History 61 (1997), 255.
10 Affairs in the Philippine Islands: Hearings before the Committee on the Philippines of the United States Senate, Senate Document 331, 57th Congress, 1st sess., 3 vols. (Washington: GPO, 1902), I:64–65.
11 Ibid., 1:70, 74, 77.
12 Ibid., 1:74, 76.
13 Ibid., 1:328, 346, 322, 323, 347, 406, 411.
14 Rudyard Kipling, "The United States and the Philippine Islands, 1899," McClure's Magazine 12 (February, 1899).
15 Both songs are compiled in Joseph L. Schott, The Ordeal of Samar (Indianapolis: Bobbs-Merrill, 1964), 65, 155.
16 Quotes from Slotkin, Gunfire Nation, 115, and Van Ells, "Assuming the White Man's Burden," 619.
17 Quoted in Slotkin, Gunfire Nation, 115.
18 Both quotes from Van Ells, "Assuming the White Man's Burden," 618. More generally see Miller, "Benevolent Assimilation," 176–218. I have discussed guerrilla hunting in Missouri during the American Civil War as "blood sport," in Inside War, 176–84.
19 George Osborn to his Parents, La Carlota, Negros, January 15, 1900, Floyd Risvold Collection, Minnesota Historical Society, quoted in Russell Roth, Muddy Glory: America's 'Indian Wars' in the Philippines, 1899–1935 (West Hanover, Mass.: Christopher Publishing House, 1981), 54, emphasis in the original.
20 Hearings, 2:1529–37, also see 2:1538–41 for another description of the same incident.
21 Hearings, 2:1537–39, 1730, 1766; 3:1971, 1975, 2062, 2256–58, 2304; and for Brownell's testimony, Letter from the Secretary of War, "Trials or Courts-Martial in the Philippine Islands in Consequence of Certain Insurrections," 57th Congress, 2nd sess., Senate Document 213, 85.
22 Hearings, 2:1927–32
23 Hearings, 3:2550–62, 2580.
24 Hearings, 3:2847–65.
25 Hearings, 3:2877–78; the best analysis of the conditions of these camps is in Glenn A. May, Battle for Batangnas: A Philippine Province at War (New Haven: Yale University Press, 1991), 262–67.
26 [Peter Finley Dunne], "Expansion," in Mr. Dooley in the Hearts of His Countrymen (Boston: Small Maynard, 1899), 3–7. Also see, "the Philippine Peace," in Observations by Mr. Dooley (New York: R. H. Russell, 1906), and several essays by Dunne reprinted in Elmer Ellis, ed., Mr. Dooley at His Best (New York: Archon Books, 1969), 59–77.
27 Quoted in Robert L. Beisner, Twelve Against Empire: The Anti-Imperialists, 1898–1900 (New York: McGraw-Hill, 1968), 235.

LESLIE BUTLER

Liberal Victorians and War in the Age of Empire

Do liberals like war? Does the respect for individual freedom, private property, and the rule of law make people more or less inclined to accept war? Leslie Butler offers an answer to these questions by exploring American and British liberal responses to war in the last decades of the nineteenth century, which helped shape a liberal foreign policy for the twentieth century. Although Gilded Age liberals vigorously opposed war in their lifetimes, they were neither antiwar nor anti-imperial: they did not always prefer diplomacy to violence; and they did not oppose the civilizing process. They critiqued aggressive foreign policy by embracing "reasoned deliberation" and a "cosmopolitan perspective." Reason fostered critical debate, which helped check the spread of manly jingoism and "the most brutal instincts of the populace," as Charles Eliot Norton phrased it. And cosmopolitan thinking encouraged a respect for other races and cultures and reflected a faith that these other cultures could become liberal.

Is there a liberal tradition in foreign policy? Or, more particularly, is there a tradition of liberal aversion to aggressive force in foreign affairs? The twentieth-century image of liberal foreign policy—from Woodrow Wilson at Versailles in 1919 to Michael Dukakis in a tank during the presidential campaign of 1988—seems to smack of a naïve idealism or well-meaning fecklessness. Where does this image come from? Is there something about the liberal tenets of individual freedom, private property, and constitutionalism that makes liberals inherently opposed to aggressive force? Are liberals "soft" on war? Is it an evil they hope human progress will eradicate?

In grappling with these (and related) questions, theorists of liberal international relations have confronted such endless complications and difficulties that we might be tempted to give up and acknowledge that liberalism, like other political idioms, is so capacious that it can be (and has been) used to defend any and all positions.[1] But a historical rather than theoretical approach to these questions can shed light on liberals' attitudes toward war. An examination of one case study in particular—the United States and Britain in the 1890s, a decade during which both nations waged imperial wars—shifts the focus from a normative discussion of "liberal societies" to an examination of liberal ideas within those societies. Liberalism has surely endured as long as it has because of the power of its ideas, but those ideas can be notoriously hard to pin down, evolving over time as well as varying within one particular historical moment. Following the historian John Burrow, we shall consider liberalism here less as a set of doctrines to which historical actors subscribed than as a vocabulary that they inhabited.[2]

We can best recover that vocabulary not by examining "liberal society" as a whole, as political scientists might, but by focusing on liberal spokesmen within that society—those opinion makers who sought to generate a coherent vision, sometimes in support of and sometimes in opposition to the larger culture. The turn of the century offers a particularly interesting historical moment in which to do this. As two liberal societies waged war, one in the Philippines and one in South Africa, a group of self-defined liberals opposed those wars and, in so doing, began to give shape to a liberal foreign policy—one that would become important for their better-known twentieth-century liberal descendants. This emerging liberal vision of international relations—which historians have not examined as fully as the context of Anglo-American "rapprochement" in which it took place—was a transatlantic phenomenon, much like the better-known nineteenth-century campaigns against slavery and for temperance and women's rights.[3] Reexamining this vision reminds us of the moral dimensions of liberalism and, in the process, reveals both the complexity and the enduring potency of liberal ideas.

Understanding this liberal vision of foreign policy requires recognizing what it was not. First, it was not an antiwar movement. Victorian liberals did indeed frequently express their preference for diplomacy over violence, supporting a number of pioneering efforts at international arbitration from the *Alabama* crisis of the 1870s to the Venezuela boundary dispute of the 1890s.[4] With E. L. Godkin, the editor of the New York *Nation*, liberals believed war was the "one great trait of barbarism" that modern nations retained from the primeval world. In their writings on diplomacy and foreign affairs, these liberals elevated the "human" plan of deciding differences by "judges, proofs, and argumentative persuasion" over the animal or "feline" method of "the tearing or rending of bodies."[5]

But while they disliked war and, at times, manifested a distinct discomfort with violence, Victorian liberals recognized that war was often necessary and, sometimes, even constructive. As John Stuart Mill wrote in 1861, "war is an ugly thing, but not the ugliest of things: the decayed and degraded state of moral and patriotic feeling which thinks nothing worth a war, is worse." Similarly, the American reformer Thomas Wentworth Higginson, a war veteran himself, bemoaned the outbreak of war with Spain in 1898 but also acknowledged that war "nurtures certain heroic qualities—courage, endurance, patient self-control, the readiness of sacrifice."[6] More concretely, by the second half of the century, liberals had waged or supported "liberal" wars throughout the world. Young British liberals came of political age amidst support for the Italian and Hungarian wars of national liberation. Perhaps the liberal most responsible for reinventing liberal foreign policy, turning it from a tradition of noninterference to one of humanitarian intervention, was William Gladstone. His 1876–78 campaign against the "Bulgarian atrocities," a touchstone of British party politics, returned the retired Liberal statesman to power and crystallized the differences between Liberals and Conservatives, under Benjamin Disraeli, on foreign policy grounds.[7] Americans followed these European movements from afar and also engaged in what they considered the ultimate "good war": the war for the Union and for emancipation in the American Civil War. Despite their ambivalence about force, British and American liberals justified these military struggles on liberal grounds. Certain powers were so antithetical to liberal civilization—the Habsburg dynasty, the southern "slave power," the Ottoman Empire—that force was required to oppose them.[8]

If Victorian liberals were not antiwar, neither were they anti-imperial in any strict sense. Though the term is often invoked, a real lack of clarity or precision attends it.[9] British Liberals, even ones often considered "anti-imperialist" by their contemporaries and subsequent scholars, all supported some version of the British empire. If they called for retrenchment, for restraint from any new obligations, or even for home rule for settler colonies such as Canada and Australia, they supported the continuation of an imperial presence in certain places of the world and felt confident that British rule had brought peace and civilization to India and parts of Africa. Goldwin Smith, the most prodigious Victorian critic of empire, typified the problem. He spent decades writing against British imperial rule—from his 1860 *The Empire* to his frequent attacks on the Boer War. But even Smith took for granted that Britain would remain in Ireland and India where, he believed, native governments would be dangerously illiberal.[10]

"Anti-imperialism" makes more sense in the American case, though some qualifications are in order there too. The United States had no overseas colonies like Great Britain, but it could boast over a century of conquest and continental expansion that many liberals, like most Americans, often took for granted. Some liberal critics of the late-century imperial expansion refused to ignore this history of violence and war. Charles Eliot Norton and Moorfield Storey, for example, often invoked history and used earlier protests of the Mexican War, the annexation of Texas, and attempts to annex San Domingo to create a tradition of liberal dissent from acquisitive foreign policy. But even if they acknowledged America's aggressive past, they always distinguished it from the colonial imperialism that Great Britain practiced and so could continue to view the United States as a republic innately hostile to empire—indeed one whose very founding, and therefore identity, stemmed from the rejection of empire.[11]

For the sake of brevity, we can highlight two concepts that were central to the liberal critique of late-century foreign policy: reasoned discussion and a cosmopolitan perspective. We can best understand these elements of the liberal vocabulary by identifying what bothered liberals about the imperial wars of the 1890s. After all, it would not have been impossible for a good liberal to champion either cause, as both conflicts sprang in part from humanitarian-liberal roots: independence for Cuba and the protection of *uitlander* rights in the Transvaal.[12] But liberals doubted the sincerity of those humanitarian claims, which they believed were undermined both by governmental policy and by the larger political and cultural climate that nurtured the wars. In place of the reasoned discussion and cosmopolitan spirit they prized, liberals found only an unthinking, often chauvinistic, patriotism. Their dissent registered their alarm that the liberal Anglo-American alliance they had hoped and worked for since the 1860s had turned instead into a transatlantic quest for world power based on brute force rather than on liberal ideals. And in abandoning those ideals, liberals feared, Britain and the United State threatened their very persistence as forces for progress. Goldwin Smith dreaded the dire consequences of "a junction of American with British Jingoism for the purpose of aggrandizement," and he wondered what "could be more strange or disastrous than this sudden relapse of humanity."[13]

Liberals viewed the jingoism sweeping through Britain and the United States as a direct threat to the reason and reasoned deliberation they prized in public life. A new word to name a new phenomenon, *jingoism* emerged in the last decades of the nineteenth century as an expression for aggressive hypernationalism that thrives on passion and emotion.[14] Goldwin Smith, a longtime observer of the phenomenon in Britain, the United States, and Canada, doubted the authenticity of any patriotism that depended on such "stimulants" as the "hoisting of flags, chanting of martial songs . . . [and] the arming and reviewing of the very children in our public schools." Liberals contrasted the "frenzied," "hasty," and "hot" manner in which imperialists went to war with the "prudent," "calm," and "sober," style they clearly preferred.[15]

The climate of overstimulated "unreason" was only compounded by the newer definitions of manhood then becoming fashionable and epitomized in the chest-thumping machismo of Teddy Roosevelt. This newer conception of masculinity, with its emphasis on action over thought and on self-assertion over self-control, played a role in international relations, as American "jingoes" eschewed supposedly "feminizing" diplomatic measures like arbitration in favor of the more aggressive foreign policy they hoped would shore up American manhood.[16] Victorian liberals also tended to speak in a rhetoric of manliness, but they used the term in a less overtly gendered way. Emphasizing the contrast with animals and boys more than with women, the liberal conception of manliness held out the possibility that all individuals could display the attributes of manliness. It was reason and maturity, they argued, not aggression or physical strength that made a man. To liberals, then, the rash wars in the Philippines and South Africa were not manly but "childish," reflecting the "boyish" notion, in Godkin's words, that one would go to war not "necessarily for a just and righteous and inevitable cause, but for the effect upon your own virility."[17]

In place of such unreflective and immature jingoism, liberals urged what they called "enlightened patriotism" or "reasoning patriotism." This was a patriotism that could remain critical and withstand the give-and-take of public debate, something a less thoughtful patriotism rejected outright. Liberals like Norton were incredulous that, without "sober reflection," the United States and Britain hurled themselves precipitously into wars the consequences of which had not been fully considered. This became most clear in the American case, where a quick victory over Spain brought with it the unexpected possibility of annexing the Philippines. Godkin found the lack of serious discussion as disturbing as the prospect of annexation: "deliberation," he explained, "is the salt of democracy; it is what keeps it democratic." Debate implied argument and disagreement, and liberals insisted that patriotism must be reasoned enough to tolerate criticism.[18]

This kind of critical patriotism could be achieved by adopting a cosmopolitan perspective, the second major feature of liberal foreign policy that we will address here. Akin to what we would today call "multilateralism," their cosmopolitanism most clearly manifested itself in their support for international institutions such as arbitration treaties, international law, and cultural exchange. Godkin argued that public leaders had a supreme duty "to cherish and exalt the idea of law as the only true controller of international relations." The very history of world progress, he believed, could be found in "the history of the growth amongst human beings of the habit of submitting their dealings with each other to the direction of rules of universal application." This emphasis on universality was the international counterpart to the liberal policy of formal equality among individuals.[19]

Liberal internationalism was marked by the sense that there was something larger than national self-interest that had to be considered, a kind of world progress to which all nations contributed and a world opinion that gave international relations legitimacy. This attitude, which also informed their cultural views, could be seen in the Harper's Weekly editor George William Curtis's insistence that "we are citizens of the world before we are citizens of any country; we are men before we are Americans."[20] In Britain, Gladstone's articulation of the "six right principles of foreign policy," during his famous "Midlothian Campaign" of 1879–80, had boldly imagined the "concert of Europe" as a source of international public opinion and even legitimate force.[21]

This cosmopolitanism or internationalism clearly reveals that liberals were no timid isolationists, as their opponents and subsequent scholars have often charged. They agreed with imperialists that the United States and Britain had an important role to play in the world, but they understood that role differently. "It is not that we would hold America back from playing her full part in the world's affairs," Norton explained, "but that we believe that her part could be better accomplished by close adherence to those high principles which are ideally embodied in her institutions." As James Bryce similarly observed in the House of Commons in 1900, it was not merely Britain's material strength and navy that "have given us our great position in the world and have extended our Empire. It has been the respect we have generally inspired for our sense of justice and for our respect for the rights of other nations." Both men feared that the arrogance and jingoism manifested in the Philippine-American and Boer Wars would harm their nations' standing in the world by raising questions about "our regard for international rights and the purity of our motives."[22]

But liberal cosmopolitanism involved more than a commitment to international rights and organizations. Being cosmopolitan also meant approaching the rest of the world from an expansive perspective, one that nurtured and was nurtured by a broad, historicist understanding of national development. Familiarity with the history and culture of the other peoples and places pushed liberals away from a provincial (one might say "exceptional") view of themselves. Such "un-exceptionalism" may sound surprising in the case of the Americans, whose very anti-imperialism depended on a stark sense of difference and departure from the "Old World." But while American liberals clearly differentiated the New World experience of the United States, their understanding of that difference was informed by a keen knowledge of history, a knowledge that led them to draw connections between national experiences. American liberals, for example, mined earlier experiences with colonial dependence for powerful arguments against acquiring the Philippines and placing the Filipinos under American rule or ending Boer independence. No one doubted, Higginson asserted, that the British had given the colonies useful representative institutions or that the "Romans governed well and were the best road-builders on this planet," but all would admit that "it helped human progress" for the United States and Britain to govern themselves, even if it had taken decades or centuries to "throw off the sense of inferiority bred by subjection."[23]

The historicist, cosmopolitan perspective led liberals to conceive of civilization in a more fluid manner than many of their contemporaries. Compared with their peers, they exhibited an uneasiness with assumptions of white Anglo-Saxon Christian superiority, or at least with the assumption that any such superiority justified aggression or violence toward others. They criticized the "cruel spirit of Christian self-righteousness," in Norton's words, that many Britons and Americans brought to the realm of international relations, and they deflated such smugness with pointed reminders of "Anglo-Saxon" deficiencies. Higginson rejected the argument that certain nations could be deemed unfit for self-government because of their instability or seeming propensity for war. Certainly no place looked less stable than the United States in 1861, he pointed out, and "we shed more blood in our own civil war than . . . [in all of South America's] 'revolutions' put together."[24] Several liberal critics noted that the most violently lawless elements of the United States population were "Anglo-Saxons" in the South, where the rash of African American lynchings represented, in Godkin's words, "surely and simply a descent into barbarism by a people who pretend to be civilized, and, not only that, but are pretending to spread civilization." Finally, liberals asserted that the cruel conduct of the wars in the Philippines and in South Africa—especially the use of concentration camps and the massive destruction of farms—most clearly undercut American and British claims to superior civilization. Such war measures were "methods of barbarism," as the Liberal leader Henry Campbell-Bannerman famously denounced them.[25]

Along with historicist and cosmopolitan thinking came a certain tolerance for other races and cultures, which was perhaps more pronounced among the aging American liberals than their British counterparts. This liberal tolerance was limited by twentieth-century standards, to be sure—reflecting not so much an embrace of difference as an insistence that differences were incidental and historical rather than permanent and biological. But given the heavily racialized context in which they were writing, this very insistence is significant. "We err," Higginson cautioned, "in assuming that any one race monopolizes all the virtues."[26]

This cosmopolitan perspective could take different forms. For Norton, a pioneer in the study of cultural history, it pushed him toward a kind of cultural relativism. "I used to tell my classes," he wrote an old friend in 1901, "that civilization was a purely relative term, meaning the sum of the acquisitions of a race at any given time, and not as white people are apt to assume a possession exclusively theirs." He repeated the sentiment to a former Japanese pupil with whom he corresponded, insisting in 1904 that he had "no such liking for our Occidental civilisation as to desire to see it extended over the East. We have as much to learn from the East as you of the East have to learn from the West, and I am not sure but that the lesson the East has to teach is the more important."[27]

More commonly, however, liberal cosmopolitanism took the form of a universalist faith in the capacity (and desire) of other peoples to become liberal, which most liberals, after all, thought was the highest goal toward which an individual or a nation should strive. Over and over again, American anti-imperialists stressed the universality of their forms of government and social organization. The platform of the Anti-Imperialist League, adopted at Chicago in 1899, declared "with Abraham Lincoln that 'no man is good enough to govern another man without the other's consent,'" and warned that "those who deny freedom to others deserve it not for themselves." Indeed, the belief in the universal applicability of liberal ideals was simply the logical extension of them, as Higginson made clear: "The test of one's real love of liberty and of republican government is that one should not believe them to be the destiny of a single race or language only, but of all nations." If the British Victorian liberals were situated quite differently, at the center of a vast global empire, and did not immediately pass Higginson's test, they too recognized the ultimate desirability of such a logical extension of liberal ideas.[28]

Those ideas, more than any structural features of liberalism, help us answer the questions posed at the beginning of this essay. Victorian liberals advocated war *and* advocated peace, depending on the circumstances, and looked to their ideas as guides. It would be those ideas—with all their "opportunities and constraints," to return to John Burrow's words— that would shape liberal foreign policy in the century that followed the Philippine-American and Boer Wars, especially in the years when the liberal internationalism that characterized the Anglo-American "special relationship" thrived. Yet those ideas are from static—they continue to evolve and adapt to new situations—and, perhaps more importantly, they are articulated and contested in history by liberals who do not always carry the day. In a liberal society, there will surely be liberal dissent. We do not need to pin down what liberalism was in the 1890s to determine what it is in our own day. But it may be useful to revisit another historical moment when liberals grappled with the question of how a nation can exercise great power and to think about how the vocabulary of nineteenth-century liberals might continue to be habitable in the twenty-first century.

NOTES

1 Theorists from Immanuel Kant to Joseph Schumpeter have weighed in the topic of liberal international relations. The scholarship is too enormous to cite here, but for a good introduction see Michael Howard, *War and the Liberal Conscience* (New Brunswick: Rutgers University Press, 1978); Michael W. Doyle, "Liberalism and World Politics," *American Political Science Review* 80 (1986): 1151–69; Doyle, *Ways of War and Peace: Realism, Liberalism, and Socialism* (New York: Norton, 1997); and Thomas L. Pangle and Peter J. Ahrensdorf, *Justice Among Nations: On the Moral Basis of Power and Peace* (Lawrence: University Press of Kansas, 1999). On the more specific subject of liberalism and imperialism, see Uday Mehta Singh, *Liberalism and Empire: A Study in Nineteenth-Century British Liberal Thought* (Chicago: University of Chicago Press, 1999), and Jennifer Pitts, *A Turn to Empire: The Rise of Imperial Liberalism in Britain and France* (Princeton: Princeton University Press, 2005).

2 "It is often more helpful, in writing the history of political thought, to think of political theories as vocabularies we inhabit, with their various claims, opportunities, and constraints, than as doctrines to which we subscribe," J. W. Burrow, *Whigs and Liberals: Continuity and Change in English Political Thought* (Oxford: Clarendon Press, 1988), 5.

3 On "rapprochement," see Lionel M. Gelber, *The Rise of Anglo-American Friendship: A Study in World Politics, 1898–1906* (London: Oxford University Press, 1938); Charles S. Campbell, *Anglo-American Understanding, 1898–1903* (Baltimore: Johns Hopkins University Press, 1957); Stuart Anderson, *Race and Rapprochement: Anglo-Saxonism and Anglo-American Relations, 1895–1904* (Rutherford, N.J.: Fairleigh Dickinson University Press, 1981). On nineteenth-century transatlantic reform, see, for example, Frank Thistlethwaite, *The Anglo-American Connection in the Early Nineteenth Century* (Philadelphia: University of Pennsylvania Press, 1959); David Brion Davis, *The Problem of Slavery in the Age of Revolution, 1770–1823* (Ithaca: Cornell University Press, 1975); David D. Hall, "The Victorian Connection," in *Victorian America*, ed. Daniel

Walker Howe (Philadelphia: University of Pennsylvania Press, 1976); David Brion Davis, *Slavery and Human Progress* (New York: Oxford University Press, 1984); Seymour Drescher, *Capitalism and Antislavery: British Mobilization in Comparative Perspective* (New York: Oxford University Press, 1986); Leila Rupp, *Worlds of Women: The Making of an International Women's Movement* (Princeton: Princeton University Press, 1997); and Bonnie S. Anderson, *Joyous Greetings: The First International Women's Movement, 1830–1860* (New York: Oxford University Press, 2000). A notable exception to the general historiographical silence on liberal foreign policy as a transatlantic phenomenon is Robert Kelley, *The Transatlantic Persuasion: The Liberal-Democratic Mind in the Age of Gladstone* (New York: Knopf, 1969).

4 Gladstone's government accepted the *Alabama* settlement, even though many in Great Britain charged him with cowardice for it. While American liberals were shocked at the tone of President Cleveland's Venezuela message, they supported the principle of arbitration that resulted from it. See Jonathan Parry, *The Rise and Fall of Liberal Government in Victorian Britain* (New Haven: Yale University Press, 1993), 270; H. C. G. Matthew, *Gladstone* (New York: Oxford University Press, 1986); Kelley, *Transatlantic Persuasion*, esp. chaps. 6 and 8.

5 Godkin, "The Absurdity of War," *Century* 53 (January 1897), 469. Victorian liberals pioneered efforts at arbitration, but recognized, in Goldwin Smith's words, that while "arbitration has done much to supersede war . . . it cannot do everything. Pride or cupidity will sometimes admit no arbitrator but the sword," *Loyalty, Aristocracy, and Jingoism* (Toronto: Hunter, Rose, 1896), 65. A peace movement, which drew from liberal and Christian roots, did emerge in the nineteenth century, but this cohort of Victorian liberals did not participate in it. Godkin, "Peace," *Nation* 11 (December 29, 1870), 432–33.

6 Mill, "The Contest in America," *Fraser's Magazine* 65 (February 1862), 268; Higginson, "War at Last," *Harper's Bazaar* (May 5, 1898). Higginson here anticipated William James's famous "moral equivalent of war" by sighing for the "day when these great gifts can be trained in ordinary life, without paying for them the terrible price of human blood."

7 On Gladstone's departure from earlier Manchester-school liberalism, see A. J. P. Taylor, *The Trouble Makers* (London: Hamilton, 1957); A. P. Thornton, *The Imperial Idea and Its Enemies* (New York: St. Martin's, 1959); Bernard Porter, *Critics of Empire: British Radical Attitudes to Colonialism in Africa* (New York: St. Martin's, 1968); and Howard, *War and the Liberal Conscience*. On the Bulgarian atrocities agitation, see Richard T. Shannon, *Gladstone and the Bulgarian Agitation, 1876* (London: Thomas Nelson, 1963). On British liberal support for national liberation movements, see Christopher Harvie, *Lights of Liberalism: University Liberals and the Challenge of Democracy, 1860–1886* (London: Allen Lane, 1976), chap. 5; Christopher Kent, *Brains and Numbers: Elitism, Comtism, and Democracy in Mid-Victorian England* (Toronto: University of Toronto Press, 1978), 22–26; and Margot Finn, *After Chartism* (New York: Cambridge University Press, 1993).

8 As David Brion Davis has shown, the language of liberalism and civilization was infinitely malleable, so that a war against slaveholders could be justified in almost the identical language slaveholders themselves used to justify the institution of slavery. See his discussion in *Slavery and Human Progress*, 257–58, and part 3 more generally.
9 On the difficulty of defining imperialism, see Richard Koebner and Helmut Dan Schmidt, *Imperialism: The Story and Significance of a Political Word, 1840–1960* (Cambridge: Cambridge University Press, 1965); Raymond Williams, *Keywords: A Vocabulary of Culture and Society* (London: Croom Helm, 1976); and Frank Ninkovich, *The United States and Imperialism* (Oxford: Blackwell, 2001).
10 On Goldwin Smith, a crucial figure in any discussion of liberal foreign policy, see Elisabeth Wallace, *Goldwin Smith: Victorian Liberal* (Toronto: University of Toronto Press, 1957).
11 On American amnesia about its imperial past, see Amy Kaplan, "'Left Alone With America': The Absence of Empire in the Study of American Culture," in *Cultures of United States Imperialism*, ed. Amy Kaplan and Donald Pease (Durham: Duke University Press, 1993), 3–21. To most Americans in the 1890s, the United States was, as Paul Kramer has memorably put it, the "empire on which the sun never rose." See his "Empires, Exceptions, and Anglo-Saxons," *Journal of American History* 88 (2002): 1315–53.
12 On the pro-empire flank of the British Liberal party, see H. C. G. Matthew, *The Liberal Imperialists: The Ideas and Politics of a Post-Gladstonian Elite* (Oxford: Oxford University Press, 1973). American imperialists never consciously embraced the term liberal, but as scholars have shown, there are several connections between liberalism and imperialism, not just ideologically but temperamentally, in the sense that both "isms" sought to reform the world. The classic work here is William Leuchtenburg, "Progressivism and Imperialism: The Progressive Movement and American Foreign Policy, 1898–1916," in *Essays in American Diplomacy*, ed. Armin Rappaport (New York: Macmillan, 1967).
13 Smith to Frederic Harrison, *A Selection of Goldwin Smith's Correspondence* (Toronto: McClellan & Goodchild), 366; Wallace, *Goldwin Smith*, 198.
14 The term *jingo* originated in Britain in the 1870s, from a song sung in London beer halls. Hugh Cunningham, "Jingoism in 1877–78," *Victorian Studies* 14 (1971): 429–53.
15 Smith, "Loyalty, Aristocracy, and Jingoism," 71.
16 On the gendered nature of foreign policy, see Harriet Hyman Alonso, *Peace as a Woman's Issue: A History of the U.S. Movement for World Peace and Women's Rights* (Syracuse: Syracuse University Press, 1993), and Kristin L. Hoganson, *Fighting for American Manhood: How Gender Politics Provoked the Spanish-American and Philippine-American Wars* (New Haven: Yale University Press, 1998). That this concern with the masculine potency of foreign policy still exists is evidenced by the neoconservative William Kristol, who distinguished the "muscular patriotism" of a TR or Ronald Reagan from the presumably flaccid and flabby "utopian multilateralism of Woodrow

Wilson and Bill Clinton," quoted in John B. Judis, "History Lesson," *The New Republic* (June 9, 2003), 22. On manliness at the end of the nineteenth century, see John Higham, "The Reorientation of American Culture in the 1890s," in his *Writing American History* (Bloomington: Indiana University Press, 1970), 73–102; Gail Bederman, *Manliness and Civilization: A Cultural History of Gender and Race in the United States, 1880–1917* (Chicago: University of Chicago Press, 1995); and Kim Townsend, *Manhood at Harvard: William James and Others* (New York: Norton, 1996).

17 Godkin, "Civilization and Barbarism," *Nation* 68 (June 1, 1899), 410–11. Claiming that Victorian liberals articulated relatively less gendered notions of manliness than many of their peers is not intended to obscure the enduring power differentials or gender hierarchies in their thought, but simply to draw important distinctions between "competing masculinities," in Catherine Hall's phrase. See her "Competing Masculinities: Thomas Carlyle, John Stuart Mill, and the Case of Governor Eyre," in Hall, *White, Male, and Middle-Class: Explorations in Feminism and History* (New York: Routledge, 1992), 280.

18 Norton, "True Patriotism"; Godkin, "Come Let Us Reason Together," *Nation* 67 (November 10, 1898), 344.

19 Godkin, "Peace," 423. On liberal support for arbitration, see Hugh Tulloch, *James Bryce's American Commonwealth: The Anglo-American Background* (Wolfeboro, N.H.: Boydell Press, 1988), 208; Robert Kelley, *Transatlantic Persuasion*, 217–27, 412–13.

20 Curtis, "Major-General John Sedgwick," in *Orations and Addresses of George William Curtis*, ed. Charles Eliot Norton (New York: Harper & Bros., 1894), 3:10.

21 Gladstone's vision of the "concert of Europe," an anticipation of the League of Nations or the United Nations, was an important development in liberal thinking about international relations. Michael Howard, *War and the Liberal Conscience*, 57.

22 Norton to Charles Waldstein, November 18, 1898, in *The Letters of Charles Eliot Norton*, ed. Sara Norton and Mark A. DeWolfe Howe (Boston: Houghton, Mifflin, 1913), 2:290–91; James Bryce speech in House of Commons, 1900, in Stephen E. Koss, *The Pro-Boers: The Anatomy of an Anti-War Movement* (Chicago: University of Chicago Press, 1973) 91–94.

23 Higginson, "The School of Jingoes," *Essays from the Chap-Book* (Chicago: Herbert S. Stone, 1899), 144.

24 Norton to Frederic Harrison, October 31, 1901, *Letters of Norton*, 2:313–14; Higginson, "Dream of the Republic," *Book and Heart* (New York: Harper and Bros., 1897), 101.

25 Norton to Frederic Harrison, October 31, 1901, *Letters of Norton*, 2:313–14; Higginson, "Dream of the Republic," 101; Godkin, "Lynching," *Nation* 69 (December 14, 1899), 440; Campbell-Bannerman quoted in Koss, *The Pro-Boers*, 194–207.

26 Higginson, "More Mingled Races?" in *Book and Heart*, 159. On the racialized context of the late nineteenth century, see Nancy Leys Stepan, *The Idea of Race in Science: Great Britain, 1800–1960* (Hamden, Conn.: Archon, 1982); George M. Fredrickson, *Racism: A Short History* (Princeton: Princeton University Press, 2002).

27 Norton to S. G. Ward, October 7, 1901, and Norton to Nariaki Kozaki, February 10, 1904, both in *Letters of Norton*, 2:311, 336.
28 Higginson, "Dream of the Republic," 101–2. See, for example, the 1899 debate between Higginson and James Bryce over the voting rights of "inferior races," Thomas Wentworth Higginson Papers, Houghton Library, Harvard University, and the James Bryce Papers, Bodleian Library, Oxford University.

ELLEN DWYER

Psychiatry and the Black Soldier during World War II

Popular memory celebrates America's involvement in World War II as a victory of the forces of democracy over those of tyranny. Yet in at least one respect, the American war effort was notably less heroic. While the American military helped to eliminate the external evil of fascism, it failed to end the internal evil of racism. Throughout World War II, at multiple sites, public and private, African American soldiers experienced relentless and often demoralizing discrimination and segregation. Judged too cowardly to engage in battle, most were assigned to "Jim Crow" service units, under the command of white officers, and given unskilled work. Black soldiers' discontent mounted until, by the midpoint of the war, even the War Department expressed alarmed. Yet little was done, even by the Army Medical Corps. To justify their inaction, the largely white psychiatrists of the Corps articulated a racial conservatism sharply at odds with the environmentalist paradigm of the day.

In response, the National Medical Association (NMA), the professional organization of African American doctors, became increasingly critical of military medicine. Especially eloquent was Rutherford Stevens. One of the few African Americans psychiatrists in the Army Medical Corps, Stevens argued that segregation and discrimination acted like "an emotional cancer" on black soldiers, destroying morale and causing psychic distress. A small but important number of his white counterparts agreed. Regrettably, once the war ended, conversations within the military about race and psychiatry also came to an end; and few black soldiers could afford treatment for neuroses or psychoses in the rapidly expanding private medical sector.

Although American psychiatrists first wrote about war neuroses during World War I, World War II generated a much larger discussion of the psychic costs of battle. Especially popular were books and articles that described, in strange and interesting detail, soldiers with "combat exhaustion" and the treatments used to return them to normalcy. Neither authors nor readers seemed to realize that the most common neuropsychiatric problems of World War II emerged not during battle, but during induction interviews, at training camps, and while soldiers worked in service units, both in the United States and overseas. Disproportionate numbers of the soldiers so afflicted were African American. Insofar as they received medical attention, it came largely in the form of efforts to explain their poor morale, not to heal their trauma.[1] Not until close to the end of the war did an important, if short-lived national conversation emerge about treatment strategies for troubled black soldiers. For the most part, that conversation was led by doctors affiliated with the National Medical Association, the African American counterpart to the all-white American Medical Association.

PREWAR ASSUMPTIONS

During the early years of World War II, two very different perspectives on the psychology of African Americans could be found in psychiatric journals. The first assumed the psychological distinctiveness and inferiority of African Americans. This biological racism had a long history, reaching back to the days of slavery, and informed the War Department's decision, during World War I, to keep African Americans in segregated units and to exclude them from combat.[2] Issues related to race loomed large in Neuropsychiatry, a history of World War I medicine published in 1929 by the Medical Corps' Division of Neurology and Psychiatry. Race dominated the many charts and tables presented in the first half of Neuropsychiatry. Apoplexy, epilepsy, enuresis, neuritis, and mental deficiency appeared to be more common among "colored" enlisted men, while neurasthenia, psychoneurosis, shell shock, dementia praecox, alcoholism, and manic depression were found more often in those considered "white." According to Neuropsychiatry, African American soldiers had lower rates of alcoholism than did white, even though both drank the same amount of alcohol. Perhaps, division psychiatrists speculated, African American soldiers' central nervous systems were less delicate and, hence, better able to resist addiction. Finally, "Negroes" were said to suffer psychoneuroses at earlier ages than "whites," in part because of the "especially unfavorable circumstances" of their educations and lives.[3]

Following World War I, American social scientists became increasingly interested in what Neuropsychiatry called "the especially unfavorable circumstances" of African Americans' lives. A number of books and articles described the ways in which segregation and discrimination hurt black self-esteem, although there was no consensus on the extent of the damage.[4] By the late 1930s, such arguments had begun to influence psychiatry as well. For example, when

Philip Wagner compared black and white psychiatric patients in the prestigious *Journal of the American Medical Association*, he footnoted the writings of the anthropologists Franz Boas and Bronislaw Malinowski, among others. Like them, Wagner argued that his research provided "much proof that individual reactions in both white and colored groups are culturally determined and modifiable." Yet the psychiatrist also believed in the possibility of race-specific psychoses, especially in the area of interracial sexual violence, and remained committed to a search for "qualities which could be considered Negroid."[5] Thus, as World War II approached, psychiatrists like Wagner generally attributed psychiatric disorders to social and economic factors but remained unwilling to abandon altogether the notion of biologically based racial difference. These two very different perspectives would continue to coexist, albeit uneasily, in mainstream medical writings and practice through the long, hard years of the war and even into the 1950s.[6]

PREPARATIONS FOR WAR

As the U.S. government prepared to enter World War II, the War Department took a number of steps intended to avoid the mistakes of World War I. In one area, however, the War Department refused to change. "Segregation is not discrimination," proclaimed Secretary of State Henry Stimson, who added that war was no time for social experiments. Of much greater concern to him and other government officials was the mounting cost of caring for the neuropsychiatric casualties of World War I. The U.S. government had spent close to $1 billion on them by the late 1930s. The best way to avoid that cost in the future, the War Department decided, was by keeping out of the military those most likely to break under the stress of battle.[7] To help draft boards do so, the Selective Service asked the prominent psychiatrist Harry Stack Sullivan to develop rigorous induction screening guidelines. Delighted by this opportunity to demonstrate psychiatry's ability to predict mental breakdown, Sullivan, with the help of colleagues, accepted the challenge. Once the new protocols were ready, he and his team ran nine two-day seminars on how to use them for psychiatrists across the country. Sullivan was convinced that a well-run, fifteen-minute interview could reveal whether an individual had the emotional stability necessary for army life.[8]

Despite Sullivan's promotional efforts, few of the general practitioners working for local draft boards had time to follow the new guidelines. Often left with only a minute or two for interviews, many asked only a few quick questions, most notoriously "Have you had a nervous breakdown?" and "Do you like girls?"[9] Yet even such superficial assessments led to the rejection of large numbers of white draft registrants in late 1940 and early 1941.[10] In need of recruits, the Selective Service asked Sullivan to modify his approach. Rather than do so, in late 1941 he quit.

In subsequent years, because of time and personnel limitations, army screeners increasingly used scores on the Army General Classification Test (most often referred to as the AGCT) as a basis for rejecting potential misfits.[11] After 1943, they also used the criminal, medical, and educational data collected under the auspices of Medical Survey Program to identify problem inductees. Not until close to the end of World War II did most military psychiatrists change their minds about the benefits of preliminary screenings.[12]

Whatever the screening protocols, between 1940 and 1945 the Selective Service consistently turned away many more African Americans than whites. As early as 1942, three Medical Corps officers, Leonard Rowntree, Kenneth McGill, and Thomas Edwards, undertook to find out why. Most often, they claimed, African Americans were rejected because of educational deficiencies and positive syphilis tests. Although the army had established special facilities for training registrants with meager schooling, these schools quickly filled to overflowing. When there were no vacancies, the Selective Service rejected poorly educated African Americans.[13] According to Rowntree and his colleagues, young African Americans also had higher rates than whites of active tuberculosis, cardiovascular conditions, and of mental problems, such as "psychopathic personality," a catchall category for "constitutional psychopathic inferiority, criminal records, and sexual psychopathy."[14]

In the early 1940s the NAACP offered a very different explanation for high African American rejection rates. After a survey of local draft boards revealed that many were all-white, the NAACP noted that all-white boards rejected African Americans 1-A registrants at a much higher rate than did mixed-race boards.[15] W. Montague Cobb, president of the (African American) Medico-Chirurgical Society of the District of Columbia, made a similar point in an essay published in the *Journal of the National Medical Association* (hereafter referred to as the JNMA). Early in the war, Montague reported, he had lobbied the Selective Service to use African American physicians as unpaid volunteers at induction centers. This change was difficult to effect, he noted, in "the southern atmosphere of the Nation's Capital," and black doctors would work only at the Freedman's Hospital at Howard University. Still, President Roosevelt appointed twenty-eight black physicians and five black dentists to the Freedmen's Examining Board. These physicians conducted about 34,400 examinations, during which they rejected 29.77 percent of the young African American males who came before them. Their rejection rate was the same as that of other District boards. However, when the men approved by the Freedman's Board subsequently were reassessed at an army induction center, an additional 30 percent were rejected, mostly on the grounds of "mental deficiency." In contrast, only 10 percent of white registrants from the District of Columbia subsequently were rejected.[16]

An essay produced by twenty-six psychiatrists from the Selective Service's Central Examining Board for Neurology and Psychiatry (also known as the C.E.B) inadvertently offered additional insights into how race shaped induction assessments. In contrast to Rowntree et al.'s reliance on aggregate data, the C.E.B. doctors presented a richly descriptive report of an experiment set up to test the reliability and validity of C.E.B. psychiatric assessments. Were C.E.B. experts able to catch and correct the errors made by local draft boards, as well as to reach agreement with one another, the testers asked? Yes, the twenty-six C.E.B. psychiatrists concluded. However, a number of comments included in this essay suggested the opposite: a high level of diagnostic uncertainty, not diagnostic consensus, especially in cases involving African American inductees. As one doctor admitted: "The colored men offered me the greatest difficulty in diagnosis. Poor cultural, occupation and educational backgrounds often made it difficult to decide whether they were defective, preschizoid, or just colored."[17]

What happened in such cases? Most often, the C.E.B. doctors resolved uncertainty about African American inductees with rejection. For example, even though two referees considered a twenty-two-year-old with a minor arrest history acceptable for full service, a third described him as "an unusually troublesome character in the community." This single negative sufficed to send the young inductee home. Race also figured in the rejection of a twenty-eight-year-old African American with a tenth-grade education, whose only major problem was a history of "nervous stomach." The initial examiner recommended his acceptance, describing the man in the following terms: "somewhat shy, diffident. No frivolity in his life. Is an ardent church-goer. Good work record." When the senior psychiatrist reexamined him, however, he diagnosed the man as "Group IV psychosomatic" and hence "wholly disqualified for military service." And so he too was disqualified. In contrast, when the referees discussed a white inductee with similar traits (he too was highly religious with a nervous stomach), they approved him on the grounds that "the service environment would offer him further opportunity for development." Other nonwhite inductees received more sympathetic treatment. For example, after one psychiatrist used his prior experience with Chinese students to relax an anxious "registrant of Chinese ancestry" who previously had been rejected as "psychoneurotic," all four C.E.B. referees decided that he would make an excellent soldier.[18]

Not until the army finally loosened its literacy standards in June of 1943 did the percentage of African Americans in the army begin to approach ten, their proportion in the population as a whole. Yet, even after 1943, African Americans continued to be rejected for military service at substantially higher rates than whites.[19] Almost all of those accepted were the bottom two intelligence grades: IV and V, as measured by the AGCT. Such individuals, army psychiatrists claimed, "could scarcely be trained to look after themselves, much less their comrades, in actual fighting." Thus, they used AGCT scores as scientific legitimation for the army's long-standing policy of assigning African Americans to service units, not combat. There they washed dishes, dug latrines, and helped dispose of garbage, all tasks considered to require little skill.[20] While African Americans were not the only poorly educated young soldiers during World War II, they were singled out for special criticism. While the War Department tried in multiple ways to keep poorly educated African Americans out of the army, it actively encouraged the recruitment of illiterate whites. So too did a navy psychiatrist who interviewed a number of illiterate young men from Tennessee. Even though these "mountain boys" often were unable to tell examiners what countries were at war, they often made very good soldiers, he claimed. The navy should pay special attention to their "peculiar philosophy of life and psychological reactions" before judging them unfit for service.[21]

FROM TRAINING CAMPS TO SERVICE

If young African Americans survived the Selective Service screenings, they then were transported to segregated training camps, many of which were located in the South and the Southwest. There young men eager to defend their country often found themselves surrounded by hostile local populations and were offered humiliatingly inferior services. Racial tensions were high and occasionally erupted into violence. As one black soldier complained in a letter sent to the editor of the *Atlantic Daily World*: "Nobody gives a d—— about what happens. Unless something is done, there will be an internal revolution. They are afraid for us to have our rifles after we leave the field. They search daily for ammunition. I swear to God it is pathetic." Equally bitter letters were sent to soldiers' families, hometown newspapers, the NAACP, the War Department, and even the president. Life in the army, several complained, was little better than life under slavery. Even the relatively fortunate black officers suffered low morale and complained of being passed over for promotion repeatedly in favor of "wash-outs" from all-white units.[22]

Army case histories published years later revealed that segregation and discrimination made military life painful, even at times impossible, for many blacks. In one instance, J.G.S., a well-educated northeasterner, became deeply distressed as a result of his treatment on southern army bases. His white superiors viewed him as a troublemaker and several times threatened him with court-martial for treason. Shortly before going overseas, he was denied a pass to return home. In its place, he was given a two-hour lecture "designed to make him give up his 'liberal' values and accept his status in the military. Subsequently, he developed a number of psychiatric problems, including severe stuttering. Nonetheless, the young soldier completed two years of overseas duty. On his return home, however, he became so upset by the frequency with which he continued to witness discriminatory actions that he ended up in a psychiatric hospital. After discharge, he went back to the northeast, married, and found stable employment.[23]

By the midpoint of the war, African American soldiers' discontent had grown so intense as to alarm even the War Department. In response, the department added to a larger study of army morale a special examination of the attitudes of the "Negro soldier." The results were grim. The army, Samuel Stouffer and his colleagues found, replicated "the same phenomena of racial subordination and superordination" that dominated so much of life outside it. This situation outraged black soldiers but was not even noticed by most white. As a result, they concluded, "almost no facet of the attitudes of Negro troops is fully intelligible without reference to the Negroes' basically racial orientation on the one hand and to the gulf between Negro and white evaluations of that orientation on the other." Stouffer and his colleagues also pointed out that enlisted men, whatever their color, as a result of being subordinates in a highly stratified social system, often engaged in behaviors considered stereotypically African American, including "laziness, boisterousness, an emphasis on sexual prowess, consciously acting stupid, [and] obsequiousness in front of superiors." The army generally ignored this provocative insight.[24]

Although still unwilling to abandon military segregation, the War Department subsequently did take several steps intended to raise black morale and increase racial harmony. Perhaps best known was the commissioning of a movie called *The Negro Soldier*. Released in 1944, the film chronicled the accomplishments of African Americans from Crispus Attucks to Joe E. Lewis and ended with a celebration of World War II as part of the fight against global injustice.[25] In 1944, the department also produced two pamphlets intended to help white officers lead more effectively by educating them about their black soldiers. *Command of Negro Troops* offered injunctions such as "Racial theories waste manpower" and "Negro Soldiers are Americans." Among the "Tips for Officers" in *Leadership and the Negro Soldier* was a list of words to be avoided, including "boy" "darky," "uncle" and "your people."[26] However, such efforts had little substantive impact on morale. While they were of symbolic importance, they came too late in the war to change substantially the behavior of white racists or to pacify angry African Americans.

RACE AND DEMOBILIZATION

As World War II drew to a close, worries about what would happen when discharged veterans began to return home increased dramatically. An entire issue of the *Journal of Clinical Psychology* focused on how best to offer what it called "civilian rehabilitation." One psychiatrist noted with alarm: "In demobilization this country must deal with several million young men who have become adult without having had time to learn adult responsibility in a socializing situation . . . trained to belong to closely knit units and filled with the experience of destroying any one who does not belong."[27] Another predicted that while many would adjust, some would become part of a "lost generation" and a small but crucial number would become hostile and aggressive.[28]

Would African American soldiers, already embittered by their wartime experiences with government-sanctioned racism, become particularly dangerous? Some feared so, arguing that "the negroes' natural aggression" was bound to increase as a result of federal fair practices employment legislation and African Americans own "feelings of aggrievement over allegedly having been repressed by whites."[29] In response to such fears, Hollywood produced a number of what David Gerber calls "reintegration dramas," including *Home of the Brave* (1949).[30] At the time of its release, *Home of the Brave* was much celebrated for its sympathetic picture of a heroic young African American soldier, broken by a traumatic wartime experience as well as by a lifetime of racial discrimination. The true hero of the film, however, was the white psychiatrist. Using hypnosis, he forcibly pulled the young soldier, crippled by rage and trauma, out of psychosomatic paralysis and back into the unpredictable mainstream of American life. Like *Home of the Brave*, John Huston's 1945 documentary *Let There be Light* demonstrated (to quote Huston) that "men who suffered mental damage in the service should not be written off but could be helped by psychiatric treatment."[31] Among the soldiers Huston followed from admission to discharge was a young African American. Like all of the soldiers profiled by Huston, this one "recovered" satisfactorily. However, because Huston's film was thought to put excessive stress on the psychic costs of war, the army forbade its release for many decades.[32]

Both of these films were set in integrated hospital units, but most African American soldiers, especially those from the South, received treatment at the all-black veterans hospital at Tuskegee.[33] As a result, as the war drew to a close, Tuskegee doctors became increasingly worried about their small number of psychiatric beds. In 1946, Prince P. Barker, chief of acute services at the Tuskegee hospital, called for national attention to "the special mental hygiene needs of Negroes," too long neglected, and noted that, like other members of minority groups, African Americans had developed "psychological and to some extent psychopathological protective and compensatory techniques" to deal with racism. While Barker did not advocate "a special psychiatry for Negroes," he argued that military psychiatrists needed to pay more attention to the damage done to African American soldiers by discrimination and segregation. For example, he warned, popular therapies such as insulin shock were especially risky for African American veterans because of their high rates of arteriosclerosis and hypertension.[34] In contrast, Alan P. Smith, Barker's successor at Tuskegee, preferred to search his black veterans' psyches, not the larger social milieu, for clues to their problems. He was particularly interested in using hypnosis to help patients release long-repressed hostilities and anger, most of which he felt were directed at family members.[35] Smith's concerns were typical of postwar American psychiatry, which, according to the historian Hans Pols, very quickly "removed trauma from the battlefield" and located its roots in the family.[36] Perhaps in part for that reason, after the early 1950s few doctors wrote about the psychological status or treatment needs of World War II's neuropsychiatric casualties, whether white or black.

FURTHER INTERPRETATIONS AND CONVERSATIONS

African American soldiers' low AGTC scores, the subject of much wartime discussion, continued to preoccupy social scientists after the war. At points, the resulting literature evoked early twentieth-century biological racism, even when its authors took care to acknowledge social forces. As Daryl Scott has noted, social scientists of the 1950s and 1960s all too easily slipped from pity to contempt in their discussion of the "damaged" black psyche.[37] In so doing, some of them, most notably Eli Ginzberg and his colleagues at Columbia University's Conservation of Human Resources Project, relied on World War II soldiers' neuropsychiatric records. In their multivolume analysis of these records, Ginzberg et al. found that "the inapt" and "the undesirable" were disproportionately African American. While harshly critical of the army's refusal to abandon segregation, in both *The Negro Potential* and the three-volume *Ineffective Soldier*, the authors claimed that African American soldiers had been handicapped not only by poor schooling but also by "stunted" ambitions. As a result, many had seen "no point in attempting to live up to the standards of the white community."[38] At least one reviewer saw in The Negro Potential support for the position that, rather than relying on fair employment practices legislation to effect social change, African Americans should take responsibility for their own "lack of motivation." Even more disquieting was the argument made by Ginzberg et al. about the best ways to maximize efficiency. Because large organizations like the army had only limited resources to spend on those who need help, they claimed, the organizations sometimes had to emphasize "effectiveness," even at the price of "equity." If the army had done so during World War II, it would have rejected more, not fewer, African Americans at induction and given more, not fewer, less-than-honorable discharges to those who broke down during service.[39]

Such recommendations grew out of the Columbia University project's mandate from its founder, Dwight Eisenhower: to explain military manpower problems during World War II. Insofar as it saw failures in military psychiatry, the project identified them as having to do with ways in which the well-being of the armed forces as a whole might better have been promoted. In this respect, military psychiatry, with its concern for the organization's health, differed markedly from civilian psychiatry, with its concern for the individual patient. Yet even within such constraints, some army psychiatrists used their encounters with troubled soldiers to rethink some traditional therapeutic issues, such as the relative efficacy of somatic and psychodynamic therapies. At induction centers, training camps, field units, and veterans' hospitals, these men, many of whom worked before the war in large psychiatric institutions, had the opportunity to interact, often for the first time, with large numbers of ordinary young males.[40] As a result, several began to think in new ways about the doctor-patient relationship. Particularly perceptive was the army psychiatrist Jerome Frank. Frank noted that many of his African American patients had been so mistreated by white doctors that they deeply distrusted them. It took much effort to break through such defenses, but if a physician were patient, eventually a "degree of confidence sufficient to be of therapeutic benefit could be established." Unfortunately, Frank's strategy required both time and empathy, qualities in short supply in many army units, and he himself reported working with only sixteen black soldiers, all of "better than average attainments."[41]

Rutherford Stevens, one of the few African American psychiatrists in the Army Medical Corps, agreed strongly with Frank. In what may have been the first article by an African American psychiatrist published in the prestigious

American Journal of Psychiatry, Stevens observed that "many military psychiatrists felt insecure when dealing with the emotional problems of Negro Soldiers." In addition, they tended to be unaware of the depth of African Americans' resentment of "the imperfections in our democracy." Army psychiatrists who failed to recognize the racial dimensions of black soldiers' emotional disturbances, Stevens argued, often were unable to help them. Because of white doctors' too-frequent assumption that all African American soldiers were the same, their prescriptions were crude, ineffective, even offensive.[42] Although he had no simple formula for rapport, Stevens suggested that much could be gained through greater sympathy and understanding. However, "the best method of treatment of emotional disturbances caused by racial factors," he concluded, "is *prevention*." If the army would eliminate segregation and discrimination, he concluded, the incidence of psychiatric illnesses among the 920,000 African Americans in uniform would fall dramatically. Stevens was especially concerned about the rate (sometimes as high as 50 percent) at which black soldiers were labeled "psychopaths." Psychiatrists needed to understand that, for many African Americans, "a history of intermittent school attendance and frequent changes of job" might have been a survival strategy, not an indicator of emotional instability. Further, high moral standards did not protect black Americans, whatever their class and behavior, from being arrested on suspicion of criminal activity. In conclusion, Stevens noted that while most black soldiers began their military experience deeply committed to the war effort and hopeful that it would improve racial conditions in the United States, the segregation and discrimination they experienced in the armed services acted as an "emotional cancer," slowly but surely embittering them and undermining their morale.[43]

The essays of Franks and Stevens were part of an important conversation about the treatment needs of troubled African American soldiers begun during World War II, largely at the instigation of civil rights activists within the National Medical Association. Regrettably, insofar as it engaged medical doctors, the conversation had a short life. After World War II, few African Americans could afford to seek treatment for neuroses or even psychoses in the rapidly expanding private medical sector. As a result, sick African Americans became an increasingly large proportion of the patients cared for in the deteriorating state and veterans hospitals across the United States. At the same time, psychiatrists' wartime concerns, both positive and negative, with issues related to race disappeared almost entirely from mainstream American medical journals. Although many African American veterans of World War II continued to struggle with neuropsychiatric problems, they got almost no attention from public policy makers. Historians have been equally neglectful. The history of troubled veterans' lives, both within and outside of Veterans Administration hospitals, has yet to be written. Such silences remind us that while there is a large and persuasive literature on how the so-called psychiatric gaze distorts and damages, especially when focused on racial others, we know much less about the consequences of its turning away.[44]

NOTES

1 For book-length studies, see Roy R. Grinker and John P. Spiegel, *War Neuroses in North Africa: The Tunisian Campaign (January–May 1943)* (New York: Josiah Macy Foundation, 1943); Grinker and Spiegel, *Men Under Stress* (Philadelphia: Blakiston, 1945); Abraham Kardiner, with Herbert Spiegel, *War Stress and Neurotic Illness* (New York: Paul B. Hoeber, 1947). Grinker and Spiegel described only white soldiers; Kardiner included one black soldier, albeit from World War I, described as "a negro of limited intelligence" who, "as is usual with his race, . . . did not admit a history of neurotic traits or of venereal disease (p. 143). See also Ben Shepherd, *A War of Nerves: Soldiers and Psychiatrists in the Twentieth Century* (Cambridge: Harvard University Press, 2001); Paul Wanke, "American Military Psychiatry and its Role among Ground Forces in World War II," *The Journal of Military History* 63(1999): 127–146; and Gerald Grob, *From Asylum to Community: Mental Health Policy in Modern America* (Princeton: Princeton University Press, 1991), 5–23.

2 J. Babcock, "The Colored Insane," *The Alienist and Neurologist* 16 (1895): 432–427; Norbert Bennett Bean, "Some Racial Peculiarities of the Negro Brain," *American Journal of Psychiatry* 9 (1906): 353–432; Franklin P. Mall, "On Several Anatomical Characters of the Human Brain, Said to Vary According to Race and Sex, with Especial Reference to the Weight of the Frontal Lobe," *American Journal of Anatomy* 9 (1909): 1–32; M. O'Malley, "Psychoses in the Colored Race," *American Journal of Insanity* 71 (1914): 309–337; A. Everts, "The Ontogenetic versus the Phylogenetic Elements in the Psychoses of the Colored Race," *Psychoanalytic Review* 3 (1916): 272–287; W. M. Bevis, "Psychological Traits of the Southern Negro," *American Journal of Psychiatry* 1 (1921): 69–76; Robert H. Foster, "Paresis in Negroes," *American Journal of Psychiatry* 5 (1926): 631–639). For historical overviews, see Peter McCandless, *Moonlight, Magnolias and Madness: Insanity in South Carolina from the Colonial Period to the Progressive Era* (Chapel Hill: University of North Carolina Press, 1996), and John S. Haller, "Labeling and Treatment Black Mental Illness in America," *Journal of Southern History* 58 (1993): 435–460.

3 Salmon, Thomas W., Williams, E. Frankwood, and Komoro, Paul O, *Neuropsychiatry in the United States*, vol. 10 of *The Medical Department of the United States in the World War* (Washington, D.C.: GPO, 1929): 153–265.

4 Daryl Michael Scott, *Contempt and Pity: Social Policy and the Image of the Damaged Black Psyche, 1880–1996* (Chapel Hill: University of North Carolina Press, 1997), 19–70.

5 Philip S. Wagner, "A Comparative Study of Negro and White Admissions to the Psychiatric Pavilion of the Cincinnati General Hospital, *Journal of the American Medical Association* 95, part 1 (July 1938): 167–183; J. E. Greene, "Analyses of Racial Differences within Seven Clinical Categories of White and Negro Mental Patients in the Georgia State Hospital, 1923–1933," *Social Forces* 17 (1938): 201–211.

6 E. Franklin Frazier, "Psychological Factors in Negro Health," *Journal of Social Forces* 3 (1925): 488–490; Charles Prudhomme, "The Problem of Suicide in the American Negro," *Psychoanalytic Review* 25 (April and July, 1938); Benjamin Malzberg, "Migration and Mental Diseases among Negroes in New York State," *American Journal of Physical Anthropology* 21 (1936): 107–113; S. C. Kaplan, "A Comparative Study of Psychoses among Negroes and Whites in the New York State Prison," *Psychiatric Quarterly* 12 (1939): 160–164.

7 There is now a large literature on the debate over military segregation during World War II. Maggi M. Morehouse, *Fighting in the Jim Crow Army: Black Men and Women Remember World War II* (Lanham, Md.: Roman and Littlefield, 2000); Mary Penick Motley, ed., *The Invisible Soldier: The Experiences of the Black Soldier in World War II* (Detroit: Wayne State University Press, 1975); Richard M. Dalfiume, *Desegregation of the U.S. Armed Forces: Fighting on Two Fronts* (Columbia, Mo.: University of Missouri Press, 1969); Neil A. Wynn, *The Afro-American and the Second World War* (London: Elek Books, 1976). For fiscal concerns, see Albert J. Glass and Robert J. Bernucci, eds., *Neuropsychiatry in World War II* (Washington, D.C.: GPO, 1966–73): 1:xiii; Shepherd, *War of Nerves*, 197.

8 For Selective Service System Medical Circular No. 1, issued on November 7, 1940, along with its rationale, see Harry Stack Sullivan, et al., "Psychiatry and the National Defense," *Psychiatry* 4 (1941): 01–264. For training efforts, see Sullivan, "A Seminar on Practical Psychiatric Diagnosis," *Psychiatry* 4 (1941): 265–283.

9 Shepherd, *War of Nerves*, 199–201; Eli Ginzberg, et al., *The Lost Divisions*, vol. 1 of *The Ineffective Soldier* (New York: Columbia University Press, 1959), 37–39.

10 Harry Stack Sullivan, "Psychiatric Aspects of Morale," *The American Journal of Psychiatry* 47 (1941): 277–301.

11 James H. Capshew, *Psychologists on the March: Science, Practice, and Professional Identity in American, 1929–1969* (Cambridge: Cambridge University Press, 1999), 97–115.

12 Grob, *From Asylum to Community*, 11; Shepherd, *War of Nerves*, 197–201. For psychiatrists' conviction that screenings needed to be more, not less, restrictive, see Ernest E. Hadley, et al., "An Experiment in Military Selection," *Psychiatry* 5 (1942): 371–402. For a slightly more critical history of the Medical Survey Program, see Ivan Berlien and Raymond W. Waggoner, "Selection and Induction," in *Neuropsychiatry in World War II*, 177–185.

13 Leonard Rowntree, Kenneth H. McGill, and Thomas I. Edwards, "Causes of Rejection and the Incidence of Defects among 18 and 19 year Old Selective Service Registrants," *Journal of the American Medical Association* 123 (September 25, 1943): 181. Rowntree et al. reported that approximately 23.8% of the white draftees and 45.5% of the black in their sample had been rejected.

14 Ibid., 184. Similar data is presented in the 1944 army manual titled *Leadership and the Black Soldier*.
15 Roy Wilkins, "No Negro Draft Board Members in Many States, says NAACP Survey," *The Crisis* 48 (1941): 22, cited in Philip McGuire, "Desegregation of the Armed Forces: Black Leadership, Protest, and World War II," *Journal of Legal History* 68 (1983): 147–158.
16 W. Montague Cobb, "Medico-Chi and the National Selective Service," *Journal of the National Medical Association* (hereafter referred to as JNMA) 37 (1945): 192–197. See also Howard Long, "The Negro Soldier in the Army of the United States," *Journal of Negro Education* 12 (1943): 315. For quote from Stimson diary, see McGuire, "Desegregation of the Armed Forces," 148–149; Richard M. Dalfiume, *Desegregation of the U.S. Armed Forces: Fighting on Two Fronts, 1939–1953* (Columbia: University of Missouri Press, 1969), 57.
17 Ernest E. Hadley, et al., "An Experiment in Military Selection," *Psychiatry* 5 (1942): 371–402.
18 Ibid., 388–400.
19 Ginzberg et al., *Lost Divisions*, 120.
20 C. Mostos Jr., "Racial Integration in the Armed Forces," *American Journal of Sociology* 72 (1966): 133. According to Mostos, there were other single-race units, e.g., the Japanese-American 442d Infantry Division, but the official Army history did not present them as having unique problems.
21 Orman C. Perkins, "Analysis of Neuropsychiatric Rejectees from the State of Tennessee," *Diseases of the Nervous System* 7 (1946): 9–18.
22 For the Army's introduction of discriminatory practices into communities that previously had lacked them, see Joseph Schiffman, "The Education of Negro Soldiers in World War II," *The Journal of Negro Education* 18 (1989): 27. For black soldiers' comparisons of military life with experience to slavery, see letter from "A Lone Soldier," to the *Pittsburgh Courier*, October 28, 1942, in McGuire, "Desegregation of the Armed Forces," 63; letter from soldiers at Fort Utah to the *Pittsburgh Courier*, April 26, 1943, in ibid., 64–65; letter from "A Soldier" to the *Chicago Defender*, January 9, 1944, in ibid., 88–89; letter from Charles F. Wilson to President Franklin Delano Roosevelt, May 9, 1944, in ibid., 134–139. In his essay "World War II and Memory," David Brion Davis also evokes the parallels between slavery and black military experiences in World War II. Recalling his experiences as a young enlisted man on board a troopship bound for France, Davis comments, "Some days out, . . . I was given a billy club and sent down into the deep hold to make sure that the blacks there 'weren't gambling.' Until then, I had not dreamed that the ship contained some two thousand black soldiers. After winding down endless circular staircases, I found myself, in effect, on board a slave ship—or at least what I imagine some slave ships to have been like." *Journal of American History* 77 (1990): 581.
23 Eli Ginzberg, et al., *Breakdown and Recovery*, vol. 2 of *The Ineffective Soldier* (New York: Columbia University Press, 1959), 105–108.

24 Samuel Stouffer, et al., *The American Soldier: Adjustment during Army Life*, vol. 1 of *Studies in Social Psychology during World War II* (Princeton: Princeton University Press, 1949), 486–513. See also Ellen Herman, *The Romance of American Psychology: Political Culture in the Age of Experts* (Berkeley: University of California Press, 1995), 72–75.

25 The film's release was delayed repeatedly by concerns that it might offend whites, and it was banned from military facilities in the South. Before release, the army cut all potentially controversial items, including footage showing black officers commanding whites and a white physiotherapy attendant massaging the back of a black soldier. Thomas Cripps and David Culbert, "The Negro Soldier (1944): Film Propaganda in Black and White," *American Quarterly* 31 (1979): 616–640; Paul Buhle and Dave Wagner, *Radical Hollywood: The Untold Story Behind America's Favorite Movies* (New York: New Press, 2002), 191.

26 War Department, *Command of the Negro Troops*, pamphlet no. 20-6 (Washington, D.C.: GPO, 29 February 1944); Army Service Forces Manual, *Leadership and the Negro Soldier*, M5 Training (Washington, D.C.: GPO, October 1944), reprinted in *Blacks in the United States Armed Forces: Basic Documents*, ed. Morris J. MacGregor and Bernard C. Nalty (Wilmington, Del.: Scholarly Resources, 1977), 307–325, 343–450.

27 George H. Preston, "Psychiatry and Demobilization," *Archives of Neurology and Psychiatry* 53 (1945): 396.

28 Howard P. Rome, "War and its Psychiatric Problems," *Journal of Nervous and Mental Disease* 101 (1945): 445.

29 Book Review, *Journal of Criminal Psychopathology* 2 (1946): 470. See also Rufus E. Clement, "Problems of Demobilization and Rehabilitation of the Negro Soldier after World Wars I and II," *Journal of Negro Education* 12 (1943): 542.

30 David Gerber, "Heroes and Misfits: The Troubled Social Reintegration of Disabled Veterans in 'The Best Years of Our Lives'," *American Quarterly* 46 (1994): 545–549. "The Best Years of Our Lives," like the much later film "PT 109," falsely suggested that the Armed Forces were integrated during World War II. (For PT 109 comment, see Mostos, "Racial Integration," 135, n. 8.

31 John Huston, *An Open Book* (New York: Knopf, 1980), 122–126.

32 After this movie was made, the U.S. Army refused to let it be released. Ibid., 122–126; see also Lawrence Grobel, *The Hustons* (New York: Macmillan, 1989), 269–271.

33 Eugene H. Dibble, "Care and Treatment of Negro Veterans at Tuskegee," *Journal of the National Medical Association* 35 (1943): 166–179.

34 Prince P. Barker, "Frontiers of Mental Hygiene," *Journal of the National Medical Association* 38 (1946): 14–17; Barker, "Results and Observations on Insulin Shock Therapy in Negro Ex-Service Men," *Journal of the National Medical Association* 35 (1943): 16–24; Jerome Frank, "Adjustment Problems of Selected Soldiers," *Journal of Nervous and Mental Disease* 105 (1947): 638.

35 Alan P. Smith, "The Role of Psychoanalytic Psychiatry in the Practice of Medicine," *Journal of the National Medical Association* 40 (1948): 147–154.

36 Hans Pols, "Repression of War Trauma in American Psychiatry after WWII," *Medicine and Modern Warfare*, ed. Roger Cooter, Mark Harrison, and Steve Sturdy (Atlanta, Ga.: Wellcome Institute, 1999), 268.
37 For a detailed analysis of the limits of postwar "damage psychology," see Scott, *Contempt and Pity*, 41–136, and Herman, *Romance of American Psychology*, 174–207.
38 Ginzberg et al. *The Negro Potential* (New York: Columbia University Press, 1955); Ginzberg, *The Ineffective Soldier: Lessons for Management and the Nation*, 3 vols. (New York: Columbia University Press, 1959); Ginzberg, *The Lost Divisions*, 120–122.
39 Ginzberg et al., *Breakdown and Recovery*, 22–24, 55–56, 86–88, 105–108, 246–248; Ginzberg, *Patterns of Performance*, vol. 3 of *The Ineffective Soldier*, 109–113; Jacob Seidenberg, "The Negro Potential: A Review," *Industrial and Labor Relations* 11 (1957): 126–127. Seidenberg went on to criticize those who thought fair employment practices legislation by itself could ensure equal job opportunity. For a very different response to the major three-volume work, see Morris Janowitz, "The Ineffective Soldier: A Review," *Administrative Science Quarterly* 5 (1960): 296–303.
40 Grob, *From Asylum to Community*, 19.
41 Jerome Frank, "Adjustment Problems of Selected Negro Soldiers," 647–660. Frank's later works, such as *Persuasion and Healing: A Comparative Study of Psychotherapy* (Baltimore: Johns Hopkins University Press, 1961), continued to explore the psychiatrist-patient relationship but without his early concern for the issue of race.
42 Rutherford Stevens, "Racial Aspects of Emotional Problems of Negro Soldiers," *American Journal of Psychiatry* 103 (1947): 493–98.
43 Ibid. Stevens' essay was immediately followed by "Mental Illness among Negro Troops Overseas" by Herbert Ripley and Stewart Wolf. However, rather than following Stevens' injunction to discard "the many false concepts of the Negro," Ripley and Wolf resurrected several dating back to the nineteenth century. H. S. Ripley and S. Wolf, "Mental Illness among Negro Troops Overseas," *American Journal of Psychiatry* (1947): 499–512.
44 While Daryl Scott, in *Contempt and Pity*, offers a persuasive critique of the therapeutic approach to the black psyche in public policy, he is more interested in the writings and activities of social scientists, including psychologists, than in those of psychiatrists.

JACK M. HOLL

Dwight D. Eisenhower
Religion, Politics, and the
Evils of Communism

When Dwight Eisenhower famously proclaimed that "our form of government has no sense unless it is grounded in a deeply felt religious faith, and I don't care what it is," one might conclude that he saw religion as an inherently moral proposition, regardless of the nature of faith or doctrinal details. But nothing could be further from what he believed, as Jack Holl notes. For Eisenhower, religious faith was inseparable from faith in democracy. In fact, religious faith *enabled* a society to become democratic. Democracy worked because God was no respecter of persons; everyone was equal in God's eyes. Eisenhower endorsed a civil religion that depended on three specific ideas: God dignified every individual; American democracy was established on this belief; and each generation needed to defend this freedom and equality against godless and evil governments.

Eisenhower's religious faith was thus wonderfully suited to cold-war ideology. He went so far as to declare that America's government was "merely a translation in the political field" of his cold-war religious doctrines. If for Carl von Clausewitz war was politics pursued by other means, for Eisenhower democratic politics was religion carried out by other means. He tested his faith against material circumstances, and it yielded positive results. Faith helped him bear the responsibility of commanding troops, fighting communism, and seeking peace in a nuclear age. As he put it, "Only by trust in one's self and trust in God can a man carrying responsibility find repose." In this sense, Eisenhower's civil religion conformed to what William James called "Healthy-Mindedness." Religion worked for him and, he thought, for democracy as well.

Bitterly criticized by liberals for not using the president's "bully-pulpit" to denounce McCarthyism or promote civil rights, Dwight D. Eisenhower dedicated himself politically, morally, and religiously to securing international peace in the nuclear age.[1] He wrestled publicly and privately with the problem of evil associated with managing a horrific, but potentially beneficial, weapons technology. As the nation's president and pastor, he played a seminal role in interpreting the West's nuclear dilemma within the context American civil religion. Eisenhower's vision was not prophetic; he preached no debilitating nuclear jeremiads, not even including his "Military-Industrial Complex" speech. He defined and explained the uses of faith in a nuclear and communistic world. His leadership was neither passive nor negative when it came to promoting American civil religion and applying its precepts to the cold war's nuclear challenge.

Soon after his election as president of the United States, Eisenhower, in December 1952, addressed the Freedom Foundation: "Our form of government has no sense," he stated, "unless it is grounded in a deeply felt religious faith, and I don't care what it is."[2] Not surprising, while Republican politicians, clergyman, and laity praised Eisenhower's piety and fervent spirituality, Democrats and liberal commentators observed that Eisenhower's religious beliefs were "bland" and "shallow." Ernest W. Lefever, for example, defined Eisenhower as a personification of American popular piety and superficial religiosity. Quoting William Lee Miller, Lefever conceded that "President Eisenhower, like many Americans, is a fervent believer in a very vague religion." The president was, in a word, "moral without being unpleasant."[3] More caustically, the radio commentator Elmer Davis observed how "unbecoming" it had been for the president to declare July 4, 1953, as a day of prayer and penance, and then go fishing in the morning, play golf in the afternoon, and play bridge with cronies into the night. Perhaps most "damning" for Lefever was the praise Eisenhower received from both the evangelist Billy Graham, who celebrated Eisenhower as the nation's spiritual leader, and the president of Republic Steel, Charles M. White, who proclaimed that Eisenhower was "the only man since Christ who [could] bring peace to the world."[4]

To the president's disadvantage, Lefever compared Eisenhower's religious beliefs to those of Adlai Stevenson. The Democratic Party's presidential candidate against Eisenhower in 1952 and 1956, Stevenson was a Unitarian (as was his mother) who joined the Presbyterian Church (his father's) just prior to the 1956 election. The fact that Stevenson maintained membership in both congregations escaped political comment. According to Lefever, membership in the mainline Presbyterian Church was about all that Stevenson and Eisenhower had in common religiously. Stevenson's religious heritage was "more intellectual and sophisticated" than Eisenhower's. Educated at Princeton and Harvard, Stevenson reportedly admired the "breadth, perception and social morality" of Reinhold Niebuhr. To his credit, Lefever did not claim that Stevenson converted to Niebuhr's worldview by reading *The Nature and Destiny of Man* or other works by the theologian: "Rather, like George F. Kennan and other men in public life, [Stevenson] found in Niebuhr an eloquent and convincing spokesman for an understanding of man and history which grew out of his own experience in practical politics. Niebuhr has often been able to articulate, clarify and enrich ideas which these men held only vague and tentatively."[5]

Predictably, in Lefever's uneven comparison of Stevenson's Niebuhr with Eisenhower's Eisenhower, the supposed simplicity and naivety of the president's religious faith was accentuated. Rather than understood it as textured and subtle, Eisenhower's thought was parodied as the antithesis of Stevenson's sensitive and ironic understanding of the human existential condition. At the White House, Special Assistant Frederic Fox was infuriated by *The Christian Century*'s partisan mixture of politics and religion at the president's expense.[6] In retrospect, the 1950s political dynamic to which Fox objected was more understandable than the scholarly willingness to attribute more substance to Stevenson's religious views than was warranted. It never occurred to Lefever to explore Eisenhower's River Brethren heritage, the Russellite influences of his youth, or his West Point education, all of which were, in their own way, both spiritual and intellectual but did not employ a religious vocabulary that Lefever understood or took seriously.

The foundation of Eisenhower's civil religion rested on three suppositions well established by the time he graduated from West Point: that the dignity of individuals was warranted by God; that American democracy was established on that faith; and that each generation was called to fight its own crusade to defend freedom against godless forces.[7] In 1947 Eisenhower offered confession of his individual faith to the Daughters of the American Revolution: "Insistence upon individual freedom springs from unshakable conviction in the dignity of man, a belief—a religious belief—that through the possession of a soul he is endowed with certain rights that are his not by the sufferance of others, but by reason of his very existence."[8] Five years later, at the dedication of the Eisenhower Museum in Abilene, Eisenhower rededicated himself to the civil faith of the Founding Fathers:

> Faith in a Provident God whose hand supported and guided them; faith in themselves as the children of God, endowed with purposes beyond the mere struggle for survival; faith in their country and its principles that proclaimed man's right to freedom and justice, rights derived from his divine origin. Today, the nation they built stands as the world's mightiest temporal power, with its position still rooted in faith and in spiritual values.[9]

In the first year of his presidency, Eisenhower greeted the governors of the National Council of Churches. Feeling uneasy addressing this religious body, the former military man compared a soldier's duty with a pastor's religious calling. This descendent of pacifist River Brethren preachers acknowledged that his military profession might seem the antithesis of the religious vocation of the assembled clergy. But even before he became president, Eisenhower believed "with very great vehemence" that military duty called him to an identical purpose of the ordained clergy. Both soldier and pastor were dedicated to the preservation of free government, which meant affirming the equality and dignity of man and, therefore, "the glory of God." [10]

Eisenhower stated his civil faith simply. The United States government was "merely a translation in the political field" of America's deeply felt civil religion. Among the sacred texts of the American civil religion, he explained to the National Council of Churches, were Magna Carta, the American Declaration of Independence, and the French Declaration of the Rights of Man. Together, these historic documents had established the principal that government recognized the equality and dignity of man. But this premise, Eisenhower stated repeatedly and consistently, would be completely baseless without the belief in a supreme being, "in front of whom we are all equal." [11]

Prayer was the central religious act of Eisenhower's civil religion. In contrast to formal liturgies, sacramental systems, worship customs, and conflicting doctrines, prayer, in Eisenhower's view, united all who believed in a supreme being. Although so-called nonsectarian prayers might not satisfy doctrinaire believers, when couched in the rhetoric of civil religion such prayers could both galvanize political will and mask ideological differences. It was prayer, Eisenhower believed, that most distinctly differentiated the communist system from the American way of life. It was religion, rather than government, economics, or strategic interests, that distinguished Americans from communists. "More precisely than in any other way, prayer places freedom and communism in opposition, one to the other," Eisenhower remarked at the 1953 lighting of the national Christmas tree. Communism can find no purpose in prayer, Eisenhower observed, because Marxist materialism and statism denied the existence of God, the foundation of America's belief in the dignity of man. The United States, on the other hand, drew hope and strength from prayer, Eisenhower believed. "As religious faith is the foundation of free government, so is prayer an indispensable part of that faith." [12]

Although prayer was central to both Eisenhower's personal faith and his civil religion, he did not believe that God eternally meddled in history or acted as a transcendent "fixer-upper." As a youth, Eisenhower had suffered a knee injury that led to blood poisoning, delirium, and a coma. Doctors believed that the boy's leg should be amputated, but with the help of his brother Edgar, Dwight insisted that his leg be spared even at the risk of death. Later grateful that his life and limb had been saved somewhat miraculously, Eisenhower nevertheless dismissed stories that his family had prayed on their knees night and day for his recovery. They were not faith healers, and he quashed rumors that the Jehovah's Witness beliefs of their parents might have rejected medicine in favor of prayer. For the Eisenhower family prayers were daily requests for God's strength and blessing, not petitions for divine intervention in human affairs."[13]

His father's death in 1942, not the war, rekindled Eisenhower's traditional religious concerns. Trapped in Washington, D.C., in March 1942 when David died, Eisenhower could not return home to bury his father or comfort his mother. He felt terrible because the war allowed no time "to indulge even the deepest and most sacred emotions." Eisenhower stole thirty minutes to meditate and pray in private, first thinking of his father and then about his mother."[14]

This prayerful interlude was his first acknowledged religious activity since leaving West Point. World War II intensified Eisenhower's religiosity. Like thousands of servicemen, during the war Eisenhower wrote to a pen pal whom he encouraged to pray for the troops in battle. In a rare public display of public religion, Eisenhower held a "little service" for his staff watching the Allied forces depart Malta for their invasion of Sicily in July 1943. Scanning the scene from a high hill top, Eisenhower suddenly snapped to attention, reverently saluted the armada below, and then bowed his head in silent prayer. Afterward, he confided to an aide: "There comes a time when you have done all that you can possibly do, when you have used your brains, training, and your technical skill, when the die is cast, and events are in the hands of God—and there you have to leave them."[15] Significantly, this comment echoed advice his mother had given him as a boy: "Do the best you can, and leave the rest to God."[16]

Similarly, prior to the D-Day invasion of Normandy in June 1944, Eisenhower asked for "the blessing of Almighty God upon this great and noble undertaking."[17] Faced with uncertain weather that could spell disaster for the invasion forces, Eisenhower knew that the decision to launch Operation OVERLORD was his alone. At this defining moment, he did not pray for God's intervention with respect to the weather or even for assured victory on the French beaches. In the early morning of June 5, with the rain still falling, Eisenhower was assured by his weather officer that the storm would abate, enabling the invasion to proceed. "Okay, we'll go," Eisenhower said simply.

Afterward, as Geoffrey Perret has reported, "On D-Day, he could only smoke and worry, hope and pray."[18] But pray about what? If Eisenhower prayed at this time, his were undoubtedly private prayers for wisdom, strength, and resolution. Subsequent mythology that Ike spent hours on his knees in prayer before the Normandy invasion conjures an image similar to that of Washington at Valley Forge. Instead, in a sentiment reflecting his River Brethren heritage, Eisenhower wrote about the hours before D-Day:

> If there is nothing else in my life to prove the existence of an almighty and merciful God, the events of the next twenty-four hours did it. This is what I found out about religion. It gives you courage to make the decisions you must make in a crisis, and then the confidence to leave the result to higher power. Only by trust in one's self and trust in God can a man carrying responsibility find repose.[19]

At Christmas 1953, Eisenhower remembered Washington at Valley Forge. During that "bitter and critical winter" when the Patriot's cause was near defeat, Washington's best reserve was "sincere and earnest prayer" from which he and the Continental troops received "new hope and new strength of purpose" in the cause of freedom. According to Eisenhower's credo, God responded to personal and community prayers petitioning his help, teaching, strength, and receipt of our thanks. Again, God helped not as a divine manager of human affairs, but rather as a transcendent Reminder of America's common heritage bequeathed by the Founders, who had cherished divinely ordained freedom. More than help, prayer provided personal and collective instruction and renewal. Prayer fostered wisdom and humility; courage and integrity; perspective and patience. Prayer should teach Americans "to shun the counsel of defeat and of despair, of self-pride and self-deceit." While prayer taught trust, hope, and self-dependence, it also taught, more importantly, "the security of faith."[20]

These religious sentiments were not simply the president's pious meanderings. Eisenhower had given deep thought to the meaning and function of prayer and had concluded that prayer was the central religious act of his personal faith and civil religion. He once confided to his White House secretary, Ann Whitman, that he did not conceive of "God as any being" but rather as a source of "affection" otherwise absent from his life. Even on a mountain top, well fed and accompanied by loved ones, a person lacked something without God. Eisenhower's "craving for affection" was not the kind solicited of family or church. It was, rather, the assurance that he was a child of God—the same sought by David and Ida. Although he "abhorred the trappings of the church as much as anyone" and believed that religion was a crutch for many, Eisenhower had no patience for atheists, whom he characterized as persons who did not think. Democracy was founded on the religious presumption that all men are created equal. "I know that I am better than lots of men," Eisenhower confessed to Ann Whitman, but democracy worked because, in the sight of God, all persons were equal. Eisenhower's reliance on God's assurance of the equality and dignity of man was the transcendent affection that lay at the core of Eisenhower's faith.[21]

Given his aversion to organized religion, prayer provided Eisenhower the spiritual equivalent of the Word and Sacrament offered by the mainline sacramental liturgical churches. His was an individualistic, robust faith, less focused on public worship of the Almighty or on securing God's blessing for the United States; and more centered on seeking community understanding of America's historic mission "under God." Eisenhower's religious concerns could not be bounded within the context of denominational or sectarian faith. His God was never as personal as that of evangelicals nor as distant as that the rationalists. Like his mother Ida, Eisenhower possessed strong Universalist inclinations, as his famous London Guildhall address revealed.[22] Whether he celebrated American national unity, extolled the commonality of the English-speaking peoples, or promoted his vision for a United States of Europe, Eisenhower's elastic civil religion included all who shared his belief in a god who helped mankind to walk in dignity, "without fear" and "beyond the yoke of tyranny." First and foremost, then, this man from Abilene, who craved God's affection, prayed to strengthen universal human brotherhood. As he stated in his Inaugural Address and repeated at Christmas, he prayed for the strength of conviction that "whatever America hopes to bring to pass in the world must first come to pass in the heart of America." Even imperfect prayer was a civic necessity, Eisenhower observed, because regardless of national shortcomings, prayer bound all Americans together in their efforts to reach out toward the Infinite.[23]

Eisenhower's Inaugural Prayer, the first written by a president, faithfully reflected his civil religion. His "little private prayer," as befitting public prayer, was universalist in tone and content. Predictably, he prayed for God's help, teaching, and strength; that is, he prayed for the power of discernment so that his administration might govern in the interests of all the people, "regardless of station, race, or calling."[24] And what was his source or authority in this? Eisenhower believed that the American Revolution marked a great turning point in history when "to establish a government for free men and a Declaration and Constitution to make it last," the Founders had professed that "We hold that all men are endowed by their Creator" with certain rights. This one sentence confirmed that American government was imbedded in a "deeply-felt religious faith." To think otherwise, Eisenhower believed, made no sense.[25]

As William Pickett has shown, Eisenhower's decision to run for president in 1952 was complex. Political mythology aside, a reluctant Eisenhower was not simply drafted by Republicans eager to place the hero/general on their ticket. Taking nothing away from the political nature of his decision to run, Eisenhower, nevertheless, experienced a religious-like transformation in this "call to duty." Perhaps, as critics have suggested, this was Eisenhower's self-serving way of transcending sordid politics, which he so much detested. At any rate, while there is no doubt that candidate Eisenhower had responded to a deeply-felt sense of duty, his understanding of his duty to America was not vague. As commanding general of the Allied Forces in World War II and as supreme commander of NATO, Eisenhower had dedicated the better part of his life to securing world peace. He ran for president in 1952 to save the United States, and the world, from falling into a nuclear abyss.[26]

Eisenhower's conversion and baptism on February 1, 1953, has largely gone unnoticed by his biographers, and it was only obliquely mentioned by Eisenhower himself in his White House memoir, *Mandate for Change*.[27] Eisenhower and Mamie (who was Presbyterian) began attending National Presbyterian Church before the 1952 election and had participated in a prayer service there on Inauguration Day. Supporters, including Clare Booth Luce, had encouraged the candidate to join a church before the 1952 presidential election, but Eisenhower angrily refused to commit such a blatantly political act. While Luce believed that the candidate's chances were weakened without church membership, Eisenhower responded that his religion was a matter strictly between himself and God. This denominational independence, of course, was in line with Eisenhower's upbringing and evidently persisted to the eve of his baptism.[28]

Why, then, did Eisenhower present himself for baptism in the Presbyterian Church shortly after his inauguration in 1953? While not intended to garner votes, no doubt Eisenhower's decision was a political act. Neither the president nor his pastor, Edward L. R. Elson, ever explained the motives behind the action. But Luce, the president's brother Milton, and the evangelist Billy Graham all commented similarly: Eisenhower believed his duty as president required membership and regular attendance at church to set a religious example and moral tone for the nation. Granting, then, a significant political incentive to his religious conversion and baptism, were there more traditionally religious concerns also motivating the baptismal decision?

Paul Tillich, writing concurrently, defined religion as the object of our "ultimate concern," usually centering on issues concerning being and nonbeing, or death.[29] Discern someone's "ultimate concern," Tillich argues, and you discover their religion: "The concern about our work often succeeds in becoming our god, as does the concern about another human being, or about pleasure. The concern about science has succeeded in becoming the god of a whole era in history, the concern about money has become an even more important god, and the concern about the nation the most important god of all."[30]

Eisenhower was not obsessed with death when he was baptized in 1953, but the former general had observed more than his share of human carnage on World War II battlefields, the Nazi death camps, and the Korean Peninsula. Almost alone among U.S. military leaders, during World War II he had opposed the atomic bombing of Hiroshima. "It was not necessary to hit them with that awful thing," he later reflected. On a postwar, low-level flight between Berlin and Moscow, Eisenhower was appalled that he saw no undamaged buildings and few living things from the Polish border to the Russian capital. Conditions in Germany differed in scale, but not in kind, from those in the Soviet Union. Millions were dead or missing.

Millions more were homeless. Cities were in ashes, and industry reduced to rubble. In aftermath unimaginable destruction and incomprehensible inhumanity Eisenhower experienced intensified stirring of religious revival.[31]

Eisenhower's moral revulsion over the atomic bomb never lessened, but rather became a major force shaping his world view, politics, and civil religion. Following his meeting with Secretary of War Henry Stimson at Potsdam in 1945, where he first learned about the successful Trinity test, Eisenhower became depressed not only because he did not believe the atomic bomb was needed to defeat Japan, but also because he did not believe the United States should be morally responsible for using a weapon of mass destruction needlessly to save American lives. He had hoped for postwar friendship with the Soviet Union, but the atomic bomb blasted any chance for peace. "I had hoped the bomb wouldn't figure in this war," he lamented. But the world had changed. "Now I don't know," Eisenhower worried, "People are frightened and disturbed all over. Everyone feels insecure again."[32] Contrasting Eisenhower with other American leaders, Gar Alperovitz later marveled at Eisenhower's moral instincts. "Why is it that some men were able to preserve their hold on ethical standards? And some were not?"[33]

Had Alperovitz known of Eisenhower's religious youth, he may have understood the origins of Eisenhower's moral compass. Eisenhower had pondered fiery Armageddon as a child and had rejected his father's apocalyptic religion. Although the prospects of nuclear holocaust were depressing, Eisenhower was an optimist. He possessed a religious-like faith that the worst circumstances could be turned toward good. In this regard, he saw divine possibility even in the most demonic events. Whether it was the unspeakable horrors of World War II or the terrible portent of the atomic bomb, Eisenhower not only believed but virtually willed that these events would work toward the ultimate benefit of mankind. Stephen Ambrose has described Eisenhower as a Wilsonian idealist—that is, a person, like Woodrow Wilson before him, who believed in the power of good will and personal diplomacy to overcome cultural, economic, and ideological differences to achieve peace, prosperity, and progress.[34] But, unlike Wilson, Eisenhower was no utopian visionary; ideas, including his religious faith, were tools to improve, not perfect, the world.[35]

In October 1953, Eisenhower graphically described the deadly horrors of nuclear warfare to the United Church Women. Although America had escaped the physical ravages of World War II, the United States' former security had disappeared with the threat of nuclear attack by intercontinental bombers. America had few choices.

> The choice that spells terror and death is symbolized by a mushroom cloud floating upward from the release of the mightiest natural power yet uncovered by those who search the physical universe. The energy that it typifies is, at this stage of human knowledge, the unharnessed blast. In its wake we see only sudden and mass destruction, erasure of cities, the possible doom of every nation and society.[36]

But Eisenhower would not abandon hope that the "titanic force" of nuclear energy could be directed to the useful service of humankind.

When Soviet premier Joseph Stalin died in March 1953, Eisenhower believed the United States stood at a turning point in history, a time of unique danger and opportunity. His father had predicted such moments of judgment. Eisenhower was neither a millenarian nor a Manichaean, but his religious worldview was informed by dialectical struggle between divine and demonic forces in history, an understanding not dissimilar to that of his father or his contemporary Paul Tillich. Typically, Eisenhower had described his struggles against the dark forces of history in the rhetoric of crusades, which was his way of highlighting the epic nature of history. But Eisenhower was not unaware of the complexities of history. His universalist beliefs regarded the Russians as "children of the same God who is the Father of all peoples everywhere." And, despite his transformation into a cold-war president, Eisenhower believed, as he had in 1945, that the Russian people genuinely longed for peace and friendship. In the spring of 1953, he saw a "chance for peace."[37] It is mystifying how scholars can read Eisenhower's "Chance for Peace" speech presented to the American Society of Newspaper Editors on April 16, 1953, and still conclude that he was bland, vague, uninformed, and disinterested. The president's estimate of "A Chance for Peace" presented a manifestly political agenda while latently revealing Eisenhower's religious transformation.

David Eisenhower had believed in three ages, or dispensations, in history, the last of which would be preceded by a fiery holocaust that foretold the second return of Christ. Eisenhower's vision of the "middle-way" in human affairs, in contrast, rejected belief in an apocalyptic end to history. Eisenhower preferred to seek salvation within nature and human history and entertained no capitulation to evil or death in this world. The theologian Paul Tillich offered a more pacific version of this historical trinity in his Protestant interpretation of history, in which ages of autonomy and heteronomy, dialectically interacting, were superseded by a theonomous age that is "directed toward" the divine principle in history revealed by the Kairos, the turning point in history that revealed the meaning and destiny of history."[38]

For Dwight Eisenhower, the spring of 1953 was just such a time of Kairos when the world was summoned to choose between peril and hope. "A Chance for Peace" described the Kairos literally: "This is one of those times in the affairs of nations when the gravest choices must be made, if there is to be a turning toward a just and lasting peace. It is a moment that calls upon the governments of the world to speak their intentions with simplicity and honesty. It calls upon them to answer the question that stirs the hearts of all sane men: is *there no other way the world may live?*"[39] What could the world hope for if there were no turning on this dreadful road, Eisenhower asked rhetorically. The *worst* was nuclear war. And the *best* that could be hoped for was a life of perpetual fear and tension; wealth and labor dissipated in an endless arms race; and governments discredited by the failure to achieve prosperity and happiness for humankind. The costs of the cold war were staggering and debilitating. "Every gun that is made, every warship launched, every rocket fired signifies, in the final sense, a theft from those who hunger and are not fed, those who are cold and are not clothed."[40] And, according to Eisenhower, the costs were not paid in cash alone. The cold war consumed the daily work of laborers, the creativity of scientists, and the future of children. In social priorities, a bomber cost thirty schools, two electric power plants, two hospitals, or fifty miles of highway. A single destroyer would buy eight thousand new homes for a small Kansas town. Paraphrasing the 1908 Democratic presidential nominee, William Jennings Bryan, Eisenhower solemnly observed, "Under the cloud of threatening war, it is humanity hanging from a cross of iron."[41]

As pessimistic as Eisenhower's remarks may have seemed, he outlined a policy for extricating the United States from the cold war. Despite the increasing intensity of the nuclear arms race, Eisenhower continued to hope for an international rapprochement with the Soviet Union. He recalled that brief moment of joyous victory in the spring of 1945 when Americans and Russians had been comrades in arms seeking to rebuild a world at peace as a fitting tribute to the millions who had died to defeat tyranny. In the aftermath of Hiroshima and Nagasaki, the United States and the Soviet Union had taken different paths, each seeking in its own way to buy security through international alliances and nuclear arms. The results were ironic and tragic. Enormous investment in weapons of mass destruction had lessened everyone's security. But Eisenhower rejected despair. Although some of his prerequisites for peace included standard cold war demands for a free Germany and a free eastern Europe that would not move the Soviet leaders, he also offered to explore more modest, incremental steps toward arms control and disarmament. Even these suggestions, including international control of atomic energy for peaceful purposes, were neither new nor original with Eisenhower. But they did represent confidence-building initiatives certain to lessen cold war animosity if adopted.[42]

"A Chance for Peace" was one of Eisenhower's finest speeches. It was not free of raw cold war propaganda in its obligatory denunciation of Soviet oppression and tyranny. Eisenhower hated Stalin's heteronomy as intensely as he had hated Hitler's. But, in contrast to the Nazis with whom no compromise had been possible, Eisenhower hoped that the new Communist leaders in the Kremlin might be amenable to making small steps toward peace. Eisenhower was not naive about the difficulty of the new path to be taken. Trust, confidence, and goodwill would be difficult to establish with the Soviets in the cold war atmosphere. If his arms-control proposals were modest, it was because Eisenhower knew full well that the "details of disarmament programs were necessarily critical and complex . . . and no nation possessed a perfect, immutable formula. But," he concluded, "the formula mattered less than the faith."[43]

Nightmares of nuclear Armageddon haunted Eisenhower. In his role as president/pastor, he wanted both to educate and assure the American people while offering hope and leadership to the world. He might not be able to dismiss his ultimate concerns about nuclear death, but he could draw on his faith that God intended for humans to employ the atom for peaceful purposes. "A Chance for Peace" was a public prayer offering a "middle-way" in public policy while reminding Americans of their historical destiny, instructing the public in the realities of nuclear arms race, and strengthening the world in its resolve to seek new, and risky, paths to peace. Characteristically, Eisenhower tried to seize an historical opportunity in 1953 rather than drift passively with the cold war tide. "A Chance for Peace" outlined an agenda for nuclear arms control and disarmament from which Eisenhower and his administration would not deviate. At the United Nations in December 1953, at the Geneva Conferences in 1955 and 1958, and during seemingly endless and fruitless negotiations to limit atmospheric nuclear testing, Eisenhower never lost sight of the historical objective envisioned in "A Chance for Peace."[44] Biographer Geoffrey Perret believes the speech was "the most trenchant criticism ever made of the Cold War."[45] Unfortunately, Eisenhower lost heart after the U-2 incident and the collapse of the Paris Peace talks just when a test-ban agreement seemed within reach. Ironically, it would be John F. Kennedy, representing a new generation, who reaped the historical and moral credit for the landmark 1963 Limited Test Ban Treaty, often cited as the most important achievement of his brief presidency.

NOTES

1 James David Barber, "Eisenhower as a 'Passive-Negative' President," in *The Eisenhower Presidency and the 1950s*, ed. Michael S. Mayer (Boston: Houghton Mifflin, 1998), 3–16; Erwin C. Hargrove, *The President as Leader: Appealing to the Better Angels of our Nature* (Lawrence: University Press of Kansas, 1998), 61–64; Fred L. Greenstein, *The Hidden-Hand Presidency: Eisenhower as Leader* (New York: Basic Books, 1982).
2 *New York Times*, December 23, 1952, p. 16, as cited in *Civil Religion and the Presidency*, ed. Richard V. Pierard and Robert D. Linder (Grand Rapids, Mich.: Academie Books, 1988), 184.
3 Ernest W. Lefever, "The Candidates' Religious Views," *The Christian Century*, September 1956, 1072.
4 Ibid.
5 Ibid., 1073.
6 Frederick Fox, White House special assistant, to Harold Frey, editor of *The Christian Century*, November 2, 1956 [not sent]. Papers of Frederick Fox, Dwight D. Eisenhower Presidential Library, Abilene, Kans [hereafter DDE].
7 Pierard and Linder, *Civil Religion and the Presidency*, 195–97.
8 Eisenhower as quoted in ibid., 195; *New York Times*, May 20, 1947, 22.
9 Eisenhower as quoted in Pierard and Linder, *Civil Religion*, 195–96; *New York Times*, June 5, 1952, 16.
10 Eisenhower, "Remarks at a Luncheon Meeting of the General Board of the National Council of Churches," Public Papers of the Presidents [hereafter PPP], DDE 1953, 791–93.
11 Ibid.
12 Eisenhower, "Remarks Upon Lighting the National Community Christmas Tree," December 24, 1953, PPP/DDE 1953, 858–59.

13 Stephen E. Ambrose, *Eisenhower: Soldier and President* (New York: Simon & Schuster, 1990), 21.
14 Dwight D. Eisenhower, *At Ease: Stories I Tell My Friends* (New York: Doubleday, 1967), 304–5.
15 Pierard and Linder, *Civil Religion*, 193.
16 Merlin Gustafson, "The Religion of a President," *Journal of Church and State* 10 (1968): 611.
17 As quoted in Ambrose, *Eisenhower*, 135.
18 Geoffrey Perret, *Eisenhower* (New York: Random House, 1999), 286.
19 Eisenhower, "Remarks at a Luncheon," PPP/DDE, 793.
20 Eisenhower, "Remarks Upon Lighting the National Community Christmas Tree," December 24, 1953, PPP/DDE 1953, 859.
21 Ann C. Whitman to E. S. Whitman, n.d, Personal Papers of Ann C. Whitman, box 1—Correspondence, Eisenhower Presidential Library.
22 Eisenhower, Guildhall Address, June 12, 1945, as noted in *At Ease*, 298–300, 388–90.
23 Eisenhower, "Inaugural Address," January 20, 1953, 7; "Remarks Upon Lighting the National Community Christmas Tree," December 24, 1953, 859; "Remarks at the Dedicatory Prayer Breakfast of the International Christian Leadership," 8; all in PPP/DDE 1953.
24 Eisenhower, "Inaugural Address," 1.
25 Eisenhower, "Remarks at the Dedicatory Prayer Breakfast of the International Christian Leadership, February 5, 1953, PPP/DDE, 7–8. For an extended modern exploration of this theme, see Robert Lowry Clinton, *God & Man in the Law* (Lawrence: University Press of Kansas, 1997).
26 William B. Pickett, "A Question of Duty," *Eisenhower Decides to Run: Presidential Politics and Cold War Strategy* (Chicago: Ivan R. Dee, 2000), 210–15.
27 Dwight D. Eisenhower, *Mandate for Change: The White House Years. 1953–1956*, (Garden City, N.Y.: Doubleday, 1963), 100.
28 Keith Bates, "Edward L. R. Elson: 'Spiritual Helper' to Dwight D. Eisenhower," Graduate Seminar on the Eisenhower Era, May 11, 2001, unpublished, 2–5. See also, Clare Booth Luce, interview by John Luter, January 11, 1968, Columbia Oral History Project, Eisenhower Presidential Library.
29 Paul Tillich, *Systematic Theology*, 3 vols. (Chicago: University of Chicago Press), 1:1951, 11–14.
30 Paul Tillich, *The New Being* (New York: Scribner's, 1955), 158.
31 Eisenhower, *Crusade in Europe* (New York: Doubleday, 1948), 443; John S. D. Eisenhower, *Strictly Personal* (Garden City, N.Y.: Doubleday, 1974), 97; Gar Alperovitz, *Atomic Diplomacy: Hiroshima and Potsdam: The Use of the Atomic Bomb and American Confrontation with Soviet Power* (New York: Penguin, 1985), 60.
32 Peter Lyon, *Eisenhower: Portrait of a Hero* (Boston: Little, Brown, 1974), 356–57, as quoted in Edgar Snow, *Journey to the Beginning* (New York: Random House, 1958), 360–61.

33 Alperovitz, *Atomic Diplomacy*, 60.
34 Ambrose, *Eisenhower*, 426–27.
35 See also, Pierard and Linder, "Woodrow Wilson and the Moralization of America's Special Mission," *Civil Religion & the Presidency*, 136–60.
36 Eisenhower, "Address at the Sixth National Assembly of the United Church Women, Atlantic City, New Jersey," October 6, 1953, PPP/DDE 1953, 636.
37 Eisenhower, *Mandate for Change*, 144.
38 Paul Tillich, *The Protestant Era* (Chicago: University of Chicago Press, 1948), 43–44.
39 Italics in the original. DDE, "The Chance for Peace" Delivered Before the American Society of Newspaper Editors, April 16, 1953, PPP/DDE 1953, 179–88.
40 Ibid.
41 Ibid.
42 Ibid.
43 Eisenhower, *Mandate for Change*, 146.
44 For an extended discussion of Eisenhower nuclear policy, see Richard G. Hewlett and Jack M. Holl, *Atoms for Peace and War. 1953–1961: Eisenhower and the Atomic Energy Commission* (Berkeley: University of California Press, 1989).
45 Perret, *Eisenhower*, 454; see also Ambrose, *Eisenhower*, 324–26.

Contributors

EDWARD BALLEISEN, associate professor of history at Duke University, is an authority on the culture of American capitalism. A former fellow at the James Willard Hurst Legal History Institute, University of Wisconsin–Madison, he is the author of *Navigating Failure: Bankruptcy and Commercial Society in Antebellum America*.

IRA BERLIN, past president of the Organization of American Historians and Distinguished University Professor of History at the University of Maryland, is author of *Slaves without Masters*, which won the Best First Book Prize from the National Historical Society; *Free at Last*, winner of the Lincoln Prize; *Freedom's Soldiers*, winner of the J. Franklin Jameson Prize; *Many Thousands Gone*, which received the Bancroft Prize, the Frederick Douglass Prize, and the Elliot Rudwick Prize; and *Generations of Captivity*, which won the Albert J. Beveridge Award.

IVER BERNSTEIN, professor of history at Washington University in St. Louis, is the author of *The New York City Draft Riots: Their Significance for American Society and Politics in the Age of the Civil War* and *Lincoln's Body Politic: How Americans Came to Sacrifice Self for Nation in the Civil War*.

ROBERT E. BONNER, a member of the history faculty at Michigan State University, has also been a visiting assistant professor of black studies and history at Amherst College. He is the author of *Colors and Blood: Flag Passions of the American South* and *Southern Slaveholders and the Crisis of American Nationhood*.

LESLIE BUTLER taught at Reed College and Michigan State University before joining the Department of History at Dartmouth College. She is the author of *Cultivating America: Victorian Intellectuals and Transatlantic Liberal Reform*.

CATHERINE CLINTON holds a chair in history at Queen's University, Belfast, Northern Ireland. She is the author of *The Plantation Mistress*, *The Other Civil War*, *Fanny Kemble's Civil War*, *Harriet Tubman: The Road to Freedom*, and many other books. She has taught at Brandeis, Brown, Harvard, Wesleyan, and Union College, and has held the Douglas Southall Freeman Visiting Chair of History at the University of Richmond, the Lewis Jones Visiting Chair of History at Wofford College, the Weissman Visiting Chair of History at Baruch College, and the Mark Clark Chair of History at the Citadel.

ELLEN DWYER, codirector of the Indiana University Center for the Study of the History of Medicine, is associate professor of criminal justice and history at Indiana University. She has served as associate editor of the *American Historical Review* and is the author of *Homes for the Mad: Life Inside Two Nineteenth-Century Asylums*.

DAVID ELTIS, the Robert W. Woodruff Professor of History at Emory University, is the author of *Economic Growth and the Ending of the Transatlantic Slave Trade*, which won the British Trevor Reese Memorial Prize, and *The Rise of African Slavery in the Americas*, awarded the Frederick Douglass Prize, the John Ben Snow Prize, and the Wesley-Logan Prize. He is editor of *Coerced and Free Migration: Global Perspectives*, coeditor of a special issue of *William and Mary Quarterly* (2001) titled *Routes to Slavery: Direction, Mortality, and Ethnicity in the Transatlantic Slave Trade, 1595–1867*, and cocreator of *The Transatlantic Slave Trade: A Database on CD-ROM*.

STANLEY L. ENGERMAN is the John Munro Professor of Economics and professor of history at the University of Rochester. He has served as Pitt Professor of American History and Institutions at Cambridge University and is past president of the Economic History Association and of the Social Science History Association. He has also been a fellow at the American Academy of Arts and Sciences and the Center for Advanced Study in the Behavioral Sciences. He is the coauthor of *Time on the Cross: The Economics of American Negro Slavery*, winner of the Bancroft Prize; and editor of *The Reinterpretation of American Economic History*; *The Cambridge Economic History of the United States*; *A Historical Guide to World Slavery*; and *Terms of Labor*.

MICHAEL FELLMAN is professor of history and director of the Graduate Liberal Studies Program at Simon Fraser University in Vancouver, British Columbia. He is the author of six books, including *Inside War: The Guerrilla Conflict in Missouri during the American Civil War* (1989); *Citizen Sherman* (1995); and *The Making of Robert E. Lee* (2000). He is also coauthor, with Daniel Sutherland and Lesley Gordon, of *This Terrible War: The Civil War and Its Aftermath* (2002).

PAUL FINKELMAN, the President William McKinley Distinguished Professor of Law and Public Policy and senior fellow in the Government Law Center at Albany Law School, has also been a fellow in law and the humanities at Harvard Law School. His many books include *A March of Liberty: A Constitutional History of the United States*, *Slavery and the Founders: Race and Liberty in the Age of Jefferson*, *Baseball and the American Legal Mind*, and *American Legal History: Cases and Materials*.

JONATHAN A. GLICKSTEIN is professor of history at the University of California, Santa Barbara. An authority on nineteenth-century U.S. intellectual, labor, and political history, he is the author of *Concepts of Free Labor in Antebellum America* (1991) and *American Exceptionalism, American Anxiety: Wages, Competition, and Degraded Labor in the Antebellum United States* (2002).

RICHARD WIGHTMAN FOX, a professor of history at the University of Southern California, studies how ideas, beliefs, and cultural practices develop in relation to social structures and individual quests for meaning. His many books include *Trials of Intimacy: Love and Loss in the Beecher-Tilton Scandal*, which received the American Association of Publishers History Award, *The Culture of Consumption*, *In Face of the Facts: Moral Inquiry in American Scholarship*, and *Reinhold Niebuhr: A Biography*.

PETER HINKS has taught at Hamilton College and been a senior research fellow at the Gilder Lehrman Center for the Study of Slavery, Resistance and Abolition at Yale. His book *To Awaken My Afflicted Brethren: David Walker and the Problem of Antebellum Slave Resistance* was a featured selection of History Book Club and the winner of the Gustavus Myers Center Award for the Study of Human Rights in North America. He is also a coeditor of the *Life of Frederick Douglass, An American Slave*.

JACK M. HOLL, professor of history at Kansas State University and director of the Institute for Military History and Twentieth-Century Studies, served as the chief historian of the U.S. Department of Energy. His books include *Atoms for Peace and War: Eisenhower and the Atomic Energy Commission*, which received the Richard Leopold Prize from the Organization of American Historians and the Henry Adams Prize from the Society for History in the Federal Government; *Argonne National Laboratory 1946–1966*, which also won the Henry Adams Prize; and *Juvenile Reform in the Progressive Era: William R. George and the Junior Republic Movement*.

PAULA KANE is associate professor and Marous Chair of Catholic Studies at the University of Pittsburgh. She is the author of *Separatism and Subculture: Boston Catholicism 1900–1920*, which examines the fate of post-immigrant Catholics in the transition from "ethnics" to assimilated Americans, and coeditor of *Gender Identities in American Catholicism*.

MARGARET M. R. KELLOW is associate professor of history and associate dean at the University of Western Ontario, where she specializes in the history of gender and race in nineteenth-century America. She is currently completing a biography of Lydia Maria Child.

WILLIAM CASEY KING taught history at Yale University before becoming the executive director of the W. E. B. Du Bois Institute at Harvard University. He has produced an acclaimed documentary, *Henry Ossawa Tanner*, and published an award-winning young adult book, *Oh, Freedom!*

STEVEN MINTZ is the John and Rebecca Moores Professor of History at the University of Houston, president of H-Net: Humanities and Social Sciences Online, and national cochair of the Council on Contemporary Families. He is the author of several books, including *Domestic Revolutions: A Social History of American Family Life*, *Moralists and Modernizers: America's Pre–Civil War Reformers*, and, most recently, *Huck's Raft: A History of American Childhood*, which won the Merle Curti Award, the R. R. Hawkins Award, and the Carr P. Collins Award.

LAURA L. MITCHELL is president of the Luther Institute, a nonprofit organization that promotes the role of faith and ethics in public life through learning, service, and leadership. She has also served as historian and project coordinator at the Smithsonian Institution's National Museum of American History, where she edited *Time Machine*, a children's history magazine, and researched and wrote on the Nobel Prize exhibition.

ORLANDO PATTERSON is the John Cowles Professor of Sociology at Harvard University. Among his many books are *The Sociology of Slavery*, *Slavery and Social Death*, *Ethnic Chauvinism*, and *Freedom: Freedom in the Making of Western Culture*. He was awarded the Distinguished Contribution to Scholarship Award of the American Sociological Association in 1983, and was cowinner of the Ralph Bunche Award of the American Political Science Association for the best scholarly work on the subject of pluralism. In 1991 he was awarded the National Book Award in nonfiction for volume one of *Freedom*. He is a fellow of the American Academy of Arts and Sciences.

RANDOLPH ROTH, associate professor of history at Ohio State University, is the author of *The Democratic Dilemma: Religion, Reform, and the Social Order in the Connecticut River Valley of Vermont, 1791–1850*. He is a member of the editorial board of *Historical Methods*, and a cofounder of the Historical Violence Database, a collaborative project to create a comprehensive database on the history of violent crime and violent death in the United States. His current research examines the history of violent crime and violent death from the 1550s to the present.

JOHN STAUFFER is chair of the Program in the History of American Civilization and professor of English and African and African American studies at Harvard University. His first book, *The Black Hearts of Men: Radical Abolitionists and the Transformation of Race*, was the cowinner of the Frederick Douglass Prize, winner of the Avery Craven Prize, and the Lincoln Prize runner-up. He has edited or coedited a number of books, including Frederick Douglass's *My Bondage and My Freedom* for the Modern Library; *Meteor of War: The John Brown Story*; and, most recently, *Black Intellectual and Abolitionist: The Selected Writings of James McCune Smith*.

SHARON HARTMAN STROM is professor of history and women's studies and chair of the Department of History at the University of Rhode Island. A former Bunting Institute fellow, she has published works on office labor, women's political movements, and the historical construction of race and gender. Her books include *Beyond the Typewriter: Gender, Class and the Origins of Modern American Office Work, 1900–1930*; *Moving the Mountain: Women Working for Social Change*; and *Political Woman: Florence Luscomb and the Legacy of Radical Reform*.

DAVID WALDSTREICHER, an associate professor of history at the University of Notre Dame, is the author of *In the Midst of Perpetual Fetes: The Making of American Nationalism, 1776–1820*, coeditor of *Beyond the Founders: New Approaches to the Political History of the Early American Republic*, and editor of *The Struggle against Slavery: A History in Documents* and *Thomas Jefferson's Notes on the State of Virginia and Related Documents*.

Acknowledgments

The editors would like to thank the following people for their comments and encouragement, and for fostering the community of ideas that helped make this book possible: David Blight, Jon Butler, Nancy Cott, Eric Foner, Alan Trachtenberg, Seymour Drescher, James Brewer Stewart, Richard Blackett, Peter Kolchin, Susanna Blumenthal, Lesley Herrmann, Christopher Brown, Willy Forbath, Elliot Gorn, Robert Forbes, Lewis Perry, Joan Shelley Rubin, Michael Salman, Barbara Savage, Clyde Spillenger, Glenn Wallach, and Steven Wilf.

Our greatest debt is to David Brion Davis, to whom we dedicate the book. As a nineteen-year-old soldier, stationed in Stuttgart, Germany, in 1946, he wrote a letter to his parents in which he spelled out a conception of history that has inspired this volume's contributors. Convinced that "the problems that surround us today" have resulted in large measure from the human race's "collective lack of perspective and knowledge of itself," he insisted that the study of history was "even more important at present" than the likes of endocrinology and nuclear fission. History's task was "an unearthing of truths long buried beneath superficial facts and propaganda; a presentation of perspective and an overall comprehensive view of what people did and thought and why they did it." Such an approach, he went on, "would make people stop and think before blindly following some bigoted group to make the world safe for Aryans or democrats or Mississippians." Now, more than six decades later, it has become even clearer that historical ignorance lies at the roots of many present-day evils and mistaken public policies.

Index

Abolition, 127–34, 148–58, 174–80, 183–94, 199; Catholics and, 199–207
American Colonization Society, 158–59
Anderson, Benedict, 261
Antinominanism, 4
Arendt, Hannah, 315
Aristotle, 102–3
Austin, James Trecothick, 245–47

Baldwin, James, 331–32
Bankruptcy, 276–84
Barrow, David, 128, 132
Beard, Charles, 130
Beecher, Henry Ward, 223, 225, 280, 298–308
Bellamy, Edward, 324–25
Bennett, James Gordon, 243, 245–46
Boaz, Franz, 368
Blair, Francis, Jr., 242, 262–63, 269
Blair, Frank, 262–64, 266–70
Blair, Montgomery, 263, 268–69
Brown, John, 251–52, 287–95
Brownson, Orestes, 179, 205
Burke, Edmund, 138, 239
Burrow, John, 354, 361

Calhoun, John C., 109, 247
Cartwright, Samuel, 107–8, 118, 233
Catholic Church, 199–207
Chandler, Elizabeth, 192–93
Child, Lydia Maria, 185, 291–92, 295
Civil War, 23, 29–30
Clay, Henry, 202, 232–34, 241–43, 247–49
Cobb, Thomas R.R., 103, 106
Colonization movement, 260–70
Conkling, Roscoe, 282–83
Conwell, Russell, 320–21

Davis, David Brion, 67, 95, 102, 120, 138–39, 142, 145, 171, 221, 223, 260
Davis, Jefferson, 117, 227–28, 231, 235, 242, 246–47, 250

DeBow, James D. B., 101, 118
Delany, Martin R., 233
Delbanco, Andrew, 3, 324
Douglas, Stephen, 242, 247, 264
Douglass, Frederick, 210–216, 224–26, 243–45, 251, 261, 266, 270, 287–89, 326, 329
DuBois, W. E. B., 227, 318–19, 328–29, 332
Dwight, Timothy, 148–58
Dyer, Christopher, 44–45

Edwards, Jonathan, Jr., 154, 159
Eisenhower, Dwight David, 329, 382–94
Emerson, Ralph Waldo, 287
Essig, James, 149–51, 154
Evil, 2–5; in American thought after the Civil War, 315–32; literature and, 3, 4; philosophy and, 4; psychological and sociological explanations of, 5; religion and, 3, 4

Finkelman, Paul, 290–91, 295
Fitzhugh, George, 99, 101, 108–10
Frank, Jerome, 375–76
Franklin, Benjamin, 162–71
Fredrickson, George, 294–95, 331
Freedom, 31–61; classical roots of, 31–36; religious roots of, 31, 35–36
Fundamentalism, 327–28

Garnet, Henry Highland, 293
Garrison, William Lloyd, 131–32, 177–78, 243, 294, 300
Garvey, Marcus, 329
Gladstone, William, 355, 358
Godkin, E. L., 354, 357–58
Goodell, William, 174–80
Graham, Billy, 383, 389
Greece, and concept of freedom, 31–34, 47
Greenberg, Kenneth, 211, 213
Gregory XVI, 199, 299
Grimké, Angelina, 184, 300
Grimké, Charlotte Forten, 226

Hammond, James Henry, 101, 105, 108–10
Hart, Levi, 154–55, 159
Hawthorne, Nathaniel, 326
Heyrick, Elizabeth, 132
Higginson, Thomas Wentworth, 226, 355, 360
Hilton, R. H., 44, 46, 56
Hitler, Adolf, 115–16, 121
Hobbes, Thomas, 231
Holt, J. C., 52–53
Hotze, Henry, 115–16, 119–20
Hopkins, Samuel, 128, 154
Howe, Julia Ward, 225, 289, 293, 325
Howe, Samuel Gridley, 188–89
Hughes, Archbishop John, 204–5

Indentured servitude, 75–76

Jackson, Andrew, 91, 102, 236
Jacobs, Harriet, 210–11, 214–16
James, William, 321–22, 350
Jefferson, Thomas, 89–91, 237; and proslavery thought, 98–99, 101–3
Jeffrey, Julie Roy, 194
Jordan, William Chester, 42–43
Jung, Carl, 3

Keimer, Samuel, 163–65, 167
Kelley, Abby, 133
Kipling, Rudyard, 344

Lay, Benjamin, 163, 168–71
Lefever, Ernest W., 383–84
Liberalism: and war, 353–61
Lieber, Frances, 236–37
Lincoln, Abraham, 25, 30, 180, 235, 238–43, 247–51, 262–63, 266–70; on John Brown, 287–88, 294
Locke, John, 59, 239
Lovejoy, Elijah, 240, 249, 251, 291

Madison, James, 238, 242, 260–61
Martin, Maria, 187–88, 194
Mather, Cotton, 162–63, 169–70
McKinley, William, 341–42

Melville, Herman, 221, 295, 326
Meyer, Donald, 320, 327
Milton, John, 143
Monroe, James, 91
Moorhead, James, 227, 326

Nazi Germany, 1, 115–16, 121, 330
Niebuhr, Reinhold, 4, 318, 327, 331–32, 383–84
Norton, Charles Eliot, 353, 356, 359–60
Nott, Josiah C., 107–8, 118

O'Brien, Richard J., 348–49
O'Connell, Daniel, 204

Paine, Thomas, 144, 235–36
Peasantry, European, 43–44, 46
Perret, Geoffrey, 387, 394
Philippines, American intervention in, 337–51, 358–59
Phillips, Wendell, 240, 287, 300
Plato, 34, 103
Proslavery thought, 95–111; religion and, 104–5; science and, 107–8

Quakers, 127–28

Race, 7–9; and science, 7, 8; shifting meaning of, 8–9; and war, 366–77
Reform, 10–14; historiography of, 11–12; gender dimensions of, 12–13; professionalization of, 11; roots of, 10–11
Rome, 96–97; and concept of freedom, 34–35
Roosevelt, Theodore, 323, 357
Rynders, Isaiah, 243–46, 250

Salvation Army, 321–22
Sandiford, Ralph, 163, 167–71
Schwarz, Philip, 74, 80
Serfdom, 39–41, 44, 55
Sewall, Samuel, 127, 162–63, 167, 170
Sherman, William Tecumseh, 339–40
Sinclair, Upton, 324–25
Slave children, 5–6

Slave culture, 26, 28–29.
Slave family life, 26–27
Slave trade, 71–72
Slavery, 5–7, 23–30, 67–73, 89–94; and American politics, 6, 24–25; and Catholics, 199–207; and the Civil War, 29–30; in colonial America, 23–24; contemporary controversies over, 23; and gender, 27–28; in North Africa, 183; resistance to, 7, 28; and sin, 138; and violence, 74–75, 76–83
Smith, Adam, 128, 238
Smith, Gerrit, 132–33, 177, 300
Smith, Goldwin, 355, 356
Smith, Jacob, 341
Smith, Samuel Stanhope, 7
Squier, E. George, 264–65, 267–68
Stanton, Elizabeth Cady, 133
St. Augustine, 4, 54, 225
Stephens, Alexander, 110–17, 119–20
Stevens, Rutherford, 366, 375–76
Stoicism, 34, 56
Stowe, Harriet Beecher, 9, 222–23, 249, 299, 324
Sumner, Charles, 251, 269, 295

Taft, William Howard, 342–45
Taney, Roger, 107, 205, 264, 319
Tappan, Arthur, 280
Tappan, Lewis, 132, 280, 303
Thoreau, Henry David, 293
Tillich, Paul, 389–92
Tise, Larry, 149–51, 154–55, 158
Townsend, John, 246–47
Truth, Sojourner, 289
Tryon, Thomas, 163–65, 167, 171
Turner, Henry M., 226, 329
Tuveson, Ernest, 223, 225
Twain, Mark, 315–20, 325, 332

Walker, Robert, 265–67
Washington, Booker T., 329
Washington, George, 143
Weber, Max, 170
Whitman, Walt, 221, 287
Whittier, John Greenleaf, 245, 291–92
Wilson, Woodrow, 353, 391
Women: and abolition, 133–34, 183–94, and slavery, 27–28
Wounded Knee, 337